P9-BYJ-595

AMERICA

The Last Best Hope

AMERICA

The Last Best Hope

Volume 2:
From *a* World *at* War
To *the* Triumph *of* Freedom
1914–1989

William J. Bennett

Thomas Nelson
Since 1798

NASHVILLE DALLAS MEXICO CITY RIO DE JANEIRO BEIJING

Published in Nashville, Tennessee. Thomas Nelson is a trademark of Thomas Nelson, Inc.

Unless otherwise noted, all interior images: Getty Images.

ISBN-10: 1-59555-057-7
ISBN-13: 978-1-59555-057-6

Printed in the United States of America

To the American soldier,
whose fidelity, patriotism, and valor
have made this land
the last best hope of earth.

Contents

Acknowledgments

As with Volume One, I would like to thank those who made this book a reality. Indeed an even better reality than the original conception. Bob Morrison was thorough, steady and overworked throughout. He is a lover of history, of good stories and anecdotes. This book is blessed with that knowledge.

Seth Leibsohn was, as always, faithful in his counsel on this project. Professor Vin Cannato offered his usual thoughtful reaction to early drafts. Professor Al Felzenberg carefully read and adjudged the final chapters with wit, humor and deep learning. Ken Watson expertly weighed in on German military strategy. Noreen Burns worried the book through to completion with concerns about how it looked, felt and would be presented. A new friend, Michael Forastiere, "the most careful of them all" deserves a special thanks for a keen eye.

Brian Kennedy, my boss at the Claremont Institute, encouraged and helped throughout. The great Kadishes—Susan and Lawrence—remind me of what was once said of James Madison "when you call on him there is always someone home."

Bob Barnett offered his invaluable counsel.

My publisher David Dunham, editor Joel Miller, and all the able people at Thomas Nelson made the production of this book a pleasure.

The callers to my radio program "Morning in America" started asking for Volume Two soon after faithfully reading Volume One.

My sons, John and Joseph, thought the book good and the project worthy.

My wife, Elayne, thought it necessary and with her wisdom and love blessed it.

Introduction

In 1921, the English writer G. K. Chesterton came to America to travel and speak. He, like other foreigners I mention in Volume 1 (think Alexis de Tocqueville and John Stuart Mill), saw us better, in many ways, than we saw ourselves. What he saw here, what he found here, is a reaffirmation of what I attempt to recapture about our country—describing it as Abraham Lincoln did: "the last best hope of earth."

The 1920s, it has been said, was a decade when many here could have really used a drink—and yet Prohibition was the law of the land. We had just come out of a war ("the War to End All Wars") that killed over one hundred thousand Americans. We had survived an influenza that killed over six hundred thousand more. It was a decade that would end with a great stock market crash. It was the decade that saw four different presidents. America was becoming more isolationist while at the same time it was fearing Socialism and anarchy. It was a decade of a presidential scandal and a rising crime wave. In a decade to come, a tyrant would arise in Europe and the world would be committed to yet another war. And yet Chesterton witnessed something altogether different here.

Chesterton saw something of and for the ages. He saw what John Winthrop saw, he saw what our Founders saw, he saw what Lincoln saw, and he saw what Ronald Reagan would see. How did he accomplish this with an outsider's view and in such a tumultuous time? He did it by taking a long and contemplative view. "There are some things about America that a man ought to see with his eyes shut," he said. In his mind's eye, he saw something about America and her founding that was wholly absent from his Great Britain or any other country and her founding. He saw us uniquely, as a country founded upon and committed to a theory: "the theory of equality." He defined this founding theory of ours simply: "the pure classic conception that no man must aspire to be anything more than a citizen, and that no man shall endure to be anything less." Lincoln could not have agreed more. Neither could our Founders.

Chesterton continued: "[C]itizenship is still the American ideal; there is an army of actualities opposed to that ideal; but there is no ideal opposed to that ideal." In explaining this to his fellow countrymen, Chesterton hoped that they might "realize that equality is not some crude fairy tale about all men being equally tall or equally tricky; which we not only cannot believe but cannot believe in anybody believing. It is an absolute of morals by which all men have a value invariable and indestructible and a dignity as intangible as death."

One could look around America and find great poverty, just as one could find great wealth—but material riches were not about what Chesterton (nor, for that matter, the Founders or Lincoln) spoke. While many, then, were deprecating our Founding and commitment to equality and freedom (and many still do); while many, then, were saying our country was based on notions of inequality and privilege (and many still do); while many, then, were arguing that our political and economic success could only last so long as it maintained a fictitious system of the favored and the disfavored (and many still do), Chesterton saw a different fact about it all in America:

> In truth it is inequality that is the illusion. The extreme disproportion between men, that we seem to see in life, is a thing of changing lights and lengthening shadows, a twilight full of fancies and distortions. We find a man famous and cannot live long enough to find him forgotten; we see a race dominant and cannot linger to see it decay. It is the experience of men that always returns to the equality of men; it is the average that ultimately justifies the average man. It is when men have seen and suffered much and come at the end of their elaborate

> experiments, that they see men under an equal light of death and daily laughter; and none the less mysterious for being many. Nor is it in vain that these Western democrats have sought the blazonry of their flag in that great multitude of immortal lights that endure behind the fires we see, and gathered them into the comer of Old Glory whose ground is like the glittering night. For veritably, in the spirit as well as in the symbol, suns and moons and meteors pass and fill our skies with a fleeting and almost theatrical conflagration; and wherever the old shadow stoops upon the earth, the stars return.

The stars always return here. That is "the glory and romance" of our history, of America's story—as the inscription atop the National Archives describes what is contained within. We have survived wars and scandals. We have survived epidemics and assassinations.

And yet.

And yet we remain a nation that can freely choose, and has freely chosen, the leaders and kinds of leaders embodied on Mount Rushmore. Mount Rushmore, I argue, is not a tribute to the leaders etched into the Black Hills of South Dakota; it is a tribute to the people who chose them—and continue to choose them time and time again, just when they are most needed. There are not enough Black Hills to embody us.

In 1943, President Franklin Delano Roosevelt dedicated the Jefferson Memorial, still one of the first tour bus stops in our nation's capital. In dedicating that memorial, Roosevelt said:

> Today, in the midst of a great war for freedom, we dedicate a shrine to freedom. . . . [Thomas Jefferson] faced the fact that men who will not fight for liberty can lose it. We, too, have faced that fact. . . . He lived in a world in which freedom of conscience and freedom of mind were battles still to be fought through—not principles already accepted of all men. We, too, have lived in such a world. . . . The Declaration of Independence and the very purposes of the American Revolution itself, while seeking freedoms, called for the abandonment of privileges. . . . Thomas Jefferson believed, as we believe, in Man. He believed, as we

believe, that men are capable of their own government, and that no king, no tyrant, no dictator can govern for them as well as they can govern for themselves.

In sum, it is the story of a great people who wisely choose how to save themselves and others, how to correct wrongs, and how to preserve what is still the greatest nation in the history of the world. This volume, taking us from World War I to the end of the 1980s, is my effort to recapture that glory and romance. I dedicate it, again, to the American soldier—and to the cause, *the idea*, and the country for which he fights.

—William J. Bennett
February 2007

America and the Great War (1914–1921)

All of Europe was a powder magazine in 1914. Secret alliances bred mistrust. And in their mistrust, the crowned heads and cabinet ministers of Europe armed against the terrible explosion they all dreaded, but which they somehow knew was coming. Sarajevo was the spark. Most Americans wanted desperately to stay out of Europe's self-immolation. They remembered warnings from Washington and Jefferson against permanent and entangling alliances. For millions of immigrants, the interminable conflicts of Europe's ruling houses were an unpleasant memory, something they left behind when they raced on deck to hail the Statue of Liberty. As horrified as they were by the Germans' unrestricted submarine warfare, average Americans still viewed ocean travel as a preserve of the rich. Only with the infamous Zimmermann Telegram—wherein the Germans secretly sought Mexico's support in carving up the Southwest U.S.—did Americans opt for war. People enthusiastically cheered the departing "Doughboys." The small but loud opponents of the war—like perennial presidential candidate Eugene V. Debs—soon found themselves facing prison terms for sedition. Americans sang "Over There," and vowed not to come back "'til it's over over there." But war-weariness soon took its toll, as it was with all American wars. Heroism and victory on the battlefield were followed only too soon by frustration and disillusionment at the Paris Peace Conference and deadlock in the U.S. Senate. In the end, the "War to End All Wars" sowed the dragon's teeth of a second and even more destructive world war.

I. "Home Before the Leaves Fall"

The immediate cause of what contemporaries called the Great War was the assassination of Archduke Franz Ferdinand and his wife, Sophie, on 28 June 1914 in the Bosnian city of Sarajevo. This autocratic Austrian was the heir to the throne of the Austro-Hungarian Empire, and reformers had high hopes he would bring greater freedom to the millions of Poles, Slavs, Magyars (Hungarians), and German-speaking Austrians who comprised this massive polyglot European Empire.

When Serbian nationalists were implicated in the murders, Austria demanded that Serbia meet stringent terms for the suspects' apprehension and prosecution. Austria was given a "free hand" by her ally, Germany, but Serbia was encouraged to resist by Russia. Russians saw themselves as protectors of the Slavs; and Serbia was a small Slavic nation.

The alliances across European countries created an intricate web. Serbia was supported by Russia, which relied on the support of the French. France had no formal treaty with England, but she did have a decade-long *entente cordiale* (cordial understanding), something skillfully advanced by the popular and pro-French King Edward VII. A clutch of secret agreements, secret war plans, and secret weapons created a tinder box in Central Europe that threatened the peace of the world. All that was needed for an earth-shattering explosion was a single spark.

The tinder in the box had been amassing for years, thanks to Germany's Kaiser Wilhelm II. In many ways, he was the most important figure in Europe in 1914. A product of royalty's preference for intermarriage, Wilhelm was the grandson of Britain's Queen Victoria. The widowed queen had so many relatives in ruling royal houses she was called "the grandmother of Europe." He proudly wore the uniforms of admiral in the Royal Navy and field marshal in the British army. He thought he knew Britain well, spoke English fluently, and visited his relatives there often. He could and should have been Britain's best hope for peace on the Continent. Instead, he was the greatest threat.

From his earliest days, Wilhelm had been a troubled and troubling child. He was bright, eager, and energetic. But he seemed to have been born with a chip on his shoulder. He was, in fact, born with a tragic birth defect. His left arm was shorter than his right, a fact about which he was deeply sensitive. He tried to conceal it, with some success, by elaborate military capes and long, elegant kid gloves that he always held in photographs. Wilhelm's willfulness terrified even his own parents.

His father was a kindly crown prince, the great hope of millions who wanted a more humane, freer German Empire. They looked to Good Fritz (Frederick) to relax the tight grip in which the Hohenzollern Imperial Household held the nation. Additionally, reformers hoped that Frederick might check the power wielded by the wily Otto von Bismarck. Though Bismarck was nominally subordinate to the German kaiser, he created the German Empire and reaped the prestige; few dared to challenge his authority. Even if he wanted to do so, Fritz barely had the chance. Tragedy struck when he died of throat cancer in 1888, barely a hundred days after becoming Kaiser Frederick III. In short order, young Kaiser Wilhelm II strained his relations with his widowed mother. When she died a few years following her beloved husband, she left orders that her body should be swathed in the British Union Jack before being placed in its coffin.[1]

Bismarck, known as the Iron Chancellor, was no democrat and no lover of peace. He had goaded the foolish Napoleon III into a war and had smashed the French army with a lightning thrust. He had proclaimed the German Empire in the Versailles Palace's famed Hall of Mirrors in 1871. But Bismarck was also shrewd, careful, and deeply aware of his country's strengths and weaknesses. "The great questions of the day are not to be settled by majority resolutions," he said, "but by blood and iron." Equally cynical and cautious, Bismarck maintained a close alliance with Europe's other autocrats—the Hapsburgs of Austria-Hungary and the Romanovs of Russia. Thus, he wisely avoided what every German dreaded, a two-front war.

Because Chancellor Bismarck had sided with the Union during America's Civil War, he was generally popular in the United States.* Former President Grant's visit to Bismarck in Berlin was lauded at home. Americans

---

* As a measure of his popularity in America, Bismarck is the only foreign leader for whom an American state capital is named: Bismarck, North Dakota.

chuckled over the chancellor's pithy sayings. "There is a Providence that protects idiots, drunkards, children, and the United States of America," he once said. Another gem attributed to him: "The Americans have contrived to be surrounded on two sides by weak neighbors and on two sides—*by fish!*" But Bismarck was less popular with Wilhelm.

Soon after he ascended the throne that Bismarck had created, Kaiser Wilhelm decided to dispense with his services. He resented the aging Bismarck's attempts to restrain him. He intended to be unchecked ruler of Germany. After all, *kaiser* is German for "caesar." So, in 1890, Wilhelm forced Bismarck into retirement.

Ridding himself of Bismarck in 1890, the thirty-one-year-old kaiser with the bold upturned mustache became the master of Germany. Britain's humor magazine *Punch* published a cartoon showing the crowned kaiser looking complacently over the railing as the steady old Bismarck descended the ladder of the ship. "Dropping the pilot" was the title of the famous cartoon.[2] They little knew that Wilhelm II would put the German ship of state on a fatal collision course with the British Empire; in dropping the pilot, he also dropped the chancellor's more prudent policies.

Wilhelm had read *The Influence of Sea Power Upon History.* This important book by American Admiral Alfred Thayer Mahan had deeply impressed not only the German ruler, but it was also devoured by such naval power theorists as Theodore Roosevelt and Winston Churchill. The leaders of the Imperial Japanese Navy translated Mahan's great work as early as 1896.

Bismarck had realized that Britain would take alarm if Germany ever amplified the power of its huge armies by building a great blue-water navy. Throwing Bismarck's caution to the winds, Wilhelm in the early 1900s raced to build a powerful fleet of dreadnought battleships and ordered every German warship to carry a copy of Mahan's masterpiece. The threat to Britain's historic isolation from European wars prompted intense fears in England—seen in the huge success of a work of popular fiction, *When William Came*, a title that reflects the English form of Wilhelm's name. This 1913 story showed the English that Kaiser Wilhelm might use his mighty High Seas Fleet to bring an overwhelming army across the English

Channel. Imaginary though that threat proved to be, the brisk sales showed that the British people truly feared invasion.

Wilhelm's throwing his weight around did not stop with building a navy. Bismarck never challenged Britain or France in the race for overseas colonies. Not so Wilhelm. Soon he was trying to grab colonies in Africa and the Pacific. He demanded Germany's "place in the sun." His rough handling managed to alienate his cousin, Tsar Nicholas. In response, Russia soon concluded an alliance with France. The watchword for the kaiser's rule was *weltmacht oder niedergang* ("world power or decline").[3] It explains the constant pushing and shoving of Wilhelm and his military chiefs that made peace so precarious for a full quarter of a century before the final outbreak of war in 1914.

Americans, shielded by three thousand miles of ocean from the kaiser's bluster, initially felt unconcerned about his militarism and his frequent saber-rattling. The interference of the German fleet with Commodore Dewey's Philippine operations in 1898 came as a rude shock. So did the kaiser's meddling in Latin America in the early Roosevelt years. But we had Teddy's Big Stick to keep us safe.

At the turn of the new century, Americans tended to view Kaiser Wilhelm II with a mixture of distrust and amused contempt. A 1903 poem published in *Harper's Weekly* reveals the attitude:

> Kaiser, Kaiser, shining bright
> You have given us a fright!
> With your belts and straps and sashes,
> And your upward-turned mustaches!
> And that frown so deadly fierce
> And those awful eyes that pierce
> Through the very hearts of those
> Whom ill fate has made your foes.
> Kaiser, Kaiser, Man of War
> What a funny joke you are.[4]

Readers recognized the satire on William Blake's line "Tyger, Tyger, burning bright." When the clash in the Balkans finally came in 1914, Wilhelm relied on his English family connection to avert war with Britain. He sent his brother, Prince Heinrich, to speak to King George V, their first cousin through their grandmother, Queen Victoria. The king said that he hoped Britain would stay out of any continental war. The kaiser mistakenly took that to mean the king would determine British policy. "I have the word of a king," he boasted.[5] Wilhelm apparently learned nothing from his mother or grandmother about the British system of governance. Britain was (and is) a constitutional monarchy. Foreign policy is made by the cabinet, not the Crown.

In July 1914, only days after the assassination of Archduke Ferdinand, the world breathed a sigh of relief as the kaiser went on his annual three-week cruise in the fjords of Norway. It seemed he was disengaging from the mounting crisis between Austria-Hungary, Serbia, and their allies. His magnificent 380-foot, 4,280-ton yacht *Hohenzollern* looked like a giant white swan gliding silently over Norway's dark, cold waters that summer.* But this peaceful image was deceptive. While the kaiser cruised these placid waters, the air was electric with radio traffic to and from the vessel. The tinder was now aflame.

Given the nature of Europe's web of alliances, the kaiser virtually guaranteed a world war in 1905 when he approved the military plan of General Alfred von Schlieffen, chief of the Imperial General Staff. According to the Schlieffen Plan, German soldiers would have to smash into Belgium and drive deep into France, knocking France out of any future war before France's Russian allies could be mobilized in the East. "Let the last man on the right brush the [English] Channel with his sleeve," it was said of the Schlieffen Plan.

Wilhelm carelessly exposed Germany to the dreaded two-front war through his own unskillful diplomacy and his regular threats to his neighbors. Further, Wilhelm seemed oblivious to the fact that the Schlieffen Plan involved violating Belgian neutrality, which Germany as well as Britain had guaranteed for a century. Britain had not clearly warned Kaiser Wilhelm that violating Belgium's neutrality would mean war. In fact, none of the Powers knew exactly what Britain's response would be if Germany marched across Belgium en route to France.[6]

---

* Uncharacteristically for a royal yacht, *Hohenzollern* was heavily armed. She carried three rapid fire, 105 mm cannons and twelve rapid fire, 50 mm cannons.

Twenty years later, Wilhelm would tell British historian Sir John Wheeler-Bennett that he never would have invaded Belgium if he had known that such a move would incite Britain to war. Subtle hints and diplomatic nuances were wasted on Wilhelm. If ever there was a case for Big Stick diplomacy, it was here.

Why did Britain fail to put the kaiser on notice with an unambiguous warning? To have announced well in advance that *any* violation of Belgian neutrality meant war with Britain might have deterred the impetuous Wilhelm. American Chesterton scholar Dale Ahlquist points to the answer in the autobiography of the noted British writer, G.K. Chesterton. Britain's ruling Liberal Party was very dependent on a small group of Manchester millionaires to finance its political campaigns. Several of these prominent industrialists were also religious pacifists (as was Andrew Carnegie in America). There was no chance that Britain would abide such clear aggression, suggests Chesterton, but the Liberal Party government could not publicly say so for fear of losing its purse. Chesterton was very close to the Liberal Party leaders of his day, and his testimony deserves serious consideration.[7]

Many later would claim that Britain gave insufficient warning to the Germans.[8] This, however, gives too little attention to the reckless conduct of Germany for the previous twenty-five years and ignores the basic fact that aggressor nations have no right to expect hand-sitting by their neighbors.[9]

The kaiser assured his ally that Germany would stand by Austria-Hungary "through thick and thin."[10] Don't worry about Russia, he told the Austrian ambassador. Russia is "in no way prepared for war."[11]

Backed by Wilhelm II, the Austrians rejected Russia's urgent plea for negotiations, even as the German military High Command was pressing the Austrians for war in response to the assassination.[12] Cousin "Nickie," Russia's tsar, desperately wrote to Cousin "Willy," the kaiser, to "beg" him to restrain Austria. Lying, Wilhelm wrote he was doing his utmost to hold his ally back.[13] Similarly, Berlin rejected Britain's call for a Four-Power conference.[14]

As July closed, Germany filled the telegraph lines of Europe with cabled ultimatums—to Russia, to France, to Belgium. A leading member of the British cabinet, Winston Churchill, was the First Lord of the Admiralty. He was responsible for the readiness of the British fleet. He worried that the

Powers were sliding into war. "I wondered whether those stupid Kings and Emperors could not assemble together and revivify kingship by saving the nations from hell but we all drift on in a kind of dull cataleptic trance."[15]

Hell was closing in. Germany declared war on France and invaded Belgium.[16] With the mutual declarations of war, Churchill cabled the Royal Navy: "Commence hostilities against Germany."

The invasion of Belgium did everything to justify the name *Hun* that the kaiser had given his troops in 1900. As early as 5 August, General von Moltke admitted that "our advance into Belgium is certainly brutal."[17] He was right. The German army murdered women and children in the towns of Andenne, Tamine, Seilles, and Dinant, over two hundred civilians in the first days of war.[18] The University in Louvain was burned and pillaged. The senseless destruction of this "Oxford" of Belgium, with its priceless medieval books and tapestries, was denounced by scholars throughout the world as "a crime against civilization."[19]

Millions in France and England who had foolishly predicted their boys would be "home before the leaves fall" were stunned as Germany's ruthless push drove the French forces and the British Expeditionary Force back to the defenses of Paris. That autumn, France was nearly defeated. France's Ferdinand Foch rallied his troops. A message—probably apocryphal—has him saying, "My center is giving way, my right [flank] is in retreat, situation excellent. I attack." Apocryphal or not, that is exactly what Foch did.[20] He was helped when hundreds of Paris taxicabs were pressed into emergency service. They brought every extra French *poilu* who could carry a rifle to the front.* Soon, the world saw "the miracle of the Marne" as the German advance was halted at the river's bank, just outside Paris.[21]

Less of a miracle was the terrible cost to France of this desperate defense. The deadly machine gun put an end to the French tactic of *offensive á outrance.* This tactic called for charging fixed gun emplacements. It was even more suicidal than the futile rushes at Fredericksburg and Gettysburg had been for the Americans. In the first three months of war alone, 350,000

* *Poilu*: literally, "a hairy one." French enlisted men had little time for haircuts and shaves under constant German bombardment in the trenches.

French soldiers died.[22] Both sides soon dug in for a long, bitter war of attrition. The trenches they built were strung with barbed wire. Between the opposing lines was a deadly "no man's land." Eventually, this ugly scar extended from Switzerland to the North Sea.

Gone were the cheering crowds who had welcomed the war. Gone, too, were the colorful flags and banners. The famous French uniforms—blue jackets with red pants and hats—were quickly replaced by dun-colored shapeless greatcoats as millions of young men descended into the blood and mud of inhuman trench warfare.

II. "Too Proud to Fight"

President Woodrow Wilson immediately declared America's neutrality. Reacting to the stories of the "rape of Belgium," Wilson said, "We must be impartial in thought as well as in action, must put a curb upon our sentiments."[23] The stance was very popular with Americans. Even the normally bellicose TR said it would be "folly to jump into the war."[24]

Besides, President Wilson was having trouble enough with Mexico. The problem was the murderous Victoriano Huerta, who had come to power by assassinating Mexico's president and vice president. Wilson refused to extend diplomatic recognition to this blood-soaked man and instead worked for his ouster. When some American sailors on shore leave were harassed by Mexican authorities, U.S. Admiral Henry Mayo demanded an apology and a proper salute to the American flag. Huerta offered to apologize and salute the American flag if the Mexican flag was rendered similar honors. This was refused.

Tensions mounted.

To prevent Huerta from rearming, Wilson ordered the seizure of the port of Veracruz. Even Mexican democrats rejected Wilson's humiliating actions. Huerta was soon forced to leave the country, but Mexico descended into chaos. Rivals fought for power: Emiliano Zapata, who represented Indians; Pancho Villa, a bandit; and General Venustiano Carranza.[25]

Wilson justified his interventions in Mexico and other Caribbean states by saying he would "teach the Latin Americans to elect good men."[26]

Secretary of State William Jennings Bryan was, as usual, mystified: "I just can't understand why those people are fighting their brothers."[27] Seeking a way, any way, out of the Mexican mess, Wilson agreed to arbitration by Latin America's "ABC" Powers: Argentina, Brazil, and Chile.[28]

All eyes turned back to Europe, however, when a German submarine sank the British luxury liner *Lusitania* on 7 May 1915 off Kinsale, Ireland. The U-boat (*unterseeboot*)* attack claimed more than twelve hundred noncombatants as the great four-stack vessel sank in just eighteen minutes.[29] Of these, 126 were American citizens who ignored the warning notices the German embassy had placed in newspapers in New York and several other major U.S. cities.[30]

The *Lusitania* was carrying munitions, which made her a legitimate target for destruction in German eyes. They had the letter of the law on their side. Even so, Americans felt a shock of horror as survivors described the babies who cried piteously as their wicker basket cradles sank slowly beneath the waves.[31] Americans were further repelled by the German reaction to the sinking. There, editorials boasted of a "joyful pride in our navy," schoolchildren were given the day off in celebration, and a Munich citizen even had a commemorative medallion struck to honor the submariners who had done this act.[32] A pro-British American living in London seized upon the medal and had three hundred thousand copies of it made. These circulated throughout the U.S. and the British Empire as evidence of German inhumanity.[33]**

President Wilson quickly responded to the outrage and the demands for war with Germany. "There is such a thing as a man being too proud to fight," he said, echoing his previous sentiments about staying out of the war.[34] Such indifference shocked former presidents Theodore Roosevelt and William Howard Taft, both Republicans. Wilson's statement left them appalled.[35] They both called for war. TR's cousin, Franklin Delano Roosevelt, agreed with their outrage.[36] But as Wilson's assistant secretary of the navy, FDR was a loyal Democrat. He could not go public with his disagreement with the president of his own party.

---

* Literally, an "under the sea boat."

** The American was Gordon Selfridge, the owner of a famous London department store. He was later to become a British subject. (Massie's, Robert K., *Castles of Steel,* 534.)

Instead of preparing for war, Wilson sent Germany a diplomatic note. When this produced no discernible reply, the next month Wilson sent a second, sterner note.

Wilson's second note provoked Secretary of State Bryan. At a Cabinet meeting, Bryan charged those present angrily: "You people are *not* neutral. You are taking sides."[37] Bryan wanted Wilson to condemn the British as well for their blockade of Germany. When Wilson refused, Bryan quit. Blockades were fully legal under international law, a minor point the pacifist secretary of state apparently had never bothered to learn. Bryan's resignation caused a domestic political crisis for the president.

Not all of Bryan's fellow evangelicals agreed with him. Rev. Billy Sunday, the most prominent preacher in the country, called the German sinking of the *Lusitania* "Damnable! Damnable! Absolutely hellish!" Another called it "a colossal sin against God and . . . premeditated murder!"[38]

Privately, Franklin Roosevelt was delighted to see the bumbling Nebraska populist go. He thought Bryan was dangerously naïve.[39] FDR agreed more with his famous cousin on the need for preparedness than with his own president. Still, FDR was determined to stay at his post to help ready the navy for the battle he thought inevitable. He knew that Secretary of the Navy Josephus Daniels had little interest in sea power or understanding of naval affairs.* (In this, FDR's relationship to his boss was not unlike TR's situation with his lackluster chief, John Long, in the McKinley administration.)

TR, of course, had no such hesitation. He turned the air blue with his words of contempt for "Professor Wilson," who represented all "flubdubs, mollycoddles and flapdoodle pacifists."[40] Wilson continued sending his feckless diplomatic notes—typed on his own typewriter—for another year.

Adding to the pressure and the drama, President Wilson was suffering deeply from the loss of his beloved wife, Ellen. All during that fateful summer of war in 1914, Ellen lay dying of cancer in the White House. Woodrow Wilson did not have close male friends, but he was exceedingly close to his wife and three daughters. With Ellen's death, he seemed to lose even his will

* Daniels's only enduring contribution to the U.S. Navy was to abolish the rum ration in favor of free coffee. FDR supported this reform. To this day, navy chief petty officers call their coffee "a cup of Joe" for Josephus.

to live. When his closest advisor, "Colonel" Edward House, joined him for a nighttime walk through Manhattan, the dejected president said he actually wished someone would kill him.[41] He even shared with his inner circle his doubts about whether he would run for reelection in 1916.

"Who *is* that beautiful lady?" the president quizzed his doctor, Admiral Cary Grayson, one day in early 1915.[42] He was asking about the shapely and attractive Washington widow, Edith Bolling Galt. She was the owner of a prominent local jewelry store. Highly intelligent and full of life, Mrs. Galt was the first woman in the capital to drive her own automobile.[43]

Soon, the widow and the widower were keeping discreet company. And the president was even observed, spring in his step, singing one of George M. Cohan's popular tunes:

O, you beautiful girl
You great, big beautiful girl

That fall, the White House quietly announced the president's intention to remarry. Before the year was out, Wilson had chosen his true running mate. And he would enter the New Year with a fresh determination to win.

As president, Wilson had to contend with deep division among Americans. As the Census of 1910 revealed, more than ten million of America's ninety-two million people had emigrated from Germany or had one or two parents from Germany or Austria-Hungary.[44] Many of these, of course, had emigrated to America because they opposed Prussian militarism and political oppression. Still, as the anti-German propaganda took on a more racial cast, these German-Americans were greatly offended. America had, as well, millions of Irish-Americans who had no love for the British Empire and who thought British claims to be fighting for freedom were the rankest form of hypocrisy.

Woodrow Wilson had other, equally compelling reasons to keep America out of Europe's war. He had racked up an impressive record of progressive reform legislation. In addition to passage of the Federal Reserve Act of 1913, Wilson had appealed to Congress to outlaw almost all child labor (even though the Supreme Court was to strike it down as unconstitutional).

He got legislative approval for limiting to eight hours a day the work of railroad workers. He had successfully pressed Congress for an income tax and a Federal Trade Commission, and he had passed an inheritance tax—over the loud objections of propertied Americans.[45] Wilson believed, and most progressives of the time agreed with him, that badly needed domestic reforms would be stalled, if not abandoned, should America be forced into the war against Germany.

One prominent dissenter from this view, however, was the philosopher John Dewey. The father of "progressive" education in America, Dewey wrote an article on, as the title had it, "The Social Possibilities of War." He recognized that war inevitably brings a vast concentration of power in the federal government, something Dewey and some leading Progressives strongly desired.

Wilson had revived the practice of delivering the State of the Union Address in person. Powerful orator that he was, Wilson mounted the podium in the well of the House of Representatives to call for a broad program of reform. "We must abolish everything that bears even the semblance of privilege or of any kind of artificial advantage," he told an enthusiastic Congress.[46]

When he said that, of course, he meant corporations. Big business—the vaunted Trusts—were the object of his reforming zeal. He clearly did not mean the artificial advantage and privilege that came from race. Many of those in Congress—especially his fellow Democrats—who applauded Wilson's denunciation of elitism gave no thought to the continued existence of racial segregation. During Wilson's first administration, not only did he not seek to end racial segregation, he affirmed it in his administration.

Wilson was willing to confront the bigotry of organizations like the Ku Klux Klan in several key appointments, however. And he did challenge ethnic and religious prejudice by installing Joseph Tumulty as his private secretary, a post comparable to the powerful position of White House chief of staff today. Tumulty was an Irish-Catholic Democrat, a friend from Wilson's brief tenure as governor of New Jersey. Because of that tie, Tumulty always called the president "governor," and Wilson accepted it as a compliment. No one served Woodrow Wilson with fiercer loyalty than Joe Tumulty.[47] Wilson also confronted prejudice when he included Louis D. Brandeis, a liberal Boston lawyer, in his inner circle of advisers. Wall Street nearly panicked when they heard that the Trust-busting Brandeis might be named attorney general.[48] Wilson wouldn't go that far, but he soon went much further. He again defied the Klan when he named Brandeis to the U.S. Supreme Court—the first Jewish appointee to that body.

The most important member of Wilson's inner circle was "Colonel" Edward M. House. This Texas millionaire was not really a colonel, but he liked the honorary title bestowed on him by a governor of the Lone Star State. Colonel House never held elective office, but preferred to serve quietly in the shadows. He saw the possibility of running Wilson for president of the United States when the ascetic scholar was still a reforming president of Princeton University. He devoted himself wholly to Wilson's political career. In return, Wilson trusted House as he trusted few men: "Mr. House is my independent self. His thoughts and mine are one."[49]

Americans were horrified by the slaughter in the trenches in France. Not only had the Germans initiated submarine warfare against passenger ships, but they were the first to introduce poison gas.[50] Hundreds of miles of the beautiful French and Belgian countryside were reduced to a hellish moonscape, a "no man's land" where rats fattened on corpses. The Germans used their powerful artillery to batter quaint towns and villages into rubble. "Big Bertha" was a forty-three-ton monster howitzer produced by the Krupp company and incongruously named for Gustav Krupp's wife. It fired a 2,200-pound shell more than nine miles.

The Germans also rained death from the air. Their hydrogen-filled dirigibles—called *zeppelins* after German Count Zeppelin—dropped bombs on civilians in London.[51] In all this, the kaiser's High Command consciously pursued a policy of *schrecklichkeit* ("frightfulness") to terrify their enemies.[52]

Wilson addressed the war in Europe in another controversial speech in 1916 in which he called for a "peace without victory" and offered to mediate.[53] Germany spurned the offer. Once again, Republicans and other supporters of the Allies were deeply affronted.

Wilson's reelection prospects brightened somewhat when the Germans offered the Sussex Pledge in May of 1916. This event followed an attack by a U-boat on the unarmed French channel steamer *Sussex* in which fifty people, including Americans, were killed. In this agreement, the Germans pledged not to attack merchant vessels unless they were carrying war contraband and unless their passengers and crew members had first been allowed to get into their lifeboats.

Wilson was renominated in 1916, but with the Republicans' divisions papered over, it appeared he would be a one-term president. TR urged his Bull Moose progressives to get behind the Republicans for the sake of national unity.[54] GOP prospects looked good; no Democrat had been reelected since Andrew Jackson.

The Republicans backed Supreme Court Justice Charles Evans Hughes. Despite the fact that the tall, bearded Hughes had once been governor of New York, however, he proved to be an inept campaigner.

Wilson's campaign stressed the theme "He Kept Us Out of War." Privately, Wilson worried that "any little German lieutenant" could put us into the war and the president could not stop it.[55] Wilson knew that relatively low-ranking submarine commanders held vastly destructive power in their hands. Any one of them could create an international incident by killing more noncombatants. What if, for example, a U-boat skipper had sunk an American liner off the shores of the president's home state of New Jersey?* But publicly, Wilson was content to campaign as the peace candidate. Democrats took out full-page ads in newspapers attacking both Hughes *and* Theodore Roosevelt:

> You are Working;
> —Not Fighting
> Alive and Happy;
> —Not Cannon Fodder!
> Wilson and Peace with Honor?
> Or Hughes with Roosevelt and War?[56]

When the British harshly put down the 1916 Easter Rebellion in Ireland, Irish-Americans were outraged. Hanging many of the romantic Irish patriots was bad enough, but the British also hanged Sir Roger Casement, a man famous for his humanitarian work in Africa. Casement was, however,

* The Germans would sink American ships within sight of the Jersey beaches in 1942.

directly implicated in gun-running from a German freighter off County Tralee. The British made their cause odious in the eyes of many Irish-Americans by releasing Casement's diaries that showed he had engaged in homosexual acts with young Africans. Irish nationalists to this day believe the British forged the so-called Black Diaries.[57]

President Wilson benefited politically from anti-British sentiment among the large Irish- and German-American communities. Meanwhile, Hughes blundered when he declined to meet California's popular progressive Governor Hiram Johnson. Johnson had been Teddy's 1912 running mate on the Bull Moose ticket.[58] TR did not help the Republicans' cause with his attacks on "hyphenated Americans."

Privately, Roosevelt dismissed Hughes as "Wilson with whiskers."

Despite his blunders, on Election Day Hughes swept the Northeast and appeared to have won. According to a story widely circulated at the time, a reporter telephoned the Hughes home and the Republican candidate's son responded that the "president" had retired for the night. "Don't wake him now," said the impish reporter, "but when he gets up, tell him he *ain't* president." The story is probably legend, but it does illustrate the cliffhanger nature of the election and the overly self-assured reputation of the Hughes campaign.

Wilson had been reelected to a second term with a plurality of the popular vote. Wilson gained 9,129,606 popular votes and 49.4 percent to win with 277 electoral votes. Hughes received 8,538,221 popular votes, 46.2 percent, and 254 electoral votes. Allan Louis Benson, the Socialist Party candidate, did not finish as strongly as Eugene V. Debs had in 1912, but he still garnered 585,113 popular votes. That was a substantial showing.

The election of 1916 was the first election decided by California's thirteen electoral votes. Wilson carried the state by fewer than four thousand votes.[59] When he heard he had lost the Golden State, Hughes probably regretted his failure to meet with Hiram Johnson.

The Allies had been bled white by the war in France. Britain alone lost 20,000 men and 40,000 wounded on the first day of the Battle of the Somme.[60] By early 1917, the Allies were near financial collapse.[61] To win the war, the Germans needed only to avoid antagonizing America.

This the reckless kaiser could not do. Early in February, he gave in to his admirals and announced a resumption of unrestricted submarine warfare. The Germans had begun to discount the American reaction to this. Because they had repeatedly provoked America and had faced no serious consequences, they haughtily assumed that America would not fight. Or, if America fought, it would not achieve much.

"They will *not* even come, because our submarines will sink them," Admiral Capelle promised Germany's parliament, the Reichstag, in January 1917. Pridefully, he continued: "Thus America from a military point of view means nothing, and again nothing, and for a third time [I say] *nothing*!"[62]

This contempt was not only an example of the German military's bloody-mindedness, it was also a reflection of President Wilson's policies and his choice of key personnel. Wilson himself had no military experience. He was certainly well respected as a scholar, but he had no deep knowledge of American diplomacy and warfare. Worse, with the sole exception of Franklin D. Roosevelt, Wilson surrounded himself with advisers similarly unqualified. He had consciously chosen pacifists as secretary of state (William Jennings Bryan) and secretary of the navy (Josephus Daniels).[63] His attorney general (A. Mitchell Palmer) was a noted Quaker, a Christian sect founded on pacifism.[64]* Even his secretary of war, Newton D. Baker, improbably, was a pacifist.[65] German diplomats stationed in Washington could not have failed to point to these incredible facts in their reports to Berlin.

As if unrestricted submarine warfare were not provocation enough, German foreign minister Arthur Zimmermann sent a secret cable to his ambassador in Mexico. The infamous *Zimmermann Telegram* proposed that Mexico and Japan should be approached to align with Germany to make war on the United States. In return for their support, the Mexicans would be given large parts of the American Southwest that the United States had seized during the Mexican war.

The Hearst Yellow Press—bitterly opposed to war with Germany—cried foul. It was all a trick of British propaganda, they charged. George Viereck was the editor of the largest German language newspaper in the United States—*Vaterland* ("Fatherland"). Viereck bluntly called the Zimmermann

---

* Initially known as "the fighting Quaker," Palmer was derided as "the quaking fighter."

Telegram "a brazen forgery planted by British agents."[66] Actually, it was Viereck and Hearst's Berlin correspondent who were paid *German* agents.[67]

Viereck was right about one thing: the British were involved. British agents had intercepted the Zimmermann Telegram—and they were at pains to keep that fact from becoming known. At first blush, this seems counter-intuitive. After all, if the telegram were made known, it would provoke America to war. But it wasn't that simple. Why? President Wilson had foolishly allowed the Germans to use official U.S. diplomatic cables because he wanted to let them discuss peace proposals without British interference. Unknown to Wilson, the British not only tapped the German cables but the American ones, too. So proficient was British intelligence that its agents could intercept, decode, and translate German cables *faster* than the Germans themselves could.[68] Americans were surely shocked by the Zimmermann Telegram. But they would have been unwilling to go to war if they had known that the British had uncovered it. They would have suspected a forgery by British intelligence—just as Hearst's men claimed—and that would have effectively kept the United States out of the war.

But then, incredibly, Foreign Minister Zimmermann admitted that the telegram was his![69]

This may have been the greatest diplomatic blunder in history.

Overnight, the American Midwest changed its view of the faraway conflict in Europe. The *Omaha World Herald* wrote, "The issue shifts from Germany against Great Britain to Germany against the United States."[70] Other Midwestern papers, including the influential German language press, dropped their neutrality.[71]

Theodore Roosevelt wrote to Massachusetts Republican Senator Henry Cabot Lodge. The older Lodge had been TR's friend and political mentor for decades. If Wilson would not fight now, TR wrote, "I'll *skin* him alive."[72]

III. Roosevelt to France?

Once the lonely decision for war was taken in the White House, Woodrow Wilson's famous gift for oratory did not desert him.

Wisely, he told a joint session of Congress on 2 April 1917: "We have no quarrel with the German people. We have no feeling towards them but one of sympathy and friendship." We were fighting, he said, because "the world must be made safe for democracy."[73]

> [The] right is more precious than peace, and we shall fight for the things we have always carried nearest our hearts—for democracy, for the right of those who submit to authority to have a voice in their own governments, for the rights and liberties of small nations, for a universal dominion of right by such a concert of free peoples as shall bring peace and safety to all nations and make the world itself at last free . . . the day has come when America is privileged to spend her blood . . . for the principles that gave her birth . . . God helping her, she can do no other.[74]

During this somber Washington Holy Week, the Senate supported the president by a vote of 82 to 6. The House passed the Declaration of War against Germany in the small hours of the morning of Good Friday, by a vote of 373 to 50.[75] Most of the fifty votes against war were cast by congressmen from the heavily German-American Midwest.[76] One of these votes was memorably cast by the only female member of Congress, Representative Jeanette Rankin, a Republican from Montana.*

Most Americans embraced America's moral cause with eagerness. Irish-American composer George M. Cohan soon wrote the lilting song that became the theme of America's first major foreign war:

> Over there, over there!
> Send the word, send the word, over there!
> That the Yanks are coming, the Yanks are coming,
> The drums rum-tumming ev'rywhere!
> So prepare, say a prayer, send the word, send the word to beware!

---

* Rankin was a leading suffragette. Other advocates for women's votes tried in vain to dissuade her from casting her unpopular vote. She was defeated in 1918 but returned to the House in 1940. There, she cast the *only* vote against war after the attack on Pearl Harbor. Capitol police had to protect her from enraged crowds. Rankin lived to lead an anti-war march to the Capitol in 1968. In 1985, the state of Montana honored her with a monument in the Capitol's Statuary Hall.

We'll be over, we're coming over,
And we won't come back 'til it's over Over There!

Not only was Tin Pan Alley*—as America's music publishing industry was then known—fully behind the war effort, millions of Americans subscribed to Liberty Loans. These were government bonds issued to help fund the war.

Theodore Roosevelt desperately wanted to get into the action. He wanted to be an American Lafayette.[77] TR swallowed his pride and went to see Wilson in the White House. He begged the president, actually *pleaded,* for permission to raise a company of volunteers to join the fight in France. Momentarily moved, the president wavered. He told his trusted aide, Joseph Tumulty, that TR was "a great big boy. . . . There is a sweetness about him that is very compelling. You can't resist the man."[78]

The two men who sat across from each other, the president of the United States and his bitter rival, the former president, could not have been more different in background, temperament, or outlook. Theodore Roosevelt was the descendant of a rich and powerful New York Dutch family. He had overcome a frail body and childhood asthma to build a powerful persona. He became America's darling as a cowboy in the Dakotas, and as a night-stalking, reforming police commissioner in his native New York City. He was the boisterous leader of the Rough Riders, his cavalry regiment of volunteers. They were Ivy League swells and Western cowpokes, drawn to the colors by personal attachment to the charismatic TR as much as they were to the thrill of combat in Cuba. Roosevelt rose unexpectedly to the presidency when an assassin felled the modest and quiet William McKinley, the last veteran of the Civil War to sit in the Executive Mansion. Pausing but a short month to mourn, "Teddy" renamed the president's home the White House and took the country by storm. This youngest of all

* Tin Pan Alley is located at 28th street in Manhattan, between 5th Avenue and Broadway. It was home to many popular music publishers. At the turn of the twentieth century, journalist Monroe Rosenfeld wrote that the sound of all the pianos banging out tunes sounded like tin pans crashing. The name stuck. (Online source: http://parlorsongs.com/insearch/tinpanalley/tinpanalley.asp.)

presidents was a dynamo. He "jawboned" mine owners and miners' union leaders until they agreed to end a devastating strike. He busted Trusts, wielded a Big Stick in diplomacy, and "made the dirt fly" to dig a canal through Panama. He won a Nobel Prize for Peace for bringing an end to the Russo-Japanese War, but he sent his Great White Fleet around the world as a warning to increasingly contentious imperial powers: Don't Tread on Me.

All that was in the past.

Now, on 7 April 1917, just one day *after* President Wilson had signed Congress's joint declaration of war against Germany, the Theodore Roosevelt who sat across the desk on this spring day was a shadow of the man he had been.

He was still suffering the effects of his 1914 expedition through the Brazilian rain forest to trace the uncharted waters of the River of Doubt. TR and his son Kermit had dashed off on the expedition almost on a dare. He *had* to go, he told doubtful friends: "It was my last chance to be a boy." Teddy left so hurriedly he couldn't even select enough reading matter. He did manage to bring Thomas More's *Utopia,* the plays of Sophocles, two volumes of Gibbons's *Decline and Fall of the Roman Empire,* and the works of Marcus Aurelius and Epictetus.[79] When he ran through these, often consuming them in a dugout canoe or sitting under mosquito netting on a rotting log, the former president seized upon Kermit's book of French poetry. "For French verse father never cared. He said it didn't sing sufficiently. 'The Song of Roland' was the one exception he granted," his son recounted.[80]

The expedition soon became a nightmare. "I don't believe [Roosevelt] can live through the night," wrote the seasoned explorer George Cherrie in his diary, as TR raved in a delirious fever.[81] At one point, TR was so weakened by infection and starvation that he actually told Kermit to push on and leave him to die. Miraculously, he survived the man-eating piranhas,* the poisonous snakes, the malarial mosquitoes, and the intense heat. He made it home, but barely. Roosevelt limped badly. He lost fifty-five pounds in the rain forest, and his clothes hung on him. He never fully regained his youthful vigor. To honor

* Ravenously hungry, TR and his party ate some surprisingly tasty piranhas. In another first, Roosevelt thus became the only former U.S. President who actually was a man eating piranha.

him, the Brazilian government renamed the one thousand-mile extent of the River of Doubt the Rio Roosevelt.[82]

How could President Woodrow Wilson find common ground with his visitor? Wilson had been raised in modest circumstances in the South, the son of a Presbyterian minister. From his earliest days, he was a man of words, not a man of action. He did not play baseball, but he wrote editorials for the student newspaper, *The Princetonian*, on how the captain of the baseball team should be selected.[83] He urged more attention to oratory, the power of rhetoric to persuade. As a Princeton undergraduate, he complained about "an excess of visible skin in the gymnasium."[84] What would the mature Wilson have thought of TR's famous "point-to-point walks" as president? During some of these, Roosevelt and his companions (senior military officers, foreign diplomats) would strip to the buff to wade through rushing streams.

Whereas Roosevelt once boasted he was proud he had not "a single drop of English blood," Wilson revered the Great Commoner, Prime Minister William E. Gladstone. Like Hamilton before him, he publicly advocated revamping the U.S. constitutional system to make it more like the British model.[85]

But now it was Teddy Roosevelt who was pleading for a chance to get into the action. He felt that history was passing him by. He may even have sensed his own mortality. Roosevelt did not care, he said, if the war killed him: "If I should die tomorrow, I would be quite content to have as my epitaph, and my only epitaph, 'Roosevelt to France.'"[86]

France's premier Georges Clemenceau was clamoring for TR. He told Wilson that the presence of Roosevelt in the trenches would do wonders for the morale of the battered French soldiers who had been fighting there for three years. "Send them Roosevelt," he pleaded.[87]

Wilson did not commit himself during their last White House meeting. At one point, even the faithful Tumulty thought the president might give in to Roosevelt's appeal.[88] Skillfully changing the subject, Wilson asked Roosevelt for his help in getting conscription legislation through Congress.[89] Americans had never liked the draft. Since TR had been loudly demanding such legislation for years, however, he could hardly refuse now.

In the end, Wilson rejected TR's plea.[90] The army brass remembered

TR's brashness in Cuba and wanted no part of him in France. Also, this grim war of attrition was to be no daring dash up San Juan Hill. TR was wasted by tropical diseases contracted from his South American trip; he was in no condition to fight in the trenches.

Roosevelt took it the only way he knew how—hard. Wilson's refusal to let him fight only deepened the former president's hostility toward the man he thought had so unworthily occupied the White House.* Bitterly, he lashed out to Kansas editor, William Allen White, a progressive Republican: "The Washington people . . . would rather make this a paper war . . . but if not that they want to make it a Democratic war."[91] TR nonetheless had the satisfaction of seeing all four of his sons bravely volunteer. Even his son-in-law, a physician, and his daughter, a nurse, faced danger in frontline medical units.

IV. Over There!

Very quickly, the Americans proved the Germans wrong about their submarine weapon. FDR moved energetically to supply the U.S. Navy with 110-foot antisubmarine vessels while Navy Admiral William S. Sims soon organized a convoy system that overcame the U-boat threat. Because of FDR and Sims's efforts, only 637 of more than one million American soldiers were lost to U-boat attacks crossing over to France.[92]

American intervention came not a moment too soon for the Allies. Britain suffered the highest loss of tonnage to submarines in *two* world wars in April 1917.[93]

General John J. Pershing was given command of the American Expeditionary Force. He made an early decision that Americans would fight under a unified command. He rejected the debilitated Allies' appeals to let American troops fill gaps in their depleted ranks.[94]** He was a resolute and

---

* With Wilson's rejection also came the end of "Roosevelt to France" as TR's epitaph. Curiously, he was the *second* U.S. President to propose putting a reference to France on his own tombstone. A century earlier, another combative man offered this: "Here lies John Adams, who took upon himself the responsibility of peace with France in the year 1800."

** President Wilson made one exception to Pershing's rule when he let black troops serve under French commanders in combat units. There, they faced no objections to keep them from taking part in the action.

Theodore Roosevelt. *Theodore Roosevelt pleaded with President Woodrow Wilson to be allowed to fight in the trenches in World War I. If he died there, the former president said, he would be content to have his tombstone read "Roosevelt to France." When Wilson rejected his appeal, the hatred between the two men deepened.*

WWI American "doughboys." *American soldiers helped turn the tide of battle for the exhausted allies in World War I. At home, Americans had a difficult time appreciating the horrors of trench warfare, where poison gas lingered in low spaces and rats fattened on corpses.*

Kaiser Wilhelm II. *Germany's Kaiser Wilhelm II was grandson to Britain's Queen Victoria. He once urged German soldiers to be as brutal as the Huns of old. The name stuck. Wilhelm's willfulness frightened even his own parents.*

Vladimir Lenin. *Lenin built Russia's Bolshevik party into a conspiratorial movement, justifying any violence that would advance the cause of world communism. He was the founder of the Soviet Union. His embalmed body remains in his Moscow mausoleum to this day.*

determined leader. The previous year, Pershing had been called upon to quell some trouble with Mexico after outlaw Pancho Villa crossed into New Mexico and murdered seventeen Americans at Columbus.[95] Wilson sent General Pershing and twelve thousand cavalry troopers to pursue the bandit leader three hundred miles into Mexico. Villa only narrowly escaped and "Black Jack" Pershing's reputation was made in the "Punitive Expedition."[96]*

Americans thrilled to stories of heroism from U.S. forces. Flying in French biplanes, the Lafayette Escadrille distinguished itself in the air. Lieutenant Eddie Rickenbacker became America's first air "Ace" by shooting down twenty-six German planes.[97] American infantrymen called "doughboys" captured French hearts, too.** Colonel Charles Stanton wowed the French at a Fourth of July ceremony in Paris. At the tomb of the Marquis de Lafayette, Stanton stepped forward, saluted smartly, and said, "*Lafayette, nous voici!*" ("Lafayette, we are here!")[98]

U.S. Marines went into action against battle-hardened German troops who soon learned to fear the Leathernecks. They called our Marines *teufelhunden*—devil dogs. When Allied generals called for a temporary withdrawal, Marine captain Lloyd Williams groused: "Retreat? *Hell,* we just got here!"[99]

It took time for U.S. industry to be converted to a wartime economy. The military was woefully ill-equipped. Secretary of War Newton D. Baker even bragged about it: "I delight in the fact that when we entered this war we were not, like our adversary, prepared for it, and inviting it. Accustomed to peace, we were not ready."[100] As a result, Americans flew in French-built Nieuports, shot British rifles, and fired French 75 mm artillery almost until the end of the war.[101]

The Allies gained major support with the arrival of the Americans, but would soon lose their Eastern partner. The tsar was overthrown in March 1917 by a democratic uprising against his long and unenlightened rule.

---

* Pershing's nickname came to him because he had proudly commanded black troops in these days of the segregated U.S. Army.

** *Doughboy* was the nickname for American infantrymen. There are several theories as to its origin, the most likely of which goes all the way back to the Civil War and the dumpling-shaped brass buttons, or "doughboys," worn on Union uniforms.

The Provisional Russian government led by Alexander Kerensky vowed to stay in the war, which opened an opportunity for Vladimir Lenin, the exiled leader of the Bolsheviks.* The Bolsheviks claimed to be the majority of Russia's revolutionary Communists. The German High Command, eager to knock Russia out of the war, placed Lenin and several top Bolshevik exiles on the famous "Sealed Train" and sent them to Petrograd, the capital of exhausted Russia.** Lenin promised "peace, land, and bread" to the starving, war-weary Russian peasants and workers. To the Germans he pledged to pull Russia out of the war. Winston Churchill described this foolhardy German move as "injecting a plague bacillus" into the Russian state.[102]

By November 1917, when Lenin seized control of the Russian government in the Bolsheviks' Red October revolution, the Germans looked forward to transferring a full *fifty* divisions of seasoned veterans to the Western Front.*** Lenin put the democratic government of Alexander Kerensky to flight, plunging Russia into Communist dictatorship for a full seventy-four years. Lenin soon signed a separate peace with Germany, permitting scores of battle-hardened divisions to join the German ranks in France.

The war produced new strains on the home front in America. The government funded the Committee on Public Information to actively promote the war with sophisticated propaganda. George Creel, head of the committee, called the effort "the world's greatest adventure in advertising."[103] Seventy-five thousand "Four-minute Men" were paid to take to public stages in movie houses and theaters to whip up sentiment against the Hun.[104] Herbert Hoover, a millionaire mining engineer, had distinguished himself with Belgian Relief at the outbreak of the war. Wilson now tapped him to head the Food Administration. The country got used to "wheatless Mondays" and "meatless Tuesdays."[105] All the while, Hoover urged us to

---

* *Bolshevik*, from *bolshoi*, means "larger" in Russian. The Bolsheviks were, in fact, the *smaller* faction among Russia's revolutionaries. It was the beginning of their propaganda success.

** The tsar had changed the name St. Petersburg to Petrograd at the outbreak of the war to give the capital city built by Peter the Great a more Russian-sounding name. It was soon to be renamed Leningrad after the founder of the USSR. In 1991, the name reverted to St. Petersburg.

*** Although the Revolution occurred on 7 November 1917, Russia was then still operating under the Julian Calendar, which the British Empire had abandoned for the Gregorian Calendar in 1752.

"clean our plates" and the government posters reminded us that "Food Will Win the War."[106]

As many progressives had warned, the war unleashed a virulent hatred of all things German. Gone was the respect for German inventive genius—like Dr. Roentgen's X-ray machine and the Diesel engine. Mozart and Beethoven were shunned, stupidly. Sauerkraut was renamed "Liberty Cabbage."[107]

Even worse things were to come. German language books were thrown out of public libraries, and a number of Midwestern states even made it *unlawful* to teach schoolchildren in the German language.[108]* The Sedition Act made any interference with the war effort a crime. More than fifteen hundred people were arrested.[109] Perennial Socialist candidate for president Eugene V. Debs was tried, convicted, and sent to prison. Whipped up anti-German sentiment unleashed a wave of suspicion as neighbors spied on neighbors. It was an opportunity, as Samuel Eliot Morison put it, for "frustrated old women of *both* sexes" to indulge their fantasies.[110]

President Wilson went before Congress in January 1918 to lay out his war aims. He spoke hopefully of the new Bolshevik government in Russia. He praised "the new voice" of the Russian people as "thrilling and compelling."[111] Few Western leaders yet understood the violence and oppression that regime would bring, but most welcomed an end to tsarist autocracy. He emphasized again his respect for the German people—as opposed to their brutal leaders. Germans, he said, were distinguished by their learning and enterprise. Their role in the world made their "record very bright and very enviable."[112]

The substance of his speech became known as the Fourteen Points. Wilson called for "open agreements openly arrived at." This was a response to secret treaties that many blamed for the war. The Bolsheviks had published these from secret tsarist archives. Wilson also called for freedom

* The Lutheran Church–Missouri Synod, a church body claiming millions of adherents, used German in its worship services and parochial schools. The Synod fought the language laws all the way to the U.S. Supreme Court, winning vindication there in 1923 in the case of *Meyer v. Nebraska*. The wartime hysteria had subsided by then. *Meyer* remains an important victory for parental rights.

of the seas. He asserted the principle of national "self-determination." He concluded with a ringing call for a "League of Nations" to defend the peace the Allies sought.[113]

The Fourteen Points represented the high idealism of progressivism. Colonel House had worked with a group of intellectuals he discreetly called "The Inquiry" to draft the principles Wilson would fashion into his soaring rhetoric.[114]* The president himself typed the eloquent address. Ironically, the group worked in secret. So did Wilson. He did not share his vision with his cabinet, with leaders of Congress, or with the democratically chosen leaders of Britain or France, his chief allies.[115]

Desperate for unity—and for American loans—the Allies did not contradict Wilson publicly. Britain, however, would never share Wilson's belief in freedom of the seas if it meant giving up her most effective weapon, the blockade. (Prime Minister David Lloyd George could have reminded Wilson that the Union had not given the Confederacy "freedom of the seas" during the American Civil War.) French premier Georges Clemenceau knew America well. He had been a reporter during our Civil War. Like Lloyd George, he refrained from publicly criticizing the Fourteen Points. Privately, however, Clemenceau "the Tiger" observed wryly that "[e]ven God Almighty has only ten."[116]

Americans began streaming into the Allied lines in great numbers in 1918. The Marines distinguished themselves in major action at Belleau Wood and Chateau Thierry. An American-led U.S.-French assault on German lines at Saint Mihiel in September led to a great breakthrough as the Allies took fifteen thousand Germans prisoner.[117] German forces were at the breaking point.

Americans sang Irving Berlin's catchy tune, "O How I Hate to Get up in the Morning," and eagerly read stories of battlefield heroism "over there." One most amazing story is that of Sergeant Alvin York. Sergeant York hailed from the hills of Tennessee. A member of a small, pacifist Christian sect, he would not even have been drafted into the U.S. Army

---

* Among the distinguished scholars of the Inquiry who would go on to greater renown were William C. Bullitt, Walter Lippmann, and Samuel Eliot Morison.

of World War II. But the draft board did not recognize York's church, so in he went. Sergeant York overcame his initial doubts about the use of deadly force. He won the Congressional Medal of Honor by saving his platoon from destruction by enemy machine gunners. York's skill with a rifle, honed by twenty years of hunting squirrels and rabbits, was unsurpassed.[118]*

Thousands of American homes received the dreaded telegram from the War Department that fall. One of those homes was Sagamore Hill, on Long Island. There, former president and Mrs. Roosevelt learned that their youngest son, Quentin, had been shot down behind German lines in France. Quentin, always the prankster in the White House, had pursued the Germans in the skies with more zeal than skill. Quentin made "repeated attacks" on seven German aircraft, their press agency reported.[119] The Germans, to their credit, buried the twenty-year-old with full military honors.[120] But somewhere a German got hold of a photograph of the dead Quentin and quickly printed thousands of ghoulish postcards. One of these even made its way back to Sagamore Hill.[121] Shaken, but unbowed, TR compared his son to Colonel Robert Gould Shaw, telling reporters, "Those alone are fit to live who do not fear to die."[122]** With similar bravery, Quentin's mother, Edith Roosevelt, said "You cannot raise your sons to be eagles and expect them to act like sparrows."

The German propagandist who circulated that picture may not have realized what he was doing. Word soon spread in the German trenches. There, soldiers who had taken inhuman punishment for four long years marveled that the sons of an American president could face danger—as they did. They knew only too well that all *six* sons of Kaiser Wilhelm II were in the German army—and all were safely embedded in staff jobs.[123] Now, for the first time in the war, unrest spread through the German ranks.

The red flag of revolution was first raised in the German High Seas Fleet as sailors mutinied.*** The fleet had been in port at Kiel ever since the

---

* As in every American war, hunters often made the critical difference on the battlefield.

** TR was referring to the Colonel Shaw who was killed at Fort Wagner, South Carolina, in 1864 as he led the soldiers of the first all-black regiment in the Union army, the 54th Massachusetts.

*** The red flag represented Communism.

climactic Battle of Jutland in 1916. There, the British Royal Navy had fought a great sea battle of *dreadnoughts.**

Although the British lost more ships and more men at Jutland, the kaiser lost his nerve. His fleet was his pride and joy. Paralyzed by fear, he kept his High Seas Fleet in port for more than two years—far from any action. But sailors idle are sailors primed for trouble.

The German people and their armed forces expected a quick victory after the Bolshevik Revolution in Russia. They had been assured they would win before the Americans could tip the balance in France. But the failure of the German army's "Big Push" in France filled the ranks with despair. Fresh American troops seemed numberless. The Yanks proved themselves again and again during the Meuse-Argonne offensive. When French marshal Ferdinand Foch, the Supreme Allied Commander, broke the Germans' Hindenburg Line on 1 October 1918, even the German High Command knew it was all over.[124]

When the liberal Prince Max, the new German civilian leader, reached out for an armistice, he communicated directly with President Wilson.[125] He wanted a peace based on the Fourteen Points. Without consulting his allies, Wilson responded that the kaiser must be overthrown before an armistice could be arranged.[126] But when the German military and civilian leaders pressed Wilhelm to abdicate, he resisted. "I wouldn't dream of abandoning the throne because of a few hundred Jews and a thousand workers," he told Prince Max.[127] Soon, however, the kaiser was forced into exile. He fled for refuge in Holland.[128]

With rumors of the imminent end of the war flying around the world, Wilson turned to the American people and appealed for their support in the congressional elections of 1918. He asked them to return Democrats to control of Congress. He addressed a message to America's voters asking them to show their backing of "*my* leadership" and to "sustain *me* with undivided minds."[129]

---

* Dreadnoughts (literally, "fear nothing") were huge and heavily armored battleships. Britain's HMS *Dreadnought* was 527 feet long, 82 feet in the beam, weighed 20,730 tons, and mounted 10 twelve-inch guns on five turrets. (Online source: http://www.worldwar1.co.uk/battleship/hms-dreadnought.html.)

Wilson was surely right that the international situation required strong American leadership. He was also right that he needed to show both the Germans and the Allied leaders that he had strong backing among the American people. Still, such self-interested and partisan emphasis was a disastrous misstep on his part. The Republicans had actually supported Wilson's war policies more wholeheartedly than Democrats had.

TR campaigned hard for Republicans in the midterm elections of 1918. "[E]very Republican vote was another nail in the Kaiser's coffin," he said.[130] When the votes were counted, the Democrats lost control of *both* Houses of Congress. Republicans returned 240 members of the House to the Democrats' 190. In the Senate, which was now elected by popular vote and not by state legislatures, the Republicans gained six seats to lead the Democrats by a narrow 49 to 47.[131]

TR had openly opposed Wilson's Fourteen Points. The only satisfactory basis for peace, he said, was the "unconditional surrender" of Germany and "absolute loyalty to France and England in the peace negotiations."[132] Was Roosevelt committing sedition here? The voters of the United States did not seem to think so.

Roosevelt wrote to French Premier Clemenceau and to Britain's foreign minister, Lord Balfour. He reminded these leaders that under a parliamentary system such as theirs, Wilson would have been voted out of office. "He demanded a vote of confidence. The people have voted a want of confidence," TR wrote.[133] Roosevelt was right about this. As a private American citizen, however, TR was guilty of gross impropriety in addressing foreign leaders this way.

TR spoke up for black Americans in uniform. He wanted civil rights for all, he said, as he demanded recognition for "the honors won and the services rendered" by America's black doughboys.[134] Wilson had refused to allow black Americans to fight alongside our white soldiers in France. He detached them from the American Expeditionary Force and put them under direct French command.[135]

Soon, the Germans set up a republic, which then sued for an armistice. Marshal Foch forced the Germans to accept harsh conditions for an end to the fighting. The agreement was signed in Foch's railway car at Compiègne, France.

The war ended at the *eleventh hour of the eleventh day of the eleventh month*—November 1918. Captain Harry S Truman was serving in an artillery battery of the Missouri National Guard. He fired his last round at 10:45 a.m. that day.[136] Finally, after four long years of the worst mass killing in human history, the guns fell silent. An estimated ten million had died in the Great War. Then, at last, it was "all quiet on the Western Front."

That night, Harry complained that the men of the neighboring French artillery battery kept him awake. They had gotten drunk and each one insisted on marching past Harry's bed to salute him and yell, "*Vive President Wilson! Vive le Capitaine d'artillerie américaine!*"[137]

On the German side, Corporal Adolf Hitler received the news in a military hospital; he had been temporarily blinded by poison gas. He cried bitter tears. For his courage under fire, Corporal Hitler was awarded the Iron Cross, First Class. He was recommended for this unusually high honor by Captain Hugo Guttman, a Jew.[138]

In Berlin, Communists attempted to set up a German *soviet* on the model of that in Moscow.* Rosa Luxemburg and Karl Liebknecht led the Red forces there. Viewing these events from the Kremlin in Moscow, Vladimir Lenin was excited.** Germany was "afire" with revolution, he reported.[139] Communists under Bela Kun set up a *soviet* government in Hungary. Soon, however, Luxemburg and Liebknecht were overthrown and killed. Bela Kun's attempt, too, failed.

Hitler, writing later in *Mein Kampf (My Struggle)*, pointed to the involvement of some prominent Jewish Communists in these events. He complained that the bloody repression of the Communists was not nearly bloody enough. He wanted to see poison gas used for "the extermination of that pestilence."[140]

---

* *Soviet* comes from the Russian word that means "to advise." A soviet, therefore, was an advisory council. In practice, the soviets did not give advice, they took it, and only from one source: the Communist Party.

** *Kreml* is the Russian word for "fortress." The Moscow *Kremlin* remains the center of the Russian government to this day.

V. Wilson in Paris

President Wilson rejected the counsel of his chief military adviser, General Pershing. The general pleaded with the president to let the American Expeditionary Force finish the job. "What I dread," the leader of American forces in France said, "is that Germany doesn't know that she was licked. Had they given us another week, we'd have *taught* them."[141]

Now, Wilson was determined to go to France for a great Peace Conference. He would confer with the leaders of the victorious Allies to craft a treaty that would officially end the war. Wilson spurned calls for him to stay home. The president of the United States had never left the country before for an extended period. The Paris Peace Conference promised to last for months. Was it even *constitutional* for the American president to absent himself? Some offered friendly advice. Journalist Frank Cobb was a strong Wilson supporter. From Paris, he wrote, "The moment the President sits at the council table with these Prime Ministers and Foreign Secretaries, he has lost all the power that comes from distance and detachment. Instead of remaining the great arbiter of human freedom, he becomes merely a negotiator dealing with other negotiators."[142] Wilson's secretary of state, Robert Lansing, also urged him not to go.[143] He could let subordinates do the detailed negotiating and take the high ground. No, Wilson objected. He had to go personally to head the American negotiating team.

Before departing aboard the troop ship *George Washington*, Wilson appointed the delegation that would accompany him.* Here he stumbled badly. Stung by the Republicans' furious response to his call for their defeat in the midterm elections, Wilson passed over every leading Republican in selecting peace negotiators. TR, obviously, was out. So, too, was Senator Henry Cabot Lodge, whom Wilson hated.[144] But the president might have chosen former President Taft or his 1916 opponent, Charles Evans Hughes. Both men were moderate Republicans and had supported Wilson's war

* Despite the Yankee Doodle name, the *George Washington* had been built by Germany as a luxury liner before the war. It had been seized by the United States at the outbreak of war and converted to a troop ship. It was to be home to the American peace delegation for the four trips across the Atlantic (*Woodrow Wilson,* Heckscher, August, 497.)

effort. They also strongly backed his call for a League of Nations. Closing the door to this kind of bipartisanship, Wilson said, "I would not dare take Taft."[145] He regarded Taft and his moderate League to Enforce Peace as mere "butters in."[146] Because the country had just given control of Congress to the Republicans, spurning such men was a grievous error.

Wilson instead chose Henry White, an aged diplomat who had Republican ties but no special influence in the party. In addition, Wilson took Secretary of State Robert Lansing, whom he did not trust, and Colonel Edward M. House, whom he did.[147] Edith Bolling Galt Wilson, the president's second wife, joined her husband. She had no official role, but her influence with her husband was great.

Britain's Prime Minister David Lloyd George had gone to the British people in a snap election. He won a huge victory by vowing to squeeze Germany for war reparations "until the pips squeak." Lloyd George said he wanted to "hang the Kaiser." Lloyd George's loyal cabinet ally, Winston Churchill, openly opposed this.[148]

Arriving in France, Wilson was invited to visit the battlefields over which so much blood had been shed. Seeing this as an attempt to manipulate him through emotion, Wilson turned down the invitation.[149] When they heard of this, the nearly one million American doughboys were deeply disappointed.[150]

Now, with the end of military combat on the Western front, came an even more deadly killer—influenza. The great pandemic of 1918–1919 swept across Europe and America and from there, around the world. Between fifty and one hundred million died in a span of mere months. Unlike previous experience with plagues, this so-called Spanish Influenza seemed to carry off the young and the fit. In a recent work on the pandemic, John M. Barry notes that "it killed more people in *twenty-four weeks* than AIDS has killed in twenty-four years, more people in a year than the Black Death of the Middle Ages killed in a century."[151] The disease was especially devastating to soldiers. More than half of U.S. casualties in World War I were attributable to influenza, not German bullets or gas. Barry also maintains that it was influenza, not a stroke, that laid President Wilson low at a critical point in the Paris peace negotiations.[152] Moreover, Barry contends that Wilson's judgment was affected by the disease.[153]

Early in 1919, the American delegation in Paris received stunning news from home. Theodore Roosevelt had died in his sleep at Sagamore Hill. TR had seen it coming. He told his son-in-law Dick Derby, "We have warmed both hands before the fire of life."[154] Roosevelt's son, Archie, cabled to his brothers in uniform around the world: "The old lion is dead."[155] No further explanation was necessary. Following the funeral party to the graveside in the January cold at Oyster Bay was Theodore's great and good friend, the ever forgiving William Howard Taft. Once again, Taft wept for his lost friend.

The nation and much of the world mourned the death of the Rough Rider. The normally frosty New Englander, Senator Henry Cabot Lodge, had been TR's colleague and friend for more than three decades. He was older than TR, and he choked up as he concluded his eulogy to Roosevelt. To Lodge, TR was "Valiant-for-Truth," the admired character in John Bunyan's *Pilgrim's Progress*. When he "passed over, all the trumpets on the other side sounded," Lodge said.[156]

In Paris, Wilson realized that death had taken his most formidable adversary. TR had been Wilson's bitter, too often hateful enemy, but the president charitably (and wisely) issued a public statement praising one of America's most beloved presidents.[157]

"A specter is haunting Europe, the specter of Communism." So begins *The Communist Manifesto* by Karl Marx. Although Marx had been dead thirty years when the victorious Allied leaders met at Paris, the specter of Communism haunted their deliberations. A leading member of the British cabinet pointed to the specter in a speech to his Scottish constituents: "Civilization is being completely extinguished over gigantic areas, while the Bolsheviks hop and caper like troops of ferocious baboons amid the ruins of cities and the corpses of their victims."[158] Winston Churchill's listeners cheered lustily as he denounced the violence and brutality of the new Bolshevik regime in Russia. Like the rest of the civilized world, the Scottish had been horrified by the Bolshevik murder of the tsar and his entire family.*

---

* Russia's deposed Tsar Nicholas II; his wife, Tsarina Alexandra; their hemophiliac teenage son, Alexei; his four older sisters, Maria, Olga, Tatiana, and Anastasia; the Imperial family doctor; and several faithful servants had been ordered into a basement in Ekaterinburg, Siberia. There, in the early hours of 18 July 1918, drunken Red Guards shot, clubbed, and stabbed them to death. Their bodies were dissolved in acid and dumped in a mine shaft.

But Scotsmen booed Churchill just as loudly as they had cheered him when he explained that the threat of Communism was why the statesmen should make a moderate peace with Germany.[159] Few people shared Winston's enthusiasm for intervening in the increasingly bloody civil war in Russia. Churchill wanted to "strangle the baby in the bath." War-weary publics in the democracies had no such vision and no such eagerness to confront the Bolsheviks.

Millions of cheering, weeping Englishmen, Frenchmen, and Italians during Wilson's victory tour of Allied capitals cried out for him. In Paris, he rode in an open car through the Arc de Triomphe. In Rome, the city streets were spread with golden sand, Wilson was hailed as "the God of Peace."[160]

When President Wilson sat down with Britain's Prime Minister Lloyd George and France's premier Georges Clemenceau, the Big Three were soon joined by Italy's Premier Vittorio Orlando. It soon became clear, however, that the Allied leaders did not stand in awe of the American president. These seasoned, wary politicians had come to Paris to claim the fruits of victory.

Lloyd George wanted Britain's share of the German overseas colonies. He wanted no interference with British rule in Ireland and India. He wanted no declarations outlawing the use of blockades during war. In fact, in order to keep the starving Germans under control, the French and the British had demanded a continuation of the blockade *until* Germany accepted a final peace treaty.[161]

France's Georges Clemenceau didn't care about Germany's colonies. He cared only about security for France. And, of course, he demanded the return of Alsace-Lorraine, the border province that Germany had seized at the end of the Franco-Prussian War in 1871. France had lost 1,300,000 men fighting the war Germany had started. All the destruction of French farming and industry must be compensated by German reparations, he insisted. If he could not persuade Allied leaders to break up the German Empire by creating an independent Rhenish state (Rhineland), he wanted at least a demilitarized Rhineland.

Because of her historically low birthrate, France had only one-half the eighteen-year-olds eligible for military service that Germany had every year. In addition, France lacked its neighbor's natural resource base and produced barely one-tenth the steel that Germany produced. France could never be safe unless steps were taken to disarm and *weaken* Germany. Clemenceau, the Tiger of France, had little or no interest in Wilson's idealistic visions. Britain had the twenty-two-mile English Channel for protection. Now that the German fleet was to be handed over to Britain, it was thought that England had little to fear. America had three thousand miles of ocean between her and German revenge. France had only fifty kilometers as a "buffer" in the Rhineland. Clemenceau demanded "the equivalent on land" of the protection Britain and the United States enjoyed at sea.[162]

Italy gained control of the Istrian peninsula, which had belonged to Austria-Hungary. Italy's Orlando also wanted the South Tyrol and the Mediterranean port of Fiume. Italy had not joined the Allies from any sense of Wilsonian idealism. Italy wanted compensation from defeated Austria-Hungary. According to agreements made with Britain during the war, Orlando felt entitled. The Allies agreed to cede the German-speaking South Tyrol* but balked at giving over the port city. (Orlando's failure to get both would lead to his political downfall at home and the rise of Fascism in Italy under Benito Mussolini.)

The Japanese got territorial concessions on the Shantung Peninsula in China. They kept the strategically important German Pacific Islands that they had quickly snatched upon declaring war. (This territorial grab was virtually Japan's only "contribution" to the Allied war effort.)

Japan was unsuccessful in getting the Peace Conference to adopt a resolution on racial equality. They resented the attitude of leading Western powers. When they defeated Russia in 1905, the Japanese expected the world to applaud. "Of course, what is really wrong with us is that we have yellow skins. If our skins were as white as yours, the whole world would rejoice at our calling a halt to Russia's inexorable aggression," said a Japanese diplomat to a European friend.[163]

It was not just the defeated kaiser who had gone on about the "Yellow Peril." The Hearst Press in the United States howled about it daily.[164] Wilson

* This is why fans of the Winter Olympics can see German-speaking skiers with very German names representing Italy to this day.

worried that any treaty the Peace Conference drafted would have to be ratified by a U.S. Senate that contained virulent racists like South Carolina Democrat "Pitchfork" Ben Tillman. Wilson therefore rejected the Japanese resolution.

When Wilson returned to the United States briefly in February 1919, signs were not good at home. Senator Lodge circulated among Republican senators a "Round Robin." It was a document that insisted that the Senate be fully included in treaty making and sternly warned Wilson that changes would have to be made in his League of Nations before the senators who signed would vote to ratify the final peace treaty.[165] Because there were more signers of the Round Robin than were required to defeat a treaty, Wilson was put on notice of the need for compromise with the Senate.* Lodge told the Senate there must be no "meddling or muddling" in every petty quarrel in Europe, that the U.S. Congress must have the ultimate decision-making authority.[166] Seeing this as a partisan attempt to embarrass him, President Wilson's hatred of Henry Cabot Lodge deepened.[167]

The president agreed to meet with Lodge's Foreign Relations Committee and answer questions about the League of Nations. Wilson's supporters thought he did well, but opponents were more determined than ever to block his plans. Republican Senator Brandegee of Connecticut would soon become one of the "Irreconcilables." This was a group of fourteen Republican and four Democratic senators who would oppose the League of Nations under *any* circumstances. Brandegee said of his meeting with the president: "I feel as if I had been wandering with Alice in Wonderland and had tea with the Mad Hatter."[168]

Returning to Paris, President Wilson's mood darkened. When his devoted friend, Colonel House, briefed him on the status of negotiations in his absence, Wilson was shocked. "House has given away everything that I had won before we left Paris."[169] The president began to be influenced by the deep-seated hostility that his wife held for Colonel House. This, and differences about the negotiations, introduced a strain in the president's relationship with his most faithful and selfless subordinate.[170]

* Before the admission of Alaska and Hawaii, there were ninety-six U.S. senators. Treaties required approval by two-thirds of the Senate to be ratified. Thus, thirty-three senators could demand amendments or the treaty would be lost.

Wilson argued against Clemenceau with vigor. At one point, he even ordered the *George Washington* made ready to depart. He was prepared to leave Paris and abandon the Peace Conference. Clemenceau privately sneered at this maneuver as Wilson's "going home to mother," but to Wilson's face he said *he* would go home. He stalked out of the conference, but soon was back.

Clemenceau said he agreed with Wilson that all men are brothers, but they are brothers "like Cain and Abel."[171] He hammered incessantly at the need for security. Even over lunch, he humorously pointed to the chicken elegantly displayed. "Why is the chicken on this plate? Because it did not have the *force* to resist us. And a good thing, too!"[172]

Clemenceau was not the only person put off by Wilson's high-minded vagaries. Australian Prime Minister Billy Hughes spoke of his frustration. He acknowledged the critical role of U.S. forces. That contribution did not entitle President Wilson to be a *deus ex machina* to rescue Europe and dictate peace terms, he said. Australia had lost more men proportionately; the Allies had sacrificed more lives and money. Hughes hoped Britain and France would stand firm and defend their interests. Besides, he said, Wilson really could not even speak for the United States.[173]

Finally, Lloyd George broke the impasse. He persuaded Wilson to give Clemenceau the assurances he sought for French security. In exchange for the Tiger's dropping the French demand for dismembering Germany, Great Britain and the United States agreed to come to France's defense if that country were attacked by Germany.[174] Only with France's safety thus protected would Clemenceau agree to Wilson's proposals for the League of Nations. Clemenceau regarded the Guarantee Treaty as the "crowning glory" of his policy.[175] Former George W. Bush speechwriter David Frum refers to the French Guarantee Treaty as an "earlier form of NATO."

The peacemakers agreed to the creation of an independent Polish state. They carved Czechoslovakia and Yugoslavia and an independent Hungary out of the now dissolved Austro-Hungarian Empire. They banned any union (*Anschluss*) between the small Austrian republic and the larger state of Germany. They forced Germany to turn over the High Seas Fleet to Britain and imposed an undetermined amount of war reparations on Germany. They demanded German disarmament. Most important to many, they inserted into the final treaty a "war guilt" clause that forced the Germans to acknowledge that they had caused the war. The French did not get an independent Rhenish state as a buffer, but the Rhineland was demilitarized and the coal-rich Saar region was stripped from Germany for fifteen years.

Woodrow Wilson's chief goal in coming to Paris was to champion his cherished League of Nations concept. He sincerely believed that many of the concessions he was forced to make to the British and the French on territory, colonies, reparations, and the war guilt of the Germans, were necessary in order to achieve his overarching purpose. The League, he thought, could correct any mistakes made by the hard-pressed negotiators in Paris. Wilson had an almost religious faith in the ability of this new "concert of nations" to operate harmoniously. This may explain his rigid refusal to compromise in any way on issues touching on the League. The Treaty of Versailles may have belonged to George and Clemenceau, but the League of Nations was *his.*

Wilson's vision was sometimes compelling but too often vague. Theodore Roosevelt had believed that his son Quentin and all the brave American soldiers had "saved the soul of the world from German militarism."[176] TR wanted an unconditional surrender of Germany to break the pride and will of the German militarists. He wanted the kaiser and his military clique punished. Roosevelt thought a peace based on Wilson's Fourteen Points—which he derided as "fourteen scraps of paper"[177]—would mean unconditional surrender, but for the United States, not Germany.[178] Surely, this last point was hyperbole. But it is no exaggeration to say that Roosevelt's concept of a league of nations—one that began with Britain and France and that did not threaten the cornerstone of American sovereignty, the Monroe Doctrine[179]—was the more realistic of the two men's postwar visions. But Roosevelt, alas, was dead, and it was the elected President Woodrow Wilson who had the constitutional authority to conduct the Paris negotiations.

In June 1919, the German High Seas Fleet steamed between massed British warships at Scapa Flow, off Scotland. But rather than surrender their magnificent dreadnoughts, German sailors opened the seacocks, set explosive charges, and scuttled their vessels. The kaiser's pride, his magnificent dreadnoughts, sank beneath the waves.[180] The race to build bigger, more powerful battleships had been a leading cause of the First World War. Now, the fleet the British so long feared simply disappeared.

Germans were outraged at the terms of the Treaty of Versailles. They considered them brutally unfair. They pointed out that they had only sought an armistice, they had not offered to surrender unconditionally. The Germans were given no part in the negotiation of the treaty. They were summoned to the great Hall of Mirrors in the historic Palace of Versailles only to sign the treaty. The signing ceremony was held on 28 June 1919. It was, ironically, the fifth anniversary of the assassinations in Sarajevo. The Hall of Mirrors was the very place where Bismarck had announced the creation of the German Empire in 1871. Now, the German delegates even brought their own fountain pens to sign the hated treaty that would end the German Empire.[181] They were unwilling to give the victors any souvenirs.

The leading delegate of the German Republic, Foreign Minister Brockdorff-Rantzau, offered his response:

> We know the power of hatred which we encounter here. . . . It is demanded of us that we shall confess ourselves to be the only ones guilty of the war. . . . Such a confession in my mouth will be a lie . . . the hundreds of thousands of noncombatants who have perished since November 11 by reason of the blockade were killed with cold deliberation after our adversaries had conquered and victory had been assured to them. Think of that when you speak of guilt and punishment.[182]

The Allied leaders were enraged at this German defiance. "The Germans really are stupid people," Wilson said.[183] Britain's foreign minister, Lord Balfour, was normally a placid man. He chimed in: "Beasts they were and beasts they are."[184]

Not all the Allies were so hardened toward the Germans, however. Colonel House confessed to a feeling of sympathy for the German delegates: "It was not unlike what was done in olden times, when the conqueror dragged the conquered in at his chariot wheels."[185]

Wilson had been the one who spoke of "a peace without victory." He had been the one who offered the Germans an armistice based on the Fourteen

Points. It was to satisfy him that the Austrians and the Germans had exiled their ruling families and become republics. They had reason to hope that Wilson would not impose a heavy burden on the starving peoples of these two war-ravaged lands. Germany and Austria-Hungary had already lost three million young men to the kaiser's warmongering.[186] But they didn't count on Wilson's willingness to compromise much for the sake of his precious League.

The harsh Treaty of Versailles was dangerous—to the victors as well as the vanquished. Germany was a great power with a great ability to recover her strength. Nothing could stop that. Winston Churchill understood this. He, too, opposed a vengeful peace with Germany. He said the hatred of the French toward the Germans was "more than human."[187] He wrote in unconcealed admiration of his fallen foe:

> For four years Germany fought and defied the five continents of the world by land, sea and air. The German armies upheld her tottering confederates, intervened in every theater with success, stood everywhere on conquered territory, and inflicted on their enemies more than twice the bloodshed they suffered themselves. To break their strength and science and curb their fury, it was necessary to bring all the greatest nations of mankind into the field against them.[188]

Wilson had become impatient, intolerant of any criticism of the peacemakers' work. This attitude extended even to the more absurd parts of the treaty. When one of his advisers complained that forcing the Germans to pay Allied soldiers' pensions would double the war reparations bill and was illogical, Wilson responded angrily: "Logic! Logic! I don't give a damn for logic! I am going to include pensions."[189]

Secretary Lansing tried to warn the president. "The terms of the treaty appear immeasurably harsh and humiliating, while many of them are incapable of performance," he wrote Wilson.[190] Once again, Wilson stiff-armed his secretary of state. "The treaty," he said, was the work of "the hand of God."[191]

The Germans were not the only ones deeply disappointed with the Treaty of Versailles and the League of Nations Covenant it contained. Some of the bright young scholars whom Colonel House had recruited for the Inquiry quit in disgust. Professor Samuel Eliot Morison was one of these. So were Adolf Berle and William C. Bullitt.[192] England's John Maynard Keynes, the liberal economist, predicted disaster from the treaty. His *Economic Consequences of the Peace* gained a wide audience and prompted much disillusion with the punitive sections on reparations.

VI. "A War to End All Wars"

Woodrow Wilson knew how the American constitutional system worked. He had enjoyed constitution-making ever since his student days at the University of Virginia's Jefferson Society.[193] He had published books on the subject. In *Constitutional Government,* he wrote that with "character, modesty, devotion and insight as well as force" a president "can bring the contending elements of the system together."[194]

Beginning in June 1919 the recently returned president would be called upon to give life to those wise words. When he visited the Senate, he bore the Treaty of Versailles in an elegant leather binding. Senator Lodge courteously offered to carry the treaty into the hearing room. "Not on your life," Wilson said, smiling broadly.[195] Everyone laughed at the president's comment, but it was not the kind of jest that breaks tension. It *increased* the tension.

The tensions between Lodge and the president were long-standing. The previous winter, Wilson had directed the *George Washington* to dock in Boston upon his first return from France. He thus threw down the gauntlet to Lodge about the Treaty of Versailles and the League of Nations in Lodge's home state.

There in Boston, the president spoke of a Paris meeting he had had with some of the scholars of Colonel House's Inquiry. "I told them I had had one of the most delightful revenges that sometimes come to men. All my life, I have heard men speak with a sort of condescension of ideals and of idealists. . . . And I have had this sweet revenge. Speaking with perfect frankness in the name of the people of the United States, I have uttered as the objects of this war great ideals, and nothing but ideals. . . ."[196]

Senator Lodge's goals for American foreign policy were simple. He wanted to win the war and curb Germany's capacity to threaten the peace.[197] Lodge was not an Irreconcilable, but like many of them he strongly supported the French Guarantee Treaty.[198] In this, Lodge shared Clemenceau's hardheaded, practical approach to peacemaking. In favoring the guarantee to France, Lodge spoke for the Republican leadership.

Senator Lodge was pressing for two amendments, or reservations, to the treaty which Wilson had negotiated: he wanted the new League of Nations to formally acknowledge America's preeminence in the Western Hemisphere by recognizing the Monroe Doctrine; and he wanted to make sure that the United States could be sent into a foreign war only if the Congress consented.

Former President Taft congratulated the president on the League of Nations Covenant.[199] He indicated his willingness to work with the president to gain acceptance. But, former Secretary of State Bryan, a leading Democrat, also appealed to the president for compromise.[200]

Wilson told the Democrats the Senate must accept the treaty as it was written. The French ambassador came to the White House to plead with him to accept some revisions to the treaty. The French were very worried about losing their Guarantee Treaty if the Versailles Treaty failed. "Mr. Ambassador," the president replied, "I shall consent to nothing. The Senate must take its medicine."[201]

Lodge demanded a reservation to Article X so that the U.S. Congress, and not a majority vote of the League of Nations in Geneva, would make final decisions on sending American boys to fight in foreign wars. Lodge strongly believed the U.S. Constitution required such congressional authorization.

President Wilson rejected any change to Article X. Revising this article, he said, "cuts the heart out of [the treaty]."[202] Wilson's ideas for the League of Nations represented a sharp break with America's history and traditions. As Henry Kissinger has written, Wilson wanted nothing less than world government and American participation in a global police force.[203] This much the Republicans were not prepared to give him. Republican Herbert Hoover had loyally served Wilson throughout the war. But Hoover thought the Treaty would be better without Article X.[204]

Wilson spurned the offers of help from Taft and such distinguished supporters as Harvard's President Charles W. Eliot.[205] Taft had offered to bring the "mild reservationists" behind the Treaty. Secretary Lansing agreed, saying the president must compromise.[206]

Colonel House told the president if he was as conciliatory with the Senate as he had been with Clemenceau and Lloyd George, the issue could be resolved favorably. "House," the president sternly responded, "I have found that one can never get anything in his life that is worth while without fighting for it." House countered that all civilization had been based on compromises. Wilson dismissed his old friend. He never saw him again.[207]

When the leader of Senate Democrats, Gilbert Hitchcock, pleaded with Wilson for compromise, Wilson told him, "I am an uncompromising partisan."[208] Wilson's unyielding position worried even some of his fellow Democrats in the Senate.[209]

Against the advice of his family and his doctor, the president decided to take his case for the unamended treaty and the League to the American people. He would undertake a lengthy tour of the Western states whose senators—men like California's Hiram Johnson and Idaho's William E. Borah—led the Irreconcilables in determined opposition to the treaty. Wilson planned to deliver scores of speeches on this railroad tour.

Wilson did not use the phrase "a war to end all wars." That unfortunate phrase was Lloyd George's. That was nonetheless the main point of Wilson's case for ratification of the treaty as it was signed in Paris. "All the elements that tended toward disloyalty are against the League, and for a very good reason," he told the people of Ogden, Utah. "If the League is not adopted, we will serve Germany's purpose."[210] He told the people of St. Louis what he would have to say to American servicemen *if* the treaty was rejected:

> You are betrayed. You fought for something that you did not get.
>
> And the glory of the armies and navies of the United States is gone like a dream in the night, and there ensues upon it . . . the nightmare of dread . . . and there will come some time, in the vengeful Providence of God, another war in which not a few hundred thousand men from American will have to die, but as many millions as are necessary to accomplish the final freedom of the peoples of the world.[211]

His opponents were not merely mistaken, they were disloyal, Wilson was saying. They did not simply oppose him, they opposed God. And if his prescription for peace was not followed without even mild reservations, another war would come and *millions* of Americans would die.

Wilson was emotionally overwrought and physically spent when he came to Pueblo, Colorado, three weeks into his speaking tour. There, on 25 September 1919, President Wilson suffered a severe nervous collapse. The remainder of the speaking tour was cancelled as, with drawn shades, the presidential train speeded east toward Washington.[212]

Days later, in the White House, Wilson suffered a massive stroke. His speech and motor skills were seriously impaired. Then, and for many long months afterward, Mrs. Wilson, Dr. Grayson, and the ever-loyal Joseph Tumulty conspired to keep the nature and extent of the president's debilitating illness concealed from a worried, anxious American public.[213] Wilson held no cabinet meetings for the next critical eight months.[214] The vice president of the United States did not meet with him. Mrs. Wilson barred him from the president's sickroom.[215] Mrs. Wilson screened all official documents and limited access to the president to a trusted few. And these few had but minutes to speak to the desperately ill chief executive.[216]

Secretary Lansing, as the senior cabinet member, was rebuked when he suggested the time had come to invoke the Constitution. Lansing wanted the vice president to assume power, at least temporarily, because of the president's disability.* When Wilson learned that the secretary of state had been meeting with the cabinet in an attempt to keep the government functioning, Wilson fired him.[217]

Desperate for American participation in the peace, Britain sent the highly respected Sir Edward Grey to plead with the president to accept some reservations. Both Britain and France were prepared to approve reservations to the treaty if that was the only way U.S. membership in the League could be secured. Mrs. Wilson refused to admit him to the White House.[218]

---

* Lansing was clearly right. Today, the Twenty-fifth Amendment provides for cabinet action to declare presidential incapacity if he stubbornly refuses to step aside.

Lloyd George, Clemenceau, and Wilson. *The victorious Allies, British Prime Minister David Lloyd George, French Premier Georges Clemenceau, and U.S. President Woodrow Wilson. This public show of good fellowship masked often rancorous negotiations behind closed doors.*

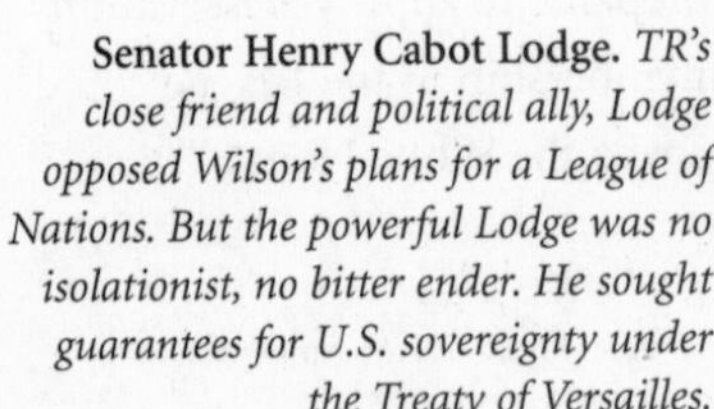

Senator Henry Cabot Lodge. *TR's close friend and political ally, Lodge opposed Wilson's plans for a League of Nations. But the powerful Lodge was no isolationist, no bitter ender. He sought guarantees for U.S. sovereignty under the Treaty of Versailles.*

Warren G. Harding 1921. *Elected by a landslide in 1920, Harding promised Americans a "return to normalcy." To voters, especially first time women voters, he represented an end to the paralysis of the later Wilson years. Privately, however, one important woman—TR's daughter Alice—dismissed him as "not a bad man, just a slob."*

Wilson's illness had not tempered his intransigence. Partially paralyzed, his speech impaired, he nonetheless ordered Democrats in the Senate to vote *against* the treaty. Why? It was no longer his treaty. Lodge had amended it to require Congress's authorization before U.S. troops could be ordered into combat by the League of Nations.[219] Senator Brandegee was happy to see the treaty and the League go down to defeat. "We can *always* depend on Mr. Wilson," he said to Senator Lodge.[220] Even so, the treaty lost by only seven votes.

The Irreconcilables were strong opponents of any form of U.S. participation in the League of Nations. The press of the day called them "bitter enders" and "the battalion of death." Some of their members became determined isolationists in later years, calling for America to shelter herself from all "foreign entanglements" and to avoid Europe's quarrels.

These men were not all blinkered reactionaries. Hiram Johnson, Robert LaFollette, and William E. Borah had been leading progressives. Many of the Irreconcilables strongly favored the French Guarantee Treaty. This, at least, was a limited U.S. commitment. But an isolated and embittered Woodrow Wilson forgot his promises to Lloyd George and Clemenceau. He refused even to submit the French Guarantee Treaty to the Senate.[221]

The world did not stop because the president was stricken. In the United States, there was a great Red Scare in 1919–20. When an anarchist attempted to assassinate Attorney General A. Mitchell Palmer, he blew himself up instead. His shin bone landed on the doorstep of Palmer's next door neighbors, Franklin and Eleanor Roosevelt.[222] Palmer used this and seven other bombings to unleash a nationwide set of raids against Communists, Socialists, and anarchists. Thousands were arrested. Wilson encouraged Palmer. At his first cabinet meeting in nearly a year, he said, "Palmer, don't let this country see red!"[223]

Two very important constitutional amendments were ratified in the waning Wilson years. The country adopted the Eighteenth Amendment to ban the sale of alcoholic beverages. Prohibition would be called a "noble experiment." It would deeply divide the country. Women achieved the goal first proclaimed at the Seneca Falls conference half a century earlier. The

Nineteenth Amendment gave all adult women the vote. America led the world in this important advance.

As the country prepared for the election of 1920, President Wilson was increasingly disconnected from reality. He dismissed his experienced, efficient aide, Joseph Tumulty, and never saw him again. Incapable of serving out a second term, Wilson absurdly expected the Democratic Party to nominate him for an unprecedented *third* term.[224] Democrats instead nominated Governor James M. Cox of Ohio and Wilson's own assistant secretary of the navy, Franklin D. Roosevelt. Wilson agreed to receive the candidates. Reassured that both men were strong supporters of the League of Nations, Wilson looked to the election as a great referendum. He hoped the American people would vindicate his hopes. "The American people will not turn Cox down and elect Harding. A great moral issue is involved," he said defiantly.[225]

The Republicans had lost TR. They had few talented men who could appeal to a broad cross-section of Americans. In a now famous "smoke-filled" room, they nominated Ohio Senator Warren G. Harding and Massachusetts Governor Calvin Coolidge. Harding had been an opponent of the Treaty of Versailles. No one viewed Harding as a leader, but he was an available compromise candidate. He promised voters not "nostrums, but *normalcy*." Americans were sick of the angry partisan warfare in Washington. Harding struck a chord. Coolidge had caught the country's imagination when he put down a police strike in Boston. "There is no right to strike against the public safety by anybody, anywhere, any time," the governor said. Americans agreed.[226]

The Republicans gained an historic victory in 1920. Harding received 16,152,200 popular votes and 404 electoral votes to 9,147,353 popular votes and 127 electoral votes for the Democratic ticket. President Wilson was shattered: "They have disgraced us in the eyes of the world."[227]

So it had come to this. Estranged from the leaders of the opposition and of his own party, his closest advisers, and his friends, Woodrow Wilson now turned on the American people themselves. It was a sad end for the man who wished to "make the world safe for democracy." He retired to a house on S Street in Washington, D.C. There, he spent his last few years occasionally writing short articles and receiving only a few visitors selected by Mrs. Wilson. He told visitors his principles would eventually win out: "I have seen fools resist Providence before."[228]

One of his visitors was Georges Clemenceau. The old Tiger's party had been voted out of office when he failed to obtain the promised French Guarantee Treaty.[229] Even so, Clemenceau was forgiving toward Wilson.

When Wilson died in 1924, Joseph Tumulty had to beg for an invitation to the funeral.[230] Barred from attending, Colonel Edward M. House stood in a cold rain outside Madison Square Garden to listen to the ceremony on a loudspeaker.[231] On Embassy Row in Washington, the German flag was the only one *not* lowered. It was the flag of the Weimar Republic, a free and democratic Germany.

America became a world power in 1898 with the war against Spain. In the following two decades, Americans made major advances toward greater personal freedom. TR carved out an important role for the government in labor-management relations and in regulating industry to provide pure food and drugs. He fought "malefactors of great wealth" and the power of the trusts. He pioneered the government's role as steward of America's precious natural resources. And always, Theodore Roosevelt stressed that America's military strength was the key to protecting America's freedom. Taft continued many of the Roosevelt reforms. Woodrow Wilson's New Freedom expanded possibilities for millions of Americans. In banking and labor legislation, he gained justifiable credit as a reformer.

Americans faced the horror of world war with courage and determination. Its armed forces and financial strength saved the Allies when they were at the point of defeat. They stopped the kaiser from imposing the rule of a haughty military clique on the free peoples of Europe.

No man was more responsible for plunging the world into World War I than Kaiser Wilhelm II. He and his small circle of military accomplices were guilty of the crimes of war. They sought it. They contemptuously regarded century-old treaties as "mere scraps of paper." They deliberately pursued a policy they called *schrechlichheit*—frightfulness. They introduced gas warfare, unrestricted submarine warfare, and aerial bombardment of civilians.

But the German people were not guilty. In his best moments, Woodrow Wilson recognized this. However his paralysis led to paralysis at the heart of the great American republic. Wilson called for a war "to make the world safe for democracy." He had a duty at least to make democracies like France and Britain safe. His failure was as much a failure of character as anything else.

Wilson gave way to Clemenceau and Lloyd George when he should have resisted them. He allowed them to turn an armistice into an unconditional surrender. He allowed them to saddle the defeated Germans with impossibly heavy reparations. But he did not even submit to the Senate the most important commitment he made to Clemenceau—the French Guarantee Treaty.

When the Germans had sought peace in late 1918, they appealed directly to Wilson, not to his allies. He pressed them to get rid of Kaiser Wilhelm II and the Hohenzollern dynasty. They did. He demanded they establish a liberal, democratic republic. They set up the Weimar Republic. They met all his conditions. And still he handed them over to the unmerciful French. Small wonder nearly all German politicians would later describe the Treaty of Versailles as "the stab in the back."

At home, Wilson alienated the Republicans utterly. He could not cooperate with the "bitter enders," those senators who opposed everything he had done. He allowed his personal distaste for the powerful Republican Senator Henry Cabot Lodge to doom any effort at collaboration. Lodge was not a bitter ender. He proposed only "mild reservations" to the Treaty of Versailles. Those mild reservations required Wilson to compromise only on two points—that Congress's consent would be required before committing U.S. troops to foreign wars and that the new League of Nations would respect the Monroe Doctrine, the cornerstone of American foreign policy for a century. This Wilson militantly refused to do.

He refused to compromise with the Mild Reservationists even when his Senate Democratic leader pleaded with him to do so and save the treaty. He refused again when the French and the British interceded, saying they would accept the Treaty of Versailles even with the reservations.

Wilson was the first Ph.D. in the White House. His doctorate was in political science. His specialty was the American constitutional system. Under that Constitution, he had to know, the president is required to accept the "advice and consent" of the Senate in order to ratify any treaty. How much stronger was the case for such cooperation after the ratification of the

Seventeenth Amendment to the Constitution that provided for direct popular election of senators. This long-sought goal of Progressives like Wilson was achieved barely a month after Wilson's own inauguration as president in 1913. Instead, Wilson spurned this people's Senate and publicly accused its majority of aiding the enemy and "betraying" American troops.

Wilson's inflexibility and disdain for others' judgment gained him the hostility of his allies in Paris. (Wilson pedantically declined even to call Britain and France allies. Instead, he said the United States was only an *associated* power.) Britain's Lloyd George and France's Clemenceau clashed with him. Italy's Orlando was so upset he left the Paris Peace conference. The Japanese, deeply offended by the rejection of their racial equality resolution, also withdrew from the conference table.

Wilson defied his Republican opponents at home, deliberately antagonizing Senator Lodge and TR. Wilson knew he could not deal with the bitter-ender opponents who also reveled in the name Irreconcilables, but he also refused to work with the much more moderate Republicans: former President William Howard Taft, the GOP's 1916 nominee Charles Evans Hughes, and TR's former secretary of state, the widely respected Elihu Root. All three of these gentlemen were put off by Wilson's intransigence.

By Wilson's collaboration with the French and British in turning a German appeal for an armistice into an unconditional surrender, the free, liberal and democratic Weimar Republic that Wilson had demanded as a negotiating partner was delegitimized in the eyes of the German people (Hitler would call the signers of the Armistice "the November criminals").

Wilson appealed to the American people for support in November 1918, but when they rejected him, he became increasingly intractable and reclusive. Following his September 1919 stroke, he shut himself up in the White House. His wife and his doctor controlled all access to him. They kept out the vice president of the United States, key cabinet members, and senators. Even important foreign emissaries like Britain's revered Sir Edward Grey were denied entry to the president's office. Wilson became estranged from his most loyal associates, men like Secretary of State Robert Lansing, Colonel House, and even the ever faithful Joe Tumulty.

Rather than yield on any disputed point, the partially paralyzed Wilson watched movie reruns of his triumphal visits to London, Paris, and Rome. The films—which had been made by the Army Signal Corps—were screened on a sheet in the East Room.[232] The flickering images of cheering millions became the embattled leader's reality. The hollow tapping of the suddenly old man's cane as he shuffled down the White House corridor symbolized the once powerful leader's impotence.[233]

Wilson resisted the entreaties of his closest political and personal friends. He summarily rejected the pleas of Senator Gilbert Hitchcock, the Democrats' leader in the U.S. Senate. Hitchcock pleaded in vain for some concession to the mild reservationists. Had Wilson had Lincoln's selfless qualities, or Washington's ability to forgive, he might have been an architect of peace. As it was, no man was more responsible for losing the peace than Woodrow Wilson. That was his tragedy—and ours.

Two

The Boom and the Bust
(1921–1933)

It is no small wonder that Americans who had been so disillusioned by the First World War, who had suffered so much during the Depression, were strongly opposed to involvement in yet another war. The rise of the dictatorships showed clearly that the next war would be more terrible than anything the world had known. That Americans argued and debated about which course to take is not surprising. What is surprising—almost miraculous—is that the critical decisions were made by elected officials whom the people could have stripped of their power simply by voting them out. How American freedom survived these desperate years is the story of this chapter.

I. The Roaring Twenties

When America sent a million soldiers to France in 1918, high idealism was the order of the day. Americans repeated the verse: "Forget us, God, if we forget, / The sacred sword of Lafayette." Lafayette's sword and many other sacred things took a beating in the brutal trench life of barbed wire, poison gas, rats, and incessant artillery bombardment. America lost forty-eight thousand young men in a short, intense period of violent combat. Another fifty thousand soldiers died from the Spanish Influenza epidemic that claimed millions of lives worldwide.

As soon as the armistice ending World War I was signed, however, a different call went up among the troops of the American Expeditionary Force:

We drove the Boche across the Rhine
The Kaiser from his throne
O Lafayette, we've paid the debt.
For Christ's sake, send us home.[1]

The hardened, cynical swagger in that doggerel speaks to the disillusionment millions of Americans felt about our first massive intervention in a foreign war.

The 1920s would regard such jaded sentiments as realism. Unwilling to sacrifice for what President Harding called "nostrums," many Americans, especially the young, believed Uncle Sam had been played for Uncle Sap. No one wanted to be taken for a sucker. Americans jumped in their "Tin Lizzies" and headed out for the open road. Jazz music was just one example of the new freedom that was a far cry from Woodrow Wilson's ideals. The proliferation of hip flasks and "bathtub gin" bespoke the attitude of millions to the new restrictions on the sale and manufacture of alcohol under Prohibition.

A new freedom could be seen in art, music, architecture, and everyday fashion. Women had succeeded in claiming the right to vote. The half-century long crusade of Susan B. Anthony and Elizabeth Cady Stanton finally achieved the suffragettes' goal with the ratification of the Nineteenth Amendment to the Constitution in 1919. These women prevailed by rejecting the tactics of radicals within their movement. Those militant crusaders who paraded outside the White House with "Kaiser Wilson" banners protesting the president's opposition to a federal suffrage amendment had not helped their cause.[2]*

In the Roaring Twenties, however, "flappers" bobbed their hair and wore dresses that came just below the knee—scandalous for the time. This frivolous form of "liberation" would have stunned many of the sober, thoughtful earlier reformers who thought women's votes would mean a

* American radical feminists were mild in comparison to their British sisters. Martin Gilbert writes that Winston Churchill was attacked by a young woman brandishing a dog whip as he accompanied his wife to the train station in 1909. The woman struggled with Churchill and tried to throw him in front of an oncoming train! Fortunately, Clementine, his wife, had no qualms about hitting a woman; she beat the assailant off with her umbrella.

purification of politics. Since the 1830s, Big City political machines had been a raucous caucus, based largely in the saloons. Women's voting and Prohibition were twin reform efforts to end all that. As we shall see, the post-World War I amendments certainly brought change, but change in unanticipated ways. No one captured the spirit of the age better than the irreverent, brassy newspaper columnist H. L. Mencken, who plied his trade at the *American Mercury* and the *Baltimore Sun.* His biting wit and mordant style made him "the god of the undergraduates." After the failure of Wilson's crusade, Americans were ripe for a writer who reveled in the role of intellectual *enfant terrible.*

> Here the general average of intelligence, of knowledge, of competence, of integrity, of self-respect, of honor is so low that any man who knows his trade, does not fear ghosts, has read fifty good books, and practices the common decencies stands out as brilliantly as a wart on a bald head, and is thrown willy-nilly into a meager and exclusive aristocracy. And here, more than anywhere else that I know of or have heard of, the daily panorama of human existence, of private and communal folly—the unending procession of governmental extortions and chicaneries, of commercial brigandages and throat-slittings, of theological buffooneries, of aesthetic ribaldries, of legal swindles and harlotries, of miscellaneous rogueries, villainies, imbecilities, grotesqueries, and extravagances—is so inordinately gross and preposterous, so perfectly brought up to the highest conceivable amperage, so steadily enriched with an almost fabulous daring and originality, that only the man who was born with a petrified diaphragm can fail to laugh himself to sleep every night, and to wake every morning with all the eager, unflagging expectation of a Sunday-school superintendent touring the Paris peep-shows.[3]

Mencken skewered respected institutions with merciless abandon. The country held President Warren Gamaliel Harding in high regard—or had been taught that it ought to. Not Mencken. Just days after Harding's grandiloquent Inaugural Address, Mencken went after the president's

"Gamalielese" with all the sadistic pleasure of a small boy pulling the wings off a butterfly:

> On the question of the logical content of Dr. Harding's harangue of last Friday, I do not presume to have views. . . . But when it comes to the style of the great man's discourse, I can speak with . . . somewhat more competence, for I have earned most of my livelihood for twenty years past by translating the bad English of a multitude of authors into measurably better English. Thus qualified professionally, I rise to pay my small tribute to Dr. Harding. Setting aside a college professor or two and half a dozen dipsomaniacal newspaper reporters, he takes the first place in my Valhalla of literati. That is, he writes the worst English that I have ever encountered. It reminds me of a string of wet sponges; it reminds me of tattered washing on the line; it reminds me of stale bean soup, of college yells, of dogs barking idiotically through endless nights. It is so bad that a sort of grandeur creeps into it. It drags itself out of the dark abysm . . . of pish, and crawls insanely up to the topmost pinnacle of posh. It is rumble and bumble. It is flap and doodle. It is balder and dash.[4]

In this assessment Mencken did not defer to the editors of the *New York Times*. The "Gray Lady" had said the president's style was "excellent." "It *looks* presidential," the *Times* said. "In the President's misty language the great majority [of Americans] see a reflection of their own indeterminate thoughts."[5]

Mencken shot back: "In other words, bosh is the right medicine for boobs."[6] It was not new for a writer to say the president was a jerk. It was somewhat novel for a popular writer to say the people were jerks. But Mencken got rich calling his fellow Americans the great "booboisie."

II. Sunrise at Campobello

The thirty-nine-year old Franklin D. Roosevelt looked forward to his summer vacation at Canada's Campobello Island, just across the U.S. border from Lubec, Maine.* His family had enjoyed the cool ocean breezes and the bracing waters of the Bay of Fundy for many years. In August 1921, however, it would be different. FDR tried to lead his family in a spirited romp after a swim. He was consciously imitating his late cousin Theodore.[7]

Suddenly, the former assistant secretary of the navy found himself stricken, unable to move. FDR had feeling in his arms, although he was temporarily unable to sign his name. (His closest political adviser, Louis Howe, would take over this job.) At the onset of the disease, he lost all feeling in his legs. FDR's wife, Eleanor, and Louis Howe took turns massaging his feet and toes.[8] They even had to insert a catheter and administer enemas so he could eliminate waste. Howe spent weeks calling up and down the East Coast, desperately seeking competent medical advice. Only after Howe wrote to Roosevelt's uncle in New York were capable physicians engaged who could even diagnose FDR's symptoms correctly: he had polio.[9] At the time, there was no known cure. The disease had blighted the lives of thousands. At its worst, polio could leave a person paralyzed from the neck down, condemned to life in an "iron lung," an unwieldy contraption that breathed for the vicitm. It was a devastating report for a vital man in the prime of life.

At least, it could have been devastating.

From the beginning, FDR was determined not to accept the verdict of his strong-willed mother, Sara Delano Roosevelt. Although devoted to his "mummy"—the Roosevelts still used that upper-class British word—FDR would not play the helpless invalid. Sara had cared selflessly for FDR's father when the older Roosevelt was diagnosed with a heart condition. But the old man's active life effectively ended when Sara took charge of his treatment.[10] FDR was having none of that.

He was determined to beat polio. When he returned to New York City in the fall of 1921, Louis Howe took pains to make sure that curious reporters didn't get the full picture of FDR's disability.[11] A smiling, buoyant Roosevelt appeared only momentarily. He had his cigarette in its familiar holder, clasped between his teeth at a jaunty angle.[12] He waved cheerily to

* The title of this section is taken from the popular three-act play written by Dore Schary. The play was first presented by The Theatre Guild on 30 January 1958 (FDR's birthday) at New York City's Cort Theatre.

onlookers. Out of public view, however, he required considerable help to perform even the most mundane tasks—getting dressed, going up stairs, shifting from a bed to a chair.*

Despite this cruel blow, FDR continued to pursue a political career. His ex-boss, Josephus Daniels, visited him in the hospital. FDR turned on his famous charm. Daniels was not to think of him as an invalid, he said. He punched the paunchy former navy secretary in the belly to make his point.[13]

Eleanor needed Franklin to succeed politically in order to continue the independent life she had made for herself. She had decided against a divorce when she discovered Franklin's affair with Lucy Mercer in 1918. In her own right, Eleanor had become a major figure in the Women's Division of the New York State Democratic Party in these first years after women received the vote.[14] Eleanor traveled the state, often in the company of two of her female friends. Journalist Nancy Cook and social worker Marion Dickerman gave solid support to Eleanor. They dismissed the inevitable gossip. Alice Roosevelt Longworth couldn't resist a pointed barb. Teddy's incorrigible daughter and Eleanor's first cousin, Alice, called Eleanor's mannish friends "female impersonators."[15] Even FDR referred to them as "she-males"—of course, only when Eleanor couldn't hear him.[16]

Roosevelt kept up his political contacts, often entertaining politicos at the family home or on board their houseboat. William Green, Samuel Gompers's successor as president of the American Federation of Labor (AFL), was one such guest.[17] Other guests in the mid-1920s were the British member of Parliament, Sir Oswald Mosley, and his wife. At this point, Mosley was a Socialist. He was captivated by FDR's charm. "This magnificent man with his fine head and his massive torso, handsome as a classic Greek," wrote Mosley of his host.[18] He noted that people were already talking of Roosevelt as the next governor of New York and possibly a future president of the United States. Mosley thought FDR had "too much will

* FDR's wheelchair had been crafted for him by a trusted Hyde Park village blacksmith. It was made from a simple kitchen chair and had no arms. Of the thirty-five thousand photos in the FDR Library at Hyde Park, only two show him in his wheelchair. (Alter, Jonathan, *The Defining Moment*, 83.)

and too little intellect."[19] His portrait of Eleanor was etched in acid: "[an] exceptionally ugly woman, all movement and vivacity with an aura of gentle kindness but without even a reflection of [FDR's] attraction."[20]

Mosley would soon find another attraction. In the 1930s, he became the leader of the British Union of Fascists, slavishly devoted to Germany's Adolf Hitler. But that was still in the future. What was remarkable about FDR's hospitality to the Mosleys at the time was they were ardent Socialists. FDR had been a member of the Wilson administration that jailed Socialist Eugene V. Debs for sedition and conducted Palmer Raids during the "Red Scare" of 1919–1920.

Against Eleanor's urgings, FDR invested nearly two-thirds of his savings in a run-down hotel and resort complex in rural Georgia that was soon to become world famous as Warm Springs.[21] Young people in the country were dancing the Charleston and riding around in automobile "rumble seats," but FDR wanted only to walk again. The soothing, sulfurous waters at Warm Springs provided Roosevelt the buoyancy he needed to exercise his withered legs. They lifted his spirits. FDR became the cheerleader-in-chief for hundreds of other polio sufferers who flocked to the resort as word of its therapeutic waters spread. Roosevelt's presence was a magnet. He took a personal interest in the progress of each of his patients. His confidence was contagious.[22]

With the help of Eleanor, Louis Howe, his faithful secretary Missy LeHand, and a host of others, Franklin Roosevelt was able to conceal the full extent of his disability. He never denied having polio, but his carefully constructed persona was a denial of reality. Obviously, polio had changed him. He was no longer tall and slender. The rigorous physical therapy he went through gave him massive strength in his neck, shoulders, and biceps. All this was necessary to compensate for his lifeless lower limbs. In his prime, FDR stood six feet two inches tall and weighed 188 pounds. Even when he had to lean on another's arm for support or grip a podium, he was a large, impressive man.

Prior to his attack, FDR was thought of by many fellow politicians as a shallow, rich young man. To them, he was an ambitious striver eager to capitalize on his famous cousin Teddy's name. After contracting polio, however, FDR had a personal story of triumph over adversity even the most hard-bitten critic had to admire. It's worth noting that FDR had won two political contests before he was afflicted with polio, both for the relatively minor post of New York State senator. He had also lost two important races, one for U.S. senator from New York and the other for vice president of the United States. After his onset of polio, however, FDR never lost an election.[23]

III. A Harlem Renaissance

Marcus Mosiah Garvey came to America from the British West Indies. By 1919, he had organized the Universal Negro Improvement Association (UNIA) and raised a black-green-red tricolor flag of black nationalism. Garvey was proud of his ancestry and liked to boast that he was pure black.[24] Garvey and his followers demanded a strict code of separation from white society. He criticized the National Association for the Advancement of Colored People (NAACP) for seeking the integration of black people into American society with full civil rights.

Garvey founded the Black Star Line, a steamship company, with the avowed purpose of carrying black Americans "back to Africa." Garvey's challenge to the black civil rights establishment made him powerful enemies. W. E. B. DuBois called him "fat, black and ugly."[25] DuBois and the NAACP leadership were deeply concerned that Garvey's separatism would kill the chances for greater acceptance of black Americans in the land of their birth. Garvey replied that "the aristocracy of the blue veins" is over.[26] That was a sly dig at some leaders of the NAACP whose skin was so fair their blue veins could be seen.

Garvey styled himself the president of a pan-African state. He hosted a convention of Negro Peoples of the World that brought twenty-five thousand delegates to New York's Madison Square Garden, and he drew attention to himself by riding in an open carriage in the uniform of a full admiral.[27]

At a time when black Americans faced discrimination in hiring, exclusion from white businesses, and segregation in many forms, Garvey's appeal for black solidarity brought hope and excitement to many. His movement newspaper, *The New Negro,* offered advertisements for black dolls and rejected ads from the makers of hair-straighteners and complexion-lightening cosmetics.[28]

His organization started grocery stores, a restaurant, a publishing house, and other businesses.[29]

In 1922, Garvey made a fatal misstep. He met secretly in Atlanta with the head of the Ku Klux Klan. He had hoped that if he persuaded the white supremacist Klan that his goal was complete separation, then UNIA might escape harassment by the KKK.[30] News of the meeting with a group that regularly terrorized black people soon leaked out. Garvey was discredited, and his opponents successfully appealed to his followers to abandon him.

Garvey's Black Star Line proved to be his greatest vulnerability. He had raised $750,000 from black Americans desperate enough to consider emigration. In 1923, Garvey and three other associates of the steamship line were tried for mail fraud. It was clear that many of Garvey's associates had their hands in the till. The Black Star Line had gone spectacularly bankrupt. Garvey was sincere in his commitment and had not enriched himself at the expense of his followers, but he was tried before Judge Julian Mack (an NAACP member) and found guilty.[31] Garvey warned of riots if he was convicted in 1923. "Hell will be turned loose all over the country," he said. Hell took a holiday. His disheartened followers took the news of his fall with quiet resignation.[32]

The Garvey episode sheds light on the state of American society in the 1920s. Black Americans had migrated north in great numbers during the war. Many looked for work in defense industries. Others sought opportunities in the burgeoning cities. New York's Harlem—named for the Dutch city of Haarlem—had been almost all white in 1900. By 1925, black people were flocking in. It was here that the NAACP established its headquarters and published its important journal, *The Crisis.* Under the leadership of James Weldon Johnson, the NAACP boldly proclaimed its purpose:

> [N]othing more or less than to claim for the Negro common equality under the fundamental law of the United States; to proclaim that democracy stultified itself when it barred men from its benefits solely on the basis of race and color.[33]

Politically, the atmosphere of Harlem gave black Americans freedom to speak, to write, to organize, to march. A photo of an early demonstration there shows young black men, smartly turned out in well-tailored suits and fashionable straw hats, bearing a banner with the famous words of the Declaration of Independence: WE HOLD THESE TRUTHS TO BE SELF EVIDENT . . . THAT ALL MEN ARE CREATED EQUAL. Below these words was a legend that read: IF OF *AFRICAN* DESCENT, TEAR OFF THIS COVER.[34]

Because of their concentration and numbers, black Americans could assert themselves freely, without fear in Harlem. The result was a literary, musical, and social "Renaissance." Johnson admired the new self-confidence of the emerging black middle class. "The Negro's situation in Harlem is without precedent in all his history in New York. Never before has he been so securely anchored, never before has he owned the land, never before has he been so well established in community life."[35]

Young New Yorkers, including white members of the so-called Smart Set, delighted in Harlem's cultural attractions. Jazz music and the blues—thoroughly unique and vital contributions of black Americans to the wider culture—thrilled these sophisticates. In 1922, Edward Kennedy "Duke" Ellington began a five-year run at Harlem's Cotton Club. There, as the bandleader, he played to all-white audiences. Soon, he composed such jazz classics as "Take the A Train," "Mood Indigo," "Sophisticated Lady," and "I Got It Bad and That Ain't Good."[36] The "A" Train, as savvy New Yorkers knew, was the subway line that led from midtown Manhattan to Harlem.

Zora Neale Hurston came from a poor Alabama sharecropper's family to graduate from Columbia University's Barnard College in 1928. She became an internationally respected writer, notably for the novel *Their Eyes Were Watching God*, and concentrated especially on black folklore from her native South. She was fully aware of injustice, but she looked steadfastly to the future. "No, I don't weep at the world," she said, "I am too busy sharpening my oyster knife."[37]

"I don't study the black man," said poet Langston Hughes, "I feel him."[38] Hughes faced the challenges that came inevitably to black writers seeking to carve out literary careers in the years of the Harlem Renaissance. "After all the deceptions and disappointments, there was always the undertow of black music with its rhythms that never betray you, its strength like the beat of the human heart."[39] In this way, the freedom of black music reinforced the yearning for freedom of black writers. And they, in turn, gave poetic expression to the soul of their community.

No small part of Harlem's attraction was the more relaxed enforcement of Prohibition laws north of 125th Street. "Speakeasy" was the name given to after-hours clubs where society "swells" could go if they were "sent by Joe."

To many black Southerners, the life and lure of Harlem beckoned like the North Star. To reach it, some poor sharecroppers fled their fields under cover of darkness. At some railroad stations, black farm workers were met by gangs of young white thugs who forcibly turned them back to their fields.[40] To check this terror, James Weldon Johnson persuaded a Republican congressman from Missouri, L. C. Dyer, to introduce the nation's first federal anti-lynching law. The Dyer bill passed the House of Representatives, but it was defeated when white Southern Democrats filibustered it to death in the Senate.[41]

In Washington, D.C., Commerce Secretary Herbert Hoover signed an order banning racial segregation in his department. Hoover's action placed pressure on other federal government agencies to overturn the Wilson administration's unfair policies on equal employment opportunity in the nation's capital.[42] Soon, Washington would become another Mecca for black Americans seeking work and dignity.

IV. Normalcy

When Warren G. Harding promised Americans "normalcy," they knew what he meant. Americans had been exhausted by years of tumult, years of reform at home and war abroad. With Harding, people expected a breathing spell. Harding named Charles Evans Hughes, the Republicans' 1916 presidential candidate, as his secretary of state. He chose Andrew Mellon, the great Pittsburgh financier, as his secretary of the treasury. Herbert Hoover's reputation as a humanitarian could not have been higher. Hoover made his name spearheading Belgian Relief when that unfortunate country was overrun by the Hun—Wilhelm's ruthless army—in 1914. After the war, Hoover led a great campaign to provide famine relief to dying Russians when the Kremlin's Communist policies led to massive starvation. Hoover was named secretary of commerce.

In a further and almost explicit bid for "normalcy," Harding brought back another reassuring Republican figure when he tapped the respected former President William Howard Taft to be chief justice of the United States—the only post Taft had really wanted. His appointment eased many troubled nerves. Taft was the only American to serve under both titles of president and chief justice of the Supreme Court.

Harding fell in with the "Ohio Gang" of cronies from the Buckeye State. Harry M. Daugherty became U.S. attorney general. Campaign manager Will Hays was postmaster general. Jess Smith became a key aide to Daugherty, and Charles R. Forbes was named to head the important Veterans Bureau.[43]

Harding encouraged Secretary of State Hughes to press for a major international disarmament conference in 1921. When delegates gathered in Washington, D.C., Hughes's bold opening announcement stunned the world. Hughes said that the United States was willing to scrap new naval construction on which the country had already spent $300 million.[44] Partially constructed warships would simply be put in "mothballs."

The Washington Treaties that were quickly negotiated outlawed the use of poison gas in war. They also ruled "piratical" submarine warfare against merchant ships, whether the ships were armed or not.[45] The most important feature of the treaties was the ratio of 5:5:3:1:1 for naval battleship and aircraft carrier construction. The United States and Britain would have the highest tonnage allowed; Japan would be allowed 60 percent of their totals; France and Italy were limited to one-fifth of the U.S.-British ratio.

Naval limitation was widely popular because the naval arms race between Britain and Germany was widely thought to have led to World War I. Still, the 5:5:3:1:1 ratio the treaties imposed was to have dire consequences when the United States was later in danger in the Western Pacific.[46] Theodore Roosevelt would have been appalled, but few Americans objected at the time. After years of sterile conflicts between the White House and Congress, the new Republican administration seemed to be working smoothly to bring an era of international peace.

Harding was a forgiving man. He quickly moved to pardon Eugene

Debs, whom Wilson had imprisoned for violating the Sedition Act. The president even hurried up the signing of Debs's pardon so he could be released from jail in time to spend Christmas with his family.[47] Even Democrat FDR was impressed by Harding's magnanimity.[48]

Harding might have fared better had he left the entire government in the hands of his abler cabinet members—Hughes, Mellon, and Hoover. He recognized his own limitations: "I can't make a damn thing out of this tax problem," he once said. "I listen to one side and they seem right, and then . . . I talk to the other side and they seem just as right. I know somewhere there is a book that will give me the truth, but hell, I couldn't read the book. . . . God, what a job!"[49]

But not everyone around him was able and trustworthy. When Senator Thomas J. Walsh, a Montana Democrat, relentlessly pursued the source of a $100,000 unsecured loan to Harding's interior secretary, he unearthed a great scandal. Albert Bacon Fall had been a U.S. senator from New Mexico, but he received no "senatorial courtesy" from his former colleague. Walsh smelled a rat. Secretary Fall had allowed the great oil reserves at Teapot Dome, Wyoming, to go to private interests in a non-bid contract. Soon, Fall was tried for corruption, convicted, and packed off to prison—the first cabinet member in history to be so disgraced.[50]

It wasn't the only impropriety. When Alice Roosevelt Longworth wandered upstairs at the White House—her former home—she came upon a recently vacated poker table. It was littered with cigar stubs and half-full whiskey glasses. Poker and tobacco were one thing, but the nation was under Prohibition. She didn't bump into Harding's young mistress, but she might have.[51]

Harding became more troubled, more harried with each passing day. He seemed to sense that his friends were not leveling with him, and he fretted about the consequences of public disclosure of some of their shady dealings. He knew he could not disentangle himself from his questionable friends. They knew too much about him. As Harding himself once confessed in a speech, his father had told him: "It's a good thing you weren't born a girl. You'd be in a family way all the time. You can't say 'no.' "[52]

He had regularly sought refuge from the White House in Jess Smith's

Washington home. He went there to drink, play poker, and escape from his mounting troubles.[53]

When Jess Smith committed suicide, the president learned that "Colonel" Forbes had been taking kickbacks on the construction of Veterans Hospitals.[54] Then, Forbes's legal adviser too committed suicide, and the stench of corruption rose over the Harding White House. In a White House meeting with Kansas editor William Allen White, Harding burst out: "I can take care of my enemies all right. But my damn friends, my G—d—— friends, White, they're the ones that keep me walking the floor nights!"[55]

The president then did what so many embattled presidents before and since have done: he took a long trip west. His escape route even took him north to Alaska. But he couldn't outrun his troubles. They caught up with him on his return swing, when he collapsed and died 2 August 1923. The country knew little of what Washington insiders had begun to suspect, so Harding was deeply and sincerely mourned. "Harding was not a bad man," said Alice Roosevelt Longworth. "He was just a slob."[56] That has been history's verdict, too.

The new president who was sworn in at 2:45 a.m. on 3 August 1923 could not have presented a stronger contrast with the man he succeeded. When word of Harding's death reached him, Calvin Coolidge was visiting his boyhood home in rural Plymouth Notch, Vermont. He took the presidential oath by the light of a kerosene lamp. His father, a local justice of the peace, swore him in.[57] It was an image of flinty integrity that Americans would cling to—and soon.

The country smiled when it heard how Calvin Jr. got word that his father had become president. The teenager reported for work at a Western Massachusetts tobacco farm where he had a summer job. The farmer told him that his father had been inaugurated in the dead of night. The boy took the report without comment, then asked, "Which shed do you want me to work today?" Amazed, the farmer said that if his father had been named president of the United States, he surely wouldn't be working twelve-hour days in a tobacco field. "You would if your father were *my* father," responded young Calvin.[58] A chip off the old block!

President Coolidge was famously reticent. His nickname, "Silent Cal," endeared him to millions. Americans delighted in stories of their new chief executive. When a young debutante approached Coolidge, one story had it, she gushed that she'd bet her friends she could get him to say more than two words. "You lose," Coolidge is reported to have replied. TR's daughter, Alice Roosevelt Longworth, typically, was less impressed. She said Coolidge looked as if he had been "weaned on a pickle."[59]

As the roof fell in on the Harding scandals, the new president moved adroitly to distance himself from them. When Attorney General Daugherty balked at providing Congress with documents for an inquiry, Coolidge might have invoked executive privilege to shield him. Instead, he sacked the tarnished Harding appointee.[60]

Prohibition was placing a great stress on law enforcement in the country. When it was passed during the war, it had seemed a great reform, and patriotic to boot. After all, many of the breweries had distinctively *German* names, among them Anheuser Busch, Piels, and Pabst.[61] But by the time Coolidge assumed leadership, Prohibition agents had grown overtly corrupt. In New York City, these agents were arriving for work in chauffeured limousines.[62] The chief of the unit resolved to clean house. He called a meeting of all his agents. Gathering them around the table in the federal building, Dan Chapin instructed them all to put their hands on the table. "Every son of a bitch wearing a diamond ring is fired!" he said.[63]

Fear of "the foreign element" spread as rum-running increased. Urban warfare broke out among gangs involved in selling bootleg whiskey; many of the members of these gangs were immigrants.

Legislation by the Republican Congresses in the 1920s sharply restricted the number of immigrants. The main part of the law was to restrict southern and eastern Europeans; the Asian restrictions were a secondary part of the law. The bill did not ban African immigration though it did impose strict quotas. The first law was passed in 1921, limiting overall immigration and creating quotas of 3 percent of each foreign-born group present based on the 1910 Census. In 1924, the immigration cap was lowered, the quotas were dropped to 2 percent, and the 1890 Census was used. This severely restricted southern and eastern Europeans. The national origins provision did not come into effect until 1929. This provision set out to determine the national origins of the entire American nation and set quotas based on that information. Ironically, the law favored immigration from our recent foe—Germany—because so many German-Americans were already in the country.

The anti-immigrant spirit was fueled by advocates of *eugenics*. Charles Darwin's cousin, Francis Galton, had developed the concept in 1883 that meant, literally, "good genes."[64] Eugenicists believed that physical and mental health came from having good genes. They sought to encourage people with good genes to have more children and discourage people with "inferior" genes from becoming parents.[65]

American William Z. Ripley, a respected economist, had published a book, *The Races of Europe*, in which he divided whites into three groups—Nordics, Mediterraneans, and Alpines. His work helped fuel anti-immigrant feeling.*

Margaret Sanger, a public health nurse who challenged laws against distributing birth control information, embraced eugenics. Sanger founded Planned Parenthood, ostensibly to encourage poor immigrants and other Americans to limit the number of children they bore. "As an advocate of birth control," she said, "I wish . . . to point out that the unbalance between the birth rate of the 'unfit' and the 'fit,' admittedly the greatest menace to civilization, can never be rectified by the inauguration of a cradle competition between these two classes. . . ."[66] She also spoke out in favor of immigration restrictions. Slowing the incoming tide of "unfits" was good policy as far as she was concerned; she did not want to pollute "the stamina of the race."[67] Soon, she would advocate a national plan to "give dysgenic groups [people alleged to have bad genes] in our population a choice of segregation or sterilization."[68]

In the twenties, Americans had a love affair with the automobile. Henry Ford made Detroit into the hub of the nation's auto industry. He introduced advanced techniques of assembly line production.[69] Although

* German scientists in the 1920s and 1930s would go beyond Ripley's work with lethal consequences for all of Europe.

Ford employees were not permitted to sit, to talk, or even to whistle while they worked, they could earn as much as $5 a day—considered a very good wage in 1924.* Ford himself became fabulously wealthy. He was probably worth $10 billion in 2004 dollars.[70]

In many ways, Henry Ford was an enlightened entrepreneur. By 1926, he had ten thousand black Americans in his work force. In the Ford Motor Corporation, black employees could rise into management.[71] Ford also opened his plant doors to workers with disabilities. His assembly line methods enabled blind men, amputees, and others to perform a single, important task. In this, he affirmed the human dignity of thousands.[72]

But Henry Ford had a dark side; his tolerance did not extend to the Jewish community in particular. His newspaper, the *Dearborn Independent*, regularly published violently anti-Semitic articles. So offensive were his attacks on the Jews that President Harding and fellow industrialist Thomas Edison had begged him to knock it off. The *Independent* reprinted the notorious invention of the tsarist secret police called *The Protocols of the Elders of Zion.* This work, long exposed as a forgery, charged there was an international conspiracy of powerful Jews to rule the world. "The International Jew: the World's Problem" was the lead article in the *Independent* that echoed the themes of the discredited *Protocols.*[73]

In 1922, a foreign correspondent for the *New York Times* visited the Munich headquarters of a new political faction, the National Socialist German Workers Party. Soon, they would be known by the German abbreviation for National Socialists—*Nazis.* The leader of the party was called *der Führer.* A decorated veteran of the Great War, young Adolf Hitler had a large portrait of Henry Ford in his office. Outside, there was a table stacked high with German translations of Ford's book *The International Jew.*[74]

Hitler expressed his admiration for another influential American, Leon Whitney. Whitney was the president of the American Eugenics

* "Whistle While You Work" was a catchy tune sung by Snow White's friends, the seven dwarfs, in the 1937 Walt Disney animated classic. Could Disney have been satirizing Ford's "no whistle" policy?

Society. The führer requested a copy of *The Passing of the Great Race*, written by a leading member of the American Eugenics Society, Madison Grant. Hitler lavished praise on the book, calling it his "Bible."[75]

V. "Keep Cool with Coolidge"

The country was shocked in 1924 by the Chicago trial of Richard Loeb and Nathan Leopold for the murder of fourteen-year-old Bobby Franks. Loeb and Leopold were teenagers, both from very wealthy families, both extremely well educated.[76] Loeb was the son of a Sears Roebuck executive and the youngest graduate of the University of Michigan. There, he had become absorbed in reading Friedrich Nietzsche's *Beyond Good and Evil.* Nietzsche argued that conventional moral codes could not apply to the "superman."[77] Leopold was attracted to Loeb and desperately sought his approval.

Loeb wanted to commit the perfect crime. The boys lured young Bobby Franks into their car, where Loeb killed him with a chisel. The boy's naked body was soon found in a culvert. The families retained the best criminal lawyer in the country, Clarence Darrow. Since evidence of the teens' guilt was overwhelming, Darrow decided to make an impassioned appeal to spare the killers' lives. Darrow recruited the best psychiatrists to testify to the nature of psychological compulsion. The prosecution derided these experts as "three wise men from the East."[78]

Darrow's closing arguments came in a hot Chicago courtroom in August 1924. He explored a world of overwhelming sexual and psychological urges. He argued for a "deterministic" view of the universe. "Nature is strong and she is pitiless."[79] Nature works in mysterious ways over which we have little control, he contended. He made a case for life imprisonment as being even harsher punishment than hanging—"In all the endless road you tread, there's nothing but the night."[80] In pleading for the lives of the two killers, Darrow passionately cried out: "If the state in which I live is not kinder, more humane, and more considerate than the mad act of these two boys, I am sorry I have lived so long!"[81] Many in the courtroom, including the presiding judge, wept openly as Darrow finished his appeal. The novel tactic worked well enough to save the pair from execution. Leopold and Loeb were sentenced to ninety-nine years in prison.[82]*

By the time the election year of 1924 arrived, few Americans tied President Coolidge to the record of Warren G. Harding. Coolidge's own honesty was beyond question. The country was enjoying peace abroad and unprecedented prosperity at home. Or at least it appeared to be. Already, there were warning signs in the farm belt as commodity prices slid. Most Americans, however, were happily experiencing boom times. Not only did Commerce Secretary Hoover and Treasury Secretary Mellon inspire confidence, the financial community looked to men like Benjamin Strong to steer the nation's economy on a safe and steady course.

Governor Strong was not the elected head of one of the forty-eight states. He was instead the governor of the Federal Reserve Bank of New York, the nation's leading banking institution. Governor Strong was respected worldwide. He had led a team to Europe to scale back German war reparations on the very sensible belief (it was actually an embarrassingly obvious observation) that if Germany were squeezed "till the pips squeak"—as Britain's Lloyd George had once demanded—she would not be able to rebuild.[83] An economically broken Germany would be bad for world trade. And that would be bad for the victorious Allies. Strong understood this.

When the Democrats met to select a presidential nominee, they faced a hard task and they knew it. They were split between "Wets" and "Drys." The Wets wanted to repeal Prohibition, and the Drys were equally determined to keep the legal cork jammed in the booze bottle. The national ban on alcohol was strongly supported in many southern and western states—where the Democratic Party had been strong since Andrew Jackson's time. Prohibition represented a genuine reform for millions of American women. For the wives of working men, a husband squandering his pay envelope in the local saloon represented a personal as well as family financial disaster.[84] These determined women now had the vote and could punish politicians who defied them.

---

* Richard Loeb was killed in 1936 by another inmate who claimed Loeb had made a sexual advance toward him. Nathan Leopold learned twenty-seven foreign languages, served as an X-ray technician in the prison hospital, and reorganized the prison library. Released in 1958, he moved to Puerto Rico and married. He wrote *The Birds of Puerto Rico.* He died in 1971 at age sixty-seven.

The leader of the Drys was William Gibbs MacAdoo. MacAdoo had served ably as Woodrow Wilson's treasury secretary and was eager to claim the populist mantle of William Jennings Bryan. He had also married President Wilson's daughter. So committed was MacAdoo to the Dry cause that he even apologized to supporters for once having eaten a piece of cake that had been soaked in sherry.[85]

MacAdoo might have sailed to the nomination had it not been revealed that he had been on retainer as a lawyer to Edward L. Doheny. Doheny was a central figure in the Teapot Dome affair, the man who had floated that unsecured $100,000 "loan" to the fallen Albert Bacon Fall in the Harding years. Though MacAdoo was personally blameless, this fact tied him in the voters' minds to the Harding scandals.[86]

Arriving in New York City for the 1924 Democratic National Convention, MacAdoo challenged the "sinister, unscrupulous, invisible government which has its seat in [this] citadel of privilege and finance. . . ."[87] It proved a poor choice of words. To many, they were a distinct echo of Henry Ford's *Dearborn Independent* in its paranoia about the Jews.

Opposing MacAdoo for the nomination was New York Governor Alfred Emanuel Smith. Al Smith's career had attracted statewide attention in 1911 when he cochaired a commission to investigate the horrible Triangle Shirtwaist Factory Fire in Manhattan. Scores of young women had been trapped on the upper floors by an inferno. Firemen were unable reach them because the doors were barred to prevent theft. New Yorkers were shocked by stories of the young women throwing themselves out of the building's windows to escape the flames. In Albany, Assemblyman Smith sponsored many reforms to provide for worker safety.[88] Soon, he was elected governor of the Empire State. When reporters quizzed him about his views on Prohibition, the clever Smith smiled and asked them: "Wouldn't you like to have your foot on the rail and blow the foam off some suds?"[89]*

There was at least one "sinister, unscrupulous, invisible government" that MacAdoo was not willing publicly to oppose: the "invisible empire" of

* Dr. Joseph Walsh, the author's grandfather, according to Bennett family lore, was Al Smith's personal physician. In any case, the governor must have been a treat to treat.

the Ku Klux Klan. Al Smith's position on the Klan could not be clearer. As a Roman Catholic, he defied the Klan. And as governor of New York, he signed legislation that virtually outlawed the KKK.

When the Democrats met in Madison Square Garden, the party was called upon to approve a Platform plank sharply condemning the Klan. Al Smith and many other Big City Democrats were determined to make an issue of it. So was Senator Oscar W. Underwood from Alabama. Underwood's candidacy for president faced two great obstacles: he was outspokenly Wet and courageously anti-KKK.*

The Convention was thrown into an uproar by the debate over the anti-Klan resolution. "Up, get up you Kleagles," anti-Klan delegates yelled at MacAdoo's supporters.** Fistfights broke out among delegates.[90] William Jennings Bryan rose to offer a watered-down resolution that condemned *violence* but carefully avoided naming the Klan.[91] In the final vote, the anti-Klan plank was defeated by one vote—543 to 542.[92] Standing on a chair in the Kentucky delegation and watching the anti-Klan resolution go down to defeat was D. W. Griffith, the producer of *The Birth of a Nation,* a film that glorified the KKK.[93] That film had been used very successfully by the Klan to recruit new members.[94]

The Democratic National Convention of 1924 met in the stifling heat of a New York summer. Tempers flared and delegates fainted in the rank air of Madison Square Garden. Then came the dramatic moment when Governor Smith's name was to be placed in nomination.

Smith had chosen Franklin Delano Roosevelt to nominate him. FDR planned this appearance as his "debut" following his polio attack. He had rehearsed and rehearsed the fifteen feet he would have to walk to the speaker's podium. Leaning on the arm of his teenage son Jimmy, FDR did not *seem* to be seeking support as giving it. He threw his head back in animated conversation, laughing heartily at some private joke. Only those very close could see the sweat pouring from his brow from his exertion and note the iron grip with which he grasped the podium.[95]

---

* John F. Kennedy saluted Underwood's valiant stand against the Klan in his 1956 best seller, *Profiles in Courage.*

** A *Kleagle* is the title of a leader in the KKK organization.

It was an incredible performance. He delivered his speech in a rich, confident tone of voice, his Harvard-inflected speech marking a strong contrast with the "Sidewalks of New York" accent of the man he was nominating. But FDR's timely support for the man he called "the happy warrior" created a bond between the patrician, Episcopalian Roosevelt and grateful Irish Catholics.[96] Thereafter, Roosevelt's personal telephone list contained the names of so many Irish pols it was said to look like "the Dublin telephone directory."[97]

The convention had been ugly, bitter, and contentious. FDR's speech was the high note in a proceeding that dragged on mercilessly for ten days. The Democrats battled for a record number of ballots before the two top contenders—Smith and MacAdoo—knocked each other out. John W. Davis, a Wall Street lawyer from West Virginia, was the compromise candidate whom exhausted delegates finally nominated on the 103rd ballot.[98]

Meanwhile in those steaming June days, at the White House, the life of sixteen-year-old Calvin Coolidge Jr. ebbed away due to a simple blister that had become infected. For a brief moment, the feuding delegates ceased their fighting to pray for the dying boy and to send a message of sympathy to the lad's heartbroken father.[99] Later, Coolidge would write about his son's death in his autobiography. With this grievous loss, Silent Cal became more silent still:

> In his suffering he asked me to make him well. I could not. When he went, the power and glory of the presidency went with him. . . . The ways of Providence are often beyond our understanding. It seemed to me that the world had need of the work that it was probable he could do. I do not know why such a price was exacted for occupying the White House.[100]

Republicans said the election was about "Coolidge or Chaos."[101] The Democrats' 1924 gathering marked the first time an American political convention had been broadcast on radio, and to many listeners the bickering and static-crackled clamor must have seemed like the antics of the popular *Katzenjammer Kids* cartoon strip.* *Katzenjammer* is German for

---

* *The Katzenjammer Kids* strip was carried by the Hearst press. Hans and Fritz were two out-of-control little hellions. Americans loved the strip and read it faithfully, even in the hysterical anti-German days of "liberty cabbage."

hangover. After the 1924 convention, both the Wets and the Drys suffered from it. Compromise candidate Davis was willing to denounce the KKK by name, despite the party's reluctance. But otherwise, he was a lackluster contender for the presidency.

Senator Robert M. LaFollette was determined to give voters a real choice in November. He took up the Progressive Party banner and mounted a vigorous campaign. Both Davis and LaFollette attacked Coolidge's tax-cutting policies as a sop to the rich. Humorist Will Rogers referred to the theory that cutting taxes for higher earners and businesses was a "trickle down" policy, a term that has stuck over the years.[102]

Republicans suffered no hangover at all from the Harding binge. Even so, they quietly shelved plans for a grand Ohio monument to the dearly departed president. Coolidge scored a nationwide victory, losing only the states of the Old Confederacy, Oklahoma, and LaFollette's Wisconsin. The president won 15,725,016 popular votes (54.1 percent) and 382 electoral votes. Davis won 8,386,503 popular votes (28.8 percent) and 136 electoral votes. LaFollette won 4,822,856 popular votes (16.6 percent) and 13 electoral votes from his home state.

The election wasn't the only contest that captured national attention then.

The state legislature of Tennessee pondered the often-frightening world conjured up by such events as the Leopold and Loeb trial. The lawmakers saw in the atheistic philosophies of such intellectuals as Charles Darwin, Friedrich Nietzsche, and Sigmund Freud cause for alarm. Nietzsche's statement that "God is dead" was widely quoted and mostly misunderstood. Actually, Nietzsche meant that people's *belief* in God had died. Shocked by such ideas, fearful Tennessee lawmakers found themselves agreeing with Russian writer Fyodor Dostoevsky, whose Ivan Karamazov said if God is dead, then everything is permitted. The lawmakers shouldered the task of making sure that not everything was permitted in Tennessee. The solution was simple and direct. They passed a law banning the teaching of Darwinism or any creed that held that man was descended from a "lower" life form.

A new group called the American Civil Liberties Union (ACLU) saw in this law an excellent opportunity to score ideological points against what they regarded as intellectually backward Christian fundamentalism. The ACLU took out ads in various newspapers and young John T. Scopes responded. The Dayton, Tennessee, science teacher indicated his willingness to test the law. In 1925, he was charged with breaking the new law, and the summer Scopes trial gripped the attention of the entire country. The famous Clarence Darrow guaranteed national focus for the case when he took up the defense.

William Jennings Bryan was eager to serve with the prosecution. Bryan was not a Tennessean, he had never made his living practicing law, and he had no knowledge of the scientific arguments likely to be at the core of the trial. But Bryan earned a good living lecturing and writing articles. Besides, the former secretary of state and the Democratic Party's three-time nominee for president of the United States loved the spotlight.[103]

Bryan succeeded in one important trial maneuver. He gained a favorable ruling from the judge that if Darrow brought in scientific experts to testify in defense of Scopes, these experts would be subject to cross-examination.[104] The ACLU's cocounsel, Arthur Garfield Hays, was distressed. "Cross examination would have shown that the scientists, while religious men—for we chose only that kind—still did not believe in the virgin birth [of Jesus] and other miracles."[105] Hays knew that the testimony of such skeptics would undermine the ACLU's broader agenda for American education.[106] Hays later wrote that the ACLU *needed* the backing of millions of Christians who believed in the basic doctrinal positions of their churches.[107] He did not want the radicalism of the ACLU to be publicly exposed by placing doubting scientists on the witness stand.[108]

Reacting to this victory for the prosecution, H.L. Mencken sneered, "All that remains of the great cause of the State of Tennessee against the infidel Scopes is the final business of bumping off the defendant."[109] Mencken was just one of hundreds of journalists who had descended on the little town of Dayton for what the press called "the monkey trial." Mencken couldn't pass up the chance to laugh at what he saw as a typical example of Southern backwardness. The South, he had written, was the "Sahara of the Bozart" (Beaux Arts).[110]*

Darrow struck next. He called to the stand "the greatest Bible expert in the world"—William Jennings Bryan![111] Poor Bryan was soon shown to be ill-equipped for the intellectual parry-and-thrust that was the experienced Darrow's courtroom stock-in-trade. And Darrow was the best in the country. Quickly tied in knots of self-contradiction, Bryan pounded his fist and pathetically cried out: "I am simply trying to protect the word of God against the greatest atheist or agnostic in the United States!"[112] The courtroom crowd wildly applauded this statement, but it was in fact an admission of defeat.[113]

When the jury found John T. Scopes guilty of having violated Tennessee's law, the judge prudently levied a fine of only $100. Bryan, unwisely again, took the verdict as a vindication and announced plans to carry the cause to other states. His wife, Mary, expressed her doubts. She did not want to see him lead an effort that would be seen as an assault on intellectual freedom.[114] Within days of the trial's end, however, the Great Commoner died in his sleep. Mencken gloated that "God aimed at Darrow and hit Bryan!"[115]

The trial came to be seen as a watershed moment in American life. An entire mythology grew up around it. The Broadway play (later a film) *Inherit the Wind* helped spread the misconceptions. Joseph Wood Krutch, a careful journalist and later a distinguished literary critic, helped to untangle the story. "The little town of Dayton behaved on the whole quite well," he wrote. "The atmosphere was so far from being sinister that it suggested a circus day. The authors of 'Inherit the Wind' made it . . . a witch hunt. . . ." Krutch pointed out that the defense, not the prosecution, sought the trial. "Thus it was a strange sort of witch trial, one in which the accused won a scholarship enabling him to attend graduate school and the only victim was the chief witness for the prosecution, poor old Bryan."[116]

There would be no such spectacular trials over troubling books in Europe. In the same year that Americans debated Darwin, German presses rolled out a new tome. Adolf Hitler published *Mein Kampf* following his release from prison. The Nazi party leader had been tried and jailed for his

* French for the fine arts.

attempt to overthrow the government of his home state of Bavaria. Hitler spent his brief, easy sentence dictating his book.*

If Darwin described a struggle among the species in which only the fittest survive, Hitler applied that struggle to the relations between nations. In his ponderous work, Hitler laid out in chilling detail his plans for the new Germany. *Aryans*—that is, those whose genes gave them fair skin, light hair, and blue eyes—were nature's fittest. They were the *Herrenvolk* ("master race"). And the only reason they had lost the First World War is that they were betrayed by Jews. Hitler referred to the armistice agreement as "the stab in the back" and those Germans who signed it as "the November criminals."

VI. "The Lone Eagle"

It seemed that Army colonel Billy Mitchell was trying to get himself court-martialed. He badgered the navy into letting him try to sink the captured German battleship, *Ostfriesland.*[117] Attacking the dreadnought with torpedoes from the air on 21 July 1921, Mitchell dramatically demonstrated how vulnerable battleships were to aerial assault. Not content with this public relations coup, however, the brash young colonel attacked army and navy brass, coolly demanded a new air force, and argued his case in widely published articles calling for air power.[118]

President Coolidge had little choice but to affirm the judgment of a military court martial in January 1926 when Mitchell at last went too far. Even though the *Ostfriesland* was anchored and not firing back, the sinking of this armored vessel by a tiny aircraft made a deep impression on the American people. Concerned, President Coolidge chose his Amherst College classmate, Dwight Morrow, to head up an aviation board to look into the issue. Morrow, a successful Wall Street financier from the House of Morgan, proved an able appointment.[119]

Another self-confident young aviator was determined to make his mark. Young Charles A. Lindbergh did not like to hustle. He didn't like having to ask businessmen and bankers for money. The twenty-four-year-old

* Hitler's Nazi Party celebrated the anniversary of the failed 1923 Munich Beer Hall *putsch* every year.

college dropout was an unlikely figure in the 1920s. He didn't smoke or drink. He avoided the girls who hung around the flight line.[120] He set high standards for himself—even setting up categories of perfection as Benjamin Franklin had done: Alertness, Altruism, Balance, Brevity, all the way through Unselfishness and Zeal.[121]

A more unrepresentative figure for the "lost generation" could hardly be imagined. But Lindbergh, son of a Minnesota congressman, did have one characteristic that he shared with F. Scott Fitzgerald's Jay Gatsby: he had an eye for the Main Chance. He knew how to get what he wanted.

Worldwide fame awaited the man who could fly nonstop across the Atlantic Ocean. Not only fame, but fortune: the $25,000 Orteig Prize led men to risk their lives. Navy commander Richard Byrd, the famous pilot who first flew over the North Pole, had crashed in April 1927 in his large trimotor plane, *America.*[122] Byrd, only slightly injured, was followed two weeks later by two other navy pilots who died in the crash of their trimotor.[123]

The prize could be won by a flight in either direction, so two French pilots started at Paris, flying westward to New York on 9 May.[124] When the great Charles Nungesser and Francois Coli were reported off the New England coast, Lindbergh's heart sank. Crowds were already cheering in Paris.[125] Suddenly, the plane carrying Nungesser and Coli went missing.

As Lindbergh watched his single engine monoplane, *The Spirit of St. Louis,* being prepared for takeoff, the drizzling rain and deeply rutted muddy road combined with the recent deaths of Nungesser and Coli to create a somber, not a celebratory scene. "It's more like a funeral procession than the beginning of a flight to Paris," Lindbergh thought.[126] He had stripped the plane to the barest of necessities. Everything not essential had to give way to fuel. The lanky aviator took only five sandwiches for the trip. Asked if this would be enough, he answered laconically: "If I get to Paris, I won't need any more. And if I don't get to Paris, I won't need any more, either."[127]

On the morning of 20 May 1927, Lindbergh took off from Long Island's Roosevelt Field.* The fuel-heavy plane missed a tractor by only ten

* It was not a good omen, for people who paid attention to such things. Roosevelt Field had been named for Quentin Roosevelt, the brave young American aviator who met his death in the skies over France.

feet, telephone wires by barely twenty as it struggled to get airborne. The country held its breath. Will Rogers did not attempt humor:

> A . . . slim, tall, bashful, smiling American boy is somewhere over the middle of the Atlantic Ocean, where no lone human being has ever ventured before. He is being prayed for to every kind of Supreme Being that ever had a following. If he is lost it will be the most universally regretted loss we ever had.[128]

Except he was not lost. And he wasn't really alone. Harold Anderson of the *New York Sun* wrote one of the most widely circulated newspaper columns of the era, "Lindbergh Flies Alone":

> Alone? Is he alone at whose side rides Courage, with Skill within the cockpit and Faith upon the left? Does solitude surround the brave when Adventure leads the way and Ambition reads the dials? Is there no company with him for whom the air is cleft by Daring and the darkness is made light by Emprise?[129]*

Delirious crowds of Frenchmen swept onto Le Bourget airdrome in Paris when Lindbergh landed, following a flight of thirty-three hours and thirty-nine minutes.[130] In an age fascinated by technical details, it was pointed out that the engine of *The Spirit of St. Louis* had to fire 14,472,000 times—without a skip or a miss—to cover the 3,735 miles from New York to Paris.[131]

Charles Augustus Lindbergh became the greatest hero of the age. He was worshipped in Paris. He received a hero's welcome and a ticker tape parade down Broadway in New York. He became such a celebrity that he could no longer send his shirts out to be laundered. They would be cut up for souvenirs. Nor could he write a check. His signature was worth more than the amount on the slip. Flying around the United States afterward, Lindbergh was feted everywhere. At one dinner, George Gershwin played his famous *Rhapsody in Blue* for the young man, only to stop midway to ask

---

* Emprise: an adventurous, daring, or chivalric enterprise. (*Merriam-Webster Online Dictionary.*)

about the dangers of the flight.[132] Lindbergh put his money in the experienced hands of the House of Morgan. There, he met Dwight Morrow, soon to become President Coolidge's ambassador to Mexico.[133]

Prohibition had strained America's relations with both our continental neighbors. Rumrunners moved across the northern and southern borders. American gangsters bribed customs officials on both sides of the border.

In the case of Mexico, however, the most troublesome seizures did not involve cases of gin. Mexican government seizures of U.S. petroleum companies' assets brought the countries close to war. President Coolidge sent Dwight Morrow to Mexico City to negotiate. Skeptical Mexicans said Morrow was just a scout for the Marines. But Morrow skillfully dealt with Mexico's various factions. He wanted to have Lindbergh invited officially to visit Mexico City.

Lindbergh had a keen eye for publicity. He said he would fly there nonstop from Washington, D.C. Morrow was unwilling to risk his famous young friend, but Lindbergh said, "You get me the invitation, and I'll take care of the flying."[134] When the man the press dubbed "the Lone Eagle" flew into Mexico City, the people went wild with joy. Thousands had slept on the runway to get a glimpse of the hero. Many prayed as Lindbergh, who had lost his bearings, arrived more than two hours late. "*Viva Lindbergh!*" they cried. Mrs. Morrow thought they might tear the young aviator's clothes off in their excitement.[135] It was, and remains, the greatest moment in U.S.-Mexican relations. President Coolidge deserves the credit for the cagey appointment of Dwight Morrow. We have only to contrast this diplomacy with Woodrow Wilson's South-of-the-Border bungling to appreciate Coolidge's achievement.

While on vacation in Mexico, "Lucky Lindy" met the young woman who was to become his wife. Anne Morrow was Ambassador Morrow's sensitive, intelligent, and beautiful daughter.

VII. Peace and Prosperity

Charles Lindbergh was not the only American who looked to Paris to make his mark. In the twenties, expatriate authors like Ernest Hemingway and F. Scott Fitzgerald flocked to the City of Light. There, Gertrude Stein and her companion Alice B. Toklas kept a literary salon that was the gathering place for young American writers eager to make their reputations. "Remarks, Hemingway, are not literature," was Stein's blunt assessment of the young American's gritty style.[136] Despite her often acerbic comments, Stein's advice was respected among writers. Even that quintessential Southerner, William Faulkner, and aspiring playwright Eugene O'Neill made their way to this home of *belles lettres.*

American secretary of state Frank B. Kellogg also looked to Paris. He responded to an offer of a treaty from the French foreign minister, Aristide Briand. The proposed treaty would ensure that the two nations would never go to war against one another. It was Briand's attempt to get U.S. backing in case France was attacked. Kellogg broadened the scope of the offer to fashion a treaty whose avowed purpose was to "renounce war as an instrument of national policy" and invited all states to sign it.[137] The Kellogg-Briand Pact would win the Nobel Prize for Peace for its two authors. Sixty-two nations would in time subscribe, including Japan, Germany, and Italy.[138]

But the Kellogg-Briand Pact was a mixed bag. In the long term, it provided the legal basis for the eventual war crimes tribunals for the makers of aggressive war. In the short term, however, it dangerously lulled the democracies into thinking they could rely on a piece of parchment for their security. Senator Carter Glass, Democrat of Virginia, said he was not "simple enough to suppose it was worth a postage stamp."[139] Nonetheless, Glass voted to ratify the so-called Pact of Paris. It sailed through the Senate on a vote of 81–1.[140] The *New York Evening Post* ridiculed the pact when Congress approved construction of fifteen new naval cruisers. How many cruisers would we need, the *Post* editorialized, "if we *hadn't* just signed a peace treaty with twenty-six nations?"[141] Apparently, the *Post* had forgotten TR's dictum: "Speak softly, but carry a big stick."

Kellogg-Briand was so popular in part because Americans preferred not to think about foreign troubles. And troubles there were. In Germany, the liberal Weimar Republic struggled to maintain democracy in the face of challenges from the Communists and the Nazis. From his exile in Holland, Kaiser Wilhelm gave interviews blaming the Jews for Germany's defeat in World War I.[142] His Dutch home at Doorn became a center of agitation against the Weimar Republic. There, he received three thousand letters on his seventieth birthday (27 January 1928) calling for his restoration.[143] The letters contained hundreds of thousands of signatures from supporters in Germany.[144] Bitterly, he told intimates that the Jews had engineered his abdication. They must be rooted out, he snarled. And the means? Wilhelm's ominous answer was blunt and savage: "*Das best wäre Gas!*" ("The best way would be Gas!")[145]

If freedom was threatened in Weimar Germany, the Bolsheviks had completely extinguished it in Soviet Russia. In the struggle for power that followed Lenin's death in 1924, Josef Stalin emerged victorious. Stalin played various factions of the ruling Communist Party of the Soviet Union off against one another.[146] Although Communist Parties throughout the world ritually denounced anti-Semitism, Stalin maneuvered successfully against his opponents among the Old Bolsheviks. First Trotsky, later Kamenev and Zinoviev would be snared. Thoughtful observers might have noticed that Stalin's "enemies" were principally Jews.*

Stalin's successful attacks on his enemies left him a free hand to bring the Ukraine under his thumb. He blamed the famine that his own policies had caused on greedy *kulaks*. *Kulak* meant fist; it was a term the Communists used to describe peasants whose own skill and hard work had brought them success in this "breadbasket." Russian novelist Vladimir Tendrayakov would describe the fate of the kulaks after their land was expropriated by the Communists:

> In the station square Ukrainian kulaks expropriated and exiled from their homeland, lay down and died. One got used to seeing the dead there in the morning, and the hospital stable-boy Abram, would come along with his cart and pile the corpses in.
>
> Not everyone died. Many wandered along the dusty, sordid alleyways, dragging dropsied legs, elephantine and bloodlessly blue, and plucked at every passer-by, begging with dog-like eyes.[147]

---

* Josif Vissarionivich Dzhugashvili was born in Georgia, not Russia proper. As a Bolshevik revolutionary, he adopted the name Stalin—Man of Steel.

While Americans knew nothing of the six or seven million who were intentionally starved to death in the Ukraine, one American did—Walter Duranty, Moscow correspondent of the *New York Times.* He would win a Pulitzer Prize for his sympathetic coverage of Josef Stalin. He chose not to report on the brutal famine. Apparently not all the news was fit to print.

In America, the love affair with the automobile proceeded apace. General Motors did not try to compete with Ford through lower prices but by giving the consumers more car for their money. The Chevrolet came with a self-starter feature that vastly increased the popularity of driving, especially among women.[148]

On the silver screen, 1927 saw the first "talkie" produced. Al Jolson starred as *The Jazz Singer.*[149] The plot centered on the son of a Jewish cantor who uses his great voice to make a fortune as a popular singer. His parents grieve because they think he has prostituted his God-given talents.[150] Most Americans were thrilled when Al Jolson spoke his signature line: "You ain't heard *nothin'* yet!"[151] But black Americans could not have been flattered by the fact that Jolson's Jazz Singer was performed in blackface.

Coolidge was at the height of his popularity in the summer of 1927. Vacationing in the Black Hills of South Dakota, the president held one of his regular not-for-attribution press conferences. As the reporters filed into a high school gym, Coolidge handed each one a slip of paper on which was typed the curt message: "I do not choose to run for President in nineteen twenty-eight."[152] Brief, blunt, direct. It was Coolidge's style.

There followed a short but intense period of speculation. Did he really mean it? Did he want to be drafted? Few insiders who had seen the president staring longingly out of the White House window at the tennis courts where Calvin Jr. had played his last game could have been surprised. Others who heard Grace Goodhue Coolidge's whispered words to her friends ("Poppa says there's a depression coming.") would have been in no doubt of his sincerity.[153] Coolidge may have sensed his own mortality. A distinguished doctor later said of him, "I have rarely known a man to have the type of heart condition such as that from which President Coolidge suffered without himself having had some of the danger signs."[154] To those who knew the president slept as many as twelve hours a day, angina may have been an explanation—perhaps even depression.

Whatever his reasons, Calvin Coolidge did his country a service in leaving office with such dignity. After the rigor mortis of Wilson and the flaccidity of Harding, he dignified his office. He was probably the only white man who could wear a full-dress Sioux war bonnet and not look ridiculous. The title Kansas editor William Allen White gave to his book on Coolidge neatly summed up this quiet man's presidency: he was *A Puritan in Babylon*.

One American who did choose to run that year was George Herman Ruth—known to millions of baseball fans as the Babe. Babe Ruth in 1927 ran the bases an astounding sixty times to set a homerun record that lasted more than thirty years. Little wonder that Yankee Stadium was called "the House that Ruth built."

Americans also thrilled that year to the exploits on the links of Bobby Jones. In his 1927 biography, *Down the Fairway,* Jones wrote, "I wish I could say here that a strange thrill shot through my skinny little bosom when I swung at a golf ball for the first time, but it wouldn't be truthful."[155] Even so, Robert Tyre Jones began to teach himself to play golf at age six and entered his first professional championship at fourteen.[156] He would come to dominate the game and represent the model of a Southern gentleman and sportsman.

Nineteen twenty-seven also saw the execution by electrocution of Nicoló Sacco and Bartolomeo Vanzetti in Massachusetts. The two Italian-born anarchists had been arrested at the height of the Red Scare in 1920. They were charged with murder and robbery, tried, convicted, and in 1921 sentenced to death. Through the long years of appeals, many intellectuals, writers, and poets protested their fate. Their fate became a *cause célèbre,* and not just among Leftists.[157] Respected Harvard professor Samuel Eliot Morison was one among thousands who signed a petition calling for clemency (even though Harvard's President A. Lawrence Lowell was one of a blue ribbon panel that had called the trial fair). Future Supreme Court justice Felix Frankfurter, then a Harvard law professor, issued a stinging report condemning the trial and the sentence. Sacco and Vanzetti met their fate with courage and simple dignity. Vanzetti's final statement to the court that condemned him, with its broken English, still moves us with its eloquence:

> If it had not been for these thing, I might have live out my life talking at street corners to scorning men. I have die unmarked, unknown, a failure. Now we are not a failure. This is our career and our triumph. Never in our full life could we hope to do such work for tolerance, for joostice, for man's onderstanding of man as now we do by accident. Our words—our lives—our pains—nothing! The taking of our lives—lives of a good shoemaker and a poor fish peddler—all! That last moment belongs to us—that agony is our triumph.[158]

This famous case still troubles our conscience. There is little doubt that a conviction for the murder of a paymaster and his guard could not be brought in a modern court on such slender evidence. Sacco and Vanzetti also point up the danger of politicized justice—both on the part of the prosecution and of the defense. The question should not have been were they radicals. Clearly, they were. The only question should have been were they guilty as charged?

VIII. "Two Chickens in Every Pot"

The Republicans felt confident about 1928. Peace and Prosperity always favors the "in" party. The obvious choice to succeed Coolidge was Commerce Secretary Herbert Hoover. President Harding had called him "the smartest gink I know."[159]

Americans admired Herbert Hoover's story. Born in poverty in Iowa, orphaned as a young boy, he had gone to Stanford University and become a world-renowned mining engineer. He made millions, and could easily have retired in luxury. Instead, he threw himself into projects like Belgian Relief, Russian famine relief, and, finally, service for eight years as commerce secretary during a time when, as President Coolidge said, "The chief business of the American people *is* business and the chief ideal of the American people is idealism."

Prohibition was bound to be an issue. Hoover called it "a noble experiment," but he said he was willing to commission a study to investigate how the experiment was going at that point. Hoover was partial to letting experts decide delicate questions of public policy. The leading Democrat, Al Smith, was notoriously Wet. "Corruption of law enforcement officials, bootlegging, lawlessness are now prevalent throughout this country," Smith charged, citing the alleged failure of Prohibition.

One poet at the time satirized what would come to be known as the "Wickersham Report":

> Prohibition is an awful flop;
> We like it.
> It can't stop what it's meant to stop.
> We like it.
> It's left a trail of death and slime,
> It don't prohibit worth a dime,
> It's filled our land with graft and crime;
> Nonetheless, we're for it.[160]

The economy, as always, was a key election issue. Hoover pointed to the Republican record of the 1920s—a 45 percent increase in national income, 3.5 million new homes, 66 percent increase in high school attendance. All of this was true.[161] Then he reached for the rhetorical heights like Icarus reaching for the sun: "We in America today are nearer to the final triumph over poverty than ever before," he said. "The poorhouse is vanishing. . . . [Given] a chance to go forward with the policies of the last eight years, we shall soon with the help of God be in sight of the day when poverty will be banished from the nation."[162]

Hoover was certainly not alone in his optimism. Even the muckraker, Lincoln Steffens, caught the buoyant spirit of the times: "Big business in America is providing what the Socialists held up as their goal: food, shelter and clothing for all. . . . It is a great country this is; as great as Rome."[163] A Republican writer, probably recruited from a Madison Avenue advertising firm, said the GOP could be relied upon to provide "two chickens in every pot and a car in every garage."[164]

Al Smith's fondness for cigars gave him a gravelly voice. He joked about his humble origins. He could not afford to go to college, but he said he had earned his F.F.M. degree (from the Fulton Fish Market). Al Smith was certainly very bright, and he had a natural dignity, but his rough accent grated on Americans' ears. He was the *foist* to address them on the *raddio.* It didn't help that candidate Smith sounded a lot like the mobsters who were being hauled before congressional committees and grand juries all over the country.

Then, there was the religion factor. Hoover would not countenance any bigotry. That didn't restrain his followers, however, for whom Smith's Catholicism was frightening. A Methodist bishop from Smith's own New York State fought Governor Smith as president of the state's Anti-Saloon League. He bluntly said, "No Governor can kiss the papal ring and get within gunshot of the White House."[165] Kansan William Allen White was the editor of the *Emporia Gazette.* He had been a progressive. Even so, White wrote, "The whole *Puritan* civilization which has built a sturdy, orderly nation is threatened by Smith."[166]

Few stopped to ask White where the *Puritan* civilization was when Washington, Jefferson, Jackson, and Cleveland were elected? Where was the Puritan in Hamilton? In Henry Clay? Or, for that matter, in the famously tolerant Lincoln?

It did not matter. No Democrat could have beaten "Peace and Prosperity." Hoover in 1928 was a very respectable candidate. He was certainly no bigot. Hoover the humanitarian was especially sensitive to the needs of women, black Americans, and Indians.[167] Al Smith, for all his courage, intelligence, and good humor, despite his solid record of progressive achievement, was doomed. Even if he had not been Catholic, he would have lost.

When the votes rolled in, Hoover was elected overwhelmingly. Hoover won 21,392,190 popular votes (58.2 percent) and 444 electoral votes from forty-one states. Smith received 15,016,443 popular votes (40.8 percent) and 87 electoral votes from just seven states. Outside of Massachusetts with its large number of Catholic voters, and Rhode Island, then the most Catholic state in the nation, Smith's other wins came, ironically, in the Deep South. He carried South Carolina, Georgia, Mississippi, Alabama, Arkansas, and Louisiana. Was this a heartening defiance of bigotry in the home of the

Calvin Coolidge. *"Silent Cal" was wildly popular after the shabby corruption of the Harding years. Called "a Puritan in Babylon," Calvin Coolidge presided serenely over America during the Roaring Twenties. At the peak of his power, though, he said, "I do not choose to run in 1928."*

Gov. Alfred E. Smith. *Alfred Emmanuel Smith, pictured with cigar, gained national attention when he investigated the horrific Triangle Shirt Company fire of 1911. He built a national reputation as a reforming Governor of New York State. Hailed by Franklin Roosevelt as "the happy warrior," Smith was the first Catholic to be nominated for President of the United States.*

Herbert Hoover. *Herbert Hoover made a fortune as a mining engineer and then set about doing good works. He rescued Americans stranded in Europe by World War I, led the Belgian relief effort, and kept millions of Russians from starvation when the Bolshevik Revolution led to famine. As President, however, he had the misfortune to preside over the Great Depression following the Stock Market Crash of 1929.*

KKK?* Or was it the result of the Solid South's willingness to vote for "a yellow dog"** so long as he was a Democrat?

After the election returns came cascading in, as papal biographer George Weigel notes, a story spread throughout the American Catholic community. Al Smith, they said, had sent this telegram to Pope Pius XI: "Unpack."[168]

An urban legend grew up around Al Smith's brave stand. It was later said he had coalesced some of the key elements of what would come to be known as the New Deal coalition—black voters, Southerners, farmers, and urban voters.[169] In fact, he did no such thing. That daunting task would be left to the man Al Smith had arm-twisted into succeeding him in the governor's chair in Albany, Franklin Delano Roosevelt.

IX. CRASH!

All Quiet on the Western Front was the literary sensation of 1929. For his classic story of the brutal impact of war on young men, German author Erich Maria Remarque was hailed throughout the Allied countries. The book sold almost half a million copies by Christmas.[170] While French critics praised the work, saying every copy sold was "a plebiscite in favor of peace," Remarque was denounced by German army officers. Later, when the Nazis came to power, his works would be burned. Remarque was forced to flee Germany and his sister, Elfriede, was killed by the Nazis.[171]

In America, Ernest Hemingway's *A Farewell to Arms* also spoke to the disenchantment so many young people felt with the failed promises of a world made safe for democracy.[172]

In Chicago, Prohibition enforcement was a sometime thing. Alfonse ("Scarface Al") Capone's gang was deep into bootlegging, speakeasy shakedowns, illegal gambling, and prostitution. On Valentine's Day 1929, they

---

* The KKK of the 1920s had expanded into Indiana and other northern states and was a strongly anti-Catholic, anti-Semitic, anti-immigrant organization.

** Since Reconstruction, white voters in the South largely backed the Democratic party. Called the Solid South, it produced the joke that they'd vote for "a yellow dog" as long as he ran on the Democratic ticket.

dealt with their competition—George ("Bugs") Moran's gang—in a way that shocked and stunned law-abiding Americans. Daniel Patrick Moynihan later wrote in his seminal essay, "Defining Deviancy Down," about the impact of that day on American life:

> In 1929 in Chicago during Prohibition, four gangsters killed seven gangsters on February 14. The nation was shocked. The event became legend. It merits not one but two entries in the *World Book Encyclopedia*. I leave it to others to judge, but it would appear that the society in the 1920s was simply not willing to put up with this degree of deviancy. In the end, the Constitution was amended, and Prohibition, which lay behind so much gangster violence, ended.[173]

During Prohibition, the government struggled to keep up with the bootleggers and rumrunners. Also in 1929, the U.S. Coast Guard chased the speedy rumrunner *Black Duck* in Rhode Island's Narragansett Bay.[174] When after repeated warnings the *Black Duck* failed to stop, the coast guardsmen opened fire, killing three of four crewmen and seizing five hundred cases of whiskey.[175] In nearby Boston, thirsty crowds were so incensed that they rioted outside Faneuil Hall and beat up a coast guard recruiter.

Still, the government was determined to uphold the rule of law. Special Agent Eliot Ness and his "Untouchables" were known for their courage, their resourcefulness, and their unwillingness to take bribes from the Mob. Ness went after Capone's gang and, by 1931, succeeded in sending Al Capone to prison for income tax evasion.[176]

On Wall Street, the Roaring Twenties roared on. No one knew better how to work the system than Boston's Joseph P. Kennedy. Kennedy once set up a "boiler room" operation in a hotel suite to save the Yellow Cab Company from ruin. He prompted hundreds of telephone calls from around the country to buy and to sell the stock of the company threatened by corporate raiders.[177] All this frenzied interest in buying and selling Yellow Cab stock made it appear the company was a hot commodity. The results so confused the raiders that the stock finally was stabilized.[178]

Millions of people rushed to get into a Bull Market, often buying stock on a "margin" as little as ten percent of face value, then reselling as a speculative "bubble" was created. In this way, stocks in poorly managed companies could nonetheless be artificially bid up in value. Hundreds of thousands acted on "hot tips" and rushed to invest their money in stocks without having any idea of their real worth. Everyone wanted to "get rich quick."

Harvard economist William Z. Ripley had warned of the Wild West atmosphere on Wall Street. He colorfully denounced the "honeyfugling, hornswoggling and skullduggery" of the corporate boardrooms.[179] Ripley's party-pooping went unheeded.

A warning tremor of hard times came in early October 1929, when the price of wheat plummeted.[180] This would have devastating consequences not only for American farmers in the Midwest but also for Canadians and Australians.[181]

Later in the month, the New York Stock Exchange recorded a serious sell-off, taking prices back to their 1927 levels.[182] President Hoover hastened to issue a reassuring statement. The "fundamentals" of American prosperity, he said, were sound.[183]

President Hoover's message could not have been more ill-timed. On that day, 24 October 1929, the Stock Market collapsed. It would forever be known as "Black Thursday." A month before, the average price of thirty leading American industrial shares was $380. When trading ended on Black Thursday, it was only $230.[184] Overnight, the investments of millions of American families were virtually wiped out.

Americans were plunged into the worst Depression they had ever known. It was an experience that scarred millions. This had always been the Land of Opportunity. And that opportunity was based in no small part on bountiful harvests. Even in the midst of civil war, President Lincoln's Thanksgiving Proclamation praised the Almighty for sending us fertile fields and bulging granaries. No more. For millions, these were the "Hungry Years."[185]

For those Americans who did not put their savings into Wall Street stocks and bonds, and they were legion, the Great Depression was felt in the unemployment figures. In 1929, unemployment had been a very low 3 percent.[186] For 1930, the jobless numbers were not as bad as they had been in the early twenties—9 percent. But in 1931, as the numbers of unemployed rose to eight million, 16 percent of the work force, the Great Fear stalked the land.[187] Was there no turnaround, no recovery in sight? In 1932, unemployment rose to a full 24 percent—twelve million out of work.[188]

Bank failures also frightened many of the most stable citizens. Trust is essential to enterprise, as Americans back to Alexander Hamilton knew. When hundreds of banks "went under," the Depression deepened. Work and thrift had always been the basis for American economic strength. Now, both work and thrift seemed to avail Americans little.

President Hoover tried manfully to buck up Americans' sagging spirits. "Any lack of confidence in . . . the basic strength of business is foolish," he said in November.[189] "We have now passed the worst," he declared on 1 May 1930.[190] "May Day," ironically, is the international distress call. The president was hurt badly in public esteem as it soon became obvious that the corner had not been turned at all. Or, if it had, it led only to harder times. Standard Oil's John D. Rockefeller, in a clumsy effort to instill confidence, announced that "the fundamental conditions of the country are sound," adding that he and his sons were *buying* stock![191]

As more and more Americans were thrown out of work, many took to the roads. "Okies" from Oklahoma piled into overburdened trucks to make the passage to Southern California, where there was said to be work. Oklahoma Native Son Will Rogers ruefully joked that America was the first country ever to "drive to the poor house in an automobile." Many a young man hit the rails, hitching rides on slow-moving freight trains. CBS News correspondent Eric Sevareid would later reflect on his experience of riding the rails. Few seeing the elegant, well-turned out newsman could imagine him bedding down in rotting straw.

John Steinbeck would later immortalize the experience of the stricken Joad family in his gritty novel, *The Grapes of Wrath.* Soup kitchens and shanty towns sprung up around the country. The shanty towns were dubbed "Hoovervilles" in a cruel riposte to the president's invincible view that "prosperity is just around the corner."

Hoover is our shepherd
We are in want
He maketh us to lie
Down on the park benches
He leadeth us beside the still factories[192]

With the deepening Depression, Americans looked to the Man in the White House for answers. President Hoover continued to maintain as much of a normal routine as he could, hoping thereby to build confidence in recovery. He dined each night at the White House wearing formal attire. He attended the opening of the baseball season (and had to endure the indignity of being roundly booed by fans in Philadelphia). When a reporter asked Babe Ruth how he could justify earning more than the president of the United States, he replied, "I had a better year than Hoover did."

In June 1930, Congress left President Hoover with an important decision: whether or not to sign the Smoot-Hawley Tariff Bill. Herbert Hoover had never been identified with isolationism, nor with a narrow, "beggar thy neighbor" view of America's economic place in the world.[193] Nonetheless, he signed Smoot-Hawley. It was to prove perhaps his worst mistake.* High tariffs on imported goods led immediately to other nations raising *their* tariffs in retaliation. Thus, at a time when all countries needed to stimulate international trade, they were choking it off.

The disastrous impact was felt almost immediately with our closest neighbor and biggest trading partner, Canada. One thousand economists had appealed to the president to veto this bill, as had the American Bankers Association.[194] As a direct result, Canada retaliated against American goods and eighty-seven branches of American factories opened up north of the 49th parallel.[195] This hurt American workers, who lost jobs and the ability to export their manufactures.

When the Republican-controlled Congress adjourned in July 1930 it was

---

* The farmers led the demands for protection and their appeal outweighed the 1,028 economists who appealed to Hoover to veto the tariff bill. The depression deepened and lengthened as a result. (Source: Taranto, James, Leonard Leo, *Presidential Leadership,* Wall Street Journal Books, 2004, 221.)

not scheduled to reconvene until December 1931.* President Hoover mistrusted Congress.[196] He resisted calls for a Special Session of Congress.[197] He replied to urgent appeals with a stern rejoinder: "We cannot legislate ourselves out of a world economic depression."[198]

The stance was unwise, even stupid. Hoover showed a fundamental lack of confidence in representative government. Since he would not work with a Congress of his own party, the voters that November gave Democrats a whopping increase of 49 seats in the House, for a total of 216. Republicans retained a paper-thin majority of 218.[199] By the time Congress sat again, more than a year after Election Day, even that would be gone.[200]

Scholars to this day debate the causes, extent, and duration of the Great Depression. Nobel Prize winner Milton Friedman calls it the Great Contraction.[201] He writes that it was caused by a disastrous *decline* in the money supply. He cites the untimely death of Governor Benjamin Strong of the New York Reserve Bank: "Once he was removed from the scene, neither the [Federal Reserve] Board nor the other Reserve Banks . . . were prepared to accept the leadership of the New York Bank."[202] Some scholars maintain that the Depression did not "really *end* until 1939–40, when America began to rearm."[203]

As always, however, people judge largely by what they can see. And in Herbert Hoover, they saw a grim, dour man utterly devoid of humor.[204] Hoover's very capable Secretary of State Henry L. Stimson said he had to flee a meeting at the White House to "get away from the ever present feeling of gloom that pervades everything connected with the Administration."[205] Even during World War I, Colonel House had confided to his diary that Hoover, "takes, as usual, a gloomy outlook. . . ."[206]

To many, Hoover seemed callously indifferent to the suffering of the common man. Although this was far from true—Hoover had in fact been a great humanitarian throughout his life—this shy, reserved man was the butt of endless bitter jokes. When out-of-work men pulled their empty pockets inside-out, they were said to be flying "Hoover Flags."[207] A story circulated that the president had asked Andrew Mellon, his secretary of the treasury,

* This antiquated schedule would later be changed by the Twentieth Amendment (The "Lame Duck" Amendment) to the Constitution in 1933. Under this amendment, Congress would meet at least annually.

for a nickel to call a friend. "Here's a dime," the Pittsburgh millionaire purportedly told Hoover, "call *all* your friends."[208]

The team of Mellon and Hoover were singled out for abuse in a thousand rhymes and satires:

> Oh, Mellon pulled the whistle, boys,
> And Hoover rang the bell,
> Wall Street gave the signal,
> And the country went to hell.[209]

The country did not, in fact, go to "hell." As bad as the Great Depression was, life expectancy increased and the death rate declined in the decade of the 1930s.[210] Because jobs were scarce, more young people stayed in school and were thereby better prepared when they graduated.[211]

Even the automobile, that symbol of American ingenuity and marketing, was proving to be something of a mixed blessing. In 1931, thirty thousand people died on America's roads, a tragic toll, and far higher proportionately than the toll in 2006.[212]

One of those who *escaped* death on the American road in 1931 was a visiting Englishman. Winston Churchill had come to America to deliver a series of lectures. He needed to. He had been pushed out of office back home and had suffered great losses in the Crash. When he stepped off a Manhattan curbside, he instinctively looked to his *right.* (The English persist in driving on the *wrong* side of the road.) He was struck by a car and landed in the hospital. With mounting medical bills, unable to complete his lecture tour, Churchill might naturally have been depressed. But the irrepressible Englishman wrote a widely syndicated article about being hit by a car.[213] When life deals out lemons, some people make lemonade. And enterprising people *sell* lemonade.

Churchill the Englishman was lucky he got knocked down in New York City. Had he visited Chicago, he might have had a run-in with "Big Bill" Thompson, the mayor of the City of Broad Shoulders. Thompson had been elected promising to "kick King George V out of Chicago."[214] The Republican candidate found his only hope of election was by twisting the lion's tale. His antics ceased being a joke, however, when he fired the city's school superintendent for being "pro-British," and burned British books that had been donated to the city following the great Chicago fire.[215]

Anti-British sentiment had been a staple of American politics for a century and a half. Millions of Americans hated the very idea of monarchy and aristocracy. Each morning, schoolchildren pledged allegiance to the flag "and to the *Republic,* for which it stands." Add to that the belief among many Irish-Americans that Britain had oppressed Ireland for centuries. German-Americans had supported the First World War only when the Zimmermann Telegram revealed Germany's aggressive designs on the U.S. Southwest. Their disillusionment with what they saw as British hypocrisy was deep and real. After the war, Britain had not given independence to India. And the Versailles Treaty had consigned Germany's African colonies to Britain and France. "A war to make the world safe for democracy"? No, to millions of Americans it was a war to make the world safe for British and French imperialism.

Americans in 1932 craved distraction from their woes. Soon, the "Crime of the Century" provided it. On the night of 1 March, little Charles A. Lindbergh Jr., a few months shy of his second birthday, was kidnapped from his parents' secluded home on their estate near Hopewell, New Jersey. The entire country was transfixed. Schoolchildren across the country were asked to pray for the baby's safe return. Boy Scouts and Princeton undergraduates volunteered to search the woods surrounding the Lindbergh's elegant home. Fearing that they might disturb footprints or other evidence, Colonel Lindbergh turned down the offer.

America's hero had received a ransom note. There were clear indications from the note's peculiar phrasing that it was written by an immigrant, probably German.

> Dear Sir!
>
> *Have 50000$ redy with 2500$ in 20$ bills 1500$ in 10$ bills and 1000$ in 5$ bills. After 2-4 days we will inform you were to deliver the Mony.*
>
> *We warn you for making anyding public or for notify the polise the child is in gute care.*
>
> *Indication for all letters are singnature and 3 holes.*[216]

Immediately, the head of the New Jersey State Police was dispatched to Hopewell to take over the investigation involving the Garden State's most famous couple. Colonel H. Norman Schwarzkopf was a thirty-seven-year old West Pointer who ran the state troopers like a military organization.* President Hoover promised all the resources of the federal government to aid in the investigation. J. Edgar Hoover, director of the Federal Bureau of Investigation, wanted badly to crack the case.[217]

Lindbergh paid the ransom money and pursued many false leads. He even went to the *Nelly* "boad" (boat), as instructed in a subsequent message from the kidnapper. But in May 1932, the badly decomposed body of the twenty-month-old son of Charles and Anne Morrow Lindbergh was found four and a half miles from their Hopewell residence. Perhaps the colonel should have accepted the offers of the Scouts and the Princeton students.

Colonel Schwarzkopf had located a ladder outside the Lindbergh home. It was cracked. Very likely, the kidnapper had scaled it successfully to enter the second floor nursery where the child slept. Then, with the baby's added weight, the ladder collapsed under him. Investigators and coroners theorized that the child had been killed by striking his head against the brick wall as the ladder broke.[218] All along, it became clear that the kidnapper had cruelly deceived the Lindberghs into thinking they might actually see their little boy again. Soon, Congress passed the Lindbergh Law to make kidnapping a federal crime.

When Hoover vetoed a bill to pay out early the bonus promised to veterans of World War I, a "bonus army" descended on Washington in 1932. The president quietly ordered tents and medical units to be made available for members of the Bonus Expeditionary Force (BEF, a clever play on the name of the U.S. force in WWI, the American Expeditionary Force, AEF). When Communist agitators prodded a small number of the men to throw bricks and stones at police, however, Hoover was determined to preserve order in the nation's capital.[219]

Hoover ordered the army to quell the riots that were breaking out

---

* Colonel Schwarzkopf's son, General Schwarzkopf, also a distinguished West Pointer, led Allied forces in Operation Desert Storm in 1991.

downtown. Hoover specified that the regular troops should *not* be armed and that the BEF men were simply to be escorted to their tent camps, or turned over to Metropolitan Police.[220]

General Douglas MacArthur, the army's chief of staff, took personal command of his troops. He used tanks, tear gas, and soldiers with fixed bayonets to clear the streets of rock-throwing bonus marchers.[221] MacArthur's aide—Major Dwight D. Eisenhower—was surprised and disappointed to see his chief preparing to storm the bonus marchers' camps. Major George S. Patton, however, eagerly led U.S. cavalry down Pennsylvania Avenue in what was to prove to be one of the last charges of mounted soldiers.[222]* Two of the bonus marchers were killed in the resulting melee. The *Washington News* was aghast. "What a pitiful spectacle is that of the great American Government, mightiest in the world, chasing unarmed men, women and children with Army tanks. . . . If the Army must be called out to make war on unarmed citizens, this is no longer America."[223]

Conditions were so desperate in the election year of 1932 that thousands of prominent writers and intellectuals openly called for Communism. F. Scott Fitzgerald, author of the vastly popular *Great Gatsby,* yearned to "bring on the revolution. . . ."[224] Other famous writers drawn to Marxist ideas were Upton Sinclair, Edmund Wilson, Sherwood Anderson, Erskine Caldwell, Malcolm Cowley, and Lincoln Steffens.[225] Many of these writers lived and worked in New York City, giving a strong leftist tilt to the state's intellectual climate, and, in effect, to the nation's atmosphere as well.

X. "Happy Days Are Here Again"

"Thank Heaven for Hoover," read the headlines in the foreign press.[226] They were welcoming President Hoover's disarmament initiative of 1932. As fifty-one nations gathered in Geneva for the World Disarmament Conference, the delegates genuinely welcomed Hoover's willingness to ban all "offensive" weapons and, further, to reduce *all* weapons stocks by one-third. With Japan

* It may have been the last charge of U.S. cavalry, unless one counts the remarkable pictures of U.S. troops in Afghanistan in 2001, pursuing the Taliban on horseback.

moving deeper into the Chinese province of Manchuria, with Italy's Fascist dictator Mussolini promising to make the Mediterranean Sea "Mare Nostrum" (Our Sea), and with Adolf Hitler's Nazis gaining strength in Germany, the foreigners were happy to have the prestige of the United States behind their efforts to call a halt to the arms race.[227]

Foreign leaders, however, do not elect American presidents. In the election year of 1932, Americans were suffering their worst economic conditions since the Panic of 1893. This virtually guaranteed that the Democrats would win the White House. Republican insiders all expected Hoover to lose. The GOP could raise only $2.5 million for their campaign, compared with nearly $7 million they had spent in the 1928 campaign.[228]

FDR was hardly the unanimous choice of the fractious Democrats. As governor of the largest state in the Union, he was the natural choice of his party, but Al Smith, the "Happy Warrior" of 1924 and 1928, had cooled toward FDR. He resented the fact that as governor, Roosevelt had ignored him.[229] Texas's John Nance ("Cactus Jack") Garner thought that as Speaker of the House he would be the strongest candidate. He tossed his Stetson into the presidential ring. Maryland had never been mother to a president, but in 1932, Governor Albert Ritchie thought she might be expecting.[230]

H.L. Mencken called FDR "Roosevelt Minor" and assured his readers that "no one, in fact, really likes Roosevelt . . . and no one quite trusts him."[231] When Roosevelt called for policies that appealed to "the forgotten man at the bottom of the economic pyramid," Al Smith was alarmed. He saw in the statement a demagogic appeal, a declaration of class warfare. And he promptly threw his *doiby* into the ring.[232]

Many of the serious thinkers of the country dismissed FDR. Columnist Walter Lippmann said he was "a pleasant man who, without any important qualifications for the office, would like very much to be President." Supreme Court justice Oliver Wendell Holmes chimed in, saying FDR had "a second class intellect, but a first class temperament."[233]

They all underestimated the New Yorker. In a dramatic move, FDR flew from Albany to the Democratic Convention in Chicago, breaking with the tradition that said a candidate never appears before the convention that nominates him. "Let it be symbolic that I broke traditions. Let it be from now on the task of our party to break foolish traditions. . . . I pledge you, I pledge myself to a new deal for the American people. . . ."[234]

The power of the appeal was mighty. Here, a man crippled by polio had dared to take to the still hazardous skies to carry his message of hope to millions who heard him via radio as he confidently addressed the party faithful. The day after FDR delivered his acceptance speech, the *New York World-Telegram* published a cartoon by Rollin Kirby. A hard-pressed farmer was shown looking up hopefully at Roosevelt's airplane. On its wings were the words "New Deal."[235]

President Hoover bravely soldiered on. He campaigned harder than he had in 1928. But he spoke in a listless, uninteresting fashion. At some of his campaign stops, he faced unfriendly audiences.[236]

If Hoover was dour but dutiful, FDR was radiant. He beamed the smile that drove his opponents crazy. He looked out at the world nearsightedly from behind *pince nez* glasses that were already out of fashion when cousin Teddy wore them. He wore a cape instead of an overcoat. It was a concession to his polio, but it gave him a rakish air. Roosevelt complained about "centralization" and called Hoover a "big spender." These were laughable charges then and hilarious now given how FDR actually governed. But he could have teamed with Walt Disney's little friend Mickey Mouse as his running mate and it wouldn't have made a difference in the outcome.*

Roosevelt won 22,821,857 popular votes (57.4 percent) and 472 electoral votes. Hoover suffered the greatest repudiation ever dealt to a sitting president. He won 15,761,845 popular votes (40.0 percent) and just 59 electoral votes. Most interesting, Socialist Party candidate Norman Thomas got only 2.2 percent of the popular vote. When the stakes were this high, few voters wanted to risk "throwing their votes away" on a futile third party protest.

"The little fella' felt that he never had a chance, and he didn't until November the Eighth. And *did* he grab it!"[237] That's how Will Rogers

* The Walt Disney studios were launched in 1928 with a black and white cartoon feature called "Steamboat Willie." It was Mickey Mouse's silver screen debut.

described the popular earthquake that overthrew not only Hoover, but the Republican majority coalition that had governed for most years between 1896 and 1932. Roosevelt not only carried a Democratic Congress in with him, he swept away Republican majorities in a score of state legislatures. Governors, mayors, even winning candidates for recorder of wills in Sleepy Eye County, Minnesota, owed their victories to Franklin Delano Roosevelt. More important, they *knew* it. For the Democrats and their millions of newly won friends, Happy Days were indeed here again.

XI. The New Deal

America had not faced such a crisis since the Secession Winter of 1860–1861. President Hoover, massively rejected by the voters, would remain in office a full *four* months until Inauguration Day on 4 March 1933. The icy grip of fear was on the land. Hoover was desperate to end his term with some action, any action, that might redeem his shattered presidency.

Hoover and FDR had been friends when they served together in the Wilson Administration. Roosevelt had never personally attacked Hoover during the 1932 campaign. He even declined to write an article against "an old personal friend."[238] Roosevelt did, however, confide to close friends that he had always found Hoover to be "cold."[239]

Then there was that incident in the White House earlier in the year. President Hoover had invited the nation's governors to a reception following a meeting of the National Governors Association. Inexplicably, the president and Mrs. Hoover left the governors *standing* in the East Room for thirty minutes before welcoming them.[240] It may have been a scheduling error by a Hoover aide, but FDR and Eleanor saw it as a *personal* slight. FDR declined the offer of a chair (some of his Democratic rivals were in the room). He determined to remain standing as long as the others did. For him, though, it was an agony. Supported by ten pounds of steel braces on his legs, FDR sweated profusely in the hot spring air.[241]

Now, as president-elect, FDR was determined not to entangle himself with the rejected Hoover or his failed policies. When Hoover asked FDR's help in reducing war debts of America's allies, he knew he needed Congress's consent. He appealed to FDR to support him in this wise and good policy. But FDR believed that until he was sworn in, he had *no* constitutional authority to give any direction to the federal government and so he declined Hoover's appeal. In this, FDR was doubtless correct. There can be only one president at a time.

As the winter deepened, so did the Depression. Hoover continued to appeal to FDR publicly for help. But to a Republican senator, he admitted, "I realize that if these declarations be made by the President-elect [the declarations Hoover had requested] he will have ratified the whole major program of the Republican Administration; that is, it means the abandonment of 90 [percent] of the so-called new deal. But unless this is done, they run a grave danger of precipitating a complete financial debacle."[242]

FDR probably did not know Hoover's mind on the subject, but he didn't need to. He suspected that he was being pressured to yield the very basis on which he had been so resoundingly elected. President Lincoln had faced precisely the same kind of pressure during the Secession Winter of 1860–1861. Like Lincoln, FDR refused the bait.

Facing a real danger of a complete breakdown in cooperation on the presidential transition, Hoover's secretary of state Henry Stimson stepped in with tact and skill to work for smoother relations. Soon, Stimson found himself serving as a de facto secretary of state for the incoming Roosevelt administration. A key Roosevelt adviser, Felix Frankfurther, was grateful to Stimson for breaking the ice between the two camps. Frankfurter would be a leading member of what was called Roosevelt's "Brain Trust." He told Stimson he might actually have more influence with the Roosevelt administration than with the man who had appointed him.[243]

The president-elect visited Miami on the evening of 15 February 1933. There, he was to meet with Chicago mayor Anton Cermak. Cermak wanted federal aid, of course, and he also wanted to make amends for having packed the convention hall the previous summer with noisy backers of Al Smith.[244] As the president-elect reached out his hand to Mayor Cermak, shots rang out in the crowd. The mayor and a policeman were hit. FDR's security detail lurched ahead, trying to leave the assassination scene behind, but Roosevelt ordered the car to go back and take the gravely wounded

Cermak to the hospital.[245] FDR's cool courage under fire thrilled the entire country. The nation soon learned that among the dying Mayor Cermak's last words were these: "I'm glad it was me instead of you."[246]

Eleanor, in New York, responded airily: "These things are to be expected."[247] Citing the danger of assassination, the Secret Service sought to assign agents to the incoming First Lady, but Eleanor valued her independence too much for that. "Well all right," said the frustrated chief of the Secret Service to Roosevelt's trusted aide, Louis Howe, "if Mrs. Roosevelt is going to drive around the country alone, at least ask her to carry this [revolver] in the car."[248]

FDR could not afford to have Eleanor's wings clipped. He depended on her too much for that. She was his eyes and ears in those places he could not go. He always questioned her extensively whenever she returned from one of her hundreds of trips:

> [W]hen I returned from a trip around the Gaspé [region of Quebec] he wanted to know not only what kind of fishing was possible in the area but what the life of the fisherman was, what he had to eat, how he lived, what the farms were like, how the houses were built, what type of education was available, and whether it was completely church-controlled like the rest of the life in the village.[249]

Eleanor's peripatetic ways would be widely lampooned in the Roosevelt years, but we see from this revealing account the extraordinary partnership they had developed. Few politicians have ever had FDR's detailed and intimate knowledge of the lives lived by very ordinary people. This was all the more remarkable because FDR was incontestably a child of privilege. His doting mother, Sara Delano Roosevelt, handled his household accounts through most of his adult life. Although Al Smith may have known the "Sidewalks of New York," thanks to Eleanor, FDR knew the lives of the people who crowded into the subways that ran *beneath* those sidewalks.

Herbert Hoover made one last attempt to bring FDR into his decision making. Hoover appealed to Roosevelt to reassure the world's banking circles that he would *not* take America off the Gold Standard. Once again,

FDR refused to comply with Hoover's increasingly urgent requests. Lacking Roosevelt's support, Hoover declined to act on his own.[250] The financial crisis worsened.

Inauguration Day 1933. The country longed for an end to the *interregnum.* (Americans, typically, rejected the fancy Latin word in favor of the more folksy term: *lame duck.*) FDR rode down Pennsylvania Avenue with the outgoing president. That was the only *outgoing* thing about poor Herbert Hoover. When he failed to engage his defeated rival in conversation, Roosevelt turned to the happy crowds cheering along the parade route. He smiled his radiant smile and waved his top hat.[251] The extraordinary scene was captured—and exaggerated—by a cartoon published in the *New Yorker* magazine. FDR was buoyant, optimistic, Hoover tight-lipped and grim. Unfortunately for the Republicans, that was to be their image for years.

"Let me assert my firm belief that the *only* thing we have to fear is fear itself"—Roosevelt intoned from the Inaugural platform—"nameless, unreasoning, unjustified terror which paralyzes needed efforts to convert retreat into advance." Then he signaled his intention of summoning Congress into special session, saying: "I shall ask the Congress for the one remaining instrument to meet the crisis—broad Executive power to wage a war against the emergency, as great as the power that would be given to me if we were in fact invaded by a foreign foe."[252]

Roosevelt's opponents seized upon the opening notes of his administration. Why were they so *fearful*? Why did FDR's appeal seem to them like a desperate power grab? To answer that, we must understand that in 1933 constitutional democracies were on the retreat all around the world. Stalin in the Soviet Union was ever tightening the vise of Communist terror and tyranny on the masses of Russians. In Germany, Adolf Hitler had no sooner been named chancellor of the Weimar Republic than a suspicious fire in the Reichstag building gave him the opportunity to blame the Communists. By outlawing the German Communist Party, Hitler's Nazis dominated elections for the new parliament. The only story on the front page of the *New York Times* on the day following FDR's inauguration that related to foreign news informed readers: "Victory for Hitler Expected Today."[253] When the new Reichstag reconvened, it passed a law allowing Hitler to rule by decree. Opposition to Hitler, the *Times* noted, was now *verboten*.[254]

The liberal Weimar Republic effectively died just weeks after Hitler came to power. Dictatorships in Hungary, Poland, and Italy had taken the place of democracies. In Japan, a prime minister who had opposed the aggressive designs of young military officers was assassinated as a warning to others not to interfere.

President Hoover, in one of his few memorable phrases, had dismissed FDR as a "chameleon on Scotch plaid."[255] To Hoover, the detail-oriented engineer, Roosevelt was shockingly unprepared for the office he had won so overwhelmingly. And here was Roosevelt, talking about asking Congress for war powers in a country still at peace. Small wonder, then, that his opponents feared Roosevelt.

Three

FDR AND THE NEW DEAL

(1933–1939)

Franklin D. Roosevelt was all at once the most powerful democratic officeholder in a world where democracy itself was increasingly threatened. Roosevelt vastly increased the power of the federal government, but he did so only with the consent of an only-too-willing elected Congress. Roosevelt created a dizzying array of "alphabet soup" agencies—the Securities and Exchange Commission (SEC), the Federal Communications Commission (FCC), the Works Progress Administration (WPA), and the Public Works Administration (PWA) to name but a few. All of these bureaucracies consumed millions of dollars and committed the government to an ever greater reliance on "tax and spend." Roosevelt's opponents feared and even loathed him. They believed he was intent on bringing Socialism to America. To be sure, thousands of Americans advocated Communism, openly sympathizing with the Bolshevik experiment then taking place in Soviet Russia. "I have seen the future—and it works," the muckraker Lincoln Steffens had said of the new Soviet Union in 1919. FDR, however, thought he was saving capitalism and democracy. Roosevelt relied on a "Brain Trust," many bright young Ivy League graduates, to staff all these new agencies. FDR committed himself to "bold experimentation," freely*

* Among those who served in FDR's Brain Trust were Raymond Moley, Rexford Guy Tugwell, A.A. Berle, and Harry Hopkins. Thomas ("Tommy the Cork") Corcoran was a durable Washington hand and early member. When this author brought the Cork his morning coffee, he cried out: "Hebe!" Questioned if he knew who Hebe was, this young office assistant replied, "Cupbearer of the gods on Mount Olympus." "You're *hired*," yelled Tommy the Cork.

admitting that some of his ideas would not work, but assuring Americans that "the immortal Dante tells us that the sins of the warm hearted and the sins of the cold blooded are weighed in different scales." He implied that his critics were the cold blooded ones. FDR's dominance of the Congress in these years, while not complete, was yet so powerful as to shape the country we live in to this day.

I. The Hundred Days . . . and After

When Franklin Roosevelt took the oath as the thirty-second president of the United States on 4 March 1933, trucks that delivered the mail had to be accompanied by armed guards in some cities. An air of crisis pervaded the country. The new president moved immediately to declare a "bank holiday," closing down the nation's savings institutions for a week. Will Rogers joked that Americans were happy at last: "We have no jobs, we have no money, we have no banks; and if Roosevelt had burned down the Capitol, we would have said, 'Thank God, he started a fire under something.'"[1]* Roosevelt needed to prevent the run on the banks that had spread panic during the long period from his election in November until his March inauguration.

When Congress assembled, the new president submitted a flurry of legislative proposals that were enacted into law so quickly that few lawmakers had even read them. Fifteen major laws were enacted between 9 March and 16 June 1933. Their very titles give us an idea of the incredible range and extent of the new powers being assumed by the federal government: Emergency Banking Act, National Industrial Recovery Act, Civilian Conservation Corps, Leaving the Gold Standard, Emergency Relief, Agricultural Adjustment Act, Emergency Farm Mortgage, Tennessee Valley Authority, Truth-in Securities, Home Owner's Loan Corporation, Glass-Steagall Banking Act, and the Farm Credit Act.[2] This fecund period

* Burning down the nation's legislature was no laughing matter in Germany, where just weeks before the Reichstag had been burned down by a Dutch anarchist. Hitler seized upon the incident to outlaw the Communists and many of their left-wing allies. From this early moment in 1933, Hitler's Germany was effectively a dictatorship.

was to be known as the Hundred Days, setting a standard of legislative accomplishment never again to be equaled.*

One of the measures easily passed by the new Congress was the Twenty-first Amendment to the Constitution, the repeal of Prohibition. Even though FDR's landslide made Prohibition's repeal a dead certainty, Congress was taking no chances. For only the second time in history, a constitutional change was submitted to state ratifying conventions rather than to the state legislatures.** At 3:32 p.m., Mountain Time, on 5 December 1933, Utah became the thirty-sixth state to vote for repeal of the Eighteenth Amendment; Prohibition thus became the only constitutional amendment ever repealed.[3]

Wet in both principle and practice during Prohibition, H. L. Mencken partook of his first *legal* beer in thirteen years at Baltimore's Rennert Hotel. "Here it goes," he said after accepting a frothy stein from barkeep Harry Roth. He tossed it back and adjudged its contents: "Pretty good, not bad at all."[4] He similarly adjudged repeal: "It isn't often that anything to the public good issues out of American politicians. This time they have been forced to be decent."[5]

Thumping Democratic majorities in both Houses of Congress provided "a rubber stamp" to FDR's proposals. So many of the members had ridden into office on FDR's coattails that it was unthinkable they would seriously oppose him.

A single paragraph from Samuel Eliot Morison is worth volumes in our understanding of the cultural and political world we inhabit, to a great extent, seventy years after the New Deal:

> A feature of the WPA [Works Progress Administration] which caught the public eye and became nicknamed "boondoggling," was the setting up of projects to employ artists, musicians, writers and other "white

---

* The Republican minority was overwhelmed in both Houses. To have filibustered against New Deal legislation at a time when everyone recognized an unprecedented national emergency would have labeled them obstructionist. Still, we can hardly claim that FDR's proposals were seriously debated in Congress. "The Hundred Days" previously had referred to Napoleon's return from Elba. Comparing an American president's agenda to that tyrant could hardly have been comforting to FDR's legions of critics.

** The original constitution was ratified by state conventions and, in 1933, this method was employed to ratify the Twenty-first Amendment.

collar" workers. Post offices and other public buildings were decorated with murals; regional and state guides were written; libraries in municipal and state buildings were catalogued by out-of-work librarians, and indigent graduate students were employed to inventory archives and copy old shipping lists, to the subsequent profit of American historians. The federal theater at its peak employed over 15,000 actors and other workers, at an average wage of $20 a week. Under the direction of John Houseman, Orson Welles, and others, new plays were written and produced, and the classics revived.[6]*

Here, in a nutshell, we see the origins of many of today's political alignments. Hollywood, academia, the press, libraries, the public universities—all are inhabited by tens of thousands of people who could trace the existence of their jobs or their institutions to a federal program begun under FDR. By bringing into government a "Brain Trust," FDR assured the allegiance of what we today call the "knowledge class" to the Democratic Party. One thing can always be assured: If you take from Peter to pay Paul, you can generally rely on the vote of Paul.

One of FDR's first ventures into foreign policy was to end the fifteen-year isolation of the Soviet Union. The president was urged to extend diplomatic recognition by William Bullitt, whose brother-in-law was the famous American Communist, John Reed. Reed's glowing account of the Bolshevik Revolution, *Ten Days That Shook the World*, was a popular book on the Left. President Woodrow Wilson had refused to recognize what he regarded as a bandit regime. He even sent U.S. troops to Russia, ostensibly to prevent U.S. war materiel from falling into German hands. Inevitably, however, U.S. forces clashed with the Reds. Following the Communist victory in the Russian Civil War, U.S. forces were evacuated. But there was lingering bitterness toward the commissars in the Kremlin.

Roosevelt assigned Bullitt to work with Soviet Commissar for Foreign

---

* Interestingly, the same John Houseman who started off in the federal WPA later became known to Americans as the curmudgeonly TV pitchman for the Wall Street investment firm of Smith-Barney. "They make money the old fashioned way," Houseman intoned; "they *earn* it."

Relations, Maxim Litvinov. Together, Bullitt and Litvinov negotiated an agreement to open relations between the two "great republics."[7] The Soviets agreed to allow religious freedom for Americans working in the USSR, an almost meaningless concession.[8] The Soviets also agreed to stop their propaganda barrage against the United States and not to send agents to America to try to subvert our government. The first condition they met, but only partially. On the third, and most important, point, Soviet attempts at subversion virtually began the day they received formal recognition.[9]

Promises of a vastly expanded trade with the resource-rich Soviet Union led to wildly exaggerated expectations for closer ties with the Communist giant. Such hopes led major American business groups, hard pressed by the Depression, to favor an open door to the USSR. Industrialist Armand Hammer spent a career promoting business ties with the Soviet Union. He was later revealed as a collaborator with the Soviets, active from the beginning in money-laundering for the Kremlin.[10] The trade promises proved just as genuine—they never materialized.[11]

Considering the overwhelming support for FDR among Catholics and labor union members, it is significant that the Catholic Conference of Bishops and the American Federation of Labor (AFL) strongly opposed diplomatic relations with the Moscow Communist regime.

When FDR announced that the two nations would exchange ambassadors after all, he named William C. Bullitt to head our Moscow Embassy. Bullitt turned out to be a hard-headed realist about Soviet-U.S. relations.[12]

The Communist Party of the United States of America (CPUSA) was politically agile and adept at advancing its aims through progressive issues. In the first half of the thirties, American Communists supported the New Deal. CPUSA agitators could be seen in a host of labor clashes, particularly where violence was employed. Textile workers in Gastonia, North Carolina, and coal miners in Harlan County, Kentucky, found their legitimate grievances being taken up by Communists sent in by the party to stir things up.[13]

Similarly, the party leapt to the defense of nine young black men falsely accused of raping a white teenager. They were known as "The Scottsboro Boys." The NAACP hesitated to take up a case so explosive. But the CPUSA gained widespread respect among idealistic Americans outraged by the continuing rule of lynch law in many Southern communities.[14]*

While many liberals mistrusted Communists, some considered them simply "liberals in a hurry." A popular slogan of the day explained away Stalin's crimes by saying "you can't make omelets without breaking a few eggs." Many liberals agreed with veteran muckraker Lincoln Steffens who had visited the new Soviet Union in 1919. Steffens said, "I have seen the future—*and it works!*" What Stalin was breaking was not eggs, but heads; and there were millions of them, not a few. We now know that the CPUSA was controlled throughout its existence by Moscow.

Some of the legislation of the Hundred Days was intended only to be temporary; other laws remain on the books to this day. One of the temporary measures was the Civilian Conservation Corps (CCC). Under the CCC, thousands of young men camped out in tents, worked on projects like completing the long, snaking Appalachian hiking trail, and received three square meals a day. They earned little, but they had health care and, importantly, a sense of achievement.[15] FDR himself stressed the spiritual and social benefits of conservation work for unemployed, restless young men. Roving bands of out-of-work, out-of-luck young men have often created combustible conditions in a nation's urban centers. Roosevelt seemed to sense this instinctively.** The Public Works Administration (PWA) dedicated itself to large projects like New York City's Triborough Bridge—still in daily use.[16]

Tens of thousands looked to the jobs provided by the Works Progress Administration (WPA) to get them through the Depression. When John Reagan became an administrator for the Dixon, Illinois, WPA, it helped the

---

* Many of the Communists and their "fellow travelers" were doubtless sincere about racial justice in America. They could see the injustices here, but they were selective about what they saw abroad. They turned a blind eye to the *millions* in the USSR who were killed outright by the Secret Police or packed off to the slave labor camps—Stalin's *Gulag*—to die of cold and starvation.

** FDR's praise for the spiritual impact of the CCC is one of the quotes chosen for his memorial in Washington, D.C. "I propose to create a Civilian Conservation Corps to be used in simple work. More important, however, than the material gains will be the moral and spiritual value of such work." (Message to Congress on Unemployment Relief, Washington, D.C., 21 March 1933.)

family stay afloat (and not incidentally made his son, Ronald, a firm supporter of the New Deal).[17]

The National Industrial Recovery Act was also not intended to be long-term. But that did not mean it was insignificant. Congress appropriated the then huge sum of $3.3 billion to set up an elaborate, nationwide system to manage the stricken economy.[18] FDR chose West Pointer Hugh Johnson to run the National Recovery Agency (NRA) set up by the legislation. The NRA provided codes for wages and hours and working conditions and discouraged women and child labor in hazardous industries. Johnson designed an Art Deco Blue Eagle as the NRA's symbol. He also organized parades and other events to rally mass support. To FDR's opponents, the NRA's symbol looked shockingly like the Nazi eagle, and Johnson's marchers looked like the Hitler Youth. When Johnson unwisely praised Mussolini's Fascist "corporatist state," even many conservative *Democrats* took alarm. They were worried about the survival of freedom in a world menaced by tyrannies of the left and the right. Both John W. Davis (1924) and Al Smith (1928), the only living former Democratic presidential candidates, joined the Liberty League to organize opposition to Roosevelt's New Deal.

Other Democrats, however, thought Roosevelt was not going far enough. Louisiana senator Huey Long was a wild-haired populist who wore a rumpled white "ice cream" suit and loved to rabble rouse. His "Every Man a King" philosophy had made him the undisputed boss of the Bayou State. When he was governor of Louisiana, his massive road-building projects and new skyscraper state capitol gave work to thousands while lining the pockets of hundreds of contractors. As U.S. senator, he loved to outrage well-bred members of Washington's social Establishment, the so-called Cliff Dwellers. When Huey Long came to the White House, he sat down to dinner *wearing his hat!*[19] Invited to the president's home in Hyde Park, New York, he was so loud and boorish at dinner that Sara Delano Roosevelt, the president's formidable mother, audibly whispered: "Who is that *awful* man sitting next to Franklin?"[20]

That awful man was the Kingfish, and Franklin was bending over backward to keep him happy. It's not that he needed his vote in the Senate, where FDR had a walloping majority. No, the president needed to keep

Long "on the reservation." The Kingfish posed a danger as a possible third party candidate advocating a "soak the rich" policy. He may have been clownish, but he was also shrewd and daring. Roosevelt knew that many of his Big Business opponents were willing to finance Long's campaign just to get *him* out of the White House.[21] "We're not for you, either," one of their representatives told the Kingfish in a secret meeting. "Just give me the money," Huey smilingly told him.[22] In the spring of 1935, Huey wrote a book, *My First Days in the White House.* His intentions were clear.[23]

An open breach occurred between New Deal supporters and radio host Father Charles Coughlin and Senator Long when, in March 1935, NRA director Hugh Johnson publicly ridiculed Coughlin. "We expect politics to make strange bedfellows, but if Father Coughlin wants to [get in bed with] Huey Long, it is only fair [that he] take off his Roman cassock."[24] Hugh Johnson's gibe risked not only driving Long into opposition to FDR, but it also threatened to alienate Catholics, a key New Deal constituency.

Senator Long returned in September 1935 to Baton Rouge, to the impressive state capitol he had built. He was shoring up his political support at home when he was confronted by Dr. Carl Austin Weiss, a brilliant young ear, nose, and throat specialist. Weiss was the son-in-law of Judge Pavy, a staunch opponent of Huey Long. The doctor shot the Kingfish, firing two bullets before his small Belgian pistol jammed. Long's enraged bodyguards immediately turned on Dr. Weiss. They shot him twenty-nine times.

The dying Long gasped, "What did he want to shoot me for?" It may have been that Weiss heard that Huey was behind a scheme to spread the word that Judge Pavy's family had black ancestors. In his time, Long was unusual because he was not a race-baiting white Southern politician. But he certainly would not hesitate to use any tactic against a political enemy. We will probably never know why Weiss killed Huey Long, but in doing so, he removed a major threat to FDR's reelection.[25]

When President Roosevelt took America off the Gold Standard in 1933, he called in gold certificates. These were replaced by greenbacks. The action had fateful consequences for the United States, the world economy, and, especially, for one immigrant carpenter in the Bronx.

Bruno Hauptmann attracted an attendant's attention when he paid for gasoline with a $100 gold certificate rarely seen in late 1934. The attendant, suspecting counterfeit, wrote down the German immigrant's license number.[26] Very quickly, police arrested Hauptmann and in an unlikely twist charged him with the kidnapping and death of Charles A. Lindbergh, Jr.

Hauptmann's trial in early 1935 in Flemington, New Jersey, quickly became a media circus. H. L. Mencken called it "the biggest story since the Resurrection."[27] Evidence introduced against him included marked gold certificates that he had stashed away; these were identified as part of Lindbergh's ransom payment. The wooden slats of the ladder he had used to enter the Lindbergh home's nursery were found to match neatly several slats in the carpenter's garage. When Charles Lindbergh took the witness stand, he showed no emotion. He gave his testimony coolly.[28] Asked if he could identify the voice of the man who spoke to him about delivering the ransom money, Lindbergh fingered Hauptmann.[29] As a measure of the intense public interest in the trial, the *New York Times* pushed aside President Roosevelt's State of the Union Address to give prime space to "Col. Lindbergh Names Hauptmann as Kidnapper and Taker of Ransom; Cool in 3-Hour Cross-Examination."[30] Turned down on appeal, Hauptmann went to his death still professing his innocence.

While Hauptmann was appealing his conviction, the Lindbergh family continued to endure intense media scrutiny of their every move. Their young son, Jon, was the new focus of kidnap threats. On Monday, 23 December 1935, the *New York Times* carried this headline: "Lindbergh Family Sails for England to Seek a Safe, Secluded Residence; Threats on Son's Life Force Decision."[31] Was such a drastic step really necessary? Might some high-profile trials of those who threatened the Lindberghs have put a stop to such intolerable harassment? We cannot know. Perhaps no one who has not suffered the traumatic loss of a beloved child to kidnapping can ever say how much threat is too much. Still, the Lindberghs' voyage into voluntary exile was a telling consequences of American press freedom. Did an irresponsible press create an intolerable madhouse atmosphere?

James Weldon Johnson. *Johnson and his fellow members of the National Association for the Advancement of Colored People (NAACP) helped to make the Harlem Renaissance and to put justice for black Americans on the nation's agenda.*

Henry Ford. *An inventive genius, Ford's assembly lines symbolized the nation's industrial might. He put America on wheels. But his* Dearborn Independent *newspaper reprinted the forged "Protocols of the Elders of Zion." His vicious anti-semitism was admired by young Adolf Hitler.*

Adolf Hitler. *Hitler won distinction as a soldier in World War I. Afterwards, he joined the National Socialist German Workers Party (Nazis). Failing to overthrow the government of his home state of Bavaria in a 1923 "Beer Hall Putsch," he wrote* Mein Kampf ("My Struggle") *during his brief, relaxed stay in prison. In it, he laid out his plans for revenge and vented his hatred of the Jews. Ten years later, on 30 January 1933, he became Germany's Chancellor. Within weeks, the legislative chamber (the Reichstag) suspiciously burned. From that point on, Hitler ruled as a dictator. He plunged Europe into a Second World War and initiated the Holocaust of the Jews.*

II. Hitler's Games: The Berlin Olympics

On 7 March 1936, Adolf Hitler told his rubber-stamp legislature that he would reoccupy the Rhineland. Even as he spoke in the Reichstag, German troops were entering this historically German region.[32]* This was a bold challenge to the Western Allies. A demilitarized Rhineland had been a key security provision demanded by the French at Versailles. Under the terms of the Treaty of Versailles, Germany was forbidden both to rearm and to reoccupy the Rhineland. Now, Hitler was throwing down the gauntlet. France reacted as if an electric shock had gone through Paris. Just as quickly, however, the conservative government of Prime Minister Stanley Baldwin in London called on France to "wait in order that both countries might act jointly and after full consideration." Winston Churchill called this move "a velvet carpet for retreat."[33] And so it was. Churchill was no defender of the Treaty of Versailles. He thought its economic clauses in particular were "malignant, silly, futile."[34] He did not go as far as France's Marshal Foch, who snorted that it was not a peace, just a twenty-year armistice.[35] Even so, if Germany could defy its disarmament and territorial provisions, the treaty would be scrapped and the fruits of victory in World War I would be lost as the world lurched toward a second clash.

Hitler was relieved when the Baldwin government talked to death any plan for French resistance. His generals feared that the still powerful French army would crush the incoming German legions. Frankly, Hitler had feared this as well. He gave his troops orders to retreat at the first sign of French resistance. If that happened, as Hitler knew, his own generals might overthrow him—a thought that had made him physically ill. When the resistance never materialized, he blustered and taunted his generals. Hitler claimed he had a superior "intuition" into the minds of his enemies.[36] He risked all and he won big.

---

* The Rhineland was always German, but it was Catholic—Germany was largely Protestant. Thus, the French had hopes that the Rhinelanders could be persuaded eventually to form their own *Rhenish* state as a buffer between France and the more powerful, largely Protestant power of Germany. The Rhineland is located on the West Bank of the Rhine River and borders France and Belgium.

Hitler shrewdly coupled his Rhineland takeover with an offer of a twenty-five-year peace pact with the Western democracies. Leading British appeasers immediately wired Prime Minister Baldwin. He should "welcome Hitler's declaration wholeheartedly," they swooned.[37] Lord Lothian, soon to become Britain's ambassador in Washington, characterized this blatant violation of the Treaty of Versailles as Hitler merely marching "into his back-garden."[38] Many of the appeasers in Britain took care to criticize Hitler's brazen violation of the terms imposed on Germany after the World War, but now some even went so far as to say, "Versailles is now a corpse and should be buried."[39]

Americans wanted desperately to stay out of Europe's quarrels. Because the United States had not ratified the Treaty of Versailles, FDR had little influence over events on the Continent. Woodrow Wilson and Lloyd George had promised aid to France if Germany ever arose to threaten France from the Rhineland. But Wilson, embittered over the Senate's rejection of his beloved League of Nations, had refused even to submit the French Guarantee Treaty for ratification. Moreover, Congress had passed a series of Neutrality Acts that would sharply reduce the president's ability to help threatened democracies in Europe. This, and their own worried electorates, prompted British and French leaders to try to keep Hitler at bay by making timely concessions to him. They realized they could not rely on American help and vainly hoped that they could satisfy Hitler's demands. Clemenceau's nightmare had sprung to life. Germany moved menacingly closer to France and the "Anglo-Saxons" did not lift a finger to stop it.

Huge majorities of Oxford undergraduates had declared by vote that "we will *not* fight for King or country." In Britain, the peace movement was strong. Still suffering from the Depression, the British upper classes, the monarchy in particular, dreaded another war.[40] King George V told Prime Minister Baldwin that if he got into another war, he would personally go down to Hyde Park and wave a red flag.* The Prince of Wales was openly pro-Hitler.[41]

Winston Churchill was at this time what British politicians call a "backbencher." In the House of Commons, those who sit in the back benches are

* The red flag always represented revolution. Even before the Communists took it up, it was the flag waved by opponents of monarchy in Europe.

those who are both physically and symbolically farthest from the Treasury Bench, the prominent place in the front where the prime minister and his cabinet sit. Churchill was in the midst of his "wilderness years," the decade when he was out of the cabinet, out of power, and increasingly out of sorts. He had turned sixty years old in 1934 and to many he was a has-been.

With the successful remilitarization of the Rhineland, Hitler was eager to redirect the world's focus. The 1936 Olympics had been awarded to Germany long before he established his Nazi dictatorship. Hitler planned to use the Games as a showcase for his regime. It was to be a propaganda blitz.

The Nazi regime stressed physical fitness, especially for the young. "Your body belongs to your country," said one fitness book that was required reading in German schools; "you are responsible to your country for your body."[42] Hitler wanted to show off the athletic prowess of German youth as a model of what National Socialist ideology taught about Aryan superiority.

Tall and statuesque, the green-eyed German Helene Mayer was living in California when the 1936 Olympics were being prepared in Berlin. She had won the gold medal for fencing while representing her native Germany in the 1928 games. Would she compete again now? Because her father was Jewish, under Hitler's new Nuremberg Laws she was officially designated as a *mischling* (person of mixed race).[43] Despite the fact that Jews had had their citizenship revoked by Hitler and were suffering all forms of political, civil, economic, and social persecution in the Nazi state, Helene was still eager to compete under the swastika flag.* She soon became immersed in a great political controversy over what some called "the Hitler Games."[44]

Predictably, Hitler's actions were producing deep unease across the Atlantic and many Americans urged a boycott of the games.[45] But Avery Brundage, head of the U.S. Olympic Committee, wanted his countrymen to compete in Berlin. He told the pro-Nazi, German-American Bund that the Olympics were "a religion with universal appeal, which incorporates all the basic values of other religions, a modern, exciting, virile, dynamic religion." Brundage opposed any talk of boycott: "Politics must not be brought

* The *swastika* was called "Hakenkreuz" (Hooked Cross) in German. Adolf Hitler personally adopted this ancient mystical sign as the symbol of his Nazi movement. It was incorporated into the German flag and was seen everywhere in Germany under the Third Reich.

into sports. I have not heard of anything to indicate discrimination of any race or religion."[46]

Brundage had not read the signs in hundreds of German towns: *Juden unerwuenscht*—"Jews Unwelcome." But thousands of others had read them and could have informed the USOC boss. Nor, apparently, was he aware that Jews had been excluded from all German sports clubs, although everyone else in the world of sports knew about this. Helene Mayer had even been excluded, but Hitler's government recognized the propaganda value of letting Helene compete for the *Vaterland*. "Helene is a good German and has nothing to do with the Jews," cabled the German consulate in San Francisco to the German Foreign Office in Berlin.[47]

Helene went on to win a silver medal in Berlin. The crowd roared as Helene stood rigidly at attention on the winner's platform, giving the stiff-armed "Heil Hitler" salute.

Not all Jewish competitors were so fortunate. American athletes Marty Glickman and Sam Stoller were yanked from their race just a day before they were to run—to appease Hitler. Frank Metcalfe and Jesse Owens would run in their place, their American coach told them. "Coach, I have won my three gold medals," Owens protested, "I have won the races I set out to win. I'm tired. I'm beat. Let Marty and Sam run." Coach Dean Cromwell pointed his finger at Owens and said: "You will do what you are told." Owens went on to win his fourth gold medal.[48]

Owens' "sunny demeanor" won him fans and friends wherever he went.[49] German crowds took up a cry of "*Oh-vens! Oh-vens*!" whenever he appeared to compete. Hitler, already having made up his mind to stop shaking each Olympic medal-winner's hand, was then asked by an aide if he wanted to make an exception for Jesse.[50] Hitler shouted at him: "Do you really think I will allow myself to be photographed shaking hands with a Negro?"[51] Much has been made of the fact that Hitler would not shake hands with Jesse Owens. But the reality was that Jesse Owens was spared the indignity of having to shake hands with Adolf Hitler.*

"No matter how Hitler and other Nazi leaders felt," writes one

* Lifelong Republican Owens spunkily pointed out that FDR never shook hands with him either! But there was never a doubt that Roosevelt would have been proud to shake Owens's hand.

author, "the Germans embraced Owens and his incredible performance. Altogether, African-American athletes won almost one-quarter of all the U.S. medals in the games. Their performance brought honor to themselves, their team, and their nation—and were a slap in the face of Hitler's racist policies."[52]

When the games opened with much fanfare, two of the surprise guests were American exiles, Charles Lindbergh and his wife, Anne. The first words that the Lindbergh's heard in Germany after a short flight from England were "Heil Hitler!" Lindbergh had come to Germany as an official guest of Hitler's new air force, the *Luftwaffe.** Anne's biographer would write of the world famous aviator: "Adolf Hitler was certain that Charles Lindbergh personified [the future of the Third Reich]. His tall frame, his sandy-haired boyishness, his piercing blue eyes, made him the quintessential Aryan. The Nazis could not have constructed a more eloquent embodiment of their vision."[53]

Lindbergh was especially impressed with the advanced state of German aeronautics. He appreciated the appearance of order and discipline he saw everywhere he went. The German press was not permitted to pester him and his wife. "Lindbergh had found the atmosphere fraternal, the people congenial, the press under control, officials deferential, discipline good, morals pure and morale high," wrote Tom Jones, a British civil servant close to Prime Minister Baldwin, of Lindbergh's reaction. "It was a refreshing change . . . from the moral degradation into which he considered the United States had fallen, the apathy and indifference of the British, the decadence of the French."[54]

Jones pointed out that Lindbergh liked what he saw because he never asked to see the concentration camps where, already, Jews, Communists, social democrats, Socialists, and any other people whom the regime chose were packed away.[55] The Nazis had opened Dachau in March 1933, just weeks after Hitler came to power. It was the first of many concentration camps that immediately began filling with opponents of the regime. By the

* According to the Versailles Treaty, Germany was also forbidden to have an air force. Hitler more or less openly defied the treaty's disarmament provisions.

end of the year, the Nazis had taken as many as one hundred thousand Germans away to these camps.[56]

As the closing ceremonies signaled the end of a very successful Olympics, the German crowd took up the chant of "*Sieg Heil!*" ("Victory, hail!")[57] Germany had won most of the medals. Nazi propagandists had labored to present a positive portrait of the Hitler dictatorship. And they largely succeeded. There was no report of any rudeness directed at any black or Jewish American Olympians.[58] The propagandists' campaign may have been helped by the timely intervention of Max Schmeling, the great German boxer. Schmeling became a "Nordic" hero when he defeated American boxer, Joe Louis, in June 1936. The "Brown Bomber" was beloved of black Americans, especially. Schmeling was not happy to be made a poster boy for the Nazis' racial views. Refusing to join the Nazi party, he nonetheless exacted a promise from Hitler that all U.S. athletes would be protected from insult during the Olympics.[59]

Because of the führer's aggressive war-making, there would not be another Olympic Games until 1948. The artificial spirit of bonhomie propagandists spread around the Games did not last. When Leni Riefenstahl, a film producer much favored by the top Nazis, showed her documentary *Olympiade 1936*, Propaganda Minister Joseph Goebbels was infuriated. Leni's camera had dwelled admiringly on Jesse Owens's muscles and a Japanese competitor's handsome face.[60] This so clashed with Goebbels's racial hatred that he banned Riefenstahl's work for eighteen months.[61]

III. "As Goes Maine . . ."

FDR's reelection in 1936 was by no means assured. The country had not fully recovered from the effects of the Depression. Economic conditions were nowhere near their pre-Crash 1929 levels. "Happy Days Are Here Again" was the Democrats' theme song, but it remained to be seen if they could capitalize on their victories of 1932 and 1934. Still, leading indicators *were* improving. The number of working Americans increased from thirty-eight million to over forty-four million. Unemployment numbers declined from thirteen million to eight million. And the economy was adding 150,000 new jobs for each month in 1936.[62]

Black Americans historically had found themselves backing the party of Lincoln. By 1936, however, many were beginning to question their ties. One black WPA worker put it this way: "I don't think it is fair to eat Roosevelt bread and meat and vote for Governor Landon."[63] Black Americans had suffered as greatly in the Depression as anyone; they looked to Washington, and FDR, for relief.

Eleanor Roosevelt was particularly sympathetic to the concerns of black Americans. In 1936, she invited the distinguished opera singer Marian Anderson to entertain at the White House. She was the first black artist to do so. While there was as yet no black cabinet member, FDR had named a record number of black appointees to subcabinet positions. When some of these officials came together under the leadership of Mary McLeod Bethune, they constituted themselves as FDR's "black Cabinet."[64] This group raised issues that the federal government might address, first to Bethune, then to the First Lady, and from there to FDR's breakfast table.

Mrs. Roosevelt's special sympathy gave rise to ugly stories and hateful attacks from racists threatened by such deliberate attempts to address racial imbalance in leadership. One vicious rhyme had FDR saying to his wife over breakfast:

> You kiss the Negroes and I'll kiss the Jews
> And we'll stay in the White House as long as we choose.[65]

In truth, FDR was building a new coalition that included *many* minorities. Catholics, Jews, blacks, Westerners, Southerners, labor union members—all were welcomed into the New Deal new majority.

When the Republicans nominated Kansas Governor Alf Landon, they spurned former President Hoover and his increasingly strident opposition to everything FDR had done. Delegates to the 1936 Republican Convention wanted to nominate New Hampshire's popular senator Styles Bridges for vice president. He looked like a sure winner for the number two slot until someone noted that "Landon-Bridges falling down" would be the inevitable response of the opposition.[66] Republicans instead turned to Frank Knox, who had been a Rough Rider with Teddy in Cuba. Most significantly, Republicans endorsed the Social Security Act FDR had introduced and Congress had quickly enacted in 1935. They also endorsed the right of labor to organize and certain forms of business regulation.[67] It was not a platform designed to appeal to conservative Republicans, and it didn't.

The press weighed in. FDR charmed the White House reporters who met regularly with him for off-the-record "background" briefings. Many of their editors, however, were solidly against Roosevelt. Colonel Robert McCormick, owner of the *Chicago Tribune*, despised FDR. He instructed his switchboard operators to answer every call with the number of days until the country was freed from Roosevelt's misrule.[68]

FDR reveled in the opposition of Big Business. He loved to tell the story of the "nice old gentleman" who had fallen into the water while wearing an expensive silk hat. In the story, the gentleman's friend ran down the pier, jumped into the water and pulled him out. But the hat floated away on the tide. At first, the old gentleman thanked his friend and praised his courage. Four years later, though, the old gentleman had begun to complain about losing that fine hat![69] FDR's telling of this story fit the caricature of the Big Businessman that even then was being popularized by the best-selling board game, *Monopoly*. People could see the "old gentleman" who wore the shiny top hat.*

In a more serious vein, FDR accepted his renomination in Philadelphia with an eloquent call: "This generation of Americans has a rendezvous with destiny."[70]

The well-respected *Literary Digest* attempted a public opinion poll. The science of polling was then in its infancy. The *Digest* polled those with telephones. In the depths of a Depression, this meant the views of millions of poverty-stricken Americans were not considered. The *Literary Digest* confidently predicted a Landon win. "A *Landon*-slide" boasted GOP campaign operatives when Maine's vote came in. The Down East

* *Monopoly* was invented in 1934. Originally rejected as too complex, it has sold more than two hundred million copies in more than eighty countries.

State traditionally had voted in September. The old saying was, "As goes Maine, so goes the Nation."

Not this year. When the votes came in, FDR had triumphed again. He won reelection with an unprecedented 27,476,673 popular votes—a stunning 60.6 percent. Landon got 16,679,583 popular votes, just 36.8 percent. In the Electoral College, Roosevelt swept the nation with 523 votes to Landon's derisory 8. Democratic National Chairman Jim Farley, one of FDR's savvy Irish political lieutenants, jibed that in view of Roosevelt's forty-six-state sweep, the old adage would have to be changed: "As goes Maine, so goes Vermont."[71] Abashed, the *Literary Digest* soon ceased publication.

Across the ocean, even people outside his Conservative Party were beginning to pay attention to Winston Churchill's warnings. Clement Atlee was the leader of the Labour Party in the House of Commons. Atlee "will support you on any rearmament programme," Winston's cousin wrote to him at this time, adding, "[Atlee] likes and admires you."[72] This support might have helped Churchill as Prime Minister Baldwin prepared to step down. But there was a crisis brewing that threatened Churchill's standing—one involving the recently crowned Prince of Wales and his American mistress.

At the end of 1936, Americans were buzzing about the new king's romance with the twice-divorced Wallis Warfield Simpson of Baltimore. Everyone in the United States knew about it, but in Britain the newspapers of Fleet Street clamped a lid on discussion of the king's plans to marry her. Thus, early in December when Prime Minister Baldwin's cabinet privately told the king he must either give up Simpson or give up the throne, few Britons knew how close they were to a sudden breach.

Churchill, ever the romantic and passionately attached to the monarchy, pleaded for time, only time. He thought he could persuade the dim-witted young king not to attempt to marry his mistress. Winston did not realize that King Edward VIII *wanted* to force the crisis as a way to escape the tiresome duties of the throne. The king had been a playboy Prince of Wales for twenty years and had no sense of responsibility. Churchill arose in Parliament pleading for "no irrevocable step," but he suffered the humiliation of being shouted down. Feeling betrayed by his prime minister, Churchill turned and shouted angrily at Baldwin: "You won't be satisfied until you've broken him, will you?"[73]

One Member of Parliament, Harold Nicolson, wrote in his diary: "[Winston] has undone in five minutes the patient reconstruction work of two years."[74] The London *Spectator* was even sharper: "[The Right Honorable Mr. Churchill] has utterly misjudged the temper of the country and the temper of the House, and the reputation which he was beginning to shake off of a wayward genius unserviceable in council has settled firmly on his shoulders again."[75]

Deciding to step down, the king made a BBC radio broadcast that was heard around the world. He said he found it "impossible to continue without the help and support of the woman I love." Women on both sides of the Atlantic wept, thrilled by his devotion and grieved for his loss of the throne. But ultimately, his decision was a blessing to both Britain and the United States. Later, as Duke and Duchess of Windsor, the royal pair flitted all too close to the flame of Nazism.

We are left to wonder: What would have happened in the world if Winston Churchill and not Neville Chamberlain had succeeded Stanley Baldwin as prime minister in 1937?

IV. FDR's "Risky Scheme"

Overwhelmingly reelected and with even stronger majorities in both Houses of Congress, FDR prepared to take on the U.S. Supreme Court.

He had reacted angrily to the Court's 1935 decision in the famous "sick chicken" case. By a vote of 9–0, the Court ruled in *Schechter Poultry Corp. v. United States* that the National Industrial Recovery Act was unconstitutional. The Court then proceeded to strike down the Agricultural Adjustment Act and other New Deal legislation. Roosevelt felt that none of his administration's achievements could be secure as long as the "nine old men" on the Supreme Court had unchecked power.

President Roosevelt tried to rally the nation behind him with his second Inaugural Address. It was delivered in a driving rain on 20 January

1937.* "I see millions denied education, recreation, and the opportunity to better their lot and that of their children," he intoned. "I see millions lacking the means to buy the products of farm and factory and by their poverty denying work and productiveness to many other millions. I see one-third of a nation ill-housed, ill-clad, ill-nourished."[76] To address these conditions, Roosevelt argued, he needed legislation. And that legislation was being attacked by an unelected, unresponsive judiciary. Roosevelt responded with a plan that soon came to be known as his "court-packing scheme."

FDR was worried that the major legislation of his first term was in jeopardy—including the Wagner Act, which governed labor relations; the Social Security Act; and his agriculture laws.[77] Roosevelt criticized Chief Justice Hughes for saying, "We are under a Constitution, but the Constitution is what the judges say it is." No, said the president, "We want a Supreme Court that will do justice under the Constitution, not *over* it. In our courts, we want a government of laws and not of men."[78] Roosevelt could wax eloquent about the power of the courts. "The [flooded] Ohio River and the Dust Bowl are not conversant with the habits of the Interstate Commerce Clause."[79] He challenged lawyers to give their opinions to "the sweating men piling sandbags on the levees at Cairo, Illinois. . . ."[80]

FDR might have succeeded with his judicial reorganization plan had he been straightforward, direct, and candid with the American people. Instead, he presented his bill as an attempt to help old or infirm judges. He would add a justice for every member of the Supreme Court who passed age seventy and did not resign. Despite its lofty-sounding justification, Americans were not taken in. FDR's scheme was a transparent plan to pack the court with compliant justices.

Congressional Democrats rebelled. "Boys, here's where I cash in," said the Texas chairman of the House Judiciary Committee to Southern colleagues.[81] Southern Democrats had come to view the Supreme Court as their bulwark against civil rights legislation. The Supreme Court's *Plessy v. Ferguson* decision of 1896 had permitted racial segregation. *Plessy* was still the "law of the land."

---

* As a result of the Twentieth Amendment, quickly ratified in 1933, the date of the Presidential Inauguration was shifted from 4 March to 20 January. Congress, too, would henceforth meet in early January every year.

The Court, perhaps recognizing it was under assault, surprised everyone by *upholding* both the Wagner Act *and* the Social Security Act. When one of the older justices resigned, FDR was given his first opportunity to name a member of the Supreme Court.

"How do you find the Court situation, Jack?" the president asked Vice President John Nance Garner about the status of the court reorganization bill. "Do you want it with the bark on or off, Cap'n?" asked Garner. "The rough way," said FDR. "You are beat," said the vice president, "you haven't got the votes."[82] Roosevelt would remember that Garner said *you* and not *we.*

When Senator Robinson of Arkansas, the Democratic majority leader, died of a heart attack, FDR's last chance of winning on his court-packing scheme died with him. Still, the Supreme Court *did* come around. It would later be called "the switch in time that saved nine." Very soon, however, FDR would make key appointments to the Supreme Court. Roosevelt would have no more trouble with the Court for the rest of his presidency. If that is defeat, he was a lucky loser.

V. "The March of Time"

Millions of Americans in the 1930s got their news from weekly newsreels in their local movie theaters. Henry R. Luce's media empire (embracing *Time*, *Life*, and *Fortune* magazines) also included *The March of Time*. These short, punchy newsreels were shown before feature films in thousands of theaters nationwide. The often shallow, frequently pompous treatment of serious subjects was lampooned by such wits as Orson Welles in his award-winning film, *Citizen Kane.* Even the cartoons that were popular with movie fans of all ages joined in poking fun at *The March of Time.* But an indication of the influence of this series can be seen in the fact that one week's segment—"Inside Nazi Germany"—was censored in two American cities. In New York, it was seen as too pro-Nazi. In Chicago, it was deemed to be anti-German![83]

"It was the pride of Germany, the way Germany showed her new aggressive flag—the swastikas on her tail. . . . It was the wonder of awed millions in cities the world over. . . . a silver whale, the symbol of luxury and speed in transatlantic travel. . . . It was landing. . . ."[84] The great German airship

Hindenburg approached the mooring station at the Naval Air Station at Lakehurst, New Jersey. Announcer Herb Morrison of Chicago's station WLS was describing its arrival to radio listeners around the country. Suddenly, the great zeppelin burst into flames. "It is burning, falling. . . . Oh! This is one of the worst. . . . Oh! It's a terrific sight," Morrison cried out in anguish. Radio announcers had not yet learned to mask their feelings behind a façade of professional *cool.* "Oh . . . the humanity!"[85] The hydrogen-filled airship's explosion was one of the great disasters of the thirties, not because of the loss of life (amazingly, only thirty-five died), but because it was so public. Americans were as yet not accustomed to disasters occurring in "real time"—recorded by newsreel cameras and carried "live" by radio announcers.

The *Hindenburg* disaster also alerted Americans to another grim reality: even though the swastika-emblazoned airship's voyage ended in flames, it demonstrated Hitler's reach. If German engineering could send a zeppelin across the ocean, might it in time send aircraft or even missiles? Thoughtful Americans realized that the broad Atlantic could no longer protect them.

Eleanor Roosevelt sought to encourage women to enter more fully into public life. She held press conferences for women journalists. She backed women in the arts. She took up the cause of women in aviation. Eleanor even invited noted aviatrix Amelia Earhart to the presidential inauguration. Once, Eleanor hosted a small dinner at Hyde Park that included Earhart and Britain's first female member of Parliament, Lady Astor. A local newspaper hailed the dinner party as a gathering of "three of the world's outstanding women."[86] Earhart was an outspoken pacifist. As the first woman ever to lecture the midshipmen of the Naval Academy, she spoke on the need for peace.[87] Along with movie stars Katharine Hepburn and Marlene Dietrich, she popularized the wearing of slacks by women. She even wore them—shockingly—downtown.[88]

Earhart had won her wings, and public adulation, by flying across the Atlantic on the fifth anniversary of Lindbergh's historic flight. Granted, she flew only from Newfoundland to Ireland—a far shorter flight than Lindy's—but she still braved the forbidding North Atlantic alone. She invited the First Lady to go up flying with her, and Eleanor quickly took her up on the offer.[89]

The American people admired young fliers like Lindbergh and Earhart because they were incredibly brave and highly skilled. Flight was still very dangerous. That fact was underscored in newspaper headlines many times throughout the decade of the 1930s. America's beloved humorist Will Rogers and journalist Wiley Post had been lost in 1935 in an air crash in Alaska.

When in 1937 Amelia announced her daring "Round the World" flight, Eleanor admitted in her syndicated column that she was anxious. "All day I have been thinking about Amelia Earhart somewhere over the Atlantic," she wrote.[90] As Amelia and her navigator Fred Noonan headed out over the Pacific, the Coast Guard cutter *Itasca* had been detailed to send weather reports to the courageous young flier.

As the first family gathered at Hyde Park for a Fourth of July picnic and a wedding, the Roosevelts' holiday was overshadowed, as was that of the whole country, by reports that Amelia Earhart had gone missing. The *Itasca* joined four thousand men in ten ships to search an area of the Pacific the size of Texas.[91] It was all in vain. Amelia was lost, just twenty-three days short of her fortieth birthday. She had said, "When I go, I would like to go in my plane. Quickly."[92] Rumors continued for years—none of them substantiated—about Amelia Earhart. Had she been taken captive by the Japanese on Saipan Island? Was she spying for the Roosevelts? Especially after Japanese planes attacked the USS *Panay* in China—an act for which they quickly apologized—Americans were jittery about the Rising Sun Flag of Japan in the Pacific.

Boston's Joseph P. Kennedy wanted to become the first Irish-American ever named as ambassador to the Court of St. James—that's how the U.S. Embassy in London is known. Kennedy had been Roosevelt's first chairman of the Securities and Exchange Commission. On the theory that "it takes a thief to catch a thief," FDR named a man known for his sharp dealing to ride herd on the sharp dealers.[93] Kennedy was an important supporter for FDR in the Catholic community.

"When I passed it to Father," said Jimmy Roosevelt, the president's son, of the Kennedy-to-London idea, "he laughed so hard he almost toppled from his wheelchair."[94] But the more the president thought about it, the more he hoped it might work. Kennedy came from Boston, where Irish-American opinion was strongly against *any* help to Britain in the event of another war. FDR thought having Kennedy in London might help to overcome that resistance should war threaten. But he also wanted to have some fun with "Old Joe."

He summoned Kennedy to the White House and told him to drop his trousers. Stunned, Kennedy complied. "Joe, just look at your legs," the president said. He explained to Kennedy that all ambassadors to Britain have to wear knee breeches and silk stockings. It's tradition. "You are the most bowlegged man I've ever seen," FDR said. "When photos of our new ambassador appear, we'll be a laughing stock."[95] Unfazed, Joe Kennedy hitched up his suspenders and appealed to the president: if he could get the British to let him present his credentials in striped pants and cutaway coat, could he go to London as ambassador? "Give me two weeks," Kennedy told the president.[96]

Roosevelt needed Joe Kennedy's help more than ever. Kennedy's friend, Father Charles Coughlin, had soured on the president. Father Coughlin's radio broadcast reached an astonishing forty million homes.[97] Initially well-disposed to FDR and the New Deal, Father Coughlin increasingly criticized Roosevelt's Brain Trust and his policies. Father Coughlin even began to sound more anti-Semitic as he attacked bankers and banking in terms not very different from those used by Henry Ford.

With Kennedy on his side, FDR would have a valuable ally should war come. Or so FDR thought at the time. As soon as Kennedy had installed his large family in the ambassador's quarters in London, he marked out an independent course. With him, he brought Rose, his wife, and his children, Rosemary, Kathleen, Eunice, Patricia, Jean, Joe Jr., John Fitzgerald, Robert, and Edward (Teddy).

Initially, the lively Kennedy clan was very popular in Britain. Joe wanted to make a social splash and kicked up an association with the socially prominent "Cliveden Set." Lady Astor's country home, Cliveden, was the social center for appeasement in Britain. The appeasement policy was based on the belief that the Treaty of Versailles had been too harsh and vindictive (which was very likely) and that better relations with Germany could be had by appeasing Hitler's territorial and economic demands (which was just as unlikely).

Hitler was unsatisfied with reoccupying the Rhineland in 1936. Early in

1938, he threatened and bullied his native Austria into submission. When he marched into Vienna on 12 March 1938, the swastika flag replaced the bold red and white striped Austrian flag at every flagpole. Hitler's power and prestige within Germany and Europe had never been higher. He had accomplished without war what not even the Iron Chancellor, Otto von Bismarck, had achieved.

The Treaty of Versailles had forbidden Germany to unite with Austria. Few of the treaty's provisions seemed to matter to him—why this one? The Austrian-born Hitler was determined to achieve this union, what he called his *anschluss*. He not only wanted to bring his homeland under his control, he also wanted to show his opponents inside Germany and outside that the victors of World War I were powerless to stop him. This made him even more powerful at home and abroad.

Hitler's every aggressive move seemed only to bring more attempts of appeasement from the British government of Prime Minister Neville Chamberlain. As soon as Nazi troops moved into Austria, they brought with them their *Gestapo*. This dreaded state police hunted down Jews, prominent Socialists, intellectuals, and Catholic opponents of Hitler.[98] One of those who fled from Nazi-ruled Vienna was Sigmund Freud, the father of psychoanalysis.

No sooner had Hitler swallowed Austria than he began to threaten Czechoslovakia. The free, democratic state created by the Allied leaders at Versailles contained a small German-speaking minority in the border region known as the *Sudetenland*. Hitler had sent money, arms, and agitators to stir up these *Sudeten* "Germans" against the Czech government in Prague. Now, he demanded that the Czechs cede the Sudetenland to him. If they wouldn't, there would be war.

Hitler spoke to a huge Nazi Party rally in Nuremberg in 1938.* He demanded that "civilized" Germans be liberated from the backward Czechs. French Prime Minister Edouard Daladier and foreign minister Georges

---

* Leni Riefenstahl, who had been in some disfavor since her Olympic film did not conform to Nazi racist notions, filmed the Nuremberg party rally. Her movie—*Der Triumph des Willins (The Triumph of the Will)*—remains a classic example of effective propaganda. It shows the awesome power unleashed by new techniques of cinematography. The Nazis were delighted with Leni's creative effort.

Bonnet were alarmed. They flew to London to plead with Chamberlain to stand firm against this new threat. They explained to Chamberlain that if Hitler gobbled up the Sudetenland, he would also get the formidable Czech border defenses and the world famous Skoda arms works. Their meeting in No. 10 Downing Street—the official residence of all British prime ministers—was a stormy one.[99]

Chamberlain would not bend. He could not bear the thought of war with Germany. "How horrible, fantastic, incredible it is that we should be digging trenches and trying on gas-masks here, because of a quarrel in a faraway country between people of whom we know nothing."[100] He was determined to do everything, *anything,* to avoid war. He dramatically proposed to meet Hitler to discuss peace—dramatic because he'd never flown and air travel was still dangerous. Nonetheless, he flew into Munich for a meeting with Hitler, Italy's Fascist dictator Benito Mussolini, and France's Premier Daladier. President Eduard Benes of Czechoslovakia was not even invited to the conference that would determine his brave little country's fate.

The Western democracies were not helped by Mussolini's presence at Munich. The Italian Fascist dictator always struck a pose of being more reasonable, less fanatic, than Hitler. As time would show, Mussolini's promises were as worthless as Hitler's.

Chamberlain agreed to give Hitler what he wanted. When he returned to London, he told an enthusiastic airport crowd that Britain would have "peace in our time." He was given the unprecedented honor of appearing on the balcony of Buckingham Palace with King George VI and his wife, Queen Elizabeth. Hundreds of thousands of weeping, cheering Britons hailed Chamberlain as the bringer of peace.

Few disagreed, but Winston Churchill was one of them. He gripped the attention of a hushed House of Commons:

> I do not grudge our loyal, brave people, who were ready to do their duty no matter what the cost, who never flinched under the strain of last week—I do not grudge them the natural, spontaneous outburst of joy and relief when they learned that the hard ordeal would no longer be required of them at the moment; but they should know the truth.

> They should know that there has been gross neglect and deficiency in our defences; they should know that we have sustained a defeat without a war . . . they should know that we have passed an awful milestone in our history, when the whole equilibrium of Europe has been deranged, and that the terrible words have . . . been pronounced against the Western democracies: "Thou art weighed in the balance and found wanting."*
>
> And do not suppose that this is the end. This is only the beginning of the reckoning. This is only the first sip, the first foretaste of a bitter cup which will be proffered to us year by year unless by a supreme recovery of moral health and martial vigor, we arise again and take our stand for freedom as in the olden time.[101]

Churchill was heard, but not heeded. He had been out of the cabinet for nearly a decade. To most Britons he was a spent force. They had booed him in Parliament when he pleaded for time for King Edward VIII to make a decision about marrying his American divorcée. They booed Churchill, too, when he stood against Indian self-government. Now, he seemed an irrelevant old warmonger, "a man of a bygone era." To many serious Britons, author John Lukacs tells us, Churchill was widely distrusted as a man of unstable temperament, unsound judgment, and rhetorical and alcoholic excess.

One of those who mistrusted Churchill was U.S. ambassador Joe Kennedy. He spoke on Trafalgar Day to a dinner hosted by the Navy League in London. This anniversary celebrated Britain's victory over the continental tyrant, Napoleon. Joe Kennedy used the occasion to urge ever more appeasement. "It has long been a theory of mine that it is unproductive for both the democratic and dictator countries to widen the divisions now existing between them by emphasizing their differences which are now self-apparent," he said. "[T]here is simply no sense, common or otherwise, in letting these differences grow into unrelenting antagonisms. After all, we have to live together in the same world whether we like it or not."[102]

---

* Winston Churchill was a man rarely found in church, but his powerful rhetoric owed much to the sonorous cadences of the King James Version of the Bible. This familiar phrase is from Daniel 5:27.

Charles A. Lindbergh. *"The Lone Eagle," young Charles A. Lindbergh flew from Roosevelt Field on Long Island across the ocean nonstop to Paris' Le Bourget air field. His flight in a single engine plane, "the Spirit of St. Louis," made him a hero on both sides of the Atlantic. So adulated was he that he could not sign a check or send his shirts out to be laundered. They would be kept as souvenirs.*

Lindbergh in the company of Nazis. *Lindbergh was a genuine pioneer of aviation. Ten years after his historic flight, however, he began consorting with leading Nazis in Germany. Here, he is shown with Reichsmarshal Herman Goering, the head of Hitler's air force. Lindbergh was a leading isolationist in the thirties, even though his own flight proved America could not stand aloof from Europe.*

Jesse Owens. *Hitler snarled at his subordinates who suggested he shake hands with the great American track star, Jesse Owens. Even so, the German crowds cheered Owens' Gold Medal victory at the Berlin Olympics of 1936. Owens' power and dignity belied the Nazis racial propaganda.*

Ambassador Joseph P. Kennedy and family. *Joseph P. Kennedy had made millions on Wall Street and in Hollywood. FDR chose him to be his Ambassador to Britain in 1938. As war clouds gathered, Joe Kennedy was an outspoken advocate for appeasement of Hitler's Nazis. He blamed World War II on Roosevelt's advisers, whom he charged were Communists and Jews.*

King George VI, Queen Elizabeth, and daughters. *The first reigning British monarch ever to visit the United States, King George VI and Queen Elizabeth (parents of Queen Elizabeth II), visited the Roosevelts at Hyde Park. There, FDR and Eleanor served them a picnic lunch of hot dogs and beans. Desperate for U.S. help as they faced the growing menace of Hitler Germany, the royals did not complain.*

Kennedy's speech provoked a firestorm of controversy.[103] He directly contradicted the president's powerful call to "quarantine the aggressors." FDR responded calmly that there can be no peace if some nations use the threat of war as a "deliberate instrument of national policy."[104] This meant Hitler, without a doubt.

Ambassador Kennedy couldn't take a hint. He ostentatiously invited Lindbergh to visit him in London. America's leading appeaser found Joe Kennedy's views on the European situation "intelligent and interesting."[105] They were exactly like his own. Lindbergh's wife described Kennedy as "an Irish terrier, wagging his tail."[106] FDR's press secretary Steve Early knew that Kennedy had his eye on the 1940 Democratic presidential nomination: "Joe wants to run for President and is dealing behind the Boss's back at the London Embassy."[107]

After the Munich conference, the irrepressible Kennedy bumped into the Czech diplomat, Jan Masaryk, in London. "Isn't it *wonderful*," Kennedy asked the heartbroken man. "Now I can get to Palm Beach after all!"[108]* To his friends, Kennedy said, "I can't for the life of me understand why anyone would want to go to war to save the Czechs."[109]

It was easier for the wealthy, socially prominent businessman-turned-diplomat to share the world with Nazis. For one, he wasn't Jewish. Just weeks after Kennedy's speech, Hitler's Nazis went on a rampage throughout Germany. Hitler had taken the measure of the leaders of Britain and France at Munich. He knew he had little to fear from them. On 9 November 1938, his Nazi thugs smashed Jewish-owned shop windows, looted merchandise, burned synagogues, beat up innocent Jews, and terrorized others. *Kristallnacht* or "night of the broken glass" was a chilling announcement that the Third Reich would brutalize any Jews who came within its grasp—and defy the opinion of the world. The hostility began to spread to sympathizers of the Jews: the Nazis roughed up Cardinal von Faulhaber and smashed windows in his Munich study in an attempt to shock him into silence.**

---

* This was a reference to the Kennedy family vacation home in the fashionable Florida community. The family still owns this estate.

** Cardinal von Faulhaber had a mixed record. He gave off-and-on-again support to the Hitler government, but he did loudly protest the Nazi euthanasia program. After the war, he ordained Joseph Ratzinger, the future Pope Benedict XVI, as a priest.

Joe Kennedy responded not with outrage against the Nazis, but with a plan to relocate all of Germany's Jews to Africa and Latin America. So impressed was *Life* magazine with the ambassador's ideas it editorialized that, if successful, the Kennedy Plan "will add new luster to a reputation that might well carry Joseph Patrick Kennedy into the White House."[110]

It was not to be. Kennedy's open clash with the president and his eagerness to appease Hitler ended his hopes for the Democratic presidential nomination—and his public career. FDR was not surprised. He had given the wily Boston pol "enough rope." Privately, Roosevelt said he was "not a bit upset over [the] final result."[111]

VI. Rebuilding America

Americans in the thirties vastly preferred to concern themselves with projects closer to home.

The dynamiting of thousands of tons of stone at South Dakota's Mount Rushmore captured the nation's imagination. Danish-American sculptor Gutzon Borglum had studied under the great French artist, Auguste Rodin.[112] He envisioned a mammoth memorial to America's greatest leaders—Washington, Jefferson, Lincoln, and Theodore Roosevelt. Selecting the site himself, Borglum declared, "American history shall march along that skyline."[113] This great work reaffirmed Americans' belief in themselves, and in the appeal of democracy in a world increasingly threatened by bloody dictatorships. Miners who at first saw the project only as steady work soon caught the spirit of the monument. Even decades later, driller "Happy" Anderson boasted, "I put the curl in Lincoln's beard, the part in Teddy's hair, and the twinkle in Washington's eye. It still gives me a thrill to look at it."[114]

New York's elegant Empire State Building was the brainchild of Al Smith after his failed presidential bid. It crowned the Big Apple's skyline as the world's tallest building until it was topped by the World Trade Center's twin towers in 1972.[115]

In California, Depression-era voters showed their confidence in the future by authorizing a bond issue to construct the graceful Golden Gate Bridge. Construction engineers stressed safety, using "hard hats" and safety goggles for the first time. Even as FDR's policies were creating a "safety net" for American workers nationwide, workers on the Golden Gate Bridge had an actual safety net that protected them from the high winds and dizzying heights. Nineteen men who were caught by the safety net formed a group they jokingly called the Half-Way-to-Hell Club.[116]

The federal government also added to the brick-and-mortar spirit of the decade. The Grand Coulee Dam in Washington State and the massive Tennessee Valley Authority are just two examples of Depression-era projects that changed the American landscape and not incidentally brought hydroelectric power to rural communities. Rural electrification had massive social, economic, and political consequences. The cultural isolation of rural America ended when power lines made radio reception possible. Electrifying the countryside made possible a huge increase in agricultural output. Politically, and FDR was certainly not unaware of this, rural electrification wired millions of farmers to the New Deal.

It's worth pointing out that Stalin's Belomor Canal, built by slave laborers in the Soviet Union, claimed tens of thousands of lives and soon silted up, becoming useless. Hitler's gargantuan Reich Chancellery was destroyed in World War II. His grotesque plans for *sportspalasts* (giant sports stadiums) and all-new planned cities never got off the drawing board. "Stalin Gothic" architecture disfigures many an urban landscape in Eastern Europe today. Hitler proudly displayed the work of his favorite architect, Albert Speer. The huge German pavilion at the Paris World Exposition of 1937 was a tower of stone and light, crowned by a Nazi eagle. This overbearing, inhuman structure, one prophetic critic said, looked "like a crematorium and its chimney."[117] Both Stalin and Hitler's architectural visions were ugly monuments to the soullessness of their authors.

Americans also rejoiced in sports in the thirties. Joe Louis had a return match with Max Schmeling in 1938. This time, Nazi ideology could not brag about another Germanic triumph over the Brown Bomber. Jimmy Carter recalled the reaction of poor black tenant farmers on his father's rural Georgia peanut farm. Allowed to approach the front porch of the big house by Carter's segregationist father, the black fans listened to the radio report Joe Louis's pounding victory. They thanked "Mr. Earl" Carter politely and quietly returned to their modest shacks. But there, Jimmy recounted, he could hear an eruption of shouts of joy and "Bless the Lords" that he remembered all his life.[118]

War jitters made Americans feel vulnerable to *any* kind of threat. On the night before Halloween 1938, the talented young Orson Welles produced a made-for-radio adaptation of H.G. Wells's science fiction classic, *War of the Worlds.* The dramatization featured musical offerings interspersed with realistic-sounding, increasingly menacing reports introduced with "we interrupt this broadcast. . . ." The radio announcer informed listeners that a meteor from the planet Mars had landed near Princeton, New Jersey. Some fifteen hundred people were reported dead. Later, it was announced that a "cylinder" had screwed itself open and that alien creatures were emerging armed with "death rays."[119] Panic struck in a number of places, showing us how great was Americans' faith in the authority of radio as a medium of communication. The Columbia Broadcasting System (CBS) and Orson Welles's Mercury Theater were threatened with millions of lawsuits, none of which came to anything. The Martian broadcast did have its humorous side, however. One hard-pressed laborer wrote to Orson Welles:

> When those things landed, I thought the best thing to do was to go away, so I took $3.25 out of my savings and bought a ticket. After I'd gone sixty miles, I heard it was a play. Now I don't have any money for the shoes I was saving up for. Would you please have someone send me a pair of black shoes, size 9B.[120]

Less than one year later, the CBS radio network and all other American media outlets would be reporting on invasions, destruction, and death on a scale hitherto unimagined. The invaders then would not be aliens from space, but the terror they spread before them would be no less horrifying.

Meanwhile, Americans had plenty to occupy their attention here at home. The New Deal had sputtered into a recession in 1937. Roosevelt could point to major legislative achievements. The Social Security Act of 1935 changed American society and politics for generations. The Wagner Act is viewed as the Magna Carta of organized labor. But Americans are result-oriented. And when FDR faced restive members of his own party in the 1938 elections, his attempts to punish conservative Democrats who opposed the New Deal were singularly unsuccessful.

Despite all this, FDR dominated the political landscape. He did so by the force of his personality. He was—as one of his biographers noted in the subtitle of his book—both "The Lion and the Fox." In Niccoló Machiavelli's classic work of 1513, *The Prince,* he famously pointed out that the prince must know how to play the part of the lion and the fox; in other words, he had to be both strong *and* clever. Franklin D. Roosevelt—while driving his critics to distraction—proved he had learned to play both parts.

America's Rendezvous with Destiny (1939–1941)

When he asked Americans to reelect him in 1936, FDR told Americans they had "a rendezvous with destiny." It was one of his most memorable phrases. Millions then knew the poem of young Alan Seeger—an American who had died fighting for France in the Battle of the Somme in 1916. It was called "I Have a Rendezvous with Death." Roosevelt, with his typical optimism, gave Seeger's short, sad poem a life-affirming turn—"a rendezvous with destiny." At the beginning of this tumultuous decade, Americans were absorbed in just making ends meet. Europe and Asia and their endless troubles seemed very far off. Through the 1930s, however, time and distance seemed to diminish. Mass media brought the sounds of dive bombers and anti-aircraft fire right into American living rooms. At the weekly cinema before the main feature, newsreels showed the march of armies. Suddenly, those thousands of miles of ocean did not seem so vast. From 1939 on, the pace of events quickened and many thought they heard the hoofbeats of the Four Horsemen of the Apocalypse. Never before had war been so terrible. Never before had destruction rained down from the sky, roiled the seas, or shaken the earth with such ferocity. Through all of this, Franklin D. Roosevelt never seemed unsteady, never betrayed doubt. No small part of his public appeal was that very self-confidence and optimism that drove his critics to distraction. "That Man in the White House," they sputtered, unable at times even to utter his name. But That Man was determined to dominate events instead of letting events dominate him.

I. Man of the Year

As 1939 dawned, *Time* magazine stunned the world by naming Adolf Hitler as its "Man of the Year" for 1938.[1] Editors of the popular newsweekly hastened to remind readers that their selection did not imply *approval* of the Nazi dictator. As they would say again and again over the decades, the "Man of the Year" (later, "Person of the Year") designation merely meant that this individual, more than any other, had influenced events for good or evil.

Hitler had assured Chamberlain and Daladier at Munich that he had "no further territorial demands in Europe." With the consent of the democracies, he had torn the German-speaking Sudetenland from a wounded Czechoslovakia. Nervous Westerners hoped it would take Hitler time to absorb his latest, almost bloodless, conquest. Still, the Nazi juggernaut showed no signs of slowing. In 1938, Hitler had expanded Germany's territory from 186,000 to 225,000 square miles and swelled the population under his control from 68 to 79 million.[2]

Whatever their rationale, *Time*'s editors gave Hitler a huge propaganda boost. Surely they knew of his brutal campaign of murder and intimidation against the Jews. And it was well known that the Nazis were pressuring parents to pull their children out of their Catholic and Lutheran church groups, and to put their young people under the control of the HJ—*Hitler Jugend.* This Hitler Youth was a state-run organization that indoctrinated the young of Germany and the occupied lands in anti-Christian beliefs. The leaders of the HJ denounced the Pope as a "half-Jew."[3] "One is either a Nazi or a committed Christian," a rally speaker told the Nazi Students' League. "We must repudiate the Old and New Testaments, since for us the Nazi idea alone is decisive. For us there is only one example—Adolf Hitler—and no one else."[4] Tragically, millions of Germans bought this teaching.

As Germany's borders expanded, so did Hitler's reach. Hitler's military assistance propelled Spain's Fascist generalissimo Francisco Franco on to victory in the Spanish Civil War. Josef Stalin backed the anti-Fascist Republicans. So did many American leftists. Hundreds of young American Communists and their "fellow travelers" volunteered to fight Fascism as members of what they called the Abraham Lincoln Brigade.

The United States, however, was bound by the terms of the Neutrality Act to keep clear from the three-year civil war. Britain and France also tried to stay out of the conflict. That left Germany, Italy, and the Soviet Union to fight by means of proxies. Writers such as Britain's George Orwell and America's Ernest Hemingway were attracted to the Republican cause and would later draw from their harrowing experiences to write such classic works as *Homage to Catalonia* and *For Whom the Bell Tolls.* The famous Spanish artist, Pablo Picasso, immortalized the first air raid on civilian targets with his painting *Guernica.* Picasso would show a lifelong affinity for Communist-backed causes. Ironically, back in the USSR, Stalin proceeded to "purge" thousands of artists and intellectuals. He also had most of his old Bolshevik comrades shot. Stalin was particularly brutal toward the Soviet military. In a two-year period (1936–1938), Stalin ordered 39,157 of his military officers to be shot or imprisoned.*

In March 1939, Hitler tore up the agreement he had signed the previous September. It was the paper Prime Minister Chamberlain proudly displayed at his airport news conference, the one with "Herr Hitler's name on it." On 15 March, the Ides of March, Hitler marched into Prague. The stricken Czechs were too stunned to resist. Hitler now made no pretense of "liberating" Germans. The Czechs were Slavs. "Shamefully abandoned," as Churchill said of them, they had put their faith in their fellow democracies and had been utterly betrayed. Fascism's march seemed unstoppable. By April, Franco had prevailed in Spain.

Pressured by members of his ruling Conservative Party, Chamberlain at last responded to Hitler's aggression by offering assurances to Poland. Britain would back the endangered nation and declare war on Germany if Hitler attacked. But this appearance of spine did not mean that Chamberlain had

* Since imprisonment in these circumstances usually meant death, too, it is always curious why Stalin bothered to make a special category of those he jailed.

renounced appeasement. To the contrary, he asked U.S. ambassador Joseph Kennedy to intervene with President Roosevelt. Chamberlain's purpose: to get FDR to secretly pressure the Poles to make concessions to Germany! Frustrated, FDR asked his ambassador to "put some iron up Chamberlain's backside."[5] Kennedy answered that the British had no iron to fight with.[6]

The following month, FDR delivered the first address ever broadcast on the new invention—television—at the opening of the New York World's Fair on 30 April 1939. Roosevelt used the occasion to celebrate the 150th anniversary of George Washington's First Inauguration. He spoke of "the vitality of Democracy and of democratic institutions." "Yes, our wagon is still hitched to a star," he said. "But it is a star of friendship, a star of progress for mankind, a star of greater happiness and less hardship, a star of international good will, and, above all, a star of peace."[7] With those words, the world's most famous scientist, Albert Einstein, threw a switch to light up fountains and floodlights. The fair was officially open.[8]

Two of the most famous fairgoers that year were King George VI and his spirited wife, Queen Elizabeth. They had never expected to sit on England's ancient thrones. But when Edward VIII abdicated rather than give up his American fiancée, his younger brother resolved to overcome his childhood stammering and do his duty.

FDR planned every detail of this first visit ever made by British monarchs to North America.[9] Snubbing Joe Kennedy in London, the president worked through William C. Bullitt, his ambassador in Paris, to bring off this historic event.[10] FDR saw this visit in many ways as a response to upper-class Americans who considered him a "traitor to his class." Their attitude was jocularly expressed in the *New Yorker* cartoon that showed well-heeled theater goers headed off to the movies. They call in to a dinner party of fellow swells: "Come on—we're going to the Trans-Lux to hiss Roosevelt." Now, FDR would play host to the biggest society "catch" in the world—the king and the queen. FDR grandly greeted the royal pair at his Hyde Park home. As soon as the royal couple had changed for dinner, FDR appeared with a pitcher of martinis that he had mixed himself. "My mother thinks you should have a cup of tea—she doesn't approve of cocktails," the president said. The king replied, "Neither does mine," as he grabbed the martini.[11] Imagine the horror of the Roosevelt hissers when they learned that FDR and Eleanor had offered the royals a picnic lunch of hot dogs and beans at Hyde Park![12]

It was not all social. FDR talked long into the night with the young king and with Canadian Prime Minister MacKenzie King about the looming danger of war.* Finally, FDR tapped the king on the knee. "Young man," he said, "it's time for you to go to bed."[13] No one seemed to notice that FDR had broken one of the oldest taboos associated with the British monarchy—that they were never to be touched by a commoner. Staring at the grim prospect of war—and the even more terrible possibility of invasion by Hitler's Germany—perhaps the young monarch was happy to have Roosevelt's reassuring touch.

The royal visit sent a vital message of Anglo-American unity as the world hurtled toward another war. For millions of Americans, however, the democracies of Europe were weak and decadent and the dictatorships were strong and dangerous. Better to stay out of the fray entirely. To the 480,000 members of the German-American *Bund*, this stance seemed especially appealing. Fritz Kuhn brazenly led twenty-two thousand members of his pro-Nazi group at a rally in Manhattan's Madison Square Garden. A giant banner held aloft the picture of George Washington, but on the floor *bundists* wore swastika arm bands and offered the "Heil Hitler" salute.[14] As far as Madison Square Garden events went, it was small. Given New York's large number of Jews, Catholics, Poles, Eastern Europeans, and black Americans, however, it was an incredibly provocative act.

Charles A. Lindbergh was no *bundist.* But he was equally determined to keep America out of Europe's troubles. He joined with others to form The Committee to Defend America First. Lindbergh had returned home from three years of self-imposed exile in Britain. He was at one time the most famous advocate for American isolation and possibly the most controversial: he had visited Hitler's Germany no less than six times while living in Britain. Lindbergh had even accepted a Nazi medal from Hermann Goering, chief of the Lufwaffe, the German air force. "If we fight [Germany]," Lindbergh had

* U.S. reporters resented the famously close-mouthed Canadian prime minister. Veteran newsman David Brinkley wrote that they made up this disrespectful doggerel: "William Lyon MacKenzie King/Never gives us a G—d— thing."

said, "our countries will only lose their best men. We can gain nothing.... It must not happen."[15] Like Ambassador Kennedy, Lindbergh had found the Cliveden Set the most congenial of Englishmen. He had urged his English hosts not to resist Germany, but to make an alliance with Hitler. At one of Lady Astor's parties, which included Joe Kennedy and the U.S. Ambassador to France, William C. Bullitt, Lindbergh "shocked the life out of everyone by describing Germany's strength."[16] Back in the United States, Lindbergh threw himself into opposition to President Roosevelt's plans.

Meanwhile, others were also trying to influence Roosevelt's plans. Leo Szilard and Eugene Wigner were atomic scientists. They had fled Germany with the rise of the Nazis. Now, in the summer of 1939, they were in America trying to find Albert Einstein.[17] Einstein had taken a summer cottage in Peconic, Long Island, where he enjoyed sailing. Wigner and Szilard, unfamiliar with American roads (or with American towns), got lost. They confused Patchogue on the South Shore, with Cutchogue, on Long Island's North Fork. Unable to locate Einstein's summer cottage, Szilard and Wigner almost gave up. Finally, Szilard leaned out of his car window and asked a little boy, "Say, do you by any chance know where Professor Einstein lives?" The eight-year-old promptly took the émigrés to Einstein's cottage.[18] There, the scientists quickly persuaded Einstein to send a letter to President Roosevelt.[19]

They almost miscalculated disastrously when they planned to ask Charles Lindbergh to be their courier to carry the Einstein letter to the White House.[20] These politically naïve men did not yet realize that Lindbergh's sympathies were not at all theirs. Instead, they asked Alexander Sachs, a man friendly to FDR.

The Einstein letter explained to the president that nuclear fission could create a chain reaction that would release vast amounts of heat and radioactivity. A bomb might be created using uranium, Einstein explained. And, he wrote, the *Germans* were known to be working on atomic fission.[21] Einstein knew all the top German scientists. Until Hitler's rise to power, he had been a respected member of the German-Swiss intellectual community. As a Jew, however, Einstein could never be accepted in the new Germany Hitler was fashioning.

FDR received Einstein's letter from scientific gadfly, Alexander Sachs.

Waving away the complex scientific jargon, FDR told Sachs: "Alex, what you are after is to see the Nazis don't blow us up."

"Precisely," Sachs answered.[22]

With that, FDR summoned General Edwin "Pa" Watson, his trusted appointments secretary. "Pa, this requires *action.*"[23] With those spare words, the largest secret weapons project in history began—the race to build an atomic bomb.

II. America on the Road to War

The world awoke to a shock on 24 August 1939. News came from Moscow and Berlin of the signing of the Nazi-Soviet Non-Aggression Pact. After the Munich agreement the previous year, Stalin had decided to protect the USSR and come to an agreement with his declared enemy, Hitler. To ease the transition, Stalin sacked his Jewish foreign minister, Maxim Litvinov, and replaced him with Vyacheslav Molotov. Molotov's name means "hammer," and the signing of the Nazi pact struck the Western democracies like a terrible blow. Now, Hitler was free to go to war in the West—free from the worst fear of all German leaders, a two-front war.

Hitler wasted no time. He demanded the Poles give in to all his demands regarding the Free City of Danzig (now Gdansk).* He wanted access through the Polish Corridor. He had gambled and won before—the Rhineland, *anschluss* with Austria, the Sudetenland, invading Czechoslovakia. Forget Chamberlain's assurances. Hitler was convinced that Britain and the decadent democracies would back down yet again.

Warning the democracies against trying to stop him, Hitler threatened to smash their cities and destroy their armies. Most ominously, he said that if "world Jewry" plunged the world into another great war, the Jews of Europe would be *annihilated.* Britain's great diplomatic historian, Sir John Wheeler-Bennett did not dismiss Hitler's words. "Except in cases where he had pledged his word, Hitler always meant what he said," said Wheeler-Bennett.[24]

* This "Free City," actually a city-state, was established by the Treaty of Versailles. Most of its population was German speaking.

Hitler's attack on Poland stunned the free peoples of Europe. After four years of bloody, exhausting fratricide in the trenches of the Great War, they could not imagine that Hitler actually wanted another conflagration.[25]

Hitler had formed an opinion of the democratic leaders from careful study of their weaknesses and from his face-to-face meeting at Munich in 1938. He could see that quick, decisive action would catch them unawares and unable to respond. Hitler had a genius for quick, decisive action. He showed this as early as 1934 when he descended on a Munich gathering of the *Sturmabteilung* (SA)—the Brownshirts, who had helped Hitler come to power. He personally arrested their leader, Ernst Röhm. Röhm was a radical Nazi, a street brawler, and an open homosexual who was a potential threat to Hitler's own power. Hitler stormed though the halls of the Munich hotel where they met and caught some of the top SA leaders in bed with boys.[26] He had Röhm shot. He used the confusion of "The Night of the Long Knives" to murder as many as four hundred opponents of his regime, including some conspicuous conservatives. One of those killed as a warning to others was Erich Klausener, a leader of the Catholic Action group.[27] Hitler struck Röhm and the others on a Saturday night and found the tactic effective enough to use again. When he marched into the Rhineland in 1936 and into Austria, 12 March 1938, he also chose to act on Saturday nights. Hitler knew how the British statesmen loved their weekends at their country estates. He told his associates that "to operate or to act quickly . . . does not come easily to the systematic French or to the ponderous English."[28]

On 1 September 1939, the armored divisions of Hitler's *Werhmacht* crashed across Poland's borders even as his Luftwaffe bombed military and civilian targets from the air. Hitler's forces showed no mercy toward hospitals, schools, or churches. He waged a war of terror designed to destroy his enemy's will to resist. This was *Blitzkrieg* —lightning war.

Poland lasted just a month. Overrun and overwhelmed, the Polish army fought bravely, often on horseback. German propaganda films emphasized the futility of Polish cavalry charging against *Panzer* tanks.*

* Three years later, however, the Soviets would use cavalry against the Germans to devastating effect. Their swift horses could attack when the *Panzer* tanks were immobilized by -50° F temperatures in the dreaded Russian winter.

Prime Minister Chamberlain, facing the ruin of all he had worked for, reluctantly declared war on Germany, but not for three days. At the end of Chamberlain's dispirited, lugubrious war announcement on the British Broadcasting Company (BBC), air raid sirens began to wail in London. Armed with a bottle of brandy, Winston Churchill accompanied his wife, Clementine, into the air-raid shelter.[29] Realizing the need for broader support in the House of Commons, Chamberlain invited his sharpest critic, Winston Churchill, once again to become First Lord of the Admiralty. On 3 September 1939, the Board of Admiralty signaled to ships in every corner of the globe: "Winston is back."[30]

Within a week, FDR was writing a personal letter to Churchill. He had taken the trouble to "clear" the communication with Prime Minister Chamberlain, he explained. But he wanted to write directly to the man who would command the world's largest navy. From then on, Chamberlain would be "out of the loop." So, not incidentally, would be Ambassador Joseph P. Kennedy. FDR would do his own diplomacy with his fellow "former naval person."

Poland's agony was extreme. When the teenager Karol Wojtyla and his ailing father joined millions of refugees fleeing bombardment by Nazi *stukas*, their flight was halted by even more terrible news: the Soviets had invaded Poland from the East. Under the barbarous rule of Nazi Governor-General Hans Frank, Poles were shot for the slightest offense, such as failing to step into the street when a German soldier passed.[31] Young Karol, the future Pope John Paul II, returned to his home to face the rigors of Nazi occupation.

In just one month, Poland was torn apart. The Soviets attacked her from the East, the Nazis from the West. With Poland's collapse, a curtain of silence descended on this ancient land. The rule of murder and repression went largely unreported in the Western press. Stalin ordered the massacre at the Katyn forest of 3,500 captured Polish army officers.[32] The West knew nothing of this until well after the war.

In the West, Britain and France settled down to a "phony war," a conflict marked by no action. The French placed their greatest reliance on a string of very modern forts known as the Maginot Line. After the bloody exhaustion of World War I, their mindset was thoroughly defensive.[33] They gave no thought to invading Germany's lightly defended Western front. Journalists mockingly called this war of preparations a *sitzkrieg*—a sitter's war.

Americans, public opinion polls showed, were strongly *opposed* to taking any part in Europe's new war. Senator William E. Borah, an Idaho Republican, was a leader of the isolationists. When the Germans attacked Poland, Borah told reporters: "Lord, if I only could have talked with Hitler, all this might have been avoided."[34]

As the 1930s ended, the movie *Gone with the Wind* reminded millions of the costs of war in death and destruction. The great Hollywood epic of the Civil War premiered in Atlanta. American matinee idol Clark Gable starred with two English actors, Leslie Howard and Vivien Leigh. Two of the movie's most memorable performers, however, did not attend. Hattie McDaniel ("Mammy") and Butterfly McQueen were not invited to the all-white Atlanta premiere.[35]

President Roosevelt faced a major decision in the new year of 1940. If he challenged the "two term" tradition established by George Washington and lost, his entire record would be tinged with failure. Ulysses S. Grant had tried and failed to win a third term. So had Cousin Theodore. But these attempts followed a period out of office. FDR, if he agreed to be a candidate, would break new ground.

Millions of Americans doubtless agreed with Joe Kennedy, who viewed the war as a disaster. "Democracy as we conceive it in the United States will not exist in England and France after the war," he warned.[36] His messages home became ever more defeatist.

Britain was fighting only for her Empire, Kennedy charged, and the British didn't stand "a Chinaman's chance" of prevailing against Germany and its Axis partners.[37] He even went so far as to express his negative opinions at a major embassy dinner. He apparently enjoyed twisting the lion's tail as he expressed his view that the British would be "thrashed" in the new war.[38]

Kennedy's all-too-gloomy predictions seemed accurate enough as the spring thaw brought action in Norway. Prime Minister Chamberlain boasted that Britain would beat Hitler to shore up a northern ally, and that

"Hitler missed the bus." This most unwarlike comment from a most unwarlike leader was soon proved spectacularly *wrong.* Hitler seized Norway almost effortlessly, giving the British a bloody nose and a terrible setback. The House of Commons erupted in stormy recriminations. Chamberlain survived a vote of "no confidence" by a comfortable margin, but the defection of some eighty members of his own Conservative Party showed, in fact, a *lack* of confidence in his leadership.

Some blamed First Lord of the Admiralty Churchill, for Norway was, after all, in his sphere of responsibility. And Churchill defended Prime Minister Chamberlain throughout the fierce Parliamentary debate. So staunchly loyal did Churchill remain to the man he had previously criticized for appeasement that former Prime Minister David Lloyd George, now past eighty but still sharp-tongued, stood to urge Churchill *not* to allow himself to become "an air-raid shelter" for an obviously failed administration.

In the midst of a political crisis in London, Hitler left Berlin on his private train, code-named *Amerika.*[39]* He struck on 10 May 1940 in the North and West. He invaded neutral Holland and tiny Denmark, crushing those peaceful little kingdoms in hours. His armored divisions, backed by air power, smashed into France. When Britain's Labour Party leaders said they would *not* join a coalition government headed by Neville Chamberlain, Chamberlain offered the king his resignation. Now, the choice was between the foreign secretary, Lord Halifax, and the first lord of the admiralty, Winston Churchill. Halifax told his best friend, Chamberlain, that he did not think he could lead the House of Commons from his position in the House of Lords. Winston, uncharacteristically, remained silent as his only possible rival took himself out of contention.

When the king called Churchill to Buckingham Palace, Churchill was invited to form a national unity government to include all of Britain's parties. He would later write of his "profound sense of relief" at that moment:

---

* Hitler's attitudes toward *Amerika* were complex. He was known to admire American ingenuity, energy, and dynamism. He loved American movies, especially Westerns and even *Gone with the Wind.* He regarded Roosevelt as a captive of the Jews, however, and in time came to despise Americans as "half negrified, half Judaized."

> At last I had authority to give directions over the whole scene. I felt as if I were walking with destiny, and that all my past life had been but a preparation for this hour and for this trial.[40]

As French and British forces in France retreated before the armored German onslaught, Churchill went before the House of Commons to offer "blood, toil, tears and sweat." His aim was simple: victory.

> Victory at all costs, victory in spite of all terror, victory however long and hard the road may be, for without victory there is no survival. . . .[41]

To many in Britain then and in the United States, Churchill's stirring speeches didn't stir. He seemed a reactionary man, unacquainted with the realities of modern life. But in his understanding of the mind of Adolf Hitler, it was Churchill who was right and the sophisticates who were wrong. Churchill knew that no negotiation was possible with such a warped and hateful man. He also knew the kind of war Hitler was determined to wage—a total war.

Sumner Welles, FDR's undersecretary of state, warned that Churchill was only a "third or fourth rate man," and a "drunken sot" to boot.[42] Joe Kennedy didn't trust him.

Roosevelt had to face an unprecedented campaign for a third term. He knew Americans were very uneasy about the war in Europe. The Gallup Poll that May showed that 51 percent were willing to sell airplanes and other war materiel to the Allies, but 49 percent were opposed.[43] Americans seemed to sense the danger. Two-thirds of them told Gallup they expected Germany to conquer Europe—and then turn on America. Two-thirds also thought the United States would eventually go to war against Hitler. Only *one in fourteen,* however, was willing to declare war on Nazi Germany in 1940, Gallup's interviewers found.[44]

As France collapsed, however, the British army in France retreated before the onrushing Germans. Within mere weeks, they had fallen back on the French port of Dunkirk. There, with their backs to the English Channel, the entire British force in France was surrounded by the triumphant

Germans. They would either be driven into the sea, annihilated where they stood, or taken prisoner.

Dunkirk is located just ten kilometers west of the Belgian border, along the English Channel.* In a maneuver code-named Operation Dynamo, Britain's Royal Navy managed the evacuation of some 340,000 soldiers—the bulk of the entire British Expeditionary Force (BEF) and many French and Allied units, as well. This incredible feat was accomplished between 26 May and 4 June.

American columnist George Will shares an amazing story from the surrounded Allied forces hunkered down in the sands of Normandy and regularly bombed and strafed by the Luftwaffe:

> [A] British officer on Dunkirk beach sent London a three-word message: "But if not." It was instantly recognized as from the Book of Daniel. When Shadrach, Meshach and Abednego are commanded to worship a golden image or perish, they defiantly reply: "Our God who we serve is able to deliver us from the burning fiery furnace, and He will deliver us out of thine hand, O king. But if not, be it known unto thee, O king, that we will not serve thy gods."[45]

A young French soldier responded to being surrounded at Dunkirk more prosaically with a humorous prayer: "O Lord, if I ever get out of this, I will learn English—*and how to swim!*"

Field Marshal Hermann Goering—the head of the Luftwaffe—had equipped his Stukas with sirens on his airplanes' wings designed solely to induce terror in their hapless victims. One British infantryman who was pounded by Stukas reported his reactions.

> An attack by Stukas cannot be described; it is entirely beyond the comprehension of anyone who has not experienced it. The noise alone strikes such terror that the body becomes paralysed, the still active mind is convinced that each and every aircraft is coming for you personally.[46]

---

* Dunkirk's un-French sounding name is really Flemish, a language closer to Dutch. Dunkirk is just a two-hour trip by ferry from the English port city of Dover.

Hitler held back, not willing to drive his enemies into the sea. Perhaps he thought the sight of defeated troops straggling back to London without their artillery, without their tanks or supplies, would demoralize the British people and bring them to sue for peace. Churchill mustered a huge "mosquito fleet" of warships, ferry boats, fishing boats, pleasure yachts, even row boats to bring off the "miracle of deliverance" of late May 1940, ever after known simply as *Dunkirk*.

As he was to do on a number of other occasions, Hitler misjudged his enemy. The sight of the soldiers coming home from Dunkirk did not demoralize the British. They were dirty and ragged. Some were missing teeth. Many still had oil over their faces from where they had been plucked out of the sea. Yet, they were cocky. They grinned and gave thumbs up signals. They said: "I'm all right, Jack." The mere sight of them thrilled the people of Britain.*

France surrendered three weeks later. On 22 June 1940, the French signed the so-called armistice with Hitler. Hitler, with a dramatic flair, had demanded that the French meet him in the same railway car that had been used when the Germans were defeated less than twenty-two years before! He came to the clearing at Compiègne, an hour's drive northeast of Paris.[47]

FDR viewed the events in Europe with mounting concern. He spoke at the University of Virginia on 10 June 1940. Without mentioning Mussolini or Italy by name, he said of the *Duce*'s** unprovoked attack on France "the hand that held the dagger has struck it into the back of its neighbor." He criticized those Americans who thought the United States could exist as a "lone island in a world dominated by the philosophy of force."[48] Clearly, FDR was talking about Defend America First, Lindbergh's group dedicated to keeping the United States out of the war.

The stunning series of events of the past weeks clearly *reversed* the outcome of World War I. On 23 June, Hitler even conducted a pre-dawn tour of the city of Paris. He admired the architectural wonders and vowed to remake

* Not all got off. Tens of thousands of valiant British and French soldiers faced capture or death forming a perimeter defense. Some of those captured by the SS were massacred.

** *Il Duce* is Italian for "the leader." Mussolini was Europe's first *Fascist* dictator. He seized power in 1922. Hitler's title—*der Führer*—was the German translation of *Duce*. *El Caudillo* was the variant adopted by Spain's general, Francisco Franco.

Berlin on an even grander scale. Americans saw Hitler's early morning victory tour in their weekly newsreels and remembered that more than 350,000 young Frenchmen had died keeping the Germans out of Paris in World War I. This time, there was no "Miracle of the Marne." For millions of Americans, this only confirmed the futility of "entanglements" in Europe's affairs.

Other Americans, however, saw Hitler's dominance of Europe as a mortal threat to the United States. Many were influential Republicans from the Northeast. They tended to be wealthier, more likely to have traveled to Europe, and more likely to have been educated in the elite universities of the Ivy League. By experience and background, these Americans knew that the United States could not survive in a world dominated by Nazi Germany and Imperialist Japan. But at this point, they were by no means a majority.

Churchill's opponent in Britain's war cabinet was Lord Halifax, the foreign secretary. This quiet, austere aristocrat was unimpressed with Winston's flowery rhetoric. To this refined man, Churchill's gravelly voice "ooze[d] with port, brandy, and the chewed cigar."[49] Americans who supported Britain, however, warmed to "Winnie's" bulldog persona. They loved his V-for-Victory salute, the cigars, the Homburg he always wore. And for this influential group, his 1940 speeches were stirring. Consider such a speech, delivered five days before Hitler toured Paris:

> What General Weygand called the Battle of France is over. I expect that the Battle of Britain is about to begin. Upon this battle depends the survival of Christian civilization. Upon it depends our own British life, and the long continuity of our institutions and our Empire. The whole fury and might of the enemy must very soon be turned on us.
>
> Hitler knows that he will have to break us in this Island or lose the war. If we can stand up to him, all Europe may be free and the life of the world may move forward into broad, sunlit uplands. But if we fail, then the whole world, including the United States, including all that we have known and cared for, will sink into the abyss of a new Dark Age made more sinister, and perhaps more protracted, by the lights of perverted science.
>
> Let us therefore brace ourselves to our duties, and so bear ourselves

that if the British Empire and its Commonwealth last for a thousand years, men will still say, "This was their finest hour."[50]*

Amid the dramatic events of the Fall of France, the Republican Party met in Philadelphia in June 1940. They had come to America's cradle of democracy to reaffirm their party's commitment to freedom. The two leading candidates for president were Ohio senator Robert A. Taft, son of the former president, and New York's Thomas E. Dewey. Dewey was young, only thirty-seven. He had made a national reputation as a fearless district attorney fighting the mob or "Murder Incorporated" as it was known to the press. When Dewey announced his intention to run for president, FDR's trusted adviser, Harold Ickes, jibed that the New Yorker had "thrown his diaper into the ring."[51]

Taft, on the other hand, lacked both his father's girth and his warmth. To elect him after FDR, said Franklin's cousin, Alice Roosevelt Longworth, would be like "drinking a glass of milk after taking a slug of Benzedrine."[52]** The delegates to the Convention must have had similar doubts about both leaders. A well-orchestrated national movement of Draft Willkie Clubs had set up a cry for the successful Wall Street utility executive Wendell L. Willkie.[53] When the two leading candidates blocked each other, a pre-arranged cry went up from the bowels of the convention hall: "We want Willkie!" In fact, this *popular* cry was wired by several communications magnates who had access to their own mass media. Henry Luce published *Time, Life,* and *Fortune* magazines. The Cowles family published *Look* magazine. The owners of the *New York Herald Tribune,* the Reid family, added their powerful endorsement.[54] They had "pumped" for Willkie as the only one who could beat FDR.[55] Republicans were desperate for a winner. Willkie was a big, bluff, outgoing man whose personal charm made him a serious rival to FDR.

The American constitutional system did not encourage the creation of

---

* General Charles de Gaulle broadcast from London on the same day. His "Appelle de l'honneur" (Appeal to Honor) was carried by the BBC to a prostrate France. He rejected the Armistice and called on the "Free French" to join him in resistance to Hitler. It was de Gaulle's "finest hour," too.

** Benzedrine is an amphetamine, a stimulant.

multi-party "national unity" coalition governments, but Lincoln had named important Democrats to his cabinet during the Civil War. Now, FDR returned the favor. He tapped two influential Republicans: Henry Stimson, Hoover's secretary of state, became his secretary of war; and Frank Knox, Alf Landon's 1936 running mate, was appointed secretary of the navy.

None of this would have helped if the Republicans had nominated for president a man dedicated to keeping the United States out of the war. Isolationist sentiment in the GOP was strong, very strong. Former President Hoover ridiculed the danger that Hitler posed to America: "Every whale that spouts is not a submarine. The 3,000 miles of ocean is still protection. . . . [To attack us, an enemy] must first pass our Navy. It can stop anything in sight now."[56]

The Republicans' former senate majority leader, James E. Watson, spoke for hundreds of GOP grassroots supporters when he scathingly expressed his opposition to Willkie, the former Democrat-turned-Republican: "Back home in Indiana we think it's alright for the town whore to join the Church, but we don't let her lead the choir on the first night."[57]

The Democrats gathered in Chicago without a serious plan. FDR had never declared he *wanted* a third term. In fact, he had encouraged a number of other men to go for the nomination. James A. Farley, his postmaster-general, took him up on it. Farley would have the undying support of at least one delegate to the Democratic National Convention of 1940: Joseph P. Kennedy, Jr. was a member of the Massachusetts delegation. Even when the young Kennedy was reminded of his own presidential ambitions, he would not budge in his support of Farley.[58]*

In the end, young Joe's stubbornness did not matter. Chicago mayor Ed Kelly had sent his superintendent of sewers into an underground passage beneath the convention arena. Kelly's man bellowed over the convention's loudspeakers. It filled the arena. "We want Roosevelt!" The delegates really had no other strong candidate to consider. FDR had played coy, encouraging

* Young Joe Kennedy had bragged that he would become America's first Catholic president. But in those days, no one with political ambitions would dare to defy his party's presidential nominee—especially on the floor of the nominating convention, and especially not one so powerful or with such a long memory as FDR!

others to run, but never taking himself out of the running. So, this "voice from the sewers" was all they needed to rush to Roosevelt. With the international situation as threatening as it had ever been, the convention delegates "drafted" FDR for an unprecedented third term.[59]

Irked at Vice President John "Cactus Jack" Garner for his weak support of the administration during the court-packing scheme and a number of other New Deal initiatives, FDR unceremoniously dumped him from the ticket.* The president informed the convention he wanted Agriculture Secretary Henry A. Wallace as his running mate. This was too much for the weary, driven delegates. Wallace was known as a disheveled, disorganized former Republican of decidedly left-wing views. He believed in "theosophy, reincarnation and food fads."[60] Only when Roosevelt threatened to decline the nomination and leave his party leaderless did the fractious delegates fall into line behind the ticket of Roosevelt and Wallace.

III. "Sail on, O Union Strong and Great"

With France's defeat, Churchill faced the imminent danger of invasion. The French government, headed by premier Paul Reynaud, had promised not to turn its powerful fleet over to the Germans. Reynaud, however, had been forced to resign. He was replaced by Marshal Philippe Pétain. Chuchill had dealt with Pétain. He knew the aged World War I hero could no longer be trusted. Pétain had left his heroism far behind. He was now the loudest French voice for capitulation. If Pétain turned the French fleet over to Hitler—or even if he allowed Hitler's SS somehow to "capture" the French fleet—Britain's very life would be threatened.

Churchill ordered his battleships to confront the French Navy at Mers-el-Kebir, off North Africa. The French commanders, under orders from Pétain, refused to come over to the British side. They were given the options

* Cactus Jack said the vice presidency was not worth "a bucket of warm spit." President John F. Kennedy visited Garner on the Texan's 95th birthday. Garner told the president, "You're my president and I love you. I hope you stay in there forever." The president was assassinated in Dallas that very day. (Online source: http://www.suite101.com/article.cfm/presidents_and_first_ladies/35366/4.)

of sailing across the Atlantic to French possessions there, joining with neutral America, or even scuttling themselves. When the French captains refused any of the options offered them, Churchill wept. But he ordered his naval commanders to *destroy* the French fleet. In five minutes of bloody action, one French battle cruiser was driven onto the beach, a cruiser was blown up, and twelve hundred French sailors were killed.[61] Churchill paid tribute to the "characteristic courage of the French Navy" in the House of Commons.[62] It was typical of him, magnanimous in victory as he always was.

But by his ruthless move, Churchill showed that a sea change had occurred in British policy. Chamberlain's government had risked fliers' lives to shower Germany with—leaflets. Now Churchill showed that he would even turn on a former ally; Britain would do whatever she had to do to survive. Churchill demonstrated forcefully that the British lion could still bare teeth and claws.

"This . . . is London." That staccato message, recited in a chain-smoker's baritone, brought the war into American living rooms. CBS's chief London correspondent, Edward R. Murrow, brought his Yankee accent and his reporter's eye for detail to the heart of London in the midst of the Blitz.

America listening to the CBS *World News Roundup* could hear the *pom-pom-pom* of London's anti-aircraft (AA) guns going off. Londoners reacted differently to the sounds of the AA guns. One man said, "You can't sleep with the guns, but it's a good sound."[63] One elderly cleaning woman groused: "Them damn guns, I could kill 'em." "It's worse than the bloody Jerries," complained a grandmother soothing a frightened child in the air-raid shelter.[64] Men, in general, liked hearing the guns giving the Germans back "some of their own." One reported: "The louder it was, the more confidence we had."[65]*

Some professional observers of the British people under the nightly bombardment of the Luftwaffe seemed surprised at their hardiness. Psychoanalysts had predicted mass hysteria—"people would revert to the pram, the womb or the tomb."[66] Individuals may have cracked, but the people of London, especially the hard-hit East Enders did not, as the Cockneys say, go "starkers." It

* In the BBC series *World at War*, a Cockney veteran of one of these AA crews was asked years later how many "Jerries" he had shot down. "Nary a one. Never 'ad a chance uv 'ittin' one," he said with a laugh. Why did they fire off those AA guns then? "It gave great 'eart to the people in the Underground!"

would not be the first time the experts were proven wrong. Still, as the bombs rained down on the just and the unjust alike, and as people generally saw the government-subsidized clergy of the Church of England failing, church attendance fell off.[67] One might have expected to see Anglican priests and nuns leading the way in pulling people out of the bombed-out rubble of their apartments, setting up canteens for the firefighters, etc. This could have been a time for the Church to lead relief efforts for the people undergoing the full rigors of the Blitz. Sadly, it was not.

A government report at the height of the Blitz noted that *only one percent* of teens out of school were involved in any kind of church activity compared with 34 percent who went to the movies.[68] It might be said that the Church of England, too, was a casualty of the London Blitz.

One Anglican layman, however, rose to the challenge. C.S. Lewis, a Cambridge don, began a series of broadcasts for the BBC.[69] The compelling author of *Mere Christianity* proved to be a dynamic speaker on "the wireless." Lewis's radio presentations were soon brought out in book form as *Broadcast Talks.* This was a tribute to the importance the Churchill government placed on civilian morale, since paper, as everything else, was strictly rationed.[70] Lewis's *Screwtape Letters* were very popular. In this book, a devil celebrates the many possibilities of snaring souls in wartime. He cited the holier-than-thou temptations of the pacifist, but he also showed the dangers of becoming brutally bloody-minded and the sin of "thinking your enemy is worse than he is." Many of Lewis's wartime writings continue to be read to this day.

Mass circulation publications like *Time*, *Life*, *Look*, *Collier's*, and the *Saturday Evening Post* printed dramatic photographs and written copy detailing every aspect of the war. The local movie theater ran newsreels of war footage from the front. At the same time that Americans desperately wanted to stay *out* of Europe's war, the mass media was inexorably drawing them *in.* Day after day, Americans sensed that the events overseas could not be kept at bay much longer. The very speed and range of the Nazi juggernaut threatened Americans' sense of security, of being set apart from European conflicts.

Even schoolchildren became familiar with the datelines of war stories—

London, Paris, Berlin, Warsaw, Moscow, Prague, Oslo, Copenhagen, Amsterdam. Never before had Europe's affairs been so much a part of Americans' daily consciousness.

It would not have been possible in World War I to *feel* the war in all its immediacy and danger. Radio now made this possible. The distance between London and New London had become negligible.

Just months before, many Americans would have agreed with Joe Kennedy that Britain was washed up. Now, in the summer of 1940, the Battle of Britain took place in the skies above "This England" that Americans remembered from their poetry books and their high school literature classes as written by Shakespeare:

> This royal throne of kings, this sceptred isle,
> This earth of majesty, this seat of Mars,
> This other Eden, demi-paradise,
> This fortress built by Nature for herself
> Against infection and the hand of war,
> This blessed plot, this earth, this realm, this England.

The Royal Air Force scrambled every day to beat off wave after wave of attacks from Hitler's Luftwaffe. "Never in the field of human conflict has so much been owed by so many to so few," Churchill said in tribute to the young men who faced death daily. Some of them may well have been among the Oxford University undergraduates who had voted overwhelmingly as recently as 1936 *against* fighting "for King and Country." Now, *everyone* had but one goal: to fling defiance in the teeth of the Hun, to resist with every ounce of human strength the "nozzie [Nazi] beast."

The Royal Air Force saved Britain from invasion that summer. In June 1940, the operational strength of RAF's Fighter Command was 1,200 planes. By November, that number had *increased* to 1,796. The German Air Force's single-engine aircraft had *decreased* from 906 at the beginning of the Battle of Britain in June to 673 in November.[71] Why this discrepancy? Many British fighters were shot down, it is true, but many of their planes could be repaired, and surviving pilots would go back into action. Also,

British aircraft production was setting records with factories working around the clock. Any planes that were not destroyed landed in British fields, where they could be retrieved. All German planes and pilots knocked out of the skies over southern England were either captured or destroyed.*

Churchill laid down concertina wire all along the threatened coastlands, creating a sharp-barbed obstacle for enemy landings. He planned to light off precious gasoline if the Germans came ashore. They would be met with a furious uprising of the whole people, he swore.

Murrow brought it all to Americans listening captive at home. He quoted William Pitt, the famous opponent of Napoleon: "England will save herself by her exertions, and Europe by her example."[72]

The bombs that fell on London killed and maimed thousands of civilians. Murrow broadcasted the sounds of fire engines racing through the night, the sound of flames crackling around St. Paul's Cathedral, the sound of Cockneys digging through the rubble of their apartment buildings.

The pleasant, shy, young King and his lively wife did not escape. Buckingham Palace was bombed. The prime minister's office let it be known that the Queen was taking shooting lessons with a revolver.[73] Perhaps Eleanor had shown her own pistol at Hyde Park! Resisting pleas from Canada to send the young princesses across the ocean, the Queen said: "The Princesses could not leave without me—and I could never leave without the King—and, of course, the King will never leave."[74]

FDR agreed to send Churchill fifty old World War I destroyers. These were desperately needed for convoy escort duty. Britain was wholly dependent on her seaborne lifeline for most of her food and war materiel and all of her oil.

In return, Britain leased to the United States a number of New World bases for ninety-nine years. Some of these, as in Gander Bay, Newfoundland, and in the British West Indies, served the U.S. Navy for decades. FDR pledged "all aid short of war." As sympathetic as Americans were to the plight of the British, polls confirmed Americans were determined not to become involved

* The Battle of Britain is generally thought of as the aerial duel between British and German fighters over Southern England from late summer to early autumn 1940. "The Blitz," Hitler's nighttime bombing raids over English cities, lasted until 10 May 1941 and resumed with V-1 and V-2 rockets in 1944.

ourselves. Still, FDR boldly proposed Lend-Lease and the first peacetime draft in American history.[75] Lend-Lease was a new policy that allowed Britain to borrow war materiel for the length of the emergency. Typically, FDR explained his policy in down-to-earth terms. He compared it to lending our "neighbah" a length of garden hose to put out a fire. In other words: We don't want the money. We just want our hose back when the fire is extinguished.[76]

As Wendell Willkie campaigned vigorously throughout the country, FDR was in the toughest campaign of his career. Shrewdly, Roosevelt decided not to take on the popular Willkie directly. Roosevelt knew he could not fairly attack Willkie's record because the businessman-turned-politician didn't have a record. Besides, Willkie was a committed internationalist whose nomination was a major defeat for the isolationist wing of the Republican Party.

Instead, Roosevelt focused on the Republican "leadahs" and how they voted in Congress. FDR ignored the magnetic Willkie and spoke of the record of top congressional Republicans on the issue of repealing an embargo of war supplies to the beleaguered Allies. Even when the Dutch, the Danes, the Norwegians, the Belgians, and the French were going down to defeat, these Republican congressional powers would not move on aid to the Allies. One of FDR's speeches, broadcast nationally, shows his masterful use of irony and wit. It made Americans realize that even if they elected Willkie president, he would still have to work with isolationist Republicans in Congress. And those Republicans opposed lifting the embargo on sending arms to the Allies:

> But how did the Republicans vote on the repeal of that embargo?
>
> In the Senate the Republicans voted fourteen to six against it. In the House the Republicans voted one hundred and forty to nineteen against it.
>
> The Act was passed by Democratic votes but it was over the opposition of the Republican leaders. And just to name a few, the following Republican leaders, among many others, voted against the Act: Senators McNary, Vandenberg, Nye and Johnson; now wait, a perfectly beautiful rhythm—Congressmen Martin, Barton and Fish.

> Now, at the eleventh hour, they have discovered what we knew all along—that overseas success in warding off invasion by dictatorship forces means safety to the United States. It means also continued independence to those smaller nations which still retain their independence. And it means the restoration of sovereignty to those smaller nations which have temporarily lost it. As we know, one of the keystones of American policy is the recognition of the right of small nations to survive and prosper.
>
> Great Britain and a lot of other nations would never have received one ounce of help from us—if the decision had been left to Martin, Barton and Fish.

Roosevelt had an ear for political speech. Overnight, the country was repeating his rhythmic ribbing of the reactionary Republicans—*Martin, Barton, and Fish!* Of special delight to FDR was the fact that Hamilton Fish was his own Duchess County, New York, congressman.

Goaded by Willkie on the issue of war, FDR told a Boston audience: "I have said this before, but I shall say it again and again and again: your boys are *not* going to be sent into any foreign wars."[77] It was too much. No president could have assured that. No president *should* have pledged that. That speech would be cited—*again and again and again*—as evidence of FDR's duplicity. But FDR did not think he was being dishonest. If America was attacked, he argued with his advisors, then of course the war was no longer a foreign war.

Hitler's unprovoked attacks on Poland, Norway, Holland, and Denmark would have an impact in the United States, too. Millions of American voters in states like Pennsylvania, Ohio, Illinois, Wisconsin, and Minnesota trace their ancestry to those overrun nations. Every one of these states wound up in FDR's column in 1940.

On 5 November 1940, there occurred an event which had never occurred before—and likely will never occur again. A president of the United States was reelected to a *third* consecutive term. Willkie had improved measurably over the previous two Republican candidates. He had won 22,304,755 popular votes (44.8 percent), nearly *six million* more votes than Landon had won in 1936. But this yielded him only 83 electoral votes. To Landon's Maine and

Vermont, Willkie added Michigan, Indiana, North and South Dakota, Iowa, Kansas, Nebraska, and Colorado.*

FDR's total in the popular vote slipped about 200,000 to 27,243,466 (54.7 percent). But his electoral vote total of 449 from thirty-eight states gave him a commanding, convincing victory. It was a demonstration of popular appeal and political skill never to be equaled.

It had not looked that way early on election night. FDR, normally the most gregarious of campaigners, closeted himself away from everyone at Hyde Park. Grim-faced and sweating, he had waited out the long hours alone until victory was assured.[78] It's a good thing for the leaders of this great republic to fear the people.

Wendell Willkie had been ridiculed by FDR's aide, Harold Ickes, as "that damned barefoot boy from Wall Street."[79] But Willkie had played a crucial role in 1940—and he would continue his service to America. Walter Lippmann said it best:

> Second only to the Battle of Britain, the sudden rise and nomination of Willkie was the decisive event, perhaps providential, which made it possible to rally the free world when it was almost conquered. Under any other leadership but his the Republican party in 1940 would have turned its back on Great Britain, causing all who resisted Hitler to feel abandoned.[80]

President Roosevelt closed out the eventful year of 1940 with one of his famous "fireside chats" to the American people. *Time* magazine reported "The President came in five minutes before the broadcast on a small rubber-tired wheelchair."[81]** He called on America to become "the great arsenal of democracy."[82] The speech was memorable and politically successful. An arsenal provides vital means of defense, but it does not take part in armed struggle. That was the policy Americans favored.

---

* Willkie received more votes than any Republican presidential candidate would get until 1952.

** *Time* was the largest circulation weekly newsmagazine in the United States. The matter-of-fact tone of this sentence shows once again that Americans were never in doubt that their president was paralyzed from the waist down.

Mount Rushmore under construction. *Gutzon Borglum, already a famous sculptor, chose this South Dakota site for a monumental depiction of the four greatest American presidents. Borglum and his party scaled Harney Peak to survey the scene. At 7,242 feet, it is the highest point between the Rockies and the Alps. "American history shall march along that skyline." It did.*

St. Paul's Cathedral surrounded by flames, 1940. *This symbol of the British Empire was wreathed in flames from near-hits by Hitler's Luftwaffe. Hitler tried to break the British people's will through his Blitzkrieg. Although Hitler's air bombardment of London and many other British cities would eventually kill 60,000 civilians, the British remained indomitable. It was, as Churchill called it, "their finest hour."*

Pearl Harbor in flames, 1941. *Japan's sneak attack on Pearl Harbor on 7 December 1941 took the U.S. Pacific Fleet and the Army Air Force base at Hickam Field by surprise. Nearly 2,500 sailors, Marines and airmen were killed on a date that President Roosevelt said "will live in infamy." Japan would pay dearly. Nearly two million of her fighting men and civilians died as a result of the war her leaders treacherously launched that quiet Sunday morning.*

Wendell Willkie. *Lampooned as "that barefoot boy from Wall Street," Wendell Willkie took the Republican National Convention in Philadelphia—and very nearly the country—by storm in the summer of 1940. In the wake of the stunning Fall of France, Willkie staunchly opposed isolationism. His support allowed FDR to extend a lifeline to embattled Britain as she stood alone against Hitler. Running against Roosevelt, Willkie nonetheless put the nation's interest ahead of his political ambitions.*

When his defeated rival, Wendell Willkie, planned a trip to embattled Britain, FDR invited him to the White House for a friendly chat. He gave Willkie a hand-written message and genially asked him to deliver it personally to Prime Minister Churchill. It was a favorite Longfellow poem the two "former naval persons" would surely appreciate, "The Building of the Ship":

> Sail on, O Ship of State!
> Sail on, O Union, strong and great!
> Humanity with all its fears,
> With all the hopes of future years,
> Is hanging breathless on thy fate.[83]

Isolationists had by no means dropped their efforts when Roosevelt was re-elected. Early in 1941, the Defend America First Committee stepped up its efforts to keep the United States out of the war. Although the group clearly attracted what Teddy Roosevelt had referred to as "the lunatic fringe," it would be a mistake to think that that is the *only* support America First received. Joe Kennedy Jr., a politically ambitious young *Democrat*, proudly signed up. So did Sargent Shriver, eventually to be a *Democratic* nominee for vice president and a candidate for president (and a Kennedy in-law). Kingman Brewster went on to become president of Yale University.* Republican Gerald Ford also joined America First, as did Olympic chairman Avery Brundage, Alice Roosevelt Longworth, and World War I flying ace Eddie Rickenbacker.[84]

Charles A. Lindbergh reached out to his friend, Henry Ford. Lindbergh, as *Life* magazine pointed out, did not even express a hope that Britain would win.[85] It might be seen as singularly ungrateful to the country that had generously provided him a safe haven in 1935, but veteran diplomat Sir John Wheeler-Bennett thought Lindy was not really anti-British; he had simply concluded that Britain was a "bad bet."[86] Ford agreed with Lindbergh. He even predicted in *Scribner's* magazine in January 1941, that the Germans would win.[87]

Lindbergh's high profile in America First gained him the attention of

* In one of the most bizarre of diplomatic postings, President Jimmy Carter sent Brewster to London as his Ambassador. It might have been argued that had the young Brewster had his way, London would have been under German occupation.

one young cartoonist named Theodore Geisel. Geisel lampooned the aviator as "the Lone Ostrich":

The Lone Eagle had Flown
The Atlantic alone
With fortitude and a ham sandwich.
Great courage that took
But he shivered and shook
At the sound of the gruff German landgwich.[88]

Geisel would become familiar to millions of Americans as the inimitable Dr. Seuss. Geisel's put-down of Lindbergh became public only following the aviator's death. When President Roosevelt publicly compared *Colonel* Lindbergh to the Civil War Copperhead Clement Vallandigham, Lindbergh reacted with anger. Unwisely, he resigned his army commission.[89]

It was a fateful move. It would alter Lindbergh's life. Never again would he have the complete trust of his government or his fellow Americans. Roosevelt's supporters pointed out that Lindbergh had never resigned as a German Knight of the Eagle. It was a distinction he shared with Henry Ford. But he had thrown back his U.S. Army commission. Defenders of the famed aviator said he had innocently received the Nazi medal and didn't know what to do with it. Unimpressed, FDR shot back: "*I* would have known what to do with it!"[90]

IV. "Sink the Bismarck!"

For a year, Britain stood alone against Hitler. She bore the brunt of his nightly fury. On the night of 10–11 May 1941, Hitler ordered a huge air raid over southern England. In the previous year, 43,000 British civilians had been killed in the Blitz and 139,000 wounded.[91] It was to be the last, terrible strike of his Luftwaffe against Britain's cities. Hitler was now massing more than three million men, tens of thousands of horses, and thousands of tanks and armored vehicles on his eastern border. His air force would be needed for the war he was planning against the Soviet Union.

Hitler had supreme confidence in his armies. Hitler's favorite commander was Erwin Rommel. Hitler made Rommel a field marshal and gave him command of the Afrika Korps. Rommel drove the British back into Egypt. Even his British enemies respected Rommel. They called Rommel "the Desert Fox." Now, he threatened Britain's lifeline through the Suez Canal. Australian and New Zealand troops (ANZAC), along with beleaguered British forces, had been withdrawn from Greece to Crete.*

In June 1941, Hitler was poised to "kick in the door" to the Soviet Union. Once he did that, he assured his generals, the whole "rotting structure will come down." Who could challenge him? Ever since his lightning victory over France, Hitler believed in the "star" of his own military genius, and none of his generals dared to question his judgment.[92]

But Hitler had no such confidence at sea. "On land, I am a hero," he boasted, "[but] at sea I am a coward."[93] Admiral Erich Raeder was certainly no coward. The head of Hitler's *Kriegsmarine* begged Hitler to get his ships into the action; he burned to erase the shame of the High Seas Fleet that scuttled itself rather than go into British captivity at Scapa Flow in 1919.[94]

Hitler was almost glum the day he went aboard the newly-launched battleship *Bismarck.* Hitler could not help noticing that Admiral Gunther Lutjens, who would command the *Bismarck,* greeted him with the proper salute of the old Imperial German Navy, not with the stiff-armed "Heil Hitler" of the committed Nazis.[95]

Raeder was an avid student of the American admiral Alfred Thayer Mahan and his *Influence of Sea Power Upon History.*[96] Raeder and Lutjens wanted the German Navy to play an important role in winning the war in the West. They wanted *Bismarck* to sink the convoys that brought critical supplies to war-ravaged Britain. Those fifty, old destroyers Roosevelt had promised Churchill would be powerless against *Bismarck,* with its eight 15-inch guns. Admiral Raeder believed in the power of blue-water navies to determine world dominance.** Hitler did not believe the powerful new

* ANZAC Day—for the Austrailia New Zealand Army Corps—is commemorated every April 25th. ANZACs distinguished themselves for courage. Austrailia has been a U.S. Ally in every war for a hundred years.

** Blue-water navies are large fleets of imposing battleships capable of ranging far and wide over the vast oceans.

warship would be effective in destroying Britain's seaborne lifeline from Canada and America. "U-boats do these things faster and better," Hitler gloomily told an aide.[97]

Hitler was afraid that the loss of a prize like *Bismarck* would shatter his aura of invincibility. The day of the battleship was past, he told his top military aide, General Admiral Jodl.[98]* When some subordinates suggested that a valuable portrait of the Iron Chancellor, Otto von Bismarck, be taken off the ship that was named for him, Hitler sourly said: "If anything happens to the ship, the picture might as well be lost too."[99]

On 21 May 1941, *Bismarck* and her smaller escort, the *Prinz Eugen*, steamed briskly out of occupied Norway and into the main shipping lanes, searching for victims.[100] Churchill wired FDR for help. "Should we fail to catch them . . . your Navy should surely be able to mark them down for us . . . Give us the news and we will finish them off."[101]

Cruising into the Denmark Strait, *Bismarck* encountered the HMS *Hood*.[102] For more than two decades, the *Hood* had steamed around the world, the symbol of Britain's mastery of the seas.** Now, at a few minutes after dawn on 24 May 1941, the *Bismarck* fired several quick, lethal salvos at the British battleship. *Bismarck*'s shells weighed 1,764 pounds each, and her range was 38,700 yards, a distinct advantage over *Hood*'s 30,000-yard range.[103] The British sailors *and* their German enemies stared dumbstruck as the *Hood* burst apart in a huge explosion. The ship sank in just minutes. Of the 1,400 men and boys who served on the *Hood*, only three men survived.[104] *Bismarck*'s murderous fire drove off the less prepared HMS *Prince of Wales*. In London, a grim but resolute Churchill received this laconic message from the HMS *Norfolk*: "Hood has blown up." Churchill, awakened for this terrible news, told President Roosevelt's personal representative, Averell Harriman: "The Hood is

---

* That Hitler recognized the vulnerability of battleships to airborne assault—seven months *before* Pearl Harbor—showed that he really did have military genius. Historian John Lukacs in *The Duel* points to Napoleon's crude dictum that in war, as in prostitution, the talented amateur is often better.

** Lord Nelson thought Viscount Samuel Hood, for whom the ship was named, "the greatest sailor he ever knew." Mount Hood in Oregon and Hood Channel in Washington State are also named for Samuel Hood. Hood suffered defeat rarely, but he failed to evacuate Cornwallis from the Yorktown Peninsula in 1781, thus assuring the independence of the United States.

sunk, hell of a battle."[105] The British responded with a torpedo attack from carrier-borne aircraft that damaged *Bismarck* sufficiently to cause her to abort her mission.[106] But the British then lost contact with *Bismarck.*

Admiral Lutjens's "Iron Mask" remained calm, his thoughts impenetrable, but he radioed his superiors at German naval headquarters in Nazi-occupied Paris: "Late in the evening of 24 May I was again detected twice by a USA-flying boat."[107] More than the American aircraft were tailing *Bismarck.* The U.S. Coast Guard Cutter *Modoc* spotted the *Bismarck* looming out of the fog.[108] Soon the British were alerted, and aircraft from the HMS *Ark Royal* torpedoed *Bismarck,* striking her rudder on 26 May and effectively crippling her.

Now, like a pack of hounds on a wounded bear, the Royal Navy warships closed in for the kill. *Bismarck* was trying desperately to get back to France, to the safety of U-boat and Luftwaffe protection. But her crippled rudder caused her to steam in larger and larger circles. On the morning of 27 May 1941, the HMS *Rodney* and HMS *King George V* began to pour fire into the dying German monster. Some of Lutjens' men thought he was a Jonah; now he proved it. He ordered the ship to be scuttled. Of the 2,222 men on board, only 115 were pulled from the frigid Atlantic waters.[109] A submarine alarm forced the British ships to leave the scene of destruction, stranding hundreds of young Germans.[110]

That same night, FDR spoke to the nation in one of his "fireside chats." He pledged to send Britain all aid short of war. "This can be done. It must be done. It *will* be done," he said with dramatic emphasis.[111] Churchill knew that Roosevelt was a religious man. He sent him a cable of thanks, quoting from 2 Corinthians 6:2: "I have heard thee in a time accepted, and in the day of salvation I have succoured thee." Then, pressing for more, Churchill added: "Behold, *now* is the accepted time; *now* is the day of salvation."[112] What Churchill wanted was for the United States to enter the war on his side.

Not yet. Not quite yet.

V. "If Hitler Invaded Hell. . ."

Americans and Britons did not know it at the time, but Hitler had decided *against* an invasion of Britain in 1941. Herman Goering's Luftwaffe had failed to destroy the Royal Air Force. He had failed to break the will of the British people by means of the Blitz. German fliers could not establish air superiority in the skies over southern England. And the German Navy could not provide safe passage for invading troops, even though the English Channel at its narrowest was only twenty-two miles.

Instead, Hitler looked East. In April, he attacked Yugoslavia and Greece. Once these states were taken down, Hitler would put into place his Operation Barbarossa: the invasion of the Soviet Union.

Churchill learned about these plans from the now-famous Enigma decrypts. These were British intercepts of Germany's coded messages. When Churchill tried to warn Stalin, the Soviet dictator brushed him off. The "Great Leader of the Peoples" had trusted only one human being in his entire life: Adolf Hitler.

Before dawn on Sunday, 22 June 1941, the full might of the German war machine was unleashed on unsuspecting Russia. The ever-so-cynical Nazi-Soviet Non-Aggression Pact signed with such ceremony on 23 August 1939 had lasted barely twenty-two months. Stalin had allowed Hitler a free hand in Poland, France, the Low Countries, and Britain. Now, his people would pay for his treachery.

Churchill hesitated not at all. His private secretary, who had once been skeptical of Churchill's leadership, now recorded the prime minister's irrepressible wit. Even at such a perilous moment, Churchill joked: "If Hitler invaded Hell, I would at least make favorable reference to the Devil" in the House of Commons.[113] He immediately bet his advisers "a Monkey to a Mousetrap that the Russians are still fighting, and fighting victoriously, two years from now."[114]* He spoke on the BBC that night:

> No one has been a more consistent opponent of Communism for the last twenty-five years. I will unsay no word I have spoken about it. But all this fades away before the spectacle which is now unfolding . . . Any

* Churchill's colorful phrase was not nonsense to his hearers. A Monkey is racetrack shorthand for 500. A Mousetrap, similarly, means a gold Sovereign, a valuable British coin. Churchill would win that bet, even giving 500:1 odds! (Gilbert, Martin, *Churchill,* 701.)

> man or State who fights on against Nazism will have our aid . . . [We] shall give whatever help we can to Russia.[115]

The most noticeable change in the American scene was the way CPUSA members and their fellow travelers changed on a dime. Ever attentive to the "party line" emanating from Moscow, Communists went from being fierce opponents of the "Imperialists' War" to clamoring for immediate U.S. entry into the war.

Meanwhile, the German thrust into Russia was opening the door to the Holocaust. The vast majority of Europe's Jews in 1941 lived in Poland, Russia, and the Ukraine. Tens of thousands of Jews were massacred as the Wehrmacht rolled almost unopposed deeper and deeper into Russia.[116] All of these Jews were soon to be targeted for destruction. Hitler wanted land in the East as *lebensraum*—"living room" for his rapidly expanding population of Germans. To achieve this, he intended to make this huge region a *judenrein*—a territory "cleansed" of Jews.

Late that summer, Churchill decided to visit President Roosevelt in North American waters. Boarding the HMS *Prince of Wales* in Scotland, Churchill steamed through U-boat-infested waters to meet Roosevelt at Placentia Bay, Newfoundland.[117]

En route, Churchill watched a movie, *That Hamilton Woman.* It starred Vivien Leigh and Lawrence Olivier. As Olivier, playing England's great naval hero, Lord Nelson, lies dying on the deck of the HMS *Victory,* he is told that he has won the Battle of Trafalgar. "Thank God!" whispers Nelson. Churchill was seen to wipe his eyes with his handkerchief. And this was the *fifth* time he had seen the movie.[118]

FDR, for his part, let reporters and family members think he was just going out on the presidential yacht for his annual fishing vacation.[119] Roosevelt, it must be admitted, loved pulling dramatic surprises of this sort. He soon transferred to the USS *Augusta* and headed for the frigid waters of Newfoundland.

Aboard the *Augusta* at 11 a.m. on 9 August 1941, Churchill approached President Roosevelt. He bore a personal letter of introduction from the king. He gave the president a slight bow.[120] He was, after all, the head of government, but Roosevelt was the chief of state.

The president stood under an awning, leaning on the arm of his son, Elliott. He smiled his broadest smile: "At last—we've gotten together." Churchill's answer: "We have."[121]

It was indeed a rendezvous with destiny. Freedom's champions met in the sheltered waters of Placentia Bay. Together, over the next four years, these two remarkable men would chart the course for the world struggle of freedom against tyranny.

Five

Leading the Grand Alliance (1941–1943)

Americans reeled in the wake of the attack on Pearl Harbor. An icy fear gripped millions, especially on the vulnerable West Coast. Little then prevented the Japanese from completing their assault. But the Japanese headed southwest, toward the Philippines, then still an American dependency. There, thousands of U.S. troops lay in their path. And thousands of U.S. sailors of the Asian squadron manned antiquated ships. These men would now pay the price in their blood and liberty for their country's enthusiastic embrace of disarmament twenty years earlier. The Washington Naval Conference of 1922 had left the United States woefully unprepared for the new enemy in the Pacific. In the midst of these stern days—Winston Churchill would never call them dark days—our new ally came to visit Washington. He was the first British prime minister ever officially to visit the United States. His reception was nearly rapturous. He was our friend in need. For President Roosevelt, Winston's White House visit would distract him from the cares of war and the personal loss of the mother to whom he had always been devoted. Together, in smoky late night sessions over maps and charts, FDR and Winston would forge the personal bond that would sustain them through four long years of war. There, they affirmed the policy of defeating Germany first. There, their subordinates got to know one another and prepared for the longest, bloodiest conflict the world had yet known. The alliance of Britain and the United States meant as well that Canada, Australia, and New Zealand would now join the American-led wartime coalition. The war would reshape the world.

I. 1941: "A Year of Holding Our Breath"

Freedom throughout the world had never seemed so imperiled as it did in 1941. Hitler used the burning of the Reichstag just weeks after he assumed power as chancellor, as a pretext to put freedom to the torch in Germany. His secret police, the *Gestapo,* hounded freedom with their dreaded midnight knock on the door. He seemed to think he could wreak the same destruction in Britain, pummeling freedom by merciless bombing raids. Despite Hitler's secret decision to postpone an invasion, the Luftwaffe crossed the Channel nightly to bomb Britain. Hitler seemed determined to break the will of the British people from the skies. But when his bombers struck at the House of Commons, the members of Parliament simply moved next door to the House of Lords and continued their debates. And the people, proud and indomitable, soldiered through. In all, sixty thousand British civilians would die under the German assault.

On 6 January 1941, Franklin D. Roosevelt rose to deliver his State of the Union message. He was determined that, in the United States, the lamp of freedom would be held high. He pledged the United States to Four Freedoms:

> We look forward to a world founded upon four essential human freedoms. The first is freedom of speech and expression—everywhere in the world. The second is freedom of every person to worship God in his own way—everywhere in the world. The third is freedom from want . . . everywhere in the world. The fourth is freedom from fear . . . anywhere in the world.

In time, these ringing phrases would be depicted in posters by the popular American illustrator, Norman Rockwell. With "Freedom from Fear," Rockwell depicted a typical American couple looking in on their peacefully sleeping children, tucked in under the covers in an attic bedroom. Mom and Dad are a picture of loving protectiveness. In his left hand, Dad trails a newspaper whose headline tells of the aerial bombardment of civilians in a faraway corner of the world. The newspaper might have told of Hitler's bombing of Rotterdam or Warsaw or a thousand Russian towns. Or it might have related the horrors of Japan's "Rape of Nanking." There, Japanese soldiers killed more than a quarter million Chinese civilians. Many were raped. Thousands were used for bayonet practice, hung up by their tongues, and eaten by vicious dogs.[1] Freedom's enemies have rarely shown themselves to be friends of mercy.

From the Arctic Circle to the Greek Isles, Europe was under the Nazi thumb. Americans sang "The Last Time I Saw Paris" and "God Bless America" with special fervor. Italy, allied with Germany, was poised to move against Albania and Greece. Inaugurated for a third term, FDR quietly ordered U.S. naval vessels to occupy Iceland and to extend ever eastward the boundaries within which American destroyers escorted convoys of merchant ships bearing supplies for embattled Britain.

In March 1941, Roosevelt finally succeeded in winning congressional approval of Lend-Lease for Britain. Churchill had told Roosevelt secretly that Britain could no longer pay for war materiel. Britain, in a word, was broke. Lend-Lease was FDR's ingenious response to keep our ally supplied. It had been touch and go. Isolationists, especially Republican senators Robert Taft of Ohio and Gerald Nye of North Dakota, bitterly opposed the measure. FDR had compared it to the garden hose one lends the neighbor whose house is burning. Taft answered the homely homily by saying that lending war supplies to a combatant was more like lending chewing gum. "We certainly do not want the same gum back."[2]

If Charles Lindbergh's historic transatlantic flight in 1927 proved anything, it was that America could not be isolated from Europe. Still, America's great aviation hero was a relentless foe of any aid to the Allies. Lindbergh mobilized the America First Committee. "I would sooner see our country traffic in opium than in bombs," he told fellow isolationists at one massive rally.[3] America Firsters, as they soon became known, flooded Congress with telegrams, petitions, and letters against U.S. aid to Britain.*

---

* Friends of democracy in France point out that the United States never even *considered* sending aid there, to our World War I ally. Even when the Third Republic was in its death throes, even when Premier Reynaud publicly pleaded with President Roosevelt to send "clouds of aeroplanes," the American response was a stony silence. Roosevelt's defenders argue, however, that only after the shock of the Fall of France would Americans listen to arguments for Lend-Lease. Even at that, the bill passed only with great difficulty.

Confronted with flaming opposition from isolationists across the nation, FDR even had to face brushfires within his own party. Joe Kennedy, just returned from his duty as U.S. Ambassador to Great Britain, dramatically broke with his party's leader. He even testifed in Congress against providing aid. Four years earlier, FDR had sent Kennedy to London in the hope that he would help him sell aid to the Allies should that become necessary. FDR needed the influential Kennedy's help among American Catholics. But his patience was wearing thin. When FDR invited Speaker of the House Sam Rayburn and his young protégé, Texas representative Lyndon Johnson, to visit him at the White House, the president took a call from Ambassador Kennedy. As usual, Kennedy complained bitterly of mistreatment by the State Department. While trying to smooth Kennedy's ruffled feathers over the phone, however, FDR drew his finger across his throat in a gesture that could mean only one thing: the president was about to drop the troublesome Boston politician. Kennedy quit as ambassador and explained that he was opposed to any and all U.S. involvement in what FDR was now calling the Second World War. "[I]f I am called an *appeaser* because I oppose the entrance of this country into the present war, I cheerfully plead guilty," Kennedy said.[4] Although he didn't know it at the time, Kennedy's public clash with FDR would prove fatal to his own political prospects. He never again held any public office.

FDR's supporters on Capitol Hill numbered the bill H.R. 1776—a clear patriotic rallying point. This maddened critics, who said the effect of Lend-Lease was to bind the United States and Great Britain ever closer together. In this they were right, although it was Britain who became dependent on the United States. Roosevelt's supporters countered, saying America's independence could only be guaranteed by propping up democracy in Britain as a counter to the Nazi menace to freedom everywhere.

William Allen White was the Republican editor of the *Emporia* (Kansas) *Gazette.* He founded the Committee to Defend America by Aiding the Allies. The group's ungainly name lacked the zing of America First. But it didn't lack clout. Soon, Americans would be wrapping bandages, folding blankets, and packaging foodstuffs for shipping. These were the famous "Bundles for Britain." It was a PR campaign that caught on. White's committee successfully fought back against America First.

With some amending and a lot of arm-twisting and horse trading on Capitol Hill, Speaker Sam Rayburn and South Carolina's Jimmy Byrnes pushed the Lend-Lease measure through a reluctant Congress.[5] FDR signed the bill 11 March 1941. It provided for $7 billion in aid to Britain, an astonishing figure considering that the entire federal budget in 1940 was only $10 billion.[6]

Even more difficult was the decision to aid the Soviet Union after 22 June 1941. Missouri's Democratic senator, Harry S Truman, spoke for millions of Americans when he said he would just as soon see the Soviets and the Nazis finish each other off. Americans had sympathized with Finland when Stalin attacked the brave little Scandinavian country in the 1939–40 "winter war."*

The Soviets' poor showing against tiny Finland helped convince Hitler that he had only to "kick open the door and the whole rotten structure [of Communism] will come crashing down."** Mechanized warfare had increased the speed of assault forces. With his typically dramatic sense of history, Hitler dubbed his invasion of the Soviet Union Operation Barbarossa, after the famous crusading German emperor of the Middle Ages, Frederick Barbarossa ("Red Beard").*** German troops raced toward Moscow and Leningrad, overrunning the ancient cities of Kiev in the Ukraine and Minsk in Byelorussia (now Belarus).

The Red Army had been almost destroyed from within during the 1930s. On Stalin's orders, thousands of Soviet army and navy officers had been falsely accused of treason, and shot. Now, millions of soldiers of the demoralized Red Army were captured. Most of these men starved to death in Nazi POW camps. Stalin had no use for the few who escaped or were released; these poor men immediately disappeared into Stalin's Gulag.****

---

* The Finns not only endeared themselves to Americans because they were brave, fierce, and independent, but they were also the *only* European state to fully repay their World War I debts. Americans dislike deadbeats.

** Outnumbered and outgunned, the resourceful Finns filled bottles with gasoline, lit their wicks, and threw them at Soviet tanks. They were called "Molotov Cocktails" and were deadly.

*** Hitler had named his abortive plan to invade England *Operation Seeloewe.* As historian John Lukacs points out, the sea lion is not a very fierce beast.

**** Gulag is the acronym for *Glavnoye Upravleniye Ispravitelno-trudovykh Lagerey*, "The Chief Directorate of Corrective Labor Camps."

The Nazis seemed to be unstoppable. In 1941, Stalin even planned to evacuate Moscow, the Soviet capital. Preparations were made for a hasty departure. Lenin's mummified body was readied for transport. Advance units of the German *Wehrmacht* reported seeing the bell towers of the Moscow Kremlin through their field glasses.

Germans besieged Leningrad (now called St. Petersburg). The German stranglehold on Tsar Peter the Great's beautiful "window on the West" began in 1941 and lasted nine hundred days. Millions of defenders starved to death or fell to disease. In Leningrad alone, more than two million Russians died. This dreadful death toll exceeded the sum of all U.S. and British losses in World War II.[7] Horrible accounts of cannibalism in the streets of the former imperial capital surfaced—but only later.* Nonetheless, Stalin never relaxed the terror that alone kept his system alive. His secret police were active throughout the war.

German troops in many areas of the Soviet Union were greeted by brutalized peasants wishing to show their lack of hostility by offering the traditional Russian gifts of bread and salt. Nazi ideology, however, regarded Slavs as *untermenschen*—subhuman. Soon it became clear that the Germans intended to reduce the Ukrainians, Byelorussians, and Russians to slaves.

The invaders brought with them Heinrich Himmler's devilish "SS." *Schutzstaffeln* translates as "protection squads." The SS was anything but protective, however. Trained to a peak of fanaticism and soulless barbarism, these black-uniformed young men with skull-and-crossbones on their peaked caps were the epitome of what philosopher Friedrich Nietzsche had called "the splendid blond beast."

German cruelty had turned these simple Russian and Ukrainian farmers and workers into dedicated enemies of the invader. Hitler's savagery drove them back into Stalin's arms. Once Stalin had recovered from his initial nervous collapse following the 22 June 1941 German invasion, he cunningly appealed to long-suppressed sentiments of patriotism and religion. He

* The full story of this most terrible siege in history is told in Harrison E. Salisbury's *900 Days: The Siege of Leningrad*. By contrast, the longest siege in American history was the Union blockade of Vicksburg, which lasted thirty-eight days in 1863.

relaxed his persecution of the Russian Orthodox Church. Soviet propaganda began to speak not of winning victories for the world Communist revolution, but of defending *Mother Russia.*

FDR sent his most trusted aide, Harry Hopkins, first to a beleaguered Britain, and then on to Moscow to assess the situation. Desperately ill for much of the war, Hopkins nonetheless was Roosevelt's eyes and ears. The British were thrilled to see him, sick or not. They were so desperate, said FDR's advisor Harold Ickes, they would have welcomed Hopkins even if he carried bubonic plague![8] Hopkins had memorably quoted from the Book of Ruth—"Wither thou goest I will go. Thy people shall be my people"—when he dined with Churchill's cabinet. He would offer no biblical maxims in the grim wartime Soviet capital. But his message was just as welcome. The United States would help anyone who resisted the Nazis.

When FDR and Churchill met secretly aboard the USS *Augusta* in Newfoundland waters in August 1941, they agreed to the Atlantic Charter. This document was unprecedented. It was not a treaty, because it contained no provisions for an alliance. (And FDR would not have wanted to submit it to a fractious Senate for ratification.) It was not the U.S. Declaration of War on Germany that Churchill had hoped for. Only Congress had that power. Yet it was a joint statement of goals the two leaders embraced. Both leaders said their nations sought no territorial aggrandizement from the war. Both asserted the right of all peoples to live under a government of their own choosing.

The meeting was high drama. Churchill planned a joint religious service aboard HMS *Prince of Wales.* British and American sailors and marines together joined the two leaders in singing "Onward Christian Soldiers" and "O God Our Help in Ages Past." Churchill chose the hymns. He was playing on FDR's American sensibilities. Afterward, awed young American sailors followed their British counterparts on a ship's tour. The Yanks gawked at the still unrepaired shell damage done to *Prince of Wales* in its recent deadly clash with the German pocket battleship *Bismarck.* It had taken all of the Royal Navy's might to sink the *Bismarck.* Churchill posed with U.S. Marines.[9] FDR presided as U.S. Marines heaved over his own "bundles for Britain." They were gift boxes from the commander in chief of the U.S. Navy to each of the men on board the British and Canadian warships. The boxes contained cigarettes, fresh fruit, cheese, and candy.[10] They were highly prized by the battle-hardened young British and Canadian sailors. Wartime rationing had deprived them of most luxuries.*

II. A Day of Infamy

If Roosevelt was concerned to stop Hitler from overrunning all of Europe, the immediate threat to the United States came in the Far East. Japan's military rulers were enraged by the oil embargo the United States had imposed. The Roosevelt administration hoped to prevent Japan from attacking the Dutch East Indies (present day Indonesia). In this instance, *economic* sanctions led directly to war.[11]

America's relations with Japan had been strained for decades. It was the United States, probably unwisely, that had pressured the British to end their treaty of cooperation with Japan following World War I. When young militarists assassinated Japanese democratic officials, the way was cleared for Japan's assault on China. Americans were outraged by the unprovoked aggression against its weaker neighbor and especially horrified by the hundreds of thousands of civilians murdered during the 1937–38 "Rape of Nanking." During this attack on China's then capital, Japanese naval aircraft struck the USS *Panay.*

The U.S. Navy's gunboat was sunk with three sailors killed and more than forty injured.

The Japanese would apologize and pay reparations, but feelings between the two Pacific powers were further embittered.

While Japan sent special emissaries in late 1941 to talk peace with Secretary of State Cordell Hull in Washington, Japan's Admiral Isoroku Yamamoto was planning a strike against the U.S. fleet anchored at Pearl Harbor on the Hawaiian Island of Oahu.

On the morning of 7 December 1941, waves of Japanese Zeroes swept in

* For hundreds of these young British sailors, FDR's box would be their last gift. HMS *Prince of Wales* and her sister ship HMS *Repulse* were sunk by the Japanese off Singapore, with heavy loss of life, barely four months later.

among the verdant hills of Oahu and struck without warning at the Navy ships tied up along "battleship row." "Pearl Harbor was asleep in the morning mist," Commander Itaya reported as his torpedoes shattered the Sunday calm of the harbor.[12] In little more than one hour, attacking Japanese aircraft had sunk the USS *Arizona*, the USS *Oklahoma*, and seriously damaged four other battleships. In all, eighteen U.S. warships were sunk or seriously damaged. One hundred eighty-eight aircraft were destroyed, most of them on the ground at Hickam Army Airfield.[13]*

Worst of all, America lost 2,403 killed and suffered 1,178 wounded. Nearly half of the deaths occurred when the *Arizona* blew up.[14] In the coming days and years, details of the sneak attack would enrage and horrify Americans. The doomed men banging on pipes with wrenches in capsized warships wrenched our hearts. But the story of navy yeoman Durrell Conner aboard the stricken *California*, engulfed in flames, lifted our spirits. When many of his fellow crewmen jumped overboard, it became impossible to fight the fires. Yeoman Conner hoisted the American flag from the battleship's stern, and sailors returned to keep her afloat.[15] *Don't give up the ship, indeed!*

An entire generation of Americans would remember where they were when they heard the shocking news of Pearl Harbor. Reverend Peter Marshall was the chaplain of the U.S. Senate. He had just preached a sermon at the Naval Academy, "What Is It Like to Die?" After the service, the young Scottish immigrant gave a lift in his car to a midshipman, only to do a U-turn and return him to duty when they heard the news on his car radio.[16]**

Brigadier General Dwight D. Eisenhower's name was known only to his many friends, fellow West Pointers, and a few thousand troops in the shrunken U.S. Army. He was sleeping in on this Sunday after weeks of grueling training exercises in the field. Despite orders to let him sleep, he was awakened with the news. He dashed out of his quarters at Fort Sam Houston, in Texas, telling his wife, Mamie, he was going to Washington and did not know when he would return.[17] Senator Henry Cabot Lodge, a

---

* Until 1947, America's air force was part of the U.S. Army.

** The inspiring story of this Presbyterian minister was told in the book, *A Man Called Peter*, by Catherine Marshall.

Republican from Massachusetts, learned of the attack as he stopped to get gas.[18] Just as his father had done with President Wilson, young Cabot Lodge now offered President Roosevelt his full support in prosecuting the war.[19]* So did the leader of Senate isolationists, Michigan Republican senator. Arthur Vandenberg. Vandenberg was pasting press clippings about his fight *against* U.S. involvement in the war in his scrapbook when word came.[20]

The next day, President Roosevelt appeared before a joint session of Congress. The attack had forged national unity as nothing else could. California senator. Hiram Johnson, who had been TR's running mate on the Bull Moose ticket in 1912, had strongly opposed intervention. Now, he marched into the chamber arm-in-arm with a Democratic colleague and voted for war.[21]

The president approached the speaker's rostrum, leaning heavily on son Jimmy's arm:

> Yesterday, December 7, 1941—a date which will live in infamy—the United States of America was suddenly and deliberately attacked by naval and air forces of the Empire of Japan.[22]

Roosevelt wore a somber expression to match the black arm band he bore for the fallen. He related the lightning strikes Japanese forces had made the same day against Hong Kong (a British Crown Colony) and the U.S. dependencies of Guam, the Philippines, and Wake and Midway Islands.[23] He concluded his call for a declaration of war with these words: "With confidence in our armed forces—with the unbounding determination of our people—we will gain the inevitable triumph—so help us God."[24]**

Few Americans realized at the moment how perilous was the condition of America's armed forces. Our army ranked in size below that of Romania. Our navy had just been dealt a near-fatal blow. Providentially, however, the U.S. aircraft carrier fleet was out to sea when Pearl Harbor was struck.

---

* The man who would eventually defeat Sen. Lodge in Massachusetts, 23-year-old John F. Kennedy, spent the morning of December 7th playing touch football on the grounds of the Washington Monument. (Source: Renehan Jr., Edward J., *The Kennedys at War.*)

** These last four words of President Roosevelt's sentence were, inexplicably, dropped from the engraved quotation on the World War II Memorial.

We need to consider, if only to dismiss it, the oft-heard charge that Roosevelt *knew* Pearl Harbor would be attacked and that he kept silent so he could get the United States involved in the Second World War. North Dakota's Republican senator was interrupted with the news of Pearl Harbor while in the middle of an anti-Roosevelt speech. "It sounds terribly fishy to me," Nye replied.[25] More guarded was Charles Lindbergh's reaction; he agreed to cancel a speech for America First. His friend and fellow isolationist General Robert E. Wood said to him: "Well, [Roosevelt] got us in through the back door."[26] Even if we could believe this of Roosevelt, we would have to believe that Secretary of War Stimson and Secretary of the Navy Knox, both loyal Republicans, colluded with the president.[27]

It is true that U.S. military intelligence believed a Japanese attack was coming *somewhere.* Because of the massing of Japanese troops, however, they predicted the attack would come to the *Southwest* of the Japanese home islands.[28] They thought the militarists in Tokyo would head for the Philippines and the British, French, and Dutch colonies in Southeast Asia. These then included Burma, Hong Kong, Singapore, Malaya, Vietnam, Cambodia, Laos, and Indonesia. In fact, that is exactly where the bulk of Japanese forces did move—and very quickly. In some of the conspiratorial literature, the conviction that Roosevelt knew can only be supported by the "unconscious suppression of vast congeries of signs pointing in every direction except Pearl Harbor."[29]

It is also true that we had broken the Japanese codes prior to the Pearl Harbor attack. We knew *something* was going to happen. The decoded messages yielded only cryptic sentences like this one from Admiral Yamamoto to Admiral Nagumo, the commander of the Japanese task force: "Climb Mount Niitaka."[30] There was a crisis atmosphere in Washington. This was less true in Pearl Harbor, where it seemed unlikely an attack might occur.[31]

The charge, often heard in later years, that Roosevelt knew the attack was coming and kept silent in order to involve us in the war does not withstand careful analysis. If FDR wanted to involve the United States in a war with Japan, he could as easily have achieved his end by alerting the Pacific fleet to the coming attack. A Japanese attack on Pearl Harbor that was beaten off would just as surely have been an act of war, and Americans undoubtedly would have demanded a declaration of war against them.[32] The main reason the sneak attack on Pearl Harbor was such a shock is because it was so stunningly *irrational.* As Samuel Eliot Morison has written: "One may search military history in vain for an operation more fatal to the aggressor."[33] Almost immediately, the planner of the Pearl Harbor attack realized how fatal that error had been; Admiral Isoroku Yamamoto said: "I fear we have awakened a sleeping giant and instilled in him a terrible resolve."[34] While America lost some 2,400 on that day of infamy, the conflict begun by Japan's warlords on 7 December 1941 would eventually cost two million of their own countrymen's lives.[35]

Most often, the charge that Roosevelt knew is coupled with the even *uglier* charge that FDR went into the war at the urging of the British and the Jews. This was the substance of Charles Lindbergh's attack on Roosevelt's pre-war policy.[36] But if Hitler had not declared war on the United States, it is hard to imagine that the American people would have tolerated adding Hitler to our list of enemies. A war with Japan, arguably, could have *prevented* a U.S. declaration of war against Hitler's Germany for years, if ever.

Franklin Delano Roosevelt was not manipulated by crafty advisors. He was very much his own man. His did not so much inhabit the White House as preside over it. As one writer has said, he regarded it almost as a family seat.[37] His mental image of the presidency was of himself occupying it.[38] Other presidents might have been shaken by the experience of Pearl Harbor. Not FDR. He had supreme self-confidence. For example, he had received Mahan's *Influence of Sea Power Upon History* as a Christmas present at age fifteen, and he boasted that he'd read it thoroughly.[39] (In this instance, however, Hitler's perception that battleships were fatally vulnerable to airborne assault *and* submarine attacks showed he was ahead of both Roosevelt *and* Churchill in his detailed knowledge of modern warfare.)

Hitler declared war on the United States on 11 December 1941. It was an act of suicidal folly equaled only by the Japanese decision four days earlier to attack Pearl Harbor.

In 1941, however, it did not look like suicide. Powerful Japanese forces were immediately unleashed on the Philippines. Churchill responded to the Japanese attacks on the Americans and British possessions by declaring war on the Japanese Empire. Churchill had gained not only a powerful ally in the United States but also a dangerous and determined enemy in the Far East where Britain's colonial empire was ripe for the picking.

Adolf Hitler's treaty with Japan required him to help his ally only if Japan was attacked. But Japan was the aggressor at Pearl Harbor. Frustrated at not being able to take Moscow in that first, bitterly cold Russian winter, Hitler lashed out at the United States: Roosevelt was controlled by the Jews, he said. Speaking from his headquarters at Rastenburg, in the German state of East Prussia, Hitler explained to an aide why he had declared war on the United States.* "[In Japan,] we now have an ally who has never been vanquished in three thousand years."[40]

FDR had called 7 December 1941 "a date which will live in infamy." His words were prophetic in another way. On that very day, Hitler began gassing the Jews of Poland.[41] His troops near Chelmno took trucks with 700 Jews and transferred them in groups of eighty to a specially modified van. The van's exhaust had been re-routed into the cargo compartment. By the time the van reached Chelmno, all eighty Jews inside were dead. It was to be the first, crude attempt at mass murder that would be known as Hitler's "Final Solution" of the "Jewish problem" in Europe. On this day of infamy, all 700 were killed. In time, 360,000 Jews from 200 surrounding villages—called *shtetls*—were killed using mobile killing vans.[42]

Hastening to Washington, Churchill spent a month in the White House in close consultation with his friend, FDR. His response to the attack on Pearl Harbor, he admitted, was not altogether mournful: that night, Churchill said he "slept the sleep of the saved and the thankful."[43] He addressed a joint meeting of Congress. There, he received a thunderous ovation. Even in the midst of these "stern days", Churchill could not resist a witticism:

> I cannot help reflecting that if my father had been American and my mother British, instead of the other way around, I might have got here

---

* East Prussia was a historically German region between Poland and Lithuania. Soviets overran the capital, Königsberg, and surrounding territories in 1945. The Germans were killed or expelled. East Prussia was divided between the Russians and the Poles. Today Königsberg is the Russian city Kaliningrad. On the Polish side, the East Prussian city Danzig is now called Gdansk.

> on my own. In that case, this would not have been the first time you would have heard my voice.[44]

He was an important guest in the White House—and memorable. Stories began to circulate about his eccentricities.

"Now, Fields," Winston told the White House usher, "we had a lovely dinner last night, but I have a few orders for you. We want to leave here as friends, right? So I need you to listen. One, I don't like talking outside my quarters; two, I hate whistling in the corridors; and three, I must have a tumbler of sherry in my room before breakfast, a couple glasses of scotch and soda before lunch and French champagne and ninety-year-old brandy before I go to sleep at night." For breakfast, Churchill ordered "eggs, bacon or ham and toast, two kinds of cold meats with English mustard and two kinds of fruit plus a tumbler of sherry."[45] We don't know what Fields thought of this—except that for the White House staff it was already a long war. They had become used to the prime minister padding around the living quarters in his "siren suit," a one-piece blue affair, flight gear for the Royal Air Force.[46]

In another story, FDR was wheeled into the prime minister's guest quarters just as Churchill had stepped out of his afternoon bath, all pink and naked. As the president signaled to be wheeled out, Churchill supposedly called out with good cheer: "The Prime Minister has nothing to hide from the President."

In another widely circulated story, Churchill asked FDR if he could bring British Marines in for a tour. "Hell no!" FDR roared without missing a beat. "The last time they were here, they burned the place"—a reference to the burning of the White House in 1814 by Royal Marines. Once he'd had his joke, FDR naturally relented.

The president asked Churchill to join him for the lighting of the White House Christmas tree. Churchill willingly obliged. By now, people were saying that FDR was the most popular politician in Britain and Churchill was the most popular in the United States.[47] Churchill's short but galvanizing speech by the tree shows why:

> Let the children have their night of fun and laughter. Let the gifts of Father Christmas delight their play. Let us grownups share to the full in their unstinted pleasures before we turn again to the stern task and the formidable years that lie before us . . . In God's mercy, a happy Christmas to you all.[48]

FDR knew there was still deep suspicion of the British, especially in the Midwest, and hostility as well toward their far-flung empire. He took important symbolic steps to assert American leadership of the new alliance. He invited Churchill to worship with him at Christ Church in Alexandria, Virginia. It was the Episcopal Church where George Washington himself had knelt in prayer. The president, it was said, took "roguish delight" in the fact that he and the British prime minister together prayed Washington's "Prayer for the United States."[49] FDR had a serious purpose in mind. The war aims were to be democratic, not imperial.

Roosevelt, Churchill, Mrs. Roosevelt, and their parties left the Alexandria church and motored ten miles out to Mount Vernon. There, Churchill was to place a wreath on the tomb of George Washington. Such important symbolism, FDR felt, might help sway public opinion.

Along the beautiful Mount Vernon Parkway, Churchill kept up a constant chatter about his favorite theme: the need for the English-speaking peoples to work together after the war for peace and security. "Yes, yes, yes," FDR kept saying along the way.[50] Roosevelt had no intention of becoming a junior partner in an alliance led by Britain, Canada, Australia, and New Zealand. Finally, Eleanor piped up: "You know, Winston, when Franklin says yes, yes, yes, it doesn't mean he *agrees* with you. It means he's listening."[51] Many an American politician had come to grief making that same mistake with FDR.

One night in the White House, Churchill felt hot. He struggled to open a window himself. The next morning, he reported to his doctor his shortness of breath and a pain over his heart. He had suffered a heart attack, but his doctor did not tell him so. He knew that Churchill would refuse bed rest and could not cancel his train trip to Ottawa. It would only add to his burden.

Until America's entry into the war, Canada had been Britain's strong right arm. The small country had built up a huge military. To help Britain stay alive, the Canadians had expanded their navy *fifty-fold.*[52] Loyally, the Canadians had declared war on Germany mere days after Britain in September 1939. Canadian forces were fighting and dying beside their British brethren. Thousands of Canadian, British, and other Commonwealth troops had just surrendered to the Japanese at Hong Kong that last week of 1941.

Churchill had to pay tribute to such a steadfast ally. Speaking to Canada's Parliament in Ottawa, he related his attempt to persuade France to stay in the war against Hitler. France's weak General Weygand had said dismissively: "In three weeks, England will have her neck wrung like a chicken." Defiantly, Churchill cried out: "*Some chicken!*" Then, when the laughter in the House of Commons had subsided, he shot back: "*Some neck!*" The hilarity of the Canadians was magnified because "neck" was Canadian slang for nerve. The Canadians loved it.

So ended 1941, the year that Dean Acheson called "the year of holding our breath."[53]

Returning to Washington by train on New Year's Day 1942, Churchill cosigned with Roosevelt a joint statement of war aims that spoke of the *United Nations'* desire to win a complete victory over Germany, Italy, and Japan. It was the first reference in American history to the United Nations as the formal name of the alliance of twenty-six nations that were fighting the Axis powers.

When he saw the newsreels of the two leaders' press conference, Hitler pronounced FDR "truly mentally ill!" and said the whole event had degenerated into a theatrical performance—"truly Jewish," he said of it.* "The Americans are the dumbest people that one can imagine," the führer snorted.[54]

Winston tried to needle FDR over the fact that the United States was still backing the pro-German Vichy regime in France while the British were backing the Free French forces of general Charles de Gaulle. FDR put him off, telling him it was a matter for Secretary of State Cordell Hull and the British ambassador Lord Halifax to work out. Churchill knew this was

---

* Hitler's party rallies—orchestrated by Albert Speer and recorded on film by Leni Riefenstahl—were nothing but *theatrical.* Only his hatred of Jews could blind the führer to the fact that his enemies had an even greater sense of history's drama than he did.

Roosevelt's way of making sure nothing would happen. "Hell, Hull, and Halifax," Churchill responded defiantly.[55]

Later after receiving 60th birthday greetings from Churchill, FDR cabled him: "It's fun to be in the same decade with you."[56] The two men were genuinely fond of one another, but they were fighting their own wars for their own objectives. Labor Secretary Frances Perkins reported a different FDR. After the Japanese attack, "he was a changed man," she said, "a more potent and dedicated personality. The terrible shock of Pearl Harbor, the destruction of his precious ships, the unknown hazards which war might bring to the people . . . acted like a spiritual purge and left him cleaner, simpler, more single-minded."[57]

Despite Roosevelt's and Churchill's good humor, the Allies' situation was grim indeed. Surrendering British and Canadian soldiers would face incredible brutality in Japanese captivity.* In the Philippines, U.S. Army and Philippine national forces under General Douglas MacArthur were increasingly isolated on the Island of Bataan. There, Japanese forces under General Homma tightened the noose. From January to April 1942, the situation worsened. Unable to relieve the fortress of Corregidor, President Roosevelt ordered MacArthur to evacuate his family and immediate staff to Australia. The Australians were an important ally. But they were shocked suddenly to find themselves in the path of the Japanese juggernaut. FDR sent MacArthur there to reassure them. As he left the Philippines by Patrol Torpedo (PT) Boat, MacArthur declared, "I shall return."

American G.I.s** felt abandoned. Bombed day and night by the Japanese, they sang a mournful tune:

> We're the Battling Bastards of Bataan
> No mama, no papa, no Uncle Sam,
> No aunts, no uncles, no cousins, no nieces,
> No pills, no planes or artillery pieces.[58]

---

* Hollywood gave *Bridge on the River Kwai* an Oscar in 1957 for its treatment of this captivity. The building of this "Railroad of Death" was even more graphically portrayed in the 2001 movie, *To End All Wars*, a powerful treatment of the horror.

** *G.I.*—short for Government Issue—was a nickname for American soldiers during World War II, just as *doughboy* had been the preferred usage in World War I.

When the American surrender finally came in April 1942, horror awaited the U.S. and Filipino POWs. Nearly 78,000 of them—the largest mass surrender in American history—were force marched to a prison camp more than sixty-five miles away. The starving, sick Americans and Filipinos were clubbed, bayoneted, and shot to death if they fell out of the line of march. It has ever after been known as the Bataan Death March.[59] (For his part in ordering the march, Japanese General Homma would later be tried, convicted, and hanged for war crimes.[60])

To lift up American morale after the disastrous defeat in the Philippines, FDR ordered an air raid on Tokyo. Colonel Jimmy Doolittle led sixteen USAAF B-25 bombers from the deck of the USS *Hornet.* Doolittle's bomber pilots practiced takeoffs from an airfield lined to the exact dimensions of a carrier deck, but they had never actually taken off from a real carrier pitching and rolling in the always stormy waters of the northern Pacific. Never before or since have bombers been launched from an aircraft carrier. Vice Admiral William F. ("Bull") Halsey's task force carried the planes to within five hundred miles of Japan's home islands. Doolittle's raid—those famous *Thirty Seconds over Tokyo*—did little damage to Japan's war machine. But it did cause the military leaders to "lose face" among the Japanese people. They now realized they were not immune to air attacks. The Doolittle Raid also electrified Americans. Just four months after Pearl Harbor, the Doolittle Raid demonstrated that the United States could strike back.[61] Nine of the eighty American flyers died in the raid, some being executed by their vengeful Japanese captors—a clear violation of the Geneva Convention.* The military felt the pressure to do something dramatic. An impatient public and an equally impatient FDR demanded action.[62]

Some Americans gave in to their fears during World War II. Widespread rumors of Japanese-American disloyalty led to panic, especially on the now-vulnerable West Coast. Responding to cries from California's Republican

---

* "A set of eighty silver goblets, each one inscribed with a Raider's name, has been kept on display at the U.S. Air Force Academy in Colorado Springs, Colorado, and flown to each reunion. There, in a private ceremony, the survivors raised their cups in a toast to Raiders departed and inverted the cups of those men who died since the previous get-together. When the last man is gone, his goblet, too, will be reversed." (Online source: http://www.historynet.com/magazines/american_history/3031641.html?showAll=y&c=y.)

attorney general Earl Warren among others, President Roosevelt signed Executive Order 9066 on 19 February 1942. EO 9066 is now generally conceded to be one of FDR's worst mistakes. It provided for the internment of some 110,000 persons of Japanese descent.[63] These included not only Japanese citizens but also those who were *Nisei* and *Sansei*, second- and third-generation Japanese Americans. Fully 64 percent of these were American citizens.[64] They were sent to internment camps in remote parts of the vast West. In no way can such camps be fairly compared with Nazi death camps or Stalin's *Gulag*, but the terrible fact remains that Americans who had done no wrong lost their property and, temporarily at least, their liberty because of the hysteria and hatred of their neighbors. It's an ugly blot on our nation's conscience.

Fortunately, the heroic combat record of the Army's all-Nisei 100th Battalion in Italy did much to bank the flames of prejudice. The 100th was integrated into the 442nd Regimental Combat Team. It was in this unit that Daniel K. Inouye, a Hawaiian Nisei, won the Congressional Medal of Honor. Years later, he was sworn in as the first Japanese-American member of Congress. When Speaker Sam Rayburn intoned the usual "raise your right hand," an awed hush came over the House of Representatives; Congressman, now Senator, Inouye had lost his right arm in service to America.[65]

FDR wasted no time or sympathy on those German-Americans who were suspected of being "fifth columnists."* Or on spies. Two parties of German saboteurs were landed by U-boat on America's shores. One came ashore in Florida, the other on Long Island. Intercepted at first by a young Coast Guardsman, John Cullen, near Amagansett, New York. Seaman Cullen soon alerted his superiors and all the Germans were quickly apprehended. FDR ordered a trial by military tribunal. Though ably defended by government attorneys, the German saboteurs were prosecuted by Francis Biddle. Biddle was attorney general of the United States. They were convicted as spies. Six members of the group were sentenced to death; two who had turned themselves in received life sentences.[66]

Roosevelt similarly turned a stern face toward Charles A. Lindbergh,

---

* The term "Fifth Column" was in widespread use during World War II. It was first used during Spain's civil war (1936–39) to describe a subversive element *within* a besieged city that would help an attacking general take it. It became shorthand for disloyalty.

whom he suspected of disloyalty. After Pearl Harbor, America First had folded and Lindbergh made it known he wanted to return to the army. Lindbergh was fully willing to fight the non-white Japanese, but he hadn't changed his mind about the desirability of coming to an agreement with Hitler. FDR was in no mood to negotiate with Lindbergh. Nor would he make any concessions to Lindbergh's oft-repeated notion that a war by Britain and America against the German *Aryans* would be suicide for the white race. Roosevelt stonily rejected Lindbergh's bid for an air force commission. "I'll clip that young man's wings," FDR told several senators.[67] And he did. Lindbergh never again enjoyed the public's trust.

Roosevelt has been criticized for what seems his vindictive treatment of a national hero. But Abraham Lincoln had personally dismissed Major John J. Key from the army in 1862. That young officer admitted to the president that he and other junior officers in General McClellan's circle did not want to decisively beat the rebels, that they preferred a negotiated settlement.[68] Roosevelt's treatment of Lindbergh was no different.

FDR was sensitive to racial unrest at home. Millions of black Americans were moving North to work in war industries. They faced discrimination in housing and in many daily activities. Race riots threatened national unity at a critical time. In one of the worst of these riots, in 1943, thirty-four people died in Detroit.

Young black men were subject to the draft, but they served in all-black units. In one such unit, the Tuskegee Airmen gained lasting fame in the skies over Germany. President Roosevelt promoted Benjamin O. Davis Sr. as the first black general in the army, a historic breakthrough.[69] The government publicized boxer Joe Louis's wry response to racial injustice in America: "There's nothing wrong with this country that Hitler is going to cure."[70]

Still, there *was* much wrong with the country. Union leader A. Philip Randolph was determined to use the war emergency to press for greater equality for black Americans. Before the outbreak of the war, Randolph had urged a great march on Washington for justice if the president did not address the issue of hiring discrimination by government defense contractors. FDR responded by creating the Fair Employment Practices Commission (FEPC). He had been urged on by Eleanor.[71] Randolph led the

Brotherhood of Sleeping Car Porters. His members were known as "civil rights missionaries on wheels."[72] Randolph would become a leading figure in the civil rights movement.

"Freedom is never granted," he said, "it is won."[73]

III. A World at War

In World War I, millions in Russia, Europe, and the wider world did not know the names of Lloyd George, Clemenceau, the kaiser, or Woodrow Wilson.[74] They had only a hazy idea of who was fighting or why. As a result of what historian John Lukacs has called the *duel,* however, the names of Hitler and Churchill were known throughout the world.

By 1942, the whole world was at war. For millions, defeat in this war would mean not only a loss of freedom, it would mean *annihilation.* This was certainly true for the Communist commissars of Soviet Russia. Hitler had issued a "commissar order" that called for the immediate murder of any of these Communist Party officials who fell into German hands. Slavs were endangered as well. Hitler wanted Poland and the Ukraine for *lebensraum*, or "living space," for the rapidly expanding population of Germans. Slavery, followed by starvation and sterilization, would be the fate of the Slavs who were in his way.

Of course, Hitler's "New Order in Europe" threatened Jews most of all. Although Allied intelligence did not know it yet, the 20 January 1942 conference held in the Berlin suburb of Wannsee planned the "Final Solution of the Jewish Problem in Europe." This *solution*—a chilling euphemism for a non-existent problem—was to be nothing less than the murder of all eleven million European Jews. The mass shootings of Jews in Russia and the gassings at Chelmno, as destructive as they were, only convinced the Nazi high command of the need for "industrial" methods of slaughter if they were to destroy all the Jews in Europe. Thus, at Wannsee, they planned to use rail transport to forcibly relocate all the Jews they could capture. Surrounding populations would be told the Jews were merely being "relocated in the East." But at remote places like Auschwitz, far from prying eyes, the monstrous mechanism of mass murder would accelerate beyond anything previously known in human history. It was the beginning of *Holocaust.* In many of the occupied states of Europe, Hitler would find willing accomplices for his plans. He sought to make all Europe *judenrein*, a land free of Jews. Hitler had publicly warned the Jews that if "they" plunged the world into another great war, they would be exterminated. Few in the West imagined he really *meant* or thought it.

Hitler spoke to a conference in Berlin, boasting that anti-Semitism was on the rise throughout the world. In this, he was correct. "In Germany, too, the Jews once laughed at my prophesies. I don't know if they are still laughing," the führer said with malicious sarcasm.[75] Meanwhile, several hundred miles to the east, at a remote Polish village, Jews from France, Belgium, and Holland were arriving in cattle cars. Many had died en route. In one group, 957 Jews had arrived from Paris on the morning of 2 September 1942. By that afternoon, 918 had already been gassed.[76]

Hitler welcomed the Grand Mufti of Jerusalem—Muslim leader Haj Amin al-Husseini—to Berlin at the outbreak of the war. There, the mufti broadcasted militantly anti-Jewish messages to the Arab world.[77] He had helped the Germans to recruit Muslims in the Balkans—the 13th *Waffen SS* Handschar Division.[78] These were certainly not Aryans. Thousands of Jews from Palestine joined the British Army in Egypt. They knew too well that if Rommel's powerful Afrika Korps crossed the Suez Canal, Hitler would call upon the Muslims to rise up and exterminate the half million Jews living precariously under the British mandate in Palestine. A distinguished Jewish educator in Jerusalem pleaded for enlistments: "If the men of the Hebrew University do not realize the urgency of this hour, who will?"[79]

FDR and Churchill had agreed on a "Germany First" strategy since both viewed Germany as the greater menace. This decision was to have profound consequences for the course of the war and for the shape of the postwar world. But agreeing on fighting Germany first did not mean that the two leaders would always agree on strategy. Nor would they find their alliance with Soviet Russia's Josef Stalin an easy one.

"I feel damn depressed," wrote Harry Hopkins from the prime minister's residence at No. 10 Downing Street in London. He said Churchill was like a cannon: great to have on your side, but devastating when he was firing away at you.[80] Hopkins had been engaged in some hard dealing with Churchill on the subject of Britain's colonies.

Churchill did not agree with Roosevelt about the future of the British Empire. When FDR had the nerve to suggest that Hong Kong be returned to the Chinese and to recommend independence for India, Churchill fired back that maybe an international team of inspection should be sent *to the American South!*[81] Churchill had traveled widely in the United States and was quite familiar with the practice of segregation. John Maynard Keynes, leading a British delegation on Lend-Lease, hated the way American lawyers condescendingly spoke to him. It was all "Cherokee" he said.* America was trying "to pick out the eyes of the British Empire," he said.[82] Keynes's fellow delegates felt like "the representatives of a vanquished people discussing the economic penalties of defeat."[83]

FDR was not willing to spend American blood and treasure to shore up what he saw as a collapsing imperial power. He would fight to save the British home islands from Hitler's ruthless tyranny, but that was all. "Billions for Britain," FDR was saying, in effect, "not a penny for Empire."

American schoolchildren of those days were used to seeing maps of the world that had great, broad bands of red (actually pink) to indicate British dominions. Canada, Australia, New Zealand, India (including modern Pakistan), as well as extensive territories in Africa, the Middle East, and Asia—all these were tied to the British Crown.

In 1942, it was still true that the "sun never set on the British Empire." With the loss of Hong Kong, Singapore, and Malaya to the Japanese, with India threatened, and with Germany's Afrika Korps moving east toward the Suez Canal, how much longer would this be true?

It must have seemed ironic indeed to Churchill that he had to battle his English-speaking Ally for the sake of his king. Hitler had pledged *not* to interfere with the British Empire. Now, here was the great democrat, Roosevelt, demanding self-government for British colonies. Churchill doubtless had FDR in mind when he declared defiantly in Parliament: "I

* Like speaking "Greek" to me.

have not become the King's first minister in order to preside over the liquidation of the British Empire."[84]

America in World War II mobilized in a way never seen before—or since. "Hitler should beware the fury of an aroused democracy," said U.S. general Dwight D. Eisenhower.[85] Hitler probably had little understanding of the vast numbers that would soon come against him. With the aid of pre-war military conscription (which had been reauthorized by a single vote in Congress), the United States quickly built up a huge military. Soon, the United States would have over twelve million men and women in uniform—surpassing all other powers, even Russia by a slight margin.[86]

Nation	Troops Fielded
Britain	4,680,000
Japan	6,095,000
Germany	10,000,000
USSR	12,300,000
U.S.	12,364,000

(Source: Stephen Ambrose, *World War II.*)

These numbers meant that one in eleven Americans was serving in the military (by comparison, in 2007, one in two hundred Americans is on active duty in the military). This incredible mobilization represented a monumental investment for a democracy—never before seen and never since surpassed.

Americans sang along with pro-military songs like the Andrews Sisters' "Boogie Woogie Bugle Boy." Irving Berlin's plaintive "God Bless America" had lifted hearts when Kate Smith sang it in the darkening years before the war. Now, in 1942, Berlin used humor to keep up morale:

This is the Army Mister Jones,
No private rooms or telephones,
You had your breakfast in bed before,
But you won't have it there any more.

Millions of young men were swept up in the draft. Few even dreamed of staying out. Conscientious objectors were shunned as "shirkers." For many, the experience of military training in boot camp was disorienting. And take this example of the drill instructor's art: "*Yew peepul're lak a bunch o' chickens. Evvy day's a nyoo day. If you keep screwin' up lak this, ahm gonna Jack Ammonia!*" Translation: "You people are like a bunch of chickens. Every day's a new day. If you keep screwing up like this, I'm going to jack them [demerits] on you!"*

On the home front, Americans lived with the rationing of many daily necessities. Meat, gasoline, automobile tires, and women's nylon stockings were but a few of the essentials in short supply. FDR let his interior secretary, Harold Ickes, mount a drive to collect rubber to repurpose for the war. The White House announced that the president's Scottish terrier, Fala, would donate his already-been-chewed rubber bones.[87] So enthusiastic was Ickes for his new assignment that he grabbed the rubber doormat outside the president's office and put it in the trunk of his limousine! One Amoco gas station in the nation's capital became carried away. They posted this sign: WE ACCEPT ANYTHING MADE OF RUBBER EXCEPT CONDOMS.[88]

Americans were exhorted daily to raise their own vegetables in backyard "victory gardens." They collected used cans and "tin" foil for reuse. With automobile production converted into tank and aircraft production, Americans could not buy new cars. Many other consumer goods were likewise unobtainable. As the government's slogan for wartime austerity put it:

Use it up
Wear it out
Make it do
Or do without

Churchill had made the V-for-Victory sign world-famous. Usually, his two-finger V sign cradled a huge cigar. His "V" was an old English gesture, going all the way back, it is believed, to King Henry V's miraculous victory

* This routine, usually spiced with salty expletives, owes much to the tradition of military boot camp company commanders going all the way back to Baron von Steuben at Valley Forge.

at the Battle of Agincourt in France in 1415. There, legend has it, the French had threatened to cut off the English archers' fingers so they could never again use their lethal longbows. Victorious English soldiers showed off their Vs to prove they still had their fingers—and their ability to fight.[89] Victory gardens, victory loans, everywhere you looked, people were being exhorted to victory. Hard-to-read V-mail (victory mail) was accepted as a matter of course. Every letter to and from America's twelve million men and women in uniform was opened, photocopied, and censored. The addressee got only the photocopy. There was barely a peep of protest at this unprecedented government intrusion.

Less savory examples of the "V" could be cited. V-girls were those young American females who hung around bases and training centers to get picked up by randy G.I.s.[90] Small wonder public health authorities fretted about a very different V—VD, for venereal disease.

In major cities of the East Coast, a wartime blackout was in effect. New York's "Great White Way"—the heart of the thriving theater district—went dark. Americans were told that nighttime blackouts were necessary, especially along the Eastern Seaboard. There, Nazi U-boats had been able to pick off U.S. merchant ships silhouetted by the lights of beach town boardwalks.

Of course, war-weary Americans could always go to the movies. Hollywood threw itself wholeheartedly into the war effort. Movie stars appeared at war-bond rallies encouraging Americans to help finance the war. Tinseltown churned out endless movies designed to bolster morale on the home front. There were several excellent movies, but hundreds of duds. *Casablanca* and *Mrs. Minniver* remain classics today. In *Desperate Journey,* Errol Flynn, Arthur Kennedy, and Ronald Reagan played three American pilots forced down behind enemy lines. It was certainly not a great role for the future president, but it did enable him to joke that he was used to people trying to upstage him. He once acted with Errol Flynn. As Reagan himself would say of the producers of some of these clunkers: "They don't want it good; they want it *Tuesday.*"

Ronald Reagan would have felt quite at home in North Platte, Nebraska. The town was a typical Midwest hamlet of 12,000 at the outbreak of the war.

But something very special happened there. Beginning on Christmas Day in 1941 and continuing through the end of the war, the town offered itself as the North Platte Canteen. There, for 365 days a year from dawn until the last troop train pulled out, volunteers from this remote Great Plains community provided hot coffee, donuts, sandwiches, and sympathy for young soldiers shipping out.

The whole effort started by mistake. Townsmen had heard that Company D of the Nebraska National Guard would be stopping over on its way to the Pacific.[91] Young Miss Rae Wilson wrote to the North Platte *Daily Bulletin* to describe what happened at the depot:

> We who met this troop train which arrived about 5 o'clock were expecting Nebraska boys. Naturally, we had candy, cigarettes, etc., but we very willingly gave those things to the Kansas boys. Smiles, tears, and laughter followed. Appreciation showed on over 300 faces. I say get back of our sons and other mothers' sons 100 percent. Let's do something and do it in a hurry. We can help this way when we can't help any other way.[92]

What began as a mistake—Kansas National Guardsmen taken for Nebraskans—ended five years later. By war's end, more than six million G.I.s had been served at the North Platte Canteen.[93]

Millions of Americans were swept into war industries. Many were prevented from leaving jobs in critical fields. When the United Mine Workers' John L. Lewis planned a strike in the coalfields that would cripple war production, FDR threatened to seize the mines and *draft* the miners.[94]

Millions of women entered the workforce for the first time in World War II. "Rosie the Riveter" became a legend. "She's a WOW," declared one poster showing an attractive young woman looking up from her assembly line at the imagined picture of her man as he headed into combat. As a Woman Ordinance Worker, she was told, she was freeing a man for the fight.[95]

Women and all other defense workers knew they were not just performing a hard, dull, routine task. They were the sinews of victory. To a stricken world, America's productive capacity seemed unlimited.

IV. The Battle of the Atlantic

Shipbuilding was a critical element in the victory of the Allies. The Nazi U-boat menace threatened Britain's very lifeblood in 1942. If Britain could not be supplied by sea, she would starve and lose the war.

FDR needed a no-nonsense industrialist to superintend shipbuilding. He tentatively turned to Joseph P. Kennedy. The National Maritime Union—a notoriously pro-Soviet outfit—wired FDR to protest any appointment for Kennedy: FATAL MISTAKE TO APPOINT THIS APOSTLE OF APPEASEMENT TO ANY SHIPPING POSITION.[96] Kennedy, still embittered toward the president, considered the job beneath him and turned it down.[97] This was a classic example of FDR's management style. He probably expected the petulant Kennedy to turn him down. But having offered Kennedy a job, he could say he had repaid his political debts to the flamboyant Boston politician.

Instead of Joe Kennedy, it would be Henry J. Kaiser who gained lasting fame as the man who built the Liberty ships. An astounding 2,751 Liberty ships were built during World War II*; one of these was built in the record time of four days, fifteen and a half hours from the time the keel was laid.[98] As plucky merchant marine sailors boasted ever after: "We could launch 'em faster than Hitler could sink 'em."

It was a brave boast, but it was the Allied seamen, not their ships, that could not be replaced. From 1939, when Britain and Canada entered the war, to 1945, 36,000 Allied sailors were killed in the Atlantic, almost all of them by U-boats. And an equal number of merchant seamen were killed.[99] Shortly after Hitler declared war on the United States, the East Coast became a hunting ground for Gross Admiral Karl Dönitz's ingenious U-boat "wolf packs."** By the middle of 1942, the Germans had sunk more Allied tonnage in the Atlantic than the Japanese had done with their more spectacular attacks on

---

* The 2,751 Liberty ships built between 1941 and 1945 were 441 feet long, 57 feet wide, and carried 10,800 tons of supplies. They each had a range of 17,000 miles. (Source: http://www.cr.nps.gov/history/online_book/butkowski1/index.htm.)

** Dönitz had conceived the idea of massing attack submarines together for attacks during his service as a junior officer in the Imperial German Navy in World War I. It was only with Hitler's backing that he was able to put his dream—*our nightmare*—into practice. Perhaps this accounts for Dönitz's incredible loyalty to Hitler.

Pearl Harbor, the Philippines, Wake, Guam, and other U.S., British, and Dutch possessions in Asia.[100] Hitler never allowed more than a dozen U-boats to operate at one time off America's Eastern seaboard, yet the damage they inflicted was frightening. Naval historian Samuel Eliot Morison compared the toll of American losses in 1942 to what we would have suffered if Nazi saboteurs had succeeded in destroying a number of our largest munitions works.[101] Dönitz believed that Germany could have won the war with the U-boat alone.[102] Considering the heavy losses the Allies sustained in a relatively short time, he was probably right.

The United States and Britain did not rely, however, merely on the overpowering productivity of their shipyards. The convoy system, destroyer escorts, submarine-destroying inventions like SONAR (ASDIC to the British, who invented it), patrol seaplanes, and dirigibles equipped for anti-submarine warfare together put an end to the U-boat menace. The U.S. Coast Guard was especially active in anti-submarine warfare in World War II. Perhaps the greatest of anti-submarine warriors was Britain's Captain F. J. "Johnnie" Walker. He sank *twenty* U-boats, employing his own tactic, the "Creeping Attack."[103] Johnnie Walker gave the Germans no chance to surrender. He would use one ship to locate the U-boat with its sonar while he "crept" up on it silently. Then he ordered the depth charges.[104] No submarine ever survived Walker's hammering blows.[105] Before the war, he had been a boxer. Pity his opponents in the ring.

By May 1943, the "happy time" the U-boat sailors fondly remembered off the coast of North Carolina was over. By war's end, three-fourths of Germany's 40,000 U-boat sailors had been killed. Little wonder, however, that Churchill feared the U-boats above everything. "The U-boat attack was our worst evil. It would have been wise for the Germans to stake all upon it."[106]

One American seaman, Leslie Morrison, described his ordeal fifty years after his merchant ship, the SS *Deer Lodge,* was torpedoed off Durban, South Africa, in February 1943. The German skipper of the U-516 submarine surfaced and asked the survivors in lifeboats their tonnage, their cargo, where they were from, and where they were bound. Morrison, relating the story to his niece, told how the German skipper, Korvetten Kapitan Gerhard Wiebe, then turned his boat around and steamed away. "Wasn't that *horrible?*" Morrison's niece asked. "Hell, no!" the old sailor laughed. "At least he didn't *shoot* us." Morrison related how the injured men were cared for in the boats as the healthier sailors took turns bailing the boats out and then holding on outside the lifeboats.

U.S. Navy seaman Basil Izzi survived an astonishing eighty-three days on a raft after the SS *Zaandam,* on which he was an armed guard, was sunk in the South Atlantic in late 1942. There were five men on the raft at the start of the ordeal; only three survived. Izzi described his time to an interviewer:

INTERVIEWER: Did you save any souvenirs from the trip?

IZZI: Yes Sir, I saved the drinking cup that we had aboard the raft.

INTERVIEWER: Beside these services for men who died, did you have any religious service on the raft?

IZZI: Yes, before anyone died we used to have services, like every night before we would go to bed. Each man would say his prayers or sometimes one man would say them for the whole party.

INTERVIEWER: Was your family notified that you were missing while you were on the raft?

IZZI: Yes, they were notified November the 18th that I was missing, and they were notified again February 1st that I was picked up.

INTERVIEWER: What was the name of the rescue ship, do you know?

IZZI: It was a PC boat 576 [U.S. Navy submarine chasers were not named—PC 576 was built in Dravo, Delaware, in 1942], an American boat, a small patrol boat. It was escorting a convoy from Trinidad.

INTERVIEWER: How about your weight?

IZZI: My regular weight is around 145 but when I got picked up I weighed something like 85 pounds. Right now I am just a few pounds out of the way [i.e., short of regular weight]. I am going to make a country tour in a few more days and after I finish that, I am going to take about two months leave and then return to the [Naval] hospital here in Bethesda [Maryland].

INTERVIEWER: You are going to talk to war plants?

IZZI: Yes Sir, I am.[107]*

Americans working in defense plants regularly heard from heroic young servicemen like Basil Izzi. It was part of the effort to "keep the home fires burning."

V. America Strikes Back

Following the Japanese sneak attack on Pearl Harbor, Navy Admiral Chester W. Nimitz was itching to hit back. The Japanese Imperial Navy had never known defeat. Each of its warships bore the sixteen-petaled chrysanthemum, the Imperial seal. A clash in May between Japanese carrier-based aircraft and American and Australian naval units became known as the Battle of the Coral Sea. The Japanese were attempting to land troops at Port Moresby, New Guinea.[108] It was the first naval battle in history in which neither fleet sighted the other. Although the Americans lost the USS *Lexington,* the Japanese were prevented from landing. They withdrew under pounding from carrier-based aircraft.[109]

The Australians and New Zealanders regard this battle as key to securing their freedom from Japanese invasion.

A Japanese attempt to take Midway Island in the South Pacific in June 1942 was turned back. American carriers, which had escaped the attack on Pearl Harbor, launched attacks on their Japanese counterparts. Miraculously, an air squadron that was headed the wrong way spotted the wake of a Japanese destroyer. They turned ninety degrees and followed the destroyer all the way back to the carrier task force. There, the U.S. Navy torpedo bombers caught Admiral Nagumo's carriers while they were preparing

---

* Dutch merchant ship SS *Zaandam*, bound for New York, carrying 8,600 tons of chrome and copper ore as well as 600 tons of general cargo, had a crew of 112, 18 armed guards, and 169 passengers including survivors from four previously sunk ships. Izzi was one of only three survivors from this particular wreck. Something separate to consider given Izzi's comments: What a marked contrast between this actual lifeboat survivor's story and the hypothetical line of conduct condoned by the infamous Lifeboat Exercise offered in some so-called Values Clarification courses.

to receive their own planes. The Japanese decks were covered with bombs and snaking hoses for aviation fuel. When the Americans struck, Nagumo suffered a catastrophe. The carriers that had carried out the sneak attack on Pearl Harbor—*Kaga, Akagi, Hiryu,* and *Soryu*—were sent to the bottom. Americans were thrilled to deal the Japanese such a stinging defeat, just six months after Pearl Harbor.[110] What Doolittle's Raid did in spirit, the Battle of Midway did in reality. The Miracle at Midway punctured the myth of Japanese invincibility. Midway was not won without suffering, however. The USS *Yorktown* was sunk. And out of forty-one planes launched by Admiral Spruance against the enemy, only six returned.[111]

Britain also enjoyed a singular victory later in 1942. Churchill was desperate to stop the "Desert Fox," Field Marshal Erwin Rommel. Rommel's Afrika Korps had pushed the British back to within just sixty miles of the Suez Canal. Not only was the canal vulnerable, and with it Britain's vital oil supply from the Persian Gulf, but so, too, was Britain's Mandate in Palestine. Jews the world over shuddered as Rommel's *panzer* tanks sped ever closer to Jerusalem.

To stop the charismatic Desert Fox, Churchill chose the equally colorful Field Marshal Bernard Law Montgomery. "Monty" and his "Desert Rats" of Britain's 8th Army defeated Rommel at El Alamein in November 1942. Britain was overjoyed. Over his wife Clementine's "violent" objections, Churchill ordered that church bells that had been silent since 1 September 1939, should now ring out all over Britain to mark the victory.* Churchill said it was not the end. "It is not even the beginning of the end. But it may be the end of the beginning." It was.

As he spoke, Hitler's unstoppable armies were stopped in North Africa and at Stalingrad in the USSR. These two Allied victories were to have worldwide consequences.

Meanwhile, in Europe, the Jews were targeted for physical annihilation under the Final Solution. Christians were to be terrorized into submission,

---

* The church bells were to be rung to signal a Nazi invasion. By this time, the danger of invasion had passed, but "Clemmie" feared further British defeats that would make Winston's impulsive act look rash. She was always trying to protect him—from himself. She need not have feared. After El Alamein, the British conquered. (Source: *Clementine Churchill: Portrait of a Marriage,* 419.)

according to documents compiled by Gen. William Donovan of the Office of Strategic Services (OSS). Donovan assembled evidence of Hitler's plan to destroy Christian churches and organizations. "Under the pretext that the Churches themselves were interfering in political and state matters, [the Nazis] would deprive the Churches, step by step, of all opportunity to affect German public life." As writer Charles A. Donovan notes: Adolf Hitler and his Nazis were "at war with God."[112]*

El Alamein was followed immediately by Operation Torch. The joint U.S.-British invasion of French North Africa was commanded by General Dwight D. Eisenhower. The victory at El Alamein helped persuade Vichy French authorities quickly to end their resistance to the Allied invasion. After some initial combat—in which 1,400 Americans and 700 French troops were killed—French authorities in North Africa sought a cease-fire.[113]** Although Operation Torch was hugely successful for the Allies in North Africa, it led to Hitler's retaliation by occupying *all* of Metropolitan France. From this point on, there would not even be the fiction that the government set up by the ancient Marshal Pétain at the little resort village of Vichy was anything but a puppet of their Nazi masters. This had disastrous consequences for millions of Frenchmen and, especially, for thousands of French Jews as Vichy complied with German demands for French slave laborers and forced the French to cooperate with the Nazis in rounding up Jews.[114]

Now, France would be completely at the mercy of Germany's secret police, the *Gestapo.* Hundreds of thousands of young French men and women would be swept up and transported across the border as forced laborers in the Third Reich. French Jews were hunted down—often in *collaboration* with Vichy police—and shipped off to German death camps.

Churchill had formed his Secret Operations Executive (SOE) with instructions to "set Europe ablaze." He wanted to disrupt and challenge Hitler's rule of the continent. Free Czech agents, trained by SOE, succeeded in May 1942, in killing Deputy Reichsprotektor Reinhard Heydrich.[115] He had

* Charles A. Donovan is the son of James R. Donovan, Sr., who served in the OSS in 1944–45. (These Donovans are no relation to OSS founder "Wild Bill" Donovan.)

** This was the only time since the Quasi-War of 1798–1800 that the French and Americans faced each other in combat.

been the one who had organized the Wannsee Conference to organize the systematic genocide of the Jews. Nazi retribution was terrible. Hitler ordered the entire Czech village of Lidie to be razed and all its male inhabitants shot. The women were sent to a concentration camp, and the children were abducted for inclusion in Himmler's notorious *lebensborn* human-breeding program.*

To bolster Allied morale, Eleanor Roosevelt visited Britain late in 1942. Clementine Churchill wrote to FDR on the amazing impact of the First Lady's tours on the young servicewomen in the British military—and of the way she handled reporters: "I was struck by the ease, friendliness and dignity with which she talked with the reporters, and by the esteem and affection with which they evidently regarded her."[116]

"Clemmie" later reported that Eleanor and Winston "had a slight difference of opinion" about Spain over dinner. Clementine was on hand to mediate differences, but she gave the president's outspoken wife little hint of her own deeply held views.[117] In the end, Winston realized he had to stay on Eleanor's good side. He wooed her with his old-fashioned charm. "You have certainly left *golden footprints* behind you," he wrote as Eleanor departed England.[118]

President Roosevelt flew seventeen thousand miles for another secret summit conference with Churchill at Casablanca in French Morocco in early 1943. The president flew aboard a commercial Boeing 314 clipper—a "flying boat." He thus became the first president to fly while in office.[119] Americans were thrilled by the danger and mystery of his dramatic wartime flight.**

Allied prospects had suddenly brightened. American soldiers, sailors, and Marines were in the final stages of taking Guadalcanal, in the Solomon Islands. Despite heavy casualties, including 1,752 dead, the Americans showed that the die-hard Japanese could be beaten, even in the steamy

---

* Under the breeding program known as Lebensborn, or Fount of Life, women deemed by the Nazis to fit the ideals of the German race were mated with selected men to "bear a child for the Füehrer." The mating places were officially disguised as maternity homes. ARD said around 7,000 children were born in the program, although numbers have never been verified. (Source: AP News story, 17 November 1999.)

** The straight-line distance between Washington, D.C. and Casablanca is just 3,794 miles, but due to wartime security and heavy load requirements, Boeing's *Dixie Clipper* made the trip in stages. FDR celebrated his 61st birthday on his return trip.

jungles of the South Pacific.[120] By contrast, in sub-zero cold, a major German army was surrounded at Stalingrad.

Among other things, FDR hoped to force his choice of General Henri-Honoré Giraud on the Free French. The president disliked and mistrusted the tall, uncooperative, self-anointed leader of the Free French, General Charles de Gaulle. When Churchill humorously said de Gaulle thought he was Joan of Arc, FDR tried to arrange a "shotgun wedding" of the two French leaders. In this, he failed. De Gaulle soon outmaneuvered Giraud in the labyrinth of French exile politics.

The most important result of the Casablanca summit was the demand for "Unconditional Surrender." Although the words do not appear in the Allies' joint communiqué, suggesting that Churchill might have been less than enthusiastic, FDR understood that the American people had to have an easily understood war aim.[121] Roosevelt has been criticized for this demand. Critics say he lengthened the war and undercut anti-Nazi elements within Germany and thus cost American lives.[124] Roosevelt knew, however, that Americans were bitterly disillusioned after World War I. He agreed with Cousin Theodore, and not with Wilson, on this point.[123] He had to reassure the American people that no "deal" would be struck with the Nazis. Churchill later softened the Allies' demand by saying: "We are no extirpators of nations, or butchers of peoples . . . We remain bound by our customs and our nature."[124] The Allies would treat defeated Germany with humanity.

Churchill suffered from pneumonia at the Casablanca summit conference. When he recovered, he ordered a picnic at a rugged retreat in the famed Atlas Mountains. Typically, he scampered down a steep gorge and tried to clamber up the biggest boulder. "Clemmie said nothing," reported a friend, Lady Diana Cooper, "but watched him like a lenient mother who does not want to spoil her child's fun nor yet his daring."[125] Later, Lady Diana spoke to Clemmie about what they would do when the war was over. "I never think of after the war," Clemmie said calmly. "You see, I think Winston will die when it's over . . . We're putting all we have into this war, and it will take all we have."[126]*

---

* Winston Churchill survived a full twenty years after World War II. His beloved, vivacious Clementine lived until 1977.

When on 30 January 1943, Hitler promoted General Friedrich von Paulus to field marshal, he reminded his commander at besieged Stalingrad that no German field marshal had *ever* been captured. Temperatures in Russia that winter had plunged to *minus* 30° C (-22° F). Starving *Wehrmacht* soldiers had to eat their horses. They even dug up dead horses to stew their bones. Over and over, the Soviets broadcast to the German troops: *Stalingrad—Massengrab* ("Stalingrad—Mass Grave"). Von Paulus surrendered his new field marshal's baton on 31 January.[127] With him, ninety thousand German soldiers, sick, cold, and hungry, passed through "the gates of Hell" into Stalin's slave-labor camps. They were all that was left of an army of a quarter million. Fewer than five thousand of these men would ever see their homes again.[128] The invading Germans had shown no mercy to the Russians. Now, they received none.

Back in Germany, state radio played dirges for days. The Nazi propaganda machine could not conceal the magnitude of the disaster and for once did not try. The brittle steel of the German *schwerpunkt*—spear tip—had broken. Hitler had determined to take Stalingrad not because of its intrinsic military value, but because of its symbolic name. For that very reason, Stalin was determined to hold it.

The city on the Volga River was little more than rubble when the Germans finally surrendered. Today, its significance is seen as the high-water mark of the German floodtide. From this point, the Germans beat a long, lugubrious but orderly retreat, harassed and pursued every step of the way by the Red Army and by thousands of partisans. And as always, the Russians had on their side their great commander whom not even Stalin could intimidate—General *Winter.* Churchill enjoyed taunting Hitler. As he told the British people:

> Then Hitler made his second grand blunder. He forgot about the Winter. There is a Winter, you know, in Russia. For a good many months the temperature is apt to fall very low. There is snow; there is frost and all that.
>
> Hitler forgot about this Russian Winter. He must have been very loosely educated. We all heard about it at school, but he forgot it. I have never made such a bad mistake as that.

This, barely three months after El Alamein, truly *was* the beginning of the end. The vaunted Nazi war machine was now seen by all to be vulnerable and headed for defeat. That did not mean, however, that the dying cobra had lost its deadly bite.

General Dwight D. Eisenhower—soon known as *Ike* to millions—followed up his North Africa success with an invasion of Sicily. Americans had gone along reluctantly with Churchill's vision for striking the "soft underbelly" of Hitler's Europe and knocking Italy out of the war. Italy did fall, but Hitler's legions soon occupied most of the Italian peninsula. There was nothing soft about Field Marshal Kesselring or his battle-hardened German troops. The fighting up Italy's rocky spine was brutal and bloody. Fortunately, Rome was declared an open city, so the Eternal City and its architectural treasures were spared. Not so Monte Cassino—which was demolished by Allied bombardment. The Allies stiff-armed protests from Pope Pius XII, believing the Germans had taken refuge in and around the historic monastery. The Allies regarded the lives of their troops as more sacred than even the greatest of monuments.* When the Fascist regime of Benito Mussolini collapsed, *Il Duce*—the leader—was taken prisoner. Hitler sent his commandos on a daring and successful mission to rescue him from his captors. Hitler proved loyal to his ally and mentor until the end.

Franklin Roosevelt lost no opportunity to remind Americans that freedom itself was at stake in the war they were fighting. On 13 April 1943, the bicentennial of Thomas Jefferson's birth, FDR spoke at the dedication of the Jefferson Memorial in Washington, D.C.:

> Today, in the midst of a great war for freedom, we dedicate a shrine to freedom . . . .
>
> [Jefferson] faced the fact that men who will not fight for liberty can lose it. We, too, have faced that fact. . . .
>
> He lived in a world in which freedom of conscience and freedom

---

* In 1969, American investigators conceded that the Germans had not, in fact, invested the monastery at Monte Cassino. Its loss, therefore, was a tragic instance of "friendly fire" in warfare. The Pope had been right. (Dear and Foot, *Oxford Companion to World War II*, 756.)

> of mind were battles still to be fought through—not principles already accepted of all men. We, too, have lived in such a world. . . .
>
> He loved peace and loved liberty—yet on more than one occasion he was forced to choose between them. We, too, have been compelled to make that choice. . . .
>
> The Declaration of Independence and the very purposes of the American Revolution itself, while seeking freedoms, called for the abandonment of privileges. . . .
>
> Thomas Jefferson believed, as we believe, in Man. He believed, as we believe, that men are capable of their own government, and that no king, no tyrant, no dictator can govern for them as well as they can govern for themselves.
>
> He believed, as we believe, in certain inalienable rights. He, as we, saw those principles and freedoms challenged. He fought for them, as we fight for them. . . .
>
> The words which we have chosen for this Memorial speak Jefferson's noblest and most urgent meaning; and we are proud indeed to understand it and share it:
>
> "I have sworn upon the altar of God, eternal hostility against every form of tyranny over the mind of man."

Roosevelt understood that Jefferson, "an Apostle of Freedom," had seen Man's inalienable rights as a gift of the Creator. This was the belief that FDR knew was threatened by the worldwide rise of Fascism and Japanese militarism.

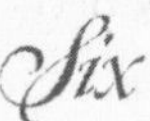

America Victorious
(1943–1945)

"Now we shall win the war!" So yelled a Soviet diplomat when he heard the list of American and British war materiel that would be delivered in 1941 to the beleaguered USSR.[1] The vast productivity of the democracies was central to the Allied victory in World War II. But production alone could not have prevailed. "They said the Americans would never come," a Japanese admiral stated ruefully after the war. "[They told us the Americans] would not fight in the jungle, that they were not the kind of people who could stand warfare," he recalled.[2] Hitler should have known better. After all, he was a corporal on the Western Front in World War I. He had seen what an impact the Americans had on the tide of battle. But he, too, thought Americans would not fight. Following the strategy of Germany first, the United States put fully 85 percent of its men and materiel into the fight against Hitler.[3] Napoleon had compared the material with the moral—and concluded that moral factors in war were ten times as important. General Marshall, ever the wise man, thought the U.S.-British Alliance was the key to victory.[4] Bismarck understood the importance of that relationship—something the kaiser and the führer never did. Josef Stalin would ever attribute his victory in The Great Patriotic War to the Marxist "correlation of forces." He had asked sarcastically, "How many divisions has the Pope?" Churchill surely knew how important it was to field well-equipped divisions, trained and willing to fight. Yet, knowing all this, Churchill still said it was Providence that brought the Allies to Victory.[5] Who are we to disagree?

I. Overlord

President Roosevelt employed every aspect of his powerful office to advance the American war effort. He was photographed personally decorating brave young warriors with the Congressional Medal of Honor. One of the more interesting of these was Lieutenant Commander Edward "Butch" O'Hare. This young naval aviator had led his squadron against Japanese bombers that were headed for his carrier, the USS *Lexington.* Butch shot down four enemy bombers in five minutes, risking his life and earning the nation's highest award for heroism. After a U.S. tour speaking at war-bond rallies, O'Hare returned to the South Pacific where he was to die during the famous "Marianas Turkey Shoot" in 1943, possibly a victim of friendly fire. After the war, Chicago's O'Hare Airport was named to honor this intrepid young Naval Academy graduate.[6]*

Soon, Butch O'Hare would be joined by other genuine heroes like army lieutenant Audie Murphy and Marine Gunnery Sergeant John Basilone. Their stories are worth retelling here. "On January 26, 1945, near Holtzwihr, France, Murphy's Company B was attacked by six [German] tanks and waves of infantry. Second Lieutenant Murphy ordered his men to withdraw to prepare positions in a woods, while he remained forward at his command post to direct the artillery. One of his company's tank destroyers received a direct hit and began to burn. Lieutenant Murphy climbed on the burning tank destroyer and trained its machine gun on the enemy, killing dozens and causing their infantry attack to waver. He held his position for more than an hour, received a leg wound, but continued the fight until his ammunition was exhausted. He then made his way to his company, refused medical attention, and organized the company in a counterattack which forced the enemy to

* Butch O'Hare's father, E. J. "Easy Eddie" O'Hare, was a business partner of the notorious gangster Al Capone. Easy Eddie turned against Capone, possibly because of the mobster's pulling off the St. Valentine's Day massacre in Chicago. Capone was sent to prison for income tax evasion, but as he was released, Easy Eddie was gunned down in 1939. Butch O'Hare had visited his dad in Chicago, but had lived his life in St. Louis. Nonetheless, *Chicago Tribune* publisher Colonel Robert McCormick wanted a local hero and "adopted" Butch. (Online source: http://www.stlmag.com/media/st-louis-magazine/july-2005/the-butch-ohare-story/.)

withdraw."[7]* Sergeant Basilone's record is similarly amazing: "Basilone was awarded the Medal of Honor during World War II for holding 3,000 Japanese soldiers at bay for 72 hours at Guadalcanal with only 15 men, 12 of whom died. Following this act of heroism, he was sent to the States to promote War Bonds. He later requested return to his unit to 'be with my boys.' Basilone was posthumously awarded the Navy Cross and Purple Heart for destroying a Japanese gun emplacement at Iwo Jima. He was killed there during a shelling attack."[8]

The government made sure that verified stories of sacrifice like those of the five Sullivan brothers were widely circulated. The Sullivans, all young sailors, were lost on the USS *Juneau.*** Also nationally known was the inspiring story of the Four Chaplains—Reverend George Fox, a Methodist minister; Rabbi Alexander Goode; the Reverend Clark Poling, a Dutch Reform minister; and Father John Washington, a Catholic priest. These brave clergymen gave up their life jackets to young soldiers and crewmen aboard the USS *Dorchester* as the overcrowded troop transport went down in the frigid waters off Greenland, the victim of a Nazi U-boat.[9]

Still, Europe writhed under the Nazi yoke of oppression. Opposition movements sprang up all over the continent. Resistance activity increased when German defeats at El Alamein and Stalingrad proved that Hitler's legions were not invincible. Underground fighters listened to clandestine broadcasts of the BBC from London. The opening notes of Beethoven's *Fifth Symphony* symbolized three dots and a dash (• • • –), the International Morse Code for the letter V. And "V" stood for Victory. One of the most dramatic incidents of resistance came on the eve of Yom Kippur, in late September 1943.[10] Informed that Hitler planned to deport all of Denmark's Jews to the Czech ghetto of *Theresienstadt*, a German diplomat named Georg Ferdinand Duckwitz passed the word to Danish authorities. They, in turn, organized a seaborne exodus to carry more than seven thousand

* Audie Murphy would go to Hollywood to star in his own story, *To Hell and Back*. The movie colony then turned out many a story of wartime heroism.

** This Waterloo, Iowa, family's loss was greater than that which prompted President Lincoln to write his famous letter to Mrs. Bixby during the Civil War. The tragedy also led the War Department to discontinue the practice of allowing brothers to serve in combat together, as the tight-knit brothers Sullivan had requested.

Danish Jews across the Skaggerak, the narrow body of water separating occupied Denmark from neutral Sweden. The oft-repeated story that Denmark's King Christian X wore a yellow Star of David is not true, but that does not detract from this heroic story of brotherhood.

FDR undertook another arduous journey in November 1943. He agreed to meet Churchill and Stalin in Tehran, the capital of Iran, for the first summit meeting of what was soon dubbed "The Big Three." Stalin feared to leave the USSR, always mistrustful, always seeing betrayal lurking everywhere. FDR turned down Churchill's invitation to stay at the British Embassy. He didn't want it to appear that the democracies were "ganging up" on Stalin. The U.S. Embassy was too far out of the city, so FDR accepted Stalin's invitation to use an entire house within the Soviet Embassy compound. Stalin told Roosevelt he had intelligence that the Germans would attempt to kidnap the American president. Later, FDR's roving ambassador, Averell Harriman, said he doubted the plot. Instead, he thought Stalin wanted the American president to stay in quarters that had already been bugged by his secret police, the NKVD.[11]

Roosevelt turned down a meeting request by Churchill and met first, instead, with Stalin. When the Big Three finally gathered, it became clear that Stalin shared Roosevelt's disdain for de Gaulle and the French because France had collapsed so quickly in 1940.* Stalin had an additional reason to dismiss de Gaulle. A vibrant, non-Communist France would impede his plans for a postwar European settlement. De Gaulle was an obstacle to the Soviets' plan of domination.[12] FDR seemed to go out of his way to tease Churchill in Stalin's presence. Harry Hopkins noted that Stalin was elegantly dressed in a field marshal's uniform, that he smoked his pipe and doodled—constantly drawing wolves—and that he spoke in a barely audible whisper.[13]

The main business was a commitment by the United States and Britain to open a "second front" in Western Europe. Stalin continually returned to the theme that the Red Army was doing all the fighting against the Nazis. In terms of numbers of troops engaged, this was largely true. He said he would

* Conveniently forgotten was the fact that French Communists, under orders from Stalin himself, had obstructed the French defense effort both in the army and in key industries. This was because Stalin in 1940 was still Hitler's ally.

be willing to break his neutrality toward Japan (the USSR was alone among the United Nations in *not* being at war with Japan), but he would only be able to come into the war in the Pacific *after* the Germans had been defeated. Roosevelt was satisfied with this. Even then, General MacArthur was brilliantly "island-hopping" in the Pacific, bringing the war closer to the Japanese home islands every day. When FDR and Churchill committed to "Overlord" early in 1944, the planned invasion of France, the mistrustful Stalin demanded to know the identity of the Allies' Supreme Commander: "What is his name?"[14]

Stalin would know soon enough. On his long way home from Tehran, FDR met with General Dwight D. Eisenhower in Tunis, North Africa. Almost casually, the president leaned over and said, "Well, Ike, you are going to command Overlord."[15] Not all of FDR's commanders relished the president's breezy informality. When he tried to call the dignified chief of staff of the army by his first name, the very able General George C. Marshall visibly recoiled. "[H]e called me 'George'—I don't think he ever did it again."[16]

Everyone revered General Marshall. Churchill called him "the noblest Roman of them all."[17] It was said of him that even if he entered his Washington office in civilian clothes, the young newsboys might not know *who* he was, but they would sure know *what* he was.[18]

Far from being put off by General Marshall's cool reserve, FDR trusted him and kept promoting him. Marshall far outranked Ike and could have had the command of Overlord simply by asking for it. Still, he told the president he would serve *wherever* the commander in chief needed him. FDR moved decisively to name Ike to command Overlord, telling Marshall, "I didn't feel I could sleep at ease if you were out of Washington."[19]*

Churchill feared the cross-Channel invasion would fail. "We might be giving the enemy the opportunity to concentrate . . . an overwhelming force against us and to inflict on us a military disaster greater than . . . Dunkirk. Such a disaster would result in the resuscitation of Hitler and the Nazi

* The man who said, "The only thing we have to fear is fear itself" did have one fear: a White House fire in the night. He regularly practiced rolling himself out of bed and propelling himself along the floor with his powerful arms.

regime."[20] He spoke darkly of "the tide running red" with the blood of young American, British, and Canadian soldiers.[21] He was remembering, too, the disaster at a French channel port in the summer of 1942. There, the Dieppe raid undertaken by a mostly Canadian force of 4,963 commandos had left 3,367 dead.[22] Stalin never had to concern himself about public opinion. He simply shot his opponents. But Churchill and Roosevelt depended on the support of free peoples.

Ike had to contend with troubles in England. General George Patton, who began the war as Ike's senior but who was now his difficult subordinate, had given a speech to a local English group in which he said the British and the Americans would together rule the world after the war. Moscow fumed and congressmen back home flamed. Newspapers demanded that Patton be fired. Ike let Patton stew for a week before telling him he could stay:

> When I gave him the verdict, tears streamed down his face and he tried to assure me of his gratitude. He gave me his promise that thereafter he would be a model of discretion and in a gesture of almost little-boy contriteness, he put his head on my shoulder as he said it.
>
> This caused his helmet to fall off—the gleaming helmet I sometimes thought he wore while in bed. As it rolled across the room I had the rather odd feeling that I was in the middle of a ridiculous situation. . . . I prayed that no one would come in and see the scene and that there were no news cameras at the window.[23]

"OK, let's go!" That was Dwight D. Eisenhower's order when his staff meteorologist gave him a brief break in the stormy weather that had forced a twenty-four-hour postponement of D-Day. General Eisenhower was the Supreme Commander of the Allied Expeditionary Force—abbreviated as SCAEF. Ike had even prepared a statement to be issued in the event the invaders were thrown back into the chilly waters of the English Channel. In it, he took complete responsibility for the failure of Overlord.[24] Fortunately, that statement was never issued.

Ike commanded a larger invasion force than the world had ever seen. Ike had assembled 150,000 men, 1,500 tanks, 5,300 ships, and 12,000 aircraft.[25]

General Dwight D. Eisenhower and G.I.s preparing for D-Day. *General Dwight D. Eisenhower's skill as a negotiator made him the clear choice for Supreme allied commander. Ike had prepared a letter accepting complete responsibility for the failure of the D-Day invasion—a letter he never had to send. When Pearl Harbor was attacked, Ike was a little-known Brigadier General. By the end of the war, he wore five stars.*

Normandy invasion, view from Landing Craft. *General Dwight D. Eisenhower commanded the largest invasion force in history. On D-Day, 6 June 1944, seven thousand ships and landing craft crossed the English Channel to land on the coast of German-occupied France. At sea, 195,701 naval personnel carried the 75,215 British and Canadian landing forces combined with 57,500 U.S. troops. They hit the Normandy beaches code named UTAH, OMAHA, GOLD, JUNO, and SWORD. British and Canadian forces suffered 4,300 casualties that day, the U.S. 6,000. France has retained these coded names to this day.*

Churchill, FDR, and Stalin at Yalta. *"The Big Three"—Prime Minister Winston S. Churchill, President Franklin Delano Roosevelt, and Soviet dictator Josef Stalin. They met at Yalta, in Soviet Crimea in January, 1945. Roosevelt, especially, has been criticized ever since for the failure of Stalin to keep his Yalta agreements. By this point in the war, however, the U.S. and Britain had few options to compel Stalin to keep his agreements.*

Atomic bomb blast. *The United States won the race to develop an atomic bomb. In 1939, world renowned nuclear physicist Albert Einstein warned President Roosevelt that Hitler's scientists might have the capacity to develop an atomic bomb. Roosevelt immediately initiated the Manhattan Project, the most costly secret weapons program in history. Japan and Germany did not learn of the U.S. effort, but Stalin surely did. From the beginning Communists and Communist sympathizers compromised the atomic bomb project.*

The Allies had gone to elaborate lengths to disguise their intended target—the beaches of Normandy. They created a false impression among the Germans that they would invade France at Calais—the closest point from Dover on the English side. Allied intelligence shuddered when, by pure coincidence, the word *Overlord* appeared in a crossword puzzle so beloved of the English newspaper readers.[26] More seriously, Ike withheld his invasion plans from General de Gaulle and the Free French until mere hours before launch.*

As Supreme Commander, Ike could give orders to millions—but not to Churchill or FDR. When the prime minister insisted on joining the invasion fleet on D-Day, Ike tried to dissuade him. Ike admired the cigar-chomping, sixty-nine-year-old leader's courage, but he didn't want him interfering. And he didn't want to bear the responsibility if Churchill were killed. Failing to dent Winston's resolve, Ike appealed to King George VI. Only when the king told Winston that he would join him on the beaches was the irrepressible Churchill finally repressed.

Ike proclaimed the expedition "a great crusade." He issued a General Order telling his men, "The eyes of the world are upon you." And so they were.

As army rangers scaled the cliffs at Pointe-du-Hoc on Omaha Beach, a toehold on the European continent had been seized.** On the night of 6 June 1944, after what many called "the longest day," President Roosevelt asked the nation to join him in prayer:

> Almighty God: Our sons, pride of our Nation, this day have set upon a mighty endeavor, a struggle to preserve our Republic, our religion, and our civilization, and to set free a suffering humanity.
>
> Lead them straight and true; give strength to their arms, stoutness to their hearts, steadfastness in their faith.
>
> They will need Thy blessings. Their road will be long and hard.

---

* It was their country, after all, that was being liberated, but the Free French had a bad reputation for leaks. This was not from any sympathy for the Axis but because a passionate people could not resist telling loved ones they would soon be home.

** President Reagan would immortalize "the boys of Pointe-du-Hoc" in his speech on the fortieth anniversary of D-Day in 1984. The Normandy landing beaches, code-named Omaha and Utah (American), Juno (Canadian), and Sword and Gold (British), retain those names to this day.

> For the enemy is strong. He may hurl back our forces. Success may not come with rushing speed, but we shall return again and again; and we know that by Thy grace, and by the righteousness of our cause, our sons will triumph.
>
> They will be sore tried, by night and by day, without rest—until the victory is won. The darkness will be rent by noise and flame. Men's souls will be shaken with the violences of war.
>
> For these men are lately drawn from the ways of peace. They fight not for the lust of conquest. They fight to end conquest. They fight to liberate. They fight to let justice arise, and tolerance and good will among all Thy people. They yearn but for the end of battle, for their return to the haven of home.
>
> Some will never return. Embrace these, Father, and receive them, Thy heroic servants, into Thy kingdom.
>
> And for us at home—fathers, mothers, children, wives, sisters, and brothers of brave men overseas—whose thoughts and prayers are ever with them—help us, Almighty God, to rededicate ourselves in renewed faith in Thee in this hour of great sacrifice.[27]

The cost of freedom was indeed great. Of the 75,215 British and Canadian troops who landed on D-Day, 4,300 became casualties. The losses suffered by Americans were even greater. The United States suffered 6,000 casualties among the 57,500 troops who stormed the beaches. President Roosevelt's prayer also went out for his own relatives. His cousin, Brigadier General Theodore Roosevelt, Jr. was on the beach. When told that he had landed at the wrong point on Utah Beach, the son of President Theodore Roosevelt gamely said, "No, we'll start the war from right here." General Roosevelt had come ashore with his son, the only father-and-son team to land that day. Exhausted by his exertions, Theodore Roosevelt, Jr. was dead of a heart attack three weeks later.

The seemingly impregnable Fortress Europa that had been strengthened substantially by Field Marshal Rommel could not be held. Rommel knew that the only way to defeat the Allied invasion was to beat it on the beaches. But he could not persuade Hitler that the invasion was actually coming in Normandy. Hitler persisted in believing that the main invasion force would come at Calais. General George S. Patton headed up Operation Fortitude for precisely that purpose—to deceive Hitler.[28] And it worked.

Soon, the Allied Expeditionary Force met stiff resistance in the hedgerow country of Normandy. These thousand-year-old obstructions were a thick undergrowth of tree roots and hedges that could hardly be bulldozed by attacking tanks. Sometimes six to eight feet high, they formed a perfect defensive works for the retreating Germans. The leading city in Normandy, Caen, was supposed to be taken on D-Day +3; it was not liberated until D-Day +31. Allied soldiers took thousands of Germans prisoner but also lost many to the Germans. When word of the murder of Canadian POWs by SS troops spread, it fired the Allies' anger.

Americans were gratified by the response of the Norman peasants. One story of the loss of an American "fly-boy" speaks across the decades. Ten days after D-Day, Lieutenant Conrad J. Netting III went into action against a German truck convoy. Lieutenant Netting and his wife were expecting their first child back in the States. He even put his unborn son's name on the nose of his plane, a P-51 Mustang. He dove down on the convoy in his "Con Jon IV," but the fighter failed to pull out of a steep dive. What happened next was related years later in a letter from a French villager: "My grandfather ran with some neighbors to the cemetery, just by the place of the crash to help the pilot, but unfortunately it was too late. . . . My grandfather [the village cabinetmaker] made the casket and took care of your father. . . . On his grave was a mountain of flowers."[29] In the village of Saint Michel, a plaque today commemorates the brave young American's sacrifice: "Lt. NETTING, CONRAD J., 8th U.S. Air Force No. 0694174. Mort pour la liberté le 10.6.1944." He died, as did all our brave, for *liberty.*

Under Eisenhower's overall command, British field marshal Montgomery struck out across occupied Holland for Germany in an attempt to shorten the war. Operation Market Garden showed the prowess of British and American elite paratroopers. The U.S. 82nd Airborne took the Nijmegen Bridge at Arnhem but suffered heavy losses. German "88s" (88 millimeter artillery pieces) devastated the Allied ranks that marched, exposed, on the high, narrow roads. These were the only paths through the flooded Dutch fields.[30] The Nijmegen Bridge proved to be "a bridge too far," as advisers had warned the brilliant but impetuous Montgomery. This bitter experience of American soldiers fighting and dying under a foreign commander continues to this day to underscore the demand that America's armed forces be led by Americans only.

Ike had more than his share of headaches from his subordinates. Field Marshal Montgomery rested on his laurels from the desert campaign. He knew that Ike couldn't fire him.[31] Eisenhower did not respect show horse generals. Montgomery had already installed one of Britain's famous painters in his headquarters for two weeks to paint his victory portrait. The finished painting was, Monty beamed, "the cat's whiskers . . . the great picture of the year."[32] Clearly, Field Marshal Montgomery was not Ike's kind of soldier. Eisenhower knew, too, that he was being sniped at by his old friend and fellow West Pointer, General George Patton. Even though Ike had gotten Patton out of numerous scrapes, Patton referred sarcastically to Ike's "D.D.E." initials (Dwight David) as "Divine Destiny."[33] In a letter to Mamie, his wife, Ike said Patton would "drive me to drink."[34] Despite this constant griping, Eisenhower demanded a "calm and cheerful" atmosphere in his Supreme Headquarters Allied Expeditionary Force—and he got it.[35]

On 20 July 1944, as German troops were retreating from Russia and fighting a losing battle in Normandy, a German officer attended a meeting at the *Wolfsschanze*—the Wolf's Lair.* It was Hitler's secret headquarters in East Prussia, near the Russian border. The officer was Colonel Claus von Stauffenberg. He was everything Hitler hated—a devout Catholic, an aristocrat, and a man of moral scruple. Stauffenberg had asked his bishop if it was permissible to kill a tyrant. Told that it was licit, Stauffenberg left a bomb in a briefcase under the table at the Wolf's Lair and left the führer's staff conference, supposedly to take a phone call. A huge explosion destroyed the building, killed several generals, and left Hitler wounded—but not dead. The widespread plot on Hitler's life soon fell apart.

* Stalin's constant doodling of *volky*—wolves—and Hitler's obvious fascination with the ravening animals was hardly the only similarity in the character of these homicidal dictators.

Stauffenberg quickly faced a firing squad. Hitler's revenge was terrible. He ordered Himmler's SS to arrest thousands of actual or suspected conspirators—including all family members. Thousands simply disappeared into *nacht und nebel* ("night and fog"). Show trials were staged to humiliate elderly generals and aristocrats. The victims were hanged from meat hooks, dying of slow strangulation. Hitler had their deaths filmed. Afterward, his health was shattered, and his arm shook uncontrollably, but his death grip on Germany continued.*

Once the Allies were ashore in Normandy, the overwhelming power of America's economic strength began to be felt by the Germans. One of their area commanders expressed his sense of futility to his superiors. It took courage to commit these words to paper in a Wehrmacht shadowed by Himmler's SS. He might have been arrested and shot for "defeatism":

> I cannot understand these Americans. Each night we know that we have cut them to pieces, inflicted heavy casualties, mowed down their transport. But in the morning, we are suddenly faced with fresh battalions, with complete replacements of men, machines, food, tools, and weapons. This happens day after day.[36]

II. "The Sun Goes Down on More Suffering . . ."

The railroad trains filled with Jews bound for the extermination camp at Auschwitz accelerated their pace as even the most fanatical Nazis must have seen the war was lost. Many Jews died of suffocation en route. The terrified survivors who emerged from the packed freight cars were marched through the gates of Auschwitz. Guards beat stragglers with truncheons or sicced dogs on them. Above the entrance gate was a sign that said ARBEIT MACHT

* Hitler's poisonous vengeance—the key to his character—knew no bounds. He forced Field Marshal Rommel to commit suicide even though Rommel was only remotely connected with the July 20th plot. And Hitler made sure the heroic Lutheran pastor Dietrich Bonhoeffer was hanged just days before the whole Nazi regime collapsed in 1945. Bonhoeffer had been a leader of the "Confessing Church" movement—Christians in Germany who refused to bend the knee to Hitler. Bonhoeffer's writings, including *The Cost of Discipleship* and *Life Together*, are classics of Christian Literature.

FREI ("work makes you free"). It was just another of the Nazi regime's lies. Millions entered those gates never to return.

The sad history of the world is replete with mass murder, sporadic persecutions, massacres, outbreaks of hatred, even genocide. Most of these, like the anti-Semitic pogroms of Tsarist Russia, were deadly outbursts of short duration. Hitler's Final Solution, however, was a systematic nightmare that applied the techniques of the factory assembly line to the project of mass murder. Hitler's willing accomplices calculated the value of the gold they could extract from the teeth of their victims. Vast gas chambers were supplied with deadly Zyklon B by seemingly legitimate German firms like I.G. Farben. Huge crematoria were constructed to dispose of the remains.

When word began to trickle out of Eastern Europe, it was sometimes brought by men who had risked their lives to document the Final Solution taking place shrouded by the fog of war. After FDR met one of these brave young men, a Polish soldier named Jan Kozielewski (Karski), the president thought the Pole's story should be heard by important American Jewish leaders. But when Karski gave his eyewitness account to Supreme Court Justice Felix Frankfurter, the jurist bluntly told the young man: "I am unable to believe you." Shocked, Frankfurter's good friend, the Polish ambassador replied: "Felix, you cannot tell this man to his face that he is lying." That was not it, Frankfurter said with a helpless gesture of his arms as if he was trying to wave the horrible news away: "Mr. Ambassador, I did not say this young man is lying. I said that I am unable to believe him. There is a difference."[37] We know that even prisoners in Auschwitz itself, people who could see the smokestacks belching flame and smoke, could not believe it.

What in human history had prepared anyone to believe it?

In a rare moment of sorrowful introspection, Churchill considered the world stage on which he played so colorful and important a part: "I do not suppose that at any moment in history had the agony of the world been so great or so widespread. Tonight the sun goes down on more suffering than ever before in the world."[38]

The Allied sweep into Germany bogged down in the summer of 1944. General Eisenhower was pressed by French general de Gaulle to divert his forces to aid in the liberation of Paris. Ike did *not* want the burden of three million extra mouths to feed.[39] But de Gaulle emphasized that if the Allies failed to free Paris, the Germans might destroy it or else the Communists among the Resistance forces might seize the city and establish a Soviet government in the heart of Western Europe. And, please, de Gaulle added, let *French* troops enter the city first. "You may be certain," Ike replied, "I wouldn't dream of taking Paris without French soldiers."[40]

Americans are used to thinking of de Gaulle as an obstructionist, a man unwilling to shoulder his fair share of the burden of the war. De Gaulle pointed out that Ike had never tried to dictate who would command *British* troops, so why were the Americans interfering in their Free French ally's command structure?[41] When Ike sought to press de Gaulle into compliance by withholding his supplies, the Free French leader pointed out that France's Marshal Foch had *never* done that to the Americans when he was the Supreme Allied Commander in World War I.[42]

In addition to de Gaulle's appeals, Ike had to consider his ally Churchill's views. The prime minister had written him: "If by the coming winter you have established yourself on the Continent with your thirty-six Allied divisions, and have the Cherbourg and Brittany peninsulas in your grasp, I will proclaim this operation to the world as one of the most successful of the war. And if, in addition to this you have . . . freed beautiful Paris . . . I will assert the victory to be the greatest of modern times. Liberate Paris by Christmas and none of us can ask for more."[43]

German general Dietrich von Choltitz had risked his life to surrender the city virtually intact. Hitler ordered his last commander of Paris to mine the Eiffel Tower, the Cathedral of Notre Dame, the Invalides, the Arc de Triomphe, and all the famous bridges and architectural treasures of the City of Light. Hitler called von Choltitz, demanding to know if his orders for blowing up the whole city had been carried out. "Is Paris burning?" Hitler barked.[44] The cagey General von Choltitz kept stalling, replying he was *preparing* to burn the city.

True to his word, Ike magnanimously approved General Omar Bradley's decision to let French general Leclerc enter Paris first. He would allow Free French soldiers the honor of retaking their capital after four long years of

German occupation.* Fulfilling his pledge to Eisenhower, de Gaulle specifically disapproved the attempt of Colonel Rol-Tanguy, the Communist leader in Paris, to claim equal credit for the surrender of the German garrison.[45] To an outburst of Gallic joy and affection, the Americans marched smartly down the Champs Elysée through liberated Paris—and right back into battle![46]

Not so happy was the fate of Warsaw. The Poles hoped to free themselves from German cruelty, just as the Parisians were doing. But Ike was nowhere near. Instead, it was the Red Army that was pressing the Germans from the East. When Warsaw rose up, however, Stalin ordered his troops to halt just outside the city. The Germans ruthlessly destroyed what was left of the beautiful medieval city, the jewel of Slavic culture and sophistication. Stalin deliberately held back while the Poles were annihilated by vengeful Germans. When Churchill and Roosevelt appealed to Stalin to allow Allied flyers to land and refuel within Soviet lines after air-dropping supplies to the desperate Polish Resistance, he bluntly refused.[47] It was the first crack in Allied wartime unity.

Britain came under renewed German attack in the summer of 1944. By this time, the vaunted Luftwaffe was almost destroyed. The few German planes that could get into the air were limited to a few minutes of flying by the shortage of fuel. Too late, Hitler introduced the world's first jet fighter aircraft. The *Messerschmidt* ME-262 could have turned the tide of war had it been employed one year earlier. Now Hitler unleashed his new Vengeance weapons, the V-1 and V-2 rockets. Launched from a site in Germany called Peenemunde, thousands of these deadly weapons landed on London, Southampton, Portsmouth, and Manchester. The vast majority of the 3,500 rockets that escaped being shot down landed on London, causing great devastation and killing 6,184 people.[48]**

---

* Ike's sensitivity to wounded French pride would be gratefully remembered when de Gaulle came to power as president of France in 1959 and Eisenhower was serving as president of the United States.

** The V-1 and V-2 were the work of the ingenious young German rocket scientist Wernher von Braun. Not only was von Braun *not* charged with war crimes for developing and deploying this indiscriminate terror weapon, he and his Peenemunde team were welcomed into the United States at the war's end. At the end of the war, von Braun led his team of rocket scientists West, hoping to surrender to the Americans. He succeeded. Von Braun would later lead America's race to the moon.

During this fateful summer of 1944, the Allies began to get reliable word on Auschwitz. Allied bombers that had flown resupply missions over Warsaw were bringing back photographs of the death camps at Auschwitz and Treblinka.

Churchill favored bombing the railroad junction that led to Auschwitz. He told his foreign minister, Anthony Eden, "This is probably the greatest and most horrible single crime ever committed in the whole history of the world."[49] Churchill called for action. "Invoke my name," he told Eden.

FDR spoke out publicly against the Holocaust and did not hide his contempt for Hitler:

> In one of the blackest crimes in all history . . . the wholesale, systematic murder of the Jews of Europe goes on unabated every hour. . . . None who participate in these acts of savagery shall go unpunished [a clear warning of postwar tribunals]. All who knowingly take part in the deportation of the Jews to their death in Poland or Norwegians and French to their death in Germany are equally guilty with the executioner himself. . . . Hitler is committing these crimes against humanity in the name of the German people.[50]

Roosevelt and Churchill were moved to outrage, but FDR had to consider Stalin's reaction. What would the grim Soviet dictator think about a joint Anglo-American action in Poland? Stalin was increasingly viewing Poland as a Soviet sphere of influence. Would Stalin be moved by humanitarian concerns? Not likely.[51]

And the American response was snarled in red tape. Samuel Rosenman, a Roosevelt speechwriter, worried that identifying the president too prominently with the plight of the Jews risked inflaming anti-Semitic outbursts in the United States.[52] FDR's advisers were stung by vile epithets—such as calling Roosevelt's New Deal the "*Jew* Deal."[53]

One of the chief obstacles to Allied action was Assistant Secretary of War John J. McCloy, who repeatedly shelved urgent appeals to intervene. "[E]ven if practicable," McCloy wrote, clearly indicating his belief that intervention was *not*, "[it] might provoke even more vindictive action by the Germans."[54] It is hard to imagine what could be worse than hundreds of railroad trains packed with innocent human beings hurtling toward their doom at Auschwitz. McCloy was in many ways an outstanding public servant; he served administrations of both parties in positions of increasing responsibility well into the 1970s. But he bears a heavy burden of responsibility for having repeatedly blocked an urgent attempt to disrupt the clickety-clack of mass murder.

Far more committed to traditional American humanitarian concerns than McCloy was the U.S. Consul in Marseilles, France. Hiram Bingham IV took grave risks when he issued visas to endangered Jews and anti-Nazis. For his pains, Bingham was demoted by State Department higher ups and transferred—this time to Argentina. Even from that remote location, however, he continued to give timely warnings on the extent of Nazi penetration in Latin America.*

FDR thought his demand for unconditional surrender was the surest way to end the mass murder of the Jews. After all, he may well have reasoned, Hitler did not want to murder only the Jews of Poland; he wanted to murder *all* the Jews. If he broke out into Palestine or counter-attacked in Russia or, worse, if he developed an atomic bomb to place on one of his V-2 rockets, the death toll could be even greater. To many, it seemed the quickest way to kill a venomous snake was to go for the head. Hitler was the head.

FDR's treasury secretary, Henry Morgenthau, had devised a plan for postwar Germany that would have reduced the country to an agricultural state. Hitler's propaganda chief, Joseph Goebbels, made much of the Morgenthau Plan. Goebbels said it proved Roosevelt was being manipulated by his Jewish cabinet secretary. The Morgenthau Plan was not all vindictiveness. After two horrible world wars caused by German aggressiveness, it might not have been a bad idea to create another Denmark inside a decentralized Germany—peaceful and pastoral—if it could have been done. But the densely populated Germany heartland could never have supported eighty million people as an

* Hiram "Harry" Bingham received a measure of vindication in 2006 when the U.S. Postal Service honored him with a stamp. Secretary of State Colin Powell gave him a posthumous award, and the U.S. Holocaust Memorial dedicated an exhibit to his heroic interventions on behalf of the Jewish people.

agricultural society. Henry Morgenthau was FDR's closest friend in the cabinet, and the Morgenthaus and Roosevelts had been neighbors and friends in the Hudson Valley for years. Still, FDR never endorsed the Morgenthau Plan.

In the summer of 1944, FDR was distracted. He would have to run for another term, an unprecedented *fourth* campaign for the White House. And he was seriously ill. Once, in his railroad car, he begged his son Jimmy to help him get out of bed to lie flat on the floor. He refused to summon a doctor and attributed the shooting pains he suffered to indigestion. We now know he was suffering from angina—a form of heart disease.[55]

FDR's maneuverings with relation to the vice presidency in 1944 did nothing to improve his reputation for straight talk (or rather the lack thereof). He seemed curiously passive and indirect. When he wrote a letter of "endorsement" for Vice President Henry Wallace, he said he would vote for the very liberal Iowan if he were a convention delegate. Then, in a move that damned Wallace with faint praise, he said, "Obviously, the Convention will do the deciding," adding that he did not want to seem to be *dictating* to the delegates.[56] So, while never technically disparaging the loyal Wallace, FDR's lukewarm backing actually helped those who wanted to throw the dreamy Wallace overboard.

The cabal that dumped Wallace was a group of mostly Irish-Catholic big-city political bosses. The "plotters" included Democratic National Chairman Bob Hannegan, New York's Ed Flynn, Mayor Ed Kelly of Chicago, party treasurer Edwin Pauley, and Postmaster General Frank Walker.* Also in on the scheme were the president's military aide, General "Pa" Watson, and White House press secretary Steve Early.[57]

The cabal did not know (but would not have been surprised to learn) that Wallace was a serious security risk. As vice president, Wallace had confided highly secret information to his brother-in-law, Dr. Charles Bruggmann.[58] Bruggmann was the Swiss envoy in Washington. Bruggmann and Switzerland may have been neutral, but the Swiss Foreign Ministry in Bern had been penetrated by the Nazis. Bruggmann sent regular, detailed messages home based on the information that Henry Wallace was giving

---

* At this time, the postmaster general was a major dispenser of political patronage.

him. His dispatches covered such supersensitive matters as the Churchill-Roosevelt summit aboard the USS *Augusta* in 1941 and the actual damage reports from Pearl Harbor.[59] Bruggmann's messages were intercepted and showed up in Berlin in mere days—and in Tokyo shortly after that. Henry Wallace was perhaps the best example of the World War II slogan: *Loose lips sink ships.*[60]

FDR would have been happy to run with South Carolina's senator, James F. Byrnes. But Byrnes was unacceptable to labor unions and black voters. As one who had turned his back on the Catholic Church of his youth, "Jimmy" Byrnes was objectionable to millions of Catholic voters upon whose unquestioned loyalty Democratic Party leaders had relied for more than a century. Still, Missouri senator Harry S Truman came to the Convention pledging not only to support Jimmy Byrnes but also to deliver his nomination speech.*

FDR thought highly of Truman. As a senator, Truman had been a loyal New Dealer and had run the select committee on war production with crisp efficiency. Finally, FDR wrote a letter saying *either* Harry Truman or the liberal Supreme Court Justice William O. Douglas would be acceptable to him. Then, almost as an afterthought, he told the plotters to "clear it with Sidney."[61]

Sidney Hillman was a textile union president and the organizer of the powerful new political action committee of the Congress of Industrial Organizations (CIO). Hillman turned his thumbs down on Jimmy Byrnes. Labor liked Vice President Wallace, Hillman told Harry Truman over breakfast: "[Labor has] a second choice, and I'm looking right at him."[62]

There was something else that gave their machinations a special urgency: FDR was clearly dying. Those who saw him face to face were shocked at how rapidly he had declined. Journalist David Brinkley would later write that in person FDR looked gray. There was no color in his sunken cheeks or his lips. In those days of black-and-white newsreels and *Time* magazine covers, FDR's deathly pallor was not so obvious.

When Bob Hannegan brought Harry to his suite in Chicago's Blackstone

* The "S" in Harry S Truman stands for just that, "S." Failing to decide which "S" grandfather to name him after, his parents just left it S.

Hotel, he called the president on the phone. FDR was in San Diego, inspecting the naval base there. The president's familiar rich tenor voice boomed out in the hotel room. "Bob, have you got that guy lined up on the Vice Presidency?"[63] Truman resisted running for vice president himself when he'd given his word to nominate Jimmy Byrnes. He knew Roosevelt was desperately ill, and he didn't *want* to be President of the United States.[64]

Hannegan's rough answer may have been intended to shake loose the reluctant Truman. "No," he growled into the receiver, as he looked directly at Harry. "He is the contrariest g—d— mule from Missouri I ever dealt with." FDR fairly shouted back, "Well, you tell the Senator if he wants to break up the Democratic Party in the middle of the war, that's *his* responsibility!"[65] With that, Roosevelt slammed down the phone. Harry's reaction, reportedly, was very human. "Oh s—!" he exclaimed.[66]

It was done. Truman's resistance wilted in the face of the president's displeasure and the pressure of the politicians Jimmy Byrnes, embittered, left Chicago for home. Kentucky's Alben Barkley, a Senate backer of the popular Byrnes, told a reporter he wanted to tear up the nominating speech he'd written for FDR's fourth bid for the White House and chuck the whole thing.[67] He soon thought better of it.

Nothing shows FDR's maddening quality of deviousness better than this important episode. And if Roosevelt could drive even his strongest political allies to distraction, imagine the reaction of his foes.

From the naval base at San Diego, FDR proceeded to Hawaii for an important war council with General Douglas MacArthur and Admiral Chester Nimitz. Nimitz wanted to drive straight for Japan. MacArthur disagreed. He proceeded to warn the president of the dangers of bypassing the Philippines: "I dare say the American people would be so aroused that they would register most complete resentment against you at the polls."[68] Once again, a leading general could not resist lecturing the commander in chief on his political responsibilities—just as McClellan had tried to instruct Lincoln. But the Philippines had been an American colony since 1898, so the case for liberating the islands from Japanese occupation—and the tens of thousands of U.S. and Filipino POWs in enemy hands—was a strong one.

Following the Pacific conference, FDR decided to visit a military hospital in Hawaii. He asked to be taken to the wards where the young amputees were. Ordinarily, Roosevelt took care *not* to be seen being wheeled about in his wheelchair. This time, however, he had himself pushed, slowly, deliberately past the bedsides of the wounded men. "He insisted on going past each individual bed. He wanted to display himself and his useless legs to those boys who would have to face the same bitterness," reported FDR's aide, Sam Rosenman.[69] Rosenman marveled that "this man who had risen from a bed of helplessness ultimately to become President of the United States and leader of the free world was living proof of what the human spirit could do."[70]

FDR was actually trailing in the polls going into the 1944 campaign.[71] The Republicans had nominated the energetic, youthful Thomas E. Dewey of New York. Dewey was given credit as a crusading district attorney for putting behind bars many members of "Murder, Inc.," an offshoot of the Mob. Dewey was intelligent and sharp-tongued. Republicans attacked what they called the "Roosevelt Recession." Americans were clearly tired after twelve years of Depression, reform, and now war.

Dewey was scoring points against Roosevelt with the public. A credible case can be made, for example, that the Democrats' historic antipathy to national banks deepened and prolonged the Great Depression. We know that FDR shared Andrew Jackson's fierce suspicion of banking. By various "reforms," the Democrats prevented the emergence of a stronger, more resilient banking system. Canada, by contrast, had vibrant national banks and did not experience a single bank failure during the Depression.[72] The national banking "holiday" FDR felt constrained to proclaim upon entering office was made necessary by the panicked reaction of a number of state governors to the failure of many local banks. This crisis of confidence led Nobel Laureate Milton Friedman to call the economic disaster of the 1930s "the Great Contraction."[73]

Economic conditions were clearly better in 1944. War production had led to high employment and improved wages, to be sure. But the tight controls and strict rationing grated on people's nerves. There was widespread resentment and suspicion that people were skirting the regulations on the black market.* Rumors spread through every town that the well-heeled or the well connected were eating T-bone steaks behind their drawn blackout curtains.

Roosevelt waited until late in the season to enter the campaign. He was at this point working shorter days, tiring easily. When he did weigh in, however, the old campaigner proved a masterful politician. "I am actually four years older—a fact that seems to annoy *some* people," he said with broad humor.[74] His listeners on a coast-to-coast radio hookup hadn't forgotten the famous *New Yorker* cartoon (mentioned previously in Chapter Four). It showed a party of wealthy theatergoers calling in through an open window to some of their well-heeled friends: "Come on—we're going to the Trans-Lux to hiss Roosevelt." Head on, he countered the Republican claim of a Roosevelt Recession. He said that just as you never mention *rope* in the house of a man who'd hanged himself: "If I were a Republican leader . . . the last word in the whole dictionary I think I'd use is that word 'depression.'"[75]

The Teamsters Union delegates whom he was addressing in Washington roared with delight. Then FDR knocked one out of the park. He had been saving up for the shrill attack of an obscure Republican congressman. The GOP critic claimed that Roosevelt had left his Scottish terrier in Alaska and had dispatched a U.S. Navy destroyer to retrieve him.

The president said he had grown used to Republican attacks on him, his wife, and his family. But Fala, the presidential dog, was less understanding: "When he learned that the Republican fiction writers had concocted a story that I had left him behind on the Aleutian Island and had sent a destroyer back to find him—at a cost of two or three or twenty million dollars—his Scotch soul was furious. He has not been the same dog since!"[76] The Teamsters, the radio audience, and in time the whole country erupted in laughter. Roosevelt had punctured the Republican campaign balloon. Though Dewey had never mentioned Fala, the Republican's tone dripped with contempt.[77] Roosevelt the heavyweight boxer had landed a knockout punch.

It didn't help, either, that a quote widely attributed to Alice Roosevelt

---

* A *black market* is the term given to any "underground" or illegal market in goods or services. Whenever rationing or government price-fixing occurs, a black market springs up almost automatically.

Longworth—that Dewey was "the little man on the wedding cake"—seemed to sum up the prim, neat, but stuffy New York lawyer.

Stuffy and prim he may have been, but Dewey was also a patriot. He had gotten word that the United States had broken Japan's military code long before Pearl Harbor. It could have been a devastating charge to lodge against Roosevelt—that he knew, or should have known, that the Japanese attack was coming.

Colonel Robert McCormick also had sources for military secrets. His newspaper, the *Chicago Tribune,* had gone so far as to publish the fact that U.S. intelligence had broken the Japanese codes.[78] Furious, FDR wanted to prosecute McCormick under the Espionage Act, but he was talked out of it by his military advisers. They noted that the Japanese were continuing to use the compromised code. Apparently, the enemy did not read the *Chicago Tribune.*

Army chief of staff General George C. Marshall cared little for politics, but he cared deeply that America's intelligence sources and methods not be compromised in the midst of a world war. General Marshall understood that if the Japanese codes became an issue in a highly charged election campaign, Tokyo would realize its code had been broken. General Marshall asked Admiral Ernest J. King, the Chief of Naval Operations, to join him in a letter to Thomas Dewey. They both pleaded with Dewey *not* to divulge the facts about *Magic*—the Top Secret decrypts of Japanese diplomatic and military communications.[79] If *Magic* had been compromised, so, too, would have been *Ultra*—the secret decrypts of German military codes. The entire war effort would have been jeopardized.

It may have been Thomas Dewey's finest hour. He continued campaigning night and day against FDR, but he never mentioned *Magic.* As if to make up for his passing up this *magic bullet,* Dewey stepped up his attacks on his fellow New Yorker. Dewey attacked the controversial and impractical Morgenthau Plan, saying it had stiffened German resistance. It was as helpful to the enemy as "ten fresh German divisions," Dewey charged.[80] Placing special emphasis on his own youth and vitality, Dewey drew attention to FDR's frail condition without saying so directly.

To dispel rumors of his fragile health, FDR took a four-hour campaign ride through the boroughs of New York City in an open car.[81]

Hundreds of thousands of Americans lined his route to cheer themselves hoarse. Blue-collar workers, in particular, yelled their heads off. FDR beamed and waved and rode through a freezing rain. He was drenched to the skin. It was a bold and dangerous gamble. If anything, however, the dying Roosevelt seemed to draw strength from the love of the people. It was to be for him his last hurrah.

Roosevelt could not bring together all the elements of his coalition, however. The irascible Joe Kennedy, threatening to endorse Dewey, met with FDR in the White House in late October. Bluntly, he told the president his advisers were disserving him. "They have surrounded you with Jews and Communists," Kennedy said angrily.[82] Later, he complained to Harry Truman about Roosevelt: "That cripple . . . killed my son Joe."[83] In fact, Joe Kennedy Jr. had volunteered for the dangerous mission of flying over the English Channel in a plane loaded with explosives. The death of Joe Jr. would mean that all of Joe Kennedy's ambitions would come to rest on his surviving twenty-seven-year-old second son, John Fitzgerald Kennedy.

On Election Day, Roosevelt triumphed a fourth time. He won 25,602,505 popular votes (53.3 percent) and 432 electoral votes to Dewey's 22,006,278 popular votes (45.8 percent) and 99 electoral votes. Roosevelt's military chiefs may have been grateful to Dewey for not revealing *Magic*, but the old contender was not appreciative: "I *still* think he's a son of a bitch," Roosevelt said of his last opponent.[84]

Freedom triumphed when the United States held national elections in the midst of World War II. No longer were people thinking that dictatorships were more efficient and clearly the wave of the future. Italy was out of the war, Germany and Japan were on the defensive, and the democracies were on the rise. The democracies *plus* the Soviet Union, that is. Few could deny that the Red Army was playing a major role in bringing down Hitler. And few could argue that Stalin was a democrat. "When are you going to stop killing people?" asked the audacious Lady Astor of the Soviet dictator at a Kremlin dinner. She was Britain's first woman member of Parliament, and it took courage to ask Stalin that question in his own den. His Communist comrades froze, but Stalin simply pulled on his pipe and mildly replied, "When it is no longer necessary."[85] "Democracy," as Churchill said, "is based on the idea that it is better to count heads than to bash them." It is not an idea Stalin the head basher ever understood.

Roosevelt was reelected and France was largely liberated by late 1944. The German rocket ranges at Peenemunde were overrun. It seemed that only "mopping up" was required to cross the River Rhine and end the war in Europe. When Allied troops advanced to Hitler's Siegfried Line, Germany lay open to invasion. Churchill visited the supposedly impregnable defensive position. He winked at the men—military and civilian journalists—who had accompanied him. Then he led them all in urinating on Hitler's famous line!

If Americans thought that the war in Europe was over, Hitler did not. He secretly planned a major counteroffensive against the Western Allies. In fact, he stripped his Eastern divisions, fatally weakening his defense against the onrushing Red Army.

Hitler's Ardennes campaign began 16 December 1944. Taking advantage of the heavy snow and low visibility, German Panzer tanks came crashing through the forests. Americans were taken by surprise. The Battle of the Bulge, as it quickly became known, was the Germans' last thrust in the West. The second day of the battle, eighty American POWs were murdered in cold blood outside the Belgian town of Malmédy. This Malmédy Massacre was the bloody work of the SS.

The Americans suffered greatly at the Bulge, and not merely from German Panzers. The merciless winter claimed casualties of its own. Night fell by 4:45 p.m. in these northerly latitudes. Even Americans from the Dakotas found the cold numbing. "Riding in a jeep through the Ardennes," recalled colonel Ralph Ingersoll, "I wore woolen underwear, a woolen uniform, armored force combat overalls, a sweater, an armored field jacket with elastic cuffs, a muffler, a heavily lined trenchcoat, two pairs of heavy woolen socks, and combat boots with galoshes over them—and I can never remember ever being warm."[86] Thousands came down with frostbite and "trench foot," a deadly disease that came from having the foot exposed to dampness for long periods. G.I.s typically hung their wet socks around their necks to provide a spare pair that would be warm and dry.[87]

The tough, battle-hardened U.S. 101st Airborne Division had landed on D-Day. Now, it was surrounded by advancing Germans in the little Belgian town of Bastogne. But when the German commander demanded surrender, the leader of the 101st, General Anthony McAuliffe, replied eloquently, "Nuts!"[88]

Ike ordered General Patton to disengage and head north to relieve Bastogne. By Christmas Eve, the cloud cover lifted. Eisenhower was able to bring to bear his overwhelming air power. That night, two thousand Allied aircraft attacked thirty-one German targets, destroying them.[89] Along with the critical shortage of fuel and the spirited American counteroffensive, the German drive was soon blunted. The Germans suffered more than a hundred thousand casualties in the Battle of the Bulge.[90]

America's victory in the Battle of the Bulge was a tribute to Eisenhower's cool courage, Patton's dash, and McAuliffe's defiance. Most of all, it was a tribute to the soldiers of democracy. The Americans' resourcefulness under the severest conditions of battle and weather was completely underestimated by Hitler and his generals.[91]

III. Democracy: "The Mustard on the Hot Dog"

When the Writers' War Board, one of the innumerable government agencies, was struggling to come up with a working definition of democracy, E. B. White set them straight in the pages of the *New Yorker:*

> Surely the Board knows what democracy is. It is the line that forms on the right. It is the don't in don't shove. It is the hole in the stuffed shirt through which the sawdust slowly trickles; it is the dent in the high hat. Democracy is the recurrent suspicion that more than half the people are right more than half of the time. It is the feeling of privacy in the voting booths, the feeling of communion in the libraries, the feeling of vitality everywhere. Democracy is a letter to the editor. Democracy is the score at the beginning of the ninth. It is an idea which hasn't been disproved yet, a song the words of which have not gone bad. It's the mustard on the hot dog and the cream in the rationed coffee.[92]

When Harry Hopkins showed him White's article, FDR burst out, "I *love* it! Them's my sentiments exactly."[93] President Roosevelt then planned a low key *fourth* Inaugural. There would be no military parade. "Who's here to parade," he asked, noting that millions of soldiers, sailors, and airmen were overseas. They were hotly pursuing the enemies of the Great Republic.[94] Even greeting the hundreds of guests at a scaled-back White House reception seemed too much for the exhausted chief executive. He asked his son Jimmy to bring him the bottle of bourbon he kept in his room in the residence, to fortify him against the wet January cold.[95] Sensing the need, he chose that historic moment to tell thirty-seven-year-old Jimmy that he had named him as executor of his will. There was a letter in his personal safe, he said, which contained instructions for his funeral. "I want you to have the family ring I wear. I hope you will wear it," he told his eldest son.[96]

FDR would need a sure sense of democracy as he approached his next Big Three summit meeting. Stalin could not have chosen a *worse* place for the leaders' conference "if we had spent ten years on research," Churchill complained when he learned of the destination: Yalta.[97]

Yalta was in the Crimea, a region of the Ukraine only recently liberated from German occupation. It was the seaside summer resort of the tsars. The meeting would be held in the Livadia Palace. For FDR, it would be torture. He would have to fly for long hours in his presidential plane from the Mediterranean island of Malta.* Then he would have to drive by car for eight hours. It was a grueling trip for the rapidly failing chief executive.

Meeting with Stalin on his home territory meant, once again, that the quarters assigned to the Allied leaders would be bugged. The maids, butlers, cooks, guards, and all others who came in contact with the Westerners would be employees of the NKVD. Stalin himself made no bones about that. In a jovial mood, he pointed out to Roosevelt one of the Soviet delegates. "That's my Himmler," he said.[98] He was speaking of Lavrentii Beria, the grim head of Stalin's secret police.

---

* The four-engine, propeller-driven plane had few of the amenities we have come to associate with today's *Air Force One*. Slow, cramped, and stuffy, the president's plane was called *The Sacred Cow*. The name was given by cynical members of the press corps. Some things never change.

FDR knew it would be difficult to deal with the Soviet dictator, especially now that the Red Army was poised for the final assault on Berlin. He had confided in Francis Cardinal Spellman, the Catholic archbishop of New York, that he expected the Soviets to dominate Eastern Europe after the war. He hoped to use diplomacy and generous U.S. aid to guarantee a mild rule.[99]

Roosevelt had to contend not only with Stalin but also with his legions of Soviet supporters in the United States. Walter Duranty, the Moscow correspondent of the *New York Times,* spoke for many of those supporters when he wrote that the "Russians are not less free than we are."[100] Americans were eager to finish the fight and bring the boys home. With twelve million in uniform, there was hardly an American family that did not have an empty place at the supper table. FDR had to consider this powerful sentiment as he sat down with Churchill and Stalin in the ornate palace of the tsars.

Churchill wanted France restored to power and influence. It was not that he found General de Gaulle easy to deal with. He said the "hardest cross I've had to bear is the Cross of Lorraine."* But Churchill wanted a strong France as a counter to rising Soviet power in Europe. Pressing hard, day after day, Stalin threw his hands up and said, "I surrender."[101] Stalin, ever the realist, let the British and the Americans give France a Zone of Occupation in Germany *provided it was carved out of the territory already allotted to the Western Allies.* His willingness to let the French sit on the European Advisory Council that would administer occupied Germany was not as generous as it seemed. He had already shown that he could influence the French through his control of the powerful French Communist Party.

If Churchill successfully held out for a restored France, FDR similarly pumped for China to be treated as a Great Power.[102] In the United Nations Organization the leaders were planning for the postwar settlement, both France and China would have permanent seats on the Security Council.

Poland was the great issue. Stalin promised "a strong, free, independent and democratic Poland."[103] The difficulty was how Stalin defined democracy. It surely was not the "mustard on the hot dog." As Stalin had said, it doesn't

---

* General de Gaulle had made the Cross of Lorraine the symbol of his Free French movement. This contrasted strongly with the atheism of the Communists who greatly influenced the French Resistance.

matter who casts the votes; what matters is who *counts* them. Wouldn't the pope be upset if atheist Communist rule were imposed on Catholic Poles? Stalin had a ready answer: "The Pope? How many divisions has he got?"[104]

Roosevelt hoped he could press the Soviets to respect the agreements they had signed on the treatment of "liberated Europe." But he believed he *had* to have Stalin's help in the coming invasion of the Japanese home islands. Stalin had held out throughout the war, claiming the urgency of defeating Hitler. Now, with the Nazis clearly on their last legs, Stalin finally agreed. The Soviets would join the war against Japan "two or three months" after the Germans surrendered. FDR and his military chiefs were jubilant. Admiral Ernest King enthused, "*We just saved two million American lives!*"[105]

Yalta was—and remains—a highly controversial summit. British field marshal Montgomery may have been the first to call it another "Munich," suggesting that Roosevelt and Churchill deliberately sold out Poland and Eastern Europe to Stalin for the sake of peace.[106] Many Roosevelt defenders try to excuse the Yalta agreements by saying FDR was deathly ill, that he really cannot be held responsible. But Averell Harriman, a Roosevelt confidant and a shrewd judge of Soviet intentions, said the president was "worn, wasted, but alert."[107]

Already in 1944, Churchill could see the problems that would be caused by millions of Stalin's troops sweeping through Eastern Europe. Churchill had gone to Moscow in 1944 and had offered Stalin an interim agreement as the Red Army overran Eastern Europe. It was not intended as a final statement on the postwar fate of those nations, but it did provide guidelines for spheres of influence. For Romania, he suggested 90 percent Soviet influence, 10 percent Western; in Greece, the shares would be reversed, 90 percent Western, 10 percent Soviet; Yugoslavia and Hungary were listed by the prime minister as 50–50. Churchill, perhaps thinking Roosevelt and Hull would reject such a division of influence, called his sheet a "naughty document." He told the Soviet dictator, "Might it be thought rather cynical if it seemed we had disposed of these issues, so fateful to millions of people, in such an offhand manner? Let us burn the paper." Stalin, who had calmly checked Churchill's figures with his blue pencil, replied with a saturnine expression, "No, you keep it."[108]

The reality was Stalin's hundreds of divisions. No one remotely contemplated war with Stalin to force him back inside the USSR's prewar boundaries. Thus, other than attempting to ply him with Lend-Lease and demonstrations of American and British goodwill, what else could the Allied leaders have done?

There is little doubt that FDR's attempt to forge a personal relationship with Stalin was—as conservative scholar Robert Nisbet has called it—"a failed courtship."[109] Franklin Roosevelt seemed to have little appreciation of the radical threat posed by aggressive, subversive Communism. There is good reason to think that Roosevelt himself recognized this courtship as failed. Two weeks before his death, FDR exclaimed in anguish, "[Stalin] has broken every one of the promises he made at Yalta!"[110]

Critics rightly point to the presence at Yalta of Alger Hiss, a Soviet agent. Hiss was a top State Department official, an FDR appointee, who would travel to Moscow after Yalta and secretly receive the Order of the Red Star.[111] And he was not the only one. Lawrence Duggan of the State Department and Harry Dexter White, Morgenthau's deputy of Treasury, were also Soviet agents.[112]

The shocking reality is that the government of the United States was dangerously penetrated by Soviet agents. To many at the time, however, this was no more sinister than the presence of many British sympathizers in high federal office.

The Soviet people were widely admired for their stubborn, brave resistance to the Nazi invaders. Stalin was seen as a stern, avuncular figure, a Russian authoritarian, but not as the ruthless, homicidal monster subsequent historical research has proved him to be. Americans had sympathy for the twenty million lives lost in the Soviet Union's "Great Patriotic War." They never saw the millions of returning Soviet POWs who were sent directly to the Gulag. If this seems insane to us, it must be remembered that these prisoners of the Nazis knew how unprepared Stalin had been for war and how much better everyone in Europe lived than the people of the Soviet Union. To Stalin, anyone who was captured was a traitor. He made no attempt to gain the release of any of the millions of Russian captives. He even let his own son, Yakov, die in a German POW camp rather than exchange him for the German field marshal von Paulus.

Returning from Yalta, President Roosevelt went immediately before Congress. There, he addressed a joint session to deliver a report on the summit. For the first time, he spoke while sitting down. It was also the first time he ever referred to his infirmity in public, referring to the "ten pounds of metal braces" on his legs. He made a point of telling the members that he had fully briefed the other participants on the U.S. Constitution and how it required Senate approval for all treaties. Wisely, he appealed to Congress for its help. He avoided the confrontational posture President Wilson had assumed after World War I.* He said there was not room in the world for "German militarism and Christian decency."[113] He spoke quite openly of the compromise on the Polish border question. The Soviet Union had been given hundreds of miles of formerly Polish territory in the East; Poland was "compensated" by being given vast German lands in East Prussia. (The Poles were not consulted on this swap.) Roosevelt showed himself committed to free elections in Eastern Europe and to a new international organization, the United Nations, to take the place of the League of Nations.[114] Few Americans would have complained if the Yalta agreements had actually been carried out.

Meanwhile, in the Pacific, General MacArthur had liberated the Philippines and was moving ever closer to Japan. Increasingly desperate, the Japanese military leaders unleashed *kamikaze* pilots. The word means "divine wind." In truth, it was a deadly wave of suicide pilots who crashed their planes into U.S. Navy ships. During the U.S. invasion of the island of Okinawa, in April 1945, kamikaze attackers destroyed thirty-six U.S. warships and inflicted damage on 368.[115] Thousands of U.S. sailors and marines were killed in these brutal attacks.

Although all the summit conferences focused primarily on the European Theater, as the war against Germany was called, the tens of thousands of casualties in the Pacific guaranteed American interest in the war against Japan. Young Lieutenant (Junior Grade) John F. Kennedy found his Patrol Torpedo boat (PT-109) cut in half one dark night by a Japanese

---

* Of course, Wilson faced a Republican-controlled Congress. FDR's fellow Democrats were in firm control of *both* Houses.

destroyer. Kennedy swam to a nearby island, pulling a wounded crewman with him and leading the others to safety. He was decorated for valor.

Another lieutenant (Junior Grade), George H. W. Bush, had dropped out of Yale to become the youngest naval aviator in history. When his plane was shot down near Chichi Jima, his two crewmen were lost. Bush frantically paddled his life raft away from the Japanese-held island. He desperately wanted to avoid capture by the savage Japanese who were known to behead downed American fliers and consume their flesh.[116] Soon, Bush was relieved to see the submarine USS *Skate* surfacing to rescue him. The suicidal resistance of the Japanese and the widely circulated stories of atrocities from our prisoners of war liberated in the Philippines made a deep, deep impression on millions of Americans.

IV. Harry Truman: "The Moon, the Stars, and All the Planets"

Still exhausted from his strenuous journey to Yalta and back, FDR went to Warm Springs, Georgia, for some rest in the balmy April breezes. There, Lucy Rutherfurd brought the painter Elisabeth Shoumatoff to do a portrait of the president. Rutherfurd had been Franklin's mistress nearly thirty years before.[117] As a condition of Eleanor's agreeing not to divorce him, FDR had promised never to see Lucy again. But here, lonely and sick, he had asked his daughter Anna to invite Lucy back. FDR needed companionship; he needed a warm, accepting friend. Eleanor, with her constant causes, projects, and endless petitioning for the less fortunate, wore Franklin out.

On the morning of 12 April 1945, while sitting for the portrait, President Roosevelt put his finger to his temple, saying, "I have a terrific headache." With that, he collapsed and died.[118] Eleanor immediately learned of Lucy's presence, but the country knew nothing of it. Eleanor coldly dismissed her daughter, whom she knew had helped her father arrange for Lucy's visit. In time, though, Anna and Eleanor were reconciled. And Eleanor later even exchanged forgiving letters with Lucy.

The country was shocked by the president's death. For millions, Franklin Delano Roosevelt had been the only president they had ever known. As he had wished, the funeral ceremonies were very simple. His casket was carried by horse-drawn caisson through Washington, D.C., and thence by train to Hyde Park, New York. America heard the news late on that Thursday afternoon. By Sunday, he had been buried. Four hundred thousand watched tearfully as the funeral caisson passed by. At the moment of interment, West Point cadets fired a rifle salute from the gravesite. Planes waited on runways, trains came to a halt, and all of America observed two minutes of silence.[119] Local newspapers carried a simple death notice just as they did for hometown boys: "Roosevelt, Franklin D., Commander-in-Chief, died at Warm Springs, Georgia." Even many Republicans who had called him "That Man" for years stilled their criticism. The famed editor of the *Emporia Gazette,* Kansan William Allen White, spoke for many of these when he wrote of FDR: "We who hate your gaudy guts salute you."[120] The country was united in grief.

The war could not wait. Aboard the USS *Tirante,* an American submarine cruising through mine-infested waters south of Japanese-occupied Korea, Lieutenant Commander George Street hunted down enemy cargo ships. Street had to take his sub into the harbor on the surface, since it was too shallow to dive. At four in the morning of 14 April 1945, Street hit a huge ammunition ship with his torpedoes. "A tremendous, beautiful explosion," Street reported, "a great mushroom of white blinding flame shot 2,000 feet into the air. . . . [At first, it was silent, but then] a tremendous roar flattened our ears against our heads." But the huge explosion exposed the *Tirante* "like a snowman in a coal pit." Instead of beating a hasty retreat, however, Street turned and coolly picked off two enemy warships, frigates of the *Mikura* class that were bearing down on his vulnerable little boat. Street and his crewmen had heard the news of President Roosevelt's death as they entered the enemy harbor. His message back to Pacific submarine command read tersely: "That's three for Franklin . . . sank ammunition ship and two escorts."[121]*

"Jesus Christ and General Jackson!" Those were Harry Truman's first words upon hearing of Roosevelt's death.[122] He had been having an after-session drink in the Capitol Hill office of the gruff, blunt Speaker of the

* Captain George Levick Street III (USN Ret.) received the Congressional Medal of Honor for this action.

House, Sam Rayburn of Texas. He hurried out of the Speaker's office, brushing past Texas Congressman Lyndon B. Johnson as he headed for the White House.[123] Here, he was quickly sworn in as the thirty-third President of the United States. Later, when President Truman met with the press for the first time, he said, "Boys, if you ever pray, pray for me now. . . . [W]hen they told me yesterday what had happened, I felt like *the Moon, the stars, and all the planets had fallen on me.*"[124]

Reaction in Britain was one of shock and dismay. Harold Nicolson, a veteran diplomat, confided to his diary: "I feel deeply for Winston, and this afternoon it was evident from his manner that it was a real body-blow. Under that bloody American Constitution they must now put up with the Vice President who was actually chosen because he was a colourless and harmless man. He may, as Coolidge did, turn out to be a person of character. But I have not heard any man say one good word in his favour."[125]

Churchill decided at the last minute not to fly to Washington. Instead, he offered this handsome tribute to Franklin D. Roosevelt in the House of Commons:

> He died in harness, and we may well say in battle harness, like his soldiers, sailors and airmen, who side by side with ours are carrying on their task to the end all over the world. What an enviable death was his. He had brought his country through the worst of its perils and the heaviest of its toils. Victory had cast its sure and steady beam upon him. . . . He was the greatest champion of freedom who has ever brought help and comfort from the New World to the Old.[126]

The leaders of democracies could understand Roosevelt. They could also understand the peaceful and orderly way in which power in a free country passed from the dying president to his constitutional successor.

Not so in Moscow. Stalin ordered all the red flags to be fringed in black, but he instructed his agents to make an appeal to FDR's son, Elliott. Stalin wanted his own doctors to examine the dead president's body. He was convinced that "Churchill and his gang" had poisoned FDR![127] As the man who had come to power by killing all his opponents, it seemed only logical.

Nor was there any mourning in Berlin. Deep under ground, in the perpetual night of the *Führerbunker,* Hitler received the news from a jubilant Goebbels: "Mein Führer, it was written in the stars! Roosevelt is dead!" Hitler, who believed in astrology, said it was the long-awaited turnabout in Germany's fortunes. Roosevelt's death was just like the death of the Russian empress that miraculously saved Hitler's hero, Frederick the Great, from defeat.[128] "Fate has removed the greatest war criminal of all time," Hitler said of FDR's death.[129]

Coming from him, it was high praise indeed.

Hitler's stars, it turns out, were anything but lucky. Two weeks after Roosevelt's death, the Red Army was closing in on Berlin. Ten thousand Soviet artillery pieces let loose an incredible barrage, reducing the historic capital to rubble.

As the ground shook above him, Hitler received news on 28 April that his mentor and friend, Benito Mussolini, had been captured. Italian partisans quickly tried *Il Duce* and shot him and his mistress along with several of his henchmen. Then they strung up their bodies heels first in a Milan gas station. Hitler was horrified and resolved never to be taken alive. He quickly married Eva Braun, his dim-witted mistress. Then, on 30 April 1945, he poisoned his favorite Alsatian dog, Blondi, and he and Eva committed suicide. Goebbels and his wife first killed their six little children by lethal injection and then joined Hitler in death.

The SS burned the bodies in the courtyard of the ruined Reich Chancellery. The grandiose Reich Chancellery, built by Hitler to overawe terrified visitors, was to have lasted a Thousand Years. It lasted barely twelve. The next day, 1 May, amid the stench of burning flesh, Red Army soldiers raised the Soviet hammer-and-sickle banner atop the remains of the Chancellery building. They were just in time to celebrate the international workers' holiday.

The hunt now began for fleeing Nazi leaders. Many were rounded up, but SS leader Heinrich Himmler was able to bite down on a cyanide capsule while in British captivity.

Determination to bring to trial all the leaders of the Third Reich stiffened as Nazi death camps were overrun and their thousands of surviving victims were liberated. Auschwitz, Treblinka, Ravensbruck, Dachau, Mauthausen—all became household words for savagery in April 1945. General Eisenhower forced enemy POWs to bury the piles of bodies that were stacked like cordwood at all the death camps in the American sector. He ordered German prisoners to watch newsreel documentation of the Holocaust.[130] He further ordered army photographers to record everything to guard against future efforts by some in the West to deny the Holocaust ever happened.* "I visited every nook and cranny of the camp," said Eisenhower, stunned by the barbarity of it all, "because I felt it my duty to be in a position from then on to testify at first hand about these things in case there ever grew up at home the belief . . . that 'the stories of Nazi brutality were just propaganda.'"[131]

President Truman pledged to carry out Franklin Roosevelt's policies. Unconditional surrender was the first among these. Within a week, German resistance collapsed. Gross Admiral Karl Dönitz, whom Hitler had designated as his successor, authorized the surrender of all German forces. On 7 May, Supreme Commander Eisenhower received the unconditional surrender of all German forces in the French city of Reims. *Received* was the carefully chosen word that described Ike's victory. So furious was the general at what he had seen in the concentration camps that he refused personally to attend the surrender ceremonies, designating a subordinate to meet the defeated Germans.[132]**

The next day, 8 May, was Harry Truman's sixty-first birthday. To the world, though, it was V-E Day—Victory in Europe Day. In London, with hundreds of thousands gathered in Trafalgar Square, Winston Churchill appeared with the King, the Queen, and Princess Elizabeth on the balcony of Buckingham Palace. Throughout the West, the peoples of the Allied and

* Despite mountains of evidence—some of those mountains in the form of eyeglasses, human hair, and children's shoes—some Holocaust deniers began their incredible work within days of the discovery of Hitler's death camps. They seem to be saying to their credulous hearers what Groucho Marx said, "Who are you going to believe—me or your own eyes?" The Iranian regime in Tehran continues to debate it to this day.

** Ike's son John recalled in 1976: "Dad hated the Nazis so much that he didn't want anything to do with them. He never forgot the horrors of the concentration camps." (Source: Neal, *Harry and Ike*, 49.)

Liberated countries celebrated the end of the greatest threat to freedom the world had ever known. In Moscow, a thousand-gun salute was fired off on 9 May to celebrate victory in "the Great Patriotic War."

The following month, Eisenhower would be given the keys to the city of London. His acceptance of the honor was the first major public speech of his life. Characteristically, in his Guildhall Speech of June 1945, he stressed his own roots in the American Midwest. In doing so, he spoke volumes about the kind of country that had sent him there. It was Ike's New World that had "stepped forth to the liberation and rescue of the Old," as Churchill always knew it would:

> Humility must always be the portion of any man who receives acclaim earned in blood of his followers and sacrifices of his friends.
>
> Conceivably a commander may have been professionally superior. He may have given everything of his heart and mind to meet the spiritual and physical needs of his comrades. He may have written a chapter that will glow forever in the pages of military history.
>
> Still, even such a man—if he existed—would sadly face the facts that his honors cannot hide in his memories the crosses marking the resting places of the dead. They cannot soothe the anguish of the widow or the orphan whose husband or father will not return.
>
> The only attitude in which a commander may with satisfaction receive the tributes of his friends is in the humble acknowledgment that no matter how unworthy he may be, his position is the symbol of great human forces that have labored arduously and successfully for a righteous cause. Unless he feels this symbolism and this rightness in what he has tried to do, then he is disregardful of courage, fortitude and devotion of the vast multitudes he has been honored to command. If all Allied men and women that have served with me in this war can only know that it is they whom this august body is really honoring today, then indeed I will be content.
>
> This feeling of humility cannot erase of course my great pride in being tendered the freedom of London. I am not a native of this land. I come from the very heart of America. In the superficial aspects by

which we ordinarily recognize family relationships, the town where I was born and the one where I was reared are far separated from this great city. Abilene, Kansas, and Denison, Texas, would together equal in size, possibly one five-hundredth of a part of great London.

By your standards those towns are young, without your aged traditions that carry the roots of London back into the uncertainties of unrecorded history. To those people I am proud to belong.[133]

Despite all the celebrations, however, all was not rosy with the wartime coalition. Passing through Washington en route to the opening of the San Francisco organizational meeting of the United Nations, Soviet foreign minister Vyacheslav Molotov—"the Hammer"—stopped by the White House to meet the new president. When Truman expressed concern that the Soviets were *not* keeping their agreements in Poland, Molotov interrupted. He said the Poles were acting *against* the Red Army. Truman cut him off, telling him to inform Marshal Stalin that the United States expected the Soviets to keep their agreements. Molotov, offended, replied he'd never been talked to that way. "Carry out your agreements and you won't get talked to like that," Truman said sharply.[134] Molotov normally was a man of pasty complexion. It was called the Kremlin pallor. Now, he looked ashen.[135] It wasn't a cold war—not yet—but there was a chill wind blowing through the corridors of power.

One of the first things Truman learned on becoming president was about the Manhattan Project. During his Senate days, Truman had repeatedly bumped up against the top secret project to develop an atomic bomb. He wasn't sure what it was, but he knew it was big. Now, twelve days after "the Moon, the stars, and all the planets had landed" on him, the new president received his first full-length briefing on the atomic bomb from Secretary of War Stimson. The sole possession by the United States of the atomic bomb was about to change everything. So, too, was the apparent willingness of the Soviets to tear up the agreements Stalin had solemnly inked at Yalta.

Truman agreed to go to Potsdam for another Big Three summit. With Roosevelt gone, it was important for the new president to establish his own relationship with Churchill and Stalin. Potsdam was a relatively undamaged, fashionable suburb of Berlin. It was behind the Soviet lines. Once again, Stalin would take pains to surround the Allied leaders with spies.

If Truman's clash with Molotov signaled a sudden chill in U.S.-Soviet relations, Truman was soon to break with FDR's most devoted personal friend and most loyal cabinet member. Henry Morgenthau, as secretary of the treasury, wanted to go to Potsdam to give new life to his Morgenthau Plan for the postwar treatment of Germany.[136]

Not only did Truman not want Morgenthau or his Morgenthau Plan in Potsdam, he didn't want him in Washington, either. With Roosevelt's death, the line of succession to the presidency went from Truman to Secretary of State James Byrnes *and then to Secretary of the Treasury Morgenthau.* Since Truman and Byrnes were both traveling to Europe on the same ship, the USS *Augusta,* an accident at sea could result in the United States having another jolting change of administration in just months. Truman saw grave danger if an unelected president, a leader committed to a most controversial plan to reduce Germany to a primitive state, came to power in this way.[137]* Truman was so insistent that he demanded Morgenthau's resignation *before* the presidential party boarded the ship for Europe.[138] Truman's crony, Fred Vinson, had his bags removed from the *Augusta* and found himself confirmed by the Senate and sworn in as the new secretary of the treasury in mere hours. It is hard to imagine a clumsier handling of a cabinet shift. Truman was certainly off to a rocky start. Henry Morgenthau surely was shabbily treated.

Despite his ham-handedness in dealing with the faithful Morgenthau, however, Truman was probably right in his judgment. The Morgenthau Plan for the permanent reduction of Germany could only have played into Soviet hands. If he had ever become president, Henry Morgenthau might have been fatally compromised when it was finally revealed that his trusted aide,

---

* Out of a profound concern that the United States not be governed by someone who had not been elected, Truman supported a change in the Presidential Succession Act. Hereafter, the Speaker of the House and the Senate President Pro Tem would come after president and vice president. Truman's reform was made less urgent, but not obsolete, by the ratification of the Twenty-fifth Amendment. It permits the president to fill a vacancy in the vice presidency by appointment, with confirmation by both Houses of Congress.

Harry Dexter White, was a Soviet agent. In the end, even Morgenthau had to admit there was "no question that White was working for the Russians."[139]

V. The Flag of Freedom

On the brink of victory, Americans could be confident that their arms and their materiel had tipped the balance of the war. All the Allied peoples had performed amazing feats of labor and devotion. Their soldiers, sailors, and airmen had performed incredible acts of heroism and sacrifice. For all that, America was the indispensable country. America made all the difference. Alistair Cooke was then a young correspondent in the United States, working for the British Broadcasting Company (BBC). In the foreword to Cooke's World War II memoir, we see in dramatic terms the American contribution to victory:

> The Allies would not have won the war in the West and the other war in the East without the way the American people, with amazing speed, created an arsenal no coalition of nations could come close to matching. Britain trebled its war output between 1940 and 1943, a ratio surpassing both Germany and Russia, who doubled theirs, though Japan excelled with a fourfold increase. And America? America stepped up its war output by a staggering twenty-five times. Instance, in 1942 a Liberty cargo ship of British design required 200 days to launch. Henry Kaiser, the dam builder from Spokane, had never before built a ship or airplane or handled steel, but he experimented with prefabrication and cut the time to 40 days. For his next trick he finished the *John Fitch* 24 hours after laying the keel. Without the fleets of Kaiser's ships carrying supplies, Britain would no doubt have starved.[140]

At Potsdam, attention centered on what to do about defeated Germany. Stalin was determined to loot the Soviet sector—soon to be known as East Germany. The Red Army had been allowed, even encouraged, to rape its way across Germany. Some two million German women—everyone from eight-year-old girls to eighty-year-old nuns—were raped in the final assault on

Germany. As many as 130,000 German women were raped in the capture of Berlin; 10,000 of these committed suicide.[141]

The Soviet secret police interrogated one German woman in East Prussia, Emma Korn, who related her experiences as the Red Army swept into East Prussia:

> Frontline troops . . . entered the town. They came into the cellar where we were hiding and pointed their weapons at me and the other two women and ordered us into the yard. In the yard, twelve soldiers in turn raped me. Other soldiers did the same to my two neighbors. The following night six drunken [Soviet] soldiers broke into our cellar and raped us in front of the children. On 5 February, three soldiers came, and on 6 February eight drunken soldiers also raped and beat us.[142]

Days later, Emma Korn and her companions could see no way out of their misery. They slit the children's wrists and then their own, but failed to kill themselves.[143]

Aleksandr Solzhenitsyn was then a thirty-four-year-old captain in the artillery in the Red Army. As his comrades looted jewels, gold and silver, and, of course, alcohol, he raced for an engineer's office to grab the famous Koh-I-Noor pencils he coveted, the only decent pencil this budding writer had ever held. He, too, committed a rape in East Prussia. His crime was committed with the nod of the head, not with a pistol, but it was rape nonetheless. Amazingly, Solzhenitsyn confessed his sins in the eight-thousand-line poem *Prussian Nights,* which he composed as he trudged off to captivity in the Gulag. Stalin's secret police had caught the young officer making reference in a letter to the Soviet dictator as "the plowman" for plowing under millions of young Russian boys.

When the victorious Big Three allied leaders finally met at Potsdam, President Truman assumed his duties as chairman with brisk efficiency. Prime Minister Churchill had arrived with his partner in the wartime coalition, Deputy Prime Minister Clement Atlee. Churchill's Conservative Party and Atlee's Labour Party had just met in an election contest. The votes had been cast, but it took weeks for the "soldier vote" to be counted from across the world. Few expected Churchill to lose.

Churchill had a sudden premonition. On 25 July 1945, he told of a dream he'd had. "I dreamed my life was over. I saw—it was very vivid—my dead body under a white sheet on a table in an empty room. I recognized my bare feet projecting from under the sheet. It was very life-like . . . Perhaps this is the end."[144]

It was not the end, not the end of Churchill's life nor of his remarkable political career. Still, it must have felt like that. The world was stunned by the Labour Party's landslide victory. Clementine, Churchill's loving and ambitious wife, tried to soothe him. "It may well be a blessing in disguise," she told him. "At the moment," Churchill said glumly, "it seems to be very *effectively* disguised."[145]

Churchill's replacement by Atlee left Stalin with two less experienced summit partners. But Truman had just received a coded message that let him know that the world's first atomic test had gone off perfectly at Alamogordo, New Mexico. One thing Truman knew he had to do at Potsdam if he was to have any hope of holding the wartime Alliance together: he must tell Stalin about the atomic bomb.

At the end of a session in which all sides had bickered, Truman casually approached Marshal Stalin. In a conversational tone, he told Stalin that the United States had developed a very powerful new weapon. Stalin did not react, at least visibly. "All he said was he was glad to hear it and hoped we would make 'good use' of it against the Japanese," Truman later remarked.[146]

Of course, Stalin already knew. Klaus Fuchs, a German-born refugee from Hitler's Germany, was a keenly intelligent nuclear scientist. He was a British subject who had been assigned to work on the Manhattan Project with the Americans. He was also a dedicated Communist and Soviet spy.[147] The Manhattan Project had probably been compromised from the beginning.

Another physicist, Ted Hall, was also spying for the USSR. Hall told one of his Soviet handlers of a conversation he'd had with another scientist at the Los Alamos nuclear lab in New Mexico. The scientist told Hall he was angered that the United States and Britain were not sharing atomic bomb-making know-how with their brave Soviet allies. The scientist said he'd be willing to do it himself if offered the occasion. Hall vociferously agreed with his colleague. Hall told him he had already begun collaborating with the Soviets. This indiscreet remark apparently scared the left-leaning scientist away, and he thereafter avoided Ted Hall. But he did not report him to the FBI.[148] The Soviets code-named their successful effort to penetrate the Manhattan Project *Enormoz*—enormous—and the consequences of their espionage were indeed enormous.[149]*

As the Potsdam conference concluded, the Allies issued another call for Japan to surrender unconditionally. The Soviets did not take part in this call, since they were not yet at war with Japan.

There was never any thought that the atomic bomb would *not* be used. It was not then seen as a weapon of a different order. Citizens had become accustomed to the terrible "thousand bomber raids" over Hamburg and Tokyo in which hundreds of thousands died. The fire-bombing of beautiful, ancient Dresden had raised a cry of alarm in some quarters. Churchill, viewing films of the attacks, bolted from his chair: "Are we *beasts?*" he cried out in anguish. But he did not order a cessation of the bombing.[150]

The indiscriminate German bombing of London and Coventry, Warsaw and Rotterdam, had hardened the hearts of the Allies toward the Germans. Similarly, stories of Japanese atrocities in Southeast Asia and the Philippines fired a vengeful mood among Americans.

The devastating American losses at Iwo Jima and Okinawa steeled American resolve to do whatever was necessary to force the Japanese to surrender. Associated Press photographer Joe Rosenthal captured an incredible scene of six American servicemen raising the Stars and Stripes above Iwo Jima.** While Americans thrilled at the raising of the flag over Mount Suribachi by five marines and a navy corpsman, the casualties lists sobered millions. The campaign took nearly three times as long as planned—thirty-six days. And it cost 5,931 marines killed and 17,372 wounded.[151]

The assault on Okinawa was even worse. Wave upon wave of kamikaze

---

* Ted Hall was discovered by the FBI in the early 1950s. Unlike Klaus Fuchs, he denied everything. Only with the publication of the *Venona* decrypts in the 1990s did the American people learn of his wartime espionage.

** Rosenthal's Pulitzer Prize–winning photograph has been converted into a massive statue across the river from Washington D.C., known now as the Marine Memorial.

planes—1,900 in all—cost 4,900 American sailors their lives. Wounded sailors numbered 4,824. U.S. Marine casualties were heavier—7,613 dead and 31,807 wounded. Further, 763 aircraft were lost.[152] The invasion of Okinawa occurred on 1 April 1945. It was not finally secured until 22 June, three of the bloodiest months of the entire war.[153]

When the Japanese military leaders stubbornly held out against the entire civilized world, Truman ordered the use of the atomic bomb. Given the events of that spring, it is hard to imagine any other president coming to any other decision. Truman feared that as many as 300,000 Americans or more could die in an invasion of the Japanese home islands. The mass suicide attacks at Okinawa, the continuing unwillingness of the Japanese military to consider surrender, and the death each month of as many as 100,000 Allied prisoners held by Japan convinced U.S. war planners of the need to drop the atomic bomb.[154]

On 6 August 1945, a USAAF bomber dropped a single atomic bomb on Hiroshima, Japan. Colonel Paul Tibbets piloted the B-29 and named it for his mother, *Enola Gay.* The powerful aircraft was able to record the event and escape the horror to return safely to base. Because the bomb was untried, there was a serious danger the atomic blast might consume aircraft and crew as well as its intended target. To guard against this happening, the bomb's descent was slowed by a parachute. The bomb resulted in 140,000 deaths. When the Japanese still had not surrendered, a second bomb was dropped on Nagasaki on 9 August 1945. An estimated 73,884 people were killed instantly. An additional 74,909 were horribly injured, alerting the world to the continuing nightmare of radiation poisoning.[155]

Keeping his word this time, Stalin declared war on Japan. Speaking on nationwide radio for the first time, the Japanese emperor Hirohito called upon his people to "endure the unendurable" and surrender. It was 15 August 1945. In all the Allied countries, the people burst forth in an outpouring of unrestrained joy known as V-J Day—Victory over Japan Day.

On 2 September 1945, the USS *Missouri* entered Tokyo Bay. There, the representatives of the Allies received the Japanese emissaries. Nothing was done to humiliate the Japanese signatories to the Instrument of Surrender.

General Douglas MacArthur made sure of that. "Let us pray that peace may be now restored to the world, and that God will preserve it always."[156]

It was not just peace that was secured in Tokyo Bay. Freedom was victorious. People all over the world had seen the democracies bounce back from the depths of defeatism and decadence in the late 1930s. Isolationism in the United States and appeasement in Britain and France were discredited. Democracy had won the war. The Great Republic of the United States had indeed become the "arsenal of democracy." American productivity overwhelmed Japanese and German industry.

To the war-weary peoples of the world, the lessons of the war should have settled forever the question of whether free people can also summon the will and the courage to defend themselves. It was the United States and Britain that held out. The United States and Britain defended the ideals of democracy to a watching world.

Even one of the most painful incidents of the war afforded an important lesson.

Winston Churchill was deeply hurt to be so unceremoniously kicked out of office by the British voters. In time, though, Churchill's famous wit would return. When King George VI offered to make him a Knight of the Garter, he replied impishly: "I can hardly accept the Order of the Garter from the King after the people have given me the Order of the Boot."[157]

The important thing is that the people were *free* to give their leaders the boot. This is what freedom is all about. It *is* the hole in the stuffed shirt. It *is* the dent in the high hat. And it is the sovereign right of the people to say who will rule over them. It was a message Americans broadcast to a watchful world. The star-spangled banner those marines and that corpsman raised above Mount Suribachi was not just a victorious battle ensign. It was the flag of freedom.

General Eisenhower inspects Nazi Death Camp, May, 1945. *As Eisenhower's troops uncovered more Nazi death camps like this one at Ohrdruf in Germany, the Supreme Commander of Allied Forces in Europe (SCAFE) personally inspected them. He wanted to be able to confront anyone who might later deny the Holocaust he had witnessed. Outraged by the Nazis' inhumanity, Ike refused to meet the defeated Germans at his headquarters at Rheims in France. His office said he merely "received" their unconditional surrender.*

Eleanor Roosevelt. *First Lady Eleanor Roosevelt made sure the President's liberal agenda was not overlooked during the war. She championed the role of women—both in the military and in war industries at home. She spoke up for the Tuskegee Airmen, black flyers who served in the still-segregated U.S. military. Mrs. Roosevelt's social conscience knew no rest. She traveled ceaselessly, often acting as her paralyzed husband's eyes and ears in remote regions.*

General Douglas MacArthur. "*I shall return,*" *pledged General MacArthur in 1942, when President Roosevelt ordered him to leave besieged Corregidor in the Philippines. Thousands of those troops who remained behind died in Japanese captivity. Here, the five-star General MacArthur presides over the Surrender of all Imperial Japanese military forces on board the USS* Missouri *in Tokyo Bay, 2 September 1945. MacArthur wisely directed the post-war occupation of Japan, creating stable and democratic institutions without destroying the best of Japanese traditions.*

Seven

Truman Defends the Free World (1945–1953)

In the troubled years following World War II, Americans would see vast changes in their country and in the world. Millions of veterans went to college on the G.I. Bill, backed by the Truman administration. Rejecting the disillusionment and isolationism that followed the First World War, Americans rallied to resist the worldwide aggression and subversion of a Communist conspiracy directed from Moscow. To prevent the USSR from extending its grasp into Western Europe, Truman rebuilt those war-torn countries through the Marshall Plan. Then he added a military component to economic help with the North Atlantic Treaty Organization (NATO), the vehicle that allowed America to lead Europe for mutual defense. At home, the response to Communism would first be too complacent. Communists, some thought, were just "liberals in a hurry." Truman stumbled badly in dismissing legitimate concerns about Communist subversion in government as merely a "red herring." Many labor unions were targeted for takeover by Communists—especially those in Hollywood. The cause of anti-Communism—which united millions of Americans and which gained the support of Democrats, Republicans, and Independents—was undermined by Senator Joe McCarthy of Wisconsin. Ronald Reagan would later say of him that he used a shotgun where a rifle was called for. Truman was not subject to the Twenty-second Amendment, which limited presidents to two terms, but its swift ratification was nonetheless seen as a rebuke to his leadership. In 1952, Americans avidly sought the reassurance offered by Republican Dwight D. Eisenhower. His landslide election brought another tested Midwesterner to national leadership.

I. A Cold War Begins

When peace finally came in September 1945, American's joy was mixed with exhaustion. The United States had been at war since 8 December 1941, her major allies even longer. Britain had been fighting for her survival since 3 September 1939. The nations of the British Empire and Commonwealth—Canada, Australia, New Zealand, India, and South Africa—had stood alongside England in the war against Hitler and the Japanese imperialists. The Soviet Union had struggled for its very existence since 22 June 1941 when Hitler unleashed a merciless *blitzkrieg* against his ally, Stalin. Stalin's blunder—trusting Hilter's word—would cost twenty million lives in the USSR. The *United Nations* was the formal title given to the wartime alliance against Hitlerism. Led by the United States, twenty-six nations pledged themselves on 1 January 1942 to fight against Hitler's Germany and not to sign a separate peace with the Nazis. Pressed by Roosevelt, forty-seven nations would eventually declare war against the man Winston Churchill liked to call the "nozzy beast."

America in World War II had become indeed what FDR named us—the arsenal of democracy. Just as General Montgomery Meigs had provided the Union armies of the Civil War with overwhelming advantages in supply, so did General Lucius D. Clay during World War II. Clay was the grandson of Confederate soldiers and a descendent of the Great Compromiser, Henry Clay. General Clay was responsible for the astonishing output of 88,000 tanks, two million trucks, and 178,000 artillery pieces.[1]

To put twelve million men and women in uniform and send millions of fighting men overseas required an unprecedented mobilization at home. The military draft conscripted healthy young men. Their places on the assembly lines were taken by millions of young women. America could accept such a massive disruption of normal life because the country was united after Pearl Harbor. Almost all Americans believed the survival of the United States and our freedoms were at stake. Rationing, wage and price controls, and war censorship of the press (and of soldiers' and sailors' letters home) were restrictions on American freedom that most accepted without grumbling.* Thousands of Americans found themselves "frozen" in critical war-related industries, unable to leave their jobs to hunt for better pay.

With the peace in 1945 came irresistible pressures. American boys in uniform who sang "Don't Sit Under the Apple Tree with Anyone Else but Me" strained to get back under that apple tree. Their mothers and fathers, their wives and girlfriends wanted them home. Just as a warship's crew cannot be held to "General Quarters" without relaxing, the American people demanded a stand down from the rigors of war mobilization. No democratic government could have ignored these pressures. Demobilization became the urgent task of the Truman administration.

In these years of an uneasy peace, however, Americans would come to accept a leadership role in the postwar world. The defense of freedom at home, most Americans believed, required a world-wide network of alliances. America's new prominence as the world leader for freedom focused a brilliant and sometimes unflattering spotlight on American institutions and practices. Racial segregation clashed with the ideal of Americans as defenders of human dignity. It was hard to celebrate the great victory over Hitler's vicious racism and then allow millions of Americans to be degraded by public water fountains labeled WHITE and COLORED. The widespread denial of the right to equal public accommodations and basic civil rights like voting and holding office seemed closer to Hitler's Nuremberg Code than to the ideals of the Founders and Abraham Lincoln. Repeatedly during this period, American presidents would point to the watching world in their appeals to Americans to live up to their highest ideals on civil rights.

Progress on civil rights, ironically, was both delayed and then, finally, accelerated by the pressures of a new, worldwide struggle with Communism. Americans in the wake of World War II were split in their views of their wartime ally, Josef Stalin. To many liberals, Stalin represented

* Examples of war censorship included not listing ships sunk by Nazi U-boats and soldiers killed in training accidents or friendly fire incidents. V-mail was the name given to photocopies of every letter sent to or from twelve million G.I.s.

the brave Soviet people. He was tough, they granted, and his methods were not our methods. But he had to be tough to survive in a world endangered by Fascists and their sympathizers in the West. Besides, they believed, Stalin's Communist system represented something hopeful for the world. Soviet propaganda regularly denounced racism and anti-Semitism. Few Americans had any real experience of the deeply ingrained racism and anti-Semitism that were a daily feature of Russian life.

American conservatives had never been comfortable with the wartime alliance of convenience with Soviet Russia. In the months immediately following V-E Day, Americans whose parents had come from Poland and Eastern Europe began to cry out against Stalin's iron grip on the "old countries." Throughout the Catholic Church in America, prayers were regularly offered for co-religionists whose freedom of worship was increasingly endangered in Eastern Europe.

President Truman struggled to maintain friendly relations with the Soviets, even as his rapid withdrawal of troops from Europe daily lessened his influence. Against conservatives' advice, he ordered U.S. troops to withdraw from advanced positions they had seized in the closing days of the war. Truman would honor FDR's wartime agreements and hope that the Soviets would honor theirs.

Stalin gave a speech in Moscow's Bolshoi Theater in February 1946 that signaled a return of the old ways. Almost matter-of-factly, Stalin rehearsed the themes he had often echoed in the prewar years: capitalism was inevitably imperialist, imperialism led to war, and the Soviet Union had to rearm to avoid being encircled and overwhelmed. There are indications as well that Truman's straightforwardness in telling Stalin about the atom bomb at Potsdam may have prompted Stalin to be more, not less, truculent. Stalin may have concluded that only a tough and unyielding stance would convince the West he could not be intimidated by the American monopoly on the bomb.

In March 1946 Truman invited former Prime Minister Winston Churchill to speak at a small liberal arts college in the president's home state of Missouri. Westminster College was proud to host the most famous man in the world—and happy to see Harry, too. Churchill and the president rode by special train from Washington to the college town of Fulton. They had plenty of time to discuss the speech during the day-and-a-half train ride.

Churchill called his address "The Sinews of Peace." As he had promised, Truman introduced the distinguished visitor. Churchill, then seventy-one, seemed to have lost none of his intellectual or physical vigor. He drew out his theme, appealing to what he called the "special relationship" between Britain and the United States in the defense of liberty.[2] He outlined the Magna Carta and England's other great documents of political liberty. With a bow to his hosts, he said these ideals "found their most famous expression in the American Declaration of Independence." Together, these English language documents constituted, he said, "the title deeds of freedom."[3]

There was much for Americans to ponder in Churchill's brilliant and profound speech, but few would ever read it in its entirety. That is because Churchill chose that moment to rivet the attention of the world by his use of a single arresting phrase:

> From Stettin in the Baltic to Trieste in the Adriatic, an iron curtain has descended across the Continent. Behind that line lie all the capitals of the ancient states of Central and Eastern Europe. Warsaw, Berlin, Prague, Vienna, Budapest, Belgrade, Bucharest and Sofia, all these famous cities . . . lie in what I must call the Soviet sphere, and all are subject . . . to an increasing measure of control from Moscow.[4]

The reaction to Churchill's "Iron Curtain" speech came like a thunder clap in a calm summer sky. Moscow was enraged, denouncing Churchill as a warmonger. Back home in Britain, the Labour government faced rebellion among its more left-wing "back bench" members.* In the United States, the speech was attacked by liberals and conservatives. How dare this foreigner propose a permanent alliance between Britain and the United States, critics howled. Liberals were incensed that that old imperialist Churchill was trying

---

* A "back bencher" is a member of Parliament who is not part of the cabinet but a member of the governing party. His support is usually necessary for the majority party to stay in office. Labour's back benchers were, and are, largely Marxist. The Conservative (Tory) back benchers were often strong supporters of the Empire, unwilling to make any concessions to the left wing. Churchill was a Tory back bencher during his "wilderness years" in the 1930s.

to stir up yet another world conflict. Former Vice President Henry Wallace, leader of the "progressives," was especially upset.[5] Few actually read what Churchill said. He called for no military or even diplomatic action to "roll back" the Iron Curtain. Instead, he urged the Western democracies to maintain their military and economic strength—and then to negotiate a better settlement with the Soviets.[6] Instead of war, Churchill wanted peace through strength. Soon, people began to speak of the "Free World," to distinguish democratic countries (and even some non-Communist autocratic states) from the vast regions behind the Iron Curtain.

Truman should not have been so surprised. He had just received "the Long Telegram" from George F. Kennan in the U.S. Embassy in Moscow. Kennan had detailed the deep roots of Soviet behavior and recommended a policy of "containment" to keep them from bringing all of Europe under their sway.[7]

Not all Americans disapproved of Churchill's electrifying speech, to be sure. Republican representative Claire Booth Luce of New York had publicly criticized Truman's failure to free the countries of Eastern Europe from Soviet domination.[8] Mrs. Luce was not only a powerful figure in her own right—one of the few women in Congress—but she was also the wife of Henry R. Luce, the publisher of *Time, Life,* and *Fortune* magazines.

Republican senator Arthur Vandenberg of Michigan had been a leading isolationist before Pearl Harbor. FDR sought Vandenberg in the postwar settlement. He had named the Midwesterner to the U.S. delegation to the founding conference of the UN in San Francisco.[9]* Now, Vandenberg urged Americans to "abandon the miserable fiction, often encouraged by our fellow travelers,** that we somehow jeopardize peace if our candor is as firm as Russia's always is."[10]

The Grand Alliance of World War II still had work to do in 1946. Even as Churchill warned of an Iron Curtain, Soviet military judges sat alongside American, British, and French jurists in the German city of Nuremberg. The city had been the scene of Hitler's monster Nazi Party rallies in the 1930s. It

* In recruiting the staunch Republican Vandenberg, FDR and later Truman showed they had learned the bitter lesson of Woodrow Wilson's attempt to exclude his political opponents from the postwar settlement.

** The term *fellow traveler* was coined by Communists themselves to describe leftist politicians and journalists in the West who tended to see world events as the Soviets did.

was also infamous because of the Nuremberg Code, which had deprived Germany's Jews of their citizenship and had prescribed the death penalty for a Jew having sexual relations with an Aryan. Truman wanted the International Military Tribunal to try the leading Nazis. He wanted a full airing of the evidence against the German leaders so that no one could ever say, "Oh, it never happened—just a lot of propaganda—a pack of lies."[11]

During the war, Stalin had brusquely said that the whole thing could be handled more easily simply by taking fifty thousand top German Nazi leaders and military officers out and shooting them. FDR responded, in a weak joke, that maybe "Uncle Joe" was too harsh and that only forty-nine should be shot. Churchill was outraged: "The British Parliament and public will never tolerate mass executions." Stalin persisted. "The Soviets must be under no delusion on this point," Churchill said, becoming more vehement. He dramatically stalked out of the Teheran conference room, saying, "I would rather be taken out into the garden here and now and be shot myself than to sully my own and my country's honor by such infamy."[12]

Truman selected Justice Robert H. Jackson, FDR's former attorney general and then a member of the U.S. Supreme Court, to lead the U.S. prosecution team at Nuremberg. The International Military Tribunal (IMT) was not without critics in the United States Senator Robert A. Taft, leader of the isolationist bloc, said the proceedings smacked of a "spirit of vengeance" and said, "The hanging of the eleven men will be a blot on America which we shall long regret."[13]* Chief Justice Harlan Fiske Stone privately even complained about "Jackson's high-grade lynching party."[14]

The Nuremberg Trials were no lynching. Overwhelming evidence was presented on the guilt of the accused Nazis. Hitler, Himmler, and Goebbels had avoided trial by committing suicide. But Hermann Goering, Rudolph Hess, Foreign Minister Joachim von Ribbentrop, Generals Keitel and Jodl, Admirals Raeder and Dönitz, and Albert Speer were among twenty-four key defendants who were confronted by irrefutable evidence of their crimes. Each of the defendants was afforded legal counsel. Each was permitted to

---

* Senator Taft's opposition to trying the Nazi leaders earned him praise in Senator John F. Kennedy's best-selling book, *Profiles in Courage*, even though Kennedy made clear he did not share the Ohioan's views.

summon witnesses to refute the charges against them. In the end, the Nuremberg Trials established an important precedent: that "following orders" was no defense against charges of mass murder, genocide, and gross violations of human rights.

At home, November 1946 meant a political shakeup. "Had enough?" was the Republican slogan in the off-year elections. Americans were impatient that the most rapid demobilization in world history was not more rapid still. As wartime price controls eased, inflation shot up. Even ground beef became too expensive for the average American dinner table. With the spike in consumer prices came wage demands from labor. Nineteen forty-six saw the most strikes in American history.[15]

President Truman's very high approval ratings during the euphoric days of victory over Germany and Japan took a tumble. His broad Missouri twang and flat delivery were compared unfavorably with FDR's elegant phrasing and patrician Hudson River accent. Normally tolerant folks who philosophically said "to err is human" now became irritable and repeated the current slam: "to err is Truman." Republicans rode this tide of voter dissatisfaction into a strong victory in both Houses of Congress. In California, Republicans elected young Richard Nixon to the House. Bucking the GOP trend, though, was Massachusetts Democrat John F. Kennedy, a decorated war hero. The unelected Truman was widely dismissed as a single-termer. Now, he would face an 80th Congress dominated by his political opponents.

His opponents underestimated the resourceful Missourian, however. Truman was a fierce political fighter, but no blind partisan. He invited former President Herbert Hoover to the White House; the much vilified Republican hurried to an Oval Office meeting. When Harry asked him to undertake a survey of world food resources, Hoover bolted and ran from the office without saying a word. Shocked by the Californian's rudeness, Truman turned angrily to his agriculture secretary for an explanation: "Don't you realize, Mr. President, the man *couldn't* answer? There were tears in his eyes." Composing himself, Hoover quickly phoned Harry to accept the assignment. He apologized for his sudden flight, saying, "Mr. President, since 1932 no one has asked me to do anything for my country. You are the *first* one."[16] It was simple human gestures like this that won Harry the tribute from Dean Acheson: "The Captain with a Mighty Heart."[17]

Truman was decisive. The presidency is supremely the institution where decisions are made. Truman even had a sign placed on his desk: "The Buck Stops Here."[18] FDR made decisions, too, but he was famously, even maddeningly indirect. Many of FDR's most important decisions were non-decisions; that is, he deliberately strung out the process of decision making so that his desired end was achieved by the exhaustion of all other alternatives. FDR's style of leadership struck the orderly, methodical Acheson as "chaotic."[19] Few could deny, however, that it kept Roosevelt at the center of every circle.

Truman never saw a problem he didn't tackle, or a hornets' nest he didn't whack. For example, when General de Gaulle was too slow in removing French troops from the American Occupation Zone of Germany, Truman bluntly told him to get out or risk an immediate cutoff of U.S. aid. The prickly de Gaulle got out.[20] To many Americans, FDR seemed to have been born in the White House; he *wore* the presidency as naturally as he wore his stylish navy boat cloak. Truman, it was said, was like having your next-door neighbor as president.

Truman used his longtime Senate friendships to good advantage. With the Republicans riding high, Truman reached out to the powerful Michigan senator Arthur Vandenberg.

Desperate to help Greece and Turkey resist Communist pressures, Truman knew he needed help from "the other side of the aisle." Vandenberg soon abandoned his isolationism, persuaded that the United States had no choice but to meet the growing Communist threat. Vandenberg reportedly advised Harry to "scare hell out of the country."[21] Having thus prepared the way, Truman's address to the Congress in 1947 was unprecedented for a nation at peace. President Truman wanted to help the Greek government resist subversion by Communist guerillas. The Turkish situation was somewhat different: there, that nominally Muslim country was faced with Soviet pressure to gain access to the Mediterranean through the Dardanelles. Stalin demanded bases on Turkish soil. Truman's appeal took on added weight because the Labour government in Britain had announced it would pull troops out of the Mediterranean as a cost-saving measure. Truman and his advisers feared the Soviets would fill the vacuum the British would leave. The Truman Doctrine pledged the United States to give financial aid to those countries struggling to resist subversion by antidemocratic forces.

Truman's "get tough with Russia" policy split the Roosevelt coalition. The "Progressives"—a group that included Communists, a much larger number of fellow travelers, and millions of sincere peace advocates—blamed the Cold War on Truman. But we now know that Stalin had his own view of East-West relations. While he was not the reckless warmonger that Hitler was, Stalin by no means wanted peace with the West. His foreign minister, Vyacheslav Molotov—"the Hammer"—was a man Churchill described as having the "smile of a Siberian winter." Molotov candidly described his boss's attitude: "Stalin looked at it this way: World War I wrested one country from capitalist slavery [the USSR]. World War II has created a socialist system [the Soviet satellites in Eastern Europe]; and the third will finish off imperialism forever."[22] So long as Stalin—or anyone else in the Soviet Union—saw security as a "zero-sum game" in which the USSR could only be secure by threatening or destroying potential adversaries, the Cold War was unavoidable.[23]

Truman showed remarkable humility in adopting the policy of his secretary of state, George C. Marshall. Truman had admired the five-star general for years. Even as a senator, Truman had called Marshall the "greatest living American."[24]* When Marshall delivered the commencement address at Harvard in 1947, he called for U.S. aid to stricken Europe. Only if America helped rebuild their shattered economies, Marshall said, could democracy be restored. Truman embraced the policy wholeheartedly. To prevent Republican opposition to him from blocking the necessary good work, he immediately dubbed the program "The Marshall Plan." Secretary Marshall had extended the offer of aid not only to the nations of Western Europe, but he also generously held out a helping hand

* That selfless comment *almost* prevented Harry's nomination as vice president. FDR was not pleased. (Source: Ferrell, *Truman: A Life*, 253.)

to the Soviet Union and Eastern Europe, too. Stalin rejected the extended hand—and forced his satellites to refuse it as well. Nonetheless, the Marshall Plan was, and remains, one of the greatest achievements of the Truman administration. If it was not "the most unsordid act in history"—Churchill had reserved that title for Lend-Lease—it was surely the *second* most unsordid act in history.

While Truman tried, with some success, to frame a bipartisan foreign policy, he continued to appeal to liberals for support of his domestic initiatives. The G.I. Bill of Rights enabled millions to go to college, buy homes, and start farms and businesses. It was an unprecedented government effort to assist returning veterans. Truman even worked with the conservative Senator Robert Taft—"Mr. Republican"—on public housing bills designed to relieve the postwar shortage.

Republicans soon responded to labor troubles, however, by passing the Taft-Hartley Bill, one of the most important pieces of labor legislation in American history. Taft was very concerned about Communist penetration of labor unions.[25] So were labor leader Walter Reuther and Minneapolis Mayor Hubert H. Humphrey. They were unwilling, however, to endorse Taft's harsh medicine. Truman had little choice but to veto the Taft-Hartley Bill.

Congress—with many Democrats joining the majority Republicans—soon overrode Truman's veto. The Taft-Hartley Act of 1947 banned the closed shop, a requirement that only union members could be hired. It mandated an eighty-day "cooling off" period if a threatened strike would affect health or safety nationwide. The law made it illegal to donate union dues to political candidates. It also required union officers to affirm under oath that they were not Communists.[26] When Taft-Hartley became law, it placed a permanent check on the growth of unions in America.[27]

With the powerful United States acting against Communist expansion in Europe and even blocking Communist influence in the American labor union movement, Stalin decided in early 1948 to apply pressure where he could. He backed a Communist *coup* in Czechoslovakia in February. Two weeks later, on 10 March 1948, Foreign Minister Jan Masaryk's body was found on the pavement outside his Prague apartment. Was the anti-Communist Masaryk—son of Czechoslovakia's first president, Tomas

Masaryk—a suicide or had he been thrown from his apartment window? History's third Defenestration of Prague sent a shiver down the spines of all friends of freedom everywhere.*

II. Red Stars in Hollywood

The collapse of the wartime alliance with the Soviets depressed and disappointed millions of Americans who had high hopes for postwar cooperation for peace. No group of Americans was more dismayed by the turn of events than the Hollywood film community. During the war, no one had been more enthusiastic to win a victory than Hollywood producers, directors, and stars. It's not surprising why. Adolf Hitler's rise in Germany had horrified liberals everywhere. His violent anti-Semitism was clear to thoughtful people. When the Communist Party's chief Hollywood recruiter, Otto Katz, came calling, doors opened for him. "Columbus discovered America," Katz would say, "but I discovered Hollywood."[28] With "Uncle Joe" Stalin as a wartime ally of America and Britain, recruitment for the Communist Party USA (CPUSA) in Tinsel Town was not difficult. Many Hollywood people were especially drawn to the Communist Party's open condemnation of anti-Semitism and racial bias. Thus, there was great anxiety when French Communist party boss Jacques Duclos publicly declared there was a *Cold War* between the United States and USSR.[29] Duclos was an obedient servant of the Kremlin. This new clash would test the loyalties of thousands of Americans.

Olivia de Havilland was known to millions of moviegoers worldwide as the beloved "Melanie" in the huge 1939 movie hit, *Gone With the Wind.* (Even Hitler had watched the movie—and liked it.) Miss de Havilland tossed away the pro-Soviet part of a speech she was scheduled to give in Seattle in June 1946. It had been written for her by Communist screenwriter Dalton Trumbo.[30] Instead, she delivered new lines written for her

* Defenestration—throwing someone to his death out of a window—had a long history in Czechoslovakia. In 1419, radical followers of Jan Hus had thrown imperial counselors out of a Prague window. Again in 1618, a second Defenestration of Prague led to the Thirty Years War in Europe.

by James Roosevelt, an anti-Communist liberal and son of the late president. De Havilland's tough speech was denounced by Hollywood's left wing. When a young actor, Ronald Reagan, spoke up in defense of Olivia de Havilland's right to express her own ideas, Reagan was denounced as "fascist scum."[31] Soon, Reagan, de Havilland, and other stars left the Communist-dominated Hollywood Independent Citizens Committee of the Arts, Sciences, and Professions, known as HICCASP.*

"Kill him! Kill him!" That was the cry of strikers on 27 September 1946 outside the MGM film studios in Culver City, California. They had just knocked down Deputy Dean Stafford with a bottle after he'd become separated from other police sent in to keep the strikers from using violence.[32] The strikers were being egged on by the head of the Conference of Studio Unions (CSU), Herb Sorrell. Sorrell was a Communist Party member who had founded the large union. The CSU was a collection of support staff—cartoonists, office workers, and skilled filmworkers. These jobs were vital to the industry, but they combined low pay, long hours, and no glamour. Sorrell flew above the fray—literally. He shouted orders to his union members on the picket lines as he flew over the MGM studios in his private plane.[33] Although Sorrell had clearly incited the violence, the Communist newspaper *People's Daily World* ran lurid headlines such as "Blood Flows as Cops Club Picketing Vets."[34]

The cops *did* use their clubs, but Sorrell had made sure there would be violence for the cameras. The Communists skillfully wrapped themselves and their cause in the honor of returning World War II veterans.

Sorrell didn't apologize for the violence he had spurred on. As the CSU strike dragged on and got worse, Sorrell confronted members of the Screen Actors Guild (SAG), demanding that the highly paid movie stars support the members of his union who were just scraping by. Sorrell told Ronald Reagan, then president of the Screen Actors Guild, that "when it ends up, there'll be only one man running labor in Hollywood, and that man will be me."[35] He refused to accept any responsibility for the violence he had sparked.

---

* In an age of acronyms, HICCASP may have been the most unwieldy. Ronald Reagan, after quitting it, joked that it sounded like "the cough of a dying man." (Source: Radosh and Radosh, *Red Star Over Hollywood,* 114.)

"We can no more control our members than [SAG] can keep your members from committing rape."[36*]

In December 1946 the Republicans had just swept control of both Houses of Congress for the first time since 1928, and all of organized labor feared the worst. Labor convened an emergency meeting in Chicago. At this session of the American Federation of Labor, many actors came together to appeal to the AFL to reject Sorrell and his CSU violence.

The SAG group included some of Hollywood's biggest names—Eddie Arnold, Gene Kelly, Robert Montgomery, George Murphy, Walter Pidgeon, Dick Powell, Robert Taylor, and, of course, SAG President Ronald Reagan and his wife, Jane Wyman.[37] Sorrell was unimpressed. At a contentious meeting in the Knickerbocker Hotel, the Communist union boss yelled at Gene Kelly, once a good friend of his.[38] Then Ronald Reagan stood up to Sorrell. "Herb, as far as I'm concerned, you have shown here tonight that you intend to welsh on your statement of two nights ago . . . *you do not want peace in the motion picture industry!*"[39] The labor union members and the actors who heard him cheered lustily. It was a dramatic clash, and it marked Reagan for leadership.

The fight over Communism in Hollywood didn't end then. It went on for many years and continues to roil the film industry to this day. Communists and ex-Communists battled over the Hollywood "blacklist"—a list of those writers who could not find work because of their ties to Moscow. It was, in fact, Communists themselves who first introduced the practice of blacklisting. Edward Dmytryk was a talented movie director and Communist. He was walking across the studio lot at RKO pictures in 1945 when he mentioned to a producer friend, Adrian Scott, an interesting new book, *Darkness at Noon.*[40] Scott, also a Communist, shushed Dmytryk, telling him party members were not allowed to read anything written by Arthur Koestler. Koestler was a disillusioned Communist, and his works lampooned the Soviet dictator. The Hungarian-born Koestler used Stalin's real name—Dzhugashvili—to satirize the heavily laden jargon of Communist writing:

---

* Reagan's famous costar, Errol Flynn, faced rape charges three times in his long career. Sorrell knew all the "dirt" there was to know about the Hollywood backlots. And he knew how to use it.

Dzhugashvilese.[41] (As it happened, it took Hollywood a full ten years to make a film of Koestler's powerful book—1955. By that time, Stalin was dead and many of the "blacklisted" Hollywood Communists were writing again.)

III. Ha Tikva—The Hope of Israel

With tensions rising in Eastern Europe, suddenly Americans and Jews throughout the world looked to the Middle East for a stunning development. On 14 May 1948 a new state was born and an ancient people restored to their land: Israel. The Jewish state had been authorized by the United Nations and created by Zionists—a movement of mainly European and American Jews who sought nationhood for the millions of Children of Israel who had been exiled for two thousand years in the *Diaspora.**

When David Ben-Gurion, the new prime minister, announced the birth of Israel, he presented their Declaration of Independence. As with the American document, the Israeli charter offered to a candid world the reasons for the new nation's being: "Here [the Jews'] spiritual, religious and political identity was shaped. Here they first attained to statehood, created cultural values of national and universal significance, and gave to the world the eternal Book of Books."[42]

Truman had to overcome the strenuous objections of the man he admired most in the world—Secretary of State Marshall.[43] During a face-to-face meeting in the Oval Office, Marshall warned the president that recognizing Israel would endanger U.S. objectives in the Middle East. Resisting Communist infiltration in that critical region would be harder if we antagonized fifty million Arabs, the State Department feared. Truman's secretary of state told him he would vote against him for president if he recognized the State of Israel.[44] This must have pained Truman deeply. Still, Harry was a shrewd Kansas City politician, too. He knew that millions of Jewish voters in America's cities would be especially relieved and grateful. Truman was in a tough contest with the Progressive Henry Wallace for the support of this traditionally liberal, very Democratic group of voters.[45]

---

* *Diaspora* (die-AHS-poor-ah), from the Greek, means a scattering.

Truman also listened to the earnest pleas of Eddie Jacobson, his partner in his first, failed haberdashery store in Kansas City. Jacobson brought Chaim Weizmann—who would become Israel's first president—to see his old friend. This time, Truman overrode General Marshall's objections.

Psalm 137 was one of Truman's favorites. "By the rivers of Babylon, there we sat down, yea, we wept, when we remembered Zion."[46] Truman as a U.S. senator had given strong support to the World War I–era Balfour Declaration of the British Government.[47] That 1917 document had promised the Jews a "national homeland in Palestine." Now in 1948 Truman felt it was time that that promise was honored.* He extended the United States' official recognition eleven minutes after Ben-Gurion's announcement. America was the first nation in the world to recognize Israel as a *defacto* state.

Truman had been influenced by a higher authority—the Bible.[48] Very simply, Truman came to believe that after the Holocaust, the Jews "deserved a home."[49] It was a view he shared with most Americans of the time. U.S. Supreme Court justice Felix Frankfurter was a man normally not given to emotional outbursts. He wrote to Chaim Weizmann: "Mine eyes have seen the glory of the coming of the Lord; happily, you can now say that . . ."[50] Truman's announcement came not a minute too soon. As soon as Israel declared her independence, she was invaded by five Arab neighbors. She was soon fighting for her very life.

IV. The Berlin Airlift of 1948

The postwar settlement in Germany had created two rival systems. Western Germany, occupied by U.S., British, and French troops, comprised more than two-thirds of Germany's territory and population. This zone was free and was quickly rebuilding a vibrant economy. Eastern Germany was a grim, totalitarian police state wholly under Stalin's heavy thumb. The Soviets had looted their occupation zone. There was little recovery in the

* Waffling on the issue of a Jewish homeland by Britain's postwar Labour Party government had led the Jews in Palestine to joke ruefully that theirs was not only "The Promised Land" but the "Twice-Promised Land."

vast, gray, dreary realm. Hitler's capital of Berlin was also divided. East Berlin was Soviet. West Berlin was free. But West Berlin was precariously located 110 miles *inside* Communist East Germany.

On 24 June 1948, Stalin applied the screws to West Berlin. He initiated a blockade by cutting off all rail and road traffic to the surrounded Free City of Berlin. Stalin was not known to be the poker player that Truman was. But he nonetheless found a way to force Truman to "put up or shut up." Here was Stalin's clever challenge to Truman's famous decisiveness. Would Harry force his way into the city, using tanks or bulldozers to knock down Soviet barriers? This would guarantee World War III, less than three years after the most terrible war in human history. Or would he surrender two and a half million West Berliners to Communist aggression and thus show the world America's powerlessness to defend freedom abroad?

General Clay was Truman's military governor in Germany. He reported that he had food stocks for only thirty-six days; coal reserves would last only forty-five days.[51] Clay said Stalin's move "was one of the most ruthless efforts in modern times to use mass starvation for political coercion."[52]

Truman decided. He would not have war *or* surrender. He refused to accept either of Stalin's forced choices. Instead, he brought the incredible power of America to bear on this most dangerous of postwar crises. Truman immediately ordered that West Berlin would be supplied *by air.* Harry would go the extra mile to keep freedom alive in its most exposed outpost.

Thus began the Berlin Airlift. Over the next nine months, the United States and Britain conducted 277,804 flights into Tempelhof Airport carrying a total of 2,325,809 *tons* of supplies into the besieged city, more than a ton for every man, woman, and child.[53] So successful was the airlift that rations for each Berliner actually *rose.*[54] Nearly one hundred U.S. and British servicemen lost their lives keeping Berliners free. Just three years earlier, American and British bombers had been pounding Berlin to rubble. Now, U.S. C-47 cargo planes were dropping candy by parachute to little German children, who scrambled to retrieve it. As a result of the Berlin airlift and the heroic struggle of the West Berliners, the free sectors of that great city were transformed in Western eyes from a citadel of Nazism to a courageous outpost of freedom.

V. "Give 'em Hell, Harry!"

As the election year of 1948 arrived, President Harry Truman should have been a strong candidate for reelection. Millions of G.I.s had returned home to find jobs, buy homes, or start college with the assistance of the G.I. Bill. They married and—this is often a sign of public optimism—fathered a huge "baby boom." The long-feared postwar depression did not occur. The American economy dominated the world. The United States, with only 6 percent of the world's people, produced more than one half of the world's goods and services.[55] Truman's Fair Deal programs, it is true, were largely frustrated by the Republican 80th Congress. Medicare, for example, was first proposed by Truman but was rejected. Despite this, millions of veterans were benefiting from the G.I. Bill, and they gave Truman and the Democrats credit for it. The generous allowances it provided often made it possible for a young married man to support a family while he went to college. Others bought homes and started farms and businesses with the help of veterans' benefits. Henry R. Luce, publisher of *Time,* labeled this "the American century."

Looking abroad, Germany had been defeated and occupied; the Western Zone was peaceful and rapidly developing as a free and democratic state. Japan, similarly, under the enlightened administration of General Douglas A. MacArthur, was quiet. MacArthur authorized war crimes tribunals that carefully excluded the Emperor Hirohito. The general introduced women's suffrage, economic and educational reforms, and even promulgated a new democratic constitution that outlawed militarism.[56] America had developed the atomic bomb but had not threatened to use it after Japan surrendered. Western Europe was enthusiastically accepting American leadership through the Marshall Plan.

Truman should have been a sure bet for reelection. In fact, few besides Harry himself thought he would win. Former Vice President Henry Wallace had left Truman's cabinet and would run for president as a Progressive Party candidate. Although Wallace could not win, he could cost Truman critical support in states like New York, Illinois, and California. Democrats feared defeat with Truman. The popular song "I'm Just Wild about Harry" had not been written to honor the Missouri Plain-Speaker. Many politicos now said, tongue-in-cheek, "I'm just mild about Harry."

If Henry Wallace spelled trouble among progressives, civil rights meant trouble in the South. For eighty years, the Democrats had relied on "the solid South" for their electoral victories. Now, however, millions of returning veterans found the antiquated strictures of racial segregation were not what they had fought for.

In 1948, both parties saw civil rights as a pressing matter. Truman had named a Civil Rights Commission the previous year whose report, *We Hold These Truths,* demanded far-reaching change.[57]

Many doubted the sincerity of Harry's commitment to civil rights. He was the proud grandson of Confederate veterans. He represented Missouri, where segregation was the law. His own mother, it was known, hated the Great Emancipator so much that she was quoted as saying she'd rather sleep on the floor than sleep in the Lincoln Bed in the White House. And there was Harry's appalling habit of referring to black people as n——s in private conversation.

Harry Truman as president soon dispelled any notion that he would not stand up for black Americans' civil rights. At a White House luncheon, a Democratic committeewoman from Alabama pleaded with him not to "ram miscegenation" down the throats of Southerners. Harry pulled a copy of the Constitution out of his pocket and read her the Civil War amendments. "I'm *everybody's* President," he said with steely determination. "I take back nothing of what I propose and I make no excuse for it."[58] A black White House waiter was so moved he accidentally knocked the president's coffee cup out of his hand.[59] Mississippi's Democratic senator James Eastland was stunned. Why, he sputtered, if Harry is right, then "Calhoun and Jefferson Davis were wrong."[60] Exactly.

The Republicans meeting in Philadelphia called for action on civil rights. They demanded the abolition of the poll tax, long used to deny black Americans access to the ballot in Southern states.[61] Governor Thomas E. Dewey of New York was again the Republicans' choice for president. Dewey was a sincere advocate of civil rights. He had done well among black voters in the Empire State.

Minneapolis's young mayor, Hubert H. Humphrey, was also a strong supporter of civil rights. He was the nominee of Minnesota's Democratic-Farmer Labor Party for the U.S. Senate in 1948. Humphrey and his fellow liberals were pressured to support *anybody but Truman* for president. Naturally, Humphrey wanted the strongest candidate possible at the head of the ticket to help him win his Senate race. Few people thought Harry Truman was the strongest candidate.

James Roosevelt, son of the late FDR, was sure Truman could not beat Dewey. He was leading a campaign to draft General Dwight D. Eisenhower as the *Democratic* Party nominee. Early in his term, Truman himself had offered to run for vice president if only Eisenhower would run for president as a Democrat.[62]

But now, Truman's fighting spirit was up. He took a train to Berkeley, California, where he confronted the younger Roosevelt: "Your father [FDR] asked me to take this job. I didn't want it. . . . But your father asked me to take it and I took it." Jabbing his finger into the younger Roosevelt's chest, Harry said, "But get this straight: whether you like it or not, *I am going to be the next President of the United States.*"[63]

It seemed to many of the professional politicians who gathered in Philadelphia for the 1948 Democratic National Convention that the Wallace campaign would cost Truman liberal support in the North. They reasoned that if Truman had any chance at all, that chance would be destroyed by any further defections from the Roosevelt coalition. That meant they had to avoid trouble on civil rights.

Hubert Humphrey didn't see it that way. He thought the Republican civil rights plank was "relatively forward looking."[64] He and his allies conducted a "floor fight" at the Democratic National Convention to adopt a strong platform plank on civil rights. Only with such a strong commitment, Humphrey reasoned, could Democrats compete with Wallace in the electoral-vote rich states in the North, the Midwest, and most importantly, California. When Humphrey arose to speak, he appealed to the Democrats to move out of the "shadow of states' rights and into the bright sunshine of human rights."[65] The adoption of the Humphrey plank offended South Carolina's Democratic Governor J. Strom Thurmond. Thurmond walked out of the convention, taking with him dozens of other Southern delegates. Thurmond pledged to run for president as the candidate of the States' Rights Democratic Party. Instantly, the press dubbed Thurmond's faction the "Dixiecrats." Thurmond vowed to maintain racial segregation.*

All public opinion polls showed Dewey easily beating Truman. The *Chicago Tribune* published a mocking tribute to the embattled Harry: "Look at little Truman now / Muddy, battered, bruised—and how!"[66]

In August, *Time* magazine editor Whittaker Chambers electrified Capitol Hill and the nation with his sensational testimony before the House Un-American Activities Committee. Chambers admitted that he had once been a Communist agent and that he had carried highly classified State Department documents to his Soviet "handler." Chambers said he obtained these secret documents from Alger Hiss, a top official of the Roosevelt and Truman administrations.[67] Speaker Sam Rayburn, a Texas Democrat, shrewdly saw "political dynamite" in Chambers's charges, but President Truman bobbled the issue badly.[68] He agreed with a reporter's description of the issue as a "red herring."[69] It was to prove one of Truman's worst political mistakes.

Republicans fairly saw the White House as theirs for the taking. They had been out of office since 1933. They ached to return to power. Thomas Dewey was now the popular and progressive governor of New York, the biggest electoral vote prize in the nation. Dewey realized that his slashing attacks on FDR in 1944 had turned voters off.[70] In his second run for the presidency, he would maintain a dignified "above the fray" pose. He would behave as if he were already president. The problem with this strategy is that it only reinforced voters' impression of Dewey as a pompous, stiff, standoffish candidate. "You have to know Mr. Dewey really well in order to dislike him," said one Republican lady, somewhat unhelpfully.[71]**

When Dewey's campaign train suddenly lurched *backward*, it narrowly

---

* Thurmond must have known that, in demanding segregation for black Americans, he was consigning his own daughter to second-class citizenship. We learned after his death that he had fathered a daughter by the family's black maid.

** Years later, a young legal intern in Governor Dewey's law firm would take a ride with the New Yorker in the elevator of the Manhattan skyscraper where both worked. When the two men were alone, the New Yorker asked Jim Compton if he was going to lunch. Excited at the prospect of dining out with the famous leader, New Mexico native Compton eagerly responded, "Yes, sir!" "Without your hat?" Dewey asked coldly, and stalked out alone.

avoided killing several people at one stop. "This is the first lunatic I have had as a train engineer," Dewey told the crowd. "He probably should be shot at sunrise, but I guess we can let him off for no one was hurt."[72] The unguarded remark might not have hurt so much if it didn't reveal what so many felt about Dewey: he was cold and arrogant.

Truman followed his August blunder over Alger Hiss with what must be seen as one of his most far-reaching decisions. Instead of going hat-in-hand to Strom Thurmond's Dixiecrats, Harry boldly issued an Executive Order *desegregating* the U.S. Armed Forces.[73]* Truman's order would take years to implement fully, but, for the first time in U.S. history, all those who risked their lives for America's freedom would do so under conditions of equality and dignity.

Harry battled through the Midwest aboard his campaign train. He had to borrow money to keep the train chugging ahead. Truman denounced the Republican Majority on Capitol Hill as the "do nothing Eightieth Congress." Senator Taft complained that the president was denouncing Congress at every "whistle stop" in the West. And even *that* statement came back to haunt the luckless Republicans. It was said to show their contempt for the people in small towns. In a fight for his political life, Truman threw away prepared texts. He was a flat speaker with a text, anyway. From the back of his train, Truman rose to the occasion. "Give 'em Hell, Harry!" yelled delighted listeners in the partisan crowds he addressed with increasing vigor. Truman's train, the *Ferdinand Magellan*, became the command center of the American government. Harry traveled an unprecedented 21,928 miles in that Whistle Stop Campaign of 1948.[74] Just as bluntly as he attacked Republicans, Harry scalded "Wallace and his Communists."[75] In fact, Wallace's campaign *was* dominated by Communists who secretly took their orders from Moscow.[76]

The last minute hustle paid off.

"Dewey Defeats Truman" read the headlines in the early edition of the *Chicago Tribune.* It remains one of the greatest embarrassments in the history

---

* "I was able to rise to the top of the Armed Forces because of those who went ahead and proved we could do it," said General Colin Powell fifty years after Executive Order 9981 was issued, "and Harry Truman who gave me the opportunity to show I could do it." (Source: Neal, *Harry & Ike,* 104.)

of journalism. Harry's grinning picture as he holds the *Tribune* up for the crowd's delight is one of the classic American political photographs.

Truman pulled off a victory few but he had predicted. Hubert Humphrey's strategy proved correct. A huge turnout of black voters and liberal supporters of civil rights had given Truman the edge. Even with Governor Earl Warren on his ticket, Dewey was unable to carry the important state of California. Friends of Israel proved grateful for Truman's timely help. And organized labor was thrilled by Harry's veto of the Taft-Hartley law. That veto won for Truman the strong support of Ronald Reagan and most of the non-Communist Hollywood Left. Pictures of Harry playing the piano while actress Lauren Bacall draped herself glamorously on top of the instrument symbolized Truman's populist appeal.*

The creation of Americans for Democratic Action (ADA), led by leading liberals like Eleanor Roosevelt, Hubert Humphrey, Arthur Schlesinger Jr., John Kenneth Galbraith, and theologian Reinhold Niebuhr, enabled Roosevelt Democrats to stand strong for labor and civil rights, while resisting the siren song of Communism. For a quarter century afterward, the ADA was to be an important leadership group for the anti-Communist left in America.

Truman's Fair Deal program was largely blocked by a coalition of Republicans and conservative Southern Democrats. One of his major agenda items was Medicare, not enacted for another twenty years. Generally, Truman was too conservative for the liberals and too liberal for the conservatives.[77] Still, his inspired leadership in foreign policy and his frenetic, aggressive campaign style enabled him to defy all pollsters and pundits and score a knockout.

Truman won 24,179,346 popular votes (49.8 percent) and 303 electoral votes to Dewey's 21,991,291 (45.1 percent) and 189 electoral votes. Former Vice President Wallace won 1,157,326 popular votes (2.4 percent) and no electoral votes. The Dixiecrats' challenge won 1,176,125 popular votes (2.4 percent) and 39 electoral votes from the Deep South.

---

* The Truman-Bacall photo, actually taken when he was briefly vice president, arguably emphasized Truman's lack of dignity. Backers, however, said he was no stuffed shirt. Cartoonist Ben Shahn, a Henry Wallace backer, used that photo to lampoon *both* major party candidates of 1948. Shahn put a smiling, seductive Dewey atop Harry's piano, suggesting that both candidates were playing music together.

VI. Under the Cloud of War

With Berlin besieged and Israel fighting for life, Eleanor Roosevelt traveled to Paris in December 1948. She was going there to address a United Nations General Assembly on Human Rights (UNDHR). Since the death of FDR, she had devoted herself tirelessly to framing a Universal Declaration of Human Rights. President Truman had named the former First Lady to lead the U.S. delegation. It was yet another example of Truman's generosity of spirit. Mrs. Roosevelt's words on that occasion still ring:

> This declaration is based upon the spiritual fact that man must have freedom in which to develop his full stature and through common effort to raise the level of human dignity. We have much to do to fully achieve and to assure the rights set forth in this declaration. But having them put before us with the moral backing of 58 nations will be a great step forward.
>
> As we here bring to fruition our labors on this Declaration of Human Rights, we must at the same time rededicate ourselves to the unfinished task which lies before us. We can now move on with new courage and inspiration to the completion of an international covenant on human rights and of measures for the implementation of human rights.[78]

It was the brazen denial of the fundamental human rights outlined in the UNDHR that would cause so many of the world tensions and so much of the bloodshed of the next fifty years. Even as Mrs. Roosevelt spoke, Communist forces were crushing human rights wherever they could extend their grip. Many of the Arab states formally signed the UNDHR, though they routinely ignored its principles in ruling over their own people. And they breathed hatred of the newborn state of Israel. They seemed to sense no inconsistency. FDR had proclaimed Four Freedoms: Freedom of Speech, Freedom of Religion, Freedom from Want, and Freedom from Fear. Now, with Eleanor's work, these freedoms would have an international basis. It was in this role that Mrs. Roosevelt earned the title "First Lady of the World."

Mrs. Roosevelt's call for *universal* human rights had no stronger supporter

Dewey Defeats Truman. *Republicans were itching for victory in 1948. They'd been out of the White House since 1933. Gov. Thomas E. Dewey of New York seemed a sure bet. Polls showed Dewey far in the lead. Truman ran a "whistle stop" campaign against the Republicans during which supporters called on him to "Give 'em Hell, Harry!" Truman's upset victory surprised everyone but Harry himself.*

Berlin Airlift. *Stalin hoped to drive the allies out of West Berlin in June, 1948, by giving them the choice of surrender or war. Truman's inspired third choice avoided surrender and prevented war. Two and a half million West Berliners were airlifted food, medical supplies, coal, and even candy. The U.S. conducted 277,804 flights into the blockaded city, carrying 2,325,809 tons of supplies. It was nearly a ton of materiel for every man, woman and child in the city.*

President Eisenhower grinning. *Americans rewarded their victorious five-star general with two landslide victories in the 1952 and 1956 elections. It was said Ike's famous grin was his philosophy, but we now know the President acted vigorously—often behind the scenes—to achieve his goals.*

Chief Justice Earl Warren. *As war-time governor of California, he called for the internment of Japanese-Americans, but he went on to become a strong voice for civil rights. It was after Warren's arrival in 1953 that the Supreme Court ruled 9–0 that "separate but equal" schools were unconstitutional—that separate could never be equal.*

than American diplomat Ralph Bunche. But as Bunche journeyed to Paris for the UN General Assembly session that fall, he was no ivory tower intellectual. He had just barely escaped assassination. Serving as a deputy to the UN's Mideast Envoy, Bunche had been scheduled to ride with Sweden's Count Folke Bernadotte to a meeting in Jerusalem. When Bunche was delayed, Bernadotte proceeded without him. The UN's Bernadotte was assassinated by members of the militant group of Zionists known as the Stern Gang. Later, a gang member said, "We knew that if Bernadotte with his magnetic personality and all his influence came and talked with his plan in Paris, the [UN] General Assembly would decide for this plan and endorse it. So we had to kill him on this day."[79] Threatened with annihilation by five invading Arab states, the Jewish side produced some extremists, too.

When Ralph Bunche took over the UN mission to bring a cease-fire in the first Arab-Israeli war, he was no stranger to danger. As a black American, he had seen violence and discrimination firsthand. He had taken full advantage of American education, however, to break down barriers. California gave him the opportunities that might have been denied him elsewhere. There he went to college on an athletic scholarship. "UCLA is where it all began for me, where, in a sense *I* began," Bunche said.[80] As early as 1928, as a professor at Washington's Howard University, Bunche stood up for one of his students who was arrested for picketing the segregated restaurant in the U.S. Capitol.*

Bunche did not hide. He plunged into his work. His final report to the UN for an Arab-Israeli cease fire was both "balanced and pragmatic."[81] The U.S. State Department's Dean Rusk welcomed Bunche's report: "Bunche's statement as a whole gives full credit to the Jewish side and should steady the nerves of those who are being bombarded by partisan propaganda."[82]

Ralph Bunche did *not* bring peace in the Mideast. That elusive goal has still not been achieved more than half a century later. But he did negotiate a cease-fire that ended the first Arab-Israeli war. He did that with skill and courage, at the risk of his life and millions of other lives.

---

* The arrested Howard student whom Bunche defended would make his *own* contribution to history. Kenneth Clark became a famous psychiatrist whose work would be cited by the U.S. Supreme Court in its landmark *Brown v. Board* decision (1954), which outlawed segregation in public education. (Source: Urquhart, *Ralph Bunche: A Life*, 44.)

For that singular achievement, Ralph Bunche was honored with the Nobel Prize for Peace in 1950. He was the first black American to be so honored. That such a man could still be denied a place teaching in many universities in his native land, or the right to vote, or the right to dine in a restaurant or visit a movie theater of his choice became all the more intolerable to millions in America. Some in the civil rights movement actually criticized Bunche for his involvement in *foreign* crises. But his very distinction on the world stage became a powerful argument against the denial of human rights at home.

With a cease-fire in the Middle East and with Stalin ending the Berlin Blockade in early 1949, the Truman administration might have hoped for a breathing spell from international crises. It was not to be.

The Soviets' aggressive moves in Eastern Europe convinced Truman that the United States had to ally more closely with the democracies of Western Europe. Truman persuaded General Dwight D. Eisenhower to take a leave of absence as president of Columbia University to lead the military effort of the North Atlantic Treaty Organization (NATO). Truman recognized that only a formal U.S. commitment to defend Western Europe from external aggression could prevent dangerous Soviet inroads. NATO was built on the idea of "collective security." An attack by the USSR on any one of the members of NATO was to be regarded as an attack on all of them. No more would dictators be able to carve up Europe piecemeal, as Hitler and Mussolini had done.

Truman knew Eisenhower was skilled at diplomacy as well as military planning. He felt that only Eisenhower's prestige as the conqueror of Hitler would bring the Europeans into full cooperation. As with his outreach to Mrs. Roosevelt, Herbert Hoover, Senator Vandenberg, and General Marshall, Truman once again showed keen insight and humility in promoting Ike. Under Truman, West Germany (The Federal Republic of Germany) was formed by uniting the Occupation Zones of France, Britain, and the United States. West German rearmament would lead, eventually, to a free and democratic German state as the second largest military member of NATO (1955). Never before had a victorious power sacrificed so much to restore and rebuild—*and defend*—a defeated enemy.

As successful as Truman's defense of freedom in Europe was, however, the U.S. position in Asia looked all the more precarious. In 1949, success with NATO was matched by the disastrous defeat of the U.S.-backed Nationalist government in China. Communist guerilla leader Mao Zedong succeeded after nearly twenty years of civil war in driving Jiang Kai-Shek's *Kuomintang* forces out of Mainland China and onto the tiny island of Formosa, known today as Taiwan.

"Who lost China?" came the anguished cry. The obvious answer, that Jiang Kai-Shek had lost China, did not satisfy. The former U.S. ambassador to Nationalist China, conservative Patrick J. Hurley, had resigned in protest. He complained that there were too many Communists in the State Department's China Desk.[83] Many Democrats and Republicans were appalled by the Communist takeover. It was an especially jarring event coming just weeks after President Truman had announced that the Soviet Union had exploded its first atomic bomb. Truman's statement was meant to reassure Americans:

> We have evidence that within recent weeks an atomic explosion occurred in the U.S.S.R.
>
> Ever since atomic energy was first released by man, the eventual development of this new force by other nations was to be expected. This probability has always been taken into account by us.[84]

Whether or not the top leaders of the government had always expected the Soviets to develop the atomic bomb, the American people were shocked that the Soviets had seemingly "caught up" in just four years. This, the Communist takeover in China, and the revelations about Alger Hiss contributed to a pervasive sense that perhaps it was not just Soviet strength but Communist perfidy that explained these disturbing events.

Congressman Richard M. Nixon had made a reputation as a tough Communist hunter when he served on the House Un-American Activities Committee (HUAC). Nixon summoned Hiss to testify. Alger Hiss denied he even knew Whittaker Chambers, although he hedged by saying he *may* have known him under another name. Chambers for his part produced microfilm copies of Top Secret State Department documents he said Hiss had given him. Dramatically, Chambers retrieved these microfilm copies from a pumpkin patch. He had hidden these "pumpkin papers" on his Westminster, Maryland, farm. Chambers's microfilmed documents seem all (with one exception) to have been typed on a Woodstock typewriter—specifically, Woodstock #N230099 owned by the Hisses.[85]

Hiss's friends—and he was *very well connected*—struck back. Rumors circulated broadly about Chambers's alleged homosexuality, insanity, imposture, and criminal behavior.[86]

Despite Hiss's firm denials he had ever cooperated with Chambers, Chambers seemed to know him very well indeed. Chambers had told HUAC of Hiss's excitement at seeing a rare bird, a *prothonotary warbler.* Later, in what seemed a relaxed interlude, a congressman asked Hiss if he'd ever seen a prothonotary warbler in the Washington area. When Hiss's eyes brightened and he confirmed his rare find, a strong link in the chain binding him to Chambers seemed to be forged. Hiss would deny for the rest of his long life what the *Venona* decrypts later proved: that he was an active Soviet agent.[87]*

Americans also worried about Communist influence in the movies. When HUAC subpoenaed several movie stars to testify, a number complied. Screen Actors Guild President Ronald Reagan testified that, yes, there *was* considerable Communist influence in Hollywood. But he urged no witch hunt. Instead, he said, "democracy is strong enough to stand up and fight against the inroads of any ideology."[88] Reagan knew what he was talking about. He had been anonymously threatened with a disfiguring acid attack if he persisted in his anti-Communist campaign. Undeterred, Reagan told the Members of Congress:

> I never . . . want to see our country become urged by either fear or resentment of this group that we ever compromise with any of our democratic principles. . . . I still think democracy can do it. . . . I believe that, as Thomas Jefferson put it, if all the American people know all of the facts they will never make a mistake.[89]

---

* The Venona Project is the name given to a supersecret U.S. intelligence effort to intercept, decode, and translate thousands of messages from Soviet agents in America to their superiors in Moscow. Only in 1995, following the collapse of the Soviet Union, did this material become available to the world.

The Cold War was splitting not only Hollywood but many American institutions. The universities, journalism, organized labor, and the military each felt pressures in different ways.

In the civil rights movement, the staunch anti-Communist Walter White exerted firm leadership in the National Association for the Advancement of Colored People (NAACP). White had rejected Henry Wallace's Communist-backed Progressive campaign and backed Harry Truman in his come-from-behind victory of 1948. When the gifted black singer-actor Paul Robeson and the famed black intellectual W. E. B. DuBois supported a Communist-inspired petition to the UN called "We Charge Genocide," White denounced the petition.[90] Yes, some state governments engaged in invidious discrimination. Some outlaw organizations like the Ku Klux Klan even engaged in lynching and other forms of terrorism to prevent black Americans from exercising their constitutional rights. But this was not the same thing as a U.S. government–backed policy of genocide, White argued. White stated forcefully that "measurable gains have been made in reducing racial bigotry."[91] Anyone who doubted that had only to look at our now integrated U.S. military or go to a baseball game and see Jackie Robinson slam a home run. (Robinson's triumphal entry into the major leagues proved to be a major turning point in a cultural revolution in America.) White made sure that the NAACP backed the Marshall Plan, rejecting "the most savage imperialism of our time: the road of Moscow and Peiping [Beijing]."[92] Walter White was not alone in fearlessly advocating freedom for black Americans at home while strongly resisting the siren song of Communism abroad. He enlisted the support of Mary McLeod Bethune, Roy Wilkins, Congressman Adam Clayton Powell Jr., and a host of other black civil rights leaders.[93] Together, they gave unyielding support to America's increasingly anti-Communist foreign policy.

VII. The Korean Conflict

Harry Truman might not have imagined how soon he would have to test the resolve of the integrated military force he had created. In addition to *racially* integrating the U.S. military, Truman was responsible for uniting *all* the armed services except the Coast Guard under the newly created Department of Defense. No longer would cabinet-level War and Navy Departments jockey with each other for a president's support.

In January 1950, Secretary of State Dean Acheson gave a fateful speech. The precise, elegant Acheson did not suffer fools gladly. His prep school background, neatly trimmed mustache, and British mannerisms were easy to caricature. Acheson was a highly capable, very dedicated diplomat. But when he addressed Asia, he made a mistake of catastrophic proportions. He spoke of a "defensive perimeter" in the Far East that pointedly did *not* include Taiwan or South Korea. "It must be clear that no person can guarantee those areas against military attack," he said.[94] To compound this grievous error, Texas's Tom Connally, the Democratic chairman of the Senate Foreign Relations Committee, announced in May that Russia might seize the Korean peninsula without U.S. response because Korea was "not very greatly important."[95]

Stalin followed these events closely. In a Kremlin meeting with the North Korean Communist ruler Kim Il-Sung, Stalin gave grudging approval to Kim's plan to invade South Korea. But Stalin warned Kim, "If you should get kicked in the teeth, I shall not lift a finger to help. You have to ask Mao for all the help."[96] That was all the word Kim needed.

Ninety thousand North Korean troops crossed the 38th Parallel into South Korea on 25 June 1950. Truman, stung by charges his administration had "lost" China to the Communists, knew he had to resist this naked aggression. General of the Army Douglas MacArthur was then in charge of the occupation of Japan as what some called a "Star-Spangled Mikado [Emperor]."* MacArthur advised Truman to send U.S. air cover from Japan to help the retreating forces of the Republic of Korea (ROK).

Only because the Soviet delegate was boycotting a UN Security Council session over another issue was it possible for the United States to get the UN to authorize action to repel the North Korean aggression. Now, just five years after MacArthur had stood on the deck of the USS *Missouri* in Tokyo

* Enormous prestige went with the exalted five-star rank held by MacArthur and only four other generals in U.S. history: George C. Marshall, Dwight D. Eisenhower, Henry H. ("Hap") Arnold, and Omar Bradley. The navy lists only four five-star Admirals of the Fleet: William D. Leahy, Ernest J. King, Chester W. Nimitz, and William F. ("Bull") Halsey.

Bay to proclaim the return of peace, the United States was involved once again in a land war in Asia.

General MacArthur was seventy years old in 1950. He might easily have begged off from yet another combat assignment and asked Truman to select a younger man. He was highly respected in the United States, not only as the victor in the Pacific war but also for his enlightened rule in occupied Japan. He had skillfully countered the threat of more than 375,000 Japanese POWs returning to the home islands from Soviet prison camps in Manchuria.[97] The Soviets had completely indoctrinated these men in Communist ideas and disruptive tactics. So strong was the Japanese respect for MacArthur, however, and so effective were the free labor unions MacArthur had established in Japan that the violent tactics of the returnees were soon overcome. Even though MacArthur had ordered war crimes tribunals that led to 720 death sentences for Japanese offenders, Japan's eighty-three million people proved deeply grateful for his mild rule.[98] Why leave all this for a dangerous assignment on the Korean peninsula? For MacArthur, the answer was one word, the most important word: *duty.*

The North Korean invasion had shocked the world. The newly created Central Intelligence Agency (CIA) failed seriously in not detecting the buildup of "Red" tanks and infantry north of the 38th Parallel. ROK forces retreated pell-mell. American troops performed badly. Poorly trained and equipped, soft from easy occupation duty in Japan, some of our soldiers allowed themselves to be overrun and taken prisoner. Within weeks, the Reds had encircled American and ROK forces in a narrow band around the South Korean port city of Pusan. MacArthur was determined to break out of this "Pusan Perimeter."

His plan was audacity itself. MacArthur planned a seaborne invasion *behind* Red lines near Inchon, the seaport for the South Korean capital of Seoul. "We drew up every conceivable natural and geographic handicap, and Inchon had them all," said one of MacArthur's military aides.[99] Not the least of the hazards were *deadly* thirty-foot tides. MacArthur's naval chief could muster no better endorsement of his plan than that it was "not impossible."[100] MacArthur kept his own counsel, puffing constantly on his trademark corncob pipe. He remembered the words of his own father, who like his son was a Medal of Honor winner: "Doug, councils of war breed timidity and confusion."[101]

MacArthur's Inchon landing succeeded brilliantly. It was one of the greatest turnarounds in American history. For breathtaking boldness, it ranked alongside Washington's crossing of the Delaware, Grant's descent on Shiloh, and Patton's relief of Bastogne. South Korea's aged President Syngman Rhee accepted the return of his liberated capital of Seoul with tearful gratitude: "We love you," he told MacArthur, "as the savior of our race."[102]

Because this was the UN's first attempt to resist aggression, the United States had the support of troops from Britain, Australia, New Zealand, Canada, and even France.[103] Truman refused to call the Korean War a war. It was a "police action," he insisted, trying to emphasize that the United Nations was being tested by international Communism. If we allowed the Reds to get away with it in Korea, then Communists would be encouraged to probe Western defenses elsewhere in Asia, Europe, and Latin America, Truman argued.

When MacArthur met Truman at Wake Island (the scene of bitter fighting in World War II) on 14 October 1950, UN forces had thrown the Reds back and were advancing toward the North Korea-China border on the Yalu River. MacArthur assured President Truman at Wake Island that there was "very little chance" of a massive intervention by Communist Chinese forces.[104]

But two hundred thousand Communist Chinese "volunteers" defied MacArthur's prediction and stormed across the frozen Yalu River. Americans were shocked and dispirited.* U.S. Marines caught by the sudden invasion took heavy casualties at the Chosin Reservoir as they "attacked in a different direction." It was Korea's coldest winter in a century. The "Frozen Chosin" was the name this Marine "band of brothers" took for themselves. Samuel Eliot Morison calls Marine General Oliver Smith's "fighting retreat" from the Chosin Reservoir "one of the most glorious in the annals of that gallant corps, recalling Xenophon's retreat of the immortal 10,000 to the sea."[105] In less flowery terms, the "grunts" on the ground called the long retreat "bugging

---

* The idea that anyone could volunteer for anything in the ruthlessly regimented Communist Chinese regime ruled by Mao Zedong was another example of the "black is white, day is night" Communist doublespeak. It left Americans deeply distrustful of Communist statements, methods, and motives.

out." Nonetheless, their courage and discipline under the harshest conditions should earn undying praise.

MacArthur wanted to carry the war north of the Yalu River, bombing the bridges and the staging areas inside Mainland China. Britain and France vetoed this idea. Britain was fighting a Communist insurgency in Malaysia; France, likewise, was bogged down battling Communists in Indo-China.[106]

Truman remembered George F. Kennan's "Long Telegram." *Containment* was the policy it recommended. Containment meant holding free territory and not yielding it up to the Communists. It did *not* mean using force to liberate territories already under Communist control. Now that Stalin, too, had the atomic bomb, that strategy might bring a nuclear World War III.

Kennan, meanwhile, had begun to see dangers *within* the West. He saw the return of the fear that had stalked free nations before World War II. He spoke to that same sense of dread that had made George Orwell's grim prophecy in his novel *1984* an international bestseller. Kennan said nuclear weapons "reach backwards beyond the frontiers of western civilization, to the concepts of warfare which were once familiar to the Asiatic hordes.[107] In a memo to his State Department superiors that was promptly ignored, Kennan quoted Shakespeare's *Troilus and Cressida*:

> Power into will, will into appetite
> And appetite, a universal wolf,
> So doubly seconded with will and power,
> Must make perforce a universal prey
> And last eat himself up.[108]

The imperious MacArthur wanted to threaten the Chinese with the atomic bomb if they did not agree to negotiate a peace in Korea. General MacArthur then committed the act that led to his summary dismissal. He released a "military appraisal" that explained why he had to carry the war to the North. He went further, writing to the Republican leader in the House of Representatives to show why his, MacArthur's, view, and not Truman's, was the correct one. "There is no substitute for victory," was MacArthur's ringing declaration.

Truman immediately fired MacArthur. It did not matter to many that Secretary of Defense George C. Marshall and Army Chief of Staff Omar Bradley—also five-star generals—recommended this course of action for rank insubordination. Truman had to endure a firestorm of protest and abuse. California Senator Richard Nixon called for MacArthur's immediate reinstatement, and Wisconsin Senator Joseph McCarthy, a notorious boozer, accused the commander in chief of sacking MacArthur while he, Truman, was drunk![109]

McCarthy had gained sudden prominence the year before when he told a Republican audience in Wheeling, West Virginia: "I have in my hand [a list of] . . . cases of individuals who would appear to be either card-carrying members or certainly loyal to the Communist party" in the State Department.[110] The exact number McCarthy used remains controversial to this day. Thus was born "McCarthyism." McCarthy addressed a real problem: disloyal elements within the U.S. government. But his approach to this real problem was to cause untold grief to the country he claimed to love.

Apparently, no one at the GOP meeting thought to call McCarthy's bluff by yelling out: "Read the names."

"Old soldiers never die," General MacArthur told a joint meeting of Congress, "they just fade away." It was an emotional moment. American soldiers were dying in frigid Korea. One of our greatest generals told us that the president and his team were not trying to win. And some strident voices were saying that that was because they didn't *want* to win, that they were influenced by Soviet agents. Small wonder that Truman's approval rating sank to an historic low of 23 percent!

Yet, we now can tell that it is precisely in such moments that a president's strength of character is tested. However brilliant and insightful MacArthur was, this country can never tolerate a military commander going over the head of the civilian authority. George Washington *wouldn't* do that. George McClellan *didn't* do that. It can *never* be allowed.

Fortunately for the country in this desperate hour, a number of leading Republicans, including Governors Thomas E. Dewey and Harold Stassen and Senators Henry Cabot Lodge Jr. and John Foster Dulles, boldly spoke up in support of the president's right as commander in chief to give orders to his military subordinates.[111] Once again, Thomas Dewey put principle above narrow partisanship.

Also critical to consider is how important the patriotic stance of Walter White and the NAACP leadership was at this critical juncture. Had there been any crack in national unity along a racial fault line, America's military position might have become untenable.

Communist propaganda tried to paint Americans as racists for fighting nonwhites in Korea. Walter White was having none of it.

Despite his successes in reaching out to the black and Jewish communities, Harry Truman as president was less successful in his attempt to extend diplomatic recognition to the Vatican. Truman, in his practical, Midwestern way, saw Pope Pius XII and his Catholic Church as a strong ally in the Cold War struggle against atheistic Communism.[112] Thus, he nominated World War II general Mark Clark, an Episcopalian, as his ambassador to Rome. Truman's own fellow Baptists were most vociferous in opposition. They held strictly to the Reformation view that the Church cannot be a State, and in these pre-Vatican II days, there was still widespread suspicion of the Catholic Church by many Protestants in the United States Truman tried to persuade the presiding bishop of the Episcopal Church in the United States in a White House meeting: "I told him that Stalin and his crowd had no intellectual honesty and no moral code, that they had broken thirty or forty treaties they made with us . . . and that all I wanted to do was to [align with Christian believers] to save morals in the world."[113] The Episcopal cleric was stubbornly unpersuaded, and Harry wrote in disgust, "If a Baptist [like me] can see what's toward—why not a high hat Church of England Bishop?"[114]* Harry was poking fun at the "high hat" of the Episcopal bishop, but his practical common sense was offended by theological disputes. He just wanted to round up all the Christians against the atheistic Communists. Truman hoped that Mark Clark's wartime prestige—and the fact that he was a Protestant—would overcome opposition to the appointment. With support from senior

* Following this Truman strategy, another Midwestern Protestant president would form an effective alliance with the Vatican thirty years later. Ronald Reagan of Dixon, Illinois, would reach out to Pope John Paul II in the 1980s.

Democrats on Capitol Hill collapsing, however, General Clark asked the president to withdraw his nomination.

VIII. The Man from Independence

Heading into the election of 1952, President Harry Truman confronted a long, grinding, bloody war in Korea. General Matthew B. Ridgeway, his replacement for the ousted MacArthur, had solidified the UN front roughly at the 38th Parallel, the prewar border between North and South Korea.

The result could hardly appeal to Americans on the ground: "Why die for a tie?" G.I.s complained. But a negotiated settlement at the 38th Parallel would at least *contain* Communism on the peninsula. And containment was the Truman administration's goal. Truman was committed to "limited war" or, as he sometimes called it, a "police action." Needless to say, such a stance was deeply unpopular in his time.

Inflation had hurt the president's domestic record. Strikes were a nagging problem. When Truman seized the steel mills to prevent a strike from crippling production during wartime, the U.S. Supreme Court handed Harry his hat. The Court struck down Truman's action by a stunning vote of 6–3 in the case of *Youngstown Sheet & Tube Co. v. Sawyer* (1952). The Supreme Court was then composed of FDR and Truman appointees, a fact that made the rejection of Truman's actions an even more stinging rebuke.

Then there was the two-term limit, passed by a Democratic-controlled Congress. Congress had passed and the states had ratified the Twenty-second Amendment to the Constitution limiting the president to only two terms. The terms of the amendment specifically exempted the current occupant of the White House, but many saw its quick passage as a vote of no confidence in Harry Truman.*

Harry Truman prized his reputation for "Plain Speaking" honesty. Once,

* The Democratic Party, going back to Jefferson and Jackson, had championed the two-term limit. It was Republicans Ulysses S. Grant and Theodore Roosevelt who seriously challenged that tradition by seeking third nonconsecutive terms (1880, 1912 respectively). But it was the Democrat FDR who sought and won third and fourth consecutive terms. Roosevelt dominated not only the Republicans but also many conservative Democrats. The Twenty-second Amendment was their response.

when a *Washington Post* music critic panned the president's daughter's singing, Harry Truman responded as an outraged, protective *father.* Harry immediately wrote the offending critic a letter, saying, "You're an eight ulcer man on four ulcer pay." He even threatened him. When I meet you, he wrote, "you'll need a new nose, a lot of beefsteak for black eyes, and perhaps a supporter below!"[115] Then, in typical Truman fashion, he affixed his own three-cent stamp to the envelope. He wouldn't abuse his presidential franking privilege when threatening a columnist with a punch in the nose!

For all his flinty personal integrity, Truman was embarrassed by attempts by some of his appointees to cash in on their offices. He had to let General Harry Vaughan go when he took up with perfume smugglers. Gifts of freezers and mink coats tainted the entire administration's reputation. By the standards of the past—the Tweed Ring, the Credit Mobilier scandal, Teapot Dome—the Truman era corruption was "small beer." Still, his party had been in power for twenty years, and people sensed a certain laxness. Truman had pulled off the most stunning political upset in history with his 1948 win. He did not want to jeopardize that feat by losing in a failed bid for a third term. So he decided not to run.

Despite his widespread unpopularity in 1952, President Truman soldiered on. While most Americans strongly disapproved of *his* performance, Winston Churchill came to Washington again and provided—as usual—a deeply insightful assessment of the Man from Independence.

Churchill had just led his Conservative Party to victory in Britain. Relaxing with Truman aboard the presidential yacht, *Williamsburg,* the seventy-seven-year-old prime minister was unusually blunt. He confessed to Harry's face that he had initially held him in "low regard" and "loathed your taking the place of Franklin Roosevelt."[116] But, he continued, that view changed:

> I misjudged you badly. Since that time, you, more than any other man, have saved Western Civilization. When the British could no longer hold out in Greece, you, and you alone, sir, made the decision that saved that ancient land from Communists. You acted in similar fashion . . . when the Soviets tried to take over Iran. . . . [Your] Marshall Plan

> . . . rescued Western Europe wallowing in the shallows and easy prey to Joseph Stalin's malevolent machinations. Then you established the North Atlantic Treaty Alliance. . . . Then there was your audacious Berlin Airlift. And, of course, there was Korea . . .[117]

It's fair to say that half a century after that chilly January cruise on the Potomac, most Americans today view Harry Truman the way Winston Churchill did—and not the way our own parents did in 1952. In refusing to allow MacArthur to use—or even threaten to use—an atomic weapon, Truman vastly increased the power of his presidency. He also reversed what had been an irreversible pattern in history: that when new weapons had been developed, they would be used.[118] And used again and again.

When Harry Truman returned with his devoted wife, Bess, to their home in Independence, Missouri, he prepared for life as a former president. There was no pension in the 1950s. There were few opportunities for him. But he returned uncomplaining to the community that had nurtured him. Asked by a television reporter what was the first thing he did on returning to the family home, Harry, plain-spoken as ever, said, "I took the grips [suitcases] up into the attic."

Eisenhower and Happy Days (1953–1961)

Dwight D. Eisenhower was just what Americans thought of when they pictured the World War II G.I.—friendly, smart, practical, decent, and fundamentally fair. That was what the U.S. Army represented in occupied Europe and Japan. Those are the characteristics Americans liked to think they embodied at home. Dwight Eisenhower's two landslide elections were personal victories. His Republican Party never fully shared in his popularity. Eisenhower's appointee as chief justice led the Supreme Court to a unanimous decision against segregation in the public schools. In response, young Dr. Martin Luther King Jr. arose to challenge Americans to live up to the ideals they professed. Dr. King's broad movement for civil rights began in Montgomery, Alabama, in 1955 with a boycott of city buses that enforced racial segregation. President Eisenhower hoped to end segregation using a combination of moral suasion and strong appointments to federal courts in the South. But the sharp resistance of Arkansas Democratic Governor Orval Faubus forced Ike to send in the U.S. Army's 101st Airborne Division in 1957 to enforce desegregation orders for Little Rock's public schools. The Soviets Union's launch of Sputnik, the earth satellite, made Americans deeply uneasy. If they could do this, they could hit the continental United States with one of the hundred megaton nuclear missiles they were testing so menacingly. Eisenhower's calm and steady response was not enough for some, including Senator John F. Kennedy. JFK vowed to "get America moving again." Kennedy spoke of a "missile gap" in his drive to establish himself as a strong and decisive leader. His heroic World War II record and his toughness in debate would mark him as a young leader to take America into the tumultuous 1960s.

I. "I Like Ike!"

The Republicans could smell victory in 1952. President Harry Truman's broad unpopularity made the GOP prospects bright. General Dwight D. Eisenhower continued to deny an interest in running. He had even told Senator Robert A. Taft he would back him if the Ohio conservative would only support NATO. Nothing doing, said Taft.[1] Ike went to Paris and kept his counsel. He had plenty to do. With the Korean war raging in Asia, the recent announcement of the Soviet A-bomb, and Stalin's attempt to starve West Berlin into submission, nerves were on edge. Ike provided a calming presence at NATO headquarters.

Back home, however, Senator Henry Cabot Lodge Jr. of Massachusetts led a "Draft Eisenhower" effort. Ike won the New Hampshire primary easily on a write-in basis. Privately, Eisenhower fumed. He said "time and again" he would not seek the Republican Party nomination. If he had really wanted to scotch the Lodge draft attempt, however, he could have reached back to the nineteenth century for a quote from his fellow West Pointer. General William Tecumseh Sherman knew how to squelch a draft: "If nominated, I will not run. If elected, I will not serve." Ike issued no such statement. Further, he was increasingly aware that he had an obligation to run. Senator Taft called publicly for the United States to bring the troops home from Europe, and Eisenhower realized such a move would be disastrous given the power vacuum it would create for the Soviets to fill. He would have to run. Fifteen thousand people gathered in New York's Madison Square Garden for an Eisenhower rally. "I Like Ike" read their signs.[2] It was a slogan that would soon sweep the country.

When Eisenhower resigned and returned home from Paris, he finally spoke out on political issues. He was opposed to Big Government, he said, to high taxes, inflation, and the "Kremlin menace."[3] Clearly, he was a Republican.

Taft was unwilling to step aside for Eisenhower. "Mr. Republican" could count on party regulars, especially in the Midwest and Far West. Eisenhower's support came from a small but influential group of Eastern Republicans. Thomas E. Dewey, the party's candidate in 1944 and 1948, lined up support for Ike. At the 1952 Republican National Convention in Chicago, Eisenhower's backers charged Taft forces with an attempt to "steal" delegates. Senator Richard M. Nixon wrested control of California's crucial delegation away from "favorite son" candidate Governor Earl Warren.* Nixon's timely intervention clinched the nomination for Eisenhower—and the vice presidential nod for himself.[4]

The Democrats were sensitive to Republican charges of "that mess in Washington." They looked outside the Truman administration for a standard bearer. Illinois Governor Adlai E. Stevenson filled the bill. Stevenson was the grandson of Grover Cleveland's vice president, but his main appeal was to liberal intellectuals within the Democratic Party. Witty and urbane, Stevenson found party regulars cool to him, but eager and active members of the faculty clubs went "Madly for Adlai."

In many ways, Stevenson was an odd choice. He was not as strong as Truman on civil rights or labor issues. He did not champion any far-reaching economic programs. But it was his *style* that most commended him. Reverend Norman Vincent Peale wrote a leading best seller of 1952, *The Power of Positive Thinking*. Peale made clear his support for the Republicans. Stevenson memorably responded, "I find Paul appealing and Peale appalling."[5] Best of all, for his followers, was Stevenson's skewering of Californian Richard Nixon. Nixon was the kind of politician, Stevenson said, who would cut down a redwood and then mount the stump to give a speech on conservation. For liberal defenders of Alger Hiss, the put-down of the Red-baiting Nixon was nothing less than thrilling.

Eisenhower proved a powerful campaigner. His smile dazzled millions of Americans. His war record was admired throughout the world. But Ike

* A "favorite son" candidacy is usually an attempt by a powerful local figure to control his party's state delegation at the national convention. The purpose of this candidacy is not to win the presidential nomination for the favorite son (although such lightning *has* struck in the past) but to allow the favorite son to "deliver" the state's delegation to the eventual nominee at a critical moment.

was leaving nothing to chance: his special train racked up its own "whistle stop" record: 51,276 miles of nonstop campaigning, more than doubling Harry Truman's 21,998 miles in the *Ferdinand Magellan* in 1948.[6]

Eisenhower's campaign train was almost derailed, however, when it was revealed that his running mate, Dick Nixon, had been supported by a "secret fund" raised for him by a small circle of California businessmen. Nixon went on national television to defend himself. He gave a tearful performance, praising his wife, Pat, for her "Republican cloth coat." (It was a dig at the Democrats' mink coat scandal.) Most effective, however, was Nixon's defiant refusal to return to donors the gift of a little dog. His young daughters called the Cocker Spaniel "Checkers," and they loved him. Nixon's "Checkers Speech" saved his political life. Public reaction was positive and overwhelming. When he met General Eisenhower behind closed doors, however, the senior man was still not sure. Nixon rudely urged him to "s— or get off the pot."[7]

Nixon stayed on the ticket, with vast consequences for American political life. He contributed to some of the campaign's uglier moments. He charged the Democrats with "twenty years of treason" and slammed "Dean Acheson's cowardly college of communist containment."[8]

Nineteen fifty-two may have been the first campaign in American history where the partisans of one party openly disdained the voters. The Federalists and the Whigs, to be sure, had at times feared the masses of voters who flocked to Jefferson and Jackson. But they generally took care not to flaunt their sense of superiority. Adlai Stevenson may have been the first to break with this tradition. When asked why he seemed to talk "over the heads of his listeners," the cerebral Adlai airily replied, "I speak to where their heads *ought* to be."*

Privately, Eisenhower's associates knew the characterization of their man as uncultured and anti-intellectual just wasn't so. C. D. Jackson, a protégé of *Time's* Henry Luce, said Ike "moved young" and was highly literate. Eisenhower is "cultured well beyond innate gentlemanliness," he said. "His

* Stevenson's partisans were lampooned as "eggheads," an unfair characterization since both Ike and Adlai sported impressive bald domes. In a further irony, Eisenhower's graceful, thoughtful memoir, *Crusade in Europe,* has never been out of print, while the presumably intellectual Stevenson's thin literary output is consigned to the back shelves of university libraries.

classical, Biblical, and mythological allusions come tumbling out when he is working with words. Even [speechwriter] Emmett John Hughes would have to agree that his capacity for unscrambling an involved paragraph and fixing it so that it says what it was supposed to say in the first place, is sometimes uncanny."[9]

Eisenhower preferred not to slug it out with his opponent. Ike led in the polls throughout the campaign, but he "put it away" in October with a simple announcement: "I shall go to Korea." Americans had confidence that Ike's military and diplomatic experience would enable him to find a way out of the bloody stalemate that then existed in that war-torn country. With that, the campaign effectively ended. Eisenhower won a smashing victory in November.

He rescued the Republican Party, and maybe America's two-party system, too. He won 33,778,963 popular votes (54.9 percent) and 442 electoral votes. Stevenson garnered 27,314,992 popular votes (44.4 percent) and just eighty-nine electoral votes. Stevenson gained three million votes on Truman's 1948 total, but it was not enough to avoid being buried by the tidal wave of "I Like Ike."

It's commonplace to say Eisenhower had no political experience before entering the White House. While it is certainly true he had held no elective office, it is also true that he had operated with distinction in the highly political atmosphere of the prewar army and had superintended the greatest international wartime coalition in history. He knew Churchill, Roosevelt, Truman, Marshall, de Gaulle, and the Soviet military leaders on a personal basis. In the dangerous new world the United States faced in the 1950s, few Americans could equal his breadth and depth of experience.

More importantly for a leader of a democracy, Ike was a man of the people. The pompous Dewey, the cold, distant Taft, the grand and glorious MacArthur—all lacked Ike's approachable manner. Dwight D. Eisenhower, the son of the American prairie, might have been Rudyard Kipling's model for his poem "If."

> If you can talk with crowds and keep your virtue,
> Or walk with Kings—nor lose the common touch . . .

II. The Kremlin's Long Shadow

Ike wasted no time in keeping his most famous campaign pledge. In November 1952, he traveled to Korea, visiting the troops and getting a firsthand assessment of the military situation. President Truman, now a "lame duck," offered the president-elect a government plane for the trip "if" he still intended to go. Eisenhower considered that *if* an insult to his integrity.[10] It was the first serious chill in the relationship between the two Midwesterners who had achieved so much together. Americans were thrilled to see their famous general eating chow off a tin tray with obviously delighted enlisted men.

As divisive as the Korean War was, there was no anti-Americanism seeping its way into popular entertainment. James Michener's *Bridges at Toko-Ri,* to be sure, explored some of the ambiguity of fighting a war that was sometimes called "the forgotten war." But Michener did not question American motives. NBC television produced the highly-rated *Victory at Sea.* This World War II series featured soaring, triumphal music by Broadway's top composer, Richard Rodgers.* For millions of returning American veterans of WWII, such fare was a way to convey to their children their answer to the question: "What did you do in the war, Daddy?"

Taking the oath at the Capitol on 20 January 1953, President Eisenhower was the first Republican in twenty years to form an administration. Americans cheered and sophisticates sneered as Ike led the nation in prayer:

> Give us, we pray, the power to discern clearly right from wrong, and allow all our words and actions to be governed thereby, and by all the laws of this land. Especially we pray that our concern shall be for all the people, regardless of station, race, or calling.[11]

Cynics were quick to point out that Ike had never joined a church prior to his coming to the White House. True, but he had never joined a political

* Richard Rodgers penned Broadway songs as young as sixteen years old, but it was his later partnership with Oscar Hammerstein that would immortalize his name. Rodgers and Hammerstein's hits include *Oklahoma!*, *Carousel*, *South Pacific*, *The King and I*, and *The Sound of Music.*

party, either. The young evangelist Reverend Billy Graham did not agree with the cynics' view of Ike. Graham knew Eisenhower well. Ike had invited him to come to Paris when Ike was the head of the Supreme Headquarters Allied Powers Europe (SHAPE). Eisenhower had even invited the young evangelical leader to come to his Chicago hotel when he was nominated for president to advise him on his acceptance speech. Graham recalls, "Eisenhower was a very religious man."[12]

Many changes were in store. Eisenhower would speak of "moral rearmament" to meet the threat of atheistic Communism and would urge Congress to add the words "under God" to the Pledge of Allegiance. The Knights of Columbus, a Catholic men's group, had been lobbying tirelessly for the change. With Ike's backing, Congress readily complied.

Just weeks after his inauguration, President Eisenhower received stunning news. On 5 March 1953, the Kremlin announced the death of Josef Vissarionovich Stalin. It is not clear even today exactly how Stalin died.* Did Nikita Khrushchev prevent the dictator from receiving medical attention? Or had Stalin's latest purge, part of the so-called Jewish Doctors' Plot, deprived him of care because all doctors were terrified to go near him? Natan Sharansky, today an Israeli cabinet member, recalled his father sending him off to a Moscow kindergarten that morning with stern instructions: When the other children cry, you cry. When they write poems to praise Stalin, you write them, too. Never reveal the joy that seized the hearts of millions of Soviet Jews in their crowded apartments. Even as he died, Stalin was preparing a new purge of highly placed Soviet Jews.

Outside the grim walls of the Kremlin, however, little of this was known. Here at home, Eisenhower was presented with a horrible decision on becoming president. Would he allow the execution of convicted atomic spies Julius and Ethel Rosenberg to proceed, or would he grant executive clemency?

---

* "Never point your finger at God," an elderly woman in a Ukrainian church scolded Dirk Mroezek, an American missionary who was pointing to the biblical passage John 3:16 carved in the church's ceiling in the 1990s. But that is exactly the last recorded gesture of the dying Stalin. His daughter Svetlana later wrote of his death bed scene: "He suddenly opened his eyes and cast a glance over everyone in the room. It was a terrible glance. Then something incomprehensible and awesome happened. He suddenly lifted his left hand as though he were pointing to something above and bringing down a curse upon all of us. The next moment after a final effort the spirit wrenched its self free of the flesh."

It had been the Truman administration that prosecuted the Rosenbergs. Judge Irving Kaufman, who presided at their trial, was a Democratic appointee, not a Republican.

Time magazine reported the verdict in its 16 April 1951 issue. In sentencing them to death, Judge Kaufman had sternly told the Rosenbergs:

> Plain, deliberate, contemplated murder is dwarfed in magnitude by comparison with the crime you have committed. I believe your conduct in putting into the hands of the Russians the A-bomb . . . has already caused the Communist aggression in Korea . . . and who knows but that millions more of innocent people may pay the price of your treason.[13]

World figures like Pope Pius XII and Albert Einstein appealed to the new president for clemency. Leftists around the world soon accused Eisenhower of anti-Semitism. International Communism raised a hue and cry against Ike personally. Communist novelist Howard Fast wrote that the "stale smell of fascism" was detected around Eisenhower by "the Jewish masses of our country."[14]

This was an obscene charge against the man who had forced German civilians to walk through liberated Nazi death camps and who had ordered army filmmakers to record for posterity the irrefutable evidence of the Holocaust. Ike maintained a dignified silence as the convicted spies went to their deaths in the electric chair at Sing Sing Prison in New York.[15]*

President Eisenhower was able to announce the ceasefire in Korea on 27 July 1953. This uneasy truce has lasted until the present day. The Korean War killed 36,000 Americans, 600,000 Chinese and some 2,000,000 North and South Koreans.[16] The De-Militarized Zone (DMZ) separating North and South Korea along the 38th Parallel remains one of the most volatile borders on earth.

In this early Cold War atmosphere of real treason, rumored treason,

---

* French Communist Party boss Jacques Duclos was a hard-line Stalinst. He attacked America, explaining that the conviction of the atomic spies in America was anti-Semitism but that the execution of *eight* Communists, all Jews, in Czechoslovakia was not. (Source: Radosh and Radosh, *Commies*, 46.)

and fear of espionage, Senator Joseph McCarthy had risen to power and prominence. Campaigning in McCarthy's home state of Wisconsin, Eisenhower failed to defend his friend and sponsor, General Marshall, from McCarthy's vicious attacks. Eisenhower privately told associates he *refused* "to get into a pissing contest with that skunk."[17] Eisenhower knew that McCarthy—like all demagogues—thrived on publicity. It was like oxygen to a fire. Eisenhower said, "I really believe that nothing will be so effective in combating his particular kind of troublemaking as to ignore him. This he cannot stand."[18] He sent to the Senate the nomination of Charles "Chip" Bohlen as his ambassador to the Soviet Union.[19] It was an indirect challenge to McCarthy and McCarthy's cohorts. Bohlen had been FDR's interpreter at Yalta. Ike's action proved he was determined to be his own man and to have his own men around him—whether McCarthy liked it or not.

President Eisenhower invoked executive privilege to keep McCarthy from going on a "fishing expedition." Whether it's fishing to "hook" embarrassing details or legitimate legislative oversight is sometimes in the eye of the beholder, but Ike had a growing number of supporters using the tools at their disposal to oppose the senator. Veteran CBS newsman Edward R. Murrow opposed McCarthy on his popular television broadcast *See it Now.* "We cannot defend freedom by *deserting* it at home," he said.[20] The Senate's only woman, Maine's Republican Margaret Chase Smith, fearlessly took on McCarthy.

When McCarthy dragged Ike's beloved army before his committee, the same television cameras that had aided McCarthy's rise would become his undoing. McCarthy tried to "investigate" the promotion of a left-wing *dentist* at Fort Monmouth, New Jersey. (And was the good dentist putting radioactive fillings in the G.I.s' teeth so the Communists could trace them on the battlefield?) Republican senator Ralph Flanders of Vermont ridiculed McCarthy:

> Whole countries are now being taken over by the Communists . . . the world seems to be mobilizing for the great battle of Armageddon. . . . [But Senator McCarthy] dons his war paint. He goes into his war dance. He emits war whoops. He goes forth to battle and proudly returns with the scalp of a pink dentist.[21]

Roy Cohn and G. David Schine were young staff members on McCarthy's committee.* They had gone on a taxpayer-funded junket through Europe, descending on U.S. Embassies and sniffing out subversive literature in U.S.-funded libraries. The president, in a commencement address at Dartmouth, denounced "book burners"—a clear reference to the antics of Cohn and Schine.[22] Unleashed by Ike's closest advisers, the army let it be known that McCarthy's attack dog, Roy Cohn, had sought special treatment for his young associate, G. David Schine, when Schine was drafted. Cohn even used his influence to have Private Schine exempted from K.P.,** the army disclosed.[23]

McCarthy's constant badgering of witnesses, his unstable personal conduct, and his general recklessness was his undoing. He interrupted a witness to make sure that some damaging information about a young lawyer was put in the record—and broadcast on national television. The lawyer in question had once belonged to the Communist-backed National Lawyers' Guild. Now he worked for the same law firm that represented the army at the Army-McCarthy hearings. The army's attorney, the proper Bostonian Joseph Welch, skewered McCarthy with this famous retort:

> Until this moment, Senator, I think I never really gauged your cruelty or your recklessness. Let us not assassinate this lad further, Senator; you've done enough. Have you no sense of decency, sir? At long last, have you left no sense of decency?[24]

McCarthy supporters were set to go after Ralphe Bunche, the Nobel Peace Prize winner. Ike was incensed. He told aides that Bunche was "a superior man, a credit to our country. I just can't stand by and permit a man like that to be chopped to pieces because of McCarthy feeling."[25] In the end, Bunche told White House aides he could handle his case alone. Dr. Bunche testified before the House Un-American Activities Committee. Still, when Ike asked Bunche to come to a quiet White House dinner, the skilled black diplomat gratefully accepted.[26]

---

* Robert F. Kennedy also served briefly on McCarthy's committee.

** K.P. means "kitchen patrol" and involves routine duties such as peeling potatoes and scrubbing pots and pans.

Eisenhower always thought McCarthy was more interested in hunting headlines than catching Communists.[27] Eisenhower surely knew the old saw: "Give a man enough rope and he'll hang himself." He gave McCarthy enough rope in the Army-McCarthy hearings, as he took command of the administration's efforts to clip McCarthy's wings.[28]

The rope this time was the coaxial cable of the television camera. Like the mythical Icarus, McCarthy flew high on wings of his own fashioning. Flying too close to the sun—in this case the glare of national publicity—the wax melted and he plummeted to earth.

McCarthy was soon censured by the full Senate by an overwhelming 67–22.[29]* The vote was taken 2 December 1954, less than two years after Eisenhower came to office. Behind the scenes, Ike urged Republicans to back the censure motion.[30] It was an outstanding example of what has been called "The Hidden-hand Presidency."

Three years later, still drinking heavily, Joe McCarthy died. He was, at forty-nine, a burnt-out case. As Michael Barone writes of him, he was "utterly *unscrupulous, untethered* to any truth, *unhampered* by any sense of fairness, and *undisciplined* by any desire to accomplish a concrete goal."[31] Worst of all, McCarthy besmirched the honorable cause of anti-Communism. He discredited *legitimate* efforts to counter Soviet subversion of American institutions. From this point on, it would only be necessary for disloyal people or groups to yell "McCarthyism" to distract public attention from real problems. For too long, McCarthy had operated with the active cooperation of mainstream Republican politicians like Senator Robert A. Taft and Senator William F. Knowland. He was even defended by the brilliant young William F. Buckley Jr. Unfortunately, McCarthy's fall did not serve as a cautionary tale to all Americans. Robert Welch, founder of the fiercely anti-Communist John Birch Society, became convinced that President Eisenhower was "a conscious agent of the Communist conspiracy."[32]

---

* Conspicuously *not* voting was young Senator John F. Kennedy. JFK had been hospitalized for a life-threatening back operation. Thus, he avoided voting to censure the man whom his father had befriended, a man who had been a guest in his home and who had dated his sister. Jack Kennedy would later joke that if reporters quizzed him while he was being wheeled into surgery on a gurney, he would cry out, "O! My back!" Mrs. Eleanor Roosevelt was not amused. She would later say JFK needed to show more courage, less *profile.*

This ridiculous charge was made against the man who had written in his memoir, with evident horror, of the Soviet method of clearing a minefield *by marching right through it*! Marshal Zhukov personally confirmed this method when Ike visited Moscow in 1945.[33] The Soviets' blatant disregard for human life—like the Nazis' concentration camps—made a deep impression on the humane Eisenhower.

III. Freedom Rising

> Communism inspires and enables its militant preachers to exploit injustices and inequity among men. This ideology appeals, not to the Italian or Frenchman or South American as such, but to men as human beings who become desperate in the attempt to satisfy common human needs. Therein it possesses a profound power for expansion. Wherever popular discontent is founded on group oppression or mass poverty or the hunger of children, there Communism may stage an offensive that arms cannot counter. Discontent can be fanned into revolution, and revolution into social chaos. The sequel is dictatorial rule. Against such tactics exclusive reliance on military might is vain.[34]

Volumes have been written on the appeal, the danger, and the appropriate responses to international Communism. No one understood its challenge better than Dwight D. Eisenhower. This passage from his best-selling war memoir, *Crusade in Europe*, makes this clear. Ike was a man widely lampooned as unintellectual, lazy, and doddering by members of an adversary culture. But this revealing passage shows his penetrating grasp of the issues and his keen insight into Communism's mesmerizing and dangerous appeal.

In this context, Eisenhower's refusal to repeal the New Deal and his encouragement of policies that brought greater material abundance to average Americans can be seen as the most effective defense of freedom. Let workers earn that new car, a television, and a summer cabin by the lake and there will be nothing to fear from Red agitation. America and Western Europe in the Eisenhower years enjoyed unprecedented prosperity.

Eisenhower went to Geneva in 1955 to meet with the new Soviet Communist leaders, Nikolai Bulganin and Nikita Khrushchev. Ike was joined by his British and French allies. He boldly offered an "Open Skies" proposal—an attempt to ease international tensions by allowing both sides to fly over each others' countries. Khrushchev, quickly emerging as the real power in the Kremlin, turned down Ike's idea. But the "thaw" in the Cold War brought about by "The Spirit of Geneva" soothed raw nerves on both sides of the Iron Curtain.

At home, Eisenhower's appointee as chief justice, Californian Earl Warren, moved quickly to respond to the issue of racial segregation in schools. What Warren lacked in legal background and constitutional subtlety he more than made up in skillful personal relations. Warren steered the Supreme Court to produce the landmark *Brown v. Board of Education* decision during his first term. By a vote of 9–0, the U.S. Supreme Court struck down racial segregation in public education.* Freedom was rising.

Eisenhower has been much criticized for his failure publicly to endorse the Court's decision. But he felt that doing so would set an undesirable precedent. If a president endorsed decisions he agreed with, might he feel compelled to oppose decisions he did not agree with? And what would that do to the rule of law? "The Supreme Court has spoken and I am sworn to uphold . . . the constitutional processes. . . . I will obey."[35] Another reason for Eisenhower's restrained response was his concern that some Southern states might close down their public school systems altogether rather than integrate them. In that event, Ike feared that all students, black as well as white, would be handicapped if this happened.[36]

For lead attorney Thurgood Marshall and other leaders of the NAACP, who had fought for so long for freedom, it was an incredible victory. Thurgood Marshall had counted no more than *four* votes for desegregation on the Court when Harry Truman's good friend, Fred Vinson, was chief justice.[37] Now, in 1954, Ike's nominee, Earl Warren, had seemingly wrought a miracle.

---

* The pre-Warren Court might have rendered a ruling favorable to integration, but strategists worried that a divided Court would strengthen resistance. The unanimous ruling Warren engineered was considered essential to popular acceptance of the Court's decision in *Brown*.

Freedom is contagious. Instead of resting on the hard-won victory of the NAACP in *Brown v. Board,* leaders pressed for more. Civil rights was in the air. The *very* next year, a black seamstress in Montgomery, Alabama, refused to give up her seat on a city bus. The young Reverend Martin Luther King Jr. immediately protested the arrest of Mrs. Rosa Parks. Her tax dollars paid for those buses, too. So did Dr. King's. Quickly, Dr. King organized a boycott of the city bus lines. He held the boycott under a tight discipline. Citing the Prophet Amos, King assured everyone there would be no violence:

> I want it to be known throughout Montgomery and throughout this nation that we are—a Christian people. . . . And we are determined here in Montgomery to work and fight, until justice runs down like water and righteousness as a mighty stream![38]

One reason Dr. King felt he had to emphasize the Christian and *constitutional* nature of his crusade for civil rights was because the civil rights movement had been dogged by charges of Communist infiltration. His statements of faith did not offend liberal supporters. The Democratic Congress had just passed and Eisenhower quickly signed a bill to make "In God We Trust" our official motto. The Republican president and Democratic congressional leaders believed—as Truman did before them—that it was important to draw a line between America's commitment to religious freedom and Soviet atheist propaganda. The Reverend Dr. King emphasized his Christian principles. He returned again and again to the Declaration of Independence and the Constitution as his sources of authority.*

Even so, Dr. King's opponents charged that his Montgomery Bus Boycott was Communist-inspired. FBI Director J. Edgar Hoover pointed to the presence of Bayard Rustin, who functioned as an adviser to Dr. King's organization. Rustin had been a member of the Young Communist League in the 1930s. By the 1950s, he had put his Communist ties behind him. An

* This author once received a compliment from Coretta Scott King for taking care to emphasize the fact that Martin Luther King Jr. was a *Reverend.*

avowed homosexual, he had been arrested on a morals charge in California.[39] Dr. King's white lawyer, Stanley Levinson, however, did have undeniable ties to the Communist Party. Clearly, however, Director Hoover had not read Dwight D. Eisenhower's thoughts on Communism. Dr. King's opponents could have no answer for his strongly *American* inspiration. King said, "The great glory of American democracy is the right of the people to protest for [their] right[s]."[40] From this perspective, how could it be maintained that Americans rejected being treated as second-class citizens only because Communist agitators had stirred them up?

The Montgomery Bus Boycott lasted more than a year, with hundreds of volunteers supplying rides to people who ordinarily needed bus transportation to get to work, to go to church, or even to shop. The city appealed to the courts to stop the carpooling. Several black churches, including that of the Reverend Ralph David Abernathy, King's closest friend, were firebombed. A white Lutheran pastor who served a black parish had his home bombed.[41] Dr. King, shaken by the violence, stunned his congregation with his tearful prayer: "Lord, I hope no one will have to die as a result of our struggle for freedom. . . . But if anyone has to die, let it be me!"[42]

With a stroke of the pen, the U.S. Supreme Court handed down a ruling declaring all segregation on public buses unconstitutional.[43]

Overnight, Dr. Martin Luther King Jr. became *the* recognized leader of the civil rights movement. He was profiled in the *New York Times* magazine and put on the cover of *Time*. President Eisenhower invited him, with other leading black Americans, to a meeting in the Oval Office. This was the first such meeting since President Lincoln had invited Frederick Douglass to confer on civil rights during the Civil War.[44]*

Most adult black and white Americans were wage earners in 1955. Whether or not they were members of organized unions, the amalgamation of the American Federation of Labor (AFL) and the Congress of Industrial Organizations (CIO) was big news for them. George Meany and Walter Reuther were both strongly anti-Communist. They were firm

* TR had famously invited Dr. Booker T. Washington to dinner at the White House in 1901—and suffered great abuse from white racists for it. But that was a social invitation, not a formal conference on civil rights.

advocates for civil rights. They knew that workers in the Soviet bloc enjoyed no right to strike and no right to bargain collectively. The new AFL-CIO would prove to be a bulwark *against* Communist expansion, both in the United States and around the world. Free labor could be relied upon in the worldwide struggle for freedom.

Suddenly, the nation was stunned to learn in the autumn of 1955 that President Eisenhower had suffered a serious heart attack. Contrasting sharply with the experience of Wilson, Harding, and FDR, however, Ike resolved to tell the American people *everything* about his illness. His press secretary, Jim Hagerty, gave full and detailed descriptions of the president's medical condition.[45] Hagerty's briefings calmed the jittery public, but they did more: they set the standard for full disclosure of the people's right to know.* "Sunshine," as Justice Brandeis said, "is the best disinfectant." Never was this wise saying truer than in the matter of presidential health.

In 1956, Eisenhower was willing to challenge politics-as-usual. He even explored the idea of running with Ohio's *Democratic* Governor, Frank Lausche. The president admired Lausche's common sense and wanted to be the first to put a Catholic on the ticket.[46]

Not surprisingly, the man who was just one heartbeat away from the presidency in 1956 did not take kindly to being nudged aside. Vice President Richard M. Nixon wasn't biting when Ike tried to lure him away. The president urged Nixon to take four years as secretary of defense to give him "executive experience." Ike prized it. Nixon prized power more and refused to step down. It is little wonder that Eisenhower responded to his doctors with irritation. They warned him to avoid "frustration, anxiety, fear, and above all anger." Ike shot back: "Just what do you think the Presidency *is*?"[47]

Frustrated or not, Eisenhower ran on a slogan of "Peace and Prosperity" in 1956. His opponent, once again, was Adlai E. Stevenson. This time, Stevenson chose not to team up with Senator John Sparkman, the Alabama segregationist who had been his 1952 running mate. Instead, he opened the vice presidential selection up to the delegates at the Democratic National

---

* Ike's example would be followed by presidents Johnson, Ford, Carter, Reagan, and both Bushes. Kennedy, Nixon, and Clinton, however, would decline to take the American people into their confidence about their health.

Convention. There was real excitement as delegates were allowed to make their own choices. Senator Estes Kefauver of Tennessee narrowly edged out Senator John F. Kennedy of Massachusetts. Kefauver had bravely resisted signing the Southern Manifesto, a segregationist petition circulated among senators from that region. Lyndon Johnson of Texas and Albert Gore Sr., also of Tennessee, had also declined to sign.

Eisenhower suffered a bout of ileitis—a potentially life-threatening disease—in June. Even so close to the election, however, Hagerty continued to fully brief reporters on the president's health. Ike recovered rapidly.

Illness wasn't the only problem facing Ike. The campaign was interrupted by simultaneous foreign crises. The British and the French responded with force when Egypt's dictator, Gamal Abdel Nasser, closed the Suez Canal. Coordinating their attack with Israel, they sought to open the canal to international shipping. Eisenhower responded with indignation. He was furious at not being consulted by his NATO allies, and he branded their action aggression. Humiliated by Eisenhower, Prime Minister Anthony Eden withdrew and soon resigned. It was the first serious split between the United States and Great Britain since Grover Cleveland's day.

Behind the Iron Curtain, the Spirit of Geneva from the year before proved ephemeral. Hungarian workers joined in a revolt just before the 1956 presidential election in the United States, trying to wrench their freedom-loving country out of the Soviet sphere. For a while, it seemed to be working as a more liberal regime under Communist Imre Nagy was installed in Budapest. Soon, however, Soviet tanks rolled in and tens of thousands of Hungarian freedom fighters were crushed. Khrushchev, now the unchallenged Soviet dictator, harshly blamed Western agitation for the revolt. It was Soviet tyranny that kindled the flames of revolution, but it is also true that the Hungarians were encouraged by Voice of America broadcasts. When they rose up and Eisenhower did not intervene, there was bitter disillusionment all over Eastern Europe. In the United States, many freedom-loving Americans reproached Ike for failing to "roll back the Iron Curtain."*

---

* Nearly fifty years after the Hungarian Revolt was crushed, a decade after the Iron Curtain came down, conservative leader Paul Weyrich still sharply condemned Eisenhower for not coming to the aid of the heroic Hungarians.

Despite Nixon's contempt on the campaign trail for that "cowardly college of Communist containment," containment was Eisenhower's policy, too. Ike was determined to avoid losing any more countries to Communist subversion. But he was equally firm about avoiding a Third World War that might have resulted from an attempt to free Eastern European satellites by force.

The initial hesitation of the Soviets to suppress the Hungarian freedom fighters gave false hopes to the world. We now know that China's Mao Zedong put fierce pressure on Khrushchev and his Kremlin comrades to crack down brutally.[48] All that Lenin achieved would be lost if they showed weakness at this critical moment.

Mao would hardly be deterred by the universal condemnation of the civilized world. He saw Stalin as his model. In the agrarian reforms, Stalin had killed seven million; Mao himself killed an estimated forty million Chinese in his reforms[49]

Stevenson had little chance to move ahead. The election returns showed another landslide for the invincibly popular Eisenhower. With typical wit, Adlai Stevenson quoted Lincoln's story of the little boy who stubbed his toe in the dark: "I'm too big to cry," said the lad, "but it hurts too much to laugh." Ike swept every region outside the Deep South. And he even won several Southern states, including Virginia, Tennessee, Kentucky, Louisiana, Texas, and Florida. It was the best showing ever for a Republican. Nationwide, Ike piled up 457 electoral votes and 35,581,003 popular votes (57.6 percent). Stevenson trailed with just 73 electoral votes from the Deep South and 25,738,765 popular votes (41.6 percent).

Eisenhower's popularity was not shared by his party, however. Unlike the Republican sweep of 1952, this time the Democrats retained control of *both* Houses of Congress. Political commentators speak of "the coattail effect" (when a candidate for president or governor pulls in candidates for lesser offices and other candidates just hang on to their leader's coattails). Political humorists were quick to jibe in 1956 that the famed Eisenhower jacket—the military style Ike made famous in World War II—"has no coattails."

Privately, Ike did not even *want* some of his fellow Republicans elected. Of the GOP Senate leader William F. Knowland, for example, Eisenhower wrote that in his case there seemed to be no final answer to the question: "How *stupid* can you get?"[50] He was impatient with some Republicans who called for eliminating Social Security, abolishing the minimum wage, and repealing farm programs and labor legislation, including unemployment compensation.[51] Ike wrote his brother Edgar *opposing* that businessman's conservative ideals. To attempt what Edgar proposed, he said, would be political suicide.[52] Eisenhower promoted what he called "Modern Republicanism." His "flaming middle of the road" positions led conservative Barry Goldwater to dismiss Eisenhower's administration as "a dime store New Deal."

Young conservatives rallied to the standard of *The National Review.* This brash, new journal was founded in 1955 by William F. Buckley Jr. Buckley took pains to avoid the extremism of the John Birchers and the anti-Semites. He rejected the racism of some who claimed to be conservatives. His feisty publication lost money, but it gained a following. And conservative books became best-sellers, too. More than six hundred thousand readers had pored over Friedrich A. Hayek's *The Road to Serfdom* since its publication in 1944. Hayek showed with admirable clarity and logic how even *democratic* socialism would lead to a loss of fundamental freedoms. Hayek was never a popular author to the extent that everyone was reading him at the corner newsstand. But the Austrian refugee showed how the *roots* of Hitler's tyranny and the bases of Marxist collectivism were one and the same. His work had a profound influence on a generation of freedom loving young conservatives.

Even Hayek might have approved of Eisenhower's pet public works projects. Early in his presidency, Ike overruled Pennsylvania and Ohio steel interests in approving the Saint Lawrence Seaway Project. Canada, impatient with decades of delay, was planning to go ahead alone with the massive effort to make the ports of the Great Lakes accessible to ocean-going vessels. President Eisenhower soon recognized the national defense implications of the project.[53] Looking beyond the narrower economic interests, Ike opted for full cooperation with the Canadians. The project is one of the world's greatest examples of peaceful international cooperation. The Soviet Union could point to no similar example of trust and mutual respect with any of its threatened neighbors.

In 1956, President Eisenhower persuaded the Democratic Congress to support his plan for an Interstate Highway System. Ever since 1920, when Major Eisenhower led an army truck convoy on a two-month expedition across the Continent, he had known that the world's richest country was hampered by seriously inadequate roads.[54] As the Supreme Allied Commander in World War II, he saw the advantages Hitler had from the excellent German autobahns. As president, he was determined to bring America into the twentieth century. Congress authorized Ike's plan, a massive road building project. The forty thousand miles of Eisenhower's Interstate Highway System was the largest public works project in our history.[55] It was comparable to the Roman roads, the pyramids, and the Great Wall of China.* It changed America forever.**

President Eisenhower faced two major crises in 1957. The locally elected school board of Little Rock, Arkansas, voted to comply with the *Brown* ruling. They began to *desegregate* the city's schools, if slowly, beginning in the fall of 1957. Nine black students were registered for classes at the city's Central High School. When some whites protested, Democratic Governor Orval Faubus called out the Arkansas National Guard to block the black students' registering. President Eisenhower ordered the Justice Department to go into federal court to demand the governor withdraw his state's troops. Faubus gave in, but riots by white protesters broke out as the black students began their classes. Quickly, Ike sent in the 101st Airborne Division to protect the black students and enforce the law. The 101st remained at the school for several months to ensure order.

Ike knew well the splendid fighting qualities of the 101st Airborne: he had ordered "the Screaming Eagles" to lead the Normandy invasion thirteen years before. The president went on national television to explain his action. Pointing to the watching world, he called on all Americans to show respect for the laws. His goal was to restore "peace and order and a blot upon the fair

---

* The Romans built more than 50,000 miles of roads; the Great Wall of China is 4,500 miles long. (2004 Edition of *World Book Encyclopedia*, Vol. 16, 361 and Vol. 8, 349, respectively.) Both projects, of course, required *centuries* to complete. And neither project was built by *free* men.

** The final estimate of the cost of the Interstate System was issued in 1991. It estimated that the total cost would be $128.9 billion, with a federal share of $114.3 billion. This estimate covered only the mileage (42,795 miles) built under the Interstate Construction Program. (Online source: http://www.fhwa.dot.gov/interstate/faq.htm#question6.)

name and high honor of our nation in the world will be removed." Eisenhower knew that Little Rock was being exploited by Soviet propaganda.[56]

Eisenhower sent in the troops to Little Rock knowing it might cause his Republican Party dearly in elections in this region. But duty came first for Ike. Leading Democrats criticized President Eisenhower's use of federal troops. Georgia's senator Richard Russell compared Eisenhower's actions to Hitler's.[57] Also, ironically, among those condemning Ike's use of force were Senators John F. Kennedy and Lyndon B. Johnson.[58]

Little Rock was knocked off the front pages by a chunk of heavy metal. The Soviet Union stunned the world by launching *Sputnik,* the first earth satellite. In Russian the word means "fellow traveler," but for Americans it meant trouble. For two hundred years, Americans felt sheltered by thousands of miles of open ocean. After Sputnik, the heartland of America was vulnerable to nuclear attack by Intercontinental Ballistic Missiles (ICBMs). Americans shuddered.

A reporter asked Eisenhower if the launch of the Sputnik didn't prove the superiority of Communism over capitalism. After all, he said, Khrushchev was boasting that the hammer-and-sickle flag was flying on the moon. "I think it's crazy," Ike responded. "We should not be hysterical when dictatorships do these things."[59]

Khrushchev saw it differently.

IV. "We Will *Bury* You!"

"We will *bury* you!" shouted the ebullient Nikita Khrushchev in 1956. Khrushchev presented a new challenge to America's political, military, and diplomatic supremacy. Unlike the cautious, secretive Joseph Stalin who rarely left his Kremlin apartments, it seemed Khrushchev was everywhere. He traveled extensively outside the USSR, especially in the nonaligned countries of Asia and Africa. The "winds of change" that followed decolonization of the British and French Empires were blowing strongly in favor of socialism.

Khrushchev exercised a rough, peasant charm and a crude sense of humor. A highly intelligent, shrewd survivor of numberless Kremlin purges and plots, he was a short, roly-poly bald man with prominent warts and a fifty-two-inch waistline. But he moved like a thin man. Khrushchev moved vigorously, creating the impression of a Soviet Union leading the way into the future. When Sputnik bleep-bleeped its way across the skies every ninety minutes, Khrushchev pointed to this coup as evidence of Soviet technological superiority. The Soviets, he said, would win the space race.

Americans did not know they were even *in* a space race. The Soviet satellite program was launched in total secrecy. That contributed to the shock. Again, Jim Hagerty's response was total openness. America would invite the world to watch the United States launch its own earth satellite. Hagerty was surely right, but this decision had disastrous consequences for American prestige—at least in the short run. As the world looked on, several U.S. rockets blew up on the launch pad. "Kaput-nik" teased irreverent headline writers. A cartoonist showed a golf ball trailing Sputnik in orbit. Maybe the president, an enthusiastic golfer, could put that in orbit! It was an international embarrassment. Senator Kennedy and Governor Nelson Rockefeller, a dissident Republican, began speaking of the "missile gap." They said the United States had fallen behind the Soviets during Eisenhower's watch. The charge was untrue.

Ike knew it was untrue. When Khrushchev had shot down Ike's "Open Skies" proposal at Geneva in 1955, the president authorized secret flights over the USSR. The high-flying American U-2 jets provided U.S. intelligence with a treasure trove of information. Ike was angry that his political opponents were taking advantage of his enforced silence.[60]

Similarly, the United States had a great advantage in submarines. In 1958, the USS *Nautilus,* the world's first nuclear-powered submarine, went from the Pacific to the Atlantic *under the polar ice cap.* (Later *Nautilus* would surface at the North Pole to claim the prize of centuries.) At last, the Northwest Passage had been discovered! Led by the genius of Admiral Hyman G. Rickover, the United States' nuclear submarine force provided America and the world with the means of "massive retaliation." In a dangerous and violent world, Rickover's "boomers" and attack submarines would provide the "nuclear umbrella" that sheltered America's freedom.

President Eisenhower named Admiral Rickover as his personal representative for New York City's ticker tape parade down Broadway to welcome home the USS *Nautilus.* It was a gracious invitation for the old West Pointer to give to a graduate of rival Annapolis. And Admiral Rickover, as usual, promised not to be an easy guest in the Big Apple. The navy brass wanted all participants to appear in sharply creased dress whites. Rickover, a three-star admiral, claimed not to have any dress whites—and, besides, he preferred his working khaki uniform.[61] It was vintage Rickover.

The "father of the nuclear navy," Rickover had been putting tacks on the chairs of navy bigwigs for nearly four decades. He had arrived at Ellis Island as a six-year-old immigrant child. His mother and siblings already had their papers marked "Deported" when his father arrived at the last minute to claim them.[62] At the Naval Academy, weighing barely 125 pounds, young Rickover had to fight with other midshipmen who insulted his Jewish background. A fellow Jewish "mid" had suffered the indignity of having his page of the Academy yearbook perforated—for easy tearing out.[63] But Rickover prevailed over pride, prejudice, and pressure.

Admiral Rickover probably wasn't kidding when he said he didn't own the ceremonial dress whites the navy loves. He typically showed up for the maiden cruises of "his" nuclear submarines in a business suit. The submarine's crew had been instructed by their skipper to provide the admiral's uniform and all toilet articles he would need. Rickover's bags contained crisp, official stationery and the prototype of a word-processing machine.

When the new submarine performed up to his most exacting standards, the admiral would unlimber his equipment and print out scores of letters from the bottom of the sea to influential members of Congress and captains of industry.[64] Rickover became a legendary figure in the navy. He rose on the basis of smarts and dedication—and carefully maintained connections on Capitol Hill. Rickover stepped on hundreds of toes. "They called me that ugly SOB; they called me that mean SOB," Rickover told his longtime aide Bill Bass, "but they never called me that dumb SOB."

Thanks to Rickover's genius and ceaseless demands for rigorous safety standards, America quickly developed a submarine force to prevail over any possibility of a sneak attack by the Soviets using nuclear weapons. It was done at comparatively low cost and with the greatest regard for the human lives of America's nuclear sailors. There would be no "marching through minefields" under Dwight D. Eisenhower.

Ike knew we were ahead of the Soviets, and he refused to give in to politically inspired panic for a raid on the Treasury. Eisenhower alone had the military expertise and prestige to stand fast. It took strength and courage. Again, Kipling could have been describing Ike:

> If you can keep your head when all about you
> Are losing theirs and blaming it on you.

V. Ike's Last Years

Eisenhower's "New Look" in defense had increased America's reliance on nuclear weapons. His secretary of state, John Foster Dulles, had spoken of "Massive Retaliation" against the Soviets if they invaded Western Europe. This reliance on nuclear supremacy also enabled Eisenhower to reduce federal spending. Ike also used the new CIA to destabilize or topple left-wing regimes he considered hostile to U.S. interests. He favored covert action in getting rid of Iran's left-wing Mohammed Mossadegh in 1953. Mossadegh had been *Time*'s Man of the Year in 1951 (it must have been a slow news year). The CIA's man in Tehran then was Kermit Roosevelt, TR's grandson.[65] Ike's CIA repeated this success by ousting Guatemala's President Jacobo Arbenz Guzmán the following year. Guzmán was working with Guatemalan Communists to take over landed estates in the Central American republic. Eisenhower was determined not to allow Communism to expand into the Western hemisphere.

With the death of Secretary of State John Foster Dulles in 1959, a famous anti-Communist leader was lost. Dulles had been very controversial. Churchill said he was a bull who carried his own china shop around with him. But Dulles had been willing, more than willing, to take the hard stances while Ike basked in the glow of international goodwill. Ike was hailed on his trip to India as the "Prince of Peace." Still, we now know that Eisenhower had approved and supported Dulles's "brinkmanship."* It was that old American game of "good cop [Ike], bad cop [Dulles]." And it worked.

Nonetheless, many people worried about war. Hollywood produced in 1959 *Pork Chop Hill*, a movie starring Gregory Peck. Just as *All Quiet on the Western Front* had done twenty years earlier, *Pork Chop Hill* stressed the futility of war.[66] It was based on the hill in Korea that had been taken by American forces, lost to the Chinese, retaken, and finally evacuated, all at the cost of 314 American lives.

Vice President Nixon was confronted by Premier Khrushchev at a U.S. trade exhibit in Moscow in 1959. Khrushchev "debated" Nixon about the gleaming American consumer goods that were displayed. Amid dishwashers and televisions, Khrushchev said the Soviets would move on past the United States in economic development. Waving his hand "bye-bye" and grinning, Khrushchev mugged for the news cameras. One Soviet citizen—and we must hope the KGB never recognized his handwriting—spoke for millions when he wrote in the U.S. guestbook: "Drop me off in America as we pass them by."

When Khrushchev shot down an American U-2 jet days before a scheduled East-West summit conference in Paris in May 1960, Eisenhower fell into an embarrassing trap. At first, the administration issued a cover story—that CIA pilot Francis Gary Powers was actually a weather reconnaissance flyer who'd been blown off course. Khrushchev then let the world know that the pilot had been taken alive, and he had confessed to spying. Ike was caught in a direct lie. When Khrushchev demanded Ike apologize as a condition for going ahead with the summit, Eisenhower refused.

This time, Britain's Prime Minister Harold MacMillan, France's President Charles de Gaulle, and West German chancellor Konrad Adenauer—the democratic leaders of NATO—fully supported President Eisenhower. Senator Kennedy stumbled when he suggested that Eisenhower apologize for the sake of peace.

The 1960 Paris summit collapsed as Khrushchev and the Soviet delegation

---

* Brinkmanship was the liberal criticism of Dulles's announced willingness to go "to the brink of war" to keep the Communists from making territorial gains.

walked out. It was Khrushchev's way of trying to tip the coming American election to the Democrats. Americans, as they so often do in crises, backed President Eisenhower completely.

Eisenhower was criticized by many writers of the adversary culture. Smart, "hip" young comedians like Mort Sahl and Lenny Bruce mercilessly lampooned the fractured syntax and confusing grammar of the old general. Serious social analysts deplored what they saw as stultifying conformity and soulless materialism. John Kenneth Galbraith derided *The Affluent Society* and Sloan Wilson's *The Man in the Grey Flannel Suit* questioned: "What price success?" Cars with wraparound chrome and outrageous fins for mom and dad, a Davy Crockett coonskin cap for Junior, and a "hoola hoop" for sister—all this represented what some saw as the mindlessness of Eisenhower's "Happy Days." Television was denounced as "a vast wasteland" by Federal Communications Commissioner Newton Minow, Adlai Stevenson's law partner. Comedian Fred Allen called television "bubble gum for the eyes."

But television was not just the well-scrubbed version of family life represented by *Ozzie and Harriet*. Host Ed Sullivan presented not only Elvis Presley's "Hound Dog" but also serious opera arias by Richard Tucker and Leontyne Price, the light wit of Victor Borge, and the artistry of mime Marcel Marceau.* Today, we view the 1950s as television's "golden era." Ronald Reagan's weekly announcement of the high-toned *GE Theater* surely contributed to television's popularity—and his.

Those same television sets transmitted Dr. Martin Luther King Jr.'s powerful cry for freedom. In not a few years, those grainy black and white TV news pictures of vicious dogs attacking peaceful civil rights demonstrators would help mightily to form the new *national* consensus for justice and freedom.

Ditto Eisenhower's beloved highway system. Before Ike, hundreds of American communities really were literally isolated. As soon as those four-lane "Interstates" were laid down, however, they could convey buses carrying

* Few who watched Marceau's silent antics on TV would have guessed that his greatest acting role was with the French Underground during World War II. He impersonated a scoutmaster who was taking children on "hikes" into the Alps. In fact, he was helping these Jewish children escape to neutral Switzerland. (Online source: http://movies2.nytimes.com/gst/movies/filmography.html?p_id=45295.)

Freedom Riders to remote towns. The revolutions in communications and transportation that Eisenhower promoted by his policies meant freedom rising. Quietly, Eisenhower filled the benches of the federal judiciary with judges who would fearlessly put an end to racial segregation.[67] Will future generations see these changes, too, as part of the Hidden-hand Presidency?

The late Stephen Ambrose sums up Ike best for us today:

> He was so comforting, so grandfatherly, so calm, so sure of himself, so skillful in managing the economy, so experienced in insuring America's defenses, so expert in his control of the intelligence community, so knowledgeable about the world's affairs, so nonpartisan and objective in his above-the-battle posture, so insistent on holding to the middle of the road that he inspired a trust that was as broad and deep as that of any president since George Washington.[68]

Eisenhower himself once responded to a complimentary letter from Henry Wallace. FDR's second vice president had made a number of speeches comparing Ike favorably with George Washington. Flattered, Ike sent this courteous reply: "My sense of pride is all the greater because I've never [agreed] with those who so glibly deprecate [Washington's] intellectual qualities. I think too many . . . confuse facility of expression with wisdom; a love of the limelight with depth of perception. I've often felt the deep wish that The Good Lord had endowed me with [Washington's] greatness of mind and spirit."[69]

Eisenhower's own assessment of his two terms was typically pithy: "[After Korea], the United States never lost a soldier or a foot of ground in my administration. We kept the peace. People ask how it happened—by God, it didn't just happen, I'll tell you that."[70] With the major exception of Cuba's falling prey to a stealth Communist revolution, Ike's defensive reaction is basically true. To top it all off, millions of Americans who grew up under his wise and good leadership can still say with genuine conviction: *I like Ike!*

Passing the Torch

(1961–1969)

"My fellow Americans: ask not what your country can do for you—ask what you can do for your country." With that thrilling exhortation, John F. Kennedy spurred Americans to action in a fresh new decade. Americans had high hopes that the energy and enthusiasm of the new Kennedy administration would "get the country moving again." JFK wowed the media with prime time press conferences that were nationally broadcast for the first time in our history. Kennedy summoned Americans to "a long twilight struggle" for liberty. He prodded us to go to the moon, and we went. His efforts were less successful in divided Berlin, imprisoned Cuba, and threatened Vietnam. Still, Kennedy faced down a mortal threat of Soviet missiles in Cuba and appealed powerfully to end a century of segregation. JFK was cruelly cut down in broad daylight in Dallas on 22 November 1963. Kennedy's successor, Lyndon B. Johnson, overcame liberal skepticism about his Texas roots. He used his formidable legislative skills to break the logjam on civil rights, signing the most far-reaching bill since Reconstruction. Johnson's landslide victory in 1964—achieved only by viciously demonizing the upright Barry Goldwater—foreshadowed the yawning "credibility gap" that would haunt his second term. LBJ wanted to do it all—fight a war on poverty at home, build a "Great Society," and nail the Communists' "coonskin to the wall" abroad. He sought much, achieved much, and wounded many. Driven from office by his own party in 1968, Johnson gave way to a warier

warrior, Richard Nixon. Johnson's rise and fall in Americans' esteem can be summed up in two Greek words: hubris and nemesis.

I. The New Frontier

John F. Kennedy's image was everywhere in 1960. Americans saw his tanned, handsome face, his beautiful, elegant wife, and their lovely little girl smiling down from thousands of magazine covers. Kennedy was in the newsreels, in the newspapers, on television. His Pulitzer Prize-winning book, *Profiles in Courage*, was reprinted for the campaign season. No one had ever campaigned so vigorously for the presidency before. *Vigah*—as he pronounced *vigor* in his Boston accent—was the key to the Kennedy magic. Another new word—*charisma*—came into general usage. Americans eagerly anticipated change.

Jack Kennedy had been planning his presidential run from the moment that he narrowly lost the Democratic vice presidential nomination to Estes Kefauver in 1956.* (Some would say that his father had been planning it since the moment Joe Jr. died in WWII.) But it would not be an easy run for the nomination.

Democrats sensed victory, and the party's best and brightest jockeyed for the position. Adlai Stevenson refused to take himself out of the running, but he would not declare a candidacy either. His indecisiveness proved fatal. Stevenson's Hamlet-like stance sapped support for the liberal champion, Senator Hubert H. Humphrey of Minnesota. Humphrey's strong record on civil rights, farm issues, and his ability to articulate liberal ideals in a commonsense way made him a hero to Midwestern populists. He proposed a Peace Corps and a Food-for-Peace program.[1] Many saw him as the most creative legislator in Senate history. Senator Lyndon B. Johnson of Texas was a powerful, skilled legislative tactician. He knew how to get things done in the fractious U.S. Senate.

---

* Kefauver, a liberal U.S. senator from Tennessee, had made a name for himself investigating gangsters in televised hearings regarding organized crime in America. Stevenson had thrown open the selection of a vice presidential nominee to the convention delegates, who had narrowly selected Kefauver. Later, when the Democratic ticket lost in a landslide, Jack Kennedy considered himself fortunate not to have been on it.

Stevenson, Humphrey, and Johnson were all older, more seasoned potential presidential candidates for the Democrats in 1960. Kennedy would not have an easy time running against these barons of the Senate.

Jack's own achievements in just eight years in the Upper Body (as the Senate was known among members of this exclusive club) were scant. No major law, no important initiative bore his name. Chronic illness and his active social life frequently kept him away from the often tedious Senate sessions. But in terms of sheer aggressiveness in the pursuit of political power, no one could match the junior senator from Massachusetts. Nor could anyone equal the hustle of Bobby Kennedy, the senator's younger brother. Bobby's lifelong reputation for political ruthlessness would be hard-earned in the 1960 campaign.

Kennedy knew he had to beat Humphrey somewhere. He needed to do this to prove to Big City Democratic party leaders—many of whom themselves were Catholic—that his religion would not hamper him from winning the White House. The Wisconsin Primary seemed a likely bet. Humphrey was known as the Badger State's "third senator." The Kennedys poured in money, talent, and their photogenic family. Humphrey complained it was like the corner drugstore trying to go up against the Rexall Chain.* Bobby Kennedy exploded on camera when CBS News's Walter Cronkite asked him if being Catholic had hurt Jack. Bobby accused the anchorman of violating the candidates' pledge *not* to inject religion into the campaign.[2] Mysteriously, campaign fliers showed up in mailboxes in heavily Catholic precincts urging voters to reject a candidate too closely aligned with Rome.

Defeated in Wisconsin, Humphrey headed for impoverished West Virginia. It was a poor state, one where Humphrey's strong ties to organized labor should have brought him victory. Humphrey would never have stooped to anti-Catholicism. He was a champion of civil rights for black Americans, and he had battled anti-Semitism as mayor of Minneapolis. Still, a state that was overwhelmingly Protestant might have leaned toward the

* It was a homely analogy and a true one. Hubert Humphrey was a trained pharmacist. The family business in Doland, South Dakota, was an old-fashioned neighborhood drugstore.

Protestant Humphrey. It didn't. The Kennedys brought glamour to the coal mining hills. Frank Sinatra sang the Kennedy campaign song. Bobby brought in Franklin D. Roosevelt Jr. FDR was still revered in West Virginia. The younger Roosevelt savaged Humphrey as a draft dodger because the Minnesotan had been rejected for military service in World War II for physical reasons.[3] Kennedy's convincing victory in the Mountain State eliminated Humphrey. Ironically, it was the mostly Catholic big city Democratic Party leaders who still fretted about Jack Kennedy's electability.[4]

Kennedy's forces dominated the 1960 Democratic National Convention in Los Angeles. It seemed that Bobby had considered every possibility. When Lyndon Johnson suggested a joint meeting before the Texas and Massachusetts delegations, he expected his maturity and experience would prevail. Kennedy pierced Johnson's campaign balloon with disarming wit by *agreeing* that Johnson was the best Senate leader in history—and promising to work closely with him when he, Kennedy, went to the White House. Johnson mistakenly thought that senators who supported him could deliver convention delegate votes. They couldn't, and John F. Kennedy was nominated on the first ballot.* Over Bobby's bitter objections, Johnson was named as the candidate for vice president. The Democrats desperately needed Texas.

The Republicans met in Chicago in 1960. Since President Eisenhower was the first president to be limited by the Twenty-second Amendment, Vice President Nixon had a huge advantage over any GOP rivals. Nixon's march to the nomination was aided by his reputation as a strong anti-Communist, his tireless efforts at party building over the eight years of the Eisenhower administration, as well as his very proper, very effective conduct during Ike's serious illnesses. Governor Nelson A. Rockefeller of New York never officially declared his candidacy. Rockefeller's popularity with minorities—Catholics, Jews, blacks, Puerto Ricans—in the Empire State was a phenomenon. He loved to wade into ethnic crowds, chew blintzes, and press the flesh. Despite his obvious campaign skills, Rockefeller was widely seen as too liberal for Republicans in the West and Midwest. Nixon chose the Eastern

* So professional was the Kennedy campaign in 1960 that it became the standard for all campaigns thereafter. Since JFK's nomination on the first ballot in Los Angeles in 1960, no nomination contest *in either party* has gone past the first ballot.

moderate Henry Cabot Lodge Jr. as his running mate and conceded major points to Rockefeller on the party's platform. Conservatives were unhappy with what they called Nixon's "sellout" on principle. Senator Barry Goldwater even called it a "Munich." But when they attempted to nominate conservative hero Goldwater as a protest, the Arizonan declined, urging conservatives to "grow up" and organize to take over the GOP.

Kennedy urged a stronger response to the Soviets and a greater federal government role in domestic programs. He eloquently called for Americans to advance toward "a New Frontier." Nixon was hampered by his pledge to visit all fifty states.* In these days before regular jet travel, flying to Alaska and Hawaii was a long, long process.

Kennedy took up the religion issue head-on in a meeting with the Protestant Ministerial association in Houston, Texas. Kennedy said he believed no Catholic president should allow a Catholic bishop to tell him how to act. He pledged to *resign* if his Church ever attempted to dictate his conduct of his office. This was intended as much as a signal to the Catholic Church to give him room as it was to the attentive Protestant pastors in the hotel ballroom. He told the ministers he did not speak for the Catholic Church and, significantly, the Catholic Church did not speak for him. The key issue then was not, as it later became, abortion or federally funded birth control, but federal aid to education. Kennedy favored federal aid that *excluded* students in Catholic parochial and other religious schools.[5]**

When Senator Kennedy met Vice President Nixon for a series of televised debates, most people expected the senior, more experienced Nixon to win convincingly. However, the tanned, articulate Kennedy performed with cool competence and flashes of wit. Nixon recently had been released from the hospital for a knee infection. He looked haggard. His much lampooned and cartooned five o'clock shadow gave him a grim appearance. Those who

* The election of 1960 was the first to include *fifty* states. The admission of Alaska (1959) and Hawaii (1960) had been the first to include noncontiguous territories as states. Hawaii's admission had been delayed by Senate segregationists who resisted admitting a state with a nonwhite majority.

** Abortion was then illegal in all fifty states, as were suicide and homosexual sodomy. No-fault divorce was illegal in forty-nine states, with only Nevada allowing for an easy end to a marriage. *All* of this was to change in the following decade.

heard the debate on radio scored it for Nixon, but *viewers* gave the contest to the young Kennedy.[6]

On Election Day, Kennedy eked out an incredibly narrow victory. Kennedy won 34,227,096 popular votes (49.7 percent) and 303 electoral votes to Nixon's 34,107,248 popular votes (49.5 percent) and 219 electoral votes. Just 119,848 votes (two-tenths of one percent) separated the two candidates. Early in the morning after the election, Nixon conceded to Kennedy. For years afterward, Republicans would cry foul over the counting of ballots in Mayor Richard Daley's Chicago and Lyndon B. Johnson's Texas.

Kennedy appeared at a simple firehouse near the family compound at Hyannis Port, Massachusetts. There, with his beautiful, expectant wife, Jacqueline, and his large, attractive family, he claimed the victory. Kennedy's charismatic appeal had helped produce a record high voter turnout. More than sixty-eight million voters trooped to the polls, a 64 percent turnout figure that has not been matched since.*

Fully 78 percent of U.S. Catholics and 81 percent of American Jews voted for Kennedy.

And a last-minute phone call from the Kennedy campaign to Reverend Martin Luther King Jr.'s wife had helped tip the balance in the black community for Kennedy. Dr. King had been jailed in Georgia on a minor traffic charge, and the Kennedys called to express their concern. Unlike other Protestants, who gave 38 percent of their votes to JFK, black Americans backed him by 70 percent.[7]**

On a sunny, frigid January day in 1961, the youngest man ever to be elected president delivered his Inaugural Address.*** In a world threatened

---

* A large part of the apparent *decline* in voter turnout has been the result of the Twenty-sixth Amendment, which permitted eighteen-, nineteen-, and twenty-year-olds to vote. It was the just thing to do, but this large group of young Americans has an historically low record of turning out to vote.

** JFK's campaign did not *change* allegiances as much as it *amplified* them. Catholics had been Democrats since Jackson's time. Jews voted heavily Democratic with FDR. Protestants outside the South had been Republicans since the party was founded in 1856. Black voters backed the Party of Lincoln until the Great Depression. JFK's unique appeal was to spike voter turnout among all minorities.

*** JFK was elected at age forty-three. TR was forty-two when he *succeeded* the assassinated McKinley. This author was seventeen in 1961, a student at a Washington, D.C., Catholic high school and attended John F. Kennedy's inauguration. As it did for millions, JFK's Inaugural Address made a lifelong impression on this young would-be Democrat.

by atheistic Communism, Kennedy reaffirmed his commitment to the ideals of the Declaration of Independence: "[The] rights of man come not from the generosity of the state, but from the hand of God." He included a ringing call to service and sacrifice that thrilled millions: "Ask *not* what your country can do for you; ask what you can do for your country."[8] He concluded with these powerful words: "With a good conscience our only sure reward, with history the final judge of our deeds, let us go forth to lead the land we love, asking His blessing and His help, but knowing that here on earth God's work must truly be our own."

He was to find no "honeymoon period" in the onrush of crises foreign and domestic. When the Eisenhower-initiated action by the CIA to overturn Cuba's Communist dictator Fidel Castro was presented to the new president, he allowed it to go forward. But, at the last minute, he withdrew the U.S. air cover for the Cuban exile army that was storming ashore. Probably, the Cuban exiles never had a chance of toppling Castro, but taking away the air cover *guaranteed* failure. The fiasco at the Bay of Pigs seemed to confirm what JFK's critics had charged: he was too young, too inexperienced, too hasty in his judgments.

Actually, Kennedy may have been trying to keep the support of his UN Ambassador Adlai Stevenson and the liberal wing of the Democratic Party in vetoing direct support to the Cuban exiles.[9] JFK came forward quickly to acknowledge fault in the Bay of Pigs episode, noting that "[d]efeat is an orphan, but victory has a thousand fathers." Americans rallied to their embattled new president, just as they had supported Ike during the U-2 affair.

The young president charmed the French people in early June when he paid a state visit to Paris. Even the normally frosty President de Gaulle warmed when the cultured young First Lady, the former Jacqueline *Bouvier*, addressed him in perfect Parisian French. JFK won hearts with his charming tribute to his lovely young wife: "I am the man who accompanied Jacqueline Kennedy to Paris."

When Kennedy met Khrushchev in Vienna in June 1961, however, the whiff of failure in the Bay of Pigs debacle was still in the air. Khrushchev told his Kremlin comrades, "Berlin is the testicles of the West. Every time I want to make the West scream, I squeeze on Berlin."[10] Behind closed doors,

Khrushchev berated and bullied the young president. Threatening war, Khrushchev did his best to intimidate his adversary. He would sign a separate treaty with his East German satellite to force the Western Allies out of Berlin, he warned. Kennedy said he could sign anything he liked with the East Germans so long as Western occupation rights were respected. "Force will be met with force," Khrushchev replied menacingly.[11] Trying to break the ice, Kennedy asked Khrushchev about a medal he was wearing. Told that it was the Lenin Peace Prize, JFK could not resist quipping: "I hope you keep it."

Changing directions, Kennedy tried to interest Khrushchev in a treaty to ban the testing of nuclear weapons in the atmosphere. It was a Stevenson proposal, and it had merit. World levels of Strontium 90—a radioactive element—had been rising; it was even being detected in children's milk. "The journey of a thousand miles begins with the first step," JFK said, quoting an ancient Chinese proverb. Khrushchev thought Kennedy was taunting him because of the just-opened public feud between Moscow and Beijing, the first split between the two Communist giants. "You seem to know the Chinese very well," Khrushchev said with a knowing smile.[12] Kennedy replied that the United States might get to know them a lot better.[13] It was one of the few times in their summit that Kennedy scored a point on the crafty Khrushchev.* The Soviet ruler ended the summit conference by saying that in six months he would sign the treaty with the East German regime. Kennedy believed that would mean war. "If that's true, it's going to be a cold winter," he said grimly.[14]

It was a baptism by fire. It was the struggling young president's first direct encounter with the brutality of the Soviet system. "He just beat hell out of me," JFK confessed to associates.[15] Kennedy told James Reston, a *New York Times* columnist—on deep background—that the Bay of Pigs fiasco had emboldened Khrushchev: "Most important, he thinks I have no guts."[16]**

---

* This was a fascinating insight, too, into the possibility that the United States might play a "China card" in a worldwide competition with the USSR. It would be left to Richard Nixon to implement that strategy.

** When a president, or other high government official, gives an interview "on background," it means he cannot be directly quoted. "Deep background" meant the journalist could not even quote the *substance* of the conversation. JFK learned to use this technique to enlist the support of influential journalists.

Khrushchev had another important reason to feel buoyant at Vienna. The Soviet Union had only recently launched the first manned spaceflight in history. On 12 April 1961, Major Yuri Gagarin orbited the earth three times in his *Vostok* space capsule. Vostok, which means "East," put the Eastern bloc far ahead in the race into space.

Soviet gains in space presented Kennedy with a serious challenge. He had come into office pledging to "get America moving again." Now, the Soviets seemed to be passing America by. Khrushchev had seen the great excitement in the West created by the appointment of seven Project Mercury astronauts.[17] The clean-cut, buttoned-down, young military pilots had what was called "the right stuff."* The U.S. media made them heroes before they set foot in space. Khrushchev was determined to steal Kennedy's thunder. And, with Gagarin's flight, he did.

Americans worried that with *Lunik 3* flying past the moon, taking photographs of the dark side, the Soviets were planning to put a man on the moon. With a cosmonaut on the moon, what would come next? Moon colonies? Missile bases on the moon that could threaten U.S. cities? Some of these fears were fanciful, to be sure, but there was no denying that the Soviets appeared to be moving far ahead of the United States.

Khrushchev thought the success of Soviet space efforts would prove the validity of Marxism-Leninism. Not the least of this system was its militant atheism. Cosmonaut Gagarin was a committed Communist. Asked what he had seen in the Heavens during his first orbital flight, he grinned in reply: "*Nyet boga!*" ("No God!")

Kennedy's response to this challenge was ingenious. Informed that there was no way the United States could catch up with the Soviets in space for the next few years, JFK demanded answers from leaders of NASA.** "Is there any place we can catch them? What can we do? Can we go around the

---

* The Project Mercury astronauts were to become America's first men in space. They were: Capt. Donald ("Deke") Slayton (USAF), Lt. Cmdr. Alan B. Shepard (USN), Lt. Cmdr. Wally Schirra (USN), Capt. Virgil I. ("Gus") Grissom (USAF), Lt. Col. John Glenn (USMC), Capt. Leroy Gordon ("Gordo") Cooper (USAF), Lt. Scott Carpenter (USN). "Deke" Slayton would be grounded for a decade for a minor heart condition, finally flying on the orbiting Apollo-Soyuz space station in 1972.

** The National Aviation and Space Administration (NASA) was Eisenhower's civilian space agency. Ike was determined to *avoid* militarizing space.

Soviet tanks in Budapest, firing on unarmed Hungarians. *The Hungarian Revolt of 1956 was ill-timed for a host of reasons. Not the least was that it occurred in the midst of a U.S. presidential election and a political crisis in the Mideast. President Eisenhower is criticized to this day for failing to "roll back" communism in Eastern Europe—as the Republican Party had pledged to do. The Hungarian Revolt proved, however, that Soviet rule in Eastern Europe was maintained only at the point of a bayonet.*

Nikita Khrushchev. *Khrushchev was a fat man who moved like a thin man. He was active, intelligent, and dangerous. He had great hopes for the Soviet space program, believing this would impress the newly de-colonized states of Africa and Asia. He was overthrown in 1964 but he was not shot or imprisoned. This was his achievement in the shadow world of communist intrigue.*

Cuban Missile Crisis, aerial photo of Cuban sites, 1962. *Khrushchev took a huge gamble by placing offensive missiles in Cuba. Kennedy's hesitation during the Bay of Pigs debacle, and his weak performance at the Vienna summit led Khrushchev to overreach. Kennedy forced Khrushchev to withdraw his missiles by ringing Cuba with American steel.*

John F. Kennedy and Jacqueline Kennedy. *The young and vigorous Kennedys cut a glamorous figure on the international stage. Jacqueline charmed the normally frosty President de Gaulle with her Parisian French. JFK earned appreciative smiles when he said: "I am the man who accompanied Jacqueline Kennedy to Paris." It may have been during this trip that Mrs. Kennedy saw the eternal flame at the Arc de Triomphe.*

moon before them? Can we put a man on the Moon before them?"[18] The new president's science advisers told him we could beat the Soviets to the moon. That was all Kennedy needed to hear. We'll do it, he said.

Instantly, Kennedy redefined the Space Race. From this point on, every Soviet first—the first woman in space, the first space walk, the first long-term orbital flight—would be measured against the overarching goal: Have they landed on the moon yet? Kennedy took a long stride toward winning the Space Race: *He moved the finish line!*

Soon, Americans would be able to hail their own space heroes, as first Navy Lieutenant Commander Alan B. Shepard and then Air Force Captain Virgil I. "Gus" Grissom rocketed into space. The heat shield on John Glenn's *Friendship 7* space capsule nearly came off, an event fully recorded and shared with the world via live-action television. The world heaved a sigh of relief and marveled at Glenn's cool courage as he faced the possibility of a flaming death.

Kennedy's bold move left the Soviets *and* his domestic opponents flat-footed.

"Why the great hurry to get to the Moon?" asked Ike in the *Saturday Evening Post.*

Still, Republican critics seemingly forgot President Eisenhower's determination *not* to militarize space when they condemned JFK for not doing so. And they criticized JFK's Apollo moon program, as well.[19]

"Why not tell the Soviets: 'Very well, you have reached the Moon, but meanwhile here in America we have been trying, however clumsily, to spread freedom and justice?'" That was William F. Buckley Jr.'s response in *Reader's Digest.*[20] Senator Barry Goldwater had initially voted for the Apollo program; now he called it "a waste."[21]

The Republicans opposed Apollo, it seemed, because Kennedy proposed it. Kennedy was more imaginative than his opponents and had an instinctive understanding of how Khrushchev was using space to challenge America in the developing world. In a stroke, Kennedy had taken away Khrushchev's air of invincibility and the Communists' illusion of *inevitability.* Khrushchev was the most dangerous of all of America's Soviet adversaries. He was the one willing to take great risks. And Khrushchev had invested *heavily* in the Soviet space program. His own political position in the Kremlin and the Soviets' position in the world were dependent on the prestige of space achievement.

By capturing that flag, John F. Kennedy contributed mightily to Khrushchev's eventual overthrow by his own conspiring Communist comrades. They would charge him with "hare-brained schemes." But that was in the future.

Here on earth, Khrushchev was still a dangerous antagonist. In August 1961, when many Western leaders were on vacation, Khrushchev moved to seal off East Berlin. He had to do something. The grim, Stalinist rump regime the Soviets had created was called the German Democratic Republic. It was neither democratic, nor republican. And it wasn't even German. It was merely a puppet state set up by the occupying Soviets. Many of the Germans who ran it for Moscow had themselves spent the Second World War in Moscow. Now, in 1961, this Soviet Zone of Germany was hemorrhaging. Thousands of trained doctors, teachers, engineers, and scientists—especially young people—were streaming into West Berlin seeking a better life. They could take an elevated tram or simply walk across the dividing line between East and West Berlin. No one dared to joke, "Will the last German to leave the Soviet Zone please turn off the searchlights?" Still, that was what was behind Khrushchev's belligerence over divided Berlin.

In late August, Khrushchev struck. Jumping his Vienna deadline of six months, the Soviet ruler ordered East Germans to string barbed wire along the entire perimeter between East and West Berlin. This was soon followed up by bulldozers and concrete sections of a long and ugly wall surrounding the entire free city of West Berlin. Kennedy, expecting another Berlin Blockade, breathed a sigh of relief. Maybe there would not be a "long, cold winter" after all. As long as Khrushchev did not block Allied access to West Berlin, the United States could protest, but it could not justify knocking down what people now called the Berlin Wall.

German families were cruelly separated. Brutal East German guards even shot their countrymen as they tried to escape from "the workers' paradise." The world watched in horror as seventeen-year-old Peter Fechter was shot by border guards. The lad lay bleeding, dying, crying out for mercy in the no-man's-land the Communists had created. East German *Volkspolizei,* or VOPOs, were said to be the "people's police." The VOPOs trained their guns on West Berliners, threatening to shoot any of them who tried to rescue young Fechter. Over the next three decades, hundreds of others would be shot down in cold blood while trying to escape.

II. "Godspeed, John Glenn!"

Marine Lieutenant Colonel John H. Glenn seemed like a figure out of central casting. Lean and strong, his "high and tight haircut" marked him as the straight arrow he was. He had met his wife, Annie, in the playpen in New Concord, Ohio. There had never been another girl in the world for him but this dark-eyed beauty. And just as Annie overcame the handicap of a speech impediment, John bested other test pilots who had completed college. At the press conference where the original *Mercury 7* astronauts were announced, Glenn stole the spotlight by speaking out about his religious faith. Even in those more religiously demonstrative times, Glenn's televised profession of faith appeared to many sophisticates as "uncool."

He almost got blackballed by his fellow astronauts when he bluntly told them to "keep it zipped." NASA officials were worried that a sex scandal might ground the famously high-flying jet jocks.

President Kennedy liked the gutsy combat pilot from the Buckeye State. He invited Glenn to the White House a few weeks before his scheduled flight in *Friendship 7*. It was to be the first U.S. effort to send a man into orbit around the earth. Kennedy had a great deal of his own political prestige riding with the Marine. Kennedy asked Glenn to roll out his charts, models, and maps in the Cabinet Room. He quizzed Glenn for more than an hour on every aspect of the flight.[22] The president was insatiably curious.

Glenn and his fellow Mercury astronauts often evoked strong feelings in Americans. Many yearned to beat the Russians and genuinely loved these brave young men who were willing to risk their lives doing it. Tax attorney Leo DeOrsey was no exception. He had agreed to represent the astronauts with the media *pro bono*.* As John Glenn prepared to rocket into space, it was revealed to his circle of family and friends that he had very little life

* *Pro bono*: "for free."

insurance. DeOrsey told John and Annie Glenn that Lloyds of London had agreed to cover the astronaut for the expected six hours of his maiden flight—for a premium of $16,000![23] Several days later, however, DeOrsey called back to recommend they turn down the Lloyds deal. He felt bad about it, he said. "I'm not going to bet against you," DeOrsey told Glenn.[24] Instead, he gave a mutual friend a check for $100,000, made out to Annie Glenn, just in case anything should happen to John.[25]

Astronaut Scott Carpenter, Glenn's backup, was obviously moved as the Atlas rocket's 367,000 pounds of thrust roared into action for liftoff. "Godspeed, John Glenn," Carpenter cried out. Tom O'Malley, the General Dynamics Corporation's project director, added his prayer: "May the good Lord ride with you all the way."[26]

Glenn could hear none of this encouragement over the sound of his rocket engines. A heart-stopping moment occurred while Glenn was in orbit when mission control began to suspect that mysterious light "butterflies" Glenn reported meant the space capsule's heat shield had deployed too soon. To test it in flight was dangerous, too. When Glenn was instructed to throw the switch, he gingerly complied—after only a slight hesitation. The temperatures outside his capsule rose to 9500°F as he reentered the earth's atmosphere, lower, but not much lower, than the surface of the sun! Without the heat shield, Glenn would be incinerated. The world held its breath.

There was a period of radio silence during re-entry. It was anticipated, but now it only increased the tension. Finally, after what seemed an eternity, John Glenn showed the right stuff as his calm, professional voice broke through the static. The heat shield held! Once again, America had fired a shot heard 'round the world.

The destroyer USS *Noa* picked up John Glenn just minutes after his splashdown in the Atlantic. The country had a new hero. Later, Glenn sparred—only verbally—with a visiting Soviet cosmonaut, Gherman Titov. Titov loudly proclaimed his view that Communist ideology was confirmed when he didn't see God in space. "The God I believe in isn't so small that I thought I would run into Him just a little bit above the atmosphere," Glenn responded with quiet dignity.[27] Then he invited Titov and his wife to join him and Annie for an all-American cookout. Glenn's skills in space exceeded his abilities with the backyard grill. As Al and Louise Shepard and the Titovs arrived in a limousine, John Glenn frantically beat out the flames that threatened to consume the steaks.[28]

III. "Eyeball to Eyeball" over Cuba

Forty thousand Soviet troops were in Cuba in 1962. We now know that.[29] When New York's Republican senator, Kenneth Keating, spoke out against the Soviet buildup "just ninety miles from our shores," President Kennedy was outraged.[30] He thought government leaks were enabling the Republicans to embarrass him and make him look weak.

In the middle of a campaign trip, the president was summoned back to Washington, D.C. There, he received confirmation from U-2 flights over Cuba that the Soviets were installing Intermediate Range Ballistic Missiles on the island fortress. These Soviet IRBMs were capable of delivering a nuclear strike against the entire Eastern Seaboard of the United States. Texas, Oklahoma, Louisiana, and Florida, in a single, secret stroke, were now also in grave danger of a nuclear Pearl Harbor.

Instantly, President Kennedy summoned his top advisers to a crisis conference. Some of his military chiefs warned him that staging a pre-emptive assault on Cuba to wipe out the missile bases before they could be made operational could lead to nuclear war.[31] Kennedy rejected that option. But he knew the Soviet missiles could not be allowed to stay in Cuba. The Kremlin turned a stony face to the world and flatly denied they had placed their offensive missiles in Cuba.

President Kennedy went on national television on 22 October 1962 to inform the American people and the world that the United States knew of the Soviets' deception, their "clandestine" and reckless nuclear arms buildup in Cuba, and to demand that the missles be removed.

> Neither the United States of America nor the world community of nations can tolerate deliberate deception and offensive threats on the part of any nation, large or small. We no longer live in a world where only the actual firing of weapons represents a sufficient challenge to a

> nation's security to constitute maximum peril. Nuclear weapons are so destructive and ballistic missiles are so swift, that any substantially increased possibility of their use or any sudden change in their deployment may well be regarded as a definite threat to peace.

Kennedy then ordered a "quarantine" of Cuba.* He would use the vast U.S. naval superiority to surround the island and intercept Soviet freighters bound for Havana with more missles.

The British were then supplying the United States with high-level intelligence from deep within the Kremlin. Colonel Oleg Penkovsky, an officer in Soviet military intelligence, was secretly spying for Britain.** Kennedy received full support from the American people, Britain's conservative Prime Minister Harold MacMillan, and, surprisingly, from France's President de Gaulle. When Kennedy's special envoy, Dean Acheson, entered de Gaulle's magnificent office in the Elysée Palace, he offered to show the austere Frenchman the U-2 photographs the United States had obtained from flights over Cuba. "Put your documents away," de Gaulle said dramatically. "The word of the President of the United States is enough for me. Tell your President that France supports him unreservedly."[32]

At the UN, Ambassador Adlai Stevenson showed the U-2 reconnaissance photos and confronted the Soviet ambassador with his lies. The Soviet claimed he had trouble with the interpretation of Stevenson's comments into Russian. "I am prepared to wait, Mr. Ambassador, *until hell freezes over* for your answer!" It was Adlai's finest hour. Watching on television, President Kennedy said, "Terrific! I never knew Adlai had it in him."[33]

When he received *two* distinct cables from the Soviet government, Kennedy ignored the harsher one and focused on the more accommodating one. He presumed that the former had been drafted by the Soviet *apparatchiks,* while gambling that Khrushchev himself had written the softer line.

---

* He avoided the term *blockade*, which is an act of war under international law. In choosing to call his action a *quarantine*, he harkened back to FDR's famous "quarantine the aggressor" speech. It was a comparison JFK welcomed.

** Penkovsky was caught and executed by the KGB. For years, the story circulated in Moscow that he had been rolled into the city's Donskoi crematorium—still alive. Recently, doubt has been cast on that part of the story, but it served its purpose.

Khrushchev offered Kennedy a *quid pro quo*—removal of Soviet missiles from Cuba in exchange for removal of U.S. missiles from NATO ally Turkey. Kennedy had to reject this, at least publicly. But he followed up another Khrushchev suggestion: that the United States agree to guarantee Cuba's territorial integrity. That meant the United States would have to drop its support for the anti-Communist Cuban exiles and agree not to invade Cuba with U.S. forces.[34]

As a Soviet freighter steamed toward the U.S. ring of steel surrounding Cuba, tension mounted around the world. Would she turn back? Would she refuse to allow an American inspection party to board her? Would there be bloodshed? Were we watching the opening act of World War III? Finally, the Soviet freighter turned away.

Khrushchev was unwilling to initiate a nuclear war over Cuba. Claiming that all he ever wanted was to protect Cuba from invasion, Khrushchev publicly backed down. On 28 October 1962, he agreed to remove his missiles from Cuba.[35] Cuba's Castro reacted with obscene abuse of his Soviet ally. Saying Khrushchev was a *maricón*, a homosexual, Castro kicked the wall and broke a mirror in his anger and frustration.[36]*

Kennedy had prevailed. As Secretary of State Dean Rusk put it, "we were eyeball to eyeball and the other guy just blinked."[37] But Rusk's comment was delivered on background. Kennedy ordered no public gloating over Khrushchev's *apparent* humiliation. Nor did JFK want it revealed that he had indeed agreed quietly to remove the U.S. missiles from Turkey.[38] Perhaps we went eyeball to eyeball over Cuba and *our* guy winked!**

"Appearances contribute to reality," Kennedy often said. And to all appearances, the brave young president had courageously backed the Soviet adversary down. Khrushchev's private letters to Kennedy now contained the word *détente*. He looked to a general relaxation of tensions, he said. Accordingly, he okayed a new "hotline" between Moscow and Washington, D.C. This was actually a teletype machine between the two

* Castro's hatred of homosexuals is wellknown. He regularly condemned homosexual Cubans to imprisonment on the Isle of Pines.

** Those missiles in Turkey are routinely described as "obsolete" in media accounts of the Cuban Missile Crisis, but they certainly weren't obsolete when they were installed, just months before Khrushchev demanded their removal.

capitals that would permit a more rapid communication in the event of a crisis. Kennedy was deeply concerned that a miscommunication might bring nuclear war. Khrushchev also dropped his opposition to the Nuclear Test Ban Treaty. It would become one of the stellar achievements of the Kennedy administration.

For American Catholics, the Kennedy years were the time of the "Two Johns." Pope John XXIII had succeeded the serious, studious Pius XII in 1958. Pope John XXIII's sunny personality charmed everyone. His warmth, his genuine affection for people, melted centuries of hostility and suspicion. The pope called for a great ecumenical council to modernize Catholic practices. *Aggiornamento* is the Italian word for bringing things up to date; the pope used it unhesitatingly to describe his planned reforms. The Vatican II Council lasted three years and stimulated sweeping changes. The Mass would be said in the language of the people. The priest would face the congregation, not the altar, when elevating the Host. No longer would Catholics be required to abstain from meat on Fridays, except during Lent. And dialogue with Protestants, Orthodox Christians, Jews, and Muslims would be encouraged. Protestants, now called "separated brethren" and not heretics, were invited to attend all sessions of Vatican II.

JFK worked to break down barriers. When he addressed the Alfred E. Smith Memorial Dinner in New York, he reminded his audience of the famous telegram Smith had supposedly sent the pope following his disastrous defeat in the presidential election of 1928: "Unpack." With a wink, Kennedy said he just received the Vatican's response to his education bill: "Pack." The audience of distinguished Catholics, Protestants, and Jews—New York's elite—laughed uproariously. A Catholic president making fun of one of the most sensitive issues in politics delighted everyone.

While the joke enhanced the president's popularity, it didn't help his education bill. Kennedy's proposal excluded any aid to children attending Catholic schools. Like so much of Kennedy's legislative program, the bill stalled in Congress.

Meanwhile, *National Review* (*NR*) criticized the Vatican for its seeming willingness to do business with the Communist occupiers of Eastern Europe. Such dissent from positions embraced by the Roman Catholic Church from the liberal JFK and the conservative and largely Catholic editors of *NR* helped put to rest fears of Catholic dominance of American political life.

War and peace were not the only issues to command attention in those heady days. A new concern, perhaps sparked by the discussion on the impact of atmospheric nuclear testing, raised questions about humans' care of the earth. "We are challenged, as mankind has never been challenged before, to prove our maturity and mastery not of nature but of ourselves," wrote Rachel Carson in her best-selling 1962 book, *Silent Spring.*[39] Americans showed renewed regard for the impact of industrialization and modernization on their surroundings. A movement arose to protect the *environment.* At first, it was a voluntary movement of individual citizens. In time, it would express itself in legislation.

IV. Freedom on the March

The fact that Americans were enjoying continuing prosperity during the affluent 1960s made the Kennedy administration seem all the more successful. JFK was generally frustrated in his attempts to get legislation he backed through Congress. He pressed the Democratic controlled Congress to cut taxes. He was the first of his party to embrace the idea that cutting taxes could actually stimulate economic growth and increase government revenues. Kennedy failed to get Medicare approved. This government program to socialize medicine for the elderly had been on the agenda since Teddy Roosevelt's failed Bull Moose effort in 1912.[40]

JFK did succeed in sending thousands of idealistic young Americans around the world in his Peace Corps. His *Alianza para Progreso* (Alliance for Progress) promised a new overture to America's long-neglected allies in Latin America.

Jacqueline Kennedy was a vastly popular First Lady. She redecorated the White House and invited leading artists to grace the old mansion. Spanish cellist Pablo Casals offered a concert for a sparkling reception. French writer André Malraux read. And always, the dashing young president and his lady brought off the ceremonial side of the White House with style and ease.

Mrs. Kennedy's love of culture and refinement added immeasurably to the appeal of this engaging young couple. The public delighted in pictures of young Caroline Kennedy riding her pony, Macaroni, and little John-John (JFK Jr.) peeking out from the kneehole of his dad's historic desk.* The popular Broadway show *Camelot* captured the imagination of the times. And Kennedy's New Frontiersmen would not have strenuously objected to any comparison of their young vibrant administration with the mythical Knights of the Round Table. We do know that Kennedy, quoting Shakespeare's *Henry V*, often used the phrase "we happy few, we band of brothers."** President Kennedy also introduced the impressive new White House arrival ceremony that we now take for granted. It was another of the Kennedy innovations that set a high cultural tone for the New Frontier presidency.

> Before the aviation age, state visitors generally arrived by train and were greeted by the president or an official delegation at Washington, D.C.'s Union Station. Presidents Truman and Eisenhower usually journeyed to Andrews Air Force Base outside of Washington to greet foreign guests. So did Kennedy in the early months of his presidency.
>
> But after a visit to London following the Vienna summit with Nikita Khruschev in June 1961, Kennedy discovered how the British royal family received its guests. Instead of the Queen going to the airport, the visitor came from the airport to the Queen at Buckingham Palace, there to be formally welcomed. When Kennedy returned to Washington, he sketched out his ideas for an event to be held on the White House lawn, featuring military bands, march-pasts by soldiers attired in colonial dress, and speeches by the president and his guest. Since that time, what has become known as the State Arrival Ceremony is a standard feature of Washington life.[41]

---

* This author's uncle, Dr. John W. Walsh, was the obstetrician who delivered John F. Kennedy Jr. John Walsh was the son of Dr. Joseph Walsh, who was said to be "Al Smith's personal physician." Both of the doctors would treat Republicans, too. Their Hippocratic Oath required it.

** Only years later, after Kennedy's death, were the tawdry tales of JFK's womanizing known to Americans. Only then might it have been pointed out that the beauty and justice of Camelot were lost because of adultery at its heart. So is the fine legacy of John F. Kennedy tinged with sorrow.

The booming economy made conditions seem all the more intolerable for black Americans who were denied equal accommodations in hotels and restaurants, who faced discrimination in jobs and housing, and who were disqualified from voting in wide areas throughout the South. People talked about the "revolution of rising expectations." The Fifteenth Amendment to the Constitution had asserted the right of the freedmen to vote, but federal enforcement was woefully lacking. Poll taxes, literacy tests, and grandfather clauses were devices routinely employed in the former Confederate states to disenfranchise black voters.*

President Kennedy's administration asked the Interstate Commerce Commission (ICC) to ban segregation at lunch counters engaged in interstate commerce along the new interstate highways. Freedom Riders from the North took buses into the South to claim the right to eat at integrated lunch counters. Some of these buses were firebombed, and the Freedom Riders were beaten. President Kennedy hesitated to endorse the Freedom Riders' effort, but he demanded order. And the ICC did ban segregation in interstate commerce.[42]

Dr. King decided to make Birmingham, Alabama, the center of his freedom movement. He called Birmingham "the most thoroughly segregated big city in the United States."[43] The local, mostly white, chamber of commerce was eager to avoid confrontation, but Police Chief Eugene "Bull" Connor vowed resistance.[44] Connor was also Alabama's Democratic National Committeeman, a man of considerable influence. Rioting broke out in Birmingham the night after Dr. King's home was hit by a bomb. Bull Connor used fierce police dogs to make sure crowds were kept in check. Television images of Bull Connor's dogs attacking demonstrators made the city notorious around the world. Alabama's Democratic Governor, George Wallace, in his 1963 inaugural address, breathed defiance. This was his understanding of freedom:

---

* The poll tax required citizens to pay a tax for the supposed maintenance of the election machines and payment of election officials. The tax had a *disparate impact* on poor black sharecroppers, most of whom could not afford to pay it. The so-called grandfather clause exempted some citizens from the literacy test if their grandfathers had been registered voters. Prior to Emancipation, of course, black people in the South could not vote. Thus, the grandfather clause was an ill-disguised ploy to let illiterate whites vote while keeping black voters from enjoying their constitutional rights.

> I have stood, where once Jefferson Davis stood, and took an oath to my people. It is very appropriate then that from this Cradle of the Confederacy . . . that today we sound the drum for freedom as have our generations of forebears before us done, time and time again through history . . . I draw the line in the dust and toss the gauntlet before the feet of tyranny . . . and I say . . . segregation today . . . segregation tomorrow . . . segregation forever.[45]

Clearly, Governor Wallace did not consider Birmingham residents and taxpayers like Dr. King and his congregation "his people."

When Wallace, as he had pledged, "stood in the schoolhouse door" to prevent two black students from enrolling at the University of Alabama, President Kennedy had no choice but to send in federal troops. Although he had criticized Eisenhower's use of federal troops at the time of Little Rock, Kennedy addressed the country on television. He called on every American to "stop and examine his conscience" about these acts of lawlessness.[46]

Kennedy praised the people of the South for their patriotism and service in peace and war, but he was determined to stand up for the civil rights of all. And he was under unremitting pressure from Roy Wilkins of the NAACP, Whitney Young of the Urban League, and A. Philip Randolph of the train car porters' union. The senior leadership of the civil rights movement expressed their frustration over the slow pace of change. Kennedy had boasted during the campaign that discrimination in housing could be ended "by a stroke of the pen." Black Americans began sending thousands of pens to the White House.

In Birmingham, though, progress would bring problems. A Nazi Party member jumped onto the stage and attacked Dr. King. King was unhurt, but there was a ceaseless drumbeat of violence directed against him and his nonviolent movement. King had already been stabbed by a deranged black woman, beaten on an airplane flight by an enraged white passenger, and pummeled at a newly integrated hotel in Selma, Alabama.[47] The thirty-three-year-old minister had to live every day as if it would be his last.

The president went on television 11 June 1963 to address the nation on civil rights. His powerful words are worth remembering today.

> If an American, because his skin is dark, cannot eat lunch in a restaurant open to the public, if he cannot send his children to the best public schools available, if he cannot vote for the public officials who represent him . . . then who among us would be content to have the color of his skin changed? Who among us would then be content with the counsels of patience and delay? We face a moral crisis as a country and as a people . . . A great change is at hand, and our task is to make that revolution peaceful and constructive for all. [48]

In Mississippi, Byron de la Beckwith did not wait to hear Kennedy's appeal for peace and justice. He shot NAACP leader Medgar Evers as the civil rights leader was returning to his home. Evers bled to death in the driveway of his home, in the presence of his wife and children.[49]

When Dr. King was jailed in Birmingham, he wrote a memorable letter that has ever afterward served as a key text of the civil rights movement. In it, he explained the need for action. "We have waited for more than 340 years for our constitutional and God-given rights," he said. "The nations of Asia and Africa are moving with jet-like speed toward gaining political independence, but we still creep at horse-and-buggy pace toward gaining a cup of coffee at a lunch counter. Perhaps it is easy for those who have never felt the stinging dart of segregation to say, 'Wait.'"[50]

Dr. King emphasized that respect for law was essential. He wrote that when he was forced to resist an unjust law as a last resort, he had to be willing to submit to the punishment that was meted out. In this, Dr. King was well within the American tradition—and the Christian tradition—of civil disobedience. King also coupled his determination to engage in civil disobedience with a firm respect for higher law and lawfulness. As a result, he obediently accepted jail sentences when courts found him in violation of law.

Kennedy's Civil Rights Bill was introduced on 19 June 1963. The Senate's famous Rule XXII had prevented meaningful action for decades. Rule XXII meant a determined minority of senators could filibuster a bill to death.* Kennedy was frustrated at the slow pace of legislation. Senator Hubert Humphrey, the prime sponsor of the Civil Rights Bill, agreed. The Constitution makes no provisions for a cloture rule in the Senate. Under

Rule XXII, a bill needed the support of two-thirds of the senators in order to be voted upon. But the Constitution, Humphrey argued, states clearly that only a majority shall be necessary to conduct business.[51] However, the legislative process was about to get a shove.

The long-promised March on Washington was the cherished idea of A. Philip Randolph. He had urged this action for more than twenty years. Earlier, however, FDR had talked him out of it. Now, in 1963, Dr. King joined the national civil rights leadership to urge hundreds of thousands to come to Washington in a blazing August sun. To Randolph's pioneering vision of a Great March was added Bayard Rustin's organizational skill. Labor joined in the effort, with George Meany and Walter Reuther of the AFL-CIO giving the March their full endorsement. Hundreds of church leaders and Jewish groups joined in.

President Kennedy's reaction was guarded. He worried that any disorder in such a huge crowd would be seized upon by Senate opponents of civil rights. He declined to meet with March organizers before the event. He did not want them to present him with any list of demands, and he wanted to keep his distance in case there was violence. But he held open the possibility of a White House meeting after the March.[52]

Gospel singer Mahalia Jackson introduced Dr. King with the words of an old Negro spiritual:

> I'm going to tell my Lord when I get home
> Just how long you've been treating me wrong.
> I've been 'buked and I've been scorned
> Trying to make this journey all alone![53]

Most white Americans had never heard the great power of the black preachers of this country. So when Dr. King mounted the podium in front

---

* From previous page. A filibuster was the title given to the Senate's tradition of "unlimited debate." In practice, senators did not have to address the merits of a bill and could even read a telephone directory of all those they claimed would be adversely affected by the pending legislation. All they had to do was keep talking. Strom Thurmond held the filibuster record of twenty-four hours and eighteen minutes for speaking against a civil rights bill in 1957. He had the help of a "Motorman's Friend"—a device that enabled him to stand and speak so long without going to the men's room.

of the massive, brooding statue of Abraham Lincoln, he asked that his children be judged "not by the color of their skin, but by the content of their character." Most of his hearers that day were unprepared for the force and the emotion that King's biblical cadences could evoke:

> I have a dream . . . I have a dream today! So let freedom ring. . . . Let freedom ring from Stone Mountain of Georgia. Let freedom ring from every hill and molehill of Mississippi, from every mountainside. And when this happens—when we allow freedom to ring from every town and every hamlet, from every state and every city, we will be able to speed up that day when all God's children—black men and white men, Jews and Gentiles, Protestants and Catholics—will be able to join hands and sing in the words of the old Negro spiritual, "Free at last, free at last, thank God Almighty, we are free at last!"[54]

So rarely can it be said that speeches change things. *Rhetoric* or *mere rhetoric* is the way knowing insiders dismiss the power of public address. But Dr. King's speech changed things. It changes things still.

And President Kennedy had inspired King and all his brothers. "Freedom is indivisible, and when one man is enslaved, all are not free," Kennedy had told hundreds of thousands in West Berlin, just weeks before the Civil Rights March on Washington. Kennedy had said, "Ich bin ein Berliner!" I am a Berliner.

If freedom truly were indivisible, as JFK said, why did it make sense to defend freedom in West Berlin but not to let freedom ring in Birmingham, Alabama? America in the 1960s still had military conscription. If young black men could be drafted and sent to West Berlin or to the De-Militarized Zone separating North and South Korea, how could anyone justify segregation at home? Why should such young Americans be denied freedom in their own home towns?

The vast throng, hot, thirsty, and tired, left in a quiet and orderly way. Some two hundred thousand marchers dispersed, leaving not so much as a piece of litter behind. Hundreds of mass demonstrations would follow in Washington, D.C. Hardly a weekend goes by without some march for this or that. None of them—arguably, not all of them combined—has had the impact that that great 1963 March on Washington had.

President Kennedy, obviously delighted by the conduct of the March, welcomed the civil rights leaders to the White House. Roy Wilkins praised the president: "You made the difference. You gave us your blessings. It was one of the prime factors in turning it into an orderly protest to help our government rather than a protest *against* our government."[55] Wilkins may have had Kennedy's behind-the-scenes influence in mind.

When young John Lewis, a fiery civil rights advocate, talked of "burning Jim Crow to the ground *nonviolently*" and marching through the heart of Dixie the way Sherman did, Washington's Catholic Archbishop drew the line.[56] Cardinal O'Boyle said if Lewis's radical rhetoric stayed in his speech, he, O'Boyle, would refuse to offer the invocation for the March. Cardinal O'Boyle, who firmly backed civil rights, was universally respected. The leaders sat on young Lewis. And the March of Freedom went into history.[57]

V. 22 November 1963

President Kennedy's political prospects looked bright in the fall of 1963. He expected his Republican opponent in 1964 to be either New York Governor Nelson A. Rockefeller or Arizona's conservative Senator Barry Goldwater. He dismissed "Rocky" as having no guts; Barry, he thought, had "no brains."[58] Though confident, he was leaving nothing to chance. Texas Democrats had split in a nasty feud between liberal Senator Ralph Yarborough and conservative Governor John Connally. JFK thought a presidential visit might help mend political fences. He was especially pleased that Jackie would go with him. Normally, the First Lady found politics a crushing bore. Texas politics was even more so. But she recognized the importance to her husband of this vital state.

The president and the First Lady rode in an open limousine down a main thoroughfare in Dallas, Texas, on a clear November day. Nellie Connally, the governor's wife, turned around in the car to comment on the large crowds who lined the way, cheering lustily: "You sure can't say Dallas doesn't love you today, Mr. President," she said.

Then shots.

They had just passed the Texas Schoolbook Depository. The shots came from behind. "I looked back and saw the president's hands fly up to his throat. He made no sound, no cry—nothing," she wrote. "I had a horrifying feeling that the president had not only been shot, but could be dead," Mrs. Connally later told the *Dallas Morning News*. "It's the image of yellow roses and red roses and blood all over the car . . . all over us," she said. "I'll never forget it. . . . It was so quick and so short, so potent."[59]

Governor Connally, riding in the "jump" seat, was struck and pitched forward. Another shot destroyed the president's skull as the limousine blazed ahead, racing for the hospital. Mrs. Kennedy, risking her own life, crawled over the seat and out of the vehicle, to help a Secret Service man get on board.

Kennedy was dead as soon as the second bullet struck him, but doctors at Parkland Memorial Hospital tried feverishly to revive him nonetheless.

The nation heard the news within moments. Walter Cronkite, CBS's veteran anchorman, broke down as he announced the president's death. The entire world seemed to stop as the casket containing the president's body was loaded onto *Air Force One*—as the presidential jet was now called. Mrs. Kennedy seemed stunned as she entered the plane, her brilliant pink suit still stained with her dead husband's blood. Lyndon Johnson asked her to stand next to him in the jet's forward cabin. With the plane still on the runway, he was sworn in as the nation's thirty-sixth president by federal district court judge Sarah T. Hughes. Judge Hughes was a longtime Johnson ally. LBJ had been instrumental in having the Dallas lawyer named to a lifetime appointment as a federal judge.

No one could be sure this was not the beginning of a plot against the government of the United States. Kenny O'Donnell, a passionate Kennedy loyalist, pointed to the new president, seated up front as the Boeing 707 jet took off for Washington. "He's got what he wants now," he said in a barely concealed whisper about LBJ. "But we take it back in '68."[60] Most Americans, however, were not interested in political comebacks. They wanted to mourn their slain leader.

Daniel Patrick Moynihan, then a young Kennedy appointee in the

Labor Department, spoke for most when he said, "I don't think there's any point in being Irish if you don't know the world is going to break your heart eventually." During those four cold, bleak November days, *all* Americans were Irish.*

The assassination and funeral were the first televised event that fused the American people together. An entire Baby Boom generation would share the memory—just as their parents' generation had been brought together by the attack on Pearl Harbor and today's young people by the terrorist attacks of 11 September 2001. Millions of American homes had photographs of President Kennedy. Millions bought and saved for their children the commemorative editions of *Time, Life,* and *Newsweek* that rolled off the presses.

The accused assassin, Lee Harvey Oswald, was quickly apprehended in Dallas. He was himself shot to death by Jack Ruby, the operator of a sleazy Dallas nightclub, as Oswald was being transferred from one prison to another. The fact that Oswald had defected to the Soviet Union, taken a Russian wife, and then returned to the United States to be employed by the Fair Play for Cuba Committee, a Communist front group, seemed to make no impression on the media of the day. Dallas was blamed, even though Judge Hughes and Mrs. Connally could have testified that they felt no fear from the good people of Dallas. In the years since the assassination, a vast right-wing conspiracy was blamed in countless articles, books, and Hollywood movies.

Conspiracy theories of the Kennedy assassination soon cropped up. President Johnson attempted to put these to rest by appointing Chief Justice Earl Warren and Republican House Conference Leader Gerald Ford to head a commission to investigate the killing. A persistent, vocal minority would not be convinced by the Warren Commission Report, issued the next year. The report said JFK was assassinated by one man—Lee Harvey Oswald—and not by a conspiracy.

Kennedy's violent death was not "the end of innocence" it is often claimed to be. How could it be? But it was a sharp dividing line in our his-

---

* Moynihan told columnist Mary McGrory, also an Irish Catholic, "We will laugh again, but we will not be young again."

tory. Lyndon B. Johnson had many strengths that Kennedy lacked, especially in dealing with a stubborn Congress. But he lacked Kennedy's special grace, and he knew it.

One example of Kennedy's beliefs is revealed in this quote from Abraham Lincoln, written in his own hand, that his faithful secretary Evelyn Lincoln had filed away for him at the time of his shattering encounter with Khrushchev in Vienna in 1961:

> I know there is a God—and I see a storm coming;
> If He has a place for me, I believe I am ready.[61]

VI. "An Idea Whose Time Has Come"

President Lyndon B. Johnson spoke at a somber joint meeting of the 88th Congress on 27 November 1963. "Let us continue," he told the lawmakers in a nationally televised broadcast. Then he gave them his number one priority for the session.

> [No] memorial oration or eulogy could more eloquently honor President Kennedy's memory than the earliest possible passage of the civil rights bill for which he fought so long. We have talked long enough in this country about equal rights. We have talked for one hundred years or more. It is time now to write the next chapter, and to write it in the books of law.[62]

Lyndon B. Johnson was widely distrusted by many supporters of civil rights. They feared his Texas origins. They distrusted his close ties to Senator Richard Russell of Georgia, Senator Harry F. Byrd of Virginia, and other segregationists among the Senate Club. Now Johnson would prove that those ties of many decades would serve him well in the White House. He would prove with deeds his sincere commitment to civil rights. In publicly committing himself to JFK's Civil Rights Bill, Johnson would go far to secure the Kennedy Legacy. His first address to the nation came just five days after the tragic events in Dallas. LBJ claimed the mantle of John F.

Kennedy as he fully embraced civil rights. Passage of Kennedy's bill would be the test of his sincerity. He would not fail.

With Johnson's strong support, Minnesota's Hubert Humphrey was made the floor leader for the Civil Rights Bill. Privately, Johnson warned Humphrey about what he saw as the historic failure of liberals to achieve their goals: "You bomb throwers make good speeches,* you have big hearts, you believe in what you stand for, but you're never on the job when you need to be there. You spread yourselves too thin making speeches to the faithful."[63]

Johnson's crude but realistic characterizations reflected his twenty-five years on Capitol Hill. He urged Humphrey to study Senator Richard Russell's skillful parliamentary maneuvers *and counter them.* He told Humphrey that the Senate's *Republican* leader, Senator Everett McKinley Dirksen of Illinois, was the key to the passage of the Civil Rights Bill.

And so he proved to be. Humphrey had to overcome the Southern Democrats' filibuster. That required sixty-seven votes.** He could only do that with Republican support. "Everett, we can't pass this bill without you," Humphrey told the Illinoisan over and over.[64] Dirksen, whose honey-coated speaking voice earned him the nickname "the Wizard of Ooze," was proud of the GOP's heritage of civil rights. He took seriously his role as Illinois's favorite son. Illinois is, after all, "the land of Lincoln." Dirksen would remain staunch for civil rights at every turn.

In June, in a key test, the Senate voted to close the debate and end the filibuster by a vote of 70–30 (a *cloture* vote). While civil rights proponents gathered to celebrate, the NAACP's Clarence Mitchell quietly walked with Richard Russell back to the Georgian's Senate office. Russell patiently explained that the Southern Democrats had to put up a fight, they had to resist passage of the bill, or it would not have been enforceable in the South. It was a curiously unconvincing argument to make. But Clarence Mitchell, the son of a distinguished black Baltimore family, smiled and listened with

* Johnson did not mean liberals were literally bomb throwers. It was his colorful expression for emotional, demonstrative people who made passionate speeches but didn't do their legislative homework.

** Today, it requires only sixty votes to invoke *cloture,* to break a filibuster. But it remains a formidable hurdle.

courtesy.[65] Mitchell's patient, steady work as the NAACP's lobbyist for civil rights for over two decades on Capitol Hill had as much to do with the final passage of the historic bill as any sitting senator. Mitchell may also have recognized what Lyndon Johnson recognized—that the bachelor Russell was really a lonely man whose whole life was the Senate.[66] For such compassion, Clarence Mitchell would be respected on all sides as "the 101st Senator."

With one major hurdle cleared, Hubert Humphrey threw himself into the effort to pass the bill. The bill required equal access in all public accommodations. It prohibited discrimination in hiring, promotion, and firing on the basis of race, color, religion, or sex. It was the most far-reaching civil rights legislation since Reconstruction.

Humphrey had to fend off criticism that the Civil Rights Bill would lead to racial quotas. He memorably shot back at his antagonists: "If the Senator can find in Title VII . . . any language which provides that an employer will have to hire on the basis of percentage or quota related to color, race, religion, or national origin, I will start eating the pages one after another, because it is not in there."[67]

In the midst of this great debate, Humphrey received word that his younger son, Bob, was headed into surgery for a cancerous tumor in his neck. Unable to leave his post at this critical moment, the weeping floor leader was consoled by his Senate colleagues.[68]

The bill went forward. Sensing his opponents had talked themselves out, Senator Humphrey brought the great Civil Rights Act of 1964 to a floor vote. Senator Dirksen, true to his word, moved for adoption of the bill. Quoting the great French liberal, Victor Hugo, Dirksen said, "Stronger than all the armies is an idea whose time has come. The time has come for equality of opportunity, in sharing in government, in education, and in employment. It will not be stayed or denied. It is here!" Hundreds of young seminarians, both Catholic and Protestant, prayed in the halls of Congress. Americans called and sent telegrams to Capitol Hill urging passage. Hundreds of organizations—religious, civic, business, professional, labor, and liberal—wrote letters of support.

Dirksen led twenty-six Republicans in voting yes. Barry Goldwater joined only five other Republicans in voting no. Among Senator Russell's segregationist supporters were current Senator Robert Byrd of West Virginia, Albert Gore Sr. of Tennessee (father of the former vice president), and Strom Thurmond, then a Democrat. The vote on final passage in the Senate was 71–29. Republicans voted 27–6 in favor of the bill; Democrats approved it 44–23.*

On 2 July 1964, President Lyndon B. Johnson signed the most far-reaching Civil Rights Act in American history. Invited to the White House for the signing ceremony were Dr. Martin Luther King Jr., Roy Wilkins of the NAACP, Whitney Young of the Urban League, A. Philip Randolph, and other major leaders of the civil rights movement. Senator Everett Dirksen, Senator Thomas Kuchel of California, and other key Republicans who had given their indispensable support to pass the bill were seated in the front row of distinguished guests.

For the rest of their lives, millions of black and white Americans would remember this day as the moment when the long delayed promise of American freedom at last became real. One of the great tragedies in modern American life is that too many critics who viewed the Civil Rights Act of 1964 as "only the first step" have diminished the epoch-making achievement of Senator Hubert Humphrey, Senator Everett Dirksen, and their colleagues. It had taken one hundred years to achieve what they achieved that day.

VII. A Choice, Not an Echo

For generations, political scientists and commentators had called for two broad parties based on philosophy—a liberal party and a conservative party. FDR had told Wendell Willkie in the White House that he wanted liberals like Willkie to come over to the Democrats and suggested he wouldn't mind trading some anti-New Deal conservative Democrats to the GOP.

In 1964, that choice was offered. Barely two weeks after LBJ signed the Civil Rights Act, Senator Barry Goldwater rose in San Francisco's Cow Palace to accept the Republican nomination for president. Goldwater's rise had been as stunning as it was unexpected.

---

* Among those voting against the Civil Rights Act on final passage were Senators J. William Fulbright (Democrat of Arkansas) and Sam Ervin (Democrat of North Carolina).

After Vice President Richard Nixon's hairbreadth loss to JFK in 1960, he would have been a natural candidate for renomination in 1964. But Nixon had unwisely agreed to run for governor of California in 1962. He had little to tell California voters that was relevant to their lives. He railed against Communism, but California had not yet adopted a foreign policy. Nixon was trounced by Democrat Pat Brown. In a bitter morning-after press conference, Nixon denounced the press for its bias and said he was quitting politics: "You won't have Dick Nixon to kick around any more." He then headed for New York City and a lucrative law practice.

New York's Governor Nelson A. Rockefeller was resoundingly reelected in 1962. Though generally considered too liberal for the GOP, Rockefeller spoke out frequently in favor of a tougher national defense. With his magnetic personality, his powerful campaign style, and his limitless wealth, "Rocky" would normally have been the leading candidate for the Republicans. A difficult divorce from his wife of thirty years and the fact that his charming new wife had lost legal custody of her children, however, caused deep concern about the example Rockefeller would set in the White House. The Republican grassroots deeply distrusted him.

Goldwater was the standard bearer for the newly assertive conservative movement. Despite the fact that some young conservative thinkers had doubts about Barry's intellectual depth, Goldwater's wildly successful book had won him thousands of eager volunteers.[69] *The Conscience of a Conservative* sold more than seven hundred thousand copies and went through twelve printings.[70] This was unheard of for a political book. With characteristic candor, Goldwater would later disavow some parts of his bestseller ("Hell, I didn't write that . . . Bozell did," he would say in exasperation).[71] This mattered little to the legions of loyal young conservatives who enlisted in Barry's movement. Against liberal charges that he was hopelessly outdated, a relic from an earlier time, Barry eloquently stated, "The laws of God and of nature have no dateline."[72] Against Lyndon Johnson, whose standard of achievement was to run up the legislative scoreboard with bills enacted, Goldwater boldly said, "I don't aim to pass laws, *but to repeal them.*"[73]

Goldwater was no Fascist, as the liberal press constantly said. He was a principled champion of freedom. He had been influenced by Friedrich A. Hayek's *Road to Serfdom* and the free-market ideas in the work of Adam Smith.[74] He was, he often said, a *Jeffersonian* who believed that that government is best that governs least. "Politics is the art of achieving the maximum amount of freedom for individuals that is consistent with the maintenance of social order," he wrote.[75]

The 1964 GOP Convention was a raucous affair. When Governor Nelson Rockefeller spoke, he was roundly booed. This was almost unprecedented. One furious Goldwater delegate, a lady, even screamed, "You lousy lover!" Rockefeller fairly taunted the hostile crowd, denouncing extremism and refusing to endorse the man the delegates would nominate. Goldwater had beaten the New Yorker in an open primary contest.

"I would remind you that extremism in the defense of liberty is no vice!" said Goldwater upon accepting the nomination. "And let me remind you also that moderation in the pursuit of justice is no virtue!"[76] Goldwater's most memorable line was a clear dig at Rockefeller and a bold exhortation to his supporters. The words were crafted by young Professor Harry Jaffa, and there was nothing in it that Thomas Jefferson or Abraham Lincoln would not have endorsed, but it was seized upon by the media and cast as a dangerous expression of radicalism.

Governor Rockefeller would go on to endorse Goldwater, but tepidly. Other moderate Republicans, like New York mayor John V. Lindsay, and New York's two Republican senators, Jacob Javits and Kenneth Keating, declined to do so. At his Gettysburg farm, former President Eisenhower angrily confronted the nominee. "What you're saying, Barry, is there's nothing wrong . . . in calling *me* 'a conscious agent of the Communists.' Well, by golly, it is wrong. It is utter tommyrot!"[77] It was the first time that Ike showed that the Birchers had gotten under his skin. Only with great difficulty was Goldwater able to persuade the former president that he didn't mean to endorse *that* kind of extremism.[78] Eisenhower finally endorsed Goldwater, but without enthusiasm. Privately, Ike shook his head. "You know, before we had this meeting, I thought Goldwater was just stubborn. Now I am convinced that he is just plain dumb."[79]

Still, Ike, faithful to his adopted party, would make a television spot for

Freedom Riders' bus on fire, 1961. *Pent-up frustrations led civil rights demonstrators to use Eisenhower's newly constructed Interstate Highway system to challenge racial segregation in hotel and restaurant accommodations. Freedom Riders from the north faced hostility in formerly isolated southern communities. But their brave rides awakened consciences.*

Martin Luther King, Jr. addressing the March on Washington. *The Reverend Dr. Martin Luther King, Jr. led demonstrations against segregation in his home region. Here, in August 1963 he appealed for national support for an historic civil rights act to put an end to all discrimination in public accommodations and hiring. "I have a dream," he cried out. The speech made him the leader of the civil rights movement.*

Assassination of John F. Kennedy. *Americans of a certain age recall exactly where they were the moment they heard President Kennedy had been assassinated in Dallas on 22 November 1963. Where their parents heard the news of Pearl Harbor on radio, baby boomers learned of President Kennedy's assassination on television. Kennedy's death dealt a major blow to the nation's self-confidence and foreshadowed a dark and brooding time in national politics.*

Lyndon B. Johnson signing Civil Rights Act of 1964. *Initially mistrusted by civil rights advocates, Lyndon B. Johnson rose to the occasion when he pledged to honor John F. Kennedy's commitment to civil rights. His in-depth knowledge of the Senate gave a strong assist to those seeking to overcome the filibuster. The Civil Rights Act of 1964 and the Voting Rights Act of 1965 transformed American public life and remain the best part of the Johnson legacy.*

Flames behind U.S. Capitol from riots after MLK assassination. *The U.S. Capitol looked like St. Paul's Cathedral at the time of the London Blitz. But these fires had been wielded by some Americans against other Americans. The failure of Lyndon Johnson's administration to stem the tide of urban violence as well as an inconclusive and bloody war in Vietnam condemned the Democrats to long years of exile from the White House.*

Goldwater in which he dismissed charges of bigotry against the rangy Arizonan as "tommyrot."

Barry Goldwater was an enormously attractive figure. A trim, tanned, athletic Westerner, he could ride and hunt, loved skiing and camping. Goldwater was a capable pilot and had risen to the rank of brigadier general in the air force reserve. "In your heart, you know he's right" was the slogan quickly adopted by his followers. "In your guts, you know he's *nuts*," his liberal critics fired back.[80]

Liberals were especially concerned with what they considered his nuclear saber rattling. As a senator, Goldwater had argued that NATO's commander should have the power to initiate a nuclear response if the Soviets invaded Western Europe. Goldwater thought we could trust solid men like Eisenhower and General Lauris Norstad with that decision. But the very idea was treated as if it were radioactive. Goldwater was widely described as recklessly advocating nuclear war. The charge was that he had once joked about "lob[bing] one into the Kremlin men's room."[81] This was at a time when leading air force generals like Curtis LeMay talked about "bombing them back to the Stone Age." Goldwater, a man's man, was blunt, direct, and funny. But presidential candidates do not joke about nuclear war, not if they hope to get elected.*

The Johnson team knew exactly how to handle the Goldwater threat. Johnson's young campaign aide, Bill Moyers, approved what was, and still is, the most vicious television ad in American history. A lovely little girl is shown pulling petals off a daisy, counting "1-2-3. . . ." Then, a man's voice reverses the count, "6-5-4. . ." giving the unmistakable impression of a *countdown* to a missile launch. Americans had grown very familiar with this rocket launch sequence because of Eisenhower's decision to broadcast our space program. But the ad showed the little girl dissolve into a picture of a nuclear explosion.

---

* The only known exception to this rule was the wisecrack Ronald Reagan offered in 1984. Warming up for his weekly radio address, Reagan said he had just signed legislation abolishing the Soviet Union and the bombing would begin in five minutes. The White House quickly put out a statement saying the president was only joking and didn't know the microphone was live. Reagan had already been president for four years at that point and had gained a reputation for calm, steady leadership. Even so, it was a heart-stopping moment for his campaign managers.

Johnson's voice was heard saying, "We must love one another or die," suggesting outrageously that Goldwater's election meant death. "Vote for President Johnson" came the white words on a funereal black screen. "The stakes are too important for you to stay home."[82] The Johnson campaign ran Moyers's Daisy ad only once, but in those days before cable and satellite, most American homes had only three or four television channels. Thus, fifty million people saw this classic negative ad. For the rest of the campaign, the networks ran the ad *for free* as they discussed the issue of nuclear responsibility in the election.

Goldwater met with Johnson in the White House. He agreed not to make an issue of riots in Harlem. He wanted to avoid injecting race into the campaign.[83] When his campaign team produced a film called *Choice* that depicted drunken white teens cavorting naked and young black men rioting, he kept his word and rejected its use. It would inflame race relations, he said.[84]

Johnson showed no such restraint in attacking Goldwater. He chose Hubert Humphrey as his running mate and encouraged the Minnesota senator to go after Goldwater with vigor. Humphrey's point-by-point dissection of the Goldwater voting record demonstrated why senators are so rarely nominated for president. Humphrey treated the delegates at the Democratic National Convention with his litany of measures supported by both Republicans *and* Democrats. "But not Senator Goldwater" was Hubert's refrain, as the delighted delegates took up the response.[85] Humphrey's attack was hard-hitting and effective, but not out of bounds. Goldwater enjoyed his reputation for flinty independence of mind. But his often eccentric voting record made it easy to depict him as an extremist.

Politics ain't beanbag.

The same could not be said for *Fact* magazine. "1189 Psychiatrists Say Goldwater is Psychologically Unfit to be President," blared the editors' alarming headline.* They neglected to tell their readers that 12,356 psychiatrists had been questioned, that only 2,417 had responded, that 571 of these had said they couldn't properly diagnose the senator without ever speaking to him.[86] (After the election, Barry Goldwater sued *Fact* for libel

* To be sure, *Fact* was not *LIFE* magazine. Still, its sensationalized story was picked up by the mainstream news organizations and given far broader circulation.

and won. The federal court found the article so false, so defamatory, so malicious, it awarded Goldwater $75,000 in punitive damages. The U.S. Supreme Court upheld the judgment.[87])*

Goldwater approved one campaign broadcast that was to have vast consequences for American history. When every poll showed Goldwater about to get buried in almost every region, Barry okayed a speech by Californian Ronald Reagan. The popular former actor and television host addressed a nationwide audience with "A Time for Choosing." The speech was the great success of the campaign. Reagan articulated smoothly, convincingly, and non-threateningly the ideals of freedom, limited government, military strength, anti-Communism, and patriotism that Goldwater had tried without success to defend in his speeches. Goldwater's campaign was cruelly cartooned as a San Francisco cable car crashing down a steep hill: "A Streetcar Named Disaster."** Reagan's speech brought a flood of donations to a campaign rapidly running out of money.

More importantly, overnight, it made Reagan the bright hope of the conservative movement. From the date of "the speech," Ronald Reagan became the *de facto* head of the conservative movement in America.

Against the caricature of Goldwater as a warmonger, Johnson claimed to be the peace candidate. "These are the stakes—to make a world in which all of God's children can live, or go into the dark. We must either love each other, or we must die," said Johnson.[88] Noble words to be sure, but there is a reason why one of Johnson's most loyal aides once called him "Machiavelli in a Stetson."[89]*** Even as the president intoned about peace and love, his men in the Pentagon prepared to initiate the bombing campaign over North Vietnam.

Johnson had rushed through the Gulf of Tonkin Resolution when

---

* The American Medical Association denounced the magazine article when it was written. Afterward, the American Psychiatric Association adopted the Goldwater Rule, calling it a violation of professional ethics to diagnose without meeting a subject.

** The caption was a satirical reference to the play by Tennessee Williams titled *A Streetcar Named Desire.*

*** Niccoló Machiavelli's Renaissance classic, *The Prince,* described the cynical, unprincipled grasping for power that characterized the Italian city states of his day. So horrified were English-speaking readers by Machiavelli's amoral policy prescriptions that they made "Old Nick" for centuries a synonym for Satan.

North Vietnamese gunboats attacked two U.S. destroyers in August 1964 in the Gulf of Tonkin. The resolution blamed the North Vietnamese for the clash and authorized the president "to take all necessary measures to repel any armed attack against the forces of the United States and to prevent further aggression." He discouraged any extensive debate and demanded immediate action. Only two senators—Wayne Morse of Oregon and Ernest Gruening of Alaska—voted no.

Vietnam was rarely discussed in the 1964 campaign. Yet it loomed, like Banquo's ghost at MacBeth's banquet, behind the seated guests.*

Goldwater tried to raise the issue of war and peace. The Democrats, he charged, had led the nation blindly into "Lyndon Johnson's war in Vietnam . . . American sons and grandsons are being killed by Communist bullets and Communist bombs. And we have yet to hear a word of truth about why they're dying."[90] His point was legitimate. But by this point in the campaign, no one was listening.

Election night 1964 produced one of the most lopsided landslides in American history. LBJ won 486 electoral votes and 42,825,463 popular votes (60.6 percent) to Goldwater's 52 electoral votes and 27,175,770 popular votes (38.5 percent). Johnson's popular vote percentage exceeded FDR's in 1936. He swept all regions except the Deep South. Goldwater had urged Republicans to "go hunting where the ducks are" in making an appeal to white Southerners. But he had surrendered the historic areas of GOP strength. Many districts that had been Republican since the party was founded elected Democrats to Congress in 1964. Johnson's coattails produced a huge Democratic majority in the 89th Congress.

Johnson critics accused him of wanting every vote and stopping at nothing to gain an overwhelming victory. Surely, Johnson's vanity was famous. He named his Texas ranch "LBJ" for himself. His wife, Lady Bird, bore the same initials, as did his daughters, Luci Baines and Linda Bird

* The Kennedy administration had okayed the ouster of South Vietnam's authoritarian president Ngo Dinh Diem. President Kennedy was shocked when military plotters not only removed Diem and his powerful brother, Ngo Dinh Nhu but murdered them both on 1 November 1963. This left U.S. planners working, uneasily, with the homicidal conspirators who had seized power in Saigon. The grim story, however, was overshadowed by JFK's own assassination just three weeks later.

Johnson.* Only his pet beagles—whom he yanked up by their ears—escaped the Texan's brand. They were called *Him* and *Her*.

Johnson's very practical reasons for wanting to bury Barry were very simple: he wanted to break the power of conservative Southern Democrats and Republicans who resisted big spending programs. Johnson knew he would need a huge victory in 1964 to make up for expected losses in the South. He had seen the FDR, Truman, and JFK administrations frustrated on Capitol Hill. He had Texas-sized plans for legislation. Only a Texas-sized victory would produce the majority he needed to enact his programs.

Johnson wanted to achieve what FDR had outlined in his 1944 State of the Union address. FDR was his political mentor and hero. Johnson wanted to expand federal programs to give government extensive new powers in housing, education, welfare, and medical care. Nor would that be enough; Johnson knew that great presidents were patrons of culture. Personally, he cared nothing for literature, music, or art, but he believed he could win the support of refined people by treating their artistic interests the way he treated other congressional colleagues' desires for a new bridge or post office. He was not entirely wrong.**

In private, Johnson railed against "all those high-falutin' Harvards."[91] At one of Jackie Kennedy's elegant White House cultural soirées, Johnson was seen in the hall with his foot up on the immaculate wall, paring his finger nails with a pocketknife, bored to death. In fairness, JFK found Jackie's cultural evenings boring, too.[92]

VIII. Operation Hope Not: Churchill's Funeral

Sir Winston Churchill was too frail to attend the White House ceremony in 1963 where President Kennedy signed Public Law 88–6. That Congressional Resolution made this half-American British statesman only the *second*

---

* Johnson did not name his wife. Born Claudia Alta Taylor, as a baby she was said to be "as purty as a lady bird." The nickname stuck.

** The patrons of the arts proved to be very supportive of federal spending on their special interests, but Johnson miscalculated in thinking they would be grateful to *him* for the generous endowments he created.

person in history to be an honorary citizen of the United States.* The president said Churchill had "marshaled the English language and sent it into battle." The younger Kennedy openly admired the man his father loathed.

Churchill died on 24 January 1965 at age ninety. It was seventy years to the day after his famous father, Lord Randolph Churchill, died.[93] Sir Winston's death was certainly not unexpected. The British government had been planning Operation Hope Not for twelve years.[94]

America's government should have been prepared. But we suffered a shocking embarrassment when President Lyndon B. Johnson announced he would not attend the funeral. Johnson's memoirs do not tell us why. Some have said he listened to State Department protocol types, who may have told him that because Churchill was only a prime minister and not a head of state, it would be inappropriate for Johnson the president to go.[95]** Or perhaps Johnson, notoriously thin-skinned, was resentful of the fact that Britain's Prime Minister Harold Wilson and the Labour Government were offering no help to Johnson in Vietnam. Johnson proposed to send instead Chief Justice Earl Warren. Warren was certainly a figure of stature and dignity, but the British were wounded.

This deep wound was salved, however, when Queen Elizabeth II invited former President Dwight D. Eisenhower to London as her personal guest. The Queen had decreed that Churchill should have a State Funeral—the first commoner ever so honored. Churchill's funeral would be an event of high drama, modeled closely on that of the Duke of Wellington, who had saved the British from Napoleon in 1815.

Historian John Lukacs had to go. The Hungarian-born American brought his eight-year-old son. He recorded the scene. The people stood in line—queued up, as they say—long, silent hours in the bone-chilling cold before the funeral began. Lukacs joined them:

---

* Churchill followed the Marquis de Lafayette. Since 1965, Mother Teresa, Raoul Wallenberg—the Swedish diplomat who died rescuing Hungary's Jews at the close of World War II—and William and Hanna Penn—the founders of Pennsylvania—have been added to the list of honorary Americans.

** Churchill himself was no stranger to such formalities. When he met FDR on board the USS *Augusta* in August of 1941 for the Atlantic Charter conference, he bowed slightly to Roosevelt and handed him a letter of introduction from the King.

> The working people. We have not made the first turn and the people are talking. The charwomen . . . in their greenish old tweed coats, the brown scarves, the little glasses resting on the bumps of their pale faces, their bad teeth, their thin mouths. "I was here in Forty." "There was St. Paul's with all the City blazing around it, you know." A hundred thousand of the working people of England, with their good nature and their knobby faces, out of a still-living feeling rather than of memory—to the bier of a man who led them not to a great victory but who saved them from the worst of possible defeats, from the collapse of English self-respect.[96]

Though few would remember in 1965, it had been the young Winston who gave these working class people their old-age pensions, their on-the-job tea breaks, and their "labour exchanges"—unemployment offices we would call them—a half-century before. This grandson of a duke was a great democrat. Churchill the Conservative was also Churchill the Liberal.

France's President Charles de Gaulle joined the mourners. Churchill loved France with a deep and romantic love. Desperate to prevent France from surrendering in 1940, Churchill had even proposed an Anglo-French Union—common citizenship for all the French and British peoples! Then, when France slipped under the jackboots of the Nazis, he broadcast to them in their native tongue—*Dieu Protège La France—God Protect France.* Churchill called de Gaulle "the Constable of France" when the Gallic giant escaped the Nazis and flew to England in 1940.* He would, with Churchill's indispensable help, lead the Free French.** Lukacs points out that the truest opponents of Hitler's evil regime were men of the right: Churchill, de Gaulle, Konrad Adenauer.[97] "[Churchill] saw the evil incarnated in Hitler instantly, immediately," he writes. "Then he rose like a hero, highest in those months of 1940 when the future of

---

* Churchill had a stormy relationship with the towering de Gaulle. Privately, he joked that the Frenchman thought he was Joan of Arc and then added, pouting: "But my bishops will not let me burn him." Noting the symbol of de Gaulle's Free French, Churchill said, "The heaviest cross I have to bear is the Cross of Lorraine."

** Each British prime minister receives as a gift from his Sovereign the red leather dispatch box he used during his time at No. 10 Downing Street. Churchill's is in Paris, at the Musée de l'Armée, a gift to the French people from his widow, Clementine.

human decency was at stake, and when Jewry and Christianity were on the same side . . . which was his side."[98]

Inside Westminster Abbey, kings and queens came to pay him homage. They stood silently, reverently, as the choir sang "The Battle Hymn of the Republic"—Churchill's favorite. As the casket was carried by RAF flyers down the steps of the Abbey, the BBC broadcast to the world these words of tribute offered by Dwight D. Eisenhower:

> At this moment, as our hearts stand at attention, we say our affectionate though sad goodbye to the leader to whom the entire body of free men owes so much.
>
> In the coming years, many in countless words will strive to interpret the motives, describe the accomplishments, and extol the virtues of Winston Churchill—soldier, statesman, and citizen that two great countries were proud to claim as their own. Among all the things so written and so spoken, there will ring out through all the centuries one incontestable refrain: Here was a champion of freedom.
>
> May God grant that we—and the generations who will remember him—heed the lessons he taught us: in his deeds, in his words, in his life.
>
> May we carry on his work until no nation lies in captivity; no man is denied opportunity for fulfillment.
>
> And now, to you Sir Winston—my old friend—farewell![99]

The British people heard these words from the heart of America—and the wound healed. As Churchill's flag-draped casket was carried down the River Thames aboard the hydrographic vessel *Havengore,* it passed the East End of London.* This is the dock area that had suffered so heavily under the Nazi blitzkrieg. There, the famously left-wing dock workers did something extraordinary. These men worked the tall cranes that move the cargo in this great world seaport. As if on cue, each of the cranes dipped in a somber salute to Winston Churchill. His casket was now transferred to a

* A hydrographic vessel is a coastal survey vessel which aids navigation.

special train named the *Winston Churchill.* It was one of the Battle of Britain class of locomotives. Finally, Churchill's body was taken to Blenheim Palace, where he had been born prematurely almost a century before. Now he sleeps there with his fathers.

IX. "We Shall Overcome!"

Johnson wasted no time in applying his greatly expanded new congressional majority. Calling his program for the country "The Great Society," Johnson pressed for new federal legislation on education and health care. Congress passed the landmark Elementary and Secondary Education Act on 9 April 1965, and the president signed it into law two days later. LBJ broke a logjam that had lasted for decades. As a Protestant, he was politically able to provide funding for students attending parochial schools (mostly Catholic). Johnson also overcame Southern opposition. With desegregation now inevitable, Southern members of Congress wanted all the federal aid they could get.

Johnson's election victory the previous November, and the Deep South's choice of Goldwater, only emphasized to Dr. King and his supporters how powerless they were without the vote. A planned march on the state capital at Montgomery began in Selma, Alabama, on a cold, blustery Sunday in March. "It's not just Negroes, but really *all* of us who must overcome the crippling legacy of bigotry and injustice. *And we shall overcome,*" King told supporters in Selma.[100] The march was interrupted by club-swinging, mounted police who barred the way to the Edmund Pettis Bridge.

Other violence broke out as well. A white minister from Boston, James Reeb, was attacked by a mob of white youths for joining in the demonstrations. He died of his wounds.[101] Later, Viola Liuzzo, a Detroit housewife, was gunned down attempting to help young black volunteers register voters.[102]

Dr. King was joined in Selma by hundreds of marchers, including leaders of the AFL-CIO, religious groups, and national civil rights organizations. With three thousand marchers in Selma demanding civil rights, President Johnson went on national television to announce his support for a far-reaching Voting Rights Bill.

When the Voting Rights Bill swept through the 89th Congress, Johnson signed it on 6 August 1965. With his signature, Johnson put an end to the political order that had dominated his native region since Reconstruction. With voting rights enacted into law, segregationist politicians "turned on a dime." Strom Thurmond, Jesse Helms, George Wallace, and hundreds of other office seekers dropped their support of racial segregation.[103] As Senator Dirksen would say of his errant colleagues, "When I feel the heat, I see the light."

Voting rights for black Americans transformed politics. America could stand before the world and assert that we were, indeed, the home of freedom. No longer could Communist and non-aligned delegates at the UN taunt America for hypocrisy.

Johnson did not rest on his laurels. He pressed Congress to enact Medicare, which it dutifully did. LBJ traveled to the Truman Presidential Library in Independence, Missouri, for the bill signing ceremony. Generously, Johnson paid tribute to Harry Truman's vision—and promptly signed up the frail senior citizen as the *first* enrollee in the vast new medical program for the elderly. LBJ demanded and got new federal departments of Housing and Urban Development and Transportation. For HUD, he tapped Robert C. Weaver as secretary. Weaver was the first black man to serve in a president's cabinet. Johnson also named Thurgood Marshall to the Supreme Court. Marshall was the first black member of the high court.

The president greatly expanded welfare. If he had read Daniel Patrick Moynihan's warnings on the crisis in the black family, he apparently paid them no mind. Moynihan warned that the illegitimacy rate among black families—then at 22 percent—posed a serious threat to community stability. But in LBJ's Great Society, marriage would no longer be the centerpiece of federal family policy. Under Johnson, many federal bureaucrats questioned whether marriage had any significance anyway. A husband, it seemed, could be replaced by a check. Johnson's "War on Poverty" resulted in billions of dollars going to Appalachian and Inner City projects. Some of these proved worthy, but many were, as their Republican critics called them, "boondoggles."

Lady Bird Johnson gained great credit for her drive to beautify federal highways. Commercial interests, including billboard advertisers, groused, but Mrs. Johnson's views prevailed.

LBJ used his vast appointive powers to give positions to consumer advocates. The consumer movement received a huge boost in 1965 following publication of the book *Unsafe at Any Speed,* a muckraking tract on General Motors' popular, sporty Corvair automobile. GM executives' clumsy attempt to discredit author Ralph Nader by prying into his private life and by trying to entice him with prostitutes was catalogued in a *New Republic* magazine article that gave the consumer activist the name "Saint Ralph."[104]*

Johnson also created the National Endowment for the Arts and the National Endowment for the Humanities. He created the Corporation for Public Broadcasting (CPB), which in time spawned the Public Broadcasting System (PBS) for television and National Public Radio (NPR). They never created a federal government monopoly on broadcasting—as is so often the case in Europe—but they helped further to institutionalize Johnson-style Big Government liberalism.

X. Vietnam

So exaggerated was LBJ's campaign against Barry Goldwater, so extreme was the denunciation of Goldwater as a warmonger, that Johnson left himself little room to serve as a wartime president. He did not have the advantage that Wilson and Roosevelt had—a clear and present danger of enemy attack. Johnson's reputation for overstatement and for successful wheeling and dealing had helped him when he was giving the famous "treatment" to colleagues on Capitol Hill. It was to prove disastrous in his efforts to persuade Americans. TR called the White House "the Bully Pulpit." He meant it was primarily a place of moral influence. Harry Truman's view of the White House was typically peppery: "I sit here all day trying to persuade people to do the things they ought to have the sense enough to do without my persuading them. . . . That's all the powers of the President amount to."[105]

---

* Nader's activism helped create the National Highway Traffic Safety Administration, which in 1973 found the Corvair not appreciably less safe than light-weight European autos favored by Nader's allies. This revelation did not dent the consumer crusader's armor. (Online source: Bailey, Ronald, "Saint Ralph's Original Sin," *National Review Online,* http://www.nationalreview.com/comment/comment062800a.html.)

At first, the Vietnam War was not Lyndon Johnson's war. The Truman Doctrine had committed the United States to help nations trying to resist Communist subversion. Accordingly, Truman sent U.S. aid to the French and anti-Communist forces in South Vietnam. Despite the vigorous attacks on containment by Vice President Richard Nixon, President Eisenhower committed the United States to contain Communist expansion.[106] Ike was the one who first used the analogy of the dominoes to explain why the United States had to support South Vietnam.[107] According to the Domino Theory, if South Vietnam fell to the Communists, so too would Laos, Cambodia, and very likely Thailand, Malaya, Singapore, and all of Southeast Asia. Given the Cold War experience with Poland, Czechoslovakia, Hungary, and the rest of Eastern Europe, it seemed a compelling theory.

As president, John F. Kennedy backed the South Vietnamese government. He increased U.S. forces from 3,164 in 1961 to 16,263 by the time of his death in 1963.[108]

When Johnson came into office, he had to deal with the chaotic aftermath of the assassination of the president of South Vietnam and his brother. Kennedy had approved their ouster, but *not* their murder.[109] The Kennedy administration suspected that Diem and his brother might be working through the French to reunify the country, neutralize it, and expel the Americans.[110]

Johnson soon found that American liberal opinion was alienated from the South Vietnamese cause, however. Journalist Stanley Karnow described the execution of a Vietnamese merchant of Chinese background. The merchant was accused of "speculation." Air Vice Marshal Nguyen Cao Ky—one of the coup plotters against the Diems—condemned the merchant to a public execution.

> Eager to demonstrate his zeal, Ky had arranged for the supposed culprit's public execution in the square facing Saigon's central market, and I joined the crowd to witness the gruesome sight. A chubby and surprisingly young man, Ta Vinh, was dragged to the stake by [South] Vietnamese soldiers as his wife and children, garbed in ritual white mourning dress, let loose bloodcurdling wails of despair. The spectators

watched numbly as the firing squad performed its task, and dispersed just as silently when the episode ended.[111]

Not only was "speculation" a specious charge to bring against anyone, the selection of an ethnic Chinese merchant was an example of Asians giving in to "the anti-Semitism of the Orient." In all countries in Southeast Asia, enterprising ethnic Chinese were often targets of envy and singled out for persecution. Yet, when LBJ met Vice Marshal Ky in Honolulu, he embraced Ky's social vision for his country. "Boy, you speak just like an American," Johnson said.[112]

Not only did Johnson fail to make the case for the Vietnam War to the American people, he also failed to gain the support of America's allies. British voters had turned out the Conservatives just weeks before Goldwater was buried. The new Labour Prime Minister Harold Wilson wanted no part of armed intervention in Southeast Asia. Johnson tried to give his famous "treatment" to Canada's Prime Minister Lester B. Pearson. He treated that nation's most respected diplomat with such contempt that the Canadian press published cartoons showing Johnson lifting "Mike" Pearson by his ears—just like a Johnson beagle!

Johnson's relations with France's Charles de Gaulle were poisoned from the start. Johnson expressed outrage when de Gaulle declined to visit the United States in 1964. The French leader said his hurried trip to Washington for JFK's funeral counted as discharging his duty to visit the United States.*

French help may not have been very helpful. After all, the French were the old imperialists of Vietnam, and they had lost ingloriously at Dienbienphu in 1954. But the active, vocal opposition of General de Gaulle

---

* Americans began to dislike France during the Johnson years. President de Gaulle was widely viewed as prickly, uncooperative, and ungrateful. So he seemed to the British, too, whom he vetoed for membership in the European Common Market. De Gaulle was notoriously touchy about France's national sovereignty. During the Second World War, de Gaulle in London had defied Churchill on a point of French national honor. His fellow Free French officers were aghast. They agreed, they assured him, but they depended on Prime Minister Churchill for every bullet, every boot, every bayonet. Stiffly pulling himself up to his full 6'5", de Gaulle frostily informed his worried subordinates: "The English must learn that you can only lean on that which offers *resistance.*" In resisting LBJ twenty years later, President de Gaulle was behaving no differently. From the Johnson years onward, the French have always given us plenty of *resistance.*

was *very* harmful to U.S. interests. De Gaulle was seen throughout the world as a conservative, nationalist leader. His opposition to U.S. policy made it respectable for anti-Communist leaders everywhere to dissent from Johnson's position. So serious was the U.S.-French split under Johnson that de Gaulle eventually expelled the American-led NATO military command from Paris.

Sensitive to troubles in their region, Australia and New Zealand provided small contingents of troops to support the U.S. effort in Vietnam.[113] As important as allies are, however, it is *American* support that is most important whenever Americans are fighting and dying in distant lands. Vice President Humphrey visited Saigon in 1967 to try to explain to President Thieu that the American people were questioning our purposes in Vietnam. "I tried to warn him that [his government] would have to make significant changes if our support was to continue. I said I wasn't sure our people would accept an indefinite long-term involvement."[114] Humphrey describes Thieu's dismissive attitude:

> Thieu listened, delicately holding a cigarette, its smoke drifting up and away from him. He broke the pose to flick the ash from his cigarette in a manner that suggested he was also flicking away what I had said.
>
> "No, you will be here for a long time. We are aware of what you say, but we realize that your support will have to continue, and perhaps even increase for the next five or six years . . ."[115]

The arrogant Thieu seemed to have little understanding that Americans were then drafting nineteen-year-olds from little towns in Minnesota to fight for *his* freedom. Even then, his government was giving draft deferments to favored young Vietnamese men. Some of them lounged around cafés in Paris discussing the existentialist writings of French philosopher Jean-Paul Sartre. On the other hand, Americans knew little of the often heroic efforts of ARVN soldiers to protect their own country.*

---

* ARVN—Army of the Republic of Vietnam. These were the anti-Communist forces in country.

When Lyndon Johnson visited American forces in Vietnam, he told our soldiers to pursue victory, to "nail the coonskin to the wall."[116] Because he could give Americans no overarching reason to fight and sacrifice, Lyndon Johnson himself increasingly became the object of opposition to the war. His coarseness and his tendency to make outrageous displays of his emotions made his critics angrier with his policies. Johnson self-pityingly decried all of this criticism as disdain for him *as a Texan*.

This was another of Johnson's self-serving exaggerations. America has had *many* Texans in public office, courtly men like Wilson's aide Colonel House, James A. Baker III, Lloyd Bentsen, and John Connally. Longtime Speaker of the House Sam Rayburn was hardly courtly, but he always maintained a gruff dignity. None of them would ever have yanked up his shirt to show an unhealed scar from a gall bladder operation as LBJ did.* Johnson was disliked for his *own* qualities and not for anything endemic to Texas. JFK and Ike could turn the air blue with barracks language, but neither man ever slipped once in public. And neither ever made a public spectacle of himself.

Johnson's personality and his administration's record became the focus of the Republican campaign of 1966. In response to *three* "long, hot summers" in which race riots had broken out in many cities, Hubert Humphrey told the NAACP convention that if *he* had to live in a ghetto, "he might lead a pretty good revolt," too. With this statement, Humphrey seemed to condone rampant lawlessness and caused many Americans to believe that liberals were "soft on crime" and disorder.[117] Thirty-four people had died in riots in the Watts section of Los Angeles in 1965.[118] Richard Nixon came out of his four-year retirement to lead the GOP attack in 1966. The Republicans gained forty-seven seats in the House of Representatives and three new U.S. senators. One of these was Massachusetts's Edward Brooke, the first black senator elected since Reconstruction.

In California, voters gave Ronald Reagan a *million vote* margin over incumbent Governor Edmund G. "Pat" Brown. Brown's campaign had

---

* One group *had* to love Lyndon—the political cartoonists. David Levine's spot-on caricature of LBJ showing his scar featured the incision in the shape of a map of Vietnam.

stupidly compared Reagan's acting career to that of John Wilkes Booth. Students who grew their hair long, smoked marijuana, and protested the war in Vietnam, the draft, and almost everything else about American life were the butt of Reagan's campaign humor. They were known as "hippies." They "act like Tarzan, look like Jane and smell like Cheetah," Reagan said good-naturedly.[119] Californians loved it.

Johnson's typical habit of exaggeration was seen in inept defenses of his war policy. We won't "pull back our defenses to San Francisco," Johnson stated.[120] LBJ himself seemed not to understand clearly what Americans were fighting for. He relied heavily on Defense Secretary Robert S. McNamara, one of the so-called "whiz kids" from the Ford Motor Company. McNamara was one of JFK's brilliant New Frontiersmen whom Johnson had retained.*

Johnson began to face a large and growing antiwar movement. Because he had never taken his case to the American people and because he had never asked Congress for a declaration of war, Johnson relied too heavily on public opinion polls. These showed support for U.S. involvement, at least until 1966. Most of the American press, especially the "prestige press," backed the Johnson administration's position on the war as late as 1966.[121]

Johnson had campaigned against Goldwater by charging the conservative senator with being reckless. Now, LBJ boasted that he kept such a tight rein on his generals "they can't bomb an outhouse" in North Vietnam without his approval.[122] The only unbelievable part of that statement is that Johnson would have said "outhouse." Although Johnson could rightly say he had not initiated the war, he was unquestionably the one who escalated American involvement in the war. It was Johnson who increased American forces "in country" to more than five hundred thousand. Most of these were draftees.

Vietnam kept American policymakers distracted. When, in June 1967, Egypt's dictator Gamal Abdel Nasser expelled UN peacekeepers from the Sinai Desert, President Johnson used the "hotline" Kennedy

* LBJ was mightily impressed by that fellow "with the sta-comb in his hair." When he told Speaker Sam Rayburn how bright McNamara and his fellow intellectuals were, Mr. Sam reportedly responded, "Maybe, Lyndon, but I'd feel a hell of a lot better if even *one* of them had ever run for sheriff."

and Khrushchev had established to argue that both nuclear superpowers should avoid direct involvement in a Mideast war. Soviet Premier Alexei Kosygin gave Johnson assurances, but the Soviets had armed Egypt and other Arab states to the teeth.[123]

When Nasser closed off the Straits of Tiran, blocking Israel's freedom of the seas, Israel decided to act. "Our basic objective," Nasser stated publicly, "will be to destroy Israel."[124] The Israelis struck back, destroying the Arab air forces on the ground and unleashing a lightning assault on the Egyptians, Jordanians, and Syrians. In six days, the Israelis threw back their Arab enemies, gaining extensive territory on the West Bank of the Jordan River, the Sinai Desert, and the Golan Heights of Syria.

Israeli jets also attacked the USS *Liberty,* killing thirty-four American sailors and wounding one hundred seventy-two. President Johnson accepted Israel's formal apology. They said they had misidentified the clearly marked intelligence ship. Israel agreed to pay $13 million in damages.

Jews around the world—and particularly in the Soviet Union—were thrilled by the State of Israel's brilliant campaign to smash the Arab armies. Friends of Israel rejoiced that the Jewish state would now have a territorial "buffer" to protect it from terrorist attacks. East Jerusalem, with its famous Western Wall, the site of Solomon's Temple, now came under Israeli control.* The occupation of the West Bank and Gaza—with more than three million Palestinian Arabs—would create massive problems for Israel that persist to this day.

The American news media wrote about "hawks" and "doves" in the administration and on Capitol Hill. *Life* magazine published three hundred photographs of young Americans who had been killed *in just one week* of fighting in Vietnam. And there were many such weeks. The media harped on Johnson's "credibility gap," accusing him of lying to take the country into war. To many Americans, the press seemed to relish its "adversarial" pose *vis à vis* the administration. Some thought the media friendlier to North Vietnam's Communist rulers than to their own government.

---

* The Israelis allowed Muslims to control the Dome of the Rock mosque, a holy site of Islam.

Woodrow Wilson had been able to defend his war policies. FDR gave eloquent expression to the need to sacrifice. Truman's defense of his Korean War policies faltered. Eisenhower had avoided a land war in Asia, or anywhere else. Judging from his World War II statements, he could have led the country in war. JFK excelled in public communication. ("Any spot is tenable if brave men will make it so" was a typical piece of Kennedy eloquence.) But none of them ever encountered the kind of bitter, intense, personal hatred that LBJ did. An example:

> Hey! Hey! LBJ!
> How many kids have you killed today?

Keenly aware of the American domestic front, North Vietnamese Communist leaders staked all on a single attack in January 1968—the Tet Offensive. They pushed their Vietcong allies to stage a suicidal series of attacks across South Vietnam.* Militarily, it was a disaster for the Vietcong as thousands were killed. But the sight of the U.S. Embassy in Saigon being invaded, of hundreds of American casualties all over the South, showed that we were nowhere near "the light at the end of the tunnel." Johnson's policy of graduated escalation seemed to millions of television viewers to be a total and bloody failure.

Tet was planned to take place during a holiday truce. But Tet was a Buddhist holiday, not an *American* one. Communists in Hué, a city in northern South Vietnam, killed between two thousand and three thousand civilians. Many of these were clubbed to death or buried alive.[125]

Little of this was shown on American television. The city was under Communist control. But when South Vietnam's police chief, General Loan, shot a Vietcong colonel in the head, the photo was shown around the world. It won a Pulitzer Prize. General Loan seemed the very picture of a brutal tyrant to shoot an unarmed man, a man whose arms were tied behind his back. We now know that Loan *knew* the man, caught him in the

---

* *Vietcong* was the name given to black pajama-clad Communist guerillas in the South. We now know that they were not independent of the North, but wholly subordinate to it.

act of terrorizing a Saigon neighborhood, and captured him in civilian clothes.[126] The man Loan shot had just killed a close personal friend of the police chief's and murdered the friend's entire family. None of this mattered then to the antiwar protesters.

Antiwar protests grew in breadth and intensity. Demonstrators burned American flags and draft cards. Three Americans, doubtless influenced by the horrific pictures of a protesting Buddhist monk in Saigon, actually *burned* themselves to death.[127] Communist agitators in the United States urged resistance to government policy. The national antiwar group, the Mobilization to End the War (known to activists as "the Mobe") was taken over by Communist followers of the violent ideas of Leon Trotsky.[128]

Writer Susan Sontag said that North Vietnam *deserved* to be idealized.[129] Actress Jane Fonda went to Hanoi and posed on North Vietnamese antiaircraft guns. This, at a time when American pilots were being shot down, killed, or imprisoned and tortured. American antiwar activists took at face value North Vietnamese claims that they actually fed U.S. prisoners *more* than they fed their own people "because they are bigger than we are."[130] Prisoner of war Jeremiah Denton was brought before television cameras. Unable to speak openly, he nonetheless sent a message. It was daring. He blinked his eyes in Morse code, and the message he sent was chilling: "t-o-r-t-u-r-e."

Defense Secretary McNamara stepped down in January 1968. He has since written a widely criticized memoir in which he claimed that he always harbored grave doubts about the U.S. involvement in Vietnam.* Johnson replaced him with Clark Clifford, who undertook a total review of U.S. policy.

Following Tet, thousands of young antiwar activists went "clean for Gene." They cut their hair and volunteered in the New Hampshire cam-

* Secretary of State Dean Rusk and National Security Adviser Walt Rostow believed in the U.S. mission in Vietnam all their days. McNamara gave no indication of his private doubts to the two presidents he served, nor to the American people, nor to the young men he sent to fight and die in Vietnam. His attempt to curry favor with the antiwar elites only further damaged his tainted reputation.

paign of Senate dove Eugene McCarthy, who had entered the Democratic presidential primaries on an antiwar platform. McCarthy, a poet and former semi-pro baseball player, had had an undistinguished career in the Senate. Now, though, the press lionized him. *St. Gene* became the great hope of activists for bringing down LBJ.

When McCarthy carried 42 percent of the vote in the New Hampshire Democratic primary, the press proclaimed him the winner.* New York senator Robert F. Kennedy now came under increased pressure to enter the race against Lyndon Johnson.

Kennedy had held back. He said he didn't want to split the Democratic Party. He said he didn't want his challenge to look like a "grudge match." (The mutual loathing between Kennedy and Johnson was famous.) At first, he didn't think Johnson was vulnerable. After New Hampshire, however, McCarthy had shown that Johnson could be brought down—maybe not by McCarthy, however. Leading antiwar Democrats feared that the aloof, scholarly McCarthy could never win a general election.

When Robert Kennedy announced that he, too, would challenge LBJ, many old Kennedy supporters were thrilled. Some of McCarthy's backers, however, were outraged. They admired their man for having had the courage to take Johnson on. Now, they resented "Bobby" for butting in. All the old stories of Kennedy's "ruthlessness" were revived.

XI. 1968: Annus Horribilis

Americans greeted 1968 with trepidation. In just five years, the nation had had to endure a nuclear showdown over Cuba, the assassination of a beloved president, violence against the movement for civil rights, riots in hundreds of cities, and a seemingly endless and bloody war. Lyndon Johnson's approval rating, on which he set such store, had plummeted. A

* Actually, Johnson won with 49 percent of the vote. His achievement was all the more amazing since he did not campaign and his name was not even on the ballot. But, as JFK said, appearances contribute to reality. In a short time, the public believed that Senator McCarthy had in fact won the New Hampshire primary election. It would not be the last time that a second-place showing in New Hampshire was "spun" into a win. Bill Clinton managed that feat in the Granite State in 1992.

naturally optimistic people, Americans hoped for a better new year. It was not to be. Nineteen sixty-eight would prove to be one of most discouraging years in our history.

After McCarthy's strong showing in New Hampshire's primary, LBJ could not bear to be bested by Bobby Kennedy, whom he despised. Johnson felt embittered and hurt. He had never wanted the Vietnam War, he told intimates. He had followed Jack Kennedy's policies—urged on by Jack Kennedy's advisers. When he entered the White House, Bobby Kennedy was still a "hawk" on Vietnam. There was a Green Beret—the symbol of America's anti-guerilla elite warriors—on JFK's grave. And the Green Berets had no greater champion in Washington than Robert Kennedy.

Meanwhile, President Johnson's Commission on Civil Disorders reported that America was becoming two societies "increasingly separate and unequal." Despite the major civil rights bills that had been passed and signed—with broad popular support—the Commission's majority blamed the urban riots on the racism of the white majority in the United States.

Johnson announced a national television address for 31 March 1968. The White House said the speech would be a review of U.S. policy in Vietnam. It was—but there was more. At the end, Johnson stunned the world by announcing that he would withdraw from the presidential race. The country was shaken. What did this mean to the troops then fighting in Vietnam? Did it mean Johnson had abandoned the policies that sent them there? Did it mean he had abandoned *them*?

Hard on the heels of this news came an even more shattering word from Memphis. Though he'd received death threats continually since 1955, Dr. Martin Luther King Jr. never shied from making public appearances. On the night of 3 April 1968 he spoke to a large crowd in a church: "I've been to the mountaintop. And I don't mind. Like anybody, I would like to live a long time. . . . But I'm not concerned about that now. I just want to do God's will. He's allowed me to go up to the mountain, and I've looked over and I've seen the Promised Land! . . . Mine eyes have seen the glory of the coming of the Lord!"[131] It was his last public address. The following day, Dr. King leaned over the railing at the Lorraine Motel and asked a friend to "sing *Precious Lord* for me tonight as you've never sung it before."[132]* At that moment, he was cut down by an assassin's bullet.

Robert Kennedy shared the news with a largely black crowd as he campaigned in Wisconsin. Crying and embracing, the crowd dispersed peacefully after he spoke these words:

> So I shall ask you tonight to return home, to say a prayer for the family of Martin Luther King . . . but more importantly to say a prayer for our own country . . . a prayer for understanding and that compassion of which I spoke.
>
> We can do well in this country. . . . It is not the end of violence; it is not the end of lawlessness; it is not the end of disorder. But the vast majority of white people and the vast majority of black people in this country want to live together, want to improve the quality of our life, and want justice for all human beings who abide in our land.
>
> Let us dedicate ourselves to . . . tame the savageness of man and make gentle the life of this world. Let us dedicate ourselves to that, and say a prayer for our country and for our people.[133]

Bobby Kennedy's words on that mournful occasion touch us down to our own day. But across America that night, riots broke out in hundreds of cities and towns. Reminiscent of the New York draft riots of 1863, rioting, looting, and burning continued for days in many cities. Hundreds died as National Guard troops had to be called in to restore order. In Washington, D.C., the Capitol looked like St. Paul's Cathedral had looked during the London Blitz. Smoke and flames rose up across the country.

America in 1968 felt like a runaway train ride. When Vice President

---

* A memorial plaque has been placed at the site of Dr. King's assassination. It says, "They said one to another,

> Behold, here cometh the dreamer . . .
> Let us slay him . . .
> And we shall see what becomes of his dreams."
> Genesis 37:19–20

The biblical inscription challenges each of us to "see what becomes of his dreams."

Humphrey declared his candidacy, he spoke of "the politics of joy." The learned Humphrey was only quoting from John Adams, but he was roundly criticized for it. Who could talk about *joy* in such a year?

And it only got worse.

Early in June, Robert Kennedy battled Gene McCarthy in the California Democratic Primary. As Kennedy went down to claim victory in Los Angeles's Ambassador Hotel, he was shot by Sirhan Sirhan, a young Palestinian immigrant who hated Senator Kennedy for his support of Israel. RFK died early the next morning.*

With King dead, the Kennedys dead, three hundred a week dying in Vietnam, our cities in flames, many of our campuses in an uproar, inflation rampant, authority itself seemed to be breaking down. The foundations of the Great Republic were tottering. Would there be no end to the horrors of this *annus horribilis*?

When the 1968 Democratic National Convention met in Chicago, Vice President Humphrey had most of the delegates' support. Humphrey later reported that his wife and children had been threatened by antiwar protesters. Red paint or, worse, excrement, would be thrown on Muriel Humphrey, the Secret Service warned.[134] No politics of joy here. Protesters were determined to break up the convention. Chicago police were just as determined to prevent that. The Democratic Party was itself bitterly divided, over the war, over the draft, over the crisis in the cities and on campuses, over the nomination of a candidate who had contested no primaries.

Only four years before, Lyndon Johnson had celebrated his fifty-sixth birthday at the Democratic Party's 1964 National Convention in Atlantic City, New Jersey. Then, throaty Carol Channing had sung "Hello, Lyndon" to the tune of "Hello, Dolly." Now, the repudiated Johnson dared not show his face at his party's nominating convention.

The riots that occurred in Chicago's Grant Park and throughout the

* Oceans of ink were spilled in these years describing the United States as a "sick" society because of these horrific assassinations. But JFK was killed by a man who had renounced his U.S. citizenship. The Reverend Dr. King was murdered by a drifter, a marginal man who spent most of his life in jail. And here, Bobby Kennedy was assassinated by an alien. Sirhan's vengeful act deserves to be described as the first instance of Arab terrorism in America.

city were fully televised to the American people. Liberal Connecticut senator Abe Ribicoff denounced the head-knocking conduct of the Chicago Police as the city's mayor, Richard J. Daley, yelled obscene abuse from his seat in the middle of the Illinois delegation. Waiting to deliver his acceptance speech, Humphrey was almost overcome by tear gas in his hotel room. Outside, demonstrators chanted "Dump the Hump!" Jerry Rubin, one of the "Chicago Seven" later tried for their activities at the convention, said his group was "guilty as hell." Rubin added, "We wanted . . . to make the city react as if it was a police state and force the attention of the whole world on us."[135]

Antiwar demonstrators claimed to believe in a "New Left." They wanted a more humane form of socialism. Behind the Iron Curtain, Czechoslovakia's Alexander Dubcek offered his people "Socialism with a *human* face."[136] His "Prague Spring" represented something new in Communist regimes and was highly popular with the Czech people. Soviet tanks rolled into Prague in August, however, putting an end to this experiment in a more liberal Communism. Dubcek and his colleagues were taken to Moscow. There, they were chained to the Kremlin walls and a drunken Leonid Brezhnev came out from a banquet to taunt them. The Czechs were shown no mercies; they were chained until they soiled themselves. The woozy dictator announced to the world his Brezhnev Doctrine. It was his version of containment: *What we have, we keep.**

The Johnson administration issued protests but took no action against the Soviets. Eighty civilians were killed as the Soviets extinguished Czech freedom for another generation. Five hundred Soviet tanks and five hundred thousand Warsaw Pact troops crushed the Czech peoples' aspirations.[137]

Following the uproarious Democratic National Convention in Chicago, it is small wonder Republican nominee Richard Nixon was more than thirty points ahead in the polls in the summer of 1968. Alabama Governor George C. Wallace jumped into the race as an independent. At the time, Wallace's entry was expected to hurt Humphrey. Many blue-collar workers sympathized

---

* Despite his ill-treatment by his Soviet captors, Dubcek returned to Czechoslovakia and lived there quietly until his death in 1992. He lived to see the collapse of the Soviet empire in Eastern Europe.

with Wallace's hawkish position on the war and his threat to "run over" demonstrators if they blocked his limousine.

As temperatures and tempers cooled in the autumn, Humphrey and his running mate, Maine's Democratic senator Edmund Muskie, rose in the polls. Humphrey had to try to appeal to antiwar voters while not losing LBJ's backing. Johnson made an attempt to get peace talks underway, but they were stalled as Nixon sent word secretly to Saigon that they should hold out for more favorable treatment under a Republican administration.[138]

There were no debates. Nixon coasted. He exuded calmness and command. "I'm not going to campaign for the black vote at the risk of alienating the suburban vote," he told campaign associates.[139] This, combined with Goldwater's stance in 1964, helped to alienate black voters from the GOP from that point on.* Burned by his experience in 1960, Nixon's goal was *not* to lose.[140] And he didn't.

Despite Humphrey's resurgence in the polls, Nixon won with 31,710,470 popular votes (43.4 percent) and 301 electoral votes. Humphrey won 30,898,055 popular votes (42.3 percent) and 191 electoral votes. Wallace's vote collapsed in the northern industrial states in the closing weeks of the campaign as organized labor came through for their friend Humphrey, but the Alabamian nonetheless carried five Deep South states. He won 9,446,167 popular votes (12.9 percent) and 46 electoral votes. Claiming victory, Nixon told the television audience of the little girl who had held up her hand-lettered sign: "Bring Us Together." Americans prayed for that.

To close out this horrible year, Americans at last had an event to bring them together. Ever since the fire on board that killed three astronauts at Cape Kennedy during a launch pad test in January 1967, it seemed doubtful that America could keep John F. Kennedy's promise to land a man on the moon by the end of the 1960s.

Now, however, in December 1968, there were concerns that the Soviets might try a "figure eight" flight to circle the moon and claim the prize. It would be a disaster for U.S. prestige at any time, but it would have been especially dispiriting after Americans had endured such a year.

---

* As recently as 1960, Nixon had been able to win 30 percent of black voters' support. Far from a majority, to be sure, but a respectable showing.

President Johnson ordered NASA to go ahead with *Apollo 8*. Astronauts Frank Borman, Jim Lovell, and Bill Anders prepared to be the first human beings to leave Earth's orbit and head out to the moon. Their wives were told by NASA that their husbands' chances of making it back alive were no better than 50–50.[141] They would not land, but their voyage would take them to within one hundred miles of the lunar surface, over the Sea of Crises, the Marsh of Sleep, and on to the Sea of Tranquility.[142] Frank Borman did not ordinarily wear his religion on his sleeve, but he said he was seized by the spiritual impact of being the first human being to see the earth as God saw it. He and his fellow astronauts broadcast to the world from sixty-nine miles above the lunar suface. They had gone where no men had gone before. And they chose to read from Genesis on Christmas Eve.

> In the beginning, God created the heaven and the earth; and the earth was without form and void, and darkness was upon the face of the deep; and the spirit of God moved upon the face of the waters.
>
> And God said, "Let there be light," and there was light.
> And God saw the light, that it was good.
> And God divided the light from the darkness.[143]

After a year of death and destruction, of tumult and war, and rumors of war, the *Apollo 8* astronauts' brave journey and their healing gesture were like a balm in Gilead. The world stood in awe of the pictures of an "earth rise" coming up over the horizon of the moon. We marveled at the beauty of this bright blue orb set in a black night. As one telegram of thanks to the astronauts put it: "You saved 1968."[144]

For Americans, *Apollo 8* held the promise that a free people and free institutions would not fail after all. Americans coming together could still achieve wonders.

Ten

NIXON'S THE ONE

(1969–1974)

In the space of just months, this Nation would achieve undreamed of heights by landing a man on the Moon, only to be plunged into the depths of discouragement as a besieged president warned against America becoming "a pitiful helpless giant." A famous political dynasty would end in the mud under a bridge at Chappaquiddick, although this was insufficiently understood at the time. America in the early 1970s experienced a protracted withdrawal from an inconclusive and bloody war. Protesting students would face National Guard bayonets and even, tragically, bullets. Crosby, Stills, Nash & Young sang a plaintive dirge: "Tin Soldiers and Nixon Comin'/We're finally on our own/This summer I hear the drumming/Four dead in Ohio." This Nation seemed to lurch from one crisis to another—the inner cities sinking in despair, court-ordered busing, gasoline shortages, abortion laws overturned, the forced resignation of a vice president and a president. As urban riots ebbed, foreign crises loomed. The war in Vietnam, terror scarring the peaceful competition of the Munich Olympics, the "oil shock" of the early 1970s, the Arabs' near-success in a war they launched against Israel on Yom Kippur—all of these menacing happenings seemed to show an America at the mercy of events. Would Americans have to adjust to an age of limits and a lesser role in world affairs? Would the younger generation face a future colder, darker, and poorer than the America their parents had known? Most importantly, would human freedom become just one of a set of competing values that

> *Americans had no right to "impose" on third-world countries? The rulers of those countries were more than willing to barter away human rights for more rapid development—so long as they stayed on top. These rulers willingly traded their peoples' freedom for bread—and they ate the bread.*

I. "Give a Damn!"

No sooner had Americans rallied to support the great Civil Rights Act of 1964, the Voting Rights Act of 1965, and a host of other measures designed to secure equal rights in housing, education, and employment than a number of major cities faced racial rioting. Los Angeles, Detroit, and Newark were among the worst of these "urban disorders," as the dominant media euphemistically called them. Hundreds of lives were lost; millions of dollars of property damage occurred. But the greatest casualty was civility.

No small amount of Richard Nixon's resurrection in the late 1960s was due to the deteriorating urban scene. Nixon pledged law and order. Liberal editorialists lambasted him as racist, saying law and order were simply code words intended to spark a white "backlash" against the just aspirations of black Americans.

No one personified the hopes of white liberals more than New York City's tall, elegant, patrician mayor, John Vliet Lindsay. As mayor, Lindsay had done all he could to keep a lid on New York. He walked the streets in shirtsleeves, seeking to cool the seething discontent with the force of his magnetic presence.

It wasn't *all* charisma, of course. The Lindsay administration in Gracie Mansion was shoveling money to some very questionable street organizers who assured frightened city officials that they—and they alone—could keep the city from erupting in flames. This process of scaring city bureaucrats was satirized by "new journalist" Tom Wolfe. "Mau-mauing the flak-catchers" was how Wolfe described the shakedown of timid city officials by radical organizers. And Wolfe gave us the term "radical chic" to note the style adopted by Manhattan's liberal social elite. Leonard Bernstein, the greatly talented director of the New York Philharmonic, was as famous for his embrace of far-left political causes as for his frenzied style with the baton. The fund-raiser he held in his posh apartment for members of the violent Black Panthers was captured forever in Wolfe's acid-etched writings.

Lindsay was the real power behind the National Advisory Commission on Civil Disorders. President Johnson had given the chairmanship to Illinois Governor Otto Kerner in 1967, but it was Lindsay who pressed members and staff to write a tough, unsparing report.* The Kerner Report, as it was called, warned that America was rapidly becoming "two societies—one black, one white—separate and unequal." For this dire state of affairs, the Commission blamed white racism. The report was widely hailed by the dominant media as "historic."[1]

Historic it certainly was. It was the first time a presidential commission had decided to blame the majority of the American people for a social condition. In effect, the commission members were trying to elect a new people. To do this, they embraced Lindsay's Manhattan liberalism. "Give a damn" was their call to end social divisions. Businesses and charities, churches and citizens were dunned to give more in time and money to solve the problems of the nation's ghettoes.

The Kerner Report received little criticism at the time it was issued. To do so would only have invited charges of racism. Looking back upon it, however, it is clear that it ignored clear signs of progress being made by black Americans in the period from 1940 to 1970—impressive gains in life expectancy (up ten years), home ownership (up 15 percent), incomes (up 150 percent), and white collar jobs (up 17 percent).[2] Also, Lindsay's prodding of those writing the report left little room to record the experiences of the *victims* of urban rioting. Thousands of small businesses were driven out of the core of our nation's cities.[3] These small businesses gave employment and life to the community. Along with churches, they made the community. By allowing violence to drive these stable citizens out, city governments and their collaborators on the national scene were sowing the seeds of poverty, violence, and hopelessness.

---

* Otto Kerner was appointed a federal judge, but was soon found to have taken bribes when he was governor. He was tried, convicted, and sent to federal prison on seventeen counts of bribery, conspiracy, perjury, and related charges.

To these people, John Lindsay turned a blind eye. Instead, Lindsay adopted the rhetoric of the radical shakedown artists. "If violence occurs in our cities," he warned when the Democratic Congress sought to scale back on federal aid to the cities, "those in Washington who have almost ignored our pleas for federal help will have to assume their share of responsibility."[4]

As if on cue, a gang of young rioters rampaged through Manhattan a week after Lindsay's invitation. These members of the Neighborhood Youth Corps broke windows in the historic Woolworth Building, stomped cars, mugged women, and looted street vendors.[5] Urban "unrest" did not stop with mere property damage and roughing up passers-by. As radical words led to ever more radical acts, the city's police increasingly became targets. The six-foot, five-inch slender mayor was famously at ease with minority citizens, but he flinched in his dealings with members of the city's other ethnic communities. For Poles, Italians, Greeks, and Slavs, he had little affinity.

He agonized over the official telephone calls to widows of slain cops—and not because of his grieving. Widows often believed what their slain husbands had been saying about His Honor and his permissive policies—that they led to more violence on the streets. "Instead of receiving his calls gracefully," one of the mayor's aides recalled, "they would rant and fulminate [against Lindsay] because their husbands had been shot in minority neighborhoods. They blamed him for the deaths. He'd come off the phone white-faced and you could see the anguish."[6] Lindsay pleaded for sympathy: "You haven't seen a dead cop in a hospital and his widow looking at me as if I'd pulled the trigger."[7]

When NYPD officers stormed a building in Harlem in April 1972, responding to a bogus call that an officer had been shot, the cops were surrounded by angry members of Louis Farrakhan's Nation of Islam. Police had not known that the building was Islam Mosque No. 7, the same place where Malcolm X had preached before he was assassinated by fellow Muslims. Shots were fired at close range in the crowded stairways of the mosque. Patrolman Philip Cardillo went down with a gunshot wound. Harlem's congressman, Charlie Rangel, and Farrakhan soon arrived. They, along with Lindsay administration officials, shooed white cops away from the scene.[8] Farrakhan and Rangel threatened the police with a riot if they stayed. Top police officials—Lindsay's men—covered up the details of Cardillo's shooting. Ballistics investigators were barred from the scene, something unprecedented for a crime investigation.[9] When Patrolman Cardillo died of his wounds, Mayor Lindsay and his hand-picked police commissioner avoided the funeral. "I don't think they dared come," said Cardillo's widow.[10] No mayor had ever before refused to attend the funeral of an officer who had died in the line of duty.

The years following the passage of the great Civil Rights Act could have been a golden age for American race relations. But by dismissing this extraordinary achievement of the entire American people, too many opinion leaders convinced ordinary people that they had no concern for the yearning of millions for safe and effective schools and for neighborhoods free from the drug dealers, prostitutes, and petty thugs. By charging decent and law-abiding Americans with racism, by condoning undoubted criminal activities of a few within the minority community, these leaders forfeited the trust and the affection of their natural constituency.

John Lindsay, long retired, charged that in the end, white Americans "didn't give a damn." Sadly for Lindsay and tragically for the country, the opportunity for genuine healing was lost. And Lindsay's fellow New Yorkers fully repaid his contempt for them.

II. "The Eagle has Landed!"

Between 750,000 and one million people crowded Florida's Cape Kennedy in the ninety-degree heat of July 1969 to witness the launch of *Apollo 11*.[11] Foreign journalists joined the throng. "This is the America we love, one so totally different than the one that fights in Vietnam," wrote a Czech reporter, whose country had the previous summer been overrun by Soviet tanks.[12] *Pravda,* the official Soviet paper, hailed "these three courageous men." *France-Soir's* special edition of 1.5 million copies sold out while Germany's *Bild Zeitung* noted, with proud precision, that seven of the fifty-seven *Apollo* managers, or twelve percent, were born in Germany.[13]

President Nixon planned to have dinner with the *Apollo 11* astronauts the night before their historic flight to the Moon. NASA's chief physician, Dr. Charles A. Berry, scotched that plan when he told the press that Nixon comes into contact with hundreds of people and might unknowingly communicate a disease to the spacemen.[14] "Totally ridiculous," was Astronaut Frank Borman's response to the doctor's exaggerated concern, but he didn't call for Berry to be countermanded. Borman thought that if "anyone sneezes on the Moon, they'd put the blame on the President."[15] Such was the atmosphere of mistrust the *Apollo* astronauts would leave behind as they departed for man's first landing on an extraterrestrial body.

Astronaut Mike Collins was orbiting the Moon alone in *Columbia.* It was Sunday, 20 July 1969. Almost casually, he had said farewell to mission commander Neil Armstrong and Buzz Aldrin as they detached in the lunar lander, an ungainly craft named *Eagle.* Armstrong and Aldrin were headed for man's first landing on the surface of the Moon. Together, *Columbia*, *Eagle,* and the three U.S. astronauts composed the *Apollo 11* mission.

"You cats take it easy on the lunar surface," Collins coolly warned his fellow astronauts. "If I hear you huffing and puffing I'm going to start bitching at you."[16] Within minutes, Armstrong would be struggling to control his spacecraft to avoid a huge crater with its jagged rocks. The rockets that slowed the *Eagle*'s descent were kicking up huge clouds of dust, obscuring his view. The efforts required to maneuver around dangerous obstacles had consumed precious fuel, leaving Armstrong within one minute of having to abort man's first landing on the Moon.[17] NASA's flight director, Gene Kranz, recalls: "There was no response from the crew. They were too busy. I got the feeling they were going for broke. I had this feeling ever since they took over manual control: 'They are the right ones for the job.' I crossed myself and said, 'Please, God.'"[18]

Almost imperceptibly, Armstrong touched down, shutting off his rockets. Without a hint of concern, he reported to a waiting world: "Houston, Tranquility Base here. The *Eagle* has landed."[19]

A decade earlier, the elite fraternity of American test pilots had laughed at the astronauts as "spam in a can." The astronauts were compared, not always favorably, with Ham, the chimp that NASA launched into space and returned safely.* Here, however, Armstrong proved he had that most admired, most elusive quality of America's best test pilots: the right stuff.** That night, at Arlington National Cemetery, someone placed a bouquet on John F. Kennedy's grave with an unsigned note: "Mr. President, the *Eagle* has landed."[20]

In Houston, Texas, Armstrong's fellow astronaut, Charlie Duke, answered Armstrong's calm voice: "Roger, Tranquility, you got a bunch of guys about to turn blue. We're breathing again. Thanks a lot."[21] Duke knew what the world did not: that the *Eagle*'s landing on the Moon was a close call. Had Armstrong failed to find a level landing site, had the *Eagle* keeled over on its side, he and Buzz Aldrin would have been condemned to die a slow, painful death as their oxygen ran out. And that nightmare would have happened in the full view of 600 million people.[22]

The landing on the Moon was a victory for the United States of America—and for freedom. President John F. Kennedy had taken up Premier Nikita Khrushchev's challenge of a space race just eight years earlier. The president redefined the space race by shooting for the Moon. "This Nation has tossed its cap over the wall of space, and we have no choice but to follow it," he said of the huge Apollo program on the last full day of his life.[23]

A landing on the Moon by the Soviets would have had incalculable results. Everything they achieved was done in secret, with the massive and single-minded redirection of resources that can only be ordered by a ruthless dictatorship. Anyone who dared to question the Soviet space program would hear the knock of the KGB at his door. If the Soviets had won the race to the Moon, millions of people around the world would have concluded that Khrushchev was right: the Soviets *had* buried the Americans.

The world knew it when Astronauts Virgil Grissom, Edward White, and Roger Chafee were killed by a fire on the launch pad in Florida on 27 January 1967. It was supposed to be a routine test, but a spark in the all-oxygen

---

* Not only had Americans been shocked by the Soviets beating the U.S. into space with *Sputnik*, but they were horrified when they learned that Laika, the Soviet space dog, would die when he consumed the last portion of his food. The Soviets had put poison in it.

** *The Right Stuff* was taken as the title of the great book on America's early astronauts by Tom Wolfe.

command module soon became an inferno. Temperatures rose in seconds to 2,500 degrees Fahrenheit.[24] The world followed the detailed investigation of the disaster that forced an eighteen-month delay in the Apollo program. The entire program had to be redesigned. It was as if the United States had broken a leg eighty yards into a hundred-yard dash. Grudgingly, the Soviets admitted that Cosmonaut Vladimir M. Komarov had been killed when the first planned Soyuz spacecraft crashed to earth, but they quickly spread the blanket of secrecy over their failure.[25]

Kennedy was dead and Khrushchev had been overthrown, but the super-power rivalry continued. Soviet Communist chief Leonid Brezhnev sought access to Western technology through the new policy of *détente*—a French word that means "an easing of tensions."[26] It was an implicit confession of weakness. To his fellow Communists in the USSR, however, Brezhnev boasted that space would lead the Soviet economy into the twenty-first century.[27] Throughout 1968, with America distracted by riots and assassinations at home, the Soviets sent *Zond* rockets around the Moon.[28] By no means had they dropped out of the space race.

And when the Soviets moved ahead in the conquest of space, Communist atheist ideology would win a great victory. "When man conquers the universe," Marxist historian Zheya Sveltilova said, "he will learn to believe in himself. It will simply be ridiculous to rely on any force other than himself. People who now believe in God will reject him. Such belief won't be logical or natural. *Man will be stronger than God*."[29]

With Armstrong's safe landing, however, the United States' victory was assured. As he descended the ladder to the lunar surface, Armstrong calmly observed: "That's one small step for man, a giant *leap* for Mankind."[30]

Meanwhile, Buzz Aldrin, inside the Lunar Excursion Module (LEM), was quietly observing the historic occasion in his own special way. Aldrin had been impressed to read that Tenzing Norgay, the Nepalese sherpa who accompanied Sir Edmund Hillary to the peak of Mt. Everest, had cleared away snow to make room for an offering of thanks to his God.[31] Now, Aldrin poured out wine that nearly overran his little cup in the one-sixth g-force of lunar gravity.[32] Holding a wafer, Aldrin read silently from a small card as he celebrated communion with these words from the Book of John:

> I am the vine and you are the branches
> Whoever remains in me and I in him will bear much fruit;
> For you can do nothing without me.[33]*

In the midst of a long, drawn-out, and inconclusive war in Vietnam, in a nation beset by seemingly irreparable divisions at home, the landing on the Moon seemed to be the one really big thing that went right. Dr. Wernher von Braun had once been Hitler's rocket scientist. Now an American citizen, he spoke with confidence of the future: "I think . . . that the Ten Commandments are entirely adequate, without amendments, to cope with all the problems that the Technological Revolution not only has brought up, but will bring up in the future."[34]

Not all Americans saw it that way. "You've been *drunk* all summer," said radical writer Norman Mailer, "and they have taken the Moon."[35] Mailer seemed to be scolding his fellow members of what was increasingly called the counterculture. This was a subculture that rejected the straight world of discipline, achievement, and drive. The radicals charged that the straight world was leading America to Fascism. Significantly, Mailer had said that "they have taken the Moon." He did not share the sense of satisfaction and pride that millions of Americans felt. He was speaking to that sense of alienation that was the banner of the rebellious youth movement.

By 1969, Norman Mailer had been speaking for an *alien nation* for more than a decade. This talented novelist wrote an influential essay called "The White Negro" in 1957. In it, he said,

> the only life-giving answer is to divorce oneself from society, to exist without roots, to set out on that uncharted journey with the rebellious imperatives of the self. . . . One is a rebel or one conforms, one is a frontiersman in the Wild West of American night life, or else a Square

* Atheist Madalyn Murray O'Hair had sued NASA following the *Apollo 8* crew's reading from the Book of Genesis during their lunar fly-by the previous Christmas Eve. Skittish NASA officials had ordered *Apollo 11* astronauts not to say anything religious from the lunar surface. But CBS's Walter Cronkite soon got word of this first communion on the Moon and told the world. The Supreme Court later dismissed O'Hair's suit. (Source: James Hansen's *First Man,* 487–88.)

> cell, trapped in the totalitarian tissues of American society. . . . Whether the life is criminal or not, the decision is to encourage the psychopath within oneself."[36]

Mailer was not issuing some abstract call to alienation, to make oneself a *philosophical outlaw.*

No, Mailer laid it out bluntly and brazenly: "It takes little courage for two strong eighteen-year-old hoodlums . . . to beat in the brains of a candy store keeper. . . . Still courage of a sort is necessary, for one murders not only a weak fifty-year-old man but an institution as well, one violates private property, one enters into a new relation with the police and introduces a dangerous element into one's life. The hoodlum is therefore daring the unknown, and no matter how brutal the act, it is not altogether cowardly."[37] Two hundred years before, such notions created a *frisson* of excitement in the salons of Paris. They led then, as they would in the years after 1969, to rivers of innocent blood. Ideas do indeed have consequences. Mailer's malevolent writings made him an American Marat.* Mailer wrote extensively about the Moon shot. His book, *Of a Fire on the Moon,* explored what he saw as the deeper meaning of the event. Mailer was widely quoted as saying the landing on the Moon was a triumph of the WASP mind. Like a laser, it could go incredible distances because it was so narrow.**

In many ways, the young rebels whom Mailer urged on showed their

---

* Jean Paul Marat was an especially vicious writer in revolutionary France. His daily demands for blood made him a "street corner Caligula." His *Ami du Peuple* (Friend of the People) "defined the language of Jacobinism." Marat wrote in his bathtub, where he spent hours daily treating some undiagnosed skin disorder. Marat was stabbed to death in his tub by the young Charlotte Corday on the eve of the revolution's holy day on 13 July 1793; the lovely *Girondist,* a moderate republican, willingly gave her life to put an end to his. Mailer was not stabbed, but he stabbed his second wife. She survived and so, in hip society, did he. He went on to win a Pulitzer Prize and marry the daughter of a duke. In 1980, he successfully campaigned for the release of convicted murderer Jack Abbott. Out of prison, Abbott murdered again. Alice Kaminsky, mother of the man Abbott murdered, wrote the unforgettable *Victim's Song.* She damned Mailer forever. Is she America's Charlotte Corday? (Source for Marat material: *A Critical Dictionary of the French Revolution,* by François Furet and Mona Ozouf.)

** WASP was the acronym the waspish Mailer used for White Anglo-Saxon Protestant. It was only partly true of the NASA scientists and engineers then and is much less true of them now.

contempt for the button-down shirts and flattop haircuts of the young engineers and technicians who had won the race to the Moon. Earlier in that summer of the *Eagle*'s landing, a riot had broken out in a New York City bar that lasted for days. The Stonewall Inn was a popular bar in Greenwich Village that was frequented by homosexuals and by male prostitutes dressed as females.[38] In 1969, it was against the law in the State of New York for a man to dress in women's clothing or for men to dance with men. It was also illegal to solicit for purposes of prostitution and to commit sodomy. Stonewall patrons resented the fact that the Mafia owned their seedy saloon.[39] They feared hepatitis that came from unclean drinking glasses that were barely even rinsed in a behind-the-bar washtub.[40] But most of all, the homosexual patrons of the Stonewall Inn hated what they saw as persecution by the cops. When a routine "bust" occurred on 28 June 1969, a mêlée erupted. The transvestite prostitutes refused to go quietly. They resisted the police in a bottle-and-brick-throwing clash that marked the beginning of the modern gay movement in America. Allen Ginsberg, famed "beat" poet of the 1950s, appeared after the riots to proclaim gay power. Ginsberg, himself a homosexual, praised the rioters, whom he said had lost "that wounded look that fags had ten years ago."[41] The new defiance alarmed many. "Things were completely changed," said a police deputy inspector, "suddenly they were not submissive anymore."[42] The inspector, his patrolmen, and millions of straight Americans resented the way the media and the "Establishment" seemed to be coddling society's rebels.

Eager to prove themselves "hip" and to profit from the rising mood of youthful rebelliousness, CBS had hired left-wing radical Jim Fouratt as its liaison to the counterculture as represented by Janis Joplin,* Chicago, and Santana—artists under contract to CBS.[43] Fouratt, a gay political activist, was at Stonewall. Friendly with radical leaders Abbie Hoffman, Allen Ginsberg, and Jerry Rubin, he took up his new job with gusto.[44]

When Norman Mailer spoke of a drunken summer, he doubtless had in mind the emblematic counterculture event of the time. In August 1969, on Max Yasgur's upstate New York dairy farm, 250,000 young people flocked

---

* In the interest of full disclosure, this author once dated the inimitable Miss Joplin, in a galaxy long ago and far away.

together to hear the leading rock bands and artists of the day. *Woodstock* was the name of the concert, even though that tony town was some fifty miles away.[45] The huge throng reveled in the rain and mud, smoked pot, and cheered every cry of defiance that came from the stage. Two deaths and two births were recorded at the festival.[46] The artists who performed at Woodstock were a virtual Who's Who of American rock 'n' roll: Joan Baez; The Band; the Jeff Beck Group; Blood, Sweat & Tears; the Paul Butterfield Blues Band; Canned Heat; Joe Cocker; Country Joe and the Fish; Creedence Clearwater Revival; Crosby, Stills, Nash & Young; the Grateful Dead; Arlo Guthrie; Keef Hartley; Richie Havens; Jimi Hendrix; the Incredible String Band; Janis Joplin; Jefferson Airplane; Mountain; Quill; Melanie; Santana; John Sebastian; Sha-Na-Na; Ravi Shankar; Sly and the Family Stone; Bert Sommer; and Sweetwater.[47] Critics dismissed this huge gathering as "rutting in the mud."*

Many "Middle Americans," those stable and solid folks who paid their taxes and obeyed the laws, had very different tastes in entertainment. They favored *Rowan and Martin's Laugh-in, Hee-Haw, Gomer Pyle USMC,* and *Bonanza* for evening viewing. When they saw the mud-spattered rock fans rejecting bedrock American values, they were put off. Lurid stories of free love and free drugs further alienated the straight from the hip. Yale Law Professor Charles Reich published a dreamy book, *The Greening of America.*[48] The reviews were rapturous. A cultural revolution was coming, Reich asserted, a new American civilization based on feeling. Reich's definition of freedom was to cast off all the old sexual and moral restraints. Sobriety and industry were for squares. "If it feels good, do it," was the cry of the radicals. And their paean to feeling good made millions of Middle Americans feel very bad indeed.

The counterculture felt justified in its contempt for American institutions when reports of the My Lai Massacre surfaced in 1969. First Lieutenant William Calley was court-martialed by the Army for the murder of twenty-two civilians in the South Vietnamese hamlet of My Lai.[49] The killings had occurred in 1968 in the wake of the murderous Communist Tet offensive, but nothing could excuse the direct targeting and killing of unarmed women, children, and

---

* In a Forrestal Lecture to the Brigade of Midshipmen at the U.S. Naval Academy in 1998, this author pointed out that if Woodstock was the defining act of an entire generation of Americans, then D-Day—a quarter century earlier—was the defining act of their parents' generation.

old men. Radicals tried to make Calley the poster boy for straight society. He was the inevitable result, these critics charged, of going along with the system. Some Americans even refused to believe the story.* Most Americans were deeply troubled by the credible charges of war crimes against our own soldiers. Still, some charged that My Lai was not an aberration, but typical of the conduct of U.S. forces in the Mekong Delta.** These critics, however, reckoned without Army Warrant Officer Hugh Thompson. It was Thompson who saw the killings and landed his helicopter *between* Calley's men and the endangered villagers. Thompson risked his own life and those of his crewmen to save hundreds of South Vietnamese villagers from certain death.[50]

Posters, in full color, that showed the My Lai dead crumpled in a ditch bore the legend: Q: AND BABIES? A: AND BABIES. It was a quote from the transcript of Calley's court martial. Thousands of these posters found their way to the walls of college dorms as opposition to the war took on the cast of a moral crusade. No posters of the thousands of South Vietnamese buried alive by the Communists in Hué are known to exist. And no posters extolled the heroism of Warrant Officer Thompson.

Another casualty of that drunken summer was the reputation of the surviving Kennedy brother. Senator Edward M. Kennedy had turned down pleas to enter the 1968 presidential race following the assassination death of his older brother, Robert. Now, in 1969, he attended a raucous party on Martha's Vineyard. Five single women and six married men—all of whom had taken part in Bobby Kennedy's presidential campaign—came together for a night of barbecue and drinks. Ted Kennedy left the party with young Mary Jo Kopechne, headed for the Edgartown Ferry. In the early hours of 19 July, Kennedy's car veered off the bridge at Chappaquiddick and sank in the dark waters.[51] Kennedy swam clear but delayed summoning police for ten hours. Kopechne was one of the "Boiler Room Girls" who had worked on brother Bobby's presidential campaign. She drowned in Kennedy's dark blue Oldsmobile.

---

* "It never happened and, besides, they deserved it," was the way one clever writer satirized the confused, disbelieving response to My Lai.

** Testimony before Congress by young Lt. (junior grade) John F. Kerry would charge that "war crimes" had been committed routinely by U.S. forces fighting in South Vietnam.

The news hit on the same day that Neil Armstrong landed the *Eagle* on the lunar surface, so the world was distracted from the full import of what had happened on Martha's Vineyard. This "lunar eclipse" prevented a penetrating media analysis of the incident. No probing questions were asked about Kennedy's unconscionable delay in calling for help, the curious decision of authorities *not* to perform an autopsy on Kopechne's body, and the "tread lightly" reaction of local Massachusetts law enforcement. What a contrast with the intense scrutiny that the errant senator, Joe McCarthy, received from Edward R. Murrow's "See it Now" broadcast of the previous decade. Clearly, Kennedy benefited from this. His pitiable speech to the people of Massachusetts was drafted for him by the protector of JFK's legacy, Ted Sorenson. It avoided as many questions as it answered. Kennedy's conduct at Chappaquiddick would not be extensively examined for another decade, until he ran for president. Even then, much of the questioning would not get to the heart of the matter.

III. The Silent Majority

Richard Nixon never said he had a "secret plan" to end the war in Vietnam. That was the charge of one of his critics. Instead, Nixon pledged to bring America out of direct involvement in combat in South Vietnam without allowing the country to fall to Communism. When Nixon took the presidential oath, there were 535,000 young Americans "in country." This huge force had been built up from 16,000 by President Lyndon B. Johnson. LBJ followed a policy of gradual escalation devised by Defense Secretary Robert Strange McNamara.

Facing massive protest demonstrations, Nixon went before the American people in November 1969 to offer his plan for *Vietnamization* of the war in Southeast Asia. By Vietnamization, Nixon meant that the Army of South Vietnam would be required to take up the defense of its own country. The United States would continue to offer air support, naval support, and, of course, a strong financial commitment to keep South Vietnam from falling to the Communist North.

General Douglas MacArthur had spoken for millions of Americans during the Korean War when he said "there is no substitute for victory." Still, top U.S. policy makers knew that there was always a danger of the "limited war" they were fighting becoming a world war, with the United States pulled into a direct conflict with a nuclear-armed Red China or Soviet Union, or both. It was to avoid this danger that both the Johnson and Nixon administrations sought the limited objective of protecting Southeast Asia.

Nixon spoke of a "silent majority" of Americans who backed his policy of gradual withdrawal from Vietnam. Nixon had ordered the return of twenty-five thousand U.S. troops in June of that year, followed by another thirty-five thousand ordered home in September.[52] The Gallup Poll showed that fully 75 percent of Americans approved of Nixon's Vietnamization policy.[53]

That fact did not dissuade antiwar protesters. It seemed only to implicate the American people in what more extreme war resisters saw as the guilt of the U.S. leaders. The radicals wrote of *Amerika.* By using the German spelling of their country's name, they sought to tie the United States to the odious Hitler regime. Even the liberal, antiwar columnist David Broder recognized the profoundly antidemocratic spirit of those who organized the mammoth antiwar protests.[54] No longer simply an expression of dissent, an effort to persuade, the giant antiwar demonstrations became in themselves an attempt to impede the carrying out of government policy. "Shut it down!" cried the youthful rebels as they ringed the Pentagon and blockaded streets in Washington, D.C. They burned American flags and even used blazing draft cards to light joints.

President Nixon found it hard to understand the youth rebellion that engulfed him. A lonely, humorless man, Nixon could not poke fun at the young protesters. In this, he was utterly unlike California Governor Ronald Reagan. When confronted by angry student rebels at Berkeley, Reagan responded lightheartedly. They warned of a "bloodbath"; Reagan replied they could start by *taking* a bath.[55] When they blocked a sidewalk and tried to stare him down, Reagan tiptoed past them with his finger to his lips. "Shhhh," he said, as even some of his adversaries broke up laughing.[56] Coming out of a meeting of the California Board of Regents, Reagan faced chanting crowds of students. They suspected, correctly, that he had come to fire their liberal chancellor and hike their tuition. "*We* are the future!" they screamed. Reagan, ever smiling, scribbled a sign on a legal pad and held it up to his limousine window: "I'll sell my bonds."[57]

Only once, in 1971, did President Nixon attempt to reach out to the protesters who besieged his White House. He went out at dawn to talk to the demonstrators who spent the night on the grounds of the Lincoln Memorial. He tried to shoot the breeze with some of them, talking about football, talking about their home towns—anything except why they had come to Washington.[58] Shy and awkward, Nixon tried, but he never could comprehend his foes.

When President Nixon invaded Cambodia in 1970, the antiwar movement howled. It was to them an insane escalation of the war. They charged that Nixon had expanded the war into another sovereign nation. The truth was the opposite. The North Vietnamese had been using Cambodia for years as a staging area for their attacks on South Vietnam. London's prestigious journal, *The Economist,* saw straight through the double standard, flagging the fact that the rest of world made "barely a chirp of protest" about Communists violating Cambodian neutrality.[59] From these Cambodian "sanctuaries," Communist forces had invaded the South, killing thousands, including many Americans. Nixon told the country that his move was only an incursion, not an invasion—only an effort to "clean out" pockets of enemy activity. American forces would leave as soon as they had achieved their aim.

The same liberal leaders who had thought Kennedy clever for using the word *quarantine* at the time of the Cuban Missile Crisis now jumped on Nixon's use of *incursion* as evidence of his duplicity. Men who had been silent, or who had muted their criticism of war policy as the Democrat Lyndon Johnson built up a huge force in Vietnam, now felt liberated as U.S. combat deaths rose to three hundred a week.[60] They attacked Nixon without restraint. Maine's Democratic senator, Edmund Muskie, charged that Nixon had decided to "seek a military method of ending this war rather than a negotiated method."[61] Normally mild-mannered Senator Walter Mondale lashed out at Nixon. "This is not only a tragic escalation, which will broaden the war and increase American casualties," he said, "but it is an outright admission of the failure of Vietnamization."[62] Mondale was proven wrong when, following the successful U.S. operation in Cambodia, American casualties actually went *down.*[63] The incursion enabled Nixon to accelerate U.S. withdrawals from South Vietnam.

But the critics were not interested in facts. They had raised their own and their followers' passions to a fever pitch. At Kent State University, Governor James Rhodes ordered Ohio National Guardsmen to contain a student uprising against the Cambodian operation. There, jittery young guardsmen fired on a menacing crowd of protesters, killing four. The country was horrified—and deeply divided over the killings at Kent State. Best-selling author James Michener came out the next year with *Kent State: What Happened and Why.* Michener defended the young guardsmen, whom he said feared for their lives.[64] They were vastly outnumbered by the cursing, screaming, rock-throwing demonstrators. I. F. Stone's angry rebuttal, *The Killings at Kent State: How Murder Went Unpunished*, sold like hotcakes.[65] Despite Stone's strident charges, however, the legal system never placed the blame for the students' tragic deaths on the guardsmen. "Izzy" Stone was later revealed to have met on a regular basis for years with Soviet intelligence agents, with full knowledge that they were Soviet operatives. They even bought his lunches. He was known to the KGB as *bliny,* or pancake.[66] Today, we might view the killings at Kent State as we view those of the Boston Massacre: a terrible and preventable tragedy.

Nixon could rightly claim that most Americans backed his war policy. He viewed the struggle in great power terms. He did not want America to become a pitiful, helpless giant.[67]

In his "Silent Majority" speech, Nixon argued strongly for a new course in Vietnam. But he warned against what he called "a precipitate withdrawal":

> The precipitate withdrawal of American forces from Vietnam would be a disaster not only for South Vietnam but for the United States and for the cause of peace.
>
> For the South Vietnamese, our precipitate withdrawal would inevitably allow the Communists to repeat the massacres which followed their takeover in the North 15 years before; they then murdered

more than 50,000 people, and hundreds of thousands more died in slave labor camps.

We saw a prelude of what would happen in South Vietnam when the Communists entered the city of Hue last year. During their brief rule there, there was a bloody reign of terror in which 3,000 civilians were clubbed, shot to death, and buried in mass graves.

With the sudden collapse of our support, these atrocities of Hue would become the nightmare of the entire nation—and particularly for the million and a half Catholic refugees who fled to South Vietnam when the Communists took over in the North.

For the United States, this first defeat in our nation's history would result in a collapse of confidence in American leadership, not only in Asia but throughout the world.

Three American presidents have recognized the great stakes involved in Vietnam and understood what had to be done.

IV. Nixon to China

Nixon was at this point preparing to play the China card. Even before he entered the White House, Nixon had written of the need for a new approach to what was then called Red China. By 1971, Nixon had determined to send National Security Advisor Dr. Henry Kissinger on a secret mission to Beijing. He wanted to take advantage of the bitter split between the Chinese and the Russians in the hope of getting China to cut off aid to the North Vietnamese. Dubbing the mission *Polo*, after the famed Italian explorer Marco Polo, the Nixon administration sent Kissinger to Pakistan. From there, Kissinger could approach Beijing more discreetly. Kissinger's July meetings with Mao Zedong and Zhou En-lai took place in strictest secrecy. China was then barely recovering from years of madness known as the Great Proletarian Cultural Revolution. The Cultural Revolution had led to the death and disgrace of millions. Mao had unleashed young Red Guards to humiliate China's intellectuals. The Red Guards brandished copies of Mao's *Little Red Book*. It was the only guide they needed, the young rebels said, to rule great China.

Kissinger stunned the world and its leaders when he announced *rapprochement* with China. Nixon had pulled off a coup. But not all were happy about it. None was more shocked and alienated than America's faithful friend, the Republic of China—the non-Communist Chinese government exiled on Taiwan. "No government less deserved what was about to happen to it than that of Taiwan," Kissinger admitted. "It had been a loyal ally; its conduct toward us had been exemplary. Its representatives . . . had behaved with that matter-of-fact reliability and subtle intelligence characteristic of the Chinese people."[68]

Kissinger the realist believed that the United States could no longer hold off majorities in the UN General Assembly who yearly voted for China to replace Taiwan in the world body and to hold a permanent seat on the Security Council. He thought that the United States could not continue to maintain the fiction that the Republic of China on Taiwan was the sole legitimate government of a billion mainland Chinese.

Soon, Nationalist China, as Taiwan had been known for decades, would be stripped of its seat on the UN Security Council, its seat in the UN General Assembly, and even abruptly downgraded from embassy status in the United States of America. Kissinger played a crucial role in drafting the Shanghai Declaration that issued from Nixon's Pacific overture. It seemed best to save what could be saved. The United States urged peaceful reconciliation of China and Taiwan, continued to maintain trade relations with the prosperous island republic, and, most important perhaps, America continued to provide arms for Taiwanese self defense. Beyond this, Nixon and Kissinger did not think they could—or should—go. President Nixon's 1972 visit to the People's Republic of China was the media highlight of his administration. He and Mrs. Nixon were shown walking on the Great Wall and toasting Mao at a splendid Beijing state dinner. Nixon had been the one who built his career denouncing liberals for "losing" China to the Communists. Now, he had come full circle. Henceforward, "Nixon to China" would be the name given to any clever political ploy in which only those who had most strenuously opposed a given policy could suddenly turn about-face to embrace it. Doubtless there were sound reasons to reassess American policy toward China. George Washington had warned against permanent alliances and permanent antagonisms. But the Nixon method—secretive, cynical, sudden—raised serious doubts about American steadfastness, American purpose, American principle.

It also raised serious questions about the meaning of freedom in the American political process. What had voters chosen when they elected Nixon, a known quantity, in 1968? What role had the people or their elected representatives had in this major turnabout? None. They were not consulted. Their views were not considered. What were the parents of young soldiers who had died fighting Chinese Communist troops in Korea in 1950 to make of their president offering a champagne toast to the long life of the bloody dictator who had made war on the United States and the entire UN? Yes, a change had to occur sometime, somehow, but did it have to happen like that? The public deception required to bring off this diplomatic coup would become a hallmark of Nixon's style. Advising Kissinger on a meeting with the press, Nixon's alter ego, H.R. "Bob" Haldeman, said, "You can only lie so far."[69] Exactly how far you could lie became the pressing concern of the Nixon administration.

Nixon and Kissinger pursued a policy of *détente* with the USSR. Nixon signed an Anti-Ballistic Missile Treaty, which prohibited both nations from deploying an antimissile defense system (except around the two super powers' capital cities). Thus, the Republicans believed they were returning to the policies of Eisenhower and Dulles, a policy known as "Mutual Assured Destruction." Fittingly, it was abbreviated MAD. Security in a dangerous world with tens of thousands of nuclear weapons held by the United States and the USSR would come to rely on what Churchill called the "balance of terror." Nixon also approved the Strategic Arms Limitation Treaty with the Soviets.

Nixon told Americans he was determined not to *bug out* of South Vietnam. To the Chinese, however, he seemed to be saying that the United States would do exactly that. Kissinger and Nixon learned that the Chinese wanted the United States to stay in Asia as a counterweight to the "hegemony" of the Soviet Union.[70] With some bitterness, Kissinger noted, the Chinese seemed to have a better understanding of American policy than the professors in Harvard Yard did.[71]

Nowhere was Nixon's penchant for shocking his opponents and stunning his friends more evident than in his economic policy. Nixon had agreed with conservative economist Milton Friedman that Lyndon Johnson's 10 percent surtax on incomes would be ineffective in wringing inflation out of the economy. By 1971 the problem was spinning out of control.[72] Inflation ate away the savings of the middle class, and it presented a special threat to the reelection of a president who depended on conservative support.

Montana's Democratic senator, Mike Mansfield, pushed legislation through both congressional houses to allow the president to set up wage and price controls. "The lesson that government price fixing doesn't work is never learned," Nixon responded, forcefully adding, "I will not take this nation down the road of wage and price controls." They could have bet he would say as much. The plan was geared to embarrass the president, because Mansfield and his fellow Democrats knew that the American people disapproved of Nixon's free-market economic policies.[73]

But the scheme did not work as planned. Nixon walked right into the trap and turned it on his opponents. Surprisingly, he backed the legislation.

Nixon's turnaround on the issue is due in part to the influence of his dynamic treasury secretary, John B. Connally. Jumping back several years, recall that Connally was the Democratic governor of Texas who survived the Kennedy assassination. Nixon fell in line with Connally's recommendations of a wage-price "freeze" and followed his protectionist policies on trade.[74] One writer has likened Connally to "a Texas cowboy in the Palace of Versailles, ignorant of who or what established the building, uncaring about what his bullets might destroy."[75] A fairer criticism would single out not the Texas in Connally, but the Connally in Texas. Most knowledgeable Texans could have told Nixon that wage and price controls are like oil-well fires: easy to start, difficult to end. Not that he would have listened. "We are all Keynesians now," said Nixon blandly.[76] He seemed not to care that the doctrines of British economist John Maynard Keynes were anathema to his conservative supporters. Keynes had advocated increased government spending in times of economic downturn as a means of "priming the pump" for recovery. Nixon was smugly satisfied that his disapproval ratings on economic issues, which had ranged higher than 70 percent, now flipped as shockingly as his own position on the issue. Americans enthusiastically embraced the idea of wage and price controls and gave Nixon more than 70 percent approval for his economic policies in public opinion polls.[77] But while the good feelings helped Nixon in the short term, it wasn't long before the economy took a dive.

The American economy in the 1970s suffered from overregulation and underinvestment. The recession of 1973–75 was the worst since the Great Depression, and it would, in time, help to undermine Nixon's standing with the American people when he faced troubles over Watergate. The bleak prospects convinced millions of Americans that their children's futures would be poorer, that there would be fewer economic opportunities for the rising generation. All of this created a sour mood in the country, and many took out their frustrations on President Nixon.

Nor were China and the economy the only areas where Nixon distressed his most loyal supporters. A presidential commission on pornography predictably recommended dropping most legal restrictions. Though many of the laws remained on the books, enforcement lagged. Soon, the nation was flooded with pornography.*

Another Nixon-appointed commission, headed by Laurance Rockefeller, studied the issue of population growth. The Rockefeller Commission backed federally-funded birth control and the repeal of the laws against abortion. Nixon *opposed* abortion-on-demand, he said, but he signed the 1970 Family Planning and Reproductive Health Act that has sluiced billions of tax dollars to Planned Parenthood ever since.**

Nixon also attempted to change federal welfare policy. He supported the initiative of his Domestic Policy Advisor, Daniel Patrick Moynihan. Moynihan was a liberal Democrat who flattered Nixon with the idea that he could be the conservative who implements a major liberal policy—as Benjamin Disraeli

* POWs returning from Vietnam were latter-day Rip van Winkles. A number of them recorded their shock at seeing—and hearing—obscenities in films, in books, and on stage. New York theater critics gushed over such offerings as the nude scenes in *Hair* and *O Calcutta!*

** The Family Planning and Reproductive Health Act of 1970 was approved by Democratic majorities in Congress. It was co-sponsored by Houston's young Republican congressman, George H.W. Bush. Bush's support provided moderate "cover" for what was essentially a radical change in federal policy toward the family. The senior Bush's key role in the bill's passage earned him the lasting mistrust of grassroots conservatives.

had done in Britain in the nineteenth century. Moynihan pressed for the Family Assistance Plan that would have given poor families cash subsidies from the government in place of welfare. Conservative economist Milton Friedman even spoke up for a Negative Income Tax. If the government could tax higher incomes, Friedman reasoned, why not supplement the incomes of the poor?[78]

Democrats who controlled the Congress blocked any action on Nixon's assistance plan. (Perhaps they agreed with Moynihan and feared that if Nixon became the American Disraeli, their majority would dissolve.) Average working Americans did not like welfare, but they disliked even more the notion that others should be paid for not working. Many asked what would happen to the "breadwinners" if their work was not needed.*

Nixon supported, or at least did not oppose, the rising environmental movement. The movement was inspired by Rachel Carson's 1962 book *Silent Spring* and given a great boost by photographs of the Earth as a "big blue marble" as taken from the Moon. Senator Edmund Muskie became a leader on Capitol Hill. Muskie crafted major legislation on Clean Air and Clean Water. Nixon dutifully signed these bills and approved creation of a new Environmental Protection Agency.[79] Some conservatives griped that the first Earth Day—22 April 1970—was also the centennial of the birth of the leading Communist revolutionary, Vladimir Lenin. The new movement was not red, however, it was *green*.

The Nixon years also saw major gains by the new feminist movement. Both parties now endorsed an Equal Rights Amendment (ERA) to the Constitution. Nixon's GOP had been supportive of it for generations. When the great Civil Rights Act of 1964 was amended by Virginia's Democratic segregationist congressman, Howard W. Smith, it also banned discrimination on the basis of sex. "Judge" Smith had hoped that outlawing sex discrimination would be a "killer amendment" that would slow down or even derail the Civil Rights Act. It did no such thing. Instead, it provided the basis *in law* for the new feminism.

* Some of the strongest evidence for a powerful effect of welfare on marriage comes, once again, from the SIME/DIME experiments [Seattle and Denver income maintenance experiments, respectively]. In response to a guaranteed income, divorce increased 36 percent among whites and 42 percent among blacks. (Source: Murray, Charles, *Losing Ground,* 151–152.)

In addition to ERA, the new feminists wanted abortion-on-demand.* Several state laws were amended to legalize what the statutes of every state had previously deemed manslaughter. Governor Nelson Rockefeller signed a radical law in New York that permitted abortion for any reason up to six months of pregnancy. California Governor Ronald Reagan agonized, but signed a bill to permit abortion for the life or health of the mother. In Washington State, voters approved a referendum to legalize abortion. Governor Dan Evans approved the change. Rockefeller, Reagan, and Evans represented a broad spectrum of the Republican Party.

Democrats were split on the abortion issue. Many black and Hispanic leaders opposed it. César Chavez, the Mexican-American leader of the California farm workers' union, strongly asserted his profound religious beliefs against abortion. Rev. Jesse Jackson denounced abortion as "black genocide." Some elected Democrats also opposed abortion. Missouri's Senator Thomas Eagleton, Wisconsin's senator, William Proxmire; Joseph Califano, a veteran of LBJ's administration; and, at least at this point in his career, Massachusetts senator, Edward M. Kennedy, vocally opposed abortion. Democrats also looked to largely-Catholic Big City political machines for support. Thus it was that the Democrats had some of the strongest opponents, as well as proponents, for liberalized abortion.

Seeing the growing *resistance* at the grassroots level to abortion-on-demand, liberal organizers recommended a strategy of going through the federal courts instead of going to the state legislatures or even directly to the voters. Washington State's Referendum 20 on abortion had produced a narrow victory—54 percent to 46 percent. Michigan voters had decisively turned down a repeal of the state's abortion law in 1972 by a vote of 61–39 percent. North Dakota's rejection of liberalized abortion was even more emphatic: voters there voted it down 77–23 percent.[80]

In New York and other states, efforts were underway to *repeal* the liberal abortion laws. Abortion advocate Judith Blake noted that nearly 80 percent of Americans opposed unrestricted abortion. Blake urged her fel-

* Many of the nineteenth-century feminists and suffragettes were strongly *anti-abortion*, most notably Susan B. Anthony.

low supporters of abortion-on-demand to go to the U.S. Supreme Court as "the only road to rapid change."[81]

On such a fundamental matter, she argued, democracy could not be trusted. Feminists held that women's fundamental reproductive rights were no more subject to voter approval than *desegregation* should depend on majority white electorates in the South. Not just American democracy was challenged by the new feminists. Repealing abortion laws would not satisfy the most extreme elements of a movement that brooked no opposition.

Radical writer Shulamith Firestone said the assault on traditional values must go further. "Feminists have to question, not just all of *Western* culture, but the organization of culture itself, and further, even the very organization of nature."[82]

V. The Election of 1972

President Nixon approached the election year of 1972 in a strong position, but he didn't *feel* strong. With his success in drawing down U.S. forces in South Vietnam and his replacement of the military draft with a draft lottery, he had brought a measure of quiet to the nation's cities and campuses.[83] He might have been the most successful of post-war presidents but for his personal characteristics. As Bryce Harlow, his close associate of many years, noted about him: Nixon was not liked by people, because he did not like people.[84]

Even so, he faced only token opposition for re-nomination in the Republican Party. Conservative congressman John Ashbrook of Ohio and liberal congressman Pete McCloskey of California got no support in their quixotic challenges to Nixon in the GOP primaries. All attention focused, instead, on the Democrats.

Senator George McGovern of South Dakota had become the leader of liberal antiwar activists. McGovern had a great advantage because he had chaired the commission that radically restructured the party's rules for nominating presidential candidates. The McGovern rules would utterly change the nominating procedures of both parties. Since 1972, the parties have selected the vast majority of their convention delegates in state primaries and caucuses. No longer would party "bosses" dictate the choice of the party's standard bearer. In the Democratic Party, this meant the nomination process would be dominated by liberal activists. For the Republicans, the conservative base would have to approve any selection.

Although Senator Edmund Muskie had broad organizational support among labor union leaders, Democratic elected officials, and among the public at large, his early support for the Vietnam War antagonized members of "the movement." They preferred McGovern whom, they said, had been "right from the start" about the war. The fact that both Senator Hubert H. Humphrey and Muskie, his 1968 running mate, had joined the antiwar faction in Congress gained them no credit with liberals who morally indicted both men.

Muskie's 1972 campaign for president collapsed, spectacularly, in New Hampshire. Muskie appeared in a February snowstorm outside the offices of *The Manchester Union Leader.* Muskie responded emotionally to an attack on his wife by the paper's combative editor, William Loeb. Television commentators wondered aloud if Muskie had the emotional stability to be president. It was an absurd argument, of course, since strong men like George Washington and Winston Churchill had famously wept in public. Still, Muskie did allow himself to be baited by the feisty Granite State editor. His front-page "editorials" called the senator "Moscow Muskie." (Worse, Loeb had labeled President Eisenhower "Dopey Dwight.")[85]

Senator Henry M. "Scoop" Jackson of Washington entered the contest for the Democratic nomination. Jackson was a "hawk," a supporter of a strong defense against Communist aggression. Jackson spoke up for persecuted Soviet Jews. He had a strong record with organized labor and civil rights groups. Significantly, Jackson opposed court-ordered busing to achieve "racial balance" in the schools. He was accused of appealing to "white backlash," but his position was supported by both white and black Americans, as all public opinion polls showed.[86] Nor would opposition to busing fade over time. "It's abusive to our children, who need to be in their own neighborhood," a black mother told the *New York Times* in 1983. "Why uproot our babies? The [whites] stay in their own neighborhood until they go to college. It's unfair. It's unsafe. It's a damn shame."[87]

Both Jackson and Hubert Humphrey, who entered the 1972 nomination race typically late and typically disorganized, were swept away by the McGovern movement. The only serious threat to George McGovern's nomination, ironically, came from former segregationist George C. Wallace. Because the nomination was taken away from party leaders, they could not veto Wallace. Wallace campaigned in the Democratic primaries, winning Michigan and—ominously—Maryland. A would-be assassin shot the Alabama governor in Laurel, Maryland, in May 1972. Wallace survived, but suffered great pain and would be wheelchair-bound for the rest of his life. His wounding cleared the path for McGovern's nomination.*

McGovern was perhaps an unusual candidate for leader of what came to be called the Peace Movement. McGovern's earliest public service had been as a twenty-two-year-old bomber pilot in World War II. He commanded respect and affection from the even younger crew members who flew on his B-24 Liberator. They had named her the *Dakota Queen,* in honor of his wife, Eleanor.[88] Married and mature, McGovern was almost a father figure to his crewmen. Mission after mission, he guided them through German flak and deadly 88-millimeter antiaircraft fire and brought them safely back to base in Italy.

On one of his missions, with several B-24s badly shot up, there were loud complaints and radio chatter about those "blasted n———s," a racist reference to the Tuskegee Airmen whose job it was to protect the slower, more vulnerable bombers. The gripes were quickly cut short when the black squadron commander of the P-51 Mustangs—who had been hovering protectively over them all the while—broke in to say: "Why don't you all shut up, white boys? We're all going to take you home."[89] The Mustangs drove off the German fighters and McGovern's squadron made it home

* George Wallace would repent of his segregationist past and appeal, quite successfully, to black voters in Alabama for their forgiveness and support. He would go on to serve several terms as governor and even take part in a re-enactment of the march on the Edmund Pettis Bridge in Selma. Wallace left segregation behind when the Voting Rights Act was signed by LBJ in 1965.

safely. Ever after, George McGovern would be one of that great generation of World War II veterans who would oppose racial discrimination wherever they saw it. As a congressman and U.S. senator, McGovern would be a strong backer of equal rights for black Americans.

McGovern's nominating convention at Miami, Florida, was far more peaceful and harmonious than the riotous party gathering in Chicago had been four years earlier. But it was no better organized. McGovern allowed Rev. Jesse Jackson to challenge and then oust a delegation headed by Chicago's powerful Mayor Dailey.

Because of scheduling delays, and the weariness of giddy delegates, the choice of a vice presidential candidate dragged out for hours. Only the most dedicated of political junkies could stay up to see Missouri senator Thomas Eagleton nominated in the wee hours of the morning. The delays masked opposition among the delegates to Eagleton. Young, attractive, Catholic, and anti-abortion, Tom Eagleton had strong ties to labor and a strong record on civil rights. As a freshman senator, he had no record on Vietnam to live down.[90] Still, liberal activists were unhappy with McGovern's choice. Their antics on the convention floor, however, announcing votes like "Wisconsin casts 235.314 delegate votes for . . . " made them look profoundly unserious and incapable as a party of governing the country.

Senator McGovern's acceptance speech before the Democratic National Convention was also thrown into the early hours of the morning. He did not speak until 3 a.m., long past the time when most voters had gone to bed.[91] The hoped-for post-convention "bounce" that successful candidates look for in public opinion polls never showed up.

McGovern's impassioned call to "come home, America" was seen as an appeal to come home from the Vietnam War. The problem for McGovern was that Nixon's policy was bringing Americans home from Vietnam. McGovern spoke to the urgent desire of his supporters for change: "We reject the view of those who say, 'America—love it or leave it.' We reply, 'Let us change it so we may love it the more.'"[92] McGovern's critics countered that he and his backers seemed to be saying they would love America only when they had transformed it in their image.

McGovern's record in World War II is one of undoubted heroism. He braved death daily for years as he fought to take the continent back from Nazism. Little of this was known, however, to the American public in 1972.* The Democratic Party was not just against the Vietnam War; it diminished the American role as the champion of freedom that FDR, Truman, and JFK had embraced.

McGovern also had to downplay his 1948 support for the Communist-duped Henry Wallace. Nixon had loyally backed the Republican Dewey that year (while Ronald Reagan, interestingly, campaigned for Harry Truman.)

Almost as soon as the McGovern-Eagleton campaign started, it ended. When it was revealed that Eagleton had been hospitalized several times for mental depression, McGovern's campaign managers shuddered. McGovern told a press conference in the aptly named Black Hills of South Dakota that he backed his running mate "1,000 percent."[93] McGovern himself was genuinely free of prejudice against those who had suffered mental illness. Then, when it was revealed Eagleton had undergone electroshock therapy, McGovern acceded to his top aides' demands that Eagleton be replaced. Because he refused to take a hint, Senator Eagleton was unceremoniously "dumped" from the ticket. One Democratic leader in New York State spoke for many party regulars when he shook his head and muttered, "They dropped the wrong nut from the ticket!" Political pros will tolerate many things from their party's leader, but they can't abide gross incompetence.

Next, McGovern engaged in an embarrassingly frantic hunt for a running mate. After being publicly humiliated by several prominent rejections, he finally settled on the ebullient Sargent Shriver, brother-in-law of the Kennedys and former director of the Peace Corps. Shriver soldiered gamely on, but there was little he could do to slow the train that was hurtling toward the washed-out bridge. McGovern was nominated by delegates chosen on a strict quota basis—so many males and females, so many minorities, so many urban and rural. This bizarre formula inevitably squeezed out delegates backed by organized labor. The AFL-CIO's president, George Meaney,

---

* By contrast, Nixon's campaign wrapped itself in the American flag. Nixon served on a navy supply ship in the South Pacific. He won the considerable sum of five thousand dollars playing poker. McGovern led the antiwar movement and therefore benefited not at all from his status as war hero. His WWII story was finally told in Stephen Ambrose's best-selling *Wild Blue.*

responded by withholding his endorsement of McGovern—something no modern Democratic nominee had been denied.[94]

Presidential politics was sidetracked, momentarily, by the Olympic Games in Munich, West Germany. It was the Germans' first chance to host the games since the Hitler Olympics of 1936. The modern, free, and democratic German Federal Republic that Konrad Adenauer had built desperately wanted to show off its tolerance and openness. As a result, it was unwilling to ring the stadium with tightened security. The Germans did not want the world's television viewers to be confronted by too many armed men. Abou Daoud was a lieutenant of Palestinian terrorist chief Yasser Arafat. Daoud and his Black September kidnappers slipped into the Olympic Village, where they took hostage eleven members of the Israeli team. When an attempt to rescue the hostages failed, Daoud's black ski-mask-wearing attackers pitched a hand grenade into the room where the Israeli athletes were being held, killing them all. The Munich Massacre bore somber witness to the rising specter of terrorism employed as an instrument of international policy. Arafat was generously supplied with funds and weapons by the USSR.[95]*

Arafat would continue his career of murder throughout the rest of his life. The year after Munich, he approved the killing of American ambassador Cleo Noel, his deputy, George Curtis Moore, and a Belgian diplomat. The three were kidnapped in Sudan's capital of Khartoum, taken to a basement, and filled with more than forty bullets each. Arafat's Black September Palestinian gunmen deliberately fired at point blank range from their victims' feet to their heads to maximize their painful deaths.[96] Meanwhile, Nixon's 1972 campaign was run smoothly but without imagination by the Committee to Reelect the President. (Even the title carefully avoided naming Nixon, a concession to Americans' lack of affection for the distant loner.) Journalists quickly dubbed the committee CREEP.

McGovern's opponents within the Democratic Party sneered at him. "Abortion, acid, and amnesty" was the taunting campaign slogan flung at

* Abou Daoud was arrested in Paris five years later, but released by French authorities. Israel's secret service, the Mossad, in time would hunt down and kill all but one of the terrorists that planned and carried out the Munich Massacre.

the party's nominee by other Democrats. They were referring to LSD (acid) and amnesty for Vietnam draft dodgers. Within the party, McGovern was dubbed "Magoo," after the near-sighted cartoon character who was forever stepping on rakes. "Let them hate, so long as they fear," went the old Roman adage. No one hated McGovern, but neither did they fear him. They mocked him, and that was fatal.

McGovern's team seemed not to comprehend the fight they were in. They distributed a bumper sticker that read REMEMBER OCTOBER 9TH. *Huh?* The mysterious message referred to a speech Nixon had given on 9 October 1968, in which the challenger said "those who have had four years to bring peace and failed do not deserve another chance." This obscure reference wasn't inside baseball; it was inside shuffleboard. Even the peace issue, that slender reed for McGovern, snapped on 26 October 1972, when Dr. Kissinger announced in his heavily accented tones: "*Ve belief zat peace iss at hand.*" Kissinger was then negotiating with the North Vietnamese representative to the Paris Peace Talks, Le Duc Tho.

On Tuesday, 7 November 1972, McGovern suffered one of the worst defeats in the history of presidential politics. Just eight years after LBJ had buried Goldwater, the Republican Nixon carried *every* state except Massachusetts and the District of Columbia. In Massachusetts, as George Will has memorably pointed out, there are more college professors than registered automobiles.

Ever afraid, Nixon had run up the score. He won 520 electoral votes and 46,740,323 popular votes (60.3 percent). McGovern won a scant 17 electoral votes and 28,901,548 popular votes. Typical of the feckless McGovern campaign operation was the breathless cry of some of his young Ivy League backers in New York State. "McGovern is leading Nixon in the City," they exulted when a *New York Daily News* poll showed the South Dakotan edging out Nixon in Gotham by 52–48 percent. No one had the heart to explain to them that a Democrat had to carry New York City by over 60 percent to be able to offset Republican strength Upstate and on Long Island. The men who knew such things, the seasoned old party pros who had nominated winners like FDR, Truman, and JFK, had been unceremoniously shown the gate by the smart young Magoos.

"I left office for reasons of health—the people got *sick* of me." That amazingly candid and funny line from a former Democratic governor of Michigan is a rarity in politics.* Most politicians are convinced they are loved and deserve to be loved. Richard Nixon had no such illusions. He knew that people did not like him.[97]

This basic insecurity led Nixon always to overcompensate. Unsatisfied with the mess Democrats were obviously making of their 1972 campaign, Nixon apparently wanted to "get something" on them. His operatives broke into the Democratic National Committee headquarters in Washington's Watergate Hotel. Then, when the relatively low-level team of burglars was caught entering the building on 23 June 1972, Nixon denied any knowledge of the affair. However, the White House tapes make it undeniably clear that he knew of it after the fact, and knew of it long before he ever admitted it to the American people. He lied about it for two full years.

Thus was born the Watergate Affair. Perhaps he saw Ted Kennedy stonewalling all attempts to get to the bottom of Chappaquiddick and still being hailed as a liberal lion.** He certainly saw Dr. Daniel Ellsberg violating federal law by giving the Pentagon Papers to the *New York Times* the previous year and being welcomed as a "whistle blower."

In a significant 1971 case surrounding the Pentagon Papers, the Supreme Court ruled that the First Amendment should stand against prior restraint in most cases. (Prior restraint is preventing the publication of information.) However, a point frequently forgotten in this history is that a plurality of the Supreme Court held that criminal prosecution of the publication could take place *after* publication. No such prosecution, however, was pursued.

Early in his administration, Nixon installed a new voice-activated audiotape system in the White House. In doing so, he would provide the documentary evidence of his own lawlessness and deceit. Presidents like

---

* The witty Jim Blanchard would serve later as Bill Clinton's ambassador to Canada.

** "I want you to stonewall it," said Nixon to his subordinates as Watergate investigators closed in. The era that gave us the Stonewall riot also gave us *stonewall* as a verb. It was Nixon's own formulation that meant to throw up a stone wall against all attempts to get at the truth.

FDR, Kennedy, and Johnson obviously had taped certain telephone conversations, but Nixon's system could pick up all discussions in the Oval Office.

Immediately after Nixon's joyless victory over McGovern, the president demanded the resignations of all his cabinet officers.* Elliot Richardson tried to break through Nixon's wall of reserve: "I wish somehow deep down inside yourself you could come to believe that you have really won . . . you won by an overwhelming margin."[98] Richardson would serve Nixon as secretary of health, education and welfare, defense secretary, and, most significantly, as attorney general. In the end, however, he couldn't penetrate the *carapace* with which Nixon surrounded himself.

There may never have been a more ungainly man in the White House than Richard Nixon. He brooded as he walked the beaches at San Clemente, California, wearing wing tips at the edge of the surf. He ate ketchup on his cottage cheese. He had coveted the Oval Office for twenty years, but as soon as he won it, he fled it for a "getaway" office in the Old Executive Office Building. There, he jacked up the air conditioning to sixty-eight degrees while sitting before a roaring fireplace. He literally had no idea how to talk to people. When campaign aides tried to introduce some comely airline flight attendants to the famous candidate, he replied: "Oh, the B-Girls." Realizing he had stumbled on a synonym for prostitute, he tried to recover by saying he meant B, for *Billings*, Montana, where the campaign jet had just landed.[99] Later, at the annual Gridiron Dinner in Washington, Nixon approached Governor Ronald Reagan and Reagan's guest. "Hello, Mr. President; this is Lou Cannon," said Reagan. "He has written a book about me." Nixon looked warily at the two men and, wagging his jowels, said, "Well, I'll skim it." When he'd left, the affable Reagan turned to Cannon and said, "Well, Lou, he just took care of you and me."[100]

It's almost painful to describe this driven man. He tried to give Reagan advice about speaking on the famous "rubber chicken circuit." Eat in your hotel room, Nixon advised the sunny Californian, and wait until the audience

* It was an unprecedented move for a triumphantly reelected president. Such reshuffles are standard practice under the British Parliamentary system, but they don't import well. Nixon had similarly tried to outfit the White House guards in new comic opera uniforms when he returned from a trip to Paris. He had been overly impressed by the *grandeur* of President de Gaulle's resplendent *garde républicaine.* For his pains, Nixon's new guards' uniforms were laughed out of town.

has eaten before you enter the hall. Preserve the sense of mystery. If you eat with them, you'll lower yourself to their level, Nixon earnestly advised. Reagan listened, smiled, and resolutely ignored Nixon's advice. Reagan genuinely liked his audiences and liked being with them before speaking to them.

Kennedy had summoned Americans to the great adventure of space exploration, but Nixon now shut the program down. He had spoken of America's need for the "lift of a driving dream." What else was space but that? Nonetheless, he announced in December 1972 that *Apollo 17* would land on the Moon for "the last time in this century."[101]

> [Astronaut Jack Schmitt] couldn't believe his ears. . . . He hated the words—hated them for their lack of vision. These words from the leader of the nation! Even if Nixon really believed them, he didn't have to say so in a public statement, taking away the hopes of a generation of young people. Schmitt was furious that in the moment of triumph he had been jolted out of the work of the mission to listen to a statement like that. He would fume silently about it for the rest of the flight.[102]*

Immediately following reelection, Nixon had to face a near breakdown of the Paris Peace talks. Not only was peace *not* at hand, it seemed more elusive than ever. Nixon reacted by unleashing a fierce bombing campaign against Hanoi, the capital of North Vietnam. Convinced he had been lying (again) just to win reelection, his critics denounced his "Christmas bombing campaign" of 1972.** American POWs held in what they jestingly called "the Hanoi Hilton" cheered the bombing campaign. They later reported it had given them hope.

Release of these prisoners of war had become a central objective of the U.S. war policy. With the aid of Texas entrepreneur H. Ross Perot, the POW

---

* Ironically, it is the failed *Apollo 13* mission that is probably most familiar to Americans. *Apollo 13* almost ended disastrously when an onboard explosion forced Astronauts Jim Lovell, Fred Haise, and Jack Swigert to circle the Moon and come back to Earth on auxiliary power. The heart-stopping story of their safe return is a tribute to Yankee ingenuity—and the Ron Howard movie is Hollywood at its best.

** Many of those who cursed Nixon for violating the spirit of the Christmas season in 1972 had offered not a word of criticism of the North Vietnamese when they launched an assault on the South in 1968 during Tet—*their* holiday.

issue became more important during the Vietnam War than in any previous American conflict. Perot, a graduate of the U.S. Naval Academy, used his wide-ranging relationships with former classmates to attempt a rescue of the POWs. Although that effort failed, Perot made sure the POWs and their families were not forgotten. The U.S. POWs from the Vietnam Era—men like Jim Stockdale, John McCain, Jeremiah Denton, and Bill Lawrence—brought honor to themselves and their country.

Americans in the 1950s were horrified when a small number of "brain-washed" young POWs in Korea turned against their own country. Now, Americans thrilled to stories of "undaunted courage" under the most extreme conditions of torture, starvation, and solitary confinement. Retired Navy Captain Gerry Coffee tells school groups that only his strong Christian faith brought him through this ordeal.[103] Former POWs would later laugh off their suffering. John McCain says "they didn't put a chocolate on the pillow at the Hanoi Hilton." Jack Fellowes even jokes about torture: "We weren't broken by it, but some of us were *bent* a good bit."

Americans have come to honor the Vietnam POWs as no previous war's prisoners have been honored. This is, in part, a tribute to their loyalty and endurance. It is also a commentary on the fact that when many questioned the old verities of duty, honor, country, these members of the U.S. military proved themselves true. They might have felt themselves abandoned by America, but they did not abandon her. They saw other young Americans burning the flag, but they cherished it. They fully merit the accolades a grateful nation has showered upon them.

President Nixon deserves credit for the attention his administration focused on the release of the POWs. Though viciously assailed for his December 1972 bombing campaign, Nixon never lost faith that the POWs would be released. By contrast, Senator George McGovern had said he would be willing "to crawl on his knees to Hanoi" if that would secure their release. Can there have been a more self-defeating verbal image in the history of American presidential campaigning?

As strongly as most Americans identified with the POWs, the reaction of many Americans to actress Jane Fonda's travels to Hanoi, her posing on a North Vietnamese antiaircraft gun, and her confrontational meeting with

U.S. POWs exposed a deep and yet unhealed wound in the nation's soul. Fonda and her fellow travelers were never charged with treason, except in the hearts and minds of millions of Americans.

Meanwhile, Nixon's critics in Congress and in Europe erupted in denunciation of him as a "mad bomber." The Democratic leader in the Senate, Mike Mansfield, called it "a Stone Age tactic." The Swedish government likened Nixon's 1972 bombing campaign to those of the Nazis.* America's NATO allies offered no help.[104] Media critics charged Nixon with "carpet bombing" civilian targets in North Vietnam. Only later, much later, did honest journalists survey the damage and report. When almost no one was paying attention, Peter Ward of the *Baltimore Sun* wrote: "Hanoi has certainly been damaged but evidence on the ground disproves charges of indiscriminate bombing."[105]

The U.S. bombing campaign worked. The North Vietnamese signed the Paris accords in January 1973. Kissinger had to press the South Vietnamese government, our reluctant ally, to accept the peace agreement he had hammered out with Le Duc Tho in Paris.

As Nixon prepared for his second inauguration as president, the world marveled at the end of the Vietnam War—or at least, the end of U.S. involvement in that war. American POWs were released to a spontaneous outburst of joy.**

VI. *Roe v. Wade*: "Raw Judicial Power"

In Texas, Lyndon B. Johnson died of a heart attack on 22 January 1973. He was sixty-four years old. The former president had lived in virtual seclusion since leaving Washington four years earlier, rarely venturing forth from his LBJ Ranch or his presidential library. He did witness the *Apollo 11* launch, a project he had so enthusiastically supported.

Johnson's death, the Paris Peace accords, and the release of the POWs

---

* The Swedes in their high dudgeon conveniently forgot how their "neutral" government had provided critical assistance to Hitler in his drive to conquer their peaceful European neighbors.

** The North Vietnamese Communists released those officially listed as POWs, but there has never been a full accounting of the MIAs—those "missing in action."

"The Eagle has Landed!" *Neil Armstrong walking on the moon with reflection in visor, 20 July 1969. John F. Kennedy's "called shot"—like that of Babe Ruth—succeeded spectacularly as the U.S. achieved his goal of putting a man on the Moon before 1970. Kennedy knew how important space was in the conflict with aggressive Soviet Communism. Jack did not live to see his triumph, but the night the lunar landing module touched down, someone placed flowers on his grave with just these words: "The Eagle has landed."*

Release of Vietnam War POWs, January 1973. *President Nixon sought "peace with honor" in Vietnam. One of his greater successes was the release of hundreds of U.S. prisoners of war by North Vietnam. Americans learned of the torture and privation these brave men endured. Three times, Navy flier John McCain refused offers of early release, remaining true to his comrades. He would say of the miserable prison the Americans called Hanoi Hilton, "they didn't put a chocolate on our pillow."*

Nixon departing from White House. *"I gave them a sword," Nixon would later tell a TV interviewer of his complicity in the cover-up of felonies involved with the Watergate break-in. Nixon spent years claiming he did not know what had happened. But when the Supreme Court ordered him to give up incriminating audio tapes, his guilt was made plain. His own words convicted him; they were "the smoking gun." Nixon became the only President to resign (but perhaps not the only one who should have resigned).*

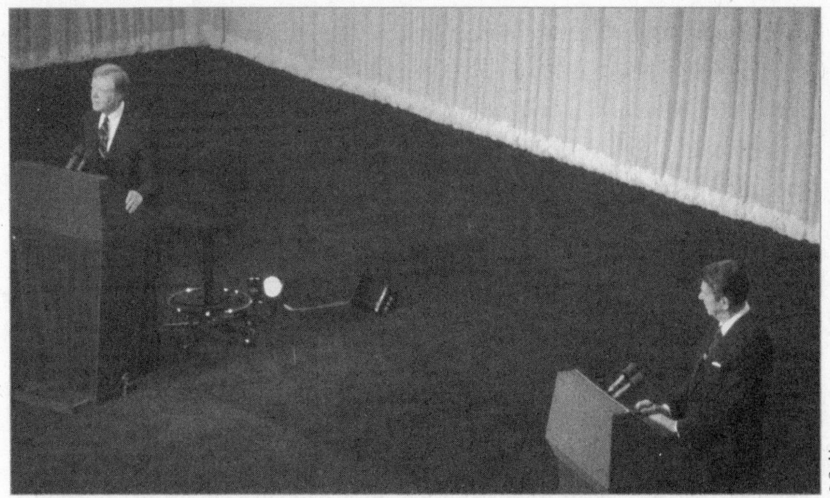

© Corbis

Jimmy Carter debating Reagan, 1980. *"There you go again," Gov. Ronald Reagan said disarmingly during his only debate with President Jimmy Carter during the 1980 campaign. Reagan was responding to Carter's repeated charges that the Californian was a reckless man and a racist. Reagan's soft answer turned away wrath. Millions of undecided voters—especially women—concluded that a man who could control himself could be trusted to run the country. Reagan swept Carter away in an unexpected landslide.*

In counsel. *The author, while serving as Secretary of Education, with President Ronald Reagan on Air Force One.*

overshadowed what otherwise would have been the major news story of 22 January 1973: the U.S. Supreme Court's 7–2 ruling in *Roe* v. *Wade.* The ruling struck down the abortion laws of all fifty states. It allowed abortion for any reason for the first three months of pregnancy. In the second three months of pregnancy, only restrictions designed to safeguard the mother's health were permitted. Only in the final three months of pregnancy, said Supreme Court Justice Harry Blackmun (a Nixon appointee), could the states restrict abortion, so long as the life and the health of the mother were protected.

In a companion case, *Doe* v. *Bolton,* decided on the same day, however, Blackmun made clear that the definition of the mother's health (including mental health) would be so broad as to provide grounds for striking down any law that placed an undue burden on a woman's choice of abortion. Henceforth, fathers would have no rights, parents of minor girls only very limited rights, and the unborn child no rights at all under the *Roe* and *Doe* line of cases. Thus, the procedure that had been a felony in most states for more than a century now became a fundamental constitutional right due to the new judicial reasoning and line of cases. Justice Byron R. "Whizzer" White, a JFK appointee, dissented, calling *Doe* an act of "raw judicial power," as it took these decisions from the states and enshrined their determination in the Supreme Court's reasoning.

Blackmun had labored for most of the previous year on the opinion the Court handed down. Justice William O. Douglas, FDR's appointee, had threatened to go public with his denunciations of Chief Justice Burger's "manipulation" in the assignment of the opinions.[106] He knew—all the justices knew—that Blackmun was the slowest writer on the Court.[107] Those who favored a broad abortion ruling knew that Douglas could not be assigned the opinion. He was seen as simply too liberal. The fact that he had been married four times would not help, either. Veteran liberal Justice Brennan was the obvious choice in terms of experience, inclination, and legal craftsmanship to write an abortion ruling, but he was the only Catholic on the Court and it was thought that would only antagonize a large segment of the American people.[108]

Eventually, Justice Douglas resigned himself to Harry Blackmun's writing the opinion.[109] In many ways, Blackmun wrote for the elite law school faculties and for the editorial board of the *New York Times.* And in those rarefied precincts, he has never lacked for defenders.

Not all scholars bowed to Blackmun's handiwork, however. John Hart Ely, a distinguished liberal constitutional scholar who favored legalized abortion, saw the flaws in the ruling's central arguments: "*Roe* lacks even colorable support in the constitutional text, history, or any other appropriate source of constitutional doctrine. . . . *Roe* is bad because it is bad constitutional law, or rather because it is *not* constitutional law and gives almost no sense of an obligation to try to be."[110]

The Court's action would drive a deep wedge between Americans. In its determination to short-circuit democratic processes, the Supreme Court would further undermine Americans' confidence in the judiciary. In the quarter of a century before *Roe*, the proportion of Americans who had "great confidence" in the judiciary plunged from 83.4 percent to just 32.6 percent.[111] And Roe was another self-inflicted wound from which the courts have not recovered. Too many people saw the Court over-reaching in its jurisdiction and power with its abortion decisions.

Liberals and feminists hailed the Court's ruling in *Roe* v. *Wade.* It was, as Lawrence Lader wrote, "central to everything in life and how we wanted to live it."[112] Lader was a founder of the National Association for the Repeal of Abortion Laws. Mainline Protestants, in general, approved the ruling. Liberal church bodies like the Presbyterian Church USA, the Protestant Episcopal Church, and the United Methodists endorsed *Roe.* Many Jewish groups also supported what they viewed as "reproductive rights."

Media sources continue to cite poll results that show majorities of Americans favor some form of liberalized abortion. And while it is true that majorities respond *no* when pollsters ask if they favor "overturning" *Roe,* critics point out that the public never favors *overturning* anything. The technical legal term sounds drastic, dangerous. Voters do not employ legal jargon in analyzing public issues. It is equally true that majorities consistently favor significant restrictions on the abortion license, restrictions that *Roe* and later Court rulings have ruled out of bounds. Over the years, since *Roe*, many Americans have become uncomfortable with the number of abortions that have taken place. (By 2005, more than forty million abortions were performed in America.)

Opposition to the Court's ruling continues to this day. For millions of Americans, the Court illegitimately stripped away the inalienable right to life from the unborn and threatened America's role as a leader of human rights in the world. The National Right to Life Committee rose up to convert opposition into lawful constitutional, legislative, and social action. Major religious groups—including the U.S. Catholic Conference, the Southern Baptist Convention, the National Association of Evangelicals, and The Lutheran Church (Missouri Synod)—would rally against the Court's rulings. Liberal and feminist groups, in turn, would rally in favor of the Court's ruling—seeing it as a litmus test for their favored brand of constitutional interpretation and as fundamental to the rights of women. Many have boiled it down, simply, this way: those opposed to *Roe* believe the Court should protect life, or the states' rights to protect life; those in favor of *Roe* believe the Court should protect a woman's right to choose an abortion—hence the terms "pro-life" and "pro-choice" have served to identify people's positions on the issue of abortion.

VII. Watergate Spills Over

In the spring of 1973, as the Watergate affair unraveled, President Nixon's political stock plummeted. Judge John J. Sirica, an Eisenhower appointee, began to apply pressure to the small fries in the burglary. They, in turn, began to implicate higher ups, who implicated still higher ups. Nixon aide John Ehrlichman suggested that the hapless director of the FBI be allowed to "twist slowly, slowly in the wind." This graphic phrase soon applied not only to L. Patrick Grey as much as to the entire Nixon administration.

The press hated Nixon. His increasingly rare press conferences challenged the notion that bear-baiting had been made illegal in America. Nixon had always had a hostile relationship with the press corps.[113] The *Washington Post*'s lead cartoonist, Herbert Block, gave Nixon a "shave" for his 1969 inauguration—a one-day reprieve. He immediately returned to savaging Nixon and his five o'clock shadow *daily* on the editorial page of the capital's hometown paper. Now, with the wolves closing in around him, Nixon was so upset, he would throw up before press conferences.[114]

By October 1973, America faced "a perfect storm." The Senate Watergate Committee had exposed widespread abuses that seemed sure to lead to the president's impeachment. The national media made a hero of the committee's Democratic chairman, North Carolina senator Sam Ervin.* Americans were impressed by the cool, lawyerly questioning of Tennessee's Republican senator, Howard Baker. "What did the President know and when did he know it," Baker asked every witness. (When the answers came to that question, the trap would be sprung.)

Vice President Spiro T. Agnew could not succeed Nixon because he was being investigated for taking massive bribes from highway contractors when he served as governor of Maryland. Agnew pleaded *nolo contendere* ("I do not contest") in Baltimore's Federal Courthouse on 10 October 1973. He resigned to escape a jail sentence.

At the same moment, Israel was invaded by Egypt. The fourth Arab-Israeli War was launched by Egypt on the Jewish High Holy Days, specifically to take advantage of the time when the Jews would be worshipping. Initially, Israeli forces were thrown back. Israel suddenly faced annihilation. The Soviets had armed the Arabs to the teeth and were egging them on. Israeli war hero Moshe Dayan—the brilliant general with the dashing patch over one eye—appeared on state television to calm Israeli fears. It would take weeks, not months, he said, for the Israeli Defense Forces (IDF) to rally and wipe out their Arab foes. "Confident words," wrote an English visitor in his diary, "but he looks more worried than he sounds."[115] Dayan had good reason to be worried. The Egyptians had never performed so well in combat. They had overwhelming numbers. If they maintained tight military discipline, they might overrun the tiny Jewish state.

"Your son is dead," read the telegram the young girls delivered to hundreds of Israeli mothers in the opening days of the Yom Kippur War.[116] Young girls were delivering the messages because so many Israeli postmen had been

* Ervin got a pass on his decades of opposition to civil rights. The canonization of this "simple country lawyer" illustrates the rule that the enemy of my enemy is my friend. So long as Ervin pursued the hated Nixon, his past sins were absolved.

called up for military duty. One of these youthful messengers watched in horror as a bereaved mother beat her head on the floor in her anguish.[117]

Besieged as he was, President Nixon immediately placed U.S. armed forces around the world on full alert. Following a practical suggestion from Governor Ronald Reagan and an urgent appeal from Prime Minister Golda Meir, he ordered American military transports to fully resupply Israel with the military equipment she so desperately needed.[118] He would not allow the Soviets to take advantage of the desperate political crisis in Washington to let their Arab clients crush Israel. Without the Nixon resupply, Israel might well have fallen.

Within weeks, the IDF had turned the tide of battle and had surrounded the Egyptian Army in the Sinai Desert. Menachem Begin and his *Likud* bloc in Israel wanted to wipe out the Egyptian Army once and for all. Henry Kissinger knew that if that happened, the Soviets would be forced to step up their support of local dictators like Khaddafi and Saddam Hussein. And they would give increased aid to terror chiefs like Yasser Arafat. Better an American-brokered ceasefire than greater Soviet influence in the Middle East, Kissinger argued. When he told Israeli Prime Minister Golda Meir that he was an American, the secretary of state, and a Jew *in that order,* she mischievously reminded Kissinger that Hebrews read from right to left!

The ceasefire Kissinger negotiated in the Middle East bought little time and no credit for Richard Nixon. When he demanded that Attorney General Elliott Richardson fire Special Prosecutor Archibald Cox, Richardson refused and resigned. Deputy Attorney General William Ruckelshaus also refused and resigned. Finally, Solicitor General Robert Bork agreed to fire Cox, if only to keep the executive branch from melting down at a time when there was no vice president. The press quickly labeled the uproar that greeted this action a "firestorm" and the firing and resignations "the Saturday night massacre."

It was an exaggeration. The Israelis could tell desk-bound reporters something about real firestorms and real massacres. Still, Nixon's authority trickled away like the sands of an hourglass. He named Michigan's Republican congressman, Gerald R. Ford, as vice president to replace the disgraced Agnew. Although a strong partisan, Ford was well-liked on both sides of the aisle. He was readily confirmed as the first vice president chosen under the Twenty-fifth Amendment to the Constitution.

The Arabs retaliated against the United States by imposing an oil embargo that caused sharp, severe gas shortages throughout North America and Europe. Prices skyrocketed.

To most Americans, their cars are their freedom.[119] With long gas lines, with odd/even days for purchase of fuel, things seemed to be falling apart. Those in charge, inevitably, were blamed.

Nixon had made no effort to share his 1972 victory with his fellow Republicans. He made no attempt to shape the coming landslide or to give it meaning. Now, he faced a hostile Congress that did not like and did not fear him.[120] Richard Nixon's political end might actually have come months before he finally resigned. In an effort to appease the pursuing investigators, he released hours and hours of carefully edited tapes. These, he argued, would prove him innocent. They proved no such thing. His antagonists sneered at them. The tapes seriously undermined Nixon's support in Middle America.

When he heard the edited tapes, the Republicans' Senate leader, Hugh Scott of Pennsylvania, called them "shabby, disgusting, immoral."[121] The silent majority that had unswervingly supported Nixon when hundreds of thousands of long-haired demonstrators converged on Washington was appalled by the foul-mouthed Nixon revealed on the tapes. Hardly a sentence was transcribed without a damning "[expletive deleted]." Nixon had always presented himself to straight Americans as a nice man. He had even prissily confronted JFK in their debates about how Ike had restored decent language to the White House.* Now, Nixon was shown to be a base, mean-spirited manipulator and, worse, an inveterate liar. "I am not a crook," he pathetically told newspaper editors. He might as well have worn a sandwich sign saying I *AM* A CROOK.[122]

Because of the deepening crisis of Watergate, Nixon's historic visit to the Soviet Union of 27 June–3 July 1974 was overshadowed by the imminent threat of his impeachment.

This first visit by a U.S. president to the Soviet Union nonetheless

---

* Candidate Jack Kennedy, with typical flair, easily fended off Nixon's attack on Harry Truman's barnyard language that Nixon voters could go to hell, Jack quipped, "I don't think we should bring up the religion issue."

produced a serious debate about *détente*. Washington's Democratic senator, Henry Jackson, strongly opposed the Soviets' anti-Semitic policies, including the Soviet refusal to allow Russian Jews to emigrate to Israel or the United States. Victims of this policy were called *refuseniks*. Senator Jackson co-sponsored the Jackson-Vanik Amendment, which limited U.S.-Soviet trade until the Jews were allowed to leave. The Nixon administration, which had very likely saved Israel during the Yom Kippur War, nonetheless strongly opposed Jackson-Vanik.

Opponents of Nixon's policy of *détente* charged that it obscured the distinction between freedom and tyranny. Ironically, the man who began his career as a fierce foe of "atheistic Communism" now seemed to see the U.S. and USSR as morally equivalent.

The House Judiciary Committee proceeded to vote out three articles of impeachment against President Nixon in June 1974. Hillary Rodham was one of the eager young Democratic staffers who helped draft the articles. Though it would avail them little, the Republican members of the committee put their country before their party and voted overwhelmingly to impeach Nixon. Veteran liberal journalist Jack Germond called the House Republicans' defense of the Constitution "magnificent."[123]

When the U.S. Supreme Court unanimously ruled in *U.S.* v. *Nixon* that the president had to surrender his White House tapes, the end was not long in coming. The tape that showed "what the President knew and when he knew it" was quickly ferreted out. It was called "the smoking gun," and it showed that Nixon had known all about the break-in at the Watergate virtually since it happened. The tape provided irrefutable evidence that Nixon had tried to get the CIA to pressure the FBI to call off its Watergtate investigation. Nixon wanted the CIA to tell the FBI it was for "national security" reasons. Furious at what Nixon had put the Congress, the country, and the Republican Party through for two years, Senator Barry Goldwater telephoned General Alexander Haig in the White House. "Al," the plain-speaking Arizonan growled, "Dick Nixon has lied to me for the very last time. And to a hell of a lot of others in the Senate and the House. We're sick to death of it all."[124] Goldwater never asked Nixon to resign when he joined the Republican leaders of the House and Senate in a last meeting with the president. But the trio made it clear Nixon had *no* support among Republicans in either House of Congress. So much for not eating rubber chicken with them!

Nixon resigned the presidency at noon on 9 August 1974. In an emotional appearance before his White House staff, he struggled to maintain his composure. This tortured man became the first president in 185 years to resign. He was also the only one to have his name engraved on a gold plate on the Moon. As Charles de Gaulle, one of the few public men Nixon admired, had said when Khrushchev was overthrown: "*Sic Transit Gloria Mundi*"—"Thus passes the glory of this world."

Eleven

The Years the Locusts Ate*

(1974–1981)

Bell-bottom trousers, platform shoes, shoulder-length hair, flowered shirts: These were the signature garb of many a man in the Western world in the 1970s. The fashion followed the times. And they were profoundly unserious times. Americans yearned for leadership, but they were sternly lectured that the fault was in themselves. It seemed as if the nation itself had been taken hostage by events. In the 1970s, freedom declined in America and in the democratic states of the Western Alliance. Workers ended the decade with less real buying power as inflation ate up wages and investments. Would America enter the decade of the 1980s as that "pitiful helpless giant" that Nixon warned about? Was the presidency too big a job for one man? A mood of profound pessimism marked the free societies. "Malaise" was the word used to describe the public mood. At the decade's end, however, there was a discernible resurgence of freedom throughout the West. It may have been heralded by acts of courage and defiance behind the Iron Curtain. "Blow the dust off the clock," cried Russian writer Aleksandr Solzhenitsyn: "Your watches are behind the times. Throw open the heavy curtains which are so dear to you—you do not

* The years that the locust hath eaten' (*Joel*, ii, 25). The British Minister of Defense, Sir Thomas Inskip, used this phrase to describe the period 1931–35 during which Britain fell further and further behind Germany in rearmament. (Quoted in Churchill, *The Second World War* (Cassell), Vol. I, 52.) This title was chosen for the period of the mid-70s to 1981 in the U.S. because the forces of freedom were in retreat and Soviet Communism was advancing.

even suspect that the day has already dawned outside."[1] *George Orwell had defined Communist totalitarianism as a boot in your face—forever. Now, Solzhenitsyn gave that boot a good hard bite. So did Andrei Sakharov and Natan Anatoly Sharansky in Russia, Lech Walesa and Karol Wojtyla in Poland, and Vaclav Havel in Czechoslovakia. These men of the East inspired and were inspired by new leaders who came to power in the West—leaders like Margaret Thatcher and Ronald Reagan. The most dramatic event of all was the advent of a new Polish pope who began his reign saying, "Be Not Afraid!" Freedom, crushed to earth, rose again.*

I. "I'm not a Lincoln, I'm a Ford"

Gerald R. Ford took the oath of office as president just as Richard Nixon's helicopter was leaving the South Lawn of the White House. "Our long national nightmare is over," he said to a relieved country. To millions of Americans, Nixon's forced resignation proved that the system of checks and balances the founders had devised two hundred years before actually worked.[2]

The first order of business for President Ford was the selection of a vice president. Quickly, he named former New York Governor Nelson Rockefeller. The country had been stunned by the resignations of an elected vice president and president. Ford wanted to reassure a worried nation and a doubtful world that Americans could competently deal with questions of governance and legitimate succession. Many people disliked Rockefeller's liberalism, but no one doubted his competence.

Conservatives who supported California Governor Ronald Reagan were deeply offended. They regarded Rockefeller as disloyal to the GOP. They blamed his lukewarm endorsement of Barry Goldwater in 1964 for the party's debacle in that election. With some difficulty, Ford was able to see Rockefeller confirmed as vice president by a sullen Democratic Congress. By choosing Rockefeller, Ford virtually guaranteed himself a serious conservative challenge in the presidential primaries of 1976.[3]

Ford was eager to put Watergate behind him. Watergate would not be over until he decided what to do about former President Nixon. The

Constitution provides that impeachment and removal from office is the greatest penalty that Congress can impose on an errant official. But *after* removal from office and the immunities of that office, a former president is subject to the same laws against obstruction of justice and subornation of perjury as any other citizen.

Nixon, in seclusion in San Clemente, California, now faced the real prospect of indictment for crimes, trial, and imprisonment. The number of legal questions that would have been raised by such proceedings would have kept law professors busy for a century. Could the tapes that Nixon had been forced to yield up be entered into evidence against him? If so, what would become of the Fifth Amendment's guarantee against self-incrimination? Where would impartial jurors be found? Had not the media feeding frenzy of the past two years bathed the country in unfavorable pre-trial publicity? More than the legal questions, what would the trial and imprisonment of a former president mean to America's position in the world? How would such a trial look in the middle of the Nation's upcoming bicentennial celebration? What would such a trial, likely coming in the middle of the 1976 presidential campaign, do to the American political system? Not least, Ford had to consider what a trial of Richard Nixon would do to his beloved Republican Party.

Ford came into the White House on a wave of public approval. Americans welcomed the plain-speaking Midwesterner with genuine affection. "Jerry" Ford had modestly and truthfully said, "I'm not a Lincoln, I'm a Ford." Few Americans could say that Lyndon Johnson or Richard Nixon were basically decent, honorable, trustworthy men. Few Americans doubted that about Jerry Ford.

If he had not been elected to the office, he had the advantage of representing Grand Rapids, Michigan, in Congress for a quarter century. Grand Rapids is virtually synonymous with the American work ethic, solid virtue, and neighborly goodwill. There, and at the University of Michigan, where he was a star football player, Jerry Ford learned to hit hard, but help his opponent up. Nixon brooded over his ever lengthening "enemies list"; Ford could have kept his on a postage stamp. The media gave him a "honeymoon." The fit, trim sixty-one-year-old was shown diving into his swimming pool. He toasted his own English muffins for breakfast.

But the honeymoon was brief. When he issued an unconditional pardon for Richard Nixon, he hoped to end the divisions and hatreds of Watergate. Instead he just mired himself in it. His approval rating dropped from 71 percent in August to 50 percent in September.[4] His presidency never fully recovered.

"Whip Inflation Now" was Ford's response to the dizzying rise in consumer prices. He wore a lapel button that said WIN. He urged Americans to limit their buying and their demands for wage hikes. He vetoed as inflationary the big-spending bills Congress put on his desk. Ford's WIN buttons provoked hoots of derision. They revived all the old, ugly LBJ stories about Ford's playing football too long without a helmet.*

The Democrats used the Nixon pardon and the worsening economic conditions to gain historic victory in the mid-term elections. The "Watergate babies"—young, smart, aggressively liberal candidates—who composed the new Congress would make substantial changes in America.** Ford's repeated attempts to use his veto were frustrated by Congress's new assertiveness. Democrats campaigned for a "veto-proof" Congress and got it.***

First to feel the impact of the liberal Democratic majority on Capitol Hill were the people of Southeast Asia. Without substantial U.S. aid to the non-Communist government in Saigon, South Vietnam could not survive. This was reality, regardless of the guarantees offered by North Vietnam in the Paris Peace accords of 1973.

Seeking to rehabilitate himself after Chappaquiddick, Senator Edward ("Ted") Kennedy had become the most outspoken leader of liberal opposition to any aid to South Vietnam. His two older brothers, Jack and Bobby,

---

* "Jerry Ford is so dumb," Johnson had said of the House Republican Leader, "he can't fart and chew gum at the same time." Johnson's crude and funny characterizations of his opponents were Washington legend. But a career of such cruel put-downs left Lyndon Johnson a lonely and dejected man at the end. The media sanitized this to have LBJ say Ford couldn't walk and chew gum at the same time. (Reeves, Richard, *A Ford, Not a Lincoln*, 25.)

** Patrick Leahy (D-Vermont) was first elected to the Senate in 1974. Among those first elected to the House that year were Sen. Tom Harkin (D-Iowa), Sen. Max Baucus (D-Montana), Rep. George Miller (D-California), Rep. Henry Waxman (D-California), Rep. James Oberstar (D-Minnesota), and Rep. John Murtha (D-Pennsylvania).

*** A veto-proof Congress is one in which the president's opponents have more than two-thirds of the seats in both Houses. It has rarely occurred in American history and, even under Ford, could be invoked only on a limited range of usually economic issues.

had done much to entangle the United States in South Vietnam. Now, Ted resorted to such devices as refusing even to allow the Pentagon to spend surplus appropriated funds in Vietnam.[5] Following Kennedy's lead, the new Democratic majority voted to cut off all aid to South Vietnam in March 1975.[6] "Do you *want* Cambodia to fall," asked a worried Ford administration official. "Yes," said liberal Democratic Rep. Don Fraser of Minnesota, "under controlled circumstances to minimize the loss of life."[7]

Sensing their opportunity with the "peace" Congress in Washington, North Vietnamese army leaders shredded their agreements and invaded the South. In short order, Americans watched while the under-equipped South Vietnamese military fell back before the armored onslaught of regular North Vietnamese army units. For decades, it had been argued that the war in the South was a civil war, that the Vietcong were "indigenous" forces. Now, the Communists of the North brazenly rolled over their Southern neighbors.

The U.S. Embassy in Saigon—soon to be renamed Ho Chi Minh City after the founder of Communist North Vietnam—was surrounded by invaders. The U.S. ambassador and his staff had to be airlifted by helicopter from the embassy roof. The ambassador bore a neatly folded U.S. flag under his arm. 30 April 1975 was the last day of American involvement in Southeast Asia. "This is not a day for recriminations," President Ford said. Ronald Reagan reportedly answered, "What *better* day?"*

Henry Kissinger records the response of a pro-American leader of Cambodia. Distraught at the collapse of American will and American allies in Southeast Asia, Kissinger offered to rescue Sirik Matak from certain death. Matak's response, in elegant French, is memorable:

> I thank you very sincerely for your letter and your offer to transport me towards freedom. I cannot, alas, leave [Cambodia] in such a cowardly fashion. As for you, and in particular your great country, I never believed for a moment that you would . . . [abandon] a people which have chosen liberty. You have refused us your protection, and we can

* A replica of the ladder used by the fleeing ambassador is on display at the Gerald R. Ford Presidential Library in Grand Rapids, Michigan. It has to be one of the strangest mementoes of any presidency. (Source: Taranto, James, *Presidential Leadership*, 185.)

> do nothing about it. You leave, and my wish is that you and your country will find happiness under the sky. [If I die here] I have committed only this mistake of believing you.[8]

When the Communist Khmer Rouge seized Phnom Penh, they shot Matak in the stomach. Unattended, it took him three days to die.[9]

It would take several years longer for masses of Matak's countrymen to die in a protracted horror known today as Cambodia's "Killing Fields." The French leftists who wrote *The Black Book of Communism* explain the numbers: When the Khmer Rouge's chief, Pol Pot, ordered all residents of Phnom Penh out into the countryside, it resulted in "400,000 deaths." The average number of all executions carried out by the Khmer Rouge forces, the *Black Book* authors find, "hovers around 500,000." Another 400,000 to 600,000 died in prison. And, of course, there was the hunger and disease that overtook city-dwellers. People were suddenly thrust into the countryside with no provisions made for them, leaving another 700,000 dead.[10]

Nothing in Sirik Matak's haunting letter proved to be wrong—except perhaps the addressee. He should have sent his letter to Senator Kennedy and Congressman Fraser.

President Ford's ability to help America's abandoned South Vietnamese allies had been seriously impaired by the congressional leadership. They cut off all funding, and Ford respected Congress's constitutional power of the purse. Still, that did not stop him from ordering the Navy to rescue as many as 130,000 "boat people," as storm-tossed refugees from the Communist terror in Southeast Asia were known. George McGovern thought they would have been better off staying in their Communist-ruled homeland.

The love of freedom, the commitment to liberty in all its forms, is hardly an American invention. Sirik Matak appealed to it. So did Aleksandr Solzhenitsyn, the Russian author imprisoned by Stalin who won the 1970 Nobel Prize for Literature.

The award of the prize greatly angered the Soviet rulers in the Kremlin. Nikita Khrushchev had permitted Solzhenitsyn to publish his short novel *One Day in the Life of Ivan Denisovich* in 1962. Khrushchev read it and saw only its indictment of Stalin's *gulag* (slave labor camps). More perceptive

Communists understood that *One Day* condemned Soviet rule, subtly, humorously, on every page. When Khrushchev was ousted in 1964, his decision to allow publication of Solzhenitsyn's masterpiece was counted as one of his "hare-brained schemes."*

By 1974, Communist Party chief Leonid Brezhnev had lost patience with the courageous Solzhenitsyn. When *The Gulag Archipelago* was published in Paris in late 1973, Brezhnev ordered Solzhenitsyn arrested. In a massive work that eventually encompassed three volumes and half a million words, Solzhenitsyn laid bare Soviet pretensions of humanity. He carefully documented the tens of millions who had lost their lives or their liberty in the slave labor camps of the USSR. These camps began under Lenin, not Stalin, and extended throughout the twelve time zones of the USSR. Some "islands" in the system were no bigger than a phone booth, and one island was bigger than France.

Throughout the world, writers and intellectuals appealed for the courageous writer's life and his freedom. American Nobel Prize winner Saul Bellow spoke for many. He said Solzhenitsyn had "redeemed" the word *hero.*[11] Bellow warned in the *New York Times* that any further Kremlin moves against Solzhenitsyn—imprisonment, deportation, or psychiatric "treatment" in one of the Soviets' notorious asylums—would prove the utter moral bankruptcy of the Soviet Union.[12]

When the KGB interrogated Solzhenitsyn, they threatened to kill his wife and his three little boys. They could make it look like a simple auto accident. They had plenty of practice at that. *Do it!* Solzhenitsyn told them defiantly. Nothing would stop him from telling the truth. At his wits' end—which was not a long trip—Brezhnev stripped him of his Soviet citizenship and kicked him out of the country. Shrewdly, other Communist party bosses figured that the West would soon tire of this stern moralist.

President Ford was embarrassed in 1975 by appeals for him to invite the exiled Russian to the White House. Turning down requests for a meeting, Ford said he did not think he could learn anything "of substance" from

* That it took a decision of the USSR's Communist Party boss to publish a single, small novel of about a hundred pages speaks volumes about the total lack of intellectual freedom in the old Soviet Union.

a meeting with Solzhenitsyn. Conservative columnist George Will agreed, but jibed that Ford's refusal said more about the president's ability to *absorb* wisdom than Solzhenitsyn's ability to *impart* it.

Henry Kissinger was widely thought to be responsible for the Solzhenitsyn turndown. As secretary of state, he doubtless knew that any triumphal White House meeting for the outspoken critic of the Kremlin and *détente* would doom efforts to get other dissident writers freed from KGB clutches. Nonetheless, one State Department bureaucrat called Solzhenitsyn practically "a fascist."[13] Such stupidity led conservative senator Jesse Helms to call for "an American desk" at the State Department.

II. 1976: A Bicentennial Election

"My name is Jimmy Carter and I'm runnin' for President," said the grinning peanut farmer from Georgia. Carter himself acknowledged that he was an unlikely candidate for president. He was a one-term governor of a mid-sized Southern state, a Naval Academy graduate who had worked under the tempestuous Admiral Hyman Rickover in the nuclear submarine program, and Carter's family income was based on the lowly "goober pea."

He was not a lawyer, not a member of Congress, not a Washington, D.C., insider. Instead of these "nots" being demerits, Carter shrewdly made them the centerpiece of his outsider campaign for the 1976 Democratic nomination for president. The McGovern rules, ironically, had opened the party up to its primary voters. This gave special influence to those who were intensely motivated. Because liberal candidates from Washington could be expected to split the support of the divided party, they created a nightmare scenario: The wheelchair-bound Governor George C. Wallace might actually come in first in a crowded primary field. Party leaders and journalists were desperate to stop Wallace. Even though the ex-segregationist had disavowed his past, Eastern liberals could neither forgive nor forget the man who had "stood in the schoolhouse door" to resist racial integration.

To stop Wallace, many liberals reasoned, they would have to find a Southerner with a good record on race. That pointed to "Jimmy" Carter. Carter communicated to voters very cleverly, perhaps especially when he chose to use only his nickname. He had several reasons for this. He wanted to emphasize a simpler, less "imperial" view of the presidency. He wanted to stress, not hide, his Southern roots. Besides, he could not use his formal name in any event. Key to Carter's quest was his strong support in the black community. *James Earl Carter Jr.* would never do in a country that had just seen the trial and conviction of *James Earl Ray Jr.* for the assassination of the beloved Dr. Martin Luther King Jr.

Carter also emphasized his evangelical Christian faith. For many Americans, their first introduction to a "born again" Christian would come through the campaign of Jimmy Carter.* In many Southern states, and in many other states with large rural populations—like Iowa, Minnesota, Wisconsin, and Pennsylvania—Carter's evangelical tone would strike a responsive chord with millions of voters.[14]

Carter took care to seek out leading members of the liberal journalistic elite. Who was this "jasper from Georgia," asked *The Baltimore Sun*'s Jack Germond dismissively.[15] Even the hard-boiled Germond, however, could not resist Carter's thoughtfulness. When Germond's fourteen-year-old daughter lay dying of leukemia, Carter sent her a thoughtful gift. He gave her Indian arrowheads he had found on his family's peanut farm—and a handwritten note asking her to share one with her sister.[16] It was a beautiful gesture.

Based on his outsider status, and his fresh appeal ("I'll never lie to you"), Carter swept past his primary opponents in the spring of 1976. As he captured the Democratic nomination for president, he even became the first candidate in history to refer publicly to his sexual drive. In an interview with *Playboy* magazine, something else unprecedented, Carter admitted he had "lusted" in his heart, but that he had never broken his marriage vows.

President Ford, meanwhile, was regularly skewered by the media. Not only did the editorial pages lambaste him, but the brilliant, irreverent young comics of television's *Saturday Night Live* lampooned him. This most athletic president since Teddy Roosevelt was depicted as a clumsy oaf.

---

* Chuck Colson had also attracted a wide audience with his best-selling book, *Born Again.* Colson went from heading Nixon's "dirty tricks" operation to serving a term in prison. From there, amazingly, he rose to lead Prison Fellowship Ministries. His is an inspiring story of conversion and commitment.

Comedian Chevy Chase made his career mocking Ford's tripping down the steps of *Air Force One.* When an errant Ford golf ball beaned a spectator, Ford once again came in for a round of ridicule. All presidents have to face ribbing. Most accept it with good nature, as Jerry Ford surely did, but the cumulative impact of the non-stop derision was to present Ford as inept and incapable. Such an impression can be fatal to a serious politician.

Ford faced a stiff challenge for the Republican nomination from former California Governor Ronald Reagan in 1976. Reagan came within 1,317 votes of defeating Ford in the New Hampshire primary. Without a cheering section in the liberal press like Gene McCarthy had in 1968, however, this near-win was played up as an embarrassing defeat.

Reagan had turned down a third party challenge to Ford by backers who wanted him to run with Alabama Governor George Wallace. Reagan appreciated the populist style in politics that both Wallace and Carter, both Southern governors, appealed to, but the Californian rejected Wallace's history of support for racial segregation.[17] Reagan also rejected a campaign flyer someone had prepared that featured a newspaper story speculating that President Ford would likely choose Massachusetts senator Edward Brooke as his running mate. To mainstream conservatives, Brooke was unacceptable because he was a Massachusetts liberal. But Reagan realized that the flyer would be used by the liberal press to suggest the Reagan forces opposed Brooke because he was black.[18] Reagan ordered the flyer shredded.

Reagan was proud of his record as governor of California. He had appointed more than 250 black officials, more than any other governor of the Golden State.[19] And he fondly recalled the story of his Eureka College football team. When bigoted hoteliers refused to let his black teammates stay in their establishments, young Ron took his friends to his home in Dixon—not far from the game. His parents would never turn away a friend in need of a bed and a hot meal.[20]

Reagan suffered several other defeats that spring. He was running out of campaign funds. Even Senator Barry Goldwater—the conservative standard bearer from 1964—urged him to drop out of the race. Journalists at a North Carolina press conference pressed Reagan, badgered him actually, to say when he was going to get out of the race.[21] Reagan's then campaign manager, John Sears, worried that Reagan's image with voters was that of a Republican George Wallace. Thus, Sears de-emphasized Reagan's strong conservative stances and ran, instead, a "résumé campaign." Sears had actually been secretly talking to President Ford's campaign manager about Reagan's expected departure from the race.[22]

A meeting held in Senator Helms' Washington office proved to be crucial. There, the North Carolina conservative pressed the Reagan campaign team to run on principle[23]—"No pale pastels." It may have been the first of many meetings whose theme was to be "Let Reagan be Reagan." They knew what many would-be "handlers" would later learn—that Reagan was at his best when hard pressed. He thrilled to the clash of ideas. He fought hardest when his back was to the wall. Reagan's pollster, Dick Wirthlin, put it best: "His enthusiasm would soar, his sights would focus and his passion would stir. He was one of the few leaders I've ever known who actually derived pleasure from confrontation."[24]

Reagan returned to North Carolina. This time he was determined that, win or lose, he would run on his own terms. There, aided by the redoubtable Helms, Reagan struck fire with the Panama Canal issue. Ford and Kissinger were preparing a treaty to turn over the canal to Panama. Reagan stood against leaders of *both* parties—and all of the Establishment press.

"We built it, we paid for it, it's ours!" was Reagan's populist cry of opposition to the giveaway. The canal negotiations represented more than they seemed. The Panama Canal issue struck millions of Americans as symbolic of America's declining power and prestige in the world. Reagan sensed this and rode the issue all the way to the Republican Convention in Kansas City, Missouri. After North Carolina, Reagan began to win primaries in the South and West.

Jerry Ford had a blessed diversion from his political woes in the celebration of the Nation's Bicentennial. Burdened by the memories of Vietnam and Watergate, the American people saw 4 July 1976 as a chance to celebrate two hundred years of freedom and independence. President Ford conducted himself with dignity and good humor at the birthday bash. With ceremonies in Washington, D.C., and Philadelphia, the president basked in the goodwill of a Nation on the mend. He told bicentennial celebrants at Independence Hall:

> The world is ever conscious of what Americans are doing, for better or for worse, because the United States today remains that most successful realization of humanity's universal hope. The world may or may not follow, but we lead because our whole history says we must. Liberty is for all men and women as a matter of equal and unalienable right. The establishment of justice and peace abroad will in large measure depend upon the peace and justice we create here in our own country, for we still show the way.[25]

In New York City, Ford presided over Op Sail, a magnificent parade of tall ships from all over the world on the Glorious Fourth. Two million people lined the shores of the Hudson River to cheer the stately procession of square-rigged sailing ships led by the U.S. Coast Guard's training ship *Eagle.** The largest fireworks display in history crowned Lower Manhattan and New York harbor as the nation rejoiced. In a blessed respite, there were no homicides in the Big Apple that historic day.

President Ford's celebratory sojourn was brief. Reagan attacked Ford's foreign policy. *Détente*, Reagan charged, ignored "the overriding reality of our time—the expansion of Soviet power in the world."[26]

Reagan tried to shake loose enough Ford delegates to capture the nomination by selecting Pennsylvania's liberal Republican senator, Richard Schweiker, as his running mate. It was either a bold move or a disastrous one. Schweiker's voting record gained him the same liberal rating as George McGovern, but Schweiker had resolutely opposed gun control and abortion and had been an outspoken defender of the "Captive Nations" held down by the USSR. Still, it was an unlikely coalition.

Reagan was trying, haltingly, to reach out to a new constituency. A year

* What the sailors of the Soviet Tall Ship, *Tovarisch*, or those of the Polish and Romanian entries—those *captive* nations—thought of this American celebration of two hundred years of freedom would make a fascinating story. Similarly, young sailors of the Chilean Tall Ship *Esmeralda* took part, even though Chile then was under the right-wing dictatorship of General Augusto Pinochet.

before he challenged President Ford, Ronald Reagan broadcast a radio commentary saying abortion was justified only in "self defense" and in which he spoke of unborn children's "human right."* In choosing Schweiker for vice president, he showed he wanted to embrace the blue collar, pro-labor stance Schweiker represented. Reagan understood that blue-collar workers were becoming disenchanted with social liberalism and accommodation of the Soviet Union as represented by *détente*.

President Ford's team used all the advantages of incumbency in beating back the Reagan challenge. Though Ford was a modest man, there was nothing modest about the Ford re-election effort. Once, when wooing some undecided Republican delegates from New York's Long Island, Ford's campaign managers invited the party wheel horses to a splendid White House State Dinner for the visiting Queen Elizabeth II. These "undecideds" quickly decided—and for the president.[27]

With such tactics, Ford beat Reagan for the nomination in 1976—barely. Ford had 1,187 delegates to Reagan's 1,070.[28] Wistfully, Reagan told his son Michael he was not bitter but he would miss not being able to sit across from the Soviet dictator at a summit, listening to his arms control demands, and then walking around to his side of the table to whisper the word "nyet" into his ear.[29]

Despite Ford's victory, Reagan stole the show when President Ford pleaded with him to come down to the victory stage and address the Republican Convention. Ford had dumped Nelson Rockefeller, taken on Senator Bob Dole as a running mate, and made major concessions to the Reagan forces on abortion and *détente* in the party platform. He needed Reagan's support. He was then behind Jimmy Carter by as much as thirty points in some polls.[30] Smiling and gracious, the tanned Californian spoke of a letter he had prepared for a time capsule that would be opened for the nation's *Tricentennial* in which Reagan was asked to enclose a letter touching on world peace:

> Those who would read this letter a hundred years from now will know whether those missiles were fired. They will know whether we met our

* (Online source: www.nytimes.com/library/magazine/home/20001231mag-reagan.html.)

> challenge. Whether they have the freedoms that we have will depend on what we do here.
>
> Will they look back with appreciation and say, "Thank God for those people of 1976 who headed off that loss of freedom, who kept our world from nuclear destruction?"
>
> And if we fail, they probably won't get to read the letter at all because it spoke of individual freedom and [they] won't be allowed to talk of that or read of it.[31]

Here was a sixty-five-year-old man talking of freedom and its future. He concluded with a stirring call to tell the world that "we [Americans] carry the message they're waiting for."[32] Delegates wept openly. Biographer Edmund Morris would later write of Reagan's "off the cuff" remarks: "The power of the speech was extraordinary. And you could just feel throughout the auditorium the palpable sense among the delegates that [they had] nominated the wrong guy." [33] Reagan consoled his heartbroken followers: "Though I am wounded, I am not slain. I shall arise and fight again."[34] Indeed, he would.

Ford campaigned vigorously. He traveled the country frenetically and narrowed the margin between himself and Carter in every poll. He was hampered, however, by his poor communication skills. As well, his message was muddled. Was he for the Nixon-Kissinger policies on détente he faithfully implemented or for the newer, more assertive Reagan policies his platform endorsed? Ford let the popular Betty speak for him on abortion—and Betty quickly disavowed the party's pro-life platform.[35]*

Ford's delivery of a speech in his hometown of Grand Rapids was described as "flat, as usual." Even here, the applause was more enthusiastic when he was introduced than when he sat down.[36] His paid advertising on television served him better. A bouncy jingle told viewers they were feeling

---

* Significantly, the Republican National Platform in 1976 *opposed* the *Roe v. Wade* ruling, offered respectful treatment of both sides in the abortion debate, but firmly endorsed "efforts of those who seek a constitutional amendment to restore protection of the right to life for unborn children." This was the party's first opportunity to respond formally to *Roe.* Although this "plank" provokes a fight—mostly in the press—every four years, the Republican Party has affirmed the right to life of unborn children ever since.

good about America. The ad showed celebrations from the Bicentennial Fourth. Carter's increasingly negative portrayal of power politics was held as a criticism of America.

Ford had challenged Carter to a debate when he was far behind in the polls. Now, for the first time in history, a sitting president would debate a challenger on national television.* During the second debate, which took place in San Francisco, Ford stumbled. It was not a physical pratfall—the kind that television comic Chevy Chase loved to spoof—but worse. Responding to Carter's attacks on his foreign policy, Ford disastrously said "there is not Soviet domination in Eastern Europe and there never will be in a Ford administration."[37] *What?* Immediately, Ford's "handlers" tried to recover from that verbal slip on a banana peel. They emphasized the enduring spirit of the Polish people, the fact that Ford's administration had pressed the Soviets to sign the Helsinki Accords on Human Rights in 1975. All of this was true, but Americans had seen Soviet tanks roll into East Berlin (1953), Hungary (1956), and Czechoslovakia (1968). If that wasn't Soviet domination then what was it? There was no recalling that gaffe. Millions of Americans concluded that honorable, good-hearted Jerry Ford was simply not up to the job. Ford was especially hurt in states with large ethnic enclaves of Poles, Hungarians, Balts, and Slavs.

Doubtless the "No Soviet Domination" gaffe damaged Ford's rising prospects in states like Pennsylvania, Ohio, and Wisconsin. There, too, Betty Ford's social liberalism hurt the president with his political base.[38]

Ford famously bore no grudges against the press. But that did not mean he got fair treatment from the members of what has been called the Fourth Estate.** A classic example was the *New York Daily News* headline: FORD TO CITY: DROP DEAD.[39] This was because President Ford refused to tax the American people to bail the city out from the bankruptcy into which profligate urban politicos had spent it. The annual income of the average

---

* They would also be only the second televised presidential debates in history. The Kennedy-Nixon debates had not been institutionalized. After Ford-Carter in 1976, every subsequent presidential election would feature debates among the major candidates.

** Fourth Estate: In pre-revolutionary France, there were said to be three estates—clergy, nobles, and the common people. Journalists sometimes consider themselves an estate outside all the others, thus a fourth estate.

American was then (and still is) far less than that of citizens of the Big Apple. A more unfair headline would be hard to imagine.

Carter received 40,830,763 popular votes, a surprisingly narrow 50.1 percent. Carter and his running mate, Minnesota's liberal senator, Walter "Fritz" Mondale, got 297 electoral votes. This was a sharp falloff for the man who once led Ford by thirty points in the polls. Ford received 39,147,793 popular votes (48.0 percent) and 240 electoral votes.*

III. "Moral Equivalent of War"

Carter was, in a sense, a member of a distinct minority. He was the first Southerner elected president since Zachary Taylor in 1848.** He was more popular with evangelicals than JFK had been, but less popular with Catholics. His strong appeal to black voters masked his relative weakness among Jews.[40]

In his Inaugural Address, President Carter renewed America's commitment to freedom. "Because we are free, we can never be indifferent to the fate of freedom elsewhere. Our moral sense dictates a clear-cut preference for these societies which share with us an abiding respect for individual human rights," Carter said. But he also warned against defining freedom in terms of material advances: "We have learned that 'more' is not necessarily 'better,' that even our great nation has its recognized limits, and that we can neither answer all questions nor solve all problems."[41]

Following his address, Carter surprised and delighted the thousands who thronged the inaugural parade route by getting out of his limousine and walking the length of Pennsylvania Avenue. He held hands with First Lady Rosalynn Carter and their daughter, Amy, as they waved to the crowds. Carter was determined to do away with the elaborate ceremony of the presidency.

---

* This was one electoral vote fewer than Ford normally would have received. Washington State's "faithless elector," Mike Padden, cast a single vote for Ronald Reagan. Padden checked to make sure Ohio's electoral vote would assure Carter's election before voting his heart. It was to be a harbinger of Reagan's coming electoral vote harvest.

** Woodrow Wilson, though born and raised in the South, was governor of New Jersey when elected president. Harry Truman, a Missourian, was from a border state. Lyndon Johnson was from Texas, but he acceded to the presidency only upon the assassination of JFK. Sensing the nation's reluctance to elect Southerners, Johnson liked to stress his W*estern* ties.

Like Thomas Jefferson, he wanted to bring the presidency to the people. He dispensed with the playing of "Hail to the Chief" and sold the presidential yacht, the USS *Sequoia.*

Jimmy Carter entered office with the great advantage of nearly 2–1 Democratic majorities in both houses of Congress. At least, it would have been a great advantage had Carter not campaigned so assiduously against Washington, D.C. His party, after all, was the party of Franklin D. Roosevelt and Lyndon B. Johnson. His was the party of Big Government. Congressional barons were not amused when he called the tax system they had so carefully crafted "a disgrace to the human race."[42]

Carter was determined to bring the Democratic leaders on Capitol Hill under *his* leadership. To show he meant business, he had Chief of Staff Hamilton Jordan consign House Speaker Thomas P. "Tip" O'Neill and his family to the farthest reaches of the inaugural banquet. It was a studied insult—and a foolish one, too.[43] Carter made the mistake of telling Tip O'Neill that he had gone over the heads of Georgia's legislature when its members blocked his programs as governor. "I can talk to your constituents easier than you can," Carter said. O'Neill could not believe Carter was comparing the part-time Georgia legislature with the U.S. Congress. "Hell, Mr. President, you're making a big mistake," Tip told the new chief executive.[44]

The real reason the 1976 election had been so close was the falling away of millions of Carter's early supporters by Election Day. That summer, Carter had led Ford by more than thirty points in most polls. He beat the incumbent in November by barely two percent of the vote (50.1 percent to 48.0 percent).

Many Americans initially drawn to Carter's high-sounding phrases ("I'll never lie to you") soon learned that you had to listen *very closely* to Carter's parsing of language. For example, Carter told voters in the Iowa caucuses in January that he "didn't like abortion." He said we needed to eliminate the "need for" abortion. When he formed an administration, however, it became clear that to Carter that meant *increasing* funding for federally-funded birth control clinics. Grassroots pro-lifers saw this as a dodge. The more birth control was used, they said, the more it failed and the more it failed, the more abortions resulted. By 1976, there were more than 1,600,000 abortions each year. Abortion was second only to circumcision as a commonly done procedure. Liberal journalist Elizabeth Drew praised Carter for wrapping a liberal policy stance in conservative rhetoric.[45] Everyday Americans, however, rejected such *legerdemain* as double talk: If you don't like something, you are expected to do something to stop it, or at least limit it.

This Carter proved willing to do. He signed the Hyde Amendment when it came to his desk in 1977. Sponsored by Congressman Henry Hyde, the amendment forbade federal funding of abortions. Carter attempted to square the circle on abortion: He would oppose any restrictions on the legality of the practice, but he would seek to avoid inflaming abortion opponents by forcing them to pay for it with their tax dollars. Carter found that this position, though sincerely held, would cause a serious rift between him and Democratic Party liberals.

Carter vigorously supported the Equal Rights Amendment (ERA) to the Constitution. First Lady Rosalynn Carter was especially energetic in pushing the ERA. Conservative leader Phyllis Schlafly denounced the ERA and Mrs. Carter's role in pressing for it. ERA foes were angered to see a First Lady exercising political pressure for an ERA when the American people had not elected her to any office.

Schlafly argued that because ERA was so vague, it could mean anything. Would young women continue to be exempt from the draft? Would they be forced into combat? Would mothers lose custody of minor children? Would child support and alimony be stripped away? Would the federal government and the states be forced to subsidize abortion-on-demand? Would homosexuals demand the right to marry? All of these questions were raised by the open-ended ERA.

Advocates of the ERA scorned Mrs. Schlafly and her grassroots activists. "Little old ladies in tennis shoes," was a familiar put-down. "They're worried about unisex public toilets," ERA supporters sneered. Well, yes, they were worried about those too.

President Carter addressed the American people on what he called the Energy Crisis. Sitting in front of a fireplace, the president wore a cardigan sweater. He warned that the United States would run out of oil by 1987 and that conservation measures were desperately needed.[46] He called this Energy Crisis "the moral equivalent of war," urging Americans to get used to an era of limits.[47] Soon, windmills and roof-mounted solar panels would qualify for federal tax breaks. Carter strongly backed the 55-mph speed limit that seriously antagonized Westerners. In the vast open spaces of the American West, a "sagebrush rebellion" was sparked first by Washington, D.C., telling residents of sparsely populated states how fast they could drive.

If Carter's policies displeased liberals, they seriously upset conservatives. During Carter's term, groups like Paul Weyrich's Free Congress Foundation, the Heritage Foundation, and the American Enterprise Institute spearheaded serious opposition to the Carter administration's domestic and foreign policies.

Defenders of free-market economics thrilled to the Nobel Prizes awarded to Friedrich von Hayek (1974) and Milton Friedman (1976).[48] Both of these distinguished scholars showed how socialism not only failed to enrich common people, but also sacrificed their freedom, too. Socialism was just a shabby way station, as Hayek put it, on "the road to serfdom." As usual, Churchill had gotten right to the nub: "Capitalism is the *unequal* sharing of blessings," he said, "while Socialism is the *equal* sharing of misery."[49] Except, in practice, it was never even that.

The continuing "stagflation" (stagnant growth, high unemployment, and high inflation) distressed average Americans. Moreover, Americans were frustrated that after billions of dollars spent in Lyndon Johnson's "War on Poverty," the percentage of poor people (12.4 percent) remained essentially what it had been in 1965.[50]

The 1970s presented many challenges to Americans' traditional understanding of freedom. In San Francisco, New York, and other major cities, gay bars and sex clubs defined a new subculture that "pushed the envelope" of promiscuity. Michel Foucault, a French philosopher and a homosexual, spoke to this overpowering sense of entitlement and liberation. "I think the kind of pleasure I would consider as *the* real pleasure would be so deep, so intense, so overwhelming that I couldn't survive it. I would die."[51] *To die for* became a slang phrase in these times—a rough American translation of Foucault's *nihilism*.

Predictably, such notions of liberation provoked a strong backlash. Ronald Reagan had resisted the Briggs Initiative in California, an attempt to run homosexual teachers out of the classroom. But the welter of personal emotions unleashed by the sexual revolution took bizarre turns. San Francisco supervisor Dan White in 1978 murdered Mayor George Moscone and his fellow supervisor, Harvey Milk. Milk was openly gay. White's use of the absurd "Twinkie defense" spared him the death penalty, but his lighter sentence led to days of nonstop rioting by San Francisco's gay protesters.*

Looking abroad, President Carter soon made clear his unwillingness to press the Soviets very hard on human rights. "We are now free of that *inordinate fear of communism* [emphasis added] that once led us to embrace any dictator who joined us in that fear," Carter told graduates of Notre Dame University in 1977.[52] From the earliest days, Carter's administration would place pressure on anti-Communist authoritarian regimes while taking a somewhat relaxed view of Soviet expansion in what was now called the third world.**

Carter chose Cyrus Vance as secretary of state. Vance told *Time* magazine in 1978 that President Carter and the Soviet Communist Party boss, Leonid Brezhnev, "share similar dreams and aspirations about the most fundamental issues."[53] Apparently agreeing with his secretary of state, Carter kissed Brezhnev during their Vienna Summit Meeting.[54] Vance was described by the seasoned New York Democrat Morris Abrams as "the closest thing to a pacifist the U.S. has ever had as secretary of state, with the possible exception of William Jennings Bryan."[55]

Carter's view sparked alarm, even by some in his own party. Washington State's Henry M. "Scoop" Jackson led opposition in the Senate to the Strategic Arms Limitation Treaty (SALT II). Jackson was convinced that Soviet cheating made enforcement impossible. Daniel Patrick Moynihan,

---

* White's attorneys argued that he acted under a diminished capacity because he had binged on Hostess Twinkies and other high-sugar junk food. It was a shocking example of the breakdown of the criminal justice system—and of common sense.

** Third-world countries generally meant "developing" countries in Asia, Africa, or Latin America. If, however, some of these countries prospered by resorting to free markets—as Singapore, South Korea and Taiwan did—then they no longer qualified as third world. In practice, therefore, third world came to mean wretchedly poor countries in those regions.

New York's junior senator, accused Carter of "trying to divert our attention from the central political struggle of our time—that between democracy and totalitarian communism."[56]

Jimmy Carter had to work hard to get his Panama Canal Treaty through the Senate in April 1978. Voting for the "giveaway," as critics called it, were many Republicans, as well as most Democrats. The Republican Senate leader, Howard Baker of Tennessee, would sacrifice his presidential hopes because he inflamed the party's conservative grassroots over the Canal. Nine senators went down to defeat, with opponents attacking them for supporting the giveaway.[57] Reagan had made the Canal giveaway a powerful symbolic issue; his position was supported by most conservatives.

Carter scored his greatest, arguably his *only*, foreign policy success with the Camp David Accords of 1978. Carter succeeded in bringing Egypt's president, Anwar Sadat, and Israel's Prime Minister, Menachem Begin, to the presidential retreat at Camp David for long and tiring negotiations on an Israeli pullout from Egypt's Sinai Peninsula. (Sadat had dramatically flown to Jerusalem to get the talks started.) He was alarmed at Carter's insistence that the Soviets be included.[58] Carter yielded on this point, and the Soviets were not invited. Sadat and Begin would win the Nobel Peace Prize for their roles in the Camp David Accords.*

Exiled Russian writer Aleksandr Solzhenitsyn spoke to Harvard's graduating class in 1978. He warned of the "loss of will" in the West to resist Soviet aggression. Intentionally provoking his audience, Solzhenitsyn said he could not recommend the West as a model for civilization to the enslaved peoples behind the Iron Curtain: "After the suffering of decades of violence and oppression, the human soul longs for things higher, warmer, and purer than those offered by today's mass living habits, introduced as a calling card by the revolting invasion of commercial advertising, by television stupor, and by intolerable music."[59] As Ethiopia, Angola, Mozambique, and Grenada slipped under Communism, Solzhenitsyn's words sparked a wounded reaction from America's liberal elite. The *New York Times*,

* Jimmy Carter would have to wait twenty-four years for his Nobel Peace Prize. His selection in 2002 was seen as a slap at President George W. Bush's plans for war against Saddam Hussein's regime in Iraq, a war Carter vehemently opposed.

the *Washington Post,* and even First Lady Rosalynn Carter criticized Solzhenitsyn.[60]

One of the Nobel laureate's few defenders was the perceptive George F. Will. In his influential column, Will wrote, "The spacious skepticism of the *New York Times* extends to all values except its own."[61] Will compared Solzhenitsyn to an Old Testament prophet whose sharp words force the nation to respond. Solzhenitsyn's ideas were those of Cicero, Augustine, Aquinas, Pascal, Thomas More, and Edmund Burke.[62] They represented the West's heritage of freedom. What did Jimmy Carter, who "shared Leonid Brezhnev's deepest values," represent? Not since Churchill at Westminster College in 1946 or George C. Marshall at Harvard in 1947 had a commencement speech stirred such a controversy.

One of President Carter's greatest strengths politically and personally was his strong identification with black Americans. This was an amazing achievement for this son of "Mr. Earl," an unyielding segregationist. Jimmy Carter moved easily among black leaders, especially those from his home state of Georgia. One of Carter's closest friends was Atlanta's Andrew Young. Young had been a disciple of Dr. King and was a dedicated champion of civil rights.

Andrew Young was singularly unsuited, however, to the role of U.S. ambassador to the UN. Young seemed determined to embarrass Carter and the United States in his very visible position. He claimed that Castro's Cuban troops in Africa were there "opposing racism."[63] Cuba had sent its armed forces to fight in Africa, he said, "because it has a shared sense of colonial oppression and domination."[64]

Ambassador Young defended the Soviet trials of prominent Jewish *refuseniks* like Natan Anatoly Sharansky. "After all," Young opined, "we also have hundreds, maybe thousands of people in our jails that I would characterize as political prisoners."[65] Young attacked Great Britain, America's closest ally, as the nation that "almost invented racism."[66] Worse, Young called Presidents Nixon and Ford racists. In a *Playboy* magazine interview, he was asked if his indictment of Republicans included Abraham Lincoln, too. "*Especially* Abraham Lincoln," he replied.[67] He criticized Israel as "stubborn and intransigent."[68] Young's stormy tenure at the UN was brought to an abrupt end when it was revealed he had held "back channel" meetings with representatives of Yasser Arafat's Palestine Liberation Organization (PLO). At that time, the State Department listed Arafat's PLO as a terrorist organization.

IV. America Held Hostage

By 1979, it was apparent that President Carter was in serious trouble. The "misery index" (derived by adding the unemployment figure and the inflation figure) which he had invented and used against Jerry Ford so effectively now weighed heavily against him. Americans had to resort to "odd and even" days to get gasoline, thanks to the Energy Crisis. Carter had grown a huge new bureaucracy in the Department of Energy, but he was unable to assure a plentiful supply of gasoline at the pump—where it counts.

Advised by his brilliant young pollster, Pat Caddell, that Americans were seriously alienated, Carter summoned groups of leaders, academics, and journalists to the scene of his great triumph, Camp David. Carter then came down from the mountain, Moses-like, to fire most of his cabinet officers. He left his inexperienced young White House staffers in place. "Good grief," said a senior Democratic congressman, "he's cut down the tall trees and left the monkeys!"[69] Carter then went on national television to deliver a major speech. In it, he deplored the "crisis of confidence" across the country that he charged was a "fundamental threat to democracy."[70]

To most Americans, the president's performance was profoundly unsettling. Gone was the toothy Carter grin. Gone was the cocky optimism of the nuclear engineer who asked, "Why not the best?" Now, Carter even had to fend off "attack rabbits" while on vacation.* Soon, his speech became known as the *malaise* speech. Though Carter never used that French word, it stuck.

Jack Germond found the whole episode disturbing—the malaise summit and the malaise speech. Surprisingly, even the feminist Germond was troubled by Rosalynn Carter's dominant role in these high-level bull sessions. "We all knew that the First Lady was a significant influence on the president

* Carter's own tale of having been attacked by a rabbit while fishing at home in Plains, Georgia, subjected the unfortunate Georgian to international ridicule.

and, because she was so obviously bright and serious, most of us probably felt comfortable about it. But I was not the only one shaken by the reality of the president's wife behaving as an official equal in these circumstances. On the way back, Joe Kraft, a columnist for the *Post,* kept shaking his head and muttering about how this was something very different indeed."[71]

Jimmy Carter and the First Lady tried to bring the country together on the growing concern about the family in America. Following the passage by many states of so-called no-fault divorce laws, divorce rates shot up. The out-of-wedlock birthrate continued to rise alarmingly. Contrary to confident predictions, the widespread availability of abortion did not reduce these numbers. The Carters genuinely sought to find common ground on these and a host of troubling issues in a series of White House Conferences on the Family. The title of these conferences was soon changed to *Families.* And therein lies a story.

Still pressing her campaign against the ERA, Mrs. Phyllis Schlafly put her organizing genius to the task of raising awareness of the implications of that word *families.* With her legal background, she recognized that the White House was on the verge of extending official recognition to a variety of domestic arrangements. She knew that the Census Bureau's decades-long definition of a family as a group of individuals joined by marriage, birth, or adoption was in jeopardy. She and other conservatives like Paul Weyrich of the Free Congress Foundation and Dr. James C. Dobson of the evangelical organization, Focus on the Family, rallied supporters. They urged their followers to get involved in the delegate selection process and take part in the substantive issues that would be raised at the local and regional preparatory meetings for the White House Conferences. Thus was born what participants call the pro-family movement. Those critical of its goals—which were clearly a defensive reaction to rapid social changes—either dismissed this grassroots movement or labeled it "the religious right." Soon, perhaps unavoidably, this movement would have an impact on national politics.

The Reverend Jerry Falwell (head of the newly formed grass-roots Moral Majority), Paul Weyrich, and Mrs. Schlafly were responding, in a sense, to the vacuum created on the conservative side of the political spectrum by the media's decades-long fascination with radical groups on the left. Students for a Democratic Society (SDS), the Congress of Racial Equality (CORE), and the Student Nonviolent Coordinating Committee (SNCC) had been formed in the sixties to generally positive media reaction. Stokely Carmichael (SNCC), H. Rapp Brown (SNCC and the Black Panthers), and Tom Hayden (SNCC) often flouted the law. Insatiable, they pushed a list of sharp demands on society. Bobby Seale and Huey Newton were leaders of the Black Panthers, one of the most militant of the left-wing groups. The Black Panthers had been implicated in extensive violence and several murders.

The Carters did not lack conviction. Jimmy and Rosalynn both rushed to the scene of the Three Mile Island nuclear power plant breakdown, calming fears.[72] Still, presidents, if they are wise, do not confess to presiding over a malaise. Carter's erratic conduct persuaded Senator Ted Kennedy that Carter might be vulnerable after all. The Democratic Party had taken a pounding in the off-year election. To Kennedy's liberal activist supporters, Carter's continued leadership would spell disaster for the party in 1980. So Kennedy declared his candidacy for the 1980 Democratic presidential nomination.*

Communist advances in Africa and Latin America were disturbing enough. While publicly embracing Carter, Leonid Brezhnev's sponsorship of terrorists like Italy's Brigadi Rossi, France's Action Direct, and West Germany's Baader-Meinhof Gang was an open secret. Nicaragua's Sandinista regime was taking a menacing turn, cracking down on freedom in that Central American republic while exporting revolution to neighboring El Salvador.

In response, many Democrats who had supported Scoop Jackson and Hubert Humphrey joined with New York writer Midge Decter to form The Committee on the Present Danger. Political Science professor Jeane Jackson Kirkpatrick wrote "Dictatorships and Double Standards," a powerful critique of Carter's foreign policy. Her article appeared in *Commentary,* and Ronald Reagan read it. In this era of limits and malaise, who would stand up for freedom? If America was crippled by doubt and guilt, who would lead the Free World? These events and concerns combined to give rise to a new

---

* Cartoonist Jeff MacNelly produced a cartoon that showed Jimmy Carter leading a revival service in a storefront mission while the uninterested winos pressed their noses longingly to the windows. Outside, Teddy as St. Bernard came shuffling through the New Hampshire snows with a keg of 100-proof liberalism around his neck.

movement called neoconservative, of which *Commentary* was the leading journal. Dr. Kirkpatrick blamed President Carter's ineptitude for the fall of many pro-American leaders, including the Shah of Iran.

On 4 November 1979, swarms of "students" in Tehran, Iran, overran the United States Embassy. They took as hostages all the Americans—diplomats and civilian employees of the embassy, even the Marine guards—fifty-two in all.* Not only did the Ayatollah Khomeini not condemn the action, he praised the hostage takers for defying America, that "Great Satan." Perhaps expecting an early resolution of the crisis, television's Walter Cronkite began ending each broadcast of the *CBS Evening News* with the number of days the Americans had been held hostage. Rival *ABC News* weighed in with Ted Koppel offering a late-night program called *America Held Hostage.* Now, Jimmy Carter would have a real malaise to contend with.

The Americans held hostage were beaten, tortured, and threatened with death as the days stretched into months. When Iranian "diplomats" came to New York City for UN sessions, they were allowed to come and go unimpeded. They had diplomatic immunity.

Initially, Americans rallied behind their commander in chief. But it soon became clear that he had no command of the situation. Carter resorted to asking his brother, Billy, a Plains, Georgia, filling station owner, to use his contacts with Libya's Muammar Khaddafi to try to get the U.S. hostages released.[73] Carter sent former U.S. attorney general Ramsey Clark on a mission to Tehran to try to gain the release of the hostages. Clark had gained notoriety for his outspoken criticism of U.S. foreign policy during the decade since he had served as LBJ's attorney general. Carter may have thought that Clark's "Third worldism" would gain him entrée to the Ayatollah's inner circle. Khomeini, apparently unimpressed by Clark's increasingly anti-American radicalism, refused even to meet with Carter's emissary.[74]

Ted Kennedy's challenge to a sitting president should have been easy. Every public opinion poll in 1979 showed Kennedy beating Carter, sometimes by margins of 2–1. Carter had few friends in the Democratic Party

* The number of hostages might have been even larger had it not been for the actions of the Canadian Ambassador Ken Taylor and his staff. The Canadians risked their lives to help six Americans escape.

establishment.* Ted had been the "heir apparent" to the Kennedy legacy ever since the death of his brother Bobby in 1968.

But now, with the Iranian hostage crisis redounding, oddly, to the president's benefit, Kennedy's support slipped. He gave a disastrous interview to CBS Newsman, Roger Mudd. In it, he stumbled and stammered and could not articulate a clear and compelling reason for his candidacy. Worse for Kennedy, many people who had not focused on his conduct at Chappaquiddick in 1969 now examined it in greater detail.[75] Despite this, Kennedy would not be deterred. He carried his challenge into New Hampshire.

When the Soviets saw that Carter would not use force to free the American hostages in Tehran, they were emboldened. Just after Christmas 1979, Soviet agents overthrew and murdered the ruler of Afghanistan. They installed a puppet ruler, Muhammed Najibullah, in Kabul, and he, obediently, invited Soviet troops to enter the country.** Carter said he was shocked by the Soviet invasion. His ambassador to the Soviet Union, Malcolm Toon, was shocked that Carter was shocked. "Apparently, he hadn't been reading the messages I had been sending him," Toon later said.[76]***

As the new decade dawned, America faced a more threatening world, and despite some victories, things only seemed to worsen. Americans went wild with joy when the U.S. hockey team beat the favored Soviets at the

---

* One exception to this, of course, was the National Education Association (NEA). The 2-million member teachers' union was grateful to Carter for creating the U.S. Department of Education. The NEA proved completely loyal to their embattled benefactor. And the NEA boasted that they sent more delegates to the Democratic National Convention than California did.

** Najibullah met his fate at the end of a rope in Kabul's soccer stadium in 1996. He was hanged by the Taliban.

*** According to a friend in attendance, Ambassador Toon began a lecture at the University of Washington in January 1982 with stiff criticism of President Reagan for characterizing Kremlin leaders as men who would lie, cheat, or commit any crime to advance world Communism. Toon said he sharply disagreed with Secretary of State Al Haig's petty harassment of Soviet Ambassador to the U.S. Anatoly Dobrynin, such as denying the envoy a parking place in the State Department garage. That was the first five minutes of the Toon address. Carter's ex-ambassador then proceeded to a devastating critique of his former boss. Toon said that the only time in his thirty years as a career diplomat that *he feared for his country* was when Jimmy Carter was president. He had never seen the Soviets so contemptuous of American weakness, Toon reported. The headline in the *Seattle Post Intelligencer* the next morning ignored Toon's scorching analysis of Carter's record, reporting instead "Toon Rips Reagan."

Winter Olympics in Lake Placid, New York. "*USA! USA!*" The crowd's chant was defiant and proud.

Misjudging the moment, Carter announced a U.S. boycott of the Summer Olympics, scheduled for the following July in Moscow. Sports fans were in a blue funk, but America's highly trained Olympic athletes were devastated. America's summer Olympic competitors saw the electrified reaction of the country to the U.S. team's victories at the Lake Placid Winter Games. These conditioned young athletes were all the more determined to bring home the gold—and the honor—for their country. Glenn Mills speaks for many of those 1980 Olympians. He was a member of the U.S. swim team:

> The better our winter athletes did, the harder our own training got. We put in 100,000 meters each week in the pool. We were reminded daily that we, too, had a chance to lift the spirits of our countrymen, just as our hockey players had. We knew the Soviets would be training hard so they could be heroes to their country. We knew we had to beat them. Many of us had relocated—far from friends and families—to intensify our training. Our parents had to tighten their belts financially to keep us competitive; friends our own age had to understand that we couldn't share the things they were doing. We were doing all we could to make ourselves worthy of America's confidence in us. And just as we were poised to go to the Olympics, President Carter announced we would not compete. The dreams of all our athletes, the years of preparation, dedication and sacrifice—all were gone in minutes.

Mills speaks without bitterness. He and most of his fellow Olympians have overcome the crushing disappointment of those days, but he says "we would have loved to be able to finish our job."[77]

Carter also cut off U.S. grain shipments to the USSR, a move that soured American farmers in the Midwest. The Soviets were not hurt by this move, since they could always buy grain from Australia, Canada, and Argentina. Only American farmers in the Midwest felt the brunt of it. Carter had begun his presidency with a walk down Pennsylvania Avenue, as Thomas Jefferson had done. Now, he adopted the worst of Jefferson's policies. Then, as in 1807, the embargo hurt Americans more than our adversaries.

When Ronald Reagan announced his candidacy in 1979, he was sixty-eight years old. He was the oldest man ever to run for the presidency, but his health seemed buoyant. He kept in shape clearing away the thick undergrowth on his California ranch—Rancho del Cielo. "People who talk about an age of limits are really talking about their *own* limitations, not America's," Reagan said.[78] He didn't mention Jimmy Carter. He didn't have to. Reagan didn't believe in an age of limits or in the limits of age.

Carter learned that he performed better in the polls when he hunkered down in the White House, attending to the crises. He began racking up primary victories against Ted Kennedy, employing this "Rose Garden Strategy."

Carter viewed it as a "positive" sign when the U.S. hostages in Tehran were transferred from the students to the direct control of the Iranian revolutionary Islamic government. Their captivity didn't end. The threats of summary execution didn't end. Their danger didn't end. What could have been positive? "He is beating on an empty drum," Khomeini mocked.[79] Secretary of State Cyrus Vance took an almost relaxed view: "Most Americans recognize that we cannot alone dictate events. This recognition is not a sign of America's decline. It is a sign of growing maturity in a complex world."[80] So the Ayatollah Khomeini and his Islamic revolutionaries could dictate events but the United States of America could not?

Carter finally roused himself to action in April 1980. Finally. For six months, Americans in Tehran had been tortured. Carter ordered a secret rescue mission, but mournfully, it failed. Several U.S. helicopters collided. Several American commandoes died. *Desert One* became a symbol of the fecklessness of the Carter administration. Cyrus Vance, outraged at the American resort to force, resigned his office.[81]

V. "USA! USA!"

Americans demanded an assertion of their country's interests and honor. The chant that arose spontaneously from the hockey crowds at Lake Placid, New York—"*USA! USA!*"—soon spread across the land. Ted Kennedy might have turned Carter out of office had he seized the moment and appealed to his brother Jack's legacy. But Ted led the "peace" faction in the Democratic Party. Four years earlier, Jimmy Carter had pledged "a government as *good* as the American people." Now, the American people demanded a government as *strong* as they were.

In the 1980 Republican primary in New Hampshire, Ronald Reagan had to make or break his last chance for the White House. George H. W. Bush claimed the "Big Mo" (momentum) after his win in the Iowa caucuses. *NBC News* reporter Tom Pettit spoke for many in the press corps. "Reagan is dead," he said after Iowa.[82]

Not quite.

Reagan agreed to debate with frontrunner George Bush, who wanted only a one-on-one confrontation. When Reagan showed up in Nashua, New Hampshire, with all the other GOP contenders—Senators Howard Baker and Bob Dole, Congressmen Phil Crane and John Anderson—Bush balked. He told the debate moderator to cut off Reagan's microphone. Angered, but controlled, Reagan used his actor's skills. He *projected* his voice so that it was picked up by the moderator's mike: "I'm *paying* for this microphone, Mr. Green!" It was Mr. *Breen*, but who cared? With that forceful gesture, Reagan captured the debate, the New Hampshire Primary, and the nomination.

Americans wanted strength. Reagan was strong.

Conservatives flocked to New Hampshire to battle for "the Gipper."* Pro-lifers pledged themselves to him. Grassroots activists were furious with Baker's support for the Panama Canal giveaway. They rejected Kissinger's détente. They cheered Reagan's support for California's Proposition 13, the beginning of the tax revolt. Ronald Reagan had been the titular leader of the conservative movement ever since he gave that strong speech for Barry Goldwater in 1964. Nineteen eighty would be Reagan's moment.

Reagan swept the spring primaries and went to Detroit as the tested leader of the Republicans. With the GOP united behind him, Reagan was almost trapped in the selection of his vice president. A movement on the

---

* Reagan had played doomed football star George Gipp in *The Knute Rockne Story.* Referring to himself, he loved to ask followers to "win one for the Gipper."

floor of Detroit's Joe Louis Arena—fanned by a bored media—took up the idea of naming former President Jerry Ford to the ticket for vice president. For Reagan to choose Ford would have been a concession that he really wasn't up to the job. The "talking heads"—the network television commentators—loved the idea. Walter Cronkite of CBS even described it, alarmingly, as a "co-presidency." But Reagan's presidency would not have training wheels. He gracefully sidestepped that booby trap by choosing George Bush as his running mate. The party's northeastern wing was mollified by the choice. Happy Republicans would beat Jimmy Carter "like a drum," vowed Party chairman Bill Brock. Brock was the highly organized and combative party leader who had helped rebuild the GOP after the debacle of Watergate.

Carter's Democrats were glum as they gathered in New York. Ted Kennedy's memorable speech ended with the powerful refrain: THE DREAM WILL NEVER DIE! Kennedy's eloquence evoked the brave promise of his slain brothers. He left thousands of delegates in tears.

The only line anyone remembered from Jimmy Carter's acceptance speech was his mangled tribute to Minnesota's late Hubert Horatio Humphrey. Carter ringingly referred to him as Hubert Horatio *Hornblower*, to audible groans.

Now desperate for Ted Kennedy's endorsement, Carter pursued the bigger man around the convention stage, in search of that elusive "photo op." It was funny—and embarrassing—how Kennedy always managed to stay a few feet away from the pursuing president.

Carter's floor managers had to give in completely to Kennedy's forces on the Democratic platform. Kennedy called for ever greater government control of key sectors of the economy. It seemed too close to socialism at a time when socialism was clearly strangling the life out of the economies of Western Europe, Canada, and the United States. Only on one subject did Jimmy Carter dissent from the very liberal platform the Kennedy delegates demanded of him. Politely but firmly, Carter *refused* to endorse federal funding of abortion-on-demand.

Walter Cronkite's nightly tally of the hostages' days in captivity in Iran had gone over 300 at the beginning of September 1980. Surely he never intended it, but Cronkite's signoff became a nightly commentary on Carter's inability to free the hostages.

One of Reagan's primary challengers, Congressman John Anderson, had moved further and further left over the years. He finally quit the GOP and vowed to run for president as an Independent. George Will puckishly noted that Anderson ran only in those primaries where he could win—and he lost there too. But despite his lack of success, for at least one shining moment he became the Great Liberal Hope.* In September, he and Reagan squared off in a televised debate. Carter was invited but declined to participate. Told again and again by their opinion leaders that Reagan was stupid and dangerous, liberals eagerly watched the Reagan-Anderson debate.

Jack Germond entertainingly described the typical Anderson voter: "She drives a Volvo. When she attends a League of Women Voters (LWV) coffee, she selects a prune Danish on purpose. She thinks wine-and-cheese parties are 'great fun.' She doesn't think Ronald Reagan and Jimmy Carter are any fun at all."[83] He was astonished to receive a phone call from a woman who exactly fit his imagined Anderson voter. She informed him that while Anderson had turned in an excellent debate performance, Reagan did not come across as scary. Most of the women in her LWV group were Republicans and they had decided to back Reagan. They didn't want to "waste" their votes.[84]

Anderson's share in the three-way polls soon collapsed. After he met Ronald Reagan in debate, his support plunged from 20 to 7 percent.[85] Anderson could not win—but he could have a massive impact on the election outcome.**

Carter's managers knew their only chance was to convince voters that Reagan was too dangerous to allow him to have access to nuclear weapons. Meanwhile, Carter's team urged industrialist Armand Hammer to make the case to his Soviet friends for concessions on the Jewish emigration issue.[86] Carter's National Security Advisor, Zbignieuw Brzezinski, signaled to Soviet

* When Congressman John Anderson was first elected, he wanted to amend the U.S. Constitution to make America an explicitly Christian nation. All that was forgotten, of course, as he sought the support of secular-minded liberals. As they say in Washington, he had grown.

** Anderson's quixotic quest is further confirmation of the fact that Third Party efforts are essentially futile. Throughout American history—with the sole exception of 1948—Third Party candidates have caused the defeat of the major party candidate closest to them in ideology. Vladimir Lenin famously said "the worse the better" to bring about a revolution; practical Americans, however, have never accepted that notion.

ambassador Dobrynin that Carter needed their help and would remember it. "[His] message was clear: Moscow should not do anything to diminish Carter's chances in the election and might even help a bit," Dobrynin reported in his memoirs.[87] They were looking for the Soviets to bail them out. Hammer, we now know, had laundered money for the Communist Party USA and was a key source for Soviet intelligence agencies.[88]

Carter and Reagan prepared for their single debate—the only time the two major party nominees would share the same stage in the 1980 presidential campaign. The Democrats' daily charges that Reagan was reckless were having an impact. Unlike all other presidential campaigns, the number of undecided voters was *increasing*. Voters knew they didn't want Carter again, but they couldn't commit to Reagan.

Onstage in Cleveland, Ohio, Carter was tense, unsmiling, Reagan relaxed. Throughout the ninety minutes, Carter tried to rattle Reagan with constant barbs. He described Reagan's views as *disturbing* six times.[89] Reagan threw the "misery index" back at Carter. It had been 12.5 in 1976 when Carter jabbed at Ford that "no man with a misery index that high had a right to seek re-election."[90] On that October night in 1980, Jimmy Carter's misery index stood at 20![91] Late in the debate, Carter again tried to provoke Ronald Reagan. The former actor looked bemused. He cocked his head to one side, shook it genially and said: "There you go again."

The media didn't get it. Some of the hardened reporters even mocked it. What a weak comeback! But they didn't understand. It was a devastating riposte. It was the perfect answer. Reagan didn't say, "There you go again, Jimmy." That would have been disrespectful to the Presidential office. He didn't say, "There you go again, Mr. President." That would have elevated Carter's stature in the viewers' eyes. Reagan had taken Carter's hits all night long. He had been called a racist, a dangerous man, a stupid man. Yet he didn't lose his dignity or his strength. Millions of Americans concluded that night that he had passed the test of leadership. Reagan's performance had the biggest impact with American women. They had been undecided. They earnestly wanted to know how this Californian would perform *under pressure.* "A soft answer turneth away wrath," says the Bible. For Reagan, that wisdom from Proverbs proved literally true.

In Carter's final statement, he said he had consulted his twelve-year-old daughter, Amy, about the most important issue facing America. Amy said she feared nuclear war. "Ask Amy," hooted Carter's critics derisively. That was cruel. There is nothing wrong with the great and powerful having a tender concern for the young and the vulnerable. Conservatives might have remembered how Whittaker Chambers wrote in *Witness* that he had gazed upon the intricate folds in his baby daughter's ear. That experience convinced Chambers there was a God, that love did exist, and that Communism was a lie. It is one of the most important passages in American political literature.

Jimmy Carter's problem was by that point in his presidency he had asked everyone in the country how he should govern. He had initiated countless town meetings. He had earnestly quizzed the "malaise summit" participants. He set up the elaborate White House Conferences on Families. He consulted Pat Caddell's poll respondents and focus groups. Process, endless process, was the order of the day. His "Amy" statement flopped because he had become a parody of himself.

Catholics said of the newly-elected Pope John Paul II that "he knew how to Pope." Jimmy Carter, Americans now ruefully concluded, did not know how to be president.

Ronald Reagan's final statement that night was also memorable. "Are you better off than you were four years ago? Are you safer than you were four years ago?" Reagan's liberal critics thought it was a base appeal to self-interest. But they didn't recognize Reagan's source: He had taken those lines from a Fireside Chat FDR delivered in 1934! They were as powerful in 1980 as they had been when they were first used.

The 1980 election took place on 4 November, the one-year anniversary of the seizure of the U.S. Embassy in Tehran. Fifty-two Americans had been held hostage for 365 days. The cascading returns shocked and awed the liberal media. Network election maps turned "Reagan blue."* Pollsters only

* The networks had assigned the colors blue and red for their election night maps to the Republicans and Democrats, respectively. In the years since, they've reversed the colors. But around the world, parties of the left are assigned the color red, conservatives are denoted by blue (except in Germany, where they are black.)

belatedly saw the tidal wave coming. John Anderson's receding numbers nationally remained higher in the most liberal states.

Carter conceded the election shortly after 8:30 p.m. eastern time. It was only 5:30 p.m. on the Pacific Coast, where several tight House and Senate races were to be decided.[92] He had been warned by Pat Caddell he would be swept out of office. He did not want to face the humiliation of a nationwide rejection as the evening wore on. Tip O'Neill screamed and cursed in his fury.[93] Carter apparently did not understand the impact his premature announcement would have on the party's candidates "down ballot." Hundreds of Democratic candidates would now lose, as millions of the party's voters in the Midwest and Far West—where the polls were still open for another hour and a half—decided not even to bother voting.

Reagan carried 489 electoral votes in 44 states. In a three-way race, he claimed an absolute majority of all voters—43,898,770 popular votes (50.8 percent). Jimmy Carter won his home state of Georgia, Fritz Mondale's Minnesota, and just four others (Rhode Island, West Virginia, Maryland, and Hawaii) for an electoral vote tally of 49. He received 35,480,948 popular votes (41 percent). It was the worst defeat for a sitting president since Herbert Hoover in 1932. John Anderson in the end was not running for the office but for the money. He won just 5,719,222 popular votes, but his 6.6 percent of the total was enough to qualify him for Federal matching funds.

John Anderson's social liberalism had important, though unintended, consequences.[94] Anderson pledged full federal funding of abortion. That was his major policy difference with Carter. The Anderson vote was decisive in tipping *ten* states to Reagan—Connecticut (12.2 percent), Delaware (6.9 percent), Maine (10.2 percent), Massachusetts (15.2 percent), Michigan (7.0 percent), New York (7.5 percent), North Carolina (2.9 percent), Oregon (9.5 percent), Vermont (14.9 percent), and Wisconsin (7.1 percent). Reagan would have won with 365 electoral votes even if Carter carried all of these states. But his victories here, some of them liberal bastions, added greatly to Reagan's aura of invincibility. He brought in a Republican Senate and made major gains in the House. It was called the Reagan Revolution.

"Dig toward freedom." That's what coal miners trapped below the surface do. They can smell the fresh air before they hear or see.[95] Americans at the end of the 1970s were digging frantically toward freedom. They weren't the only ones.

In Britain, Margaret Thatcher had won an unexpected landslide in 1979. She had to stare down the Communist trade unionists and beat back the battered Labour Party. Most of all, Thatcher had to overcome the weak knees of her fellow Tories. Often at Conservative Party gatherings, it was said, Thatcher was "the only *man* in the room." Her policy was as simple as it was urgent: She wanted to restore freedom. She wanted to put the *Great* back in Great Britain.

Behind the Iron Curtain, Poland's Lech Walesa had started the only free labor union anywhere in the Soviet bloc. *Solidarity* boldly challenged the Polish Communist regime—and the Soviets who propped it up. When Pope John Paul II returned to his native Poland in 1979, he held an open-air Mass for a million Poles. Walesa was there, wearing a lapel pin of the Blessed Virgin. "We want God! We want God!" cried the Poles. Watching on television, his eyes misting up, Ronald Reagan the candidate said of the new pope: "I want to work with him." In the coming decade, these four—the Pope, Thatcher, Reagan, and Walesa—would take their stand for freedom. They and their loyal, liberty-loving followers would change the world.

The Freedom Revolution that began in the late 1970s knocked fatalism into a cocked hat. People who are free can choose to take history by the tail and give it a good yank. And so they did. America, and hope, were coming back.

Twelve

Reagan and Revival (1981–1989)

When General Victor "Brute" Krulak asked President Reagan what advice he would give young Marine officers, Reagan didn't hesitate: "Plant your flag." He meant find those principles, those ideals, that plan or project on which you will stake your reputation, and plant your flag there. Brute Krulak had done just that in World War II when he fought for the landing craft that made amphibious assaults possible. In the years from 1981 until 1989 Americans planted their flag with the world-wide advance of freedom. But the effort was by no means a smooth and easy path. At many points during the eighties, the story might well have turned to tragedy. When Franklin D. Roosevelt said "the only thing we have to fear is fear itself," he well understood the power of fear to frustrate Americans' aspirations for freedom. As the new year of '81 dawned, the country feared for the fifty-two Americans who had been held as hostages for more than a year in Tehran. The captive Americans had spent two Christmases there, subjected to beatings and threatened daily with violent death. Americans were frustrated with the slow pace of negotiations with Muslim extremists in Tehran. Then, suddenly, the fifty-two hostages were freed—and a nation felt liberated.*

---

* "Brute" Krulak related this story at a ceremony honoring him and four other Distinguished Graduates of the U.S. Naval Academy (10 September 2004.) The legendary General Krulak, 90, had earned the nickname Brute when he arrived in Annapolis in 1930 at age 16. Slightly over five feet tall, Krulak weighed just 121 pounds.

I. 1981: A New Beginning

When Ronald Reagan mounted the inaugural stands on 20 January, he looked out on a vast throng from the west front of the Capitol. It was the first time an Inauguration had been held there. It was singularly appropriate that this Californian should look westward.

The U.S. economy was in serious trouble at that moment. "Stagflation" meant high unemployment and punishing interest rates. Americans grumbled as they lined up for rationed gasoline. The Iranian militants had been holding fifty-two of their fellow citizens in cruel captivity for 444 days.

Reagan took the oath and quoted from Dr. Joseph Warren. Warren is among the least-known of the founding fathers because he was killed at Bunker Hill in 1775. Yet Warren, the president of the Massachusetts Congress, had told his fellow patriots: "Our country is in danger, but not to be despaired of. . . . On you depend the fortunes of America. You are to decide the important questions upon which rests the happiness and liberty of millions yet unborn. Act worthy of yourselves."[1] Reagan spoke of his confidence that Americans were indeed ready to act worthy of themselves. As he stepped from the Inaugural platform, Reagan signed an Executive Order. With that stroke of his pen, he dismantled the price controls on oil that had stood for a decade. The next day, he went further. He abolished the Council on Wage and Price Stability. The energy crisis that had consumed the Carter presidency ended that day.[2] Americans have never lined up for gasoline since.

That evening, at one of the resplendent Inaugural Balls, President Reagan made a momentous announcement: Finally, the American hostages had been freed! He asked former President Carter to fly to Wiesbaden, West Germany, as his personal representative. There, Reagan's defeated rival would welcome the former hostages to freedom.

During the transition from Carter to the Reagan administration, the Iranians sent feelers to the incoming Reagan team. They might need another six months to release the Americans, they said. Reagan's Secretary of State-designate was Alexander Haig, former military commander of NATO. Haig's answer lacked the concision of General McAuliffe's at

Bastogne, but it conveyed the same idea: Nuts! Americans joked, "What is green and glows on January 20th? Answer: Iran." Brave talk. The reality was that the United States combined various concessions—like releasing the Iranian assets President Carter had frozen and giving the Ayatollah Khomeini's regime immunity from lawsuits in international courts—with the newer, harder Reagan line. The Iranians thought it best to end the impasse quickly.

President Reagan soon announced his plan for the largest tax cut in American history. Speaker Tip O'Neill, Democrat from Massachusetts, vowed to block it. Massachusetts' other powerful liberal, Senator Edward Kennedy, also opposed Reagan's move. This, despite the fact that his late brother had slashed taxes for business and top earners. "In the 1960s, President John F. Kennedy proposed a cut of the top rate to 70 percent from 91 percent," writes economist Dan Mitchell. "Between 1961 and 1968, as the economy expanded by more than 42 percent and tax revenues rose by one-third, the rich saw their share of the tax burden climb to 15.1 percent from 11.6 percent."[3]

Reagan defended his economic plan before a labor union audience at the Washington Hilton on 30 March 1981. After the event, he walked to his waiting limousine. Bursting out of the crowd, a deranged young man fired six shots at the president. John Hinckley Jr. grievously wounded the president's press secretary, Jim Brady, but it was not immediately clear that the president had been hit. Hinckley also hit a police officer and a secret service agent. Reagan thought he had just broken a rib when his secret service agent shoved him into the limo and jumped on top to shield him with his body. As the president arrived at George Washington University Hospital, he forced a wan smile. Once inside, however, his knees buckled and he was rushed into surgery.

It would be years before Americans learned how close Ronald Reagan came to dying that day, barely two months into his presidency. The assassin's bullet lodged within just an inch of his heart, and he suffered terrible blood loss.* But that night a relieved country laughed as Reagan's words to First

* Surgeons at George Washington University Hospital who opened the president's chest marveled at his musculature. One said he'd never seen a seventy-year-old man with such well-developed pectorals.

Lady Nancy were quoted on every news broadcast: "Honey, I forgot to duck." Even at the point of death, the affable trouper could not resist cracking a joke.*

Reagan's sense of humor never lagged. He often repeated Churchill's witticism: "Nothing is so exhilarating as to be shot at without result." When Reagan staffers James A. Baker III, Ed Meese, and Mike Deaver came into the recovering president's room to assure him everything was running smoothly at the White House, Reagan cracked, "What makes you think I'd be happy to hear *that*?"[4]

The new president's spiritual side showed as well. At one point, Reagan requested a visit from a clergyman. Deaver summoned New York's Terence Cardinal Cooke. When the eminent Catholic leader hurried to Reagan's bedside, the president told him: "I have decided whatever time I may have left is left for Him."[5]

Journalist Sam Donaldson believes that Reagan became truly isolated from the American people after the assassination attempt.[6] Donaldson probably never met Anne Higgins and Chuck Donovan. These quiet, dedicated Reagan loyalists headed up his Presidential Correspondence Unit. They made sure that the president did *not* lose touch with the American people. Higgins and Donovan saw to it that every letter received was promptly answered. They regularly sent the president dozens of letters culled from the hundreds of thousands received. Lincoln had called his immersion in such letters and local newspapers his "public opinion baths." Reagan even wrote a longhand letter to Soviet Communist Party boss Leonid Brezhnev as he recuperated from his gunshot wound. Although the literary salons would find it laughable, Reagan was indeed "a man of letters."

Reagan rebounded from the assassination attempt and spoke to a joint session of Congress to press his economic recovery plan. He was the first president ever to survive after being shot. "He reacted better," one writer noted, "to being shot than most politicians do to a bad headline." "There he

* Avid boxing fans knew that Reagan's quote—like so many of his best lines—was not original. Heavyweight Champion Jack Dempsey had first used that line half a century earlier. Just as appropriate at this grim moment in history was another classic Dempsey line: "A champion is someone who gets up when he can't."

stood, Lazarus-like," said Tip O'Neill's young aide, Chris Matthews. "He ran his vote total over the top that night."[7] Americans enthusiastically backed him when he asked for their help. Speaker O'Neill was frustrated when twenty-nine of his Democratic representatives supported the president. Most of these congressmen were Southern "Boll Weevils" from districts where Reagan had run well ahead of the hapless Jimmy Carter. As the old Capitol Hill expression goes, "if they didn't see the light, they surely felt the heat." One of these Southerners, Louisiana's senator, John Breaux, even joked that his vote was not for sale—"but it might be for rent."[8]

Even though Reagan had to wrestle the Democratic Speaker O'Neill for every vote in the House, he never let their competition become personal or bitter. When the time came to celebrate Tip O'Neill's seventieth birthday, Reagan invited him to the White House to apply the soft soap. Toasting the Speaker with champagne, the Irish president saluted his very Irish sparring partner:

> If I had a ticket to heaven
> And you didn't have one, too
> I'd sell mine, Tip
> And go to hell with you![9]

President Reagan signed the Economic Recovery Act—a combination of massive tax cuts and spending cuts—at his Western White House, his Rancho del Cielo. Richard Darman later noted the symbolism of the heavy fog that rolled in, making it hard for press and invited guests to find their way to the event.[10] "It was a river boat gamble," said the Republicans' Senate Leader, Howard Baker of Tennessee.[11]

Congressman Jack Kemp beat the drums for supply-side economics. The Kemp-Roth bill was based on the simple idea that when taxes are too high, they discourage enterprise and constrict economic activity. Thus, as the supply-side model shows, lowering taxes stimulates economic growth and generates more revenue in the long run. While Presidents Kennedy and Johnson had shown that the theory worked in practice years before, in those early days of the Reagan administration there was bitter disagreement over the theory. Kemp mocked Kansas Republican senator Bob Dole's high-tax policies as "root canal" economics, and maverick congressman Newt Gingrich called Dole "the tax collector of the Welfare State."[12] Dole responded with a story of a bus full of supply side economists that went over a cliff. "It was a great tragedy," Dole deadpanned. "Why? Well, there were two empty seats on that bus!"[13]

Most politicians didn't really know who was right, but they did know that while Reagan was sweeping the New Hampshire Primary in 1980, the heroic Dole was garnering only 597 votes statewide.

Reagan concentrated on a few, easily comprehended objectives. Columnist George Will summed up the Reagan agenda: "Government is too big, it taxes too much, and the Soviets are getting away with murder."[14] Howard Baker noted how Jimmy Carter had never been able to prioritize his legislative goals. He "sent up dozens of initiatives and lost his focus."[15]

In the summer of 1981, the Professional Air Traffic Controllers Union (PATCO) went out on strike. Reagan had been proud to claim the support of this union in 1980. He bragged about having been the only union president ever to run for the White House. But now he issued a stern warning: If PATCO members—government employees—violated federal law by walking off the job, he would fire them all. Few people believed the president would carry out that threat. But he did. It was an incredibly daring move. If even one midair collision had occurred, Reagan's presidency might have been fatally damaged.[16]

At the time, it was not clear what impact firing PATCO workers would have. There had been 795,000 workers in all fields on strike in 1980; by 1987, that number declined nationally to 174,000.[17] Not only did the reaction to the PATCO strike give Americans a measure of labor peace at home, but many in the chanceries of Europe and in the Kremlin watched and marveled that Reagan really meant what he said. Even the KGB noted it. With Reagan, they wrote in a background paper for the Soviet Communist leadership, "word and deed are the same."[18]

Reagan also had to contend with international terrorism. The young, vigorous Pope John Paul II was shot in St. Peter's Square. Mehmet Ali Agca, the Turkish assassin, was widely believed to be an agent of the Bulgarian secret police. That meant he was an agent of the Soviet KGB. Reagan wrote to the pope, assuring him of his prayers for a quick recovery. Though grievously wounded, the pontiff did recover. Both leaders would attribute their survival of these near-death experiences to God's protection. It would form a bond between them.

When Libya's dictator, Muammar Khaddafi, sent several Soviet-made MiG jet fighters to threaten U.S. Navy jets in the international waters of the Gulf of Sidra, Reagan ordered them shot down.[19] Reversing Carter-era policies, Reagan told his military chiefs they could pursue harassing Libyan jets. When asked if they could pursue them into Libyan territory, he responded: "You can follow them into their damned hangars."[20] His answer was repeated throughout the Pentagon and, indeed, throughout the entire military.

Stories of Reagan's resolve—coupled with the largest peacetime military buildup in American history—spread through the ranks of the nation's military like an electric current. Reagan greatly improved military pay. Under Carter, in the years of "the hollow military," enlisted men and their families had had to resort to food stamps to make ends meet.[21] Now, morale in the military soared.

At least the military had jobs. For nearly ten million unemployed Americans, *Reaganomics* was proving to be a cruel joke. It seemed Reagan had gambled on tax cuts stimulating the economy, and lost. Inflation was coming down rapidly as Carter's appointee, Paul Volcker, and the Federal Reserve Board applied a tourniquet to the money supply. Gasoline prices, after an initial spike, were coming down and supply was plentiful. Reagan pledged to "stay the course" and resisted advice to raise taxes again. The loud demands of his opposition on Capitol Hill were to be expected. The contempt of the liberal press for Reagan and his policies was palpable. Reagan's problem was that most members of his own party, even most members of his own administration, counseled retreat. Reagan stubbornly refused.

By 1982, the recession deepened, and Reagan looked like a one-termer. "The stench of failure" was rising above the Reagan White House, wrote the editors of the *New York Times* with obvious *schadenfreude.* That German word precisely captures their hand-warming "malicious joy." Still, Reagan soldiered on. He did what so many embattled presidents do when domestic crises threaten to overwhelm them. He changed the subject—and the scenery. In June, President Reagan became the first U.S. president to address the British House of Commons. Of the 225 Labour Party members, 125 boycotted the historic speech.[22] He was undeterred:

> In an ironic sense, Karl Marx was right. We are witnessing today a great revolutionary crisis, a crisis where the demands of the economic order are conflicting directly with those of the political order. But the crisis is happening not in the free, non-Marxist West, but in the home of Marxist-Leninism, the Soviet Union . . . . [T]he march of freedom and democracy . . . will leave Marxism-Leninism on the ash heap of history as it has left other tyrannies which stifle the freedom and muzzle the self-expression of the people.[23]

Many of the British members of Parliament were stunned by Reagan's toughness—and his mastery.[24] They had been led by U.S. news media to expect something of a dodderer, an elderly and confused man. Reagan in Parliament was in command. And he employed a new style teleprompter which the British had never seen. They thought he had committed the entire speech to memory.[25] One Labour Party leader, David Owen, was impressed: "Maybe he'll go down as a much better President than any of us are yet prepared to admit."[26]

Reagan also had a chance during this trip to meet with Queen Elizabeth II. The president and the Queen were both avid riders. Reagan's men were especially eager to get "visuals" of the president and the Queen riding at the royal estate at Windsor. As the two heads of state galloped up a steep hill, however, the Queen's horse let out a long, loud blast of gas.

"Oh, I'm so sorry, Mr. President," the Queen said.

Without hesitation, Reagan responded: "It's alright, Your Majesty; I thought it was the horse."[27]

Republicans in the House and Senate were little interested in the clash between East and West. They worried about high rates of unemployment. Although inflation was being wrung out of the economy, interest rates were still painfully high. They dreaded facing the voters.

© Corbis

Pope John Paul II. *"Be not afraid." Those were the words of the angel to the Blessed Virgin Mary in the Bible and those were the first words of Karol Wojtyla upon his election as Pope John Paul II in 1978. The Polish pontiff was not afraid to challenge Soviet domination of his homeland—or to challenge the domination of any godless philosophy over the mind and hopes of man.*

© Corbis

Prime Minister Thatcher with Reagan. *The "Special Relationship" between Britain and the U.S. had never been closer than it was under Prime Minister Margaret Thatcher and President Ronald Reagan. She provided him with a staunch ally against Soviet expansionism. When the Soviets called her "the iron lady," Mrs. Thatcher retorted that "the lady's not for turning."*

Reagan at the Brandenburg Gate—"Tear Down this Wall!" *The U.S. State Department and the National Security Council repeatedly rejected Reagan's draft of his speech at the Brandenburg Gate. Career diplomats would—at most—call for the Berlin Wall to disappear "some day." At each turn, Reagan put this line back in the speech: "Mr. Gorbachev, tear down this wall!" And he delivered it with emphasis. It remains at the heart of his greatness.*

Bush, Reagan, and Gorbachev at Governors Island, New York, December 1988. *There could have been no stable ending of the Cold War without major Soviet disarmament of conventional weapons as well as nuclear weapons. Here, at Governors Island, Gorbachev had just come from his UN speech where he announced major conventional arms cutbacks. Only with these cuts could Europe's threatened democracies breathe easily. Reagan's steady pressure and negotiating skill helped bring about this peaceful miracle.*

The president went out on the hustings, urging voters to "win one for the Gipper." In New Haven, Connecticut, Reagan spoke to the Knights of Columbus' Centennial convention. He told the plumed, caped delegates a Hollywood story of sorts. "I am proud to have been an actor," the president said. "In those days, there was a lot to be proud of." The Knights cheered. Then he described the disappointment he and his brother Neal felt when their father refused to allow them to see a hit movie that was coming to Dixon. The teenagers wanted to see the film that all the kids were talking about. "That movie glorifies the Ku Klux Klan," said Jack Reagan. "They're not heroes; they're murderers and bigots and we're not going." Reagan concluded, saying, "That's one movie I've never seen and I never will." The Knights' emotional response was explosive. They could identify with Jack Reagan's brave stand against an organization that terrorized black Americans and hated Jews, Catholics, and immigrants. They doubtless knew that Jack Reagan had suffered all his life from alcoholism. Ronald Reagan was holding his father up, honoring him in the midst of thousands of his dad's fellow Catholics. In the presence of dozens of Cardinals—Princes of the Church—Reagan honored his father.[28]

This fine moment was one of the few for Reagan in that winter of our discontent. Many Republican candidates feared to embrace Reagan's staunch stand against the Communists. They were skittish about his economic plans. And many feared the impact on voters of his pro-life position.

Tip O'Neill was ready to take back Reagan's victory over taxes. With a slashing attack, O'Neill seized on the Social Security issue and hammered away. In November 1982, the Republicans barely hung on in the Senate and lost twenty-seven seats in the House.[29]

II. An Evil Empire

Reagan did not trim or backtrack on his core principles once he entered the White House. He made no attempt to "run to the middle," as conventional political commentators argued he must do. Most journalists continued to be stunned by Reagan's stubborn commitment to his bedrock beliefs.

Central to those beliefs was his anti-Communism. At one time a "bleeding-heart liberal," Reagan became an unyielding opponent of Communism while serving as president of the Screen Actors Guild. He soon saw Communism's violence, its hostility to democracy, its hatred of God. He knew the Communist record of crushing human rights—and its undeniable record of mass murder.

When Leonid Brezhnev died in 1982, Reagan recognized that the new Soviet Communist Party general secretary, Yuri Andropov, was a more dangerous figure. Unlike Brezhnev, Andropov was known to be highly intelligent. He was the former head of the Soviet secret police, the KGB.* Western liberals greeted his appointment. Some press profiles gushed over Andropov's supposed fondness for jazz and American movies.

Andropov was determined to block the U.S. effort to put Cruise and Pershing II missiles in Europe. He hoped to split forever the NATO alliance. The KGB supported the Western Peace Movement that called for a nuclear "freeze." No more missiles would be built; none would be placed in Europe to counter the Soviet SS-19 and SS-20 missiles that had already been put in place. Ronald Reagan offered his "Zero Option." If the Soviets would only withdraw their offensive missiles, the United States would hold back. Ironically, the Cruise missiles were not a Ronald Reagan initiative. Jimmy Carter had pledged to supply them when nervous NATO allies feared Soviet advances. Now, however, millions in Europe and the United States worried that the "cowboy" Reagan would blunder into war. The president was determined to follow through on Carter's pledge. He pressed wavering European governments to stand by their commitments.

British Prime Minister Margaret Thatcher stood firmly with Reagan on this. So did West German chancellor Helmut Kohl. Even France's Socialist president, Francois Mitterrand, came around. The NATO alliance held.

Reagan's rhetoric frightened many liberals on both sides of the Atlantic. That didn't slow him down. In 1983, he went further than he had gone in his 1982 commencement speech at the University of Notre Dame. He even

---

* Komitet Gosudarstvennoy Bezopasnosti—the Committee for State Security—was the last name of the dreaded secret police apparatus first established by Lenin in 1918. It went by various names throughout Soviet history—the *Cheka*, the OGPU, the NKVD among them— but its signature was always the single bullet at the base of the skull. The KGB is responsible for taking literally *millions* of innocent lives.

went further than he had gone in his speech to the British Parliament. In March, he spoke to the convention of the National Association of Evangelicals. Warning of the growing trend in religious circles to see "moral equivalence" between the two "Super Powers," Reagan asked the delegates not to turn a blind eye to the aggressive acts of an "evil empire."

Those two words ricocheted around the world. Reagan used them only once. But they were picked up and repeated endlessly. Deep within the bowels of the USSR, where he was held as a prisoner, Natan Anatoly Sharansky learned of Reagan's words. He tapped them out in prison code on the sewer pipes. Reagan had said what they all knew to be true! "One word of truth can move the world," says an old Russian proverb. *Two* words of truth shook it to the foundations.

Later in March, President Reagan addressed the nation on the subject of ballistic missile defense. He proposed a new Strategic Defense Initiative (SDI), urging a technological breakthrough that would allow the United States to defend itself and its allies from a Soviet missile attack, or, importantly, from a stealth attack by a "rogue" state like Iran or North Korea. "Isn't it better to defend lives than to avenge them?" Reagan asked. Some conservatives approved SDI, but only as a "bargaining chip" to trade away for Soviet concessions on arms control. Liberals uniformly detested the idea. "How high do you want to make the *rubble* bounce?" asked Senator Ted Kennedy. He immediately derided SDI as "Star Wars"—a sly reference to Reagan's Hollywood background and a suggestion that the president was once again confusing fantasy with reality.*

On 1 September 1983, the anniversary of the outbreak of World War II in 1939, a South Korean passenger airliner strayed into Soviet territory over the Kamchatka Peninsula. Soviet MiGs scrambled to intercept it. The jet was clearly marked. Soviet pilots reported they could see the civilians inside. They made no attempt to force the airliner to land. Instead, they shot it down,

* Conservatives were furious with Kennedy's attack on SDI, but President Reagan never complained. *Star Wars* was one of the most imaginative and popular movies ever made, he knew, and it featured brave warriors of the "Republic" fighting and winning against an unquestionably evil "Empire." Reagan believed that the same advances in computer technology that could produce *Star Wars* could also outmaneuver the "Heavy Metal" of a ponderous, bureaucratic war machine in the USSR.

killing 269 men, women, and children, including U.S. congressman Larry MacDonald of Georgia.

Reagan flew back to Washington from California. His military and civilian advisers recommended a wide array of defensive measures. Trade and cultural sanctions against the Soviet Union, condemnation in the UN, and heightened military alerts were among the suggestions. "Fellas," Reagan interrupted, "I don't think we need to do a damned thing. The entire world will rightly and vigorously condemn the Soviets for this barbarism. We need to remember our long-term objectives."[30] Shrewdly, Reagan now knew that those who had praised the jazz-loving movie fan in the Kremlin were the ones who looked foolish. The Soviet bear had shown his fangs for all the world to see. Who could deny it was an evil empire?

The following month, a suicide truck bombing of the Marine barracks in Beirut, Lebanon, shocked America. Killed in their sleep were 241 Marines and Navy corpsmen. They had been sent to the war-torn city to keep peace between the Lebanese, the Palestinians, and the Israelis. Reagan ordered U.S. battleships to shell terrorist strongholds but quickly ordered remaining U.S. forces out of the bomb-cratered Arab capital. It was to be the deadliest attack and the worst failure of the Reagan years.

There was unrest elsewhere as well. The tiny Caribbean island of Grenada experienced a tumultuous uprising within its own government in 1983. The Marxist Prime Minister, Maurice Bishop, was overthrown by his deputy, Bernard Coard. Bishop had led the island's New Jewel movement for four years when Coard deposed him. Coard ordered Bishop and seven of his followers shot at Fort Rupert. English-speaking peoples all over the former British West Indies were shocked.[31] Six mini-states appealed to President Reagan for help. Reagan had been viewing this creation of yet another Communist tyranny in the Western Hemisphere with mounting suspicion.

He acted quickly, but he had to overcome the reluctance of the Joint Chiefs of Staff. Former Secretary of State George Schultz recalls that "Cap [Weinberger] was continuing to say that there had to be far greater preparation and a much larger force before an operation [in Grenada] could begin."[32] Reagan had what Napoleon sought in his marshals—luck. Grenada might have turned out badly. Then, he would have learned what

JFK said at the time of the Bay of Pigs: "Victory has a thousand fathers but defeat is an orphan."

U.S. and allied forces invaded Grenada on 19 October. They quickly overwhelmed the Cuban "engineers" who had been helping island Communists build a huge airstrip capable of landing Boeing 747s—or, Reagan warned, Soviet long-range bombers. Most of Grenada's hundred thousand natives cheered the six thousand United States troops who liberated them. American medical students who were rescued by the invading forces returned to the U.S. and kissed the ground on their arrival home.[33] Many of Reagan's opponents loudly denounced Operation Urgent Fury as a violation of international law, but the American people were delighted to boot the Soviets and Cubans out of a nearby island—especially when the invasion was accomplished almost bloodlessly.

Grenada was part of Reagan's worldwide strategy of pushing back at the periphery of the Soviet empire. He continued Carter's aid to the Afghan Mujahaddin. He sent aid to the Nicaragua anti-Communist Contras. He also worked with anti-Communist forces in Poland. Reagan met with the Polish-born pope and pledged to aid Poland's Solidarity movement. Lech Walesa, an electrician, led the first free-trade union behind the Iron Curtain. He had been imprisoned by Poland's Communist government. Reagan delivered stern warnings that the United States would react sharply if Walesa was harmed. Secretly, Reagan supplied Solidarity with Xerox machines and fax machines. Not so secretly, Reagan worked with the AFL-CIO to bolster the role of free-trade unions behind the Iron Curtain.

Unlike the secular elites of the United States and most of Europe, President Reagan took seriously the role of faith in people's lives. He strongly believed in God. He spoke out in defense of freedom of religion everywhere. Under Reagan, the United States government's *Voice of America* began to broadcast religious programs into the Soviet bloc. Catholic Masses from U.S. parishes were beamed into heavily Catholic Poland. Father Viktor Potapov, a Russian Orthodox priest, broadcast his program into Russia. "Religion in Our Lives" was carried to believers in the USSR six times a week in seven languages.[34]

Nor did Reagan doubt the role of faith in Americans' lives. He met with leaders of the Right to Life Movement on 22 January, the anniversary of the Supreme Court's *Roe* v. *Wade* ruling. Reagan maintained close ties with Rev. Billy Graham, the leading evangelist in the country, and he had an especially close relationship with New York's Catholic leader, Terence Cardinal Cooke. Cooke, dying of cancer, was often welcomed to the Reagan White House. So was Mother Teresa, the Nobel Peace Prize winner who had served the poor of Calcutta for decades. Reagan took care to send many church conventions videotaped messages of support and empathy. It was a way for him to bypass the major television networks whose anchors and reporters arrogated to themselves the role of information "gatekeepers" and deliver his message unfiltered and uncensored.

Reagan's Office of Public Liaison repeated the drill with business groups and friendly professional associations. Reagan earned the title of Great Communicator because of his skill on television, but his detractors hardly realized the manifold ways he would reach out to Americans through such traditional organizations as the Boy Scouts, 4H, and the Future Farmers of America.

New organizations, collectively dubbed "the religious right," appealed to conservative Catholics, Jews, and evangelicals in the Reagan years. Rev. Jerry Falwell's Moral Majority worked on voter registration. Paul Weyrich's Free Congress Foundation and Phyllis Schlafly's Eagle Forum specialized in grassroots organization. Schlafly undertook to defeat the Equal Rights Amendment (ERA). When it was originally approved by more than two-thirds of Congress, the ERA had the support of both parties, the national news media, corporate and labor leaders, professional groups, and virtually all the nation's colleges and universities. Nonetheless, Schlafly rallied other women against this feminist objective. Specifically, she appealed to women as wives and mothers.

A Harvard graduate with a law degree from St. Louis's Washington University, Schlafly did not suffer fools or feminists gladly. She showed how the ERA's open-ended and purposely vague language could be used by liberal activist judges to force Congress and the state legislatures to pay for abortions with tax dollars and how the ERA would require women to be drafted if the United States ever reinstituted conscription. She showed how child custody and alimony would be affected, to the likely disadvantage of women. Despite the fact that thirty-five of the required thirty-eight states had ratified the ERA, Schlafly reversed the trend, blocked any further ratifications, and even raised the intriguing possibility of a number of states rescinding their earlier ratifications. "Can that even be done?" constitutional scholars asked. The fact that they were asking the question was a tribute to Schlafly's organizing skill. She was playing ball on her opponents' side of the gridiron.

III. "Morning in America"

In many respects, Grenada was when the tide of the Cold War turned. Just as the little town of Gettysburg was the "high-water mark" of the Confederacy, Grenada was the high-water mark of Soviet expansion.

Before October 1983, the Soviets had advanced steadily, sometimes stealthily, from the Bolshevik Revolution of 1918. Sometimes, they seemed to pull back—as from Iran in 1946 or Austria in 1955. But it was always "two steps forward, one step back," as Stalin had said, and the Brezhnev Doctrine was always in play. "What we have, we keep," said the late Soviet dictator. The Soviets never abandoned the idea of world Communism. The entire world, sooner or later, would be brought under the "dictatorship of the proletariat." Totalitarian rule of the international workers' movement, of which the Communist Party of the Soviet Union was the "vanguard," was their *raison d'être.*

The lovely island of Grenada is only fifty-one square miles. Barely one thirty-ninth the size of Rhode Island, it contains just one tenth of our smallest state's population. Given its diminutive size, it is easy to miss its importance in the Cold War. Reagan's liberation of the island shattered the myth of Soviet invincibility and delivered a powerful blow to the idea of its inevitability. No longer did it seem so sure that Soviet-style Communism was "the wave of the future." Reagan showed that he could snatch a delightful morsel from the maw of the Russian bear—and the bear could do nothing about it.

Importantly for Reagan, October 1983 was not only the turning point for the world struggle between freedom and Communism, it was also the turning point in his flagging political fortunes. The real October Revolution that year was Reagan's. The economic renewal that he had long proclaimed began sparking to life, and a land held in the icy grip of recession felt a thaw. Housing starts went up. Laid-off workers moved back to work.

As for his critics, Reagan just teased them. He told the story of two old friends invited to a fancy costume party. One asked the other what he should wear: "I suppose you could just slap an egg on your face and go as a liberal *economist.*" More seriously, Reagan on the hustings grinned as he said, "I notice they don't call it *Reaganomics* anymore."[35]

Despite Reagan's renewed popularity, Democrats eagerly looked forward to the 1984 elections. To them, 1980 was an aberration—more a factor of Jimmy Carter's great unpopularity than anything innately appealing about Ronald Reagan. As to Carter's low esteem, many Democrats themselves despised him. To them, he was the most conservative Democrat since Grover Cleveland.

The Democratic primaries offered a wide array of talent. Former Vice President Walter "Fritz" Mondale was respected if not enthusiastically embraced. Senator John Glenn of Ohio, the former Project *Mercury* astronaut, was a national hero. Insiders predicted that Glenn's candidacy would receive a big bounce when Hollywood released the movie *The Right Stuff*, based on Tom Wolfe's bestselling book, just before the primaries. Senator Gary Hart's tall, lean demeanor and craggy good looks evoked his Colorado roots. His role as George McGovern's campaign manager had gained him many contacts and followers among the now dominant "reform wing" of the Democratic Party. Then there was Rev. Martin Luther King Jr.'s former deputy, Rev. Jesse Jackson. "Run, Jesse, Run," urged black audiences and many white liberals.

Mondale had an impressive command of facts and figures, a skill honed from nearly twenty years in the Senate and in Carter's Oval Office, but he lacked charisma. When Senator Hart's emphasis on "new" began to catch fire, Mondale countered, "Where's the beef?" echoing a then-popular television ad in which a crabby old lady demanded to know why she was being short-changed by her local burger joint. It worked because there was little of substance in Hart's appeal for "newness," but it was telling that

Mondale's most memorable and effective line was pinched from Madison Avenue ad writers. It was the brightest his rhetorical star could shine. New York's colorful Democratic Governor, Mario Cuomo, conceded Mondale's weakness here, quoting his Italian mother, who said the Minnesotan was like polenta: "Filling, but not thrilling."

Mondale's lackluster image was further damaged in his misunderstanding about voter outreach. He mistakenly thought that the endorsements he was lining up—from the AFL-CIO and the powerful teachers' union, the NEA—could substitute for real strength at the grassroots.[36] He moved easily on Capitol Hill and with the leading lobbyists of liberal interest groups, but he was increasingly out of place at the Minnesota State Fair.

John Glenn suffered from similar problems, though his shortcomings were more acute. His soporific speaking style and poor organization soon forced him out of the running. It didn't help that the actor who portrayed Glenn, the compelling Ed Harris, was a much more interesting figure. By comparison, Glenn clearly had the wrong stuff.

In the meantime, Jesse Jackson had problems of his own. He provoked a firestorm of criticism when he was overheard referring to New York City as "Hymietown." This crude, anti-Semitic remark shocked millions. Jackson was a Christian minister, an associate of the sainted Martin Luther King Jr., whose own relations with Jews had been exemplary. Jews had famously supported the movement for black civil rights. Three of the most famous martyrs to civil rights were Michael Schwerner, Andrew Goodman, and James Chaney. The first two, young Jewish men from the North, had joined with James Chaney, a black Mississippian, during the summer of 1964, to fight for voters' rights. All three had been cruelly murdered and buried together in a shallow grave. For many Americans, the very thought of anti-Semitism in the black community was a *non sequitur.* And when Minister Louis Farrakhan, the notoriously Jew-bating leader of the Nation of Islam, stepped forward to defend Jackson, the situation looked even worse.

After edging out Hart and Jackson for the nomination, Mondale started his hunt for a running mate. In no time, he converted the vice presidential selection process into a "quota parade" as he invited all the usual prospects to visit him at his Minnesota home.[37] He added nearly every black big-city mayor, every Hispanic officeholder of note, and an array of women politicians. He no doubt meant well, but his outreach to each group became almost a *parody* of inclusiveness. People who would never be considered for vice president under normal conditions were interviewed, seemingly to give their racial, sex, or ethnic "affinity group" the impression that their concerns were close to Mondale's heart.[38]

His final selection of Democratic congresswoman Geraldine Ferraro from New York seemed a stroke of genius. Running behind a rebounding Reagan in every poll, Mondale knew he had to throw a "Hail Mary" pass to shake up the race and pick up serious yardage. Ferraro was smart, sassy, New York brash, attractive, and funny. Though a very junior member of the House, she was a quick study. As the first woman on a major national party ticket, she created a stir among feminists. The Democratic ticket was compared to the famous Hollywood dance team of Fred Astaire and Ginger Rogers: He gave her class and she gave him sex appeal, something Mondale was sorely lacking.

Unfortunately, they had to face the music and dance rather abruptly. Investigative reporters at the Wall Street Journal zealously dug up financial scoops on Ferraro's businessman husband. They looked, if not criminal, then highly unsavory. Ferraro's total unawareness of the sources and methods by which her family's income was procured dented her image of cool competence.

She faced additional problems among the base. Ferraro was the first Catholic on a national ticket since Sargent Shriver in 1972. Much had changed since then, most notably, the Supreme Court's *Roe* v. *Wade* decision. Ferraro tried to square the circle of loyalty to the National Organization for Women and abortion-on-demand while saying she remained a faithful Catholic. New York's Cardinal John O'Connor was having none of it. He publicly rebuked Ferraro and bluntly instructed her on the Catholic Church's unyielding defense of innocent human life.

Despite the difficulties, the campaign had its moments. Governor Mario Cuomo's powerful keynote speech to the Democratic National Convention meeting in San Francisco thrilled the country.* More than any politician of

---

* This author has had occasion to debate many leading Democrats—Howard Dean, Robert Reich, Geraldine Ferraro among them. Mario Cuomo is by far the best of the bunch.

his time, Cuomo spoke for the millions whose ancestors had come to this country in steerage. They yearned to breathe free; they were determined to have a better life for their children. Cuomo's speech was the highlight of his career. But in that summer of 1984, it only served as a dispiriting contrast for Democrats whose nominee, the worthy, plodding Fritz, could never bring his audiences to their feet.

President Reagan had had no primary opponent. He bided his time. On 6 June 1984, Reagan spoke at the Ranger Monument on a cliff overlooking Omaha Beach at Normandy. There, he pointed to the grizzled veterans of that fateful day forty years before, and paid tribute to the courage and dedication of those "boys of Pointe du Hoc":

> Behind me is a memorial that symbolizes the Ranger daggers that were thrust into the top of these cliffs. And before me are the men who put them there.
>
> These are the boys of Pointe du Hoc. These are the men who took the cliffs. These are the champions who helped free a continent. These are the heroes who helped end a war.
>
> Gentlemen, I look at you and I think of the words of Stephen Spender's poem. You are men who in your "lives fought for life . . . and left the vivid air signed with your honor. . . ."
>
> Forty summers have passed since the battle that you fought here. You were young the day you took these cliffs; some of you were hardly more than boys, with the deepest joys of life before you. Yet you risked everything here. Why? Why did you do it? What impelled you to put aside the instinct for self-preservation and risk your lives to take these cliffs? What inspired all the men of the armies that met here? We look at you, and somehow we know the answer. It was faith, and belief; it was loyalty and love.
>
> The men of Normandy had faith that what they were doing was right, faith that they fought for all humanity, faith that a just God would grant them mercy on this beachhead or on the next. It was the deep knowledge—and pray God we have not lost it—that there is a profound moral difference between the use of force for liberation and

> the use of force for conquest. You were here to liberate, not to conquer, and so you and those others did not doubt your cause. And you were right not to doubt.
>
> You all knew that some things are worth dying for. One's country is worth dying for, and democracy is worth dying for, because it's the most deeply honorable form of government ever devised by man. All of you loved liberty. All of you were willing to fight tyranny, and you knew the people of your countries were behind you.[39]

When a Mondale campaign aide watched Reagan's speech, he groused to veteran political reporters Jack Germond and Jules Witcover that *his* man had slogged through the long, wearying primaries of the spring only to see Ronald Reagan get thirty minutes of free air-time. It didn't seem fair that Reagan was "grabbing all the coverage."[40] But, of course, it wasn't just the president's ability to command media coverage; it was the powerful and creative uses to which he put that advantage that made him so formidable. Reagan's stirring "Boys of Pointe du Hoc" speech bears comparison with Churchill's tribute to the Royal Air Force ("Never . . . was so much owed by so many to so few."), Pericles' Funeral Oration, and even the Gettysburg Address.

It must be remembered that Reagan was then in the midst of a great transatlantic debate on the defense of freedom against Soviet tyranny. His opponents not only wanted to "freeze" the production and deployment of nuclear weapons to match the Soviets' attempts to intimidate free societies, they also wanted to chill his moral indictment of totalitarianism. Consequently, national defense played a vital role in Reagan's reelection bid. Opponents bitterly denounced his huge defense buildup. It was contributing to the ballooning deficit, they charged. The defense buildup was undoubtedly expensive, but it was never more than a six or seven percent increase. Reagan sided with his staunch defense secretary, Caspar "Cap" Weinberger, in every administration battle over defense spending. Faced with the choice between balancing the federal budget and, for example, building a six-hundred-ship Navy, Reagan opted for the Navy.

Reagan never publicly argued for more defense spending; instead he spoke out for a "defense *second to none.*" Recalling the disaster of Carter's failed

"Desert One" attempt to rescue the hostages in Iran, Reagan argued that our young servicemen and women needed the best equipment the Nation could provide. The maneuver helped Reagan skirt the unpopularity associated with defense spending. He let Cap Weinberger make the case on Capitol Hill for more money and for specific weapons systems. Reagan stayed with the big picture. As a result, *Washington Post* cartoonist Herb Block ("Herblock") pilloried the faithful Weinberger for the inevitable defense cost overruns. Herblock never drew Weinberger without a $600 military toilet seat around his neck.

National defense was also the subject of one of the most successful campaign ads in history. The Reagan campaign presented "The Bear" in 1984. The announcer informed viewers that there was a bear in the forest. Some people don't see the bear. Some don't believe there are bears in the woods. All the while, viewers can hear but not see a huge bear, rustling in the branches, grunting. As the camera panned out and showed a very threatening looking grizzly faced by a single resolute man, the announcer asked if it was not a good idea to be prepared—"*If there is a bear.*" Not since the infamous "Daisy" commercial of 1964, which had savaged the supposed recklessness of Barry Goldwater, had a campaign ad achieved so much notice. The ad played on what viewers already knew: Republicans thought Mondale was naïve and weak on defense. The bear, of course, was the historic symbol of Russia. That only made the ad more pointed.

Another memorable television ad showed Americans going back to work, raising the flag, celebrating at the Olympics. The announcer said it's *Morning in America.* It evoked a mood of golden reverie, of renewal, of optimism and growth. In a subtle way, it challenged Governor Cuomo's depiction of an America still held in the grip of recession.

Mondale attacked Reagan's repeated appeals to Christian fundamentalists. The former vice president had said yes to virtually every organized liberal interest group in Washington, but tried to rule the opinions of millions of evangelicals "out of order."

In an influential essay in *Commentary* magazine, the Rev. Richard J. Neuhaus defended the right of evangelicals and fundamentalists to argue for their public policy preferences in a liberal democracy. Neuhaus had warned against the attempt to drive religiously derived moral beliefs out of public life in a well-reviewed book, *The Naked Public Square.* Neuhaus was then a Lutheran minister who had marched with Dr. King for civil rights. His article, "What the Fundamentalists Want," spelled out their agenda:

> The list includes prayer and Bible reading in public schools, a "pro-life" amendment (or some instrument for overruling *Roe v. Wade*), legal restrictions on pornography, an end to state "harassment" of Christian schools, resistance to feminist and gay-rights legislation, increased defense spending, and terminating social programs that, it is believed, only increase the dependency of the poor.[41]

Neuhaus argued that even if liberals opposed every point on the evangelicals' agenda, they could not claim that all those issues had been settled by a democratic consensus. It was not illegitimate to raise questions about them. In fact, liberals came increasingly to rely on the unelected judiciary to force compliance with their agenda when they could no longer persuade legislative majorities.

Faith continued to function as a lighting rod during the campaign. Mondale raised alarms about Reagan's alleged reliance on the Bible's Book of Revelation and the frightening image of a final battle of Armageddon at the end of history. Reagan acknowledged that he had read and did believe in biblical prophecy, but he had not allowed any particular doomsday interpretation to guide his policies toward the Soviet Union.

Mondale was never quizzed about his uncritical acceptance of the Nuclear Freeze concept put forward by Australia's Dr. Helen Caldicott. Caldicott openly claimed that her views on "nuclear winter" had been formed as a teenager when she read the Australian novel, *On the Beach.* In that novel, author Neville Shute writes about how the end of the world comes to the Southern Hemisphere following a nuclear war between the United States and USSR. Caldicott had met the president's radical daughter, Patti Davis, at Hugh Hefner's Playboy Mansion.[42] Davis got Caldicott a White House meeting with her father, but the Australian antinuclear activist described it as "the most disconcerting of my life."[43]

Entering the fall campaign, Reagan was well ahead of Mondale in all the polls. But, when the two candidates met for their first debate in Louisville, Kentucky, the seventy-three-year-old Reagan seemed slightly confused. He had to correct himself in mid-sentence once or twice—a rarity for the smoothly articulate old Hollywood pitchman. To make matters worse, Reagan ran over time in his closing statement, leaving viewers stranded as he spoke about the Pacific Coastal Highway.

Democratic campaign aides handed Fritz a baseball bat, a "Louisville Slugger," as they claimed victory in the debate. The Mondale-Ferraro campaign was infused with new life as the press took up the "buzz" of Reagan's age for weeks. No president had ever run for reelection in his seventies before. Politely, and sometimes bluntly, columnists began to ask if the president had begun to show signs of dementia.

When the two candidates met for a second debate in Kansas City, it was late in the campaign. One of the panel of journalists posed the question to the president—delicately. Henry Trewhitt of the *Baltimore Sun* had asked the *Sun*'s liberal pundit, Jack Germond, how to frame the question that would highlight Reagan's greatest vulnerability. Germond worked with Trewhitt for "several hours" crafting a question that would be hard for Reagan to avoid. But watching the debate from the television pressroom monitor, Germond recalls Trewhitt's question:

> Mr. President, I want to raise an issue that I think has been lurking out there for two or three weeks, and cast it specifically in national security terms. You already are the oldest President in history, and some of your staff say you were tired after your most recent encounter with Mr. Mondale. I recall, yes, that President Kennedy, who had to go for days on end with very little sleep during the Cuba missile crisis. Is there any doubt in your mind that you would be able to function in such circumstances?

Germond saw the windup and the pitch, but he recalls: "I could see the hint of a smile on Reagan's face, and I thought, Oh, s—, he's all ready for it and he's going to hit it out of the park." And, of course, that is what the president did.

"Not at all, Mr. Trewhitt," answered Reagan. "And I want you to know that I will not make age an issue in this campaign. I am not going to exploit, for political purposes, my opponent's youth and inexperience."[44]

Trewhitt laughed. The panel of journalists laughed. The country laughed. Even Mondale laughed—as his only hope of winning the election went up in smoke.*

Reagan's joke was played and replayed on every television station. Often, it was the only "clip" from the debate that was featured. Reagan's wit was taken as a sure sign that the Old Gipper was mentally agile and fully capable of conducting the affairs of state.

Soviet Communist Party boss Yuri Andropov had died earlier that year, only to be succeeded by the moribund Konstantin Chernenko. Challenged by U.S. reporters for being the first president since Hoover who had failed to meet with the leader of the Soviet Union, Reagan good-naturedly responded: "How can I? They keep *dying* on me!"[45]

Reagan used humor as a weapon. He knew such quips pointed to the larger truth about the USSR: It was a dying empire. It was the Communist system that was sclerotic, ossified. But Reagan knew that even a grizzly bear dying of stomach cancer could be dangerous.

The Soviets could read the polls. They knew they would have to deal with Reagan for a second term. They sent Foreign Minister Andrei Gromyko to visit President Reagan in the White House that October. Gromyko, normally a dour, humorless *apparatchik*, even managed a wan smile for reporters.

On Election Day, Ronald Reagan defeated Walter Mondale. He racked up the greatest popular vote total in history. Reagan won 54,451,521 popular votes (58.8 percent) to Mondale's 37,566,334 popular votes (40.5 percent). Reagan won every state except Mondale's Minnesota, giving him 525 electoral votes.** The former vice president also carried the District of Columbia to

* Jack Germond's honest relating of this campaign story shows the often intimate connection between liberal journalists and their preferred candidates. Would Germond have spent three hours prepping one of the debate panelists with a well-honed question to exploit Mondale's greatest weakness?

** President Reagan came within 3,100 votes of carrying Minnesota, too. That state has only 3,200 election precincts; thus, Reagan lost it by less than one vote per precinct. Reagan had spent only forty-five minutes in the state at an airport rally.

yield thirteen electoral votes. Mrs. Ferraro had not helped. Women voters chose the president. Catholic voters, Italian-American voters, New Yorkers, and even the voters of Mrs. Ferraro's Queens constituency voted for Reagan.*

In Washington, D.C., that November day the weather was blustery and gray and the mood was somber. Reagan's team was not jubilant as they waited for the election returns. They were scared. All the public opinion polls looked favorable, but no one can ever be completely sure who will show up at the polling stations or what will motivate them. Voter turnout is everything. Recalling FDR hunkered in Hyde Park during the uncertain election of 1940, the fact bears repeating: In a democracy, it is good for the governors to fear the people.

When the networks reported the nationwide romp, however, Reagan's people relaxed. The Republican Party did not share in Reagan's "lonely landslide." The "Morning in America" mood deliberately created by the Reagan campaign operation tended to favor incumbents generally, and that was not good for Republicans seeking to oust Democrats in Congress. Reagan had been elected with the support of 24 percent of the Democrats. His fellow Republicans could not match that cross-party appeal. Many of them didn't even try.

The day after Reagan's reelection, leading Democrats began a series of illegal sit-in demonstrations outside the Washington embassy of the apartheid government of South Africa. Getting arrested in protests of the racist policies of the Pretoria regime became a badge of honor among liberal Democratic activists.

IV. "We Can Do Business . . ."

Ronald Reagan had barely been sworn in for a second term when the Soviet Union once again buried a leader of the Communist Party. Konstantin

---

* This is not especially *unusual.* Vice presidential nominees are chosen more for their ability to unify and excite various elements of the party. This Ferraro clearly did. Voters generally consider the vice presidential nominee only as a reflection of the presidential candidate's seriousness and ability. Thus, Goldwater's choice of Congressman Bill Miller "because he drives Lyndon Johnson nuts" was seen as a mark against Goldwater, and George McGovern's failure to do a background check on Senator Tom Eagleton was evidence of his general fecklessness.

Chernenko died 10 March 1985 of emphysema. He was seventy-four years old. Three Soviet rulers had followed each other to the grave in less than three years. Nothing better symbolized the hardening of the arteries of the Soviet Communist order.

This would change—abruptly. Mikhail Sergeivich Gorbachev was only fifty-four when he was elected to lead the Communist Party of the Soviet Union. He had been groomed by a dying Yuri Andropov for his intelligence, his polished manners, his youthful vigor, and his affability. If Communism was to survive, if the USSR was to survive, an infusion of new blood was desperately needed. Gorbachev and his educated, stylish, articulate wife, Raisa, were that new blood.*

Even before his selection, Gorbachev had shrewdly made a visit to London. If he could make headway with Prime Minister Margaret Thatcher—Britain's *Iron Lady*—Gorbachev felt confident that would enhance his prestige in Moscow and would later help him deal with Ronald Reagan. Not since Churchill and FDR had there been such a close transatlantic partnership as that between Thatcher and Reagan. Gorbachev succeeded brilliantly. Thatcher was duly impressed. She announced after their first meeting: "I like Mr. Gorbachev. We can do business together." From the no-nonsense, all-business Margaret Thatcher, there was no higher compliment.**

President Reagan knew he would have to meet with Gorbachev, but he was not willing to appear too eager. Aides privately pressed the president to meet. Gorbachev was different from all those other Communist Party hacks, they said. Gorbachev was interested in relaxing tensions. There was no time to lose. Gorbachev was different. According to stories

* Raisa Gorbachev's Ph.D. dissertation had advocated national state-run child care centers because too many working Soviet mothers were leaving their children in the care of grandparents who were religious. This author had occasion to use this information in congressional hearings where committee members demanded action on day care from the Reagan administration.

** The press was right to play up this Thatcher comment, since her closeness with Ronald Reagan was already the stuff of legend. So close were they that Ronald Reagan had a gag film poster in the saddle room of his Rancho del Cielo. The poster showed Reagan as Rhett Butler carrying Margaret Thatcher as Scarlett O'Hara upstairs to the bedroom of their Atlanta mansion. Reagan would not bring the satirical poster into the ranch house, he said blushingly, because Britain's first female prime minister, a frequent visitor to the ranch, might see it. A special relationship, indeed! (Source: Edmund Morris, *Dutch*, 592.)

that circulated in Washington, Reagan responded to all this prodding with typical humor. "I know he's different. . . . He's the first Soviet leader who weighs more than his wife!"

Reagan had to make sure the Western Alliance was secure before he engaged in any high-level summitry with the vigorous new leader of the Kremlin. No one was more important in NATO than West German chancellor Helmut Kohl. Kohl had taken huge political risks in backing Reagan on Pershing II Missile deployment. West Germany was fighting against the Bader-Meinhof gang of Communist terrorists, among the world's most violent. Reagan felt we "owed Helmut one."[46]

President Reagan planned a visit to West Germany to support his stalwart ally. It was planned that the president would lay a wreath at the Bitburg Military Cemetery to symbolize the Federal Republic of Germany's commitment to Western democracy. Reagan's aide, Michael Deaver, traveled to West Germany to do the "advance" work on the presidential visit. What Deaver did *not* see among the snow-covered gravestones of eighteen- and nineteen-year-olds were several dozen markers for members of Heinrich Himmler's dreaded Waffen SS.[47]

When word of this ghastly detail leaked out, a worldwide controversy erupted.

Nancy Reagan was appalled. She called Mike Deaver and tearfully complained that he had ruined "Ronnie's" presidency.[48] Within the administration, most advisors urged Reagan to cancel the Bitburg appearance. Communications Director Pat Buchanan urged him to stand firm. Holocaust survivor Elie Wiesel, a winner of the Nobel Peace Prize, came to the White House to receive an award. He lectured the president to his face, telling him his place was with the victims, not with the Nazis. Reagan could be very stubborn, especially when patronized. And he felt he was being patronized now. "The final word has been spoken, as far as I'm concerned," Reagan grimly told his subordinates.[49]*

General Matthew Ridgeway, the legendary commander of the 82nd

* This author was at that meeting and can testify to Reagan's grim determination not to be pressed on a matter where he had made up his mind.

Airborne, called the White House and volunteered to lay the wreath in Reagan's stead. The president gratefully took the call and accepted the ninety-year-old's gracious offer, but they would go together. Reagan would not let the old warrior take upon himself the odium of the event, but he was proud to stand with him.[50]

To soothe frayed nerves, President Reagan also included a trip to the Bergen-Belsen concentration camp. There, he spoke movingly of the cruel injustice done to the Jewish people by the Nazis. He invoked Abraham Lincoln's words, appealing to "the better angels of our nature."

Bitburg was, and remains, one of the worst missteps of Reagan's presidency. Almost lost in the controversy of the time was the idea expressed by the American Legion and other veterans' groups: The President of the United States has no business honoring enemy soldiers *ever.* Even if there had been no SS graves at Bitburg, no American president should lay a wreath at a cemetery for soldiers who had been ordered to kill young Americans.

The United States did indeed "owe one" to the faithful Chancellor Kohl. But that debt could have been generously discharged by having President Reagan lay a wreath at the grave of the architect of West German *freedom*—the late Konrad Adenauer. Adenauer, the devout Catholic; Adenauer, the prisoner of Hitler; Adenauer, the reconciler of the ancient hatreds with France. *Das ist der Mann!**

Reagan had domestic business to attend to before meeting with the newly named Kremlin leader, Gorbachev. During the first term, conservatives had failed to disestablish the newly-created U.S. Department of Education. Liberal Republicans in the Senate—including Connecticut's Lowell Weicker and Vermont's Robert Stafford—teamed with ranking Democrat Ted Kennedy to prevent that. Reagan's first education secretary, Terrell Bell, had appointed a National Commission on Excellence in Education. The commission produced a report that warned of "a rising tide of mediocrity" and called for greater emphasis on "the basics" in education.

---

* "Der alte Jude, das ist der Mann!" ("The old Jew, there is the man!") So said Chancellor Otto von Bismarck admiringly of Britain's prime minister Benjamin Disraeli at the Congress of Vienna in 1878. How much happier Europe's history would have been if all the German chancellors had held to that admiration.

Reagan's second-term secretary of education was William J. Bennett, a Democrat and the former chairman of the National Endowment for the Humanities.* Bennett updated the traditional "Three Rs" of education (reading, 'riting, and 'rithmetic) by adding the "Three Cs"—*content, character,* and *choice.* Following the commission report, Bennett wanted to beef up the content of academic curriculum. He wanted to stress the importance of character development. "What is noble, what is base?" he asked rhetorically. "Who said 'I have a dream'? What does 'I am the state' mean? 'Where is the Mississippi?' 'Why is there a Berlin Wall?' Students should know," he said. By choice, Bennett meant that parents should be able to choose the public, private, or religious school that best meets their children's needs. To this end, he backed a voucher proposal for students languishing in ineffective federally-financed programs for lower income families.

Bennett also supported the rising movement for home-schooling. When home-school lawyer-advocate Mike Farris was challenged for encouraging a religious cult movement, he always responded that James Madison, the father of our Constitution and the author of our Bill of Rights, was home schooled.

Secretary Bennett proved a media lightning rod for the administration. When he suggested that students had a moral duty to repay their college loans, liberal editorial pages denounced him as a heartless skinflint. Under heavy criticisms, Bennett emphasized that the American taxpayers had underwritten those loans and that part of any student's education must involve learning to meet one's moral obligations.

At Bennett's first cabinet meeting, the president opened the session by reading from a file of harsh newspaper criticisms of the group's newest and youngest member. Then, with a smile, Reagan looked around and said, "Now, what's wrong with the *rest* of you?" As the meeting concluded, Reagan told Bennett he'd learned in Hollywood the difference between the box office and the critics.

The death of actor Rock Hudson in 1985 introduced the general public to Auto-Immune Deficiency Syndrome (AIDS). The Reagans, of course, knew Rock Hudson from their Hollywood days. They also knew of his

* For purposes of narrative flow, the author refers to himself in this chapter in the third person.

homosexuality. Socially tolerant, the Reagans had never shunned friends because they were gay. But when the disease spread, claiming thousands of lives, President Reagan faced a rising chorus of criticism for not delivering a major address on the issue.

The criticism illustrated a striking change in Americans' expectations of their presidents. Millions had died of influenza in 1919 and 1920 and President Wilson never spoke out on the subject. FDR at Warm Springs contributed mightily to treatment and acceptance of polio victims, but he did not deliver presidential addresses on the disease. Eisenhower never spoke about heart disease, even after suffering two heart attacks. JFK never even admitted he had Addison's Disease. Still, Reagan's silence about AIDS for nearly two years was charged against him by liberal critics as cruel indifference to the plight of sufferers.

It was not that the federal government was not spending huge amounts on research and treatment of the disease. When young Ryan White, a hemophiliac, contracted AIDS through a blood transfusion, Congress moved quickly to fund research and education on the subject. Reagan supported this legislation. Additionally, the second leading cause of AIDS was intravenous drug use. Mrs. Reagan's spirited and effective promotion of the "Just Say No" campaign against drug use was given added urgency by the epidemic.

Meanwhile, back in the USSR, Mikhail Gorbachev became "the new broom that sweeps clean"—or at least he tried to. He denounced alcoholism and absenteeism in the workplace. He spoke out against corruption in the Communist Party *apparat*. He recognized that the USSR must reform or collapse. Pressed hard by Reagan's military buildup and especially concerned about SDI, Gorbachev started two simultaneous initiatives—*perestroika* ("restructuring") and *glasnost* ("openness"). Under glasnost, horrifying stories that had been suppressed since the founding of the Soviet state began to flood the Soviet media. One of these stories made it into print in the West:

> Tens of thousands of people, perhaps even a quarter of a million, were executed in the prisons of Kiev with a bullet through the temple, brought to Bykivnia by the truckload, and cast into quicklimed pits. Four official commissions have investigated this annihilation in the last

forty-five years. Yet the full story of who the victims are, who killed them, and how they came to be buried here has yet to be exhumed.[51]

Gorbachev allowed these stories to come out because he needed to undercut his hard-line Communist opponents in the Kremlin's perennial power struggles. He may not have realized that in so doing, he was undermining the legitimacy of the Soviet state in the eyes of its own people.

When he met Ronald Reagan in Geneva in late 1985, the Western media fairly swooned for Gorbachev. Conservative radio personality Rush Limbaugh would later style these glowing reports "gorbasms," but there was little doubt that the Western press was pulling for the vigorous new Soviet party leader to succeed.

The get-acquainted summit produced no diplomatic breakthroughs, nor was it intended to. It did, however, melt the ice between the two heads of government. For the first time since Carter met Brezhnev in Vienna nearly a decade earlier, the Soviet and American chiefs were talking. Some in the American delegation worried that the seventy-four-year-old president would be outmaneuvered by his much younger rival. But Reagan appeared hatless and coatless in the chill air to welcome the Soviet general secretary to the American Embassy. Gorbachev fiddled uncomfortably with his muffler as he got out of his *Zil* limousine.[52] Reagan mixed personal warmth and good fellowship with a tough, almost aggressive negotiating style. "Let me tell you *why* we mistrust you," he said in a one-on-one session.[53] Soon, though, Reagan was insisting that they address each other as "Ron and Mike." Many of Reagan's strongest supporters worried that he would allow personal relationships to blind him to the Soviets' seventy-year record of bad faith. This attempt to build a personal rapport had been the source of FDR and JFK's difficulties in dealing with a shrewd and unscrupulous foe, they believed.

Events beyond improved Soviet relations demanded Reagan's attention then. Early in the New Year, the president was alerted to a tragedy unfolding on national television. In a mere seventy-three seconds, the Space Shuttle *Challenger* was launched into a chilly blue sky only to explode spectacularly. Seven *Challenger* astronauts, including the teacher-volunteer

Christa McAuliffe, were instantly killed.* Their family members witnessed in horror from the reviewing stands, and children throughout the nation watched in their classrooms. President Reagan went on national television that night—28 January 1986—to console and comfort a grieving people. He explained to the frightened children that courage is required to face the dangers of space exploration. We honor those brave astronauts and men and women in every field whose daring and personal sacrifice alone make progress possible. Then, he quoted from *High Flight*, a poem written in honor of World War I aviators: "We will never forget them, nor the last time we saw them, this morning, as they prepared for the journey and waved goodbye and 'slipped the surly bonds of earth' to 'touch the face of God.'"

House Speaker Tip O'Neill was moved to tears by the president's eloquence. "He may not be much of a debater," O'Neill observed, "but with a prepared text he's the best public speaker I've ever seen. . . . I'm beginning to think that in this respect he dwarfs both Roosevelt and Kennedy."[54] This was high praise from the fiercely partisan Democratic speaker.

Reagan captured—or perhaps he shaped—a national mood of firm resolve. Public opinion polls recorded that Americans strongly supported continuing the space program, despite the worst disaster in history. Significantly, despite the trauma of a nationally televised explosion of a space shuttle, NASA remained committed to the policy of openness first mandated by President Eisenhower in 1959.

1986 marked more joyous events as well, including the centennial celebration of New York's Statue of Liberty. Reagan had used the upcoming hundredth anniversary of the Lady in the Harbor to recruit Chrysler Corporation president Lee Iacocca to lead a private fund-raising drive. Reagan hoped to commemorate the event by restoring the worn, storm-stressed statue. A joint French-American team took on the work of restoration, carefully replacing every one of thousands of individually-wrought steel support struts. The great symbol of "Liberty Enlightening the World" had been in danger of collapse.

---

* This author had the privilege of meeting Christa McAuliffe and teaching her New Hampshire class.

On 3 July 1986, President Reagan invited French President Francois Mitterrand to join him and Mrs. Reagan for the statue's rededication. It was to be a tribute, as well, to American ideals of liberty. Reagan treated the Socialist Mitterrand with elaborate courtesy—even as he was doing his best to consign socialism "to the ash heap of history."

Oddly, Reagan was indebted to Mitterrand. The French leader had collaborated with France's powerful Communist Party in 1981–82. He tried to impose Marxism democratically on the French people. This Gallic effort was widely viewed as the polar opposite of Reagan's renewed commitment to free enterprise. The success of Reagan's policies contrasted powerfully with the soon abandoned disaster of Mitterrand's policies. The failure of this attempt at democratic Socialism had deeply impressed the free peoples of Europe and the world.

For the celebration, President Reagan strode the deck of the USS *Iowa,* a World War II-era battleship retrofitted for service in the nuclear age. In New York's darkened harbor, he sent a laser beam to the tip of the Statue of Liberty, dramatically signaling the unveiling. With Solidarity alive in Poland, with the Mujahaddin harassing the Soviets in Afghanistan, with Grenada liberated and the Nicaraguan Contras pressing the Communist Sandinistas in Central America,* Reagan felt confident in saluting "the cause of human freedom" and relighting Lady Liberty's torch.

With peace and prosperity, Reagan could be forgiven for thinking he had restored America's rightful place of leadership in the world.

V. Reykjavik: The Clash

The Soviet Union was not just going to collapse, said the leading experts on the Kremlin. Former President Richard Nixon had spoken of seeking "hard-headed détente" as the best we could realistically hope for.[55] But Reagan saw things differently.

His critics always accused him of being *simplistic.* Veteran Washington

* When the majority of House Democrats in 1986 voted against aid to the anti-Communist Nicaraguan contras, this author, a life-long Democrat, finally switched parties and became a Republican.

wise man Clark Clifford called the president "an amiable dunce."[56] They did not know what Reagan had told Richard Allen a decade earlier. Allen would become Reagan's national security advisor in the White House. Years before Reagan was elected, he spoke with Allen: "My idea of American policy toward the Soviet Union is simple, and some would say simplistic. It is this: We win and they lose. . . ."[57] The problem was that Reagan's critics mistook clarity for simplicity.

The hastily-called Summit at Reykjavik, Iceland, in late 1986 was Gorbachev's idea, If Hollywood had searched for a location in which to dramatize visually the East-West clash, it could not have chosen a better one. Iceland is a volcanic island midway between Europe and North America. Instead of green grass, there is black volcanic ash. Höfdi House is the modest nineteenth century mansion where the two Super-Power leaders would meet. It is an unadorned, white building with a dark slate roof. Some local residents even claim that Höfdi House is haunted.[58] The island's capital city is surrounded by dark gray crags.

In mid-October the stark Icelandic landscape was almost devoid of color. The scene was dominated by black and white. It was even like those Hollywood movies that Reagan had starred in, the ones that sharply contrasted good and evil. Those were the films that nauseated the sophisticates. To make the contrast even more compelling, Gorbachev showed up in his black limousine, wearing a heavy black overcoat and a black snap-brim Fedora. Reagan arrived wearing a light tan raincoat, which on television appeared to be white.

Very quickly, both summit participants went far beyond the agenda. Gorbachev, we now know, was desperate to end the arms race. Perestroika was not working. The Soviet system was being crushed by the burden of keeping up with the U.S. military buildup. If he could cut defense spending, Gorbachev could divert desperately needed funds to perestroika and his effort to save the Communist system. "He has a nice smile," the grim-faced Foreign Minister Andrei Gromyko said of their young champion, "but he has *iron* teeth."[59]

Like two poker players, they faced each other across a table. Gorbachev made daring offers to Reagan. He offered major weapons cutbacks.

Everything Reagan had offered five years earlier in his Zero Option proposal, he could now have. Reagan suggested that both sides scrap all offensive missiles within ten years. Gorbachev saw Reagan's bid and raised him: Why not get rid of *all* strategic weapons, he asked.[60] It was a breathtaking offer. It went far beyond anything ever proposed, ever even imagined, in the entire history of arms-control negotiations between the United States and USSR. But there was a condition: the United States would have to agree not to continue work on the Strategic Defense Initiative.

Ronald Reagan could have the most successful summit in American history. He could sign the most far-reaching agreement ever with the Soviets. He could return home—just in time for the mid-term congressional elections—as the Peacemaker. All he had to do was give up SDI. He could explain to the American people that it had *always* been his intention to use SDI as "a bargaining chip" and that he had held out for the best agreement the United States had ever won.

He would not do it. He had eerily described this scene fully ten years earlier. In 1976, he told his son Michael that he was not so sorry he had lost the Republican nomination for president. His only regret was now he would never have the chance to hear out a Soviet ruler's arms control demands. These demands would surely have left the free countries at a disadvantage. Then, Reagan said, he would quietly walk around the table and whisper *nyet.* Here, that scene, exactly as Reagan had described it, was being played out. And as president, Ronald Reagan whispered *nyet.*

With hopes dashed, the two unsmiling leaders left Höfdi House. "I don't know what else I could have done," Gorbachev told Reagan through an interpreter as they parted. "You could have said yes," Reagan answered with uncharacteristic bitterness. At the time, Reykjavik seemed to be a failed summit. In the off-year elections of 1986, the Republicans lost control of the Senate. For the rest of Reagan's term, he would face an increasingly fractious Congress.

VI. Iran-Contra

"Do whatever you have to do to keep the Contras alive," President Reagan had told his National Security Staff.[61] Gung-ho figures like Admiral John

Poindexter and Marine lieutenant colonel Oliver North were prepared to carry out that order.

Reagan wanted to help the Contras weather the seesawing efforts in Congress to cut off their funding. Liberals were determined to avoid a Vietnam in this hemisphere. They made repeated runs at defunding the Contras, occasionally succeeding in passing amendments to appropriations bills. Congressman Eddie Boland, a Democrat from Massachusetts, offered an amendment that prevented U.S. intelligence agencies from seeking to overthrow the government of Nicaragua. The Reagan administration narrowly interpreted this amendment as applying to the Central Intelligence Agency and the Defense Intelligence Agency, but not to the National Security Council where Poindexter and North worked. They were deemed free to seek outside support for the Contras. "Ollie" North was thus left free to solicit funds from such anti-Communist stalwarts as the Sultan of Brunei.

Beirut came back to haunt the administration. The Marines and Navy Corpsmen who died in 1982 were deeply mourned in the Reagan White House. CIA Station Chief William Buckley had been kidnapped, tortured, and murdered by Hezbollah terrorists. So had Navy diver Bobby Stethem. Reagan anguished over these deaths. George Will says this was "the soft side of Ronald Reagan." He was incapable of putting these American captives out of his mind and regarding them as casualties of war.[62] Reagan had spoken wistfully of the days when an American had only to put an American flag in his lapel to be able to walk safely anywhere in the world. He yearned to intervene on behalf of endangered Americans—especially those who were serving the United States.

Reagan was persuaded that there were "moderates" in Iran. These moderates were jockeying for power in a post-Ayatollah Khomeini regime. They said they wanted better relations with the United States But they would be strong-armed out of power unless they could buy weapons. If they were armed, they claimed they could influence the hostage takers in Beirut.

Thus was born the fateful linkage between the sale of arms to Iran, the ransoming of hostages in Beirut, and the diversion of profits from the arms sales to support the Nicaraguan Contras.

What is so clear to critics now was not so clear then. Americans have repeatedly joined civilized nations all over the world in negotiating for the release of hostages held in the Middle East. Hostage-taking and ransom demands are a highly developed art in the Mideast. As long ago as the eighteenth century, no lesser figures than President Washington and President Adams became involved in paying for the release of American sailors held captive in North Africa. They did it because the Europeans did it. Jefferson determined to use force rather than pay ransom. He sent U.S. warships and Marines "to the shores of Tripoli."

The day before the 1986 mid-term elections in the United States, a Beirut newspaper reported that the United States was involved in paying for the release of hostages. Initially, the Reagan White House dismissed the notion as ridiculous. When White House chief of staff Donald Regan first informed President Reagan that the profits from arms sales were being diverted to support the Contras, Reagan became pale. "Why would they do that?" he asked, apparently forgetting his orders to Poindexter and North.[63]

Iran-Contra, as the burgeoning scandal was soon known, erupted. Reagan was described in the press as culpable if he was aware—and thus liable to impeachment. Or, if he really did not know what his subordinates were doing, then he was clearly disengaged. The famous Reagan management style was to sketch the broad outlines of policy in clearly communicated terms and then let his subordinates handle the details. This style had been highly successful in the first term. Now, especially with Donald Regan making many of the day-to-day decisions himself, Reagan's hands-off management style was seen as a failure.

Reagan appointed former senator John Tower of Texas to investigate Iran-Contra. Admiral Poindexter testified that he had *not* told the president of the diversion of funds.[64] CIA director William Casey had played a key role in Reagan's foreign policy. Casey was an old hand at intelligence. During World War II, he had served in the OSS. He had followed Churchill's order to "set Europe ablaze" against Hitler. A genuine patriot, a man of deep religious faith, Casey flew around the world in the 1980s in his unmarked black jet transport. He orchestrated the Reagan administration's global squeeze on the hard-pressed Soviet Union. Casey doubtless knew a great deal about Iran-Contra, but he suffered a debilitating stroke in November 1986 and died in May 1987. This man who kept the secrets may have taken many of them to his grave. With Casey's death and Poindexter's testimony, the possibility of a Reagan impeachment lost steam. Liberals were visibly disappointed. At the height of the media firestorm, *Washington Post* editor Ben Bradlee exulted, "I haven't had so much fun since Watergate."

President Reagan suffered a loss of twenty points in his approval rating by the American people. He was dispirited. When he finally agreed to fire Chief of Staff Donald Regan, he did not realize how close he was himself to being deposed. Regan's departing assistants told staffers for the incoming White House chief of staff, Howard Baker, that Reagan was incapacitated. Baker should be prepared, they said, to invoke the Twenty-fifth Amendment to the Constitution. Reagan was too old, too forgetful, too passive to serve in the nuclear age.[65]

On arriving for work, former senator Baker stationed various staff members at different points in the Cabinet Room. Their assigned task was to observe closely how the president interacted with others.

They found Reagan stimulated by the new faces, fully engaged, and with a total grasp of the issues at hand. The president rose to the occasion. He may never have known he was being measured for a political casket when he gamely refused to die. Senator Baker concluded that he was "fully competent" and the crisis passed.[66] When the president went on national television to take responsibility for Iran-Contra, his approval rating buoyed up once again.*

VII. "Tear Down This Wall!"

Reagan was scheduled to visit West Germany again in June 1987. He wanted to speak there as part of Berlin's 750th anniversary celebration. Less interested in history, the media were obsessed with Iran-Contra. Commentators spoke of Reagan as a "lame duck."** There was a sense that his trip to Europe was merely an effort to avoid the political heat at home.

* This author had encouraged the president to take this course that day.

** Formally, a "lame duck" officeholder is one who is retiring or who has been defeated but who is still serving out his term. More recently, a lame duck is any politician the media is tired of.

The president was determined to make a strong statement about divided Berlin. Nothing could be worse, the State Department thought. Prepping for the president's trip in May 1987, White House speechwriter Peter Robinson traveled to the divided city and met with John Kornblum, the top U.S. diplomat in West Berlin. Don't bash the Soviets, Kornblum counseled. Don't come off as a "cowboy." And whatever you do, don't mention the Berlin Wall. Berliners, Kornblum advised, are worldly, sophisticated, and left-wing. And besides, they've grown *used* to the Berlin Wall.[67]

Robinson listened carefully. Then he took a ride in a U.S. Army helicopter.

The sixty-mile-long wall didn't just separate a city, Robinson later wrote, but "separated two different modes of existence. On one side . . . lay movement, color, modern architecture, crowded sidewalks, traffic. On the other side, all was drab."[68] In East Berlin, buildings still showed evidence of bomb and bullet damage from World War II. In 1987, the war had been over for forty-two years. Two hundred fifty people had been killed by East German border guards since the wall went up in 1961.[69]

That evening, Robinson went to a dinner party hosted by Dieter and Ingeborg Etz. Herr Etz had lived in Washington when he worked at the World Bank and Frau Etz taught German language at Georgetown Prep in suburban Bethesda, Maryland.[70] Emboldened by his helicopter ride, Robinson asked his hosts and their German guests if West Berliners had, as he had been told, "gotten used to the Wall."

The dinner party became very quiet. Robinson thought he'd committed a faux pas even asking the question.[71] Then, one of the German men looked very serious and said: "My sister lives twenty miles in that direction. I have not seen her in more than two decades. Do you think I can get used to that?"[72] Another German described his morning walk to work, past a guard tower where a soldier—always the same soldier—stares at him through binoculars. "That soldier and I speak the same language. We share the same history. But one of us is a zookeeper and the other is an animal, and I'm never certain which one is which."[73] Finally, Ingeborg Etz broke in, her face reddening. She pounded a fist into her palm and said: "If this man Gorbachev is serious with his talk of *glasnost* [openness] and *perestroika* [restructuring], he can prove it. He can get rid of this wall!"[74]*

Returning to Washington, Peter Robinson was determined to put a line in the president's speech about the Berlin Wall. But it would not be easy. Robinson put in a line urging General Secretary Gorbachev to tear down the wall. Robinson met in the Oval Office with Reagan and the speechwriting team. Robinson told the president that the speech would be heard on radio, not just in West Berlin, but in East Berlin, East Germany and as far away as Moscow.[75] "That wall has to come down," Reagan reiterated. "That's what I'd like to say to them."[76]

The State Department, the National Security Council, even Secretary of State George Schultz all weighed in *against* putting that line in the president's speech.

Grudgingly, they suggested that Reagan might say something vague, like "some day this ugly wall will disappear." Some day?

Reagan knew the western media was swooning over Mikhail Gorbachev. He also knew something about upstaging a rival. If Gorbachev really meant *openness,* he could start by opening the Brandenburg Gate.

> General Secretary Gorbachev, if you seek peace, if you seek prosperity for the Soviet Union and Eastern Europe, if you seek liberalization: Come here to this gate! Mr. Gorbachev, open this gate! Mr. Gorbachev, tear down this wall!

Though Reagan's speech at the Brandenburg Gate stands today as one of history's great speeches, at the time, the American press paid little attention. It seemed almost rude to mention Gorbachev's connection to the Iron Curtain. There was far more interest in the Senate's Iran-Contra hearings. But the drive to criminalize policy differences was dealt a serious blow when Colonel Oliver North used his testimony before the committee to vigorously defend his actions. Appearing ramrod straight in full uniform, with a chestful of combat

---

* The story of Ingeborg Etz and her role in Reagan's historic speech has been related by Peter Robinson and by Dr. Stephen J. Ochs, history instructor at Georgetown Prep. Ochs taught both the author's sons.

ribbons, North thrilled the country. "Olliemania" swept the land.[77] Not only did he not repent, he intimidated and flummoxed committee members. Even North's attorney, the redoubtable Brendan Sullivan, managed to back down the committee. When one senator tried to elicit a statement from witness North without advice of his counsel, Sullivan shot back irreverently: "I'm not a potted plant!"

The summer of 1987 also saw a great fight over a vacancy on the U.S. Supreme Court.

President Reagan had named the first woman to the high court. Justice Sandra Day O'Connor was a keen disappointment to the president's conservative backers. They were happier when he elevated Associate Justice William Rehnquist to Chief Justice and named Federal Judge Antonin Scalia to fill the Rehnquist vacancy in 1986. Of course, all three of those nominations had been made while the Republicans controlled the Senate.

Reagan's opponents, led once again by Senator Kennedy, were determined to deny him his choice of Supreme Court justices. When Reagan named the controversial Federal Judge Robert Bork, Kennedy lit up the Capitol with his impassioned rhetoric. "In Robert Bork's America," Kennedy roared, women would have to resort to back-alley abortions. Even worse, he claimed, "In Robert Bork's America . . . blacks would sit at segregated lunch counters; rogue police would break down citizens' doors in midnight raids."[78]

Never before had a Supreme Court nomination been made the subject of such a vast, well-financed public campaign of vilification and character assassination. Lifelong friends of the scholarly, bearded former Yale law professor could not recognize the devil figure Kennedy had created. The idea of a single member of the Supreme Court having the power Kennedy conjured was ridiculous on its face, but Bork's opponents would stop at nothing to discredit the witty, learned man. Liberal activists who had virtually invented the constitutional doctrine of privacy found nothing wrong with invading the judge's privacy; even records of his video rentals were gone over for evidence to use against him. (The judge, it seemed, had a predilection for Broadway musicals.)

On 17 September 1987, the day of the Bicentennial of the U.S. Constitution, Bork had to endure being grilled by Senator Kennedy before the Judiciary Committee. Kennedy asked the judge hostile questions about his ruling in an interstate trucking decision.*

In a gross violation of the Constitution's provisions on a religious test, Judge Bork was asked by Alabama's Democratic Senator, Howell Heflin, to discuss his religious beliefs—under oath. Robert Bork, then a conventional Protestant, had married a Jewish woman. Following her death from cancer after a long and devoted marriage, Bork had married a former Catholic nun. If ever a man had demonstrated his complete lack of religious bigotry, it was Robert Bork. The mere asking of such a question directly violated the Constitution's prohibition. Had the committee chairman, Senator Joseph Biden, a Democrat from Delaware, cared about fairness, he would instantly have ruled the question out of order.**

Bork was rejected 58–42 by the Senate. This entire ugly and discreditable episode was dragooned by Edward M. Kennedy. The country's politics and jurisprudence continue to be poisoned by the dishonorable methods used in that Bicentennial summer of 1987 by Robert Bork's opponents.

VIII. Into the Sunset

Ronald Reagan was by far the oldest president to serve. He had survived a serious assassination attempt, colon cancer, and skin cancer. Politically, he had survived the loss of control of Congress and an international arms-for-hostages scandal that threatened to result in his impeachment. The stock market had crashed dizzily in October 1987, sending shock waves through financial markets, but it soon rebounded. The prestige press emphasized every political embarrassment and hyped such issues as homelessness and income disparity as crises that the administration was unwilling or unable to handle.

Still, the economy continued to boom, generating millions of new jobs.

---

* One wag at the time suggested that it was the judge who should be arraigning the Senator from Chappaquiddick on *his* driving safety record.

** Article VI, Section 3 of the Constitution says, "[B]ut no religious test shall ever be required as a qualification to any office or public trust under the United States." Heflin's improper grilling of Judge Bork may have been the most public and flagrant flouting of this vital constitutional provision.

Tax revenues doubled on Reagan's watch—a tribute to the success of supply side economics.[79] Still his critics didn't call it *Reaganomics.*

When Mikhail Gorbachev came to Washington, D.C., in December 1987, the press delighted in showing him wading into lunchtime crowds on the capital's fashionable Connecticut Avenue. His obvious boyish delight in mixing with Americans on the streets reminded some of the popular movie of the day—*Ferris Bueller's Day Off.* It would have seemed churlish to point out that half a billion people held at bayonet point under Soviet rule had no similar freedom of movement.

So, too, was Reagan determined to break through the "bubble" that protected him and get a real sense of the Russian people. Unexpectedly, in 1988, the president and Mrs. Reagan got out of their limousine to walk around Moscow's famed Arbat district. The Russian crowd responded with delight. The Arbat is a district known for its greater commercial and artistic freedom. Very quickly, however, the KGB muscled its way into the friendly crowd, pushing, punching, manhandling the Reagans' admirers.[80] They kicked and shoved everyone, including American reporters. "Leave them alone, these are Americans," cried Reagan White House staffer Mark Weinberg. Reagan recorded in his diary that night his reaction to the Soviets' brutalizing their own people: "Perestroika or not, some things have not changed."[81]

Despite all the surface bonhomie, Gorbachev was miffed that Reagan persisted in calling him "Mikhail." If he knew anything about Russian ways, he would have known to call him *Mikhail Sergeivich,* the Soviet ruler told his friends.[82]

The tensions were broken somewhat when presidential biographer Edmund Morris sat with two Soviet intellectuals at a formal lunch at the Writers House. Felix Kuznetsov, the head of the Gorky Institute, pointed out a reporter behind the velvet rope. "Who is that man . . . staring at us with such malevolence?" the fearful Soviet asked. "Don't worry about Sam Donaldson," Morris replied, explaining that the ABC News reporter was "a thorn in the President's flesh." Kuznetsov did not recognize the biblical expression. When it was explained to him, he said the Russian phrase was better. The Russians would call Sam Donaldson "a splinter in the president's ass," Kuznetsov said.[83]

Reagan, politically weakened and consigned by the political pundits to "lame duck" status, signed an Intermediate Nuclear Forces (INF) agreement with Gorbachev. Under the terms of the agreement, the United States would remove the Pershing II missiles Carter had promised NATO as a counterweight to the placement of Soviet SS-19 and SS-20 missiles in Eastern Europe. INF was the Zero Option that Reagan had proposed in 1983. The mere suggestion of this Zero Option had caused the Soviets to react with outrage. In protest, the Soviet Delegation walked out of arms control talks at Geneva. For that portion of the Western intelligentsia that sees arms control as an indicator of East-West relations, this Soviet move had spread panic. Nuclear war—with its attendant horrors of megadeaths and nuclear winter—loomed before them. Terrified, Western anti-war demonstrators rallied in their millions to demand a nuclear freeze. Reagan had held firm.

Now, Gorbachev was coming to him *and on his terms.* As Churchill might have said: "Some lameness! Some Duck!" All previous arms control agreements had merely sought to slow the rate of growth of weapons systems. This was the first agreement that actually *reduced* the number of offensive nuclear weapons.

If Reagan's historic achievement was not appreciated by his opponents in the United States, it had many in his own party muttering. The eminent columnist George Will was one of the most highly respected "adults" in the Washington press corps. Will lamented that Reagan had "bought into the arms control *chimera.*"[84] The longtime conservative activist Howard Philips called the president "a useful idiot."[85]* "Let Reagan be Reagan," conservative grassroots began to cry.

But Reagan was being Reagan. He had always had a horror of nuclear warfare. He had always said that the United States must negotiate out of strength. He was now putting into practice those eloquent words from John F. Kennedy's Inaugural addres: "Let us never negotiate out of fear. But let us never fear to negotiate."

* This was an especially cruel taunt. "Useful idiot" was the term Lenin had used for credulous Western businessmen like Armand Hammer who helped build up the Soviet Communist state. "How will we hang the Capitalists," asked one of Lenin's Bolshevik comrades, "we don't have enough rope!" "They will sell it to us—on credit," Lenin famously replied.

Reagan's skilful negotiating strategy paid off. Following the Soviets' withdrawal from Afghanistan, Reagan visited Moscow in late May 1988.* While press attention at home was focused overwhelmingly on the upcoming presidential campaign, Reagan pressed on, carrying his appeal for freedom to the heart of the Soviet Empire.

The pressures unleashed by Gorbachev's perestroika continued to build. The 1986 meltdown of a nuclear power plant at Chernobyl, in the Ukraine, had caused thousands of deaths. The Soviet state was shown to be corrupt, inefficient, and heedless of human life. The environmental impact of Communist rule was seen to be nothing less than catastrophic.

Now, Reagan stood in the resplendent St. George's Hall in the Kremlin. He responded to a formal welcoming speech from Gorbachev. There, amid the gold and crystal and rich tapestries of the Tsars—and among the paintings of saints—Reagan looked steadily at the General Secretary of the Communist Party of the Soviet Union and said, "God *bless* you." It was the first time the name of God had been uttered aloud in that place in seventy years. And it was heard by every citizen across twelve times zones of the Soviet Union.

Some of the Communist leaders who heard these words "visibly blanched." A Soviet diplomat later recalled the moment: "The . . . impregnable edifice of Communist atheism was being assaulted *before* [our] *very eyes.*"[86]

Reagan insisted on meeting with Jewish refuseniks. When one of them was denied permission to visit the U.S. Embassy, Reagan told his Soviet hosts he would go to the man's apartment. Embarrassed, the KGB backed down. Reagan invited hundreds of religious believers to a reception at Spaso House.[87] He stressed the need for religious freedom to be part of any meaningful perestroika.

Invited to address students at Moscow State University, Reagan leaped at the chance to talk to the sons and daughters of the Soviet ruling class—the *nomenklatura.* He praised "the first breath of freedom" they had seen in

---

* After the Fall of Communism, this author informally polled top Reagan defense officials. Asked what single thing led to the collapse of the Soviet system, they answered most frequently: Stingers—those mobile, shoulder-fired missiles the Afghan *Mujahaddin* used to deadly effect against the Soviet invaders.

this "Moscow Spring." These knowledgeable young students could not miss his reference. Many of their parents had had their hopes for a relaxation of tyranny in the Eastern bloc dashed when Soviet tanks rolled into Czechoslovakia in 1968. That was the brutal end of the "Prague Spring."

Now, standing under a huge, scowling bust of Lenin, Reagan patiently laid out the case for freedom in the information age. Marx was wrong to see materialism at the center of human existence, he said. The new computer revolution was powered by the silicon chip—whose material basis was the same as the most plentiful substance on earth—sand. In order for a state to compete in the modern world, though, the computer revolution demanded free minds. No state could enjoy progress when every fax machine, every photocopier, every computer hard drive had to be controlled by the secret police.

He returned again and again to the spiritual basis of freedom. To these young people who had been schooled in atheist materialism from kindergarten, he boldly proclaimed:

> Even as we explore the most advanced reaches of science, we are returning to the age-old wisdom of our culture, a wisdom contained in the Book of Genesis in the Bible. In the beginning was the spirit, and it was from this spirit that the material abundance of creation issued forth. But progress is not foreordained. The key is freedom—freedom of thought, freedom of information, freedom of communication.

He ended his address with an appeal to these future leaders of Russia:

> We do not know what the conclusion of this journey will be, but we're hopeful that the promise of reform will be fulfilled. In this Moscow spring, this May 1988, we may be allowed that hope—that freedom, like the fresh green sapling planted over Tolstoi's grave, will blossom forth at least in the rich fertile soil of your people and culture. We may be allowed to hope that the marvelous sound of a new openness will keep rising through, ringing through, leading to a new world of reconciliation, friendship, and peace.

Thank you all very much and *da blagoslovit vas gospod*! God bless you.[88]

As Reagan departed the Soviet Union, he gave the first nationally televised address to the Soviet people. He had been prepped by America's leading Russian scholar, James Billington. Reagan reached out to the *babushkas* (grandmothers). These aged women were the true spiritual leaders of Mother Russia, Billington said. Reagan praised them—and blessed them.

There would be no Appomattox, 1865, or Surrender Ceremony on board the USS *Missouri,* 1945, to mark the end of the Cold War. If we search for the defining moment when the USSR ceased to threaten the life and liberty of the world, it might be seen at Reykjavik. Secretary of State George Schultz thought this was the turning point. So did Mikhail Gorbachev.* Although the press in 1986 lamented the "failure" to sign an arms control agreement, Gorbachev noted that it was the first time they had engaged in deep discussions on the future of nuclear weapons and the future of the Super Power relationship.[89]

But even without tens of thousands of nuclear tipped missiles, the Soviet Union could still be a deadly menace. The massive preponderance of Soviet troops and tanks was the reason the Western democracies had sought protection under their "nuclear umbrella" from the earliest days of the Cold War. Margaret Thatcher knew this. She worried that Reagan and Gorbachev would be carried away by their nuclear-arms-cutting enthusiasms and forget the threat of Soviet conventional armed strength.[90] With her keen sense of history, with her passion for freedom in Europe, she was a true heir of Winston Churchill. There could be no secure peace in which the United States abandoned its truest ally.

If therefore, we seek that defining moment when the Cold War ended, we might look to New York harbor on 7 December 1988. Mikhail Gorbachev had just delivered his speech to the UN General Assembly. In it, the Soviet ruler announced massive cuts in *conventional armed forces in Europe.* He

* Reagan's friend Charles Z. Wich congradulated him on the plane ride home. "You just won the Cold War," Wich said. (Source: http://nrd.nationalreview.com/article/?q,13 February 2007.)

would cut his troop strength by 500,000 men, his tanks divisions by a quarter, and his combat aircraft by 500. Now, Mrs. Thatcher could affirm the course of human events.[91]

President Reagan and President-elect George H.W. Bush awaited their Soviet guest on Governors Island, just south of Manhattan Island. Reagan strongly approved of Gorbachev's speech to the UN that morning. Reagan had always said there was not distrust in the world because there are arms; there are arms because there is distrust. Now, Reagan and his designated successor welcomed the Soviet initiative. To be sure, the *need* to cut his conventional forces was forced on Gorbachev in no small measure by the internal failings of Communism and by the economic pressure that Reagan had been applying since the day he came to office. Ronald Reagan had planted his flag and now Gorbachev was coming to him.

The worldwide Communist system had made a charnel house of the twentieth century. Fully 100 million people had been killed by Communism.[92] The red flag never brought any of its chained peoples closer to peace, justice or equality. Gorbachev seemed to understand this—at least at some level. While claiming all along to be a loyal Communist, Gorbachev reveled in the greater freedom he saw in the West. The Soviet rulers had come in their grim succession—Lenin, Stalin, Khrushchev, Brezhnev, Andropov, Chernenko. But Gorbachev was different—and not just because as Reagan joked that he weighed more than his wife. He was the first Soviet ruler with whom we could speak about peace with freedom, peace with safety, peace with justice. He was the Soviet ruler who had not waded through blood in his path to power.

As Mikhail Sergeivich Gorbachev left the United Nations headquarters at Turtle Bay, he would have proceeded south along FDR Drive to South Ferry. His limo swept him past Wall Street, the dynamo of America's powerful free market economy. There, George Washington had taken the oath of office as the first elected president nearly two centuries before Gorbachev's arrival. There George Washington had kissed the Bible.

The Communist Party's general secretary would embark for Governors Island at the ferry terminal, in the shadow of the World Trade Center. As it plowed its way ponderously across the narrow divide that separates Governors Island from Manhattan, the ferry would take just five or six minutes to carry the distinguished Soviet visitor to his meeting with two American presidents. During the short trip, Gorbachev would have a commanding view of New York harbor. He would have time to think about that Lady in the Harbor—Lady Liberty. He would see Ellis Island, where millions had come, yearning to breathe free. Here they found America, the last best hope of earth.

That white, squat, lumbering Coast Guard ferry was the furthest thing we might imagine from the power and pomp of that 1945 surrender ceremony aboard the USS *Missouri.* There would be no surrender in the Cold War. But there would be something better. On that chilly day in New York harbor, peace glided into that ferry slip, quietly, almost unannounced, almost unperceived. Not bad, as Reagan would say—not bad at all.

Epilogue

A Personal Reflection

As I write this, the United States of America is at war. It is a war whose means and ends have become controversial, but it is a war for our very existence nonetheless. And yet I close on the high-note of the presidency of Ronald Wilson Reagan. I have three reasons for doing this.

First, it is no secret that I am a great admirer of Ronald Reagan. He was my first government employer, a mentor, and a friend.

Second, in looking back over the past two decades, I cannot find the right words yet to dispassionately describe the relevant history of what we have gone through since his presidency ended. This is not because of my partisan or ideological convictions. Rather, it is because I believe more time needs to pass for us to fully and completely digest the history of the past two decades. Many of the players and actors of the past twenty years are still alive, and I wish to be fair to the times and root out any possible prejudice occasioned by my own association with the actors in this drama.

But the third reason for ending with Ronald Reagan is the most important. Reagan was an amateur historian who spoke often about our own history and what future generations would inherit of and in America. Those questions were always on his mind.

Readers of Volume I of this project will recall Reagan's final speech as our fortieth president, where he warned of "an eradication of the American memory that could result, ultimately, in an erosion of the American spirit." We suffer from too much of that today. It is sad but true that American students know less about American history than any other subject they study.

And yet we are a resilient people, caretakers of a blessed nation. It has become a commonplace that we always rise to the occasion in this country. That is still true. And we surprise ourselves, never knowing with exact certainty from whence our next leader or hero will come—good reason to respect and defend one another as Americans, as fellow countrymen dedicated to a great proposition.

Allow me a few simple illustrations. If you were sitting in a saloon in 1860, and someone told you that while he did not know who would win that year's presidential election, the next elected president after him was right then a little known leather tanner in Galena, Illinois, he would be laughed out of the saloon. But then came Ulysses S. Grant. If you were sitting at Franklin D. Roosevelt's inauguation, in 1933, and someone told you the next president was a little-known judge in Jackson County, Missouri, he would have been made to look the fool. But then came Harry S Truman. If you were a political consultant in California in 1950 watching the bitter Senate race between Richard Nixon and Helen Gahagan Douglas (where Nixon labeled Douglas "the pink lady"), and you said that actor Ronald Reagan (who was then campaigning *for* Douglas) would someday be a Republican president and would crush the Soviet Union, your career would have been over.

As I wrote in the Introduction, we Americans have a knack for choosing rightly, just when we need to choose rightly. This has been true of our Lincolns, our Roosevelts, our Trumans, our Reagans, and so many others—from soldiers, to generals, to heroes in every walk of life, in every city in America.

As early as 1974, Ronald Reagan was already thinking about our history and our timeless mission. He concluded a major address, then, when Americans were not feeling too good about their country or their institutions, saying,

> We are not a sick society. A sick society could not produce the men that set foot on the moon, or who are now circling the earth above us in the Skylab. A sick society bereft of morality and courage did not produce the men who went through those years of torture and captivity in Vietnam. Where did we find such men? They are typical of this

> land as the Founding Fathers were typical. We found them in our streets, in the offices, the shops and the working places of our country and on the farms.
>
> We cannot escape our destiny, nor should we try to do so. The leadership of the free world was thrust upon us two centuries ago in that little hall of Philadelphia. In the days following World War II, when the economic strength and power of America was all that stood between the world and the return to the dark ages, Pope Pius XII said, "The American people have a great genius for splendid and unselfish actions. Into the hands of America God has placed the destinies of an afflicted mankind."
>
> We are indeed, and we are today, the last best hope of man on earth.

Indeed we are.

That is the thesis and the conclusion of my project here. I would like to think it is a thesis all of us can take to heart—whether we are immigrants or natural born citizens; whether we are Democrats, Republicans, or Independents; whether we are governors or the governed. Each and every one has played a role in making this country, after all, and it is each and every one of us who is given the task to keep it.

Notes

CHAPTER ONE:
America and the Great War (1914–1921)

1. Massie, Robert K., *Dreadnought*, Random House: 1991, 110.
2. Massie, *Dreadnought*, 128–129.
3. Online source:
http://www.ibiblio.org/HTMLTexts/Albert_Frederick_Pollard/A_Short_History_Of_The_Great_War/chapter01.html.
4. Bailey, Thomas Andrew, *A Diplomatic History of the American People*, Prentice-Hall: 1980, 501.
5. Gilbert, Martin, *A History of the Twentieth Century: Volume One, 1900–1933*, William Morrow and Company, Inc.: 1997, 25.
6. Martel, Gordon, *The Origins of the First World War*, Longman: 1996, 85.
7. Chesterton, G. K., "The Case Against Corruption," *Collected Works of G.K. Chesterton*, Vol. 16, IgnatiusPress: 1986, 200–01.
8. Remak, Joachim, *The Origins of World War I: 1871–1914*, Harcourt Brace College Publishers: 1995, 138.
9. Remak, 138.
10. Gilbert, *A History of the Twentieth Century: Volume One*, 19.
11. Gilbert, *A History of the Twentieth Century: Volume One*, 19.
12. Gilbert, *A History of the Twentieth Century: Volume One*, 26.
13. Gilbert, *A History of the Twentieth Century: Volume One*, 26.
14. Gilbert, *A History of the Twentieth Century: Volume One*, 23.
15. Gilbert, *A History of the Twentieth Century: Volume One*, 25.
16. Keegan, John, *An Illustrated History of the First World War*, Hutchinson: 2001, 65.
17. Keegan, 71.
18. Keegan, 74.
19. Keegan, 74.
20. Keegan, 103.
21. Keegan, 100–101.
22. Keegan, 119.
23. Leckie, Robert, *The Wars of America*, Harper & Row: 1981, 599.

24. Leckie, 599.
25. Morison, Samuel Eliot, *The Oxford History of the American People, Volume Three: 1869 Through the Death of President Kennedy, 1963*, Penguin, New York: 1965, 171.
26. Bailey, 555.
27. Morison, *The Oxford History of the American People, Volume Three*, 171.
28. Morison, *The Oxford History of the American People, Volume Three*, 172.
29. Massie, Robert K., *Castles of Steel: Britain, Germany and the Winning of the Great War at Sea*, Random House: 2003, 530.
30. Massie, *Castles*, 530.
31. Massie, *Castles*, 532.
32. Massie, *Castles*, 532.
33. Massie, *Castles*, 534.
34. Morison, *The Oxford History of the American People, Volume Three*, 179.
35. Massie, *Castles*, 535.
36. Black, Conrad, *Franklin D. Roosevelt: Champion of Freedom*, Public Affairs: 2003, 73.
37. Massie, *Castles*, 541.
38. Bailey, 578.
39. Black, 74.
40. Bailey, 579.
41. Brands, H.W., *Woodrow Wilson*, Henry Holt and Company: 2003, 65.
42. Brands, *Woodrow Wilson*, 65.
43. Brands, *Woodrow Wilson*, 65.
44. Bailey, 564.
45. Brands, *Woodrow Wilson*, 71.
46. Brands, *Woodrow Wilson*, 32.
47. Brands, *Woodrow Wilson*, 29.
48. Brands, *Woodrow Wilson*, 27.
49. Brands, *Woodrow Wilson*, 27.
50. Keegan, 176.
51. Gilbert, Martin, *A History of the Twentieth Century: Volume One*, 457.
52. Tuchman, Barbara W., *The Zimmermann Telegram*, The Macmillan Company: 1966, 172.
53. Black, 77.
54. Morison, *The Oxford History of the American People, Volume Three*, 183.
55. Black, 77.
56. Bailey, 588.
57. Online source: http://homepage.eircom.net/~seanjmurphy/irhismys/casement.htm.
58. Morison, *The Oxford History of the American People, Volume Three*, 183.
59. Morison, *The Oxford History of the American People, Volume Three*, 183.
60. Tuchman, 4.
61. Tuchman, 23.
62. Keegan, 351.
63. Tuchman, 40.
64. Morison, *The Oxford History of the American People, Volume Three*, 217.
65. Renehan, Edward J., *The Lion's Pride: Theodore Roosevelt and his Family in Peace and War*, Oxford University Press, New York, 1998, 125.
66. Tuchman, 181.
67. Tuchman, 181, 185.
68. Tuchman, 14.

69. Tuchman, 183.
70. Tuchman, 184.
71. Tuchman, 184–186.
72. Tuchman, 187.
73. Heckscher, August, *Woodrow Wilson*, Scribner: 1991, 440.
74. Heckscher, 441.
75. Morison, *The Oxford History of the American People, Volume Three*, 189.
76. Bailey, 593.
77. O'Toole, Patricia, *When Trumpets Call: Theodore Roosevelt After the White House*, Simon & Schuster: 2005, 310.
78. Black, 82.
79. Millard, Candice, *River of Doubt: Theodore Roosevelt's Darkest Journey*, Random House: 2005, 480.
80. Millard, 481.
81. Millard, 1.
82. Brands, *TR: The Last Romantic*, 743.
83. Brands, *Woodrow Wilson*, 6.
84. Brands, *Woodrow Wilson*, 6.
85. Brands, *Woodrow Wilson*, 7.
86. Brands, *TR: The Last Romantic*, 784.
87. Brands, *TR: The Last Romantic*, 783.
88. O'Toole, 310.
89. O'Toole, 310.
90. Brands, *TR: The Last Romantic*, 783.
91. O'Toole, 311.
92. Gilbert, *A History of the Twentieth Century: Volume One*, 461.
93. Gilbert, *A History of the Twentieth Century: Volume One*, 455.
94. Leckie, 634.
95. Bailey, 561.
96. Leckie, 625.
97. Morison, *The Oxford History of the American People, Volume Three*, 199.
98. Leckie, 635.
99. Keegan, 375.
100. Renehan, 160.
101. Leckie, 632.
102. Online source: http://www.loc.gov/exhibits/churchill/wc-affairs.html.
103. Heckscher, 466.
104. Morison, *The Oxford History of the American People, Volume Three*, 205.
105. Leckie, 641.
106. Leckie, 641.
107. Leckie, 641.
108. Morison, *The Oxford History of the American People, Volume Three*, 206.
109. Morison, *The Oxford History of the American People, Volume Three*, 206.
110. Morison, *The Oxford History of the American People, Volume Three*, 206.
111. Heckscher, 471.
112. Heckscher, 472.
113. Bailyn, Bernard, et al, *The Great Republic: A History of the American People*, Little & Brown: 1977, 1039.
114. Heckscher, 470.

115. Heckscher, 471.
116. Morison, *The Oxford History of the American People, Volume Three*, 192.
117. Morison, *The Oxford History of the American People, Volume Three*, 204.
118. Leckie, 653.
119. Renehan, 197.
120. Renehan, 197.
121. Renehan, 197.
122. Renehan, 200.
123. Renehan, 217.
124. Heckscher, 482.
125. Leckie, 654.
126. Bailey, 599.
127. Gilbert, *A History of the Twentieth Century: Volume One*, 520.
128. Keegan, 395.
129. Heckscher, 485.
130. Gould, Lewis L., *The Grand Old Party: A History of the Republicans*, Random House: 2003, 213.
131. Gould, 215.
132. Brands, *TR: The Last Romantic*, 809.
133. Brands, *Woodrow Wilson*, 102.
134. Renehan, 216.
135. Macmillan, Margaret, *Paris 1919: Six Months that Changed the World*, Random House: 2001, 319.
136. Gilbert, Martin, *The First World War: A Complete History*, Harold Holt and Company: 1994, 501.
137. Gilbert, *First World War*, 503.
138. Gilbert, *First World War*, 447.
139. Gilbert, *First World War*, 494.
140. Gilbert, *A History of the Twentieth Century: Volume One*, 534.
141. Gilbert, *First World War*, 503.
142. Brands, *Woodrow Wilson*, 103.
143. Brands, *Woodrow Wilson*, 103.
144. Gould, 217.
145. Ambrosius, Lloyd E., *Woodrow Wilson and the American Diplomatic Tradition: The Treaty Fight in Perspective*, Cambridge University Press: 1987, 82.
146. Ambrosius, 38.
147. Heckscher, 491.
148. Gilbert, *First World War*, 503.
149. Gilbert, *First World War*, 507.
150. Gilbert, *First World War*, 507.
151. Barry, John M., *The Great Influenza*, Viking: 2004, flyleaf.
152. Barry, 387.
153. Barry, 387.
154. Renehan, 218.
155. Brands, *TR: The Last Romantic*, 811.
156. O'Toole, Patricia, *When Trumpets Call: Theodore Roosevelt After the White House*, Simon & Schuster: 2004, 404.
157. Heckscher, 512.
158. Gilbert, Martin, *Churchill: A Life*, Henry Holt and Company: 1991, 403.

159. Gilbert, *Churchill: A Life*, 403.
160. Brands, *Woodrow Wilson*, 104.
161. Gilbert, *First World War*, 509.
162. Macmillan, 198.
163. Macmillan, 311.
164. Macmillan, 314.
165. Gould, 217.
166. Gould, 218.
167. Gould, 217.
168. Bailey, 606.
169. Heckscher, 545.
170. Heckscher, 546.
171. Will, George, "Can We Make Iraq Democratic?" City Journal, Winter 2004.
172. Will, George, "Can We Make Iraq Democratic?" City Journal, Winter 2004.
173. Hoover, Herbert, *The Ordeal of Woodrow Wilson*, McGraw-Hill Book Company, Inc.: 1958, 256.
174. Kissinger, Henry, *Diplomacy*, Simon & Schuster: 1994, 237.
175. Lentin, Antony, *Lloyd George and the Lost Peace, From Versailles to Hitler, 1919–1940*, St. Martin's Press: 2001, 48.
176. Brands, *TR: The Last Romantic*, 804.
177. Miller, Nathan, *Theodore Roosevelt: A Life*, William Morrow and Company, Inc.: 1972, 563.
178. Brands, *TR: The Last Romantic*, 805.
179. O'Toole, 403.
180. Gilbert, *First World War*, 517.
181. Macmillan, 476.
182. Mee, Charles L., Jr., *The End of Order: Versailles 1919*, E.P. Dutton: 1948, 215–216.
183. Mee, *The End of Order*, 216.
184. Mee, *The End of Order*, 216.
185. Bailey, Thomas A., *Woodrow Wilson and the Lost Peace*, The Macmillan Company: 1944, 302.
186. Gilbert, *First World War*, 541.
187. Macmillan, 469.
188. Churchill, Winston S., *The World Crisis, Volume IV*, Charles Scribner's Sons: 1927, 275–276.
189. Bailey, 609.
190. Macmillan, 467.
191. Black, 114.
192. Mee, *The End of Order*, 226.
193. Heckscher, 533.
194. Heckscher, 608.
195. Knock, Thomas J., *To End All Wars: Woodrow Wilson and the Quest for a New World Order*, Oxford University Press: 1992, 251.
196. Brands, *Woodrow Wilson*, 108.
197. Ambrosius, 48.
198. Ambrosius, 109; Stone, Ralph, *The Irreconcilables*, The University Press of Kentucky: 1970, 180.
199. Ambrosius, 88.
200. Ambrosius, 97.

201. Watt, Richard M., *The Kings Depart: The Tragedy of Germany, Versailles, and the German Revolution*, Simon and Schuster: 1968, 511.
202. Macmillan, 492.
203. Kissinger, *Diplomacy*, 234.
204. Hoover, 267.
205. Heckscher, 539.
206. Ambrosius, 164.
207. Bailey, *Woodrow Wilson and the Lost Peace*, 307–308.
208. Ambrosius, 83.
209. Ambrosius, 181.
210. Brands, *Woodrow Wilson*, 122.
211. Heckscher, 598.
212. Heckscher, 609–610.
213. Brands, *Woodrow Wilson*, 125.
214. Hoover, 276.
215. Witcover, Jules, *Party of the People: A History of the Democrats*, Random House: 2003, 330.
216. Brands, *Woodrow Wilson*, 126–127.
217. Stone, 162.
218. Egerton, George W., "Britain and the 'Great Betrayal': Anglo-American Relations and the Struggle for Ratification of the Treaty of Versailles, 1919–1920," the *Historical Journal*, 21, 4 (1978), 885–911.
219. Mee, *The End of Order*, 263.
220. Mee, *The End of Order*, 263.
221. Lentin, 146.
222. Black, 77.
223. Morison, *The Oxford History of the American People, Volume Three*, 217.
224. Heckscher, 632.
225. Bailey, Thomas A., *Woodrow Wilson and the Great Betrayal*, The Macmillan Company: 1945, 344.
226. Morison, *The Oxford History of the American People, Volume Three*, 219.
227. Bailey, *Woodrow Wilson and the Great Betrayal*, 344.
228. Mee, *The End of Order*, 263.
229. Watt, 513.
230. Watt, 512.
231. Watt, 512.
232. Heckscher, 628.
233. Heckscher, 628–629.

CHAPTER TWO:
The Boom and the Bust (1921–1933)

1. Online source: http://encarta.msn.com/related_761569981_59.129/World_War_I_We_drove_the_Boche_across.html.
2. Online source: http://www.archives.gov/digital_classroom/lessons/woman_suffrage/woman_suffrage.html.

3. Kramer, Hilton, "Who Reads Mencken Now?" Online source: http://www.newcriterion.com/archive/21/jan03/mencken.htm.
4. Weigel, George, "God, Man, and H.L. Mencken," *First Things* vol. 53, May 1995, 50–59.
5. Weigel, 50–59.
6. Weigel, 50–59.
7. Black, Conrad, *Franklin D. Roosevelt: Champion of Freedom*, Public Affairs: 2003, 137.
8. Black, 139.
9. Black, 138–139.
10. Black, 143.
11. Alter, Jonathan, *The Defining Moment: FDR's Hundred Days and the Triumph of Hope*, New York: 2006, 83.
12. Black, 141.
13. Black, 141.
14. Black, 161.
15. Black, 146.
16. Black, 146.
17. Black, 171.
18. Black, 171.
19. Black, 171.
20. Black, 171.
21. Black, 171.
22. Black, 170.
23. Black, 143.
24. Perret, Geoffrey, *Eisenhower*, Random House: 1999, 239.
25. Marks, Carole, and Diana Edkins, *The Power of Pride: Stylemakers and Rulebreakers of the Harlem Renaissance*, Crown Publishers, Inc.: 1999, 65.
26. Marks and Edkins, 65.
27. Marks and Edkins, 65.
28. Perret, 243.
29. Perret, 240.
30. Perret, 240.
31. Perret, 241.
32. Marks and Edkins, 65.
33. Marks and Edkins, 83.
34. Marks and Edkins, 100.
35. Marks and Edkins, 63.
36. "Harlem 1900–1940," Schomburg Exhibit Timeline. Online source: http://www.si.umich.edu/CHICO/Harlem/timex/timeline.html.
37. Gates, Henry Louis, Jr., and Cornel West, *The African-American Century: How Black Americans Have Shaped Our Country*, The Free Press: 2000, 131–132.
38. Gates and West, 100.
39. Gates and West, 100.
40. Perret, 244.
41. Perret, 245.
42. Perret, 244.
43. Morison, Samuel Eliot, *The Oxford History of the American People, Volume Three*, Oxford University Press: 1994, 260.
44. Morison, *The Oxford History of the American People, Volume Three*, 263.

45. Gilbert, Martin, *A History of the Twentieth Century: Volume One, 1900–1933*, William Morrow and Company, Inc.: 1997, 625.
46. Morison, *The Oxford History of the American People, Volume Three*, 263.
47. Morison, *The Oxford History of the American People, Volume Three*, 262.
48. Black, 162.
49. Morison, *The Oxford History of the American People, Volume Three*, 262.
50. Morison, *The Oxford History of the American People, Volume Three*, 277.
51. Morison, *The Oxford History of the American People, Volume Three*, 261.
52. Witcover, Jules, *Party of the People: A History of the Democrats*, Random House: 2003, 338.
53. Morison, *The Oxford History of the American People, Volume Three*, 261.
54. Morison, *The Oxford History of the American People, Volume Three*, 276.
55. Gould, Lewis L., *The Grand Old Party: A History of the Republicans*, Random House: 2003, 235.
56. Noonan, Peggy, "Why the Speech Will Live in Infamy," *TIME*, 31 August 1998.
57. Perret, 179.
58. Smith, Richard Norton, "The Price of the Presidency," *Yankee Magazine*, January, 1996.
59. Perret, 193.
60. Perret, 186.
61. Perret, 168.
62. Perret, 170.
63. Perret, 170.
64. Wallace, Max, *The American Axis: Henry Ford, Charles Lindbergh, and the Rise of the Third Reich*, St. Martin's Press: 2003, 95.
65. Wallace, 95.
66. Wallace, 96.
67. Wallace, 96.
68. Wallace, 96.
69. Perret, 256.
70. Perret, 256.
71. Perret, 260.
72. Perret, 260.
73. Wallace, 244–245.
74. Perret, 258.
75. Wallace, 97.
76. Linder, Douglas O., "The Leopold and Loeb Trial: A Brief Account." Online source: http://www.law.umkc.edu/faculty/projects/ftrials/leoploeb/Accountoftrial.html, 1997.
77. Linder, "The Leopold and Loeb Trial: A Brief Account."
78. Linder, "The Leopold and Loeb Trial: A Brief Account."
79. Linder, "The Leopold and Loeb Trial: A Brief Account."
80. Linder, "The Leopold and Loeb Trial: A Brief Account."
81. Linder, "The Leopold and Loeb Trial: A Brief Account."
82. Linder, "The Leopold and Loeb Trial: A Brief Account."
83. Gilbert, *A History of the Twentieth Century: Volume One*, 630.
84. Morison, *The Oxford History of the American People, Volume Three*, 237.
85. Witcover, 340.
86. Witcover, 340.
87. Witcover, 340.
88. Online source: http://encyclopedia.thefreedictionary.com/Alfred%20E.%20Smith.
89. Witcover, 337.

90. Perret, 188.
91. Witcover, 340.
92. Perret, 188.
93. Perret, 188.
94. MacLean, Nancy, *Behind the Mask of Chivalry: The Making of the Second Ku Klux Klan*, Oxford University Press: 1994, 13.
95. Black, 164.
96. Black, 164.
97. Black, 166.
98. Witcover, 341.
99. Smith, Richard Norton, "The Price of the Presidency," *Yankee Magazine*, January, 1996.
100. Smith, Richard Norton, "The Price of the Presidency," *Yankee Magazine*, January, 1996.
101. Perret, 190.
102. Morison, *The Oxford History of the American People, Volume Three*, 293.
103. Larson, Edward J., *Summer for the Gods: The Scopes Trial and America's Continuing Debate Over Science and Religion*, BasicBooks: 1997, 97.
104. Larson, 181.
105. Larson, 181.
106. Larson, 181.
107. Larson, 181.
108. Larson, 181.
109. Larson, 181.
110. Mencken, H.L., "Sahara of the Bozart," *New York Evening Mail*, 13 November 1917.
111. Larson, 182.
112. Larson, 190.
113. Larson, 190.
114. Larson, 199.
115. Larson, 200.
116. Larson, 241.
117. Perret, 278.
118. Perret, 280.
119. Perret, 280.
120. Perret, 280.
121. Perret, 280.
122. Perret, 281.
123. Perret, 282.
124. Perret, 282.
125. Perret, 282.
126. Berg, A. Scott, *Lindbergh*, G.P. Putnam's Sons: 1998, 114.
127. Berg, 115.
128. Berg, 121.
129. Berg, 122.
130. Morison, *The Oxford History of the American People, Volume Three*, 232.
131. Berg, 118.
132. Berg, 172.
133. Berg, 172.
134. Berg, 172.
135. Berg, 173.
136. Online source: http://www.brainyquote.com/quotes/authors/g/gertrude_stein.html.

137. Morison, *The Oxford History of the American People, Volume Three*, 263
138. Morison, *The Oxford History of the American People, Volume Three*, 264.
139. Bailey, Thomas A., *A Diplomatic History of the American People*, Prentice-Hall, Inc.: 1980, 650.
140. Morison, *The Oxford History of the American People, Volume Three*, 263.
141. Bailey, 650.
142. Gilbert, *A History of the Twentieth Century: Volume One*, 631.
143. Waite, Robert G. L., *Kaiser and Fuhrer: A Comparative Study of Personality and Politics*, University of Toronto Press: 1998, 200.
144. Waite, 200.
145. Waite, 122.
146. Gilbert, *A History of the Twentieth Century: Volume One*, 702.
147. Gilbert, *A History of the Twentieth Century: Volume One*, 761.
148. Perret, 298.
149. Perret, 297.
150. Perret, 297.
151. Perret, 297.
152. Gould, 246.
153. Gould, 245.
154. White, William Allen, *A Puritan in Babylon: The Story of Calvin Coolidge*, The Macmillan Company: 1938, 437.
155. Online source: http://www.harvard-magazine.com/on-line/030220.html.
156. Online source: http://www.harvard-magazine.com/on-line/030220.html.
157. Online source: http://www.assumption.edu/users/McClymer/his394/sacco%20and%20%20vanzetti/Shahn%20Passionsacco_vanzetti.jpg.
158. Online source: http://www.assumption.edu/users/McClymer/his394/sacco%20and%20%20vanzetti/Shahn%20Passionsacco_vanzetti.jpg.
159. Gould, 248.
160. Perret, 405.
161. Perret, 312.
162. Perret, 312.
163. Morison, *The Oxford History of the American People, Volume Three*, 282.
164. Perret, 315.
165. Perret, 310.
166. Perret, 313.
167. Perret, 306.
168. Online source: http://www.detnews.com/2001/religion/0108/12/religion-250986.htm.
169. Perret, 316.
170. Gilbert, *A History of the Twentieth Century: Volume One*, 770.
171. Gilbert, *A History of the Twentieth Century: Volume One*, 770.
172. Gilbert, *A History of the Twentieth Century: Volume One*, 771.
173. Online source: http://www2.sunysuffolk.edu/formans/DefiningDeviancy.htm.
174. Perret, 404.
175. Perret, 404.
176. Gilbert, *A History of the Twentieth Century: Volume One*, 802. For the seminal biography about Ness see Heimel, Paul W., *Eliot Ness: The Real Story*, 2nd ed., Cumberland House: 2000.

177. Morison, *The Oxford History of the American People, Volume Three*, 283.
178. Morison, *The Oxford History of the American People, Volume Three*, 283.
179. Morison, *The Oxford History of the American People, Volume Three*, 285.
180. Gilbert, *A History of the Twentieth Century: Volume One*, 768.
181. Gilbert, *A History of the Twentieth Century: Volume One*, 768.
182. Gilbert, *A History of the Twentieth Century: Volume One*, 768.
183. Gilbert, *A History of the Twentieth Century: Volume One*, 768.
184. Gilbert, *A History of the Twentieth Century: Volume One*, 768.
185. Watkins, T. H., *The Hungry Years: A Narrative History of the Great Depression in America*, Henry Holt and Company: 1999.
186. Barone, Michael, *Our Country: The Shaping of America from Roosevelt to Reagan*, The Free Press: 1990, 43.
187. Barone, 43.
188. Barone, 43.
189. Morison, *The Oxford History of the American People, Volume Three*, 291.
190. Morison, *The Oxford History of the American People, Volume Three*, 291.
191. Morison, *The Oxford History of the American People, Volume Three*, 291
192. Online source:http://www.ukans.edu/carrie/docs/texts/brother.htm.
193. Gilbert, *A History of the Twentieth Century: Volume One*, 753.
194. Morison, *The Oxford History of the American People, Volume Three*, 275
195. Morison, *The Oxford History of the American People, Volume Three*, 275.
196. Barone, 46.
197. Fausold, Martin L. Ed., *The Hoover Presidency: A Reappraisal*, State University of New York Press: 1974, 88.
198. Fausold, Ed., 88.
199. Barone, 46.
200. Gould, 257.
201. Friedman, Milton, and Anna Jacobson Schwartz, *A Monetary History of the United States: 1867–1960*, Princeton University Press, National Bureau of Economic Research: 1963, 301.
202. Friedman and Schwartz, 413.
203. Morison, *The Oxford History of the American People, Volume Three*, 287.
204. Fausold, Ed., 91.
205. Fausold, Ed., 91.
206. Fausold, Ed., 91.
207. Gould, 256.
208. Gould, 256.
209. Ketcham, Richard M., *The Borrowed Years: 1938–1941, America on the Way to War*, Random House: 1989, 19.
210. Morison, *The Oxford History of the American People, Volume Three*, 291.
211. Morison, *The Oxford History of the American People, Volume Three*, 291.
212. Gilbert, *A History of the Twentieth Century: Volume One*, 803.
213. Gilbert, Martin, *Churchill: A Life*, Henry Holt and Company: 1991, 504.
214. Gilbert, *A History of the Twentieth Century: Volume One*, 719–720.
215. Gilbert, *A History of the Twentieth Century: Volume One*, 719–720.
216. Berg, 244.
217. Berg, 246.
218. Berg, 241.
219. Perret, 480.

220. Perret, 480.
221. Perret, 481.
222. Perret, 481.
223. Witcover, 355.
224. Alter, 82.
225. Alter, 82.
226. Bailey, 653.
227. Bailey, 653.
228. Gould, 261.
229. Barone, 52.
230. Barone, 52.
231. Barone, 54.
232. Barone, 52.
233. Fausold, Ed., 90–91.
234. Jenkins, Roy, *Franklin Delano Roosevelt*, Times Books: 2003, 61.
235. Alter, 119.
236. Gould, 261.
237. Morison, *The Oxford History of the American People, Volume Three*, 296.
238. Fausold, Ed., 137.
239. Fausold, Ed., 137.
240. Fausold, Ed., 137.
241. Fausold, Ed., 137.
242. Fausold, Ed., 145.
243. Fausold, Ed., 144.
244. Black, 263.
245. Black, 263.
246. Black, 264.
247. Black, 263.
248. Nishi, Dennis, Ed., *The Great Depression*, Greenhaven Press, Inc.: 2001, 206.
249. Nishi, Ed., 207.
250. Fausold, Ed., 149.
251. Black, 270.
252. Witcover, 361.
253. Alter, 218.
254. Alter, 218.
255. Alter, 218.

CHAPTER THREE:
FDR AND THE NEW DEAL (1933–1939)

1. Witcover, Jules, *Party of the People: A History of the Democrats*, Random House: 2003, 362.
2. Morison, Samuel Eliot, *The Oxford History of the American People, Volume Three*, Oxford University Press: 1994, 303.
3. Allen, Frederick Lewis, *Since Yesterday: The Nineteen Thirties in America*, Harper & Brothers Publishers: 1940, 139–140.
4. Johns, Bud, *The Ombibulous Mr. Mencken*, Synergistic Press: 1968, 36.

5. Kobler, John, *Ardent Spirits*, Putnam: 1973, 340.
6. Morison, *The Oxford History of the American People, Volume Three*, 306.
7. Black, Conrad, *Franklin D. Roosevelt: Champion of Freedom*, Public Affairs: 2003, 314.
8. Black, 314.
9. Morison, *The Oxford History of the American People, Volume Three*, 318.
10. Klehr, Harvey, John Earl Haynes, and Kyrill M. Anderson, *The Soviet World of American Communism*, Yale University Press: 1998, 34.
11. Morison, *The Oxford History of the American People, Volume Three*, 318.
12. Nisbet, Robert, *Roosevelt and Stalin: The Failed Courtship*, Regnery Gateway: 1988, 6.
13. Klehr, Harvey, John Earl Haynes, and, Fridrikh Igorevich Firsov, *The Secret World of American Communism*, Yale University Press: 1995, 8.
14. Klehr, et al, *The Secret World of American Communism*, 8.
15. Hamby, Alonzo, *For the Survival of Democracy: Franklin Roosevelt and the World Crisis of the 1930s*, The Free Press: 2004, 240–241.
16. Hamby, 240–241.
17. Online source: http://www.leg.wa.gov/pub/billinfo/2001-02/senate/8600-8624/8618_02162001.txt.
18. Barone, Michael, *Our Country: The Shaping of America from Roosevelt to Reagan*, The Free Press: 1990, 67.
19. Barone, 82.
20. Barone, 82.
21. Williams, T. Harry, *Huey Long*, Alfred A. Knopf: 1970, 845.
22. Williams, 845.
23. Williams, 845.
24. Leuchtenburg, William E., *Franklin D. Roosevelt and the New Deal, 1932–1940*, Harper Torchbooks: 1963, 102.
25. Williams, 870–871.
26. Berg, A. Scott, *Lindbergh*, G.P. Putnam's Sons: 1998, 298.
27. Wallace, Max, *The American Axis: Henry Ford, Charles Lindbergh, and the Rise of the Third Reich*, St. Martin's Press: 2003, 103.
28. Berg, 315.
29. Berg, 315.
30. Berg, 315.
31. Berg, 341.
32. Churchill, Winston S., *The Second World War, Vol. One: The Gathering Storm*, Houghton Mifflin Company: 1948, 192.
33. Churchill, *The Second World War, Vol. One: The Gathering Storm*, 194.
34. Churchill, *The Second World War, Vol. One: The Gathering Storm*, 7.
35. Churchill, *The Second World War, Vol. One: The Gathering Storm*, 7.
36. Churchill, *The Second World War, Vol. One: The Gathering Storm*, 199.
37. Gilbert, Martin and Richard Gott, *The Appeasers*, Phoenix Press: 1963, 41.
38. Gilbert and Gott, 41.
39. Gilbert and Gott, 41.
40. Bernier, Olivier, *Fireworks at Dusk: Paris in the Thirties*, Little, Brown and Company: 1993, 36–37.
41. Bernier, 36.
42. Hart-Davis, Duff, *Hitler's Games: The 1936 Olympics*, Harper & Row: 1986, 68.
43. Hart-Davis, 75.
44. Online source: http://www.jewishmag.com/36MAG/olympic/olympic.htm.

45. Hart-Davis, 79.
46. Online source: http://www.jewishmag.com/36MAG/olympic/olympic.htm.
47. Online source: http://www.jewishmag.com/36MAG/olympic/olympic.htm.
48. Online source: http://www.jewishmag.com/36MAG/olympic/olympic.htm.
49. Hart-Davis, 188.
50. Interview with Guy Walters, author, *Berlin Games: How the Nazis Stole the Olympic Dream*, William Morrow: 2006.
51. Hart-Davis, 177.
52. Burgan, Michael, "Great Moments in the Olympics," *World Almanac Library*, 2002, 13.
53. Wallace, 114–115.
54. Hart-Davis, 128.
55. Hart-Davis, 128.
56. Gilbert, Martin, *A History of the Twentieth Century: Volume Two: 1933–1951*, William Morrow and Company, Inc.: 1998, 15.
57. Hart-Davis, 225.
58. Hart-Davis, 221.
59. Online source: http://www.auschwitz.dk/schmeling.htm.
60. Hart-Davis, 241–242.
61. Hart-Davis, 242.
62. Black, 381.
63. Witcover, 375.
64. Witcover, 374.
65. Troy, Gil, http://www.arts.mcgill.ca/history/faculty/troyweb/CanThisMarriageBeSaved.htm.
66. Gould, Lewis L., *The Grand Old Party: A History of the Republicans*, Random House: 2003, 272.
67. Gould, 272.
68. Gould, 272.
69. Barone, 96.
70. Barone, 101.
71. Gould, 273.
72. Gilbert, Martin, *Churchill: A Life*, Henry Holt & Co.: 1991, 568.
73. Gilbert, *Churchill: A Life*, 569.
74. Gilbert, *Churchill: A Life*, 569.
75. Gilbert, *Churchill: A Life*, 569.
76. Hunt, John Gabriel, Ed., *Inaugural Addresses of the Presidents*, Gramercy Books: 1995, 383.
77. Barone, 113.
78. Black, 411.
79. Black, 411.
80. Black, 411.
81. Barone, 113.
82. Witcover, 378.
83. Online source: http://xroads.virginia.edu/~MA04/wood/mot/html/censor.htm.
84. Mooney, Michael Macdonald, *Hindenburg*, Dodd, Mead & Company: 1972, 234.
85. Mooney, 239.
86. Rich, Doris L., *Amelia Earhart: A Biography*, Smithsonian Institution: 1989, 161.
87. Rich, 229.
88. Rich, 212.
89. Rich, 162.

90. Rich, 259.
91. Rich, 271.
92. Rich, 270.
93. Beschloss, Michael R., *Kennedy and Roosevelt: The Uneasy Alliance*, W.W. Norton & Company: 1980, 157.
94. Beschloss, *Kennedy and Roosevelt: The Uneasy Alliance*, 153.
95. Beschloss, *Kennedy and Roosevelt: The Uneasy Alliance*, 154.
96. Beschloss, *Kennedy and Roosevelt: The Uneasy Alliance*, 154.
97. Beschloss, *Kennedy and Roosevelt: The Uneasy Alliance*, 113.
98. Gilbert, *A History of the Twentieth Century, Volume Two*, 177.
99. Gilbert, *A History of the Twentieth Century, Volume Two*, 199.
100. Gilbert, *A History of the Twentieth Century, Volume Two*, 201.
101. Gilbert, *Churchill: A Life*, 601.
102. Beschloss, *Kennedy and Roosevelt: The Uneasy Alliance*, 178.
103. Beschloss, *Kennedy and Roosevelt: The Uneasy Alliance*, 178.
104. Beschloss, *Kennedy and Roosevelt: The Uneasy Alliance*, 179.
105. Beschloss, *Kennedy and Roosevelt: The Uneasy Alliance*, 176.
106. Beschloss, *Kennedy and Roosevelt: The Uneasy Alliance*, 176.
107. Beschloss, *Kennedy and Roosevelt: The Uneasy Alliance*, 171.
108. Beschloss, *Kennedy and Roosevelt: The Uneasy Alliance*, 177.
109. Beschloss, *Kennedy and Roosevelt: The Uneasy Alliance*, 174.
110. Beschloss, *Kennedy and Roosevelt: The Uneasy Alliance*, 180.
111. Beschloss, *Kennedy and Roosevelt: The Uneasy Alliance*, 178.
112. Online source: http://www.americanparknetwork.com/parkinfo/ru/history/carve.html.
113. Online source: http://www.americanparknetwork.com/parkinfo/ru/history/carve.html.
114. Online source: http://www.americanparknetwork.com/parkinfo/ru/history/carve.html.
115. Online source: http://www.pbs.org/wgbh/buildingbig/wonder/structure/empire_state.html.
116. Online source: http://www.goldengatebridge.org/research/ConstructionBldgGGB.html.
117. Evans, Richard J., *The Third Reich in Power*, The Penguin Press: 2005, 302 (illus).
118. Online source: http://www.pbs.org/wgbh/amex/carter/peopleevents/p_jcarter.html.
119. Gilbert, *A History of the Twentieth Century, Volume Two*, 221.
120. Ketchum, Richard M, *The Borrowed Years, 1938–1941: America on the Way to War* (sound recording), Books On Tape: 1999.

CHAPTER FOUR:

AMERICA'S RENDEZVOUS WITH DESTINY (1939–1941)

1. Online source: http://history.sandiego.edu/gen/USPics27/75297h.jpg.
2. Gilbert, Martin, *A History of the Twentieth Century: Volume Two: 1933–1951*, William Morrow and Company, Inc.: 1998, 205.
3. Evans, Richard J., *The Third Reich in Power*, The Penguin Press: 2005, 250.
4. Evans, 250.

5. Beschloss, Michael R., *Kennedy and Roosevelt: The Uneasy Alliance*, W.W. Norton & Company: 1980, 189.
6. Beschloss, *Kennedy and Roosevelt: The Uneasy Alliance*, 189.
7. Online source: http://www.presidency.ucsb.edu/site/docs/pppus.php?admin=032&year=1939&id=73.
8. Ketchum, Richard M., *The Borrowed Years: 1938–1941, America on the Way to War*, Random House: 1989, 161.
9. Black, Conrad, *Franklin D. Roosevelt: Champion of Freedom*, Public Affairs: 2003, 522.
10. Black, 523.
11. Ketchum, 156.
12. Ketchum, 157.
13. Black, 523.
14. Online source: http://history.acusd.edu/gen/ww2Timeline/Prelude10a.html.
15. Berg, A. Scott, *Lindbergh*, G.P. Putnam's Sons: 1998, 370.
16. Berg, 372.
17. Ketchum, 283.
18. Ketchum, 280.
19. Ketchum, 281.
20. Ketchum, 283.
21. Ketchum, 283.
22. Ketchum, 284.
23. Ketchum, 285.
24. May, Ernest R., *Strange Victory: Hitler's Conquest of France*, Hill & Wang: 2000, 453.
25. May, 453.
26. Evans, 32.
27. Evans, 34.
28. May, 456.
29. Meacham, Jon, *Franklin and Winston: An Intimate Portrait of an Epic Friendship*, Random House: 2003, 42.
30. Gilbert, *Churchill: A Life*, 624.
31. Weigel, George, *Witness to Hope: The Biography of Pope John Paul II*, Cliff Street Books: 1999, 50–51.
32. Courtois, Stéphane, Nicolas Werth, Jean-Louis Panné, *The Black Book of Communism: Crimes, Terror, Repression*, Harvard University Press: 1999, 6.
33. Kagan, Donald, *On the Origins of War*, Doubleday: 1995, 414.
34. Krauthammer, Charles, "Short-Term Gain, Long-Term Pain," *Washington Post*, 11 August 2006, A19.
35. Online source: http://ngeorgia.com/feature/gwtwpremiere.html.
36. Beschloss, *Kennedy and Roosevelt: The Uneasy Alliance*, 193.
37. Beschloss, *Kennedy and Roosevelt: The Uneasy Alliance*, 193.
38. Beschloss, *Kennedy and Roosevelt: The Uneasy Alliance*, 195.
39. Lukacs, John, *The Duel: 10 May–31 July: The Eighty-Day Struggle Between Churchill and Hitler*, Ticknor & Fields: 1991, 1.
40. Gilbert, *Churchill: A Life*, 645.
41. Gilbert, *Churchill: A Life*, 646.
42. Meacham, 51.
43. Ketchum, 471.
44. Ketchum, 471.
45. Will, George F., "Readers' Block," *Washington Post*, 23 July 2004, A29.

46. Jackson, Julian, *The Fall of France: The Nazi Invasion of 1940*, Oxford University Press: 2003, 211.
47. Black, 554.
48. Jackson, *The Fall of France*, 181.
49. Jackson, *The Fall of France*, 210.
50. Online source: http://www.winstonchurchill.org/i4a/pages/index.cfm?pageid=418.
51. Gould, Lewis L., *The Grand Old Party: A History of the Republicans*, Random House: 2003, 281.
52. Gould, 281.
53. Gould, 284.
54. Barone, Michael, *Our Country: The Shaping of America from Roosevelt to Reagan*, The Free Press: 1990, 136.
55. Gould, 284.
56. Peters, Charles, *Five Days in Philadelphia*, PublicAffairs: 2005, 82.
57. Peters, 95.
58. Beschloss, *Kennedy and Roosevelt: The Uneasy Alliance*, 209.
59. Barone, 140.
60. Barone, 140.
61. Gilbert, Churchill, 667.
62. Gilbert, Churchill, 667.
63. Harrisson, Tom, *Living Through the Blitz*, Schocken Books, New York: 1976, 101.
64. Harrisson, 101.
65. Harrisson, 101.
66. Harrisson, 308.
67. Harrisson, 310.
68. Harrisson, 310.
69. Jacobs, Alan, *The Narnian: The Life and Imagination of C.S. Lewis*, Harper: 2005, 223.
70. Jacobs, 223.
71. Overy, Richard, *The Battle of Britain: The Myth and the Reality*, W.W. Norton & Company: 2000, 162.
72. Murrow, Edward R., *This Is London*, Simon and Schuster: 1941, 135.
73. Ketchum, 342.
74. Ketchum, 343.
75. Barone, 140.
76. Barone, 146.
77. Barone, 141.
78. Barone, 143.
79. Peters, 111.
80. Peters, 194.
81. Peters, 182.
82. Barone, 147.
83. Meacham, 95.
84. Wallace, Max, *The American Axis: Henry Ford, Charles Lindbergh, and the Rise of the Third Reich*, St. Martin's Press: 2003, 249.
85. Wallace, 275.
86. Wallace, 277.
87. Wallace, 257.
88. Wallace, 260.

89. Wallace, 277.
90. Wallace, 285.
91. Bercuson, David J., and Holger Herwig, *The Destruction of the Bismarck*, The Overlook Press: 2001, 2.
92. May, *Strange Victory*, 480.
93. Bercuson and Herwig, 14.
94. Bercuson and Herwig, 24.
95. Bercuson and Herwig, 18.
96. Bercuson and Herwig, 15.
97. Bercuson and Herwig, 14.
98. Bercuson and Herwig, 16.
99. Bercuson and Herwig, 15.
100. Online source: http://www.history.navy.mil/photos/events/wwii-atl/batit-41/bismk-a.htm.
101. Bercuson and Herwig, back cover.
102. Online source: http://www.history.navy.mil/photos/events/wwii-atl/batit-41/bismk-a.htm.
103. Bercuson and Herwig, 29.
104. Gilbert, Martin, *The Second World War*, Henry Holt and Company: 1989, 185.
105. Bercuson and Herwig, 221.
106. Online source: http://www.history.navy.mil/photos/events/wwii-atl/batit-41/bismk-a.htm.
107. Bercuson and Herwig, 178.
108. Bercuson and Herwig, 177.
109. Dear, I.C.B, General Editor, and Foot, M.R.D., Consulting Editor, *The Oxford Companion to World War II*, Oxford University Press, New York: 1995, 133.
110. Gilbert, *Second World War*, 186.
111. Gilbert, *Second World War*, 186.
112. Gilbert, Martin, *Churchill and America*, The Free Press: 2005, 225.
113. Jenkins, Roy, *Churchill: A Biography*, Farrar, Straus and Giroux: 2001, 659.
114. Gilbert, *Churchill and America*, 701.
115. Gilbert, *Churchill and America*, 702.
116. Gilbert, Martin, *A History of the Twentieth Century: Volume Two: 1933–1951*, William Morrow and Company, Inc.: 1998, 380.
117. Gilbert, *Churchill and America*, 705.
118. Meacham, 107.
119. Meacham, 105.
120. Meacham, 108.
121. Meacham, 108.

CHAPTER FIVE:
Leading the Grand Alliance (1941–1943)

1. Ferguson, Niall, *Empire: The Rise and Demise of the British World Order and the Lessons for Global Power*, Basic Books: 2002, 332.
2. Barone, Michael, *Our Country: The Shaping of America from Roosevelt to Reagan*, The Free Press: 1990, 147.

3. McDougall, Walter A., *Promised Land, Crusader State: The American Encounter with the World Since 1776*, Houghton Mifflin: 1997, 151.
4. Beschloss, Michael, *Kennedy and Roosevelt: The Uneasy Alliance*, W.W. Norton & Company: 1980, 238.
5. Barone, 147.
6. Barone, 147.
7. *The World at War*, Film Documentary produced by Thames Television, Ltd., London: 1974, Vol. II, Barbarossa.
8. Wilson, Theodore A., *The First Summit: Roosevelt and Churchill at Placentia Bay, 1941*, University Press of Kansas: 1991, 12.
9. Wilson, 91.
10. Wilson, 91.
11. Acheson, Dean, *Present at the Creation*, Books-on-tape, Cassette 1, Side 1.
12. Morison, Samuel Eliot, *The Oxford History of the American People, Volume Three: 1869 Through the Death of President Kennedy, 1963*, Penguin: 1965, 357.
13. Lord, Walter, *Day of Infamy*, Henry Holt and Company: 2001, 212.
14. Lord, 212.
15. Lord, 158.
16. Online source: http://www.crossroad.to/Victory/stories/woman.htm.
17. Lord, 217.
18. Lord, 217.
19. Lord, 217.
20. Lord, 217.
21. Lord, 218.
22. Black, Conrad, *Franklin Delano Roosevelt: Champion of Freedom*, PublicAffairs: 2003, 692.
23. Black, 692.
24. Black, 692.
25. Fleming, Thomas, *The New Dealers' War: F.D.R. and the War within World War II*, Basic Books: 2001, 40.
26. Fleming, 40.
27. Morison, Samuel Eliot, *The Two-Ocean War*, Little, Brown and Company: 1963, 69.
28. Wohlstetter, Roberta, *Pearl Harbor: Warning and Decision*, Stanford University Press: 1962, 386.
29. Wohlstetter, 387.
30. Online source: http://www.geocities.com/dutcheastindies/december1.html.
31. Morison, *The Two-Ocean War*, 74.
32. Morison, *The Two-Ocean War*, 69.
33. Leckie, Robert, *The Wars of America*, Harper & Row, Publishers: 1981, 735.
34. van der Vat, Dan, *Pearl Harbor: Day of Infamy—An Illustrated History*, Basic Books: 2001, 158.
35. Online source: http://www.historyplace.com/worldwar2/timeline/statistics.htm.
36. Berg, A. Scott, *Lindbergh*, G.P. Putnam's Sons: 1998, 425.
37. Larrabee, Eric, *Commander in Chief: Franklin D. Roosevelt, His Lieutenants, and Their War*, U.S. Naval Institute Press: 1987, 3.
38. Larrabee, 3.
39. Larrabee, 3.
40. Gilbert, Martin, *The Second World War: A Complete History*, Henry Holt & Co.: 1989, 275.

41. Gilbert, *The Second World War*, 274.
42. Gilbert, *The Second World War*, 274–275.
43. Brookhiser, Richard, "Book of the Century," *Finest Hour* No. 103. Online source: http://www.winstonchurchill.org/i4a/pages/index.cfm?pageid=469.
44. Gilbert, Martin, *Churchill: A Life*, Henry Holt and Company: 1991, 714.
45. Bercuson, David, and Holger Herwig, *One Christmas in Washington*, Overlook Press: 2005, 129.
46. Bercuson and Herwig, *One Christmas*, 130.
47. Brinkley, 101.
48. Brinkley, 103.
49. Bercuson and Herwig, *One Christmas*, 212.
50. Bercuson and Herwig, *One Christmas*, 213.
51. Bercuson and Herwig, *One Christmas*, 214.
52. *World at War*, a film documentary by Thames Ltd., Vol. Four, "The U-Boat War, Wolf Pack in the Atlantic,"1974.
53. Acheson, *Present at the Creation*.
54. Bercuson and Herwig, *One Christmas*, 143.
55. Bercuson and Herwig, *One Christmas*, 215.
56. Berthon, Simon, and Joanna Potts, *Warlords: An Extraordinary Re-creation of World War II Through the Eyes and Minds of Hitler, Roosevelt, Churchill, and Stalin*, DaCapo Press: 2006, 131.
57. Berthon and Potts, 131.
58. Leckie, 741.
59. Dear, I.C.B, General Editor, and Foot, M.R.D., Consulting Editor, *The Oxford Companion to World War II*, Oxford University Press, New York: 1995, 115.
60. Dear and Foot, 115.
61. Dear and Foot, 309.
62. Dear and Foot, 309.
63. Dear and Foot, 632.
64. Dear and Foot, 633.
65. "The Medal of Honor: Bravest of the Brave." Online source: http://www.medalofhonor.com/DanielInouye.htm.
66. Williams, Nathan, "What Happened to the 8 Germans Tried by a Military Court in World War II?" Online source:http://hnn.us/articles/431.html.
67. Berg, 437.
68. Guelzo, Allen, C., *Lincoln's Emancipation Proclamation: The End of Slavery in America*, Simon & Schuster: 2004, 163.
69. Gates, Henry Louis, Jr., and Cornel West, *The African-American Century: How Black Americans Have Shaped Our Country*, The Free Press: 2000, 53.
70. Quoted in Thomas Sowell, "Enemies Within," *Jewish World Review*, 9 January 2002, Online source: http://www.jewishworldreview.com/cols/sowell010902.asp.
71. Barone, 160.
72. Barone, 159.
73. Gates and West, 183.
74. Lukacs, John, *The Duel, 10 May–31 July 1940: The Eighty-Day Struggle Between Churchill and Hitler*, Ticknor & Fields: 1991, 52.
75. Gilbert, Martin, *Auschwitz and the Allies: A Devastating Account of How the Allies Responded to the News of Hitler's Mass Murder*, Henry Holt: 1981, 72.
76. Gilbert, *Auschwitz*, 73.

77. Online source: http://www.palestinefacts.org/pf_mandate_during_ww2.php.
78. Online source: http://www.palestinefacts.org/pf_mandate_during_ww2.php.
79. Gilbert, Martin, *Jerusalem in the Twentieth Century*, John Wiley & Sons, Inc.: 1996, 162.
80. Meacham, Jon, *Franklin and Winston: An Intimate Portrait of an Epic Friendship*, Random House: 2003, 192.
81. Ferguson, 344.
82. Ferguson, 344.
83. Ferguson, 346.
84. Ferguson, 346.
85. Ambrose, Stephen E., *American Heritage New History of World War II*, Viking: 1997, 365.
86. Ambrose, *World War II*, 365.
87. Brinkley, 131.
88. Brinkley, 131.
89. Lacey, Robert, *Great Tales from English History*, Volume II [sound recording]: "Chaucer to the Glorious Revolution."
90. Dear and Foot, 1246.
91. Greene, Bob, *Once Upon a Town: The Miracle of the North Platte Canteen*, HarperCollins: 2002, 13.
92. Greene, 14–15.
93. Greene, back jacket.
94. Barone, 162.
95. Ambrose, *World War II*, 419.
96. Beschloss, *Kennedy and Roosevelt: The Uneasy Alliance*, 246.
97. Beschloss, *Kennedy and Roosevelt: The Uneasy Alliance*, 246.
98. Dear and Foot, 689.
99. White, David Fairbank, *Bitter Ocean: The Battle of the Atlantic, 1939–1945*, Simon & Schuster: 2006, front jacket.
100. Hickam, Homer H., Jr., *Torpedo Junction*, Naval Institute Press: 1989, xi.
101. Hickam, vii.
102. Hickam, vii.
103. White, 247.
104. White, 247.
105. White, 247.
106. Hickam, vii.
107. Online source: http://www.history.navy.mil/faqs/faq87-3j.htm.
108. Dear and Foot, 271.
109. Dear and Foot, 271.
110. Dear and Foot, 748–749.
111. Dear and Foot, 748–749.
112. Donovan, Charles A., "At War with God," *Citizen Magazine*, Focus on the Family, © 2002.
113. Dear and Foot, 815.
114. Deer and Foot, 527.
115. Deer and Foot, 527.
116. Soames, Mary, *Clementine Churchill: The Biography of a Marriage*, Houghton Mifflin: 1979, 420.
117. Soames, 420.
118. Soames, 421.
119. Online source: http://www.wpafb.af.mil/museum/annex/an27.htm.

120. Dear and Foot, 515.
121. Dear and Foot, 1174.
122. Fleming, 188.
123. Fleming, 183.
124. Gilbert, Martin, *Churchill: A Life*, 815.
125. Soames, 420.
126. Soames, 461.
127. Dear and Foot, 1059.
128. Ambrose, *World War II*, 254.

CHAPTER SIX:
America Victorious (1943–1945)

1. Overy, Richard, *Why the Allies Won* (W.W. Norton & Co., 1995), 316.
2. Overy, *Why the Allies Won*, 317.
3. Overy, *Why the Allies Won*, 321.
4. Overy, *Why the Allies Won*, 317.
5. Overy, *Why the Allies Won*, 320.
6. Offner, Larry, "The Butch O'Hare Story," online source: www.stlmag.com/media/st-louis-magazine/july-2005/the -butch-ohare-story.
7. From a speech by Rep. Ralph Hall (Texas), 30 May 1996, *The Congressional Record.*
8. Online source: http://www.audiemurphy.com/stamp p1.htm.
9. Online source: http://www.dcdiocese.org/swkregister/Nov_7_04/fourchaplainstv.htm.
10. Online source: http://www.ushmm.org/outreach/denmark.htm.
11. Nisbet, Robert, *Roosevelt and Stalin: The Failed Courtship*, Regnery Gateway: 1988, 45.
12. Meacham, Jon, *Franklin and Winston: An Intimate Portrait of an Epic Friendship*, Random House: 2003, 250.
13. Meacham, 251.
14. Barone, Michael, *Our Country: The Shaping of America from Roosevelt to Reagan*, The Free Press: 1990, 168.
15. Ambrose, Stephen E., *American Heritage New History of World War II*, Viking: 1997, 282.
16. Pogue, Forrest C., *George C. Marshall: Interviews and Reminiscences for Forrest C. Pogue*, George C. Marshall Research Foundation: 1991, 108–9.
17. Larrabee, Eric, *Commander in Chief: Franklin D. Roosevelt, His Lieutenants, and Their War*, U.S. Naval Institute Press: 1987, 99.
18. Larrabee, 98.
19. Eisenhower, John S. D., *General Ike: A Personal Reminiscence*, The Free Press: 2003, 99.
20. Gilbert, Martin, *Churchill: A Life*, Henry Holt and Company: 1991, 756.
21. Eisenhower, Dwight D., *Crusade in Europe*, Johns Hopkins University Press: 1948, 194.
22. Dear, I.C.B, General Editor, and Foot, M.R.D., Consulting Editor, *The Oxford Companion to World War II*, Oxford University Press, New York: 1995, 298.
23. Eisenhower, Dwight D., *At Ease: Stories I Tell to Friends*, Doubleday & Co., Inc.:1967, 270.
24. Beschloss, Michael R., *Eisenhower: A Centennial Life*, HarperCollins Publishers: 1990, 66.
25. Leckie, Robert, *The Wars of America*, Harper & Row: 1981, 796.
26. Leckie, 796.

27. Online source: http://www.presidency.ucsb.edu/site/docs/pppus.php?admin=032&year=1944&id=37.
28. Ambrose, *World War II*, 487.
29. Netting, Conrad J., IV, "Delayed Legacy," *USAA Magazine*, 2004, No. 2, 24.
30. Ambrose, *World War II*, 498.
31. Perret, Geoffrey, *Eisenhower*, Random House: 1999, 325.
32. Perret, 312.
33. Perret, 324.
34. Perret, 359.
35. Perret, 324.
36. Overy, *Why the Allies Won*, 319.
37. Source: http://www.remember.org/karski/kaudio.html.
38. Soames, Mary, *Clementine Churchill: The Biography of a Marriage*, Houghton Mifflin: 1979, 479.
39. Eisenhower, Dwight D., *Crusade in Europe*, 296–97.
40. Perret, 308.
41. Eisenhower, John S. D., *General Ike: A Personal Reminiscence*, The Free Press: 2003, 156.
42. Eisenhower, John S. D., *General Ike: A Personal Reminiscence*, 156.
43. Eisenhower, John S. D., *General Ike: A Personal Reminiscence*, 197.
44. Ambrose, *World War II*, 488.
45. De Gaulle, Charles, *The Complete Memoirs*, Carroll & Graf Publishers, Inc.: 1998, 647.
46. Eisenhower, Dwight D., *Crusade in Europe*, 298.
47. Meacham, 295.
48. Dear and Foot, 1252.
49. Gilbert, Martin, *Auschwitz and the Allies*, Henry Holt and Company: 1981, 341.
50. Beschloss, Michael, *The Conquerors: Roosevelt, Truman and the Destruction of Hitler's Germany, 1941–1945*, Simon & Schuster: 2002, 59.
51. Beschloss, *Conquerors*, 41.
52. Beschloss, *Conquerors*, 59.
53. Online source: http://www.townhall.com/columnists/SuzanneFields/2006/04/20/recycling_anti-semitism.
54. Gilbert, *Auschwitz*, 303.
55. Black, Conrad, *Franklin D. Roosevelt: Champion of Freedom*, Public Affairs: 2003, 974.
56. Witcover, Jules, *Party of the People: A History of the Democrats*, Random House: 2003, 404.
57. Witcover, 401.
58. Persico, Joseph E., *Roosevelt's Secret War: FDR and World War II Espionage*, Random House: 2001, 149.
59. Persico, 149.
60. Persico, 149.
61. Witcover, 404.
62. Witcover, 405.
63. McCullough, David, *Truman*, Simon & Schuster: 1992, 314.
64. McCullough, 308.
65. McCullough, 314.
66. McCullough, 314.
67. McCullough, 313.

68. Goodwin, Doris Kearns, *No Ordinary Time: Franklin and Eleanor Roosevelt, The Home Front in World War II*, Simon & Schuster: 1994, 532.
69. Goodwin, 532.
70. Goodwin, 532.
71. Barone, 176.
72. Powell, Jim, *FDR's Folly: How Roosevelt and His New Deal Prolonged the Great Depression,* Crown Forum, Random House: 2003, ix.
73. Powell, 33.
74. Barone, 177.
75. Barone, 177.
76. Gould, Lewis L., *Grand Old Party: A History of the Republicans*, Random House: 2003, 297–98.
77. Barone, 178.
78. Paul Greenberg, "A General In Charge of the CIA?" Online source: Townhall.com, http://www.townhall.com/columnists/column.aspx?UrlTitle=a_general_in_charge_of_the_cia_shocking!&ns=PaulGreenberg&dt=05/15/2006&page=1.
79. Pogue, 411.
80. Beschloss, *Conquerors*, 163.
81. Barone, 178.
82. Beschloss, Michael R., *Kennedy and Roosevelt: The Uneasy Alliance*, W.W. Norton & Company: 1980, 257.
83. Beschloss, *Kennedy and Roosevelt*, 259.
84. Gould, 299.
85. "Stalin, Man of the Year: 1939," *Time Magazine*, 1 January 1940, online source: http://www.time.com/time/special/moy/1939.html.
86. Ambrose, Stephen E., *The Victors: Eisenhower and His Boys: The Men of World War II*, Simon & Schuster: 1998, 299–300.
87. Ambrose, *World War II*, 300–1.
88. Leckie, 816.
89. Dear and Foot, 52.
90. Dear and Foot, 52.
91. Eisenhower, John S. D., *The Bitter Woods*, G.P. Putnam's Sons: 1969, 462.
92. Meacham, 368–69.
93. Meacham, 369.
94. Brinkley, David, *Washington Goes To War*, Ballantine Books: 1988, 265.
95. Brinkley, 265.
96. Brinkley, 265.
97. Black, 1043.
98. Black, 1062.
99. McDougall, Walter A., *Promised Land, Crusader State: The American Encounter with the World Since 1776*, Houghton Mifflin: 1997, 156.
100. McDougall, *Promised Land, Crusader State*, 155.
101. Black, 1066.
102. Black, 1058.
103. Black, 1070.
104. Churchill, Winston, *The Gathering Storm: The Second World War*, Houghton Mifflin: 1948.
105. Meacham, 317.
106. Black, 1074.

107. Black, 1074.
108. Gilbert, *Churchill*, 796.
109. Nisbet, Robert, *Roosevelt and Stalin: The Failed Courtship*, Regnery Gateway: 1988.
110. Gaddis, John Lewis, *The Cold War: A New History*, Penguin Press: 2005, 22.
111. Weinstein, Allen and Alexander Vassiliev, *The Haunted Wood: Soviet Espionage in America—the Stalin Era*, Random House: 1999, 269.
112. Weinstein and Vassiliev, 196–97.
113. Roosevelt, Franklin, D., "Address to Congress on the Yalta Conference," 1 March 1945, online source: http://www.presidency.ucsb.edu/site/docs/pppus.php?admin=032&year=1945&id=16.
114. Roosevelt, "Yalta Address," 1 March 1945.
115. Dear and Foot, 642.
116. Bush, George H. W., "Forrestal Lecture," U.S. Naval Academy, Annapolis, Md., 4 March 2004.
117. Collier, Peter, and David Horowitz, *The Roosevelts: An American Saga*, Simon & Schuster: 1994, 430.
118. Collier and Horowitz, 430.
119. Collier and Horowitz, 432.
120. Online source: http://hnn.us/articles/1834.html.
121. Online source: http://www.history.navy.mil/cgi-bin/htsearch.
122. Black, 1112.
123. Black, 1112.
124. McCullough, 353.
125. Nicolson, Nigel, Ed., *Harold Nicolson Diaries, The War Years: 1939–1945*, Atheneum: 1967, 447.
126. Gilbert, *Churchill*, 836.
127. Collier and Horowitz, 442.
128. Black, 1119
129. Black, 1119.
130. Ambrose, *World War II*, 457.
131. Ambrose, *World War II*, 80.
132. Neal, Steve, *Harry and Ike: The Partnership that Remade the Postwar World*, Scribner: 2001, 48.
133. Online source: http://www.eisenhower.archives.gov/guild.htm.
134. McCullough, 375–76.
135. McCullough, 375.
136. Beschloss, *Conquerors*, 248.
137. Beschloss, *Conquerors*, 249.
138. Beschloss, *Conquerors*, 249.
139. Beschloss, *Conquerors*, 153.
140. Cooke, Alistair, *The American Home Front: 1941–1942*, Atlantic Monthly Press: 2006, xi.
141. Online source: http://news.bbc.co.uk/1/hi/world/europe/1939174.stm.
142. Beevor, Antony, *The Fall of Berlin: 1945*, Penguin Books: 2002, 29.
143. Beevor, 29.
144. Mee, Charles L., Jr., *Meeting at Potsdam*, M. Evans & Company: 1975, 224.
145. Gilbert, *Churchill*, 855.
146. McCullough, 442.
147. McCullough, 443.
148. Weinstein and Vassiliev, 209.

149. Weinstein and Vassiliev, 208.
150. Harmon, Christopher, "Are We Beasts? Churchill and the Moral Question of World War II 'Area Bombing,'" *Finest Hour* 76, online source: http://www.winstonchurchill.org/i4a/pages/index.cfm?pageid=680.
151. Dear and Foot, 604.
152. Dear and Foot, 836.
153. Dear and Foot, 836.
154. Frank, Richard B., "Why Truman Dropped the Bomb," Weekly Standard, 8 August 2005.
155. Dear and Foot, 773.
156. Ambrose, *World War II*, 597.
157. Online source: http://www.johndilbeck.com/genealogy/orderofthegarter.html.

CHAPTER SEVEN:

Truman Defends the Free World (1945–1953)

1. Beschloss, Michael, *The Conquerors: Roosevelt, Truman and the Destruction of Hitler's Germany, 1941–1945*, Simon & Schuster: 2002, 271.
2. Muller, James W., Ed., *Churchill's Iron Curtain Speech Fifty Years Later*, University of Missouri Press: 1999, 6.
3. Muller, 96.
4. Muller, 66.
5. Barone, Michael, *Our Country: The Shaping of America from Roosevelt to Reagan*, The Free Press: 1990, 187.
6. Muller, 79.
7. Muller, 102.
8. Graebner, Norman A., *Cold War Diplomacy, 1945–1960*, D. Van Norstrand Company, Inc.: 1962, 28.
9. Barone, 206.
10. Graebner, 28.
11. Beschloss, *Conquerors*, 275.
12. Harris, Whitney R., *Tyranny on Trial*, Southern Methodist University Press: 1999, 497.
13. "Robert Jackson's Place in History," Chautauqua Institution, Chautauqua, New York, 13 June 2003, online source: http://robertjackson.org.
14. Online source: http://robertjackson.org.
15. Barone, 187.
16. Ferrell, Robert H., *Harry S. Truman: A Life*, University of Missouri Press: 1994, 194–95.
17. Ferrell, 181.
18. Ferrell, 181.
19. Ferrell, 185.
20. Beschloss, *Conquerors*, 276.
21. Ferrell, 251.
22. Gaddis, John Lewis, *We Now Know: Rethinking Cold War History*, Oxford University Press: 1997, 14.
23. Gaddis, *We Now Know*, 15.
24. Ferrell, 253.
25. Barone, 192.

26. Morison, Samuel Eliot, Henry Steele Commager, and William E. Leuchtenberg, *A Concise History of the American Republic*, Oxford University Press: 1977, 676.
27. Barone, 193.
28. Radosh, Ronald, and Allis Radosh, *Red Star Over Hollywood: The Film Colony's Long Romance with the Left*, Encounter Books: 2005, 48.
29. Radosh and Radosh, 112.
30. Radosh and Radosh, 114.
31. Radosh and Radosh, 115.
32. Billingsley, Kenneth Lloyd, *Hollywood Party: How Communism Seduced the American Film Industry in the 1930s and 1940s*, Forum: 2000, 152.
33. Billingsley, 153.
34. Billingsley, 155.
35. Billingsley, 157.
36. Billingsley, 157.
37. Billingsley, 157.
38. Billingsley, 158.
39. Billingsley, 158.
40. Billingsley, 125.
41. Billingsley, 125.
42. Gilbert, Martin, *Israel: A History*, William Morrow and Company, Inc.: 1997, 187.
43. Ferrell, 311.
44. Spalding, Elizabeth Edwards, *The First Cold Warrior: Harry Truman, Containment, and the Remaking of Liberal Internationalism*, University Press of Kentucky: 2006, 98.
45. Spalding, 96.
46. Spalding, 97.
47. Spalding, 96.
48. Ferrell, 311.
49. Ferrell, 311.
50. Gilbert, *Israel*, 191.
51. Clay, Lucius D., *Decision in Germany*, Doubleday & Company, Inc.: 1950, 365.
52. Clay, 365.
53. Ferrell, 259.
54. Ferrell, 259.
55. Barone, 208.
56. Ferrell, 314.
57. Humphrey, Hubert H., *The Education of a Public Man: My Life and Politics*, Doubleday and Company, Inc.: 1976, 111.
58. Ferrell, 295.
59. Ferrell, 295.
60. Ferrell, 297.
61. Gould, Louis L., *Grand Old Party: A History of the Republicans*, Random House: 2003, 316.
62. Beschloss, Michael, *Eisenhower: A Centennial Life*, An Edward Burlingame Book: 1990, 94.
63. Ferrell, 268–69.
64. Humphrey, 111.
65. Humphrey, 110.
66. McCullough, David, *Truman*, Simon & Schuster: 1992, 467.
67. McCullough, 467.

68. McCullough, 652.
69. McCullough, 652.
70. Gould, 315.
71. Gould, 315.
72. Barone, 219.
73. Barone, 214.
74. McCullough, 654.
75. Barone, 220.
76. Haynes, John Earl, and Harvey Klehr, *Venona: Decoding Soviet Espionage in America*, Yale University Press: 1999, 156.
77. Brands, H. W., *Cold Warriors: Eisenhower's Generation and American Foreign Policy*, Columbia University Press: 1988, 7.
78. Online source: http://www.americanrhetoric.com/speeches/eleanorrooseveltdeclarationhumanrights.htm.
79. Urquhart, Brian, *Ralph Bunche: An American Life*, W.W. Norton & Company: 1993, 179.
80. Urquhart, 37.
81. Urquhart, 193.
82. Urquhart, 193.
83. Ferrell, 253.
84. Online source: http://www.atomicarchive.com/Docs/SovietAB.shtml.
85. Online source: http://www.law.umkc.edu/faculty/projects/ftrials/hiss/hisschronology.html.
86. Weinstein, Allen, *Perjury: The Hiss-Chambers Case*, Alfred A. Knopf: 1978, 67.
87. Haynes and Klehr, *Venona*, 156.
88. Schweizer, Peter, *Reagan's War: The Epic Story of His Forty-Year Struggle and Final Triumph Over Communism,* Random House: 2002, 16.
89. Schweizer, 16.
90. Janken, Kenneth Robert, *White: The Biography of Walter White, Mr. NAACP*, New Press: 2003, 320.
91. Janken, 320.
92. Janken, 320.
93. Janken, 322.
94. Barone, 237.
95. Leckie, Robert, *The Wars of America*, Harper & Row Publishers, Inc.: 1981, 849.
96. Gaddis, John Lewis, *The End of the Cold War*, Penguin Press: 2005, 74.
97. Morison, Samuel Eliot, *The Oxford History of the American People, Volume Three: 1869 through the Death of John F. Kennedy, 1963*, The Penguin Group: 1994, 430.
98. Morison, *The Oxford History of the American People, Volume Three*, 430.
99. Leckie, 877.
100. Leckie, 878.
101. Leckie, 878.
102. Leckie, 881.
103. Leckie, 856.
104. Morison, *The Oxford History of the American People, Volume Three*, 436.
105. Gaddis, *The End of the Cold War*, 47.
106. Gaddis, *The End of the Cold War*, 47.
107. Morison, *The Oxford History of the American People, Volume Three*, 438.
108. Gaddis, *The End of the Cold War*, 55.
109. Morison, *The Oxford History of the American People, Volume Three*, 436.

110. Morison, *The Oxford History of the American People, Volume Three*, 439.
111. Gould, 322.
112. Morison, *The Oxford History of the American People, Volume Three*, 438.
113. Spalding, 217.
114. Spalding, 217.
115. Spalding, 217.
116. McCullough, 829.
117. Spalding, 228.
118. Spalding, 228.

CHAPTER EIGHT: EISENHOWER AND HAPPY DAYS (1953–1961)

1. Beschloss, Michael R., *Eisenhower: A Centennial Life*, HarperCollins Publishers: 1990, 100.
2. Beschloss, *Eisenhower*, 106.
3. Beschloss, *Eisenhower*, 106.
4. Beschloss, *Eisenhower*, 108.
5. Online source: http://www.firstthings.com/ftissues/ft9411/reviews/briefly.html.
6. Beschloss, *Eisenhower*, 111.
7. Beschloss, *Eisenhower*, 111.
8. Barone, Michael, *Our Country: The Shaping of America from Roosevelt to Reagan*, The Free Press: 1990, 258.
9. Brands, H. W., *Cold Warriors: Eisenhower's Generation and American Foreign Policy*, Columbia University Press: 1988, 185.
10. Beschloss, *Eisenhower*, 115.
11. Hunt, John Gabriel, Ed., *The Inaugural Addresses of the Presidents*, Gramercy Books: 1995, 412.
12. America Online Transcript, 6 July 1999, http://www.time.com/time/community/transcripts/1999/070699grahamtime100.html.
13. Online source: http://www.fortunecity.com/tinpan/parton/2/julius.html.
14. Radosh, Ronald, *Commies*, Encounter Books: 2001, 46.
15. Barone, 267.
16. Gaddis, John Lewis, *The End of the Cold War*, Penguin Press: 2005, 50.
17. Gould, Lewis L., *The Grand Old Party: A History of the Republicans*, Random House: 2003, 336.
18. Beschloss, *Eisenhower*, 127.
19. Barone, 266.
20. Powers, Richard Gid, *Not Without Honor: The History of American Anticommunism*, The Free Press: 1995, 268.
21. Powers, 268.
22. Powers, 264.
23. Barone, 269.
24. Online source: http://itre.cis.upenn.edu/~myl/languagelog/archives/001036.html.
25. Ambrose, Stephen E., *Eisenhower: The President*, Simon & Schuster: 1984, 81.
26. Ambrose, *Eisenhower: The President*, 81.
27. Ambrose, *Eisenhower: The President*, 81.
28. Powers, 268.
29. Barone, 270.

30. Beschloss, *Eisenhower*, 128.
31. Barone, 269.
32. Barone, 271.
33. Eisenhower, Dwight D., *Crusade in Europe*, The Johns Hopkins University Press: 1997, 468.
34. Eisenhower, *Crusade in Europe*, 476.
35. Wicker, Tom, *Dwight D. Eisenhower*, Times Books, Henry Holt & Company: 2002, 47.
36. Wicker, 53.
37. Wicker, 50.
38. Frady, Marshall, *Martin Luther King, Jr.*, The Penguin Group: 2002, 35.
39. Frady, 42.
40. Frady, 35.
41. Frady, 49.
42. Frady, 50.
43. Frady, 48.
44. Frady, 52.
45. Beschloss, *Eisenhower*, 137.
46. Beschloss, *Eisenhower*, 140.
47. Beschloss, *Eisenhower*, 138.
48. Gaddis, *The End of the Cold War*, 109.
49. Gaddis, *The End of the Cold War*, 111–112.
50. Beschloss, *Eisenhower*, 122.
51. Beschloss, *Eisenhower*, 126.
52. Beschloss, *Eisenhower*, 126.
53. Ambrose, *Eisenhower: The President*, 80.
54. Parrett, Geoffrey, *Eisenhower*, Random House: 1999, 74–75.
55. Beschloss, *Eisenhower*, 126.
56. Barone, 299.
57. Wicker, 99.
58. Wicker, 99.
59. McDougall, Walter A., *The Heavens and the Earth: A Political History of the Space Age*, Basic Books, The Johns Hopkins University Press: 1985, 221.
60. Beschloss, *Eisenhower*, 153.
61. Duncan, Francis, *Rickover: The Struggle for Excellence*, Naval Institute Press: 2001.
62. Duncan, 5.
63. Duncan, 14.
64. Personal interview, Capt. John Gallis (USN Ret.), 17 July 2006.
65. Gizzi, John, "Should the U.S. Have Overthrown Iran's Mossadegh?" *Human Events*, 13 October 2003.
66. Gilbert, Martin, *A History of the Twentieth Century: Volume Three—1952–1999*, William Morrow and Company, Inc.: 1999, 222.
67. Bischof, Gunther and Stephen E. Ambrose, eds. *Eisenhower: A Centenary Assessment*, Louisiana State University Press: 1995, 100.
68. Taranto, James and Leonard Leo, *Presidential Leadership: Rating the Best and the Worst in the White House*, The Free Press: 2004, 164.
69. Ambrose, Stephen E., *Eisenhower: The President*, Simon & Schuster: 1984, 393.
70. Bischof and Ambrose, eds., 251.

CHAPTER NINE:
Passing the Torch (1961–1969)

1. Barone, Michael, *Our Country: The Shaping of America from Roosevelt to Reagan*, The Free Press: 1990, 312.
2. Collier, Peter and David Horowitz, *The Kennedys: An American Drama*, Summit Books: 1984, 236.
3. Barone, 323.
4. Barone, 322.
5. Barone, 331.
6. Barone, 332.
7. Barone, 335.
8. Hunt, John Gabriel, Ed., *The Inaugural Addresses of the Presidents*, Gramercy Books: 1995, 428, 431.
9. Beschloss, Michael R., *The Crisis Years: Kennedy and Khrushchev, 1960–1963*, HarperCollins Publishers: 1991, 465.
10. Gaddis, John Lewis, *The End of the Cold War*, Penguin Press: 2005, 71.
11. Reeves, Richard, *President Kennedy: Profile of Power*, Simon & Schuster: 1993, 171.
12. Reeves, 168.
13. Reeves, 168.
14. Reeves, 224.
15. Beschloss, *Crisis Years*, 211.
16. Reeves, 172.
17. Schefter, James, *The Race: The Uncensored Story of how America Beat Russia to the Moon*, Doubleday: 1999, 81.
18. McDougall, Walter A., *The Heavens and the Earth: A Political History of the Space Age*, Basic Books, The Johns Hopkins University Press: 1985, 318.
19. McDougall, *The Heavens and the Earth*, 391.
20. McDougall, *The Heavens and the Earth*, 392.
21. McDougall, *The Heavens and the Earth*, 400.
22. Glenn, John and Nick Taylor, *John Glenn: A Memoir*, Bantam: 1999, 253.
23. Glenn and Taylor, 255.
24. Glenn and Taylor, 255.
25. Glenn and Taylor, 255.
26. Glenn and Taylor, 255.
27. Glenn and Taylor, 288.
28. Glenn and Taylor, 289.
29. Reeves, 345.
30. Reeves, 345.
31. Gilbert, Martin, *A History of the Twentieth Century: Volume Three—1952–1999*, William Morrow and Company, Inc.: 1999, 280.
32. LaCouture, Jean, *De Gaulle: The Ruler, 1945–1970*, W.W. Norton & Company: 1991, 375.
33. Reeves, 406.
34. Gilbert, *A History of the Twentieth Century: Volume Three*, 282.
35. Gilbert, *A History of the Twentieth Century: Volume Three*, 282.
36. Beschloss, *Crisis Years*, 543.
37. Barone, 346.
38. Beschloss, *Crisis Years*, 547.

39. Gilbert, *A History of the Twentieth Century: Volume Three*, 275.
40. Reeves, 327.
41. Barnes, John A., "John F. Kennedy on Leadership," quoted in David Frum's National Review Online column, 29 August 2005, online source: http://frum.nationalreview.com/post/?q=ZDYwYTZmZDFkYzQ2ZmY4MzAzY2VlO TRiYjdmODA1MDc=.
42. Online source: http://www.pbs.org/wgbh/amex/eyesontheprize/story/05_riders.html.
43. Gilbert, *A History of the Twentieth Century: Volume Three*, 301.
44. Gilbert, *A History of the Twentieth Century: Volume Three*, 301.
45. Online source: http://www.archives.state.al.us/govs_list/inauguralspeech.html.
46. Gilbert, *A History of the Twentieth Century: Volume Three*, 301.
47. Frady, Marshall, *Martin Luther King, Jr.*, The Penguin Group: 2002, 51.
48. Reeves, 522.
49. Reeves, 523.
50. Online source: http://almaz.com/nobel/peace/MLK-jail.html.
51. Humphrey, Hubert H., *The Education of a Public Man: My Life and Politics*, Doubleday and Company, Inc.: 1976, 269.
52. Reeves, 581.
53. Reeves, 583.
54. Frady, 124.
55. Reeves, 585.
56. Reeves, 581.
57. Reeves, 581.
58. Reeves, 320–321.
59. Online source: http://web.lconn.com/mysterease/connally.htm.
60. Beschloss, *Crisis Years*, 675.
61. Reeves, 174.
62. Humphrey, 273.
63. Humphrey, 274.
64. Humphrey, 278.
65. Humphrey, 284.
66. Humphrey, 284.
67. Online source: http://www.opinionjournal.com/diary/?id=110009275.
68. Humphrey, 285.
69. Edwards, Lee, *Goldwater: The Man Who Made a Revolution*, Regnery Publishing, Inc.: 1995, 115.
70. Edwards, 150.
71. Edwards, 116.
72. Edwards, 123.
73. Edwards, 122.
74. Edwards, 274.
75. Online source: http://www.theatlantic.com/issues/95dec/conbook/conbook.htm.
76. Edwards, 275.
77. Edwards, 276.
78. Edwards, 277.
79. Edwards, 278.
80. Edwards, 317.
81. Barone, 376.
82. Edwards, 300.